Y0-BQJ-588

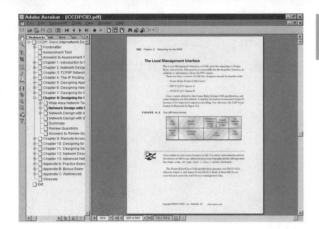

Search the CCDP: CID Study Guide ebook in PDF!

✔ Access the entire *CCDP: CID Study Guide*, complete with figures and tables, in electronic format.

✔ Use Adobe Acrobat Reader (included on the CD-ROM) to view the electronic book.

✔ Search chapters to find information on any topic in seconds.

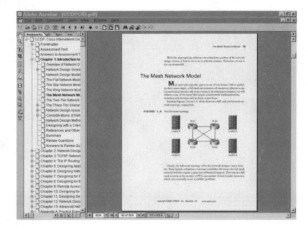

Evaluation copies of award-winning network utilities from the AG Group

✔ Preview some of the best network monitoring tools in the industry, including NetSense and AGNetTools.

SYBEX

CCDP: Cisco Internetwork Design Study Guide

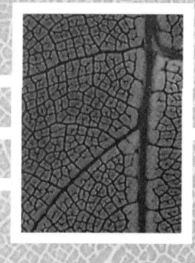

CCDP™: Cisco®
Internetwork Design
Study Guide

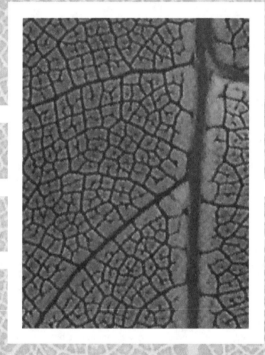

Robert Padjen
with Todd Lammle

San Francisco • Paris • Düsseldorf • Soest • London

SYBEX

Associate Publisher: Neil Edde
Contracts and Licensing Manager: Kristine O'Callaghan
Acquisitions & Developmental Editor: Linda Lee
Associate Developmental Editor: Dann McDorman
Editors: Linda Recktenwald and Emily K. Wolman
Project Editor: Julie Sakaue
Technical Editors: David Rajala and Lance Skok
Book Designer: Bill Gibson
Graphic Illustrator: Tony Jonick
Electronic Publishing Specialist: Nila Nichols
Project Team Leader: Shannon Murphy
Proofreaders: Jennifer Campbell, Molly Glover, Patrick J. Peterson, Dave Nash, Alison Moncrieff, and Laurie O'Connell
Indexer: Ted Laux
CD Coordinator: Kara Schwartz
CD Technician: Keith McNeil
Cover Designer: Archer Design
Cover Illustrator/Photographer: Tony Stone Images

SYBEX and the SYBEX logo are trademarks of SYBEX Inc. in the USA and other countries.

Screen reproductions produced with Collage Complete.
Collage Complete is a trademark of Inner Media Inc.

The CD interface was created using Macromedia Director, © 1994, 1997-1999 Macromedia Inc. For more information on Macromedia and Macromedia Director, visit http://www.macromedia.com.

This study guide and/or material is not sponsored by, endorsed by or affiliated with Cisco Systems, Inc. Cisco®, Cisco Systems®, CCDA™, CCNA™, CCDP™, CCNP™, CCIE™, CCSI™, the Cisco Systems logo and the CCIE logo are trademarks or registered trademarks of Cisco Systems, Inc. in the United States and certain other countries. All other trademarks are trademarks of their respective owners.

TRADEMARKS: SYBEX has attempted throughout this book to distinguish proprietary trademarks from descriptive terms by following the capitalization style used by the manufacturer.

The author and publisher have made their best efforts to prepare this book, and the content is based upon final release software whenever possible. Portions of the manuscript may be based upon pre-release versions supplied by software manufacturer(s). The author and the publisher make no representation or warranties of any kind with regard to the completeness or accuracy of the contents herein and accept no liability of any kind including but not limited to performance, merchantability, fitness for any particular purpose, or any losses or damages of any kind caused or alleged to be caused directly or indirectly from this book.

Library of Congress Card Number: 99-69764

ISBN: 0-7821-2639-1

Manufactured in the United States of America

10 9 8 7 6 5 4 3 2 1

Dedicated to the memories of David Grosberg and Scott Pfaendler

Acknowledgments

I want to thank my family for their patience and assistance in this effort.

Kris, I love you, it's as simple as that.

Eddie and Tyler, you're both fascinating and I learn more from each of you each day. I love you both very much.

I also need to thank:

- Bob Collins

- Sean Stinson, Deb McMahon, Theran Lee, and the Schwabies

- George, Steve, Milind, and the rest of the Cisco kids

While there are times where I don't know if I should thank him or kick him, I need to acknowledge Todd for making my life even more of a hectic event.

Thanks to all of the copy editors and technical editors—there were a lot. A special note of thanks to Dave, who kept me on my toes and challenged me to the point of irritation, and Emily, who may have persuaded me to never go down to Australia. It's a better book because of all of the editors, and I am grateful for their insight and diligence. I also want to thank Julie, Linda R., Lance S., Dann, Neil, and Linda L. for their assistance.

Then, of course, there is the whole Production crew—Shannon M., Nila N., Tony J., Keith M., Kara S., Patrick P., Dave N., Alison M., and Laurie O. Without them, this book would be nothing but a bunch of files.

Contents at a Glance

Table of Contents

Introduction

This book is intended to help you continue on your exciting new path toward obtaining your CCDP and CCIE certification. Before reading this book, it is important to have at least studied the Sybex *CCNA Study Guide*. You can take the tests in any order, but the CCNA exam should probably be your first test. It would also be beneficial to have read the Sybex *ACRC Study Guide*. Many questions in the CID exam build upon the CCNA and ACRC material. We've done everything possible to make sure that you can pass the CID exam by reading this book and practicing with Cisco routers and switches. Note that compared to most other Cisco certifications, the CID exam is more theoretical. Practical experience will help you, especially in regard to Chapters 3, 4, 5, 6, 7, and 10. You'll benefit from hands-on experience in the other chapters, but to a lesser degree.

Cisco—A Brief History

Many readers may already be familiar with Cisco and what it does. However, the story of the company's creation and evolution is quite interesting.

In the early 1980s, Len and Sandy Bosack worked in different computer departments at Stanford University and started cisco Systems (notice the small *c*). They were having trouble getting their individual systems to communicate (like some married people), so they created a gateway server in their living room to make it easier for their disparate computers in two different departments to communicate using the IP protocol.

In 1984, Cisco Systems was founded with a small commercial gateway server product that changed networking forever. Some people think that the name was intended to be San Francisco Systems, but that the paper got ripped on the way to the incorporation lawyers—who knows? But in 1992, the company name was changed to Cisco Systems, Inc.

The first product it marketed was called the Advanced Gateway Server (AGS). Then came the Mid-Range Gateway Server (MGS), the Compact Gateway Server (CGS), the Integrated Gateway Server (IGS), and the AGS+. Cisco calls these "the old alphabet soup products."

In 1993, Cisco came out with the then-amazing 4000 router, and later created the even more amazing 7000, 2000, and 3000 series routers. While the product line has grown beyond the technologies found in these platforms, the products still owe a substantial debt of gratitude to these early systems. Today's GSR product can forward millions more packets than the 7000, for example. Cisco Systems has since become an unrivaled worldwide leader in networking for the Internet. Its networking solutions can easily connect users who work from diverse devices on disparate networks. Cisco products make it simple for people to access and transfer information without regard to differences in time, place, or platform.

Cisco Systems' big picture is that it provides end-to-end networking solutions that customers can use to build an efficient, unified information infrastructure of their own or to connect to someone else's. This is an important piece in the Internet/networking-industry puzzle because a common architecture that delivers consistent network services to all users is now a functional imperative. Because Cisco Systems offers such a broad range of networking and Internet services and capabilities, users needing regular access to their local network or the Internet can do so unhindered, making Cisco's wares indispensable. The company has also challenged the industry by acquiring and integrating other technologies into its own.

Cisco answers users' need for access with a wide range of hardware products that are used to form information networks using the Cisco Internet Operating System (IOS) software. This software provides network services, paving the way for networked technical support and professional services to maintain and optimize all network operations.

Along with the Cisco IOS, one of the services Cisco created to help support the vast amount of hardware it has engineered is the Cisco Certified Internetworking Expert (CCIE) program, which was designed specifically to equip people to manage effectively the vast quantity of installed Cisco networks. The business plan is simple: If you want to sell more Cisco equipment and have more Cisco networks installed, you must ensure that the networks you installed run properly.

However, having a fabulous product line isn't all it takes to guarantee the huge success that Cisco enjoys—lots of companies with great products are now defunct. If you have complicated products designed to solve complicated problems, you need knowledgeable people who are fully capable of installing, managing, and troubleshooting them. That part isn't easy, so Cisco began the CCIE program to equip people to support these complicated networks. This program, known colloquially as the Doctorate of Networking, has also been very successful, primarily due to its stringent standards. Cisco continuously monitors the program, changing it as it sees fit, to make sure that it remains pertinent and accurately reflects the demands of today's internetworking business environments.

Building upon the highly successful CCIE program, Cisco Career Certifications permit you to become certified at various levels of technical proficiency, spanning the disciplines of network design and support. So, whether you're beginning a career, changing careers, securing your present position, or seeking to refine and promote your position, this is the book for you!

Cisco's Network Support Certifications

Cisco has created new certifications that will help you get the coveted CCIE, as well as aid prospective employers in measuring skill levels. Before these new certifications, you took only one test and were then faced with the lab, which made it difficult to succeed. With these new certifications that offer a better approach to preparing for that almighty lab, Cisco has opened doors that few were allowed through before. So, what are these new certifications, and how do they help you get your CCIE?

Cisco Certified Network Associate (CCNA)

The CCNA certification is the first in the new line of Cisco certifications, and it is a precursor to all current Cisco network support certifications. With the new certification programs, Cisco has created a type of stepping-stone approach to CCIE certification. Now, you can become a Cisco Certified Network Associate for the meager cost of the Sybex *CCNA Study Guide,* plus $100 for the test. And you don't have to stop there—you can choose to continue with your studies and achieve a higher certification called the Cisco Certified Network Professional (CCNP). Someone with a CCNP has all the skills and knowledge required to attempt the CCIE lab. However, because no textbook can take the place of practical experience, we'll discuss what else you need to be ready for the CCIE lab shortly.

Why Become a CCNA?

Cisco has created the certification process, not unlike those of Microsoft or Novell, to give administrators a set of skills and to equip prospective employers with a way to measure skills or match certain criteria. Becoming a CCNA can be the initial step of a successful journey toward a new, highly rewarding, and sustainable career.

The CCNA program was created to provide a solid introduction not only to the Cisco Internet Operating System (IOS) and Cisco hardware, but to internetworking in general. This program can provide some help in understanding networking areas that are not exclusively Cisco's. At this point in the certification process, it's not unrealistic to imagine that future network managers—even those without Cisco equipment—could easily require Cisco certifications for their job applicants.

If you make it through the CCNA and are still interested in Cisco and internetworking, you're headed down a path to certain success.

To meet the CCNA certification skill level, you must be able to do the following:

- Install, configure, and operate simple-routed LAN, routed WAN, and switched LAN and LANE networks.

- Understand and be able to configure IP, IGRP, IPX, Serial, AppleTalk, Frame Relay, IP RIP, VLANs, IPX RIP, Ethernet, and access lists.

- Install and/or configure a network.

- Optimize WAN through Internet-access solutions that reduce bandwidth and WAN costs, using features such as filtering with access lists, bandwidth on demand (BOD), and dial-on-demand routing (DDR).

- Provide remote access by integrating dial-up connectivity with traditional remote LAN-to-LAN access, as well as supporting the higher levels of performance required for new applications such as Internet commerce, multimedia, etc.

How Do You Become a CCNA?

The first step is to pass one "little" test and poof—you're a CCNA! (Don't you wish it were that easy?) True, it's just one test, but you still have to possess enough knowledge to understand (and read between the lines—trust us) what the test writers are saying.

We can't say this enough—it's critical that you have some hands-on experience with Cisco routers. If you can get hold of some 2500 routers, you're set. But in case you can't, we've worked hard to provide hundreds of configuration examples throughout the Sybex CCNA *Study Guide* book to help network administrators (or people who want to become network administrators) learn what they need to know to pass the CCNA exam.

One way to get the hands-on router experience you'll need in the real world is to attend one of the seminars offered by GlobalNet System Solutions, Inc. Please check www.lammle.com for more information and free router giveaways every month! Cyberstate University also provides hands-on

Cisco router courses over the Internet using the Sybex Cisco Certification series books. Go to www.cyberstateu.com for more information. In addition, Keystone Learning Systems (www.klscorp.com) offers the popular Cisco video certification series, featuring Todd Lammle.

For online access to Cisco equipment, readers should take a look at www.virtualrack.com.

It can also be helpful to take an Introduction to Cisco Router Configuration (ICRC) course at an authorized Cisco Education Center, but you should understand that this class doesn't meet all of the test objectives. If you decide to take the course, reading the Sybex *CCNA Study Guide*, in conjunction with the hands-on course, will give you the knowledge that you need for certification.

A Cisco router simulator that allows you to practice your routing skills for preparation of your Cisco exams is available at www.routersim.com.

For additional practice exams for all Cisco certification courses, please visit www.boson.com.

Cisco Certified Network Professional (CCNP)

This Cisco certification has opened up many opportunities for the individual wishing to become Cisco-certified, but who is lacking the training, the expertise, or the bucks to pass the notorious and often-failed two-day Cisco torture lab. The new Cisco certification will truly provide exciting new opportunities for the CNE and MCSE who just don't know how to advance to a higher level.

So, you're thinking, "Great, what do I do after I pass the CCNA exam?" Well, if you want to become a CCIE in Routing and Switching (the most popular certification), understand that there's more than one path to that much-coveted CCIE certification. The first way is to continue studying and become a CCNP. That means four more tests—and the CCNA certification—to you.

The CCNP program will prepare you to understand and comprehensively tackle the internetworking issues of today and beyond—not just those limited to the Cisco world. You will undergo an immense metamorphosis, vastly increasing your knowledge and skills through the process of obtaining these certifications.

Remember that you don't need to be a CCNP or even a CCNA to take the CCIE lab, but it's extremely helpful if you already have these certifications.

What Are the CCNP Certification Skills?

Cisco demands a certain level of proficiency for its CCNP certification. In addition to those skills required for the CCNA, these skills include the following:

- Installing, configuring, operating, and troubleshooting complex routed LAN, routed WAN, and switched LAN networks, and Dial Access Services.

- Understanding complex networks, such as IP, IGRP, IPX, Async Routing, AppleTalk, extended access lists, IP RIP, route redistribution, IPX RIP, route summarization, OSPF, VLSM, BGP, Serial, IGRP, Frame Relay, ISDN, ISL, X.25, DDR, PSTN, PPP, VLANs, Ethernet, ATM LAN emulation, access lists, 802.10, FDDI, and transparent and translational bridging.

To meet the Cisco Certified Network Professional requirements, you must be able to perform the following:

- Install and/or configure a network to increase bandwidth, quicken network response times, and improve reliability and quality of service.

- Maximize performance through campus LANs, routed WANs, and remote access.

- Improve network security.

- Create a global intranet.

- Provide access security to campus switches and routers.

- Provide increased switching and routing bandwidth—end-to-end resiliency services.

- Provide custom queuing and routed priority services.

How Do You Become a CCNP?

After becoming a CCNA, the four exams you must take to get your CCNP are as follows:

- **Exam 640-503:** Routing continues to build on the fundamentals learned in the ICND course. It focuses on large multiprotocol internetworks and how to manage them with access lists, queuing, tunneling, route distribution, route summarization, and dial-on-demand.

- **Exam 640-504:** Switching tests your understanding of configuring, monitoring, and troubleshooting the Cisco 1900 and 5000 Catalyst switching products.

- **Exam 640-505:** Remote Access tests your knowledge of installing, configuring, monitoring, and troubleshooting Cisco ISDN and dial-up access products.

- **Exam 640-506:** Support tests you on the troubleshooting information you learned in the other Cisco courses.

If you hate tests, you can take fewer of them by signing up for the CCNA exam and the Support exam, and then taking just one more long exam called the Foundation R/S exam (640-509). Doing this also gives you your CCNP—but beware, it's a really long test that fuses all the material listed previously into one exam. Good luck! However, by taking this exam, you get three tests for the price of two, which saves you $100 (if you pass). Some people think it's easier to take the Foundation R/S exam because you can leverage the areas in which you score higher against the areas in which you score lower.

Remember that test objectives and tests can change at any time without notice. Always check the Cisco Web site for the most up-to-date information (www.cisco.com).

Cisco Certified Internetwork Expert (CCIE)

You've become a CCNP, and now you've fixed your sights on getting your CCIE in Routing and Switching—what do you do next? Cisco recommends that before you take the lab, you take test 640-025, Cisco Internetwork Design (CID), and the Cisco authorized course called Installing and Maintaining Cisco Routers (IMCR). By the way, no Prometric test for IMCR exists at the time of this writing, and Cisco recommends a *minimum* of two years of on-the-job experience before taking the CCIE lab. After jumping those hurdles, you then have to pass the CCIE-R/S Exam Qualification (exam 350-001) before taking the actual lab.

To become a CCIE, Cisco recommends the following:

1. Attend all the recommended courses at an authorized Cisco training center and pony up around $15,000–$20,000, depending on your corporate discount.

2. Pass the Drake/Prometric exam ($200 per exam—so let's hope you'll pass it the first time).

3. Pass the two-day, hands-on lab at Cisco. This costs $1,000 per lab, which many people fail two or more times. (Some never make it through!) Also, because you can take the exam only in San Jose, California; Research Triangle Park, North Carolina; Sydney, Australia; Halifax, Nova Scotia; Tokyo, Japan; or Brussels, Belgium, you might need to add travel costs to this figure.

The CCIE Skills

The CCIE Router and Switching exam includes the advanced technical skills that are required to maintain optimum network performance and reliability, as well as advanced skills in supporting diverse networks that use disparate technologies. CCIEs have no problems getting a job. These experts are basically inundated with offers to work for six-figure salaries! But that's because it isn't easy to attain the level of capability that is mandatory for Cisco's CCIE. For example, a CCIE will have the following skills down pat:

- Installing, configuring, operating, and troubleshooting complex routed LAN, routed WAN, switched LAN, and ATM LANE networks, and Dial Access Services.

- Diagnosing and resolving network faults.

- Using packet/frame analysis and Cisco debugging tools.

- Documenting and reporting the problem-solving processes used.

- Having general LAN/WAN knowledge, including data encapsulation and layering; windowing and flow control and their relation to delay; error detection and recovery; link-state, distance-vector, and switching algorithms; and management, monitoring, and fault isolation.

- Having knowledge of a variety of corporate technologies—including major services provided by Desktop, WAN, and Internet groups—as well as the functions, addressing structures, and routing, switching, and bridging implications of each of their protocols.

- Having knowledge of Cisco-specific technologies, including router/ switch platforms, architectures, and applications; communication servers; protocol translation and applications; configuration commands and system/network impact; and LAN/WAN interfaces, capabilities, and applications.

Cisco's Network Design Certifications

In addition to the Network Support certifications, Cisco has created another certification track for network designers. The two certifications within this track are the Cisco Certified Design Associate and Cisco Certified Design Professional certifications. If you're reaching for the CCIE stars, we highly recommend the CCNP and CCDP certifications before attempting the lab (or attempting to advance your career).

These certifications will give you the knowledge to design routed LAN, routed WAN, and switched LAN and ATM LANE networks.

Cisco Certified Design Associate (CCDA)

To become a CCDA, you must pass the DCN (Designing Cisco Networks) test (640-441). To pass this test, you must understand how to do the following:

- Design simple routed LAN, routed WAN, and switched LAN and ATM LANE networks.

- Use network-layer addressing.

- Filter with access lists.

- Use and propagate VLAN.

- Size networks.

The Sybex *CCDA Study Guide* is the most cost-effective way to study for and pass your CCDA exam.

Cisco Certified Design Professional (CCDP)

It is surprising that the Cisco's CCDP track has not garnered the response of the other certifications. It is also ironic, because many of the higher paying jobs in networking focus on design. In addition, the other certifications, including the CCIE, tend to focus more on laboratory scenarios and problem resolution, while the CCDP and CID exams look more at problem prevention. It is important to note that Cisco highly recommends the CID examination for people planning to take the CCIE written exam.

What Are the CCDP Certification Skills?

CCDP builds upon the concepts introduced at the CCDA level, but adds the following skills:

- Designing complex routed LAN, routed WAN, and switched LAN and ATM LANE networks.

- Building upon the base level of the CCDA technical knowledge.

CCDPs must also demonstrate proficiency in the following:

- Network-layer addressing in a hierarchical environment.

- Traffic management with access lists.

- Hierarchical network design.

- VLAN use and propagation.

- Performance considerations, including required hardware and software, switching engines, memory, cost, and minimization.

How Do You Become a CCDP?

Attaining your CCDP certification is a fairly straightforward process, although Cisco provides two different testing options once a candidate passes the CCDA examination (640-441), which covers the basics of designing Cisco networks, and the CCNA (640-507). Applicants may then take a single Foundation Exam (640-509) or the three individual exams that the Foundation Exam replaces: Routing, Switching, and Remote Access (640-503, 640-504, and 640-505, respectively). The Foundation Exam will save you some money if you pass, but it is a much longer test that encompasses the material presented in the three other examinations. Note that the CCNP requires these same tests, except for the CCDA.

Following these two certifications and the noted exams, applicants must pass only the CID examination (640-025) to earn their CCDP. In the process, applicants will have earned three different certifications. Furthermore, many of the tests are applicable to the CCNP certification track.

What Does This Book Cover?

This book covers everything you need to pass the CCDP: Cisco Internetwork Design exam. In concert with the objectives, the exam is designed to test your knowledge of theoretical network design criteria and the practical application of that material. Each chapter begins with a list of the CCDP: CID test objectives covered.

Chapter 1 provides an introduction to network design and presents the design models that are used in the industry, including the hierarchical model. The benefits and detriments of these models are discussed.

The tools used in network designs are introduced in Chapter 2. These include switches, routers, hubs, and repeaters.

Chapter 3 addresses the IP protocol and the many challenges that can confront the network designer, including variable-length subnet masks and IP address conservation.

The various IP routing protocols are presented in Chapter 4, including IGRP, EIGRP, and OSPF. This chapter is augmented with information on ODR and new routing techniques that are becoming important for the modern network designer.

Chapter 5 presents AppleTalk networking, including the benefits and detriments of the protocol. It is important to note that while the AppleTalk protocol is losing market share in production networks, it is still covered in the CID exam.

Chapter 6 focuses on Novell networking and the IPX protocol. Like AppleTalk, IPX provides the designer with many benefits. The protocol is also being slowly phased out in favor of IP, but, like AppleTalk, it is still part of the CID examination.

Windows networking and the NetBIOS protocol are presented in Chapter 7. This popular operating system requires knowledge of address and name management (DHCP, WINS, and DNS), in addition to an understanding of the protocols that can transport NetBIOS packets, including IPX, IP, and NetBEUI. The issue of broadcasts in desktop protocols is also covered in this chapter.

Chapter 8 presents the wide-area network (WAN) technologies, including SMDS, Frame Relay, and ATM. This presentation focuses on the characteristics of each technology.

Chapter 9 addresses the remote-access technologies, including asynchronous dial-up, ISDN, and X.25. In addition, this chapter adds to the Cisco objectives by including DSL and cable-modem technologies.

SNA networking and mainframes are covered in Chapter 10. This chapter introduces the ways to integrate SNA networks into modern, large-scale routed environments, using technologies including STUN, RSRB, DSLW+, and APPN.

Chapter 11 focuses on security as a component of network design. This includes the placement and use of firewalls and access lists in the network.

Chapter 12 summarizes the text and provides an overview of the network management.

Chapter 13 departs from the somewhat dated CID exam objectives and introduces a few of the more current issues and challenges facing modern network designers. This section covers IP multicast, VPN technology, and encryption.

Within each chapter there are a number of sidebars titled "Network Design in the Real World." This material may either augment the main text or present additional information that can assist the network designer in applying the material. Each chapter ends with review questions that are specifically designed to help you retain the knowledge presented.

We've included an objective map on the inside front cover of this book that helps you find all the information relevant to each objective in this book. Keep in mind that all of the actual exam objectives covered in a particular chapter are listed at the beginning of that chapter.

Where Do You Take the Exam?

You may take the exams at any of the more than 800 Sylvan Prometric Authorized Testing Centers around the world. For the location of a testing center near you, call (800) 755-3926, or go to their Web site at www.2test.com. Outside of the United States and Canada, contact your local Sylvan Prometric Registration Center.

To register for a Cisco Certified Network Professional exam:

1. Determine the number of the exam you want to take. (The CID exam number is 640-025.)

2. Register with the nearest Sylvan Prometric Registration Center. At this point, you will be asked to pay in advance for the exam. At the time of this writing, the exams are $100 each and must be taken within one

year of payment. You can schedule exams up to six weeks in advance or as soon as one working day prior to the day you wish to take it. If you need to cancel or reschedule your exam appointment, contact Sylvan Prometric at least 24 hours in advance. Same-day registration isn't available for the Cisco tests.

3. When you schedule the exam, you'll get instructions regarding all appointment and cancellation procedures, the ID requirements, and information about the testing-center location.

Tips for Taking Your CID Exam

The CCDP CID test contains about 100 questions to be completed in 90 minutes. You must schedule a test at least 24 hours in advance (unlike the Novell or Microsoft exams), and you aren't allowed to take more than one Cisco exam per day.

Unlike Microsoft or Novell tests, the exam has answer choices that are really similar in syntax—although some syntax is dead wrong, it is usually just *subtly* wrong. Some other syntax choices may be right, but they're shown in the wrong order. Cisco does split hairs and is not at all averse to giving you classic trick questions.

Also, never forget that the right answer is the Cisco answer. In many cases, more than one appropriate answer is presented, but the *correct* answer is the one that Cisco recommends.

Here are some general tips for exam success:

- Arrive early at the exam center, so you can relax and review your study materials.

- Read the questions *carefully*. Don't just jump to conclusions. Make sure that you're clear about *exactly* what each question asks.

- Don't leave any questions unanswered. They count against you.

- When answering multiple-choice questions that you're not sure about, use a process of elimination to get rid of the obviously incorrect answers first. Doing this greatly improves your odds if you need to make an educated guess.

- As of this writing, the CID exam permits skipping questions and reviewing previous answers. However, this is changing on all Cisco exams, and so you should prepare as though this option will not be available.

After you complete an exam, you'll get immediate, online notification of your pass or fail status, a printed Examination Score Report that indicates your pass or fail status, and your exam results by section. (The test administrator will give you the printed score report.) Test scores are automatically forwarded to Cisco within five working days after you take the test, so you don't need to send your score to them. If you pass the exam, you'll receive confirmation from Cisco, typically within two to four weeks.

Appendix C lists a number of additional Web sites that can further assist you with research and test questions.

How to Use This Book

This book can provide a solid foundation for the serious effort of preparing for the Cisco Certified Network Professional CID (Cisco Internetwork Design) exam. To best benefit from this book, use the following study method:

1. Study each chapter carefully, making sure that you fully understand the information and the test objectives listed at the beginning of each chapter.

2. Answer the review questions related to that chapter. (The answers are in Appendix A.)

3. Note the questions that confuse you, and study those sections of the book again.

4. Before taking the exam, try your hand at the practice exams that are included on the CD that comes with this book. They'll give you a complete overview of what you can expect to see on the real thing. Note that the CD contains questions not included in the book.

5. Remember to use the products on the CD that is included with this book. Visio, EtherPeek, and the EdgeTest exam-preparation software have all been specifically picked to help you study for and pass your exam.

To learn all the material covered in this book, you'll have to apply yourself regularly and with discipline. Try to set aside the same time period every day to study, and select a comfortable and quiet place to do so. If you work hard, you will be surprised at how quickly you learn this material. All the best!

What's on the CD?

We worked hard to provide some really great tools to help you with your certification process. All of the following components should be loaded on your workstation when studying for the test.

The EdgeTest for Cisco CID Test Preparation Software

Provided by EdgeTek Learning Systems, this test-preparation software prepares you to pass the Cisco Internetwork Design exam. To find more test-simulation software for all Cisco and NT exams, look for the exam link on www.lammle.com.

AG Group NetSense and AGNetTools

Two AG Group products appear on the CD that accompanies this book: the Windows demonstration software of NetSense and the freeware version of AGNetTools. With NetSense, you can perform expert analysis of peer-to-peer conversations in packets captured from EtherPeek or TokenPeek, both of which are available as demonstration software at www.aggroup.com. You'll find a link to their Web site on the CD interface. AGNetTools is an interface- and menu-driven IP tool compilation.

You can find out more information about AG Group and its products at www.aggroup.com.

How to Contact the Authors

To reach Robert Padjen, send him e-mail at networker@popmail.com. Robert provides consulting services to a wide variety of clients, including Charles Schwab and the California State Automobile Association.

You can reach Todd Lammle through GlobalNet Training Solutions, Inc. (www.lammle.com)—his Training and Systems Integration Company in Colorado—or e-mail him at todd@lammle.com.

Assessment Test

1. A LANE installation requires what three components?

2. In modern networks, SNA is a disadvantage because of what limitation?

3. The native, non-routable encapsulation for NetBIOS is _____.

4. The FEP runs VTAM. True or false?

5. Switches operate at _____ of the OSI model.

6. ATM uses _____ in AAL 5 encapsulation.

7. Clients locate the server in Novell networks by sending a _____ request.

8. Most network management tools use _____ to communicate with devices.

9. The address 127.50.0.14 is part of what class?

10. The formula for determining the number of circuits needed for a full-mesh topology is _____.

11. A remote gateway provides support for _____ application/applications.

12. An IP network with a mask of 255.255.255.252 supports how many hosts per subnet?

13. ISDN BRI provides _____.

14. The RIF is part of a/an _____ frame.

15. Local acknowledgment provides _____ system response for remote nodes.

16. OSPF is a _____ protocol.

17. AppleTalk networks automatically define the node number. The administrator or designer assigns a _____ to define the network number.

18. EIGRP does not support variable length subnet masks. True or false?

19. It is most practical to establish a remote _____ configuration so that all services are available to remote users.

20. RSRB allows SNA traffic to traverse non-_____ segments.

21. Networks with a core, access, and distribution layer are called _____.

22. Multilink Multichassis PPP uses what proprietary protocol?

23. Hub-and-spoke networks could also be called _____.

24. What datagrams are typically forwarded with the `ip helper-address` command?

25. Type 20 packets are used for what function?

26. A user operates a session running on a remote workstation or server from home as if they were physically there. What is this called?

27. What is Cisco's product for IPX-to-IP gateway services called?

28. What is the routing protocol of the Internet?

29. What is a link with 2B and 1D channels called?

30. Multicast addresses are part of what class?

31. Information about logical groupings in AppleTalk is contained in _____.

32. What are L2TP, IPSec, and L2F typically used for?

33. TACACS+ and RADIUS provide what services?

34. What is an FEP?

35. For voice, video, and data integration, designers should use which WAN protocol?

36. What is the default administrative distance for OSPF?

37. Network monitoring relies on what protocol?

38. What is a connection via dial-up, ISDN, or another technology that places a remote workstation on the corporate network as if they were directly connected called?

39. What does HSRP provide the designer?

40. VLSM is supported in which of the following routing protocols?

A. EIGRP

B. IGRP

C. RIP v2

D. RIP v1

E. OSPF

Answers to Assessment Test

1. LES, LEC, and BUS. *See Chapter 8.*

2. It is not routable. In addition, it is very sensitive to delay. *See Chapter 10.*

3. NetBEUI. *See Chapter 7.*

4. False. *See Chapter 10.*

5. Layer 2. *See Chapter 2.*

6. 53-byte cells, 48 of which are used for user data. *See Chapter 8.*

7. Get Nearest Server. *See Chapter 6.*

8. SNMP. *See Chapter 12.*

9. None. This network is reserved for the loopback function. *See Chapter 3.*

10. $N * (N-1) / 2$. *See Chapter 8.*

11. A single. *See Chapter 9.*

12. Two. *See Chapter 3.*

13. Two B channels of 64Kbps each and one D channel of 16Kbps. *See Chapter 9.*

14. Token Ring. *See Chapter 10.*

15. Improved. *See Chapter 10.*

16. Link-state. *See Chapter 4.*

17. Cable-range. *See Chapter 5.*

18. False. *See Chapter 4.*

19. Node. *See Chapter 9.*

20. Token Ring. *See Chapter 10.*

21. Hierarchical. *See Chapter 1.*

22. Stackgroup Bidding Protocol (SGBP). *See Chapter 9.*

23. Star. *See Chapter 1.*

24. DHCP, although this command also forwards seven additional datagrams. *See Chapter 7.*

25. NetBIOS over IPX. *See Chapter 6.*

26. Remote control. *See Chapter 9.*

27. IP eXchange. *See Chapter 6.*

28. BGP. *See Chapter 4.*

29. ISDN BRI. *See Chapter 9.*

30. Class D. *See Chapter 13.*

31. Zone Information Protocol (ZIP) packets. *See Chapter 5.*

32. VPNs. *See Chapter 9.*

33. Centralized authentication. *See Chapter 11.*

34. A front-end processor for a mainframe. *See Chapter 10.*

35. ATM. *See Chapter 8.*

36. 110. *See Chapter 4.*

37. SNMP. RMON would also be applicable. *See Chapter 12.*

38. Remote node. *See Chapter 9.*

39. Router redundancy. *See Chapter 4.*

40. A, C, E. *See Chapter 3.*

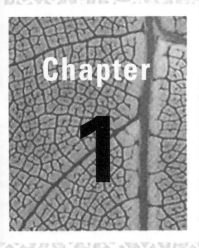

Chapter 1

Introduction to Network Design

CISCO INTERNETWORK DESIGN EXAM OBJECTIVES COVERED IN THIS CHAPTER:

- ✓ Demonstrate an understanding of the steps for designing internetwork solutions.

- ✓ Analyze a client's business and technical requirements and select appropriate internetwork technologies and topologies.

- ✓ Construct an internetwork design that meets a client's objectives for internetwork functionality, performance, and cost.

- ✓ Define the goals of internetwork design.

- ✓ Define the issues facing designers.

- ✓ List resources for further information.

- ✓ Identify the origin of design models used in the course.

- ✓ Define the hierarchical model.

Network design is one of the more interesting facets of computing. While there are many disciplines in information technology, including help desk, application development, project management, workstation support, and server administration, network design is the only one that directly benefits from all these other disciplines. It incorporates elements of many disciplines into a single function. Network designers frequently find that daily challenges require a certain amount of knowledge regarding all of the other IT disciplines.

The network designer is responsible for solving the needs of the business with the technology of the day. This requires knowledge of protocols, operating systems, departmental divisions in the enterprise, and a host of other areas. The majority of network design projects require strong communication skills, leadership, and research and organizational talents. Project management experience can also greatly benefit the process, as most network design efforts will require scheduling and budgeting with internal and external resources, including vendors, corporate departments, service providers, and the other support and deployment organizations within the enterprise.

This text will both provide an introduction to network design and serve as a reference guide for future projects. Its primary purpose is to present the objectives for the CCDP: Cisco Internetwork Design examination and to prepare readers to pass this certification test. However, it would be unfortunate to read this book only in the context of passing the exam. A thorough understanding of network design not only assists administrators in troubleshooting, but enables them to permanently correct recurrent problems in the network. An additional perk is the satisfaction that comes with seeing a network that you designed and deployed—especially a year later when only minor modifications have been needed and all of those were part of your original network design plan.

Having said that, it is important to note that in "real world" network designs virtually no individual does all the work. Vendors, business leaders, and other administrators all will, and should, play a significant role in the design process. This is obviously true when planning server-based services, such as DHCP (Dynamic Host Configuration Protocol). Though many beautiful network designs have been conceived without consideration and consultation of the user community, the end result is an expensive "It should have worked!" After reading this text, and specifically this chapter, no one should ever make this mistake.

Overview of Network Design

It has been stated that network design is 50 percent technology, 50 percent diplomacy, and 50 percent magic. While written examinations will likely ignore the last item, mastery of the first two is critical in exam preparation.

In actuality, network design is simply the implementation of a technical solution to solve a nontechnical problem. Contrary to expectations, network design is not as basic as configuring a router, although we will address this critical component. Rather, as presented in this first chapter, network design is a multifaceted effort to balance various constraints with objectives.

Network design encompasses three separate areas: conception, implementation, and review. This chapter will elaborate on these areas and expand the scope of each. It's important to remember that each phase is unique and requires separate attention. The final phase of network design—review—is perhaps more important than any other phase, as it provides valuable information for future network designs and lessons for other projects. Readers should consider how they might design networks deployed with the technology referenced in this text—the easiest methodology is to establish a list of metrics from which to make a comparison. Designers who meet the original metrics for the project usually find that the network is successful in meeting the customer's needs.

Each design, whether the simple addition of a subnet or the complete implementation of a new international enterprise network, must address the same goals: scalability, adaptability, cost control, manageability, predictability, simplicity of troubleshooting, and ease of implementation. A good design will both address current needs while effectively accommodating future needs. However, two constraints limit most designs' ability to address these goals: time and money. Typical network technology lasts only 24 to 60 months, while cabling and other equipment may be *expected* to remain for over 15 years. The most significant constraint, though, will almost always be financial.

The actual expected life of a cable plant is subject to some debate. Many networks are already coming close to the 15-year mark on the data side, and the voice side already has upwards of 60 years. The trend has been for copper cable to have some built-in longevity, and such efforts as Digital Subscriber Line (DSL), Category 5E, and Gigabit Ethernet over copper are solid evidence that corporations will continue to regard this copper infrastructure as a long-term investment.

With that said, let's focus on some of the theory behind network designs.

Network Design Goals

Network designers should strive to address a number of objectives in their designs. Readers should focus on these goals and consider how they might relate to the typical corporate environment. (Later in this chapter, we will more fully explore the importance of the business relationship.) In addition, designers should pay specific attention to the relationships between the design goals, noting that addressing one goal will frequently require compromising another. Let's look at these goals in detail.

Scalability

Scalability refers to an implementation's ability to address the needs of an increasing number of users. For example, a device with only two interfaces will likely not provide as much service and, therefore, not be as scalable as a device with 20. Twenty interfaces will likely cost a great deal more and will undoubtedly require greater amounts of rack space, and so scalability is often governed by another goal—controlling costs. Architects are often challenged to maintain *future-proof* designs while maintaining the budget.

Factors that augment scalability include high-capacity backbones, switching technology, and modular designs. Additional considerations regarding scalability include the number of devices in the network, CPU utilization, and memory availability. For example, a network with one router is likely to be less scalable than a network with three, even if the three routers are substantially smaller than the one.

Adaptability

While similar to scalability, adaptability need not address an increase in the number of users. An adaptable network is one that can accommodate new services without significant changes to the existing structure, for example, adding voice services into the data network. Designers should consider Asynchronous Transfer Mode (ATM) where the potential for this adaptive step exists. For example, the possibility of adding voice service later would negate the use of Fiber Distributed Data Interface (FDDI) in the initial network design. Making this determination requires a certain amount of strategic planning, rather than a purely short-term tactical approach, and could therefore make a network more efficient and cost-effective. However, this section is not intended to advocate the use of any specific technology, but rather to show the benefits of an adaptable network.

Adaptability is one aspect of network design where using a matrix is beneficial. A matrix is a weighted set of criteria, designed to remove subjectivity from the decision-making process. Before reviewing vendors and products, a designer will typically work with managers, executives, and others to construct a matrix, assigning a weight to each item. While a complete matrix should include support and cost, a simple matrix could include only the adaptability issues. For example, the use of variable-length subnet masks might be weighted with a five (on a scale from one to five), while support for SNMP (Simple Network Management Protocol) v.3 might only garner a weight of one. Under these conditions, the matrix may point to a router that can support Enhanced Interior Gateway Routing Protocol (EIGRP) or Open Shortest Path First (OSPF) over one with a higher level of manageability, assuming that there is some mutual exclusivity.

Cost Control

Financial considerations often overshadow most other design goal elements. If costs were not an issue, everyone would purchase OC-192 SONET (Synchronous Optical Network) rings for their users with new equipment installed every three months. Clearly this is not the "real world." The network designer's role is often similar to that of a magician—both must frequently pull rabbits from their hats, but the network designer has the added responsibility of balancing dollars with functions. Therefore, the designer is confronted with the same cost constraints as all other components of a business. The fundamental issue at this point must be how to cope with this limitation without sacrificing usability. There are a number of methods used in modern network design to address this problem.

First, many companies have a network budget linked to the IT (Information Technology) department. This budget is typically associated with such basic, general services as baseline costs—wiring, general desktop connectivity, and corporate access to services such as the Internet. There is typically also a second source of funding for the IT department from project-related work. This work comes in the form of departmental requests for service beyond the scope of general service. It may involve setting up a workgroup server or lab environment, or it may involve finding a remote-access solution so that the executives can use a newer technology—DSL, for example. These projects are frequently paid for by the requesting department and not IT. In such cases, the requesting department may even cover costs that are not immediately related to its project. In the DSL project, for example, few companies would argue with the logic of setting up a larger scalable installation to address the needs of the few executives using the first generation of the service. It may be possible to have the requesting department fund all or part of a more-expensive piece of equipment to avoid a fork-lift upgrade in the future. (A fork-lift upgrade is one that requires the complete replacement of a large component—a chassis, for example.) Even if IT may need to fund a portion of the project, this is usually easier than funding the entire effort.

Second, a good network design will include factors that lend themselves to scalability and modularity. For example, long-range (strategic) needs may prompt the conversion of an entire network to new technologies, while immediate needs encompass only a small portion of such a project. By addressing tactical needs with an eye toward the strategic, the network designer can accomplish two worthy goals—a reduction in costs and the creation of an efficient network. In reality, the costs may not be reduced; in fact, the costs will likely rise. However, such costs will be amortized over a longer period of time, thus making each component appear cost effective. Such an undertaking is best approached by informing management of the schedule and long-range plan. Budgets frequently open up when a long-term plan is presented, and designers always want to avoid having a budget cut because a precedent was set by spending too little in the previous year.

The third approach to balancing network cost with usability is to buy cheaper components. A brief word of advice: avoid this approach at all costs. The net impact is that additional resources are required for support, which erodes any apparent savings.

The last approach is to use a billing model. Under this model, all purchases are pooled and then paid for by the other departments. This method can be quite limiting or quite fair, depending on its implementation. Such a model does away with the problem caused by concurrent usage but may leave the IT group with no budget of their own.

Concurrent Usage

Concurrent usage is an interesting concept in network design, as it ignores most other concerns. Imagine that the IT department has a single spare slot on its router and another department (Department A) wants a new subnet. One approach would be to have Department A purchase the router card and complete the project. However, this approach fails to consider the next request. A month later, another department (Department B) wants the same special deal on a new network segment, but, alas, there are no open slots. Department B would need to pay for a new router, power supplies, rack space, wiring, maintenance, and so forth. Department A may have paid $2,000 for their segment, but Department B will likely generate a bill for ten times that figure. Of course, Department C, making their request after Department B, would benefit from Department B's generosity—their new segment would cost only $2,000, since there would now be a number of open slots.

Another solution is to fund all network projects from a separate ledger—no department owns the interface or equipment under this model. Unfortunately, this solution often leads to additional requests—it is always easier to spend someone else's money. Bear in mind that this solution focuses only on the technical costs. If the designer is asked to spend 30 hours a week for six months on a single department's effort, there will likely be additional expenses.

With all of these approaches, the goal is to obtain the largest amount of funding for the network (within the constraints of needs) and then to stretch that budget accordingly. There will likely be points in the design that have longer amortization schedules than others, and this will help to make the budget go further. For example, many corporations plan for the cable plant to last over fifteen years (an optimistic figure in some cases), so you shouldn't skimp on cabling materials or installation. Such expenses can be amortized over a number of years, thus making them appear more cost effective. Plus, a few pennies saved here will likely cost a great deal more in the long run. Ultimately, it's best to try and work with the business and the corporate culture to establish a fair method for dealing with the cost factors.

Network Design in the Real World: Cabling

A network designer installed three live Category 5 wires to each desktop along with a six-pair Category 3 for voice services in a campus installation that I eventually took over. A live connection meant that it was terminated to a shared media hub or switch. Cross-connects were accomplished virtually, using VLANs (virtual LANs). This design cost a great deal to implement, but saved thousands of dollars in cabling and cross-connects. MAC (move, add, and change) costs were greatly reduced and theoretically could have been eliminated with dynamic VLAN assignments. By the way, this particular shop had three different platforms—Macintosh, Windows, and Unix—on almost every desktop, lending itself to the three-drop design.

This is a great demonstration of the importance of considering corporate needs and, to a certain degree, culture. Various efforts to remove even some of the machines from each desktop were largely unsuccessful, primarily because of the corporate culture at the time. IT was unable to resolve this conflict, which resulted in spending a great deal on network, workstation, and software equipment and licenses. While the network designer should be able to work with other IT groups and management to prevent such waste, a good designer should also be able to accommodate their demands. We'll come back to this network when discussing broadcasts and other constraints. For now, just note that multiple networks were desirable for each desktop—Macintosh and Windows on one and Unix on the other—adding another expense to the design criteria.

The Bottom Line

It helps to have a bit of accounting experience or at least a relationship with the Accounting department when calculating network design costs. Forgoing options such as leasing, there are a couple of ways to assess the cost of a network design.

Basically, costs will appear in two general categories. The first is initial costs—those costs that appear once, typically at the beginning of the purchasing process. For example, the acquisition of a router or switch would likely be an initial cost. Initial costs are important for a number of reasons. However, these costs can be a bit misleading. Larger corporations will incorporate an amortization on equipment based on the projected lifespan of the device. Thus, a router may actually be entered as a cost over 30 months instead of just one month. This variance can greatly impact the budgets of both the network and the corporation. It's important to consult with the Accounting group in your organization so that you understand how such costs are treated.

The second category is recurring costs. These costs frequently relate to circuits and maintenance contracts and are typically paid on a monthly or annual basis. These costs can frequently overshadow the initial costs—a $100,000 router is cheap compared to a monthly $50,000 telecommunications bill. Consider that the monthly cost for a $100,000 router is only 18 percent of the cost for a $50,000-a-month circuit after the first year—and that router will have residual value for years beyond.

A significant amount of this material is written in the context of large corporations and enterprise-class businesses. In reality, the concepts hold true for even the smallest companies.

Additional Design Goals

While Cisco typically refers to the three goals of network design, our discussion would be incomplete if the list was not augmented. In addition to scalability, adaptability, and cost control, designers must be familiar with predictability, ease of implementation, manageability, and troubleshooting. These goals integrate well with the three-tier model and will be presented in greater detail in the section, "The Three-Tier (Hierarchical) Network Model," later in this chapter.

Scalability refers to the ability to add additional nodes and bandwidth to the network, and its characteristics typically interrelate with those of predictability. Predictable networks provide the administrator with a clear traffic flow for data and, combined with baselining and monitoring, solid capacity-planning information.

A well-designed network is easily implemented. This characteristic also applies to modular designs, but it does not have to. Implementations typically work best when the developer draws upon prior experience and introduces the design in phases. Prior to deploying any new design, the developer should test it in a lab or discuss the installation with others in the field. The adage "Why reinvent the wheel?" is particularly valuable here.

The last network design goal encompasses the recurrent demand for diagnostics. Unfortunately, even the best designs fail, and sometimes these failures are the result of the design itself. A good design should focus on solid documentation and be as straightforward as possible. For example, a design that uses network address translation (NAT) when it is not required would likely be more difficult to fix in a crisis than one without NAT. Designers should refrain from adding features just because they are available and focus on simplicity of design.

Troubleshooting capabilities can be enhanced by placing monitoring tools in the network. Protocol analyzers and remote monitoring (RMON) probes should be available for rapid dispatch if permanent installations are not an option at critical points in the network, including the core and distribution layers. This chapter will later define the core and distribution layers, in addition to the hierarchical model. For now, simply consider the core and distribution layers as the backbone of the network.

Network Design Models

At this point, most readers preparing for the CID examination are undoubtedly well versed in the OSI (Open Systems Interconnection) model for network protocols.

If you need additional information regarding the OSI model and its relationship to the networking protocols, please consult one of the many texts on the subject, including the Sybex Network Press publications.

This model (the OSI model) explains the functions and relationships of the individual protocols. Similarly, a number of other network design models have been established. Most of these models now focus on a single three-tier methodology. This approach preserves many of the criteria necessary for effective network design and will be presented later in this chapter.

Recall that the OSI model provides benefits in troubleshooting because each layer of the model serves a specific function. For example, the network layer, Layer 3, is charged with logical routing functions. The transport layer, Layer 4, is atop Layer 3 and provides additional services. In the TCP/IP world, Layer 3 is served by IP, and Layer 4 is served by TCP (Transmission Control Protocol) or UDP (User Datagram Protocol).

As a humorous aside, some network designers have added two additional layers to the OSI model—Layer 8, which refers to the political layer, and Layer 9, which represents the financial one. These layers are particularly appropriate in the context of this chapter.

In the same manner, the network design models provide an overview of the function and abilities of each theoretical network design. The most common large network design, the three-tier approach, further defines functions for each tier. To move from one tier to another, packets should traverse the intermediate tier. Note that in this model the definitions are nowhere near as precise as they are in the OSI model, but the model should be adhered to as closely as possible.

This section will first present some of the alternatives to the OSI model and end with a detailed examination of the three-tier model. The caveats and guidelines for the three-tier approach will be examined in more detail than the other approaches, but readers and designers should consider the positive and negative impacts of each design.

The Flat Network Model

The flat network may assume many forms, and it is likely that most readers are very comfortable with this design. In fact, most networks develop from this model.

A flat network contains no routers or Layer 3 awareness (Layer 3 of the OSI model). The network is one large broadcast domain. This does not preclude the incorporation of switches or bridges to isolate the collision domain boundaries and, depending upon the protocols in use, it could support up to a few hundred stations. Unfortunately though, this design rarely scales to support the demands of most networks in terms of users, flexibility, and security.

Performance may be only one concern. Typically, the need for access lists (ACLs) and other benefits at Layer 3 in the OSI model will require the incorporation of routers. The flat network model fails to address many of the important factors in network design—the most significant of which is scalability. Consider the impact of a single network interface card (NIC) sending a broadcast onto the network. At Layer 2, this broadcast would reach all stations. Should the NIC experience a fault where it continued to send broadcasts as fast as possible, the entire network would fail.

The Star Network Model

The traditional star topology typically meets the needs of a small company as it first expands to new locations. A single router, located at the company's headquarters, interconnects all the sites. Figure 1.1 illustrates this design.

FIGURE 1.1 The star topology

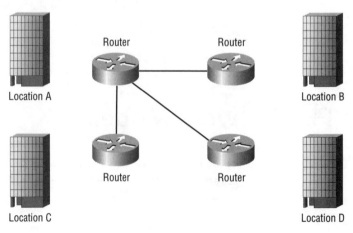

The following list encompasses both the positive and negative aspects of such a topology, but the negative aspects should be somewhat obvious:

- Low scalability

- Single point of failure

- Low cost

- Easy setup and administration

Star topologies are experiencing a resurgence with the deployment of private remote networks, including Digital Subscriber Line (DSL) and Frame Relay solutions. While the entire network will likely mesh into another model, the remote portion of the network will use the star topology. Note that the star topology is also called the hub-and-spoke model.

The Ring Network Model

The ring topology builds upon the star topology with a few significant modifications. This design is typically used when a small company expands nationally and two sites are located close together. The design improves upon the star topology, as shown in Figure 1.2.

FIGURE 1.2 The ring topology

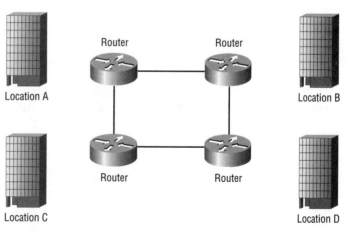

As you can see, the ring design eliminates one of the main negative aspects of the star topology. In the ring model, a single circuit failure will not disconnect any location from the enterprise network. However, the ring topology fails to address these other considerations:

- Low scalability

- No single point of failure

- Higher cost

- Complex setup and configuration

- Difficulty incorporating new locations

Consider the last bullet item in the list and how the network designer would add a fifth location to the diagram. This is perhaps one of the most significant negative aspects of the design—a circuit will need to be removed and two new circuits added for each new location. Figure 1.3 illustrates this modification. Note that the thin line in Figure 1.3 denotes the ring configuration before Location E was added.

FIGURE 1.3 Adding a site in the ring topology

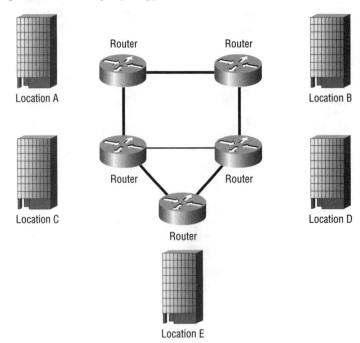

While the ring topology addresses the redundancy portion of the network design criteria, it fails to do so in an efficient manner. Therefore, its use is not recommended.

The Mesh Network Model

Mesh networks typically appear in one of two forms—full or partial. As their names imply, a full mesh interconnects all resources, whereas a partial mesh interconnects only some resources. In subsequent chapters, we will address some of the issues that impact partial-mesh implementations, including split-horizon and multiple-router hops.

Examine Figures 1.4 and 1.5, which illustrate a full- and partial-mesh network topology, respectively.

FIGURE 1.4 The full-mesh topology

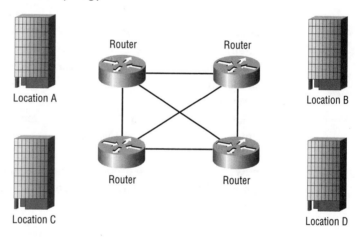

Clearly, the full-mesh topology offers the network designer many benefits. These include redundancy and some scalability. However, the full-mesh network will also require a great deal of financial support. The costs in a full mesh increase as the number of PVCs (permanent virtual circuits) increases, which can eventually cause scalability problems.

FIGURE 1.5 The partial-mesh topology

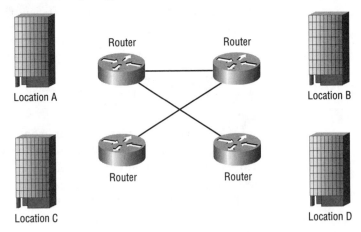

Assume that a designer is architecting a seven-site solution. Under the hub-and-spoke model, a total of six PVCs are needed (N-1). Under a full-mesh design, the number of PVCs equals 21 [N(N-1)/2]. For a small network without a well-defined central data repository, the costs may be worth the effort. In larger networks, the full-mesh design is a good tool to consider, but the associated costs and scalability issues frequently demand the use of other strategies.

The partial-mesh model does not constrain the designer with a predefined number of circuits per nodes in the network, which permits some latitude in locating and provisioning circuits. However, this flexibility can cause reliability and performance problems. The benefit is cost—fewer circuits can support the entire enterprise while providing specific data paths for higher priority connections.

The Two-Tier Network Model

The two-tier model shares many attributes with the partial-mesh model, but the design has some additional benefits. This design typically evolves from the merger of two companies—each of small size and using historical star topologies. However, the design may also merit use in the initial deployment of a medium-sized network. Figure 1.6 illustrates the two-tier model. This model is sometimes used in metropolitan settings where a number of buildings require connectivity but only two buildings have WAN connections—this design reduces total costs yet provides some redundancy. The two core installations in Figure 1.6 would incorporate the WAN links.

Notice that the two-tier model introduces a single, significant point of failure: the link between the primary locations. However, if designed for each side (east/west) to be independent of the other, the model can work effectively.

This solution works best when both locations have strong support organizations and the expenses associated with complete integration are high. Because of the limited connectivity between the two primary sites and the lack of any other connections, this solution typically provides the lowest cost and is the simplest approach. When a single core location is selected, the alternate primary location can move to the distribution layer (explained in the next section) or can provide a distributed core for redundancy.

FIGURE 1.6 The two-tier model

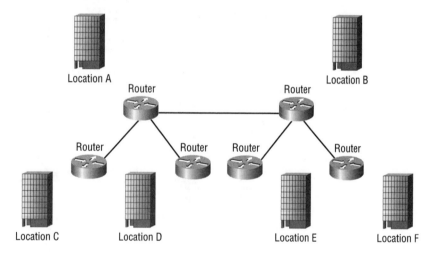

The Three-Tier (Hierarchical) Network Model

Most modern networks are designed around a form of the three-tier model. As shown in Figure 1.7, this network model defines three levels (functions) of the network: core, distribution, and access. The highest level is the network core, which interconnects the distribution layer resources. Access routers connect to the distribution layer moving up the model and to workstations and other resources moving down the model.

This design affords a number of advantages, although the costs are greater than those for the previous models. The biggest advantage to this design is scalability.

FIGURE 1.7 The three-tier model

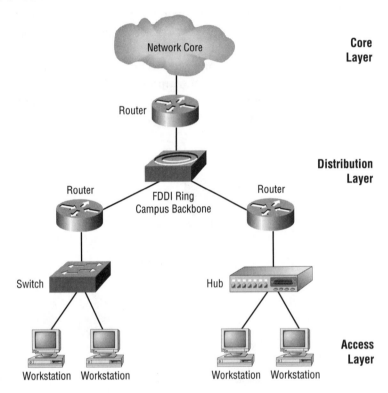

Virtually all scalable networks follow the three-tier model for network design. This model is particularly valuable when using hierarchical routing protocols and summarization, specifically OSPF, but it is also helpful in reducing the impact of failures and changes in the network. The design also simplifies implementation and troubleshooting, in addition to contributing to predictability and manageability. These benefits greatly augment the functionality of the network and the appropriateness of the model to address network design goals. These benefits, which are typically incorporated in hierarchical designs, are either not found inherently in the other models or not as easily included in them. Following is a closer look at the benefits just mentioned:

Scalability   As shown in the previous models, scalability is frequently limited in network designs that do not use the three-tier model. While there may still be limitations in the hierarchical model, the separation of functions within the network provides natural expansion points without significantly impacting other portions of the network.

Easier implementation   Because the hierarchical model divides the network into logical and physical sections, designers find that the model lends itself to implementation. A setback in one section of the network build-out should not significantly impact the remainder of the deployment. For example, while a delay in connecting a distribution layer to the core would affect all of the downstream access layer nodes, the setback would not preclude continued progress between the access layer and the distribution layer. In addition, other distribution and access layers could be installed independently. Project managers typically build out the core and distribution layers first in a new deployment and then proceed with the access layer; however, if immediate service is needed at the access layer, the designer may adopt a plan that focuses on that tier and then interconnects with the infrastructure at a later time. This means that the designer may be required to provide a connection between two locations that are remote—locations that would typically be located in the access layer. When the core and distribution layers are completed, the designer can move the circuits used for the temporary connection, bringing the smaller network into the larger one. Better still, many architects try to place the distribution in one of the two temporary link locations—reducing the expense and providing a termination point for other access layer locations.

Easier troubleshooting   Given the logical layout of the model, hierarchical networks are typically easier to troubleshoot than other networks of equal size and scope. Reducing the possibility of routing loops further aids troubleshooting, and hierarchical designs typically work to reduce the potential number of loops.

Predictability   Capacity planning is generally easier in the hierarchical model, since the need for capacity usually increases as data moves toward the core. Akin to a tree, where the trunk must carry more nutrients to feed the branches and leaves, the core links all the other sections of the network and thus must have sufficient capacity to move data. In addition, the core typically connects to the corporate data center via high-speed connections to supply data to the various branches and remote locations.

Manageability   Hierarchically designed networks are usually easier to manage because of these other benefits. Predictable data flows, scalability, independent implementations, and simpler troubleshooting all simplify the management of the network.

Table 1.1 provides a summary of the functions defined by the hierarchical model.

TABLE 1.1   The Three Tiers of the Hierarchical Model

Tier	Function
Core	Typically inclusive of WAN links between geographically diverse locations, the core layer is responsible for the high-speed transfer of data.
Distribution	Usually implemented as a building or campus backbone or a limited private MAN (metropolitan-area network), the distribution layer is responsible for providing services to workgroups and departments. Policy is typically implemented at this layer, including route filters and summarization and access lists. However, the Cisco CID textbook answer for access lists is to place them in the access layer.
Access	The access layer provides a control point for broadcasts and additional administrative filters. The access layer is responsible for connecting users to the network and is regarded as the proper location for access lists and other services. However, network designers will need to compare their needs with the constraints of the model—it may make more sense to place an access list closer to the core, for example. The rules regarding each model are intended to provide the best performance and flexibility in a theoretical context.

It is very important that designers understand the significance of the model's three tiers. Therefore, let's elaborate on the cursory definitions provided in Table 1.1. For reference, Figure 1.8 provides a logical view of the three-tier hierarchy.

FIGURE 1.8   Logical view of the hierarchical model

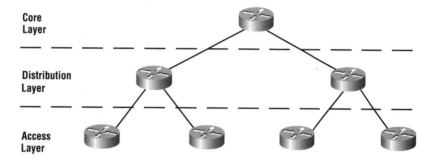

The Core Layer

In generic terms, a core refers to the center of an object. In network design, this concept is expanded to mean the center of the network. Typically focused on the WAN implementation, the network core layer is responsible for the rapid transfer of data and the interconnection of various distribution and access layers. Therefore, the core routers typically do not have access lists or other services that would reduce the efficiency of the network. The core layer should be designed to have redundant paths and other fault-tolerance criteria. Without the core, all other areas would be isolated. Convergence and load balancing should also be incorporated into the core design. Note that servers, workstations, and other devices are typically not placed in the core.

Figure 1.9 illustrates the use of the core to interconnect three sites in the enterprise. This core is composed of a WAN medium—possibly Frame Relay, ATM, or point-to-point links.

FIGURE 1.9 The core layer

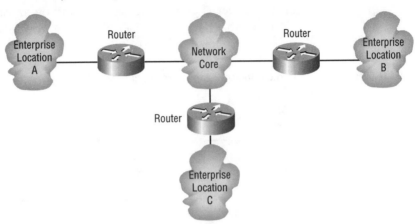

The Distribution Layer

In a pure three-tier model, the distribution layer serves as the campus backbone. For the exam, you should think of the core as being a WAN service that interconnects all of the sites to each other.

The distribution layer thus becomes a point in the network where policy and segregation may be implemented. Typically, the distribution layer assumes the form of a campus backbone or MAN. Access lists and other security functions are ideally placed in the distribution layer, and network advertisements and other workgroup functions are ideally contained in this layer as well.

Throughout this chapter the distribution and access layers are noted to be acceptable locations for access lists. This placement depends on the function of the list in question and the reduction in processing or administration that the placement will cause. Generally access lists are not included in the core layer, as historically this placement has impacted router performance substantially. The goal is to limit the number of lists required in the network and to keep them close to the edge, which encourages access-layer placement. However, given the choice of implementing 50 access-layer lists or two distribution-layer lists-all things being equal-most administrators would opt for fewer update points. Performance issues for ACLs are nowhere as significant as they once were, so this concern, especially with advanced routing such as NetFlow or multilayer switching, is substantially reduced.

For the purposes of the CID exam, the proper placement of access lists is the access layer. For production networks, it is acceptable, and sometimes desirable, to place them in the distribution layer. For the CCNA/CCDA small-to-medium business examination, the proper placement of the access lists is always the distribution layer, which is different than the CID recommendation.

For example, it would be appropriate for a SAP (Service Advertising Protocol) filter to block Novell announcements of printer services at the distribution layer because it is unlikely that users outside of the distribution layer would need access to them. The textbook answer, however, is to place access lists at the access layer of the model.

Route summarization and the logical organization of resources are also well aligned with the distribution layer. A strong design would encompass some logical method of summarizing the routes in the distribution layer. Figure 1.10 displays the IP (Internet Protocol) addressing and DNS (Domain Name Service) names for two distribution layers attached to the core. Note how 10.11.0.0/16 and 10.12.0.0/16 are divided at each router. Thus, routing tables in the core need only focus on one route, as opposed to the numerous routes that might be incorporated into the distribution area. In the same manner, the DNS subdomains are aligned with each distribution layer, which, along with IP addressing standards, will greatly augment the efficiency of the troubleshooting process. Troubleshooting is simplified when administrators can quickly identify the location and scope of a network outage—a benefit of addressing standards. In addition, route summarization, a concept presented in Chapter 4, can help avoid recalculations of the routing table that might lead to problems on lower-end routers.

The final advantage of using this distribution layer design in the three-tier model is that it will greatly simplify OSPF configurations. The network core becomes a natural area 0, while each distribution router becomes an area border router between area 0 and other areas.

FIGURE 1.10 The hierarchical model with addressing

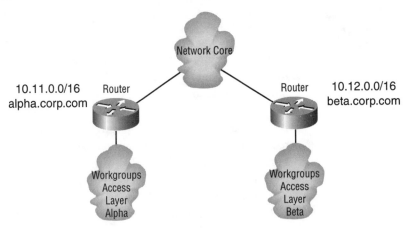

Designers should use the distribution layer with an eye toward failure scenarios as well. Ideally, each distribution layer and its attached access layers should include its own DHCP (Dynamic Host Configuration Protocol) and WINS (Windows Internet Naming Service) servers, for example. Other critical network devices, such as e-mail and file servers, are also best included in the distribution layer. This design promotes two significant benefits. First, the distribution layer can continue to function in the event of core failure or other concerns. While the core should be designed to be fault-tolerant, in reality, network changes, service failures, and other issues demand that the designer develop a contingency plan in the event of its unavailability. Second, most administrators prefer to have a number of servers for WINS and DHCP, for example. By placing these services at the distribution layer, the number of devices is kept at a fairly low number while logical divisions are established, all of which simplify administration.

The Access Layer

The network's ultimate purpose is to interconnect users, which is how the access layer completes the three-tier model. The access layer is responsible for connecting workgroups to backbones, blocking broadcasts, and grouping users based on common functions and services. Logical divisions are also maintained at the access layer. For example, dial-in services would be connected to an access layer point, thus making the users all part of a logical group. Depending on the network's overall size, it would likely be appropriate to place an authentication server for remote users at this point, although a single centrally located server may also be appropriate if fault tolerance is not required. It is helpful to think of the access layer as a leaf on a tree. Being furthest from the trunk and attached only via a branch, the path between any two access layers (leaves) is almost always the longest. The access layer is also the primary location for access lists and other security implementations. However, as noted previously, this is a textbook answer. Many designers use the distribution layer as an aggregation point for security implementations.

Guidelines for the Three-Tier Model

The three-tier model can greatly facilitate the network design process so designers should closely follow the guidelines. Failure to do so may result in a suboptimal design. There may be good cause to waver from these guidelines, but doing so is not recommended and usually will cause additional compromises. The main reason these rules are broken is for financial considerations.

Interconnect Layers via the Layer Just Above

There will be a great temptation to connect two access layers directly in order to address a change in the network. Figure 1.11 illustrates this implementation with the bold line between Routers A and B.

There are many arguments in favor of this approach, although all of them are in error. The contention will be made that the interconnection will reduce hop count, latency, cost, and other factors. However, in reality, connecting the two access groups will eliminate the benefits of the three-tier model and will ultimately cost more, which is something most designers try to avoid. Most of the hop count and other concerns are moot in modern networks, and if they are legitimate issues, the designer should address those problems before deploying a work-around. Connecting access layers, or distribution layers, without using the core complicates troubleshooting, routing, economies of scale, redundancy, and a host of other factors. It can be done, and the arguments may be quite persuasive, but avoid doing it.

FIGURE 1.11 Interconnection of access layers

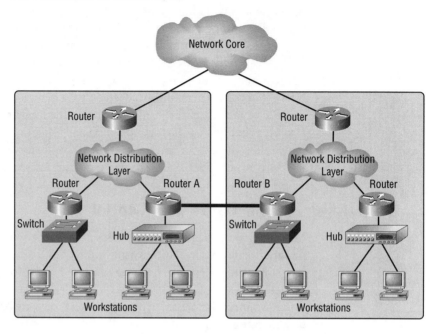

Connect End Stations to Access Layers

Ideally, the backbone should be reserved for controlled data flow. This includes making as few changes as possible in the core and, to a lesser degree, the distribution layer. While an exception might be made for a global service, such as DHCP, it is usually best to keep the core and distribution layers as clean as possible. Reliability, traffic management, capacity planning, and troubleshooting are all augmented by this policy.

Design around the 80/20 Rule When Possible

Historically, networks were designed around the 80/20 rule, which states that 80 percent of the traffic should remain in the local segment and the remaining 20 percent could leave. This was primarily due to the limitations of routers.

Today, the 80/20 rule remains valid, but the designer will need to factor cost, security, and other considerations into this decision. New features, including route once/switch many technologies and server farms have altered the 80/20 rule in many designs. The Internet and other remote services have also impacted these criteria. While it is preferable to keep traffic locally bound, in modern networks it is much more difficult to do so, and the benefits are not as great as before.

While the 80/20 rule does remain a good guideline, it is important to note that most modern networks are confronted with traffic models that follow the corollary of the 80/20 rule. The 20/80 rule acknowledges that 80 percent of the traffic is off the local subnet in most modern networks. This is the result of centralized server farms, database servers, and the Internet. Designers should keep this fact in mind when designing the network—some installations are already bordering on a 5/95 ratio. It is conceivable that less than five percent of the traffic will remain on the local subnet in the near term as bandwidth availability increases.

Network Design in the Real World: Outsourcing

In 1998 and 1999, the networking industry saw an explosion of outsourcing efforts to move responsibility for the data center away from the enterprise. The intent was to reduce costs and allow the organization to focus on their core business. While some of these efforts were less than successful, there is little doubt that contracting and outsourcing will remain acceptable strategies for many companies.

The need for high-speed connections is one consequence of off-site data centers. A number of companies place their file servers in a remote, outsourced location, moving all of their data away from the user community. It is likely that this trend, should it continue, will take data off not only the user subnet (the origin of the 80/20 rule), but the local campus network as well.

Make Each Layer Represent a Layer 3 Boundary

This is possibly one of the easier guidelines to understand, as routers are included at each layer in the model and these routers divide Layer 3 boundaries. Therefore, this rule takes on a default status. It also relates to the policy of not linking various layers without using the layer just above in that switches (Layer 2 devices) should not be used to interconnect access layer groups. Later in this text the issues of spanning tree and Layer 3 designs will be presented—they relate well to this policy.

Note that this guideline also incorporates a separation of the broadcast and collision domains. Network design model layers cannot be isolated by only collision domains—a function of Layer 2 devices, including bridges and switches. The layers must also be isolated via routers, which define the borders of the broadcast domain.

Implement Features at the Appropriate Layer

This guideline is one of the most difficult to enforce, yet it is one of the most important. Included in this policy is the recommendation that access lists remain outside of the core layer. While Cisco has greatly improved the performance of their router products, access lists and other services still impose a substantial burden on resources (depending on router type and features). By keeping these functions at a deeper layer of the model, the designer should be able to maintain performance for the majority of packets. Each design will require some interpretation of this guideline—there clearly may be exceptions where a feature must be deployed at a specific point in the network.

Network Design Issues

All good network designs will address at least one of the following questions. Excellent designs will answer all of them:

- What problem are we trying to solve?
- What future needs do we anticipate?
- What is the projected lifespan of this network?

What Problem?

New networks are typically deployed to solve a business problem. Since there is no legacy network, there are few issues regarding the existing infrastructure to address. Existing networks confronted by a potential upgrade are typically designed to resolve at least one of the problems discussed below, under "Considerations of Network Design."

Future Needs?

It is unlikely that anyone with the ability to accurately predict the future would use such ability to design networks. Ignorance is a likely enemy of efforts to add longevity to the network design. An assessment of future needs will incorporate a number of areas that will help augment the lifespan of the network, but success is frequently found in "gut feelings" and overspending.

Network Lifespan?

Many would classify this topic as part of the future needs assessment; however, it should be viewed as a separate component. The lifespan of the network should also not be viewed in terms of a single span of time. For example, copper and fiber installations should be planned with at least a 10-year horizon, whereas network core devices that remain static for more than 36 months are rare. Given these variations, it is important to balance the costs of each network component with the likelihood that it will be replaced quickly. Building in expandability and upgradability will affect the lifespan of a network installed today. Designers should always consider how they might expand their designs to accommodate additional users or services before committing to a strategy.

Considerations of Network Design

The network design considerations addressed in this section are the solutions to the network design issues addressed earlier. For example, the first network design consideration below addresses excessive broadcasts. The designer will need to understand the concept of broadcasts in the network, how they are impacting the existing network, how they may increase in the future, and how broadcasts may be dealt with in the lifespan of the network.

Excessive Broadcasts

Recall that broadcasts are used in networking to dispatch a packet to all stations on the network. This may be in the form of an Address Resolution Protocol (ARP) query or a NetBIOS name query, for example. All stations will listen and accept broadcast packets for processing by an upper-layer process—the broadcast itself is a Layer 2 process.

While the broadcast packet is no larger than any other packet on the media, it is received by all stations. This results in every station halting the local process to address the packet that has been forwarded from the network interface card. This added processing is very inefficient and, for the majority of stations, unnecessary.

A general network design guideline says that 100 broadcasts per second will reduce the available CPU on a Pentium 90 processor by two percent. Note that this figure does not compare the percentage of broadcasts on the network to user data (typically unicast). While most modern networks are now using much more powerful processors and larger amounts of bandwidth per workstation, broadcasts are still an area warranting control by the network designer and administrator.

There are two methods for controlling broadcasts in the network. Routers control the broadcast domain. Thus, a router could be used to divide a single network into two smaller ones. This would theoretically reduce the number of broadcasts per segment by 50 percent. This technique would also affect bandwidth and media contention, so it might be the correct solution. However, it's now much easier to use a router to reduce broadcasts. In reality, the total number of broadcasts will almost always increase when using two networks instead of one. This is due to the nature of the upper-layer protocols. For example, a single network could use a single Service Advertising Protocol (SAP) packet (Novell), whereas a dual network installation will require at least two. The number of broadcasts per network will decrease, but not by 50 percent.

Another method for controlling broadcasts is to remove them at the source—typically servers and, to a lesser extent, workstations. This is one aspect of network design that greatly benefits from the designer having a detailed knowledge of both protocols and operating systems. For example, Apple computer has offered an IP-based solution for its traditional Apple-Talk networks for a long time. Implementation of this service would greatly reduce the number of broadcasts in the network for a number of reasons, including the elimination of an entire protocol and AppleTalk's intensive use of broadcasts. Assuming that most workstations are also running IP for Internet connectivity, this design could easily be incorporated into the network. Removing AppleTalk provides two benefits—a reduction in background broadcasts compared with IP and in the amount of overhead demanded by the network.

Contention for the Media

Media contention is frequently associated with 10Mbps Ethernet, where a large number of stations are waiting for access to the physical layer and a large number of collisions are likely to occur. However, media contention can also occur in FDDI and Token Ring. While both of these technologies negate the possibility of collision, each station must wait for receipt of the token before transmitting. This can cause significant delays.

Historically, access to the media was controlled by installing additional router ports and hubs. Installing new routers may result in network-wide IP readdressing, which may have a large up-front cost factor. While installing these routers reduced the number of stations on the segment, it did not eliminate contention issues; rather, it reduced the impact and frequency of them. With the advent of switching technology in the network, designers were offered the opportunity to virtually eliminate contention at a low cost. Discounting buffering issues and other advanced considerations, a full-duplex connection presents no contention points. This is a marked improvement that may be implemented with no change to the user workstation (with the possible exception of a full-duplex-capable network card). Designers should consider the use of switching technologies to resolve media-contention issues.

Security

Security is one of the overlooked components of network design. Typically, the security procedures and equipment are added to the network well into the implementation phase. This usually results in a less-secure configuration that demands compromises. For example, access lists are one component of network security. Assuming a hierarchical design, if the network designers were to use bit boundaries to define security domains, a single access-list wildcard mask could be used in different areas of the network. In addition, extranet (non-internal) connections could be placed in a secure, centralized location, freeing greater bandwidth for the rest of the enterprise. This design contrasts with installations where these connections are distributed throughout the network. While centralization may lead to more significant outages, it is often easier to administer resources in a protected, central location close to the support organization.

Consider for a moment a fairly benign network design decision. A company elects to deploy an ATM WAN for a new network upgrade. The network requires some security, because the data is privileged and involves financial information. Rather than isolating extranet connections, the company decides to place these less-secure links on the same physical interface as their internal connections. While this setup can work, think about the limitations that such a design would impose on security. The designer would be unable to restrict the PVC before the circuit entered the core router, thus making the only line of defense a subinterface access list. Denial-of-service attacks and other intrusion techniques would be much more likely than if the extranet PVC were isolated from the enterprise network by a separate router and a firewall.

Having identified security as a design consideration, the designer must evaluate the role of the network in the security model. There is little question that firewalls and bastion hosts (a bastion host is a secure public presence—it may be the firewall itself or a server in the transition area between the public and private networks, also called a DMZ) are part of the network, but some schools of thought argue that the network, in and of itself, is not a security device. While there are compelling arguments to support the stance that the network is not a security solution, most designers take a simpler view of security. In practical terms, anything that can protect the data in the network—be it a lock on a door, an access list, or the use of fiber instead of copper—is part of an overall solution and should be considered in the design of the network.

Some of the tools available to the network architect are:

- Fiber links

- Firewalls

- Access lists

- Bastion hosts

- Encryption

- Authentication, including CHAP (Challenge Handshake Authentication Protocol)

- Accounting

- Secure physical media, including data rooms and cables

- Auditing tools

All available tools should be considered when formulating a design. By including them in the initial phases, appropriate budgetary and technology allocations may be made.

A complete presentation of network security and design considerations for architects is presented in Chapter 11.

Addressing

Addressing issues frequently involve the IP protocol, which uses user-defined addresses. Many networks evolved without regard to the strategic importance of the infrastructure. In addition, corporations occasionally acquire another organization, resulting in the duplication of network addresses even with careful planning. Whatever the cause, readdressing IP addresses is a significant process in the life of the network. And while DHCP, NAT, and dynamic DNS can reduce the impact, there will likely be a point where some determined effort is necessary.

Subsequent chapters will discuss the art of network readdressing; however, there are a few points that should be presented here. First, plan for connectivity to other companies and the Internet. Second, consider the impact of readdressing on the corporation's servers and workstations and have a plan in mind on how to deploy any remedial effort. Third, know the limitations of the various tools that would be used in readdressing, including the fact that NAT cannot cope with NetBIOS traffic—an important function of the Windows and OS/2 operating systems. Chapter 7 presents the NetBIOS protocol in detail. In addition, designers will need to consider the use of RFC 1918 addresses—a collection of addresses specifically reserved from appearing on the Internet. Finally, consider the impact of the classful network address and the routing protocols that you might need.

 Don't be concerned if some of the issues presented here are new. In later chapters they will be presented in greater detail.

Bandwidth

There are two schools of thought regarding bandwidth in network design. The first believes that the network is built to withstand peaks and then some. Historically, this has resulted in throwing bandwidth at poor application behavior and, ultimately, poor network performance. The second school believes in building for the average usage and allows a certain amount of degradation during peak times—the morning login, for example. As shown in Figure 1.12, the typical network experiences peaks between 8:00 and 9:00 A.M. and 1:00 and 2:00 P.M. Another peak may occur in the evening as backups and other automated processes start.

FIGURE 1.12   A typical network load curve

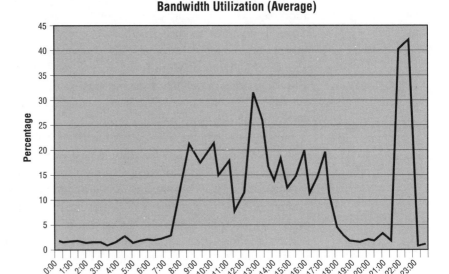

Fortunately, the two schools of thought on this subject are coming together. Designers should avoid the temptation to add bandwidth for no reason and not keep a network so close to the edge of the performance curve that it cannot handle any changes. This balance will compel programmers and server administrators to consider the far-reaching impact of poor application programming and will preserve the network budget for new services and value-added initiatives.

As a final point, careful consideration of the network backbone is critical to the health of the network. This is one area where excess bandwidth may be the perfect solution, but only if consideration is given to cost and over-head. For example, many companies jumped on the ATM LANE (LAN Emulation) platform for backbone technology in the late 1990s. While a good solution, LANE greatly adds to the cost of the network and the over-head associated with it. Gigabit Ethernet and other technologies may provide better solutions, equal or greater bandwidth, and lower cost. Of course, if voice and other services geared toward ATM are needed, the effort may be warranted.

New Payloads

Networks are frequently called upon to supply services beyond those originally anticipated. Not that long ago, video and voice over data networks (LAN systems) were costly and lacked sufficient business drivers for implementation. As the technology advances, more and more firms are exploring these services.

In addition, there may be enhancements to existing systems that greatly add to the network's burden. Consider a simple database that contains the names and addresses of a company's customers. Each record might average 2,000 characters—less than 10,000 bits, including overhead. When the database is enhanced to include digital images of the customers and their homes in addition to a transcript of their previous five calls, it is easy to see the potential impact. What was 2,000 characters may exceed 2 million, possibly resulting in millions of bits per transaction. No protocol was added to the network nor were additional users placed in the switch, but the impact would greatly tax even the best designs.

Configuration Simplification

One of the most significant costs in the network results from the move, add, and change (MAC) process. This process refers to the effort involved in installing new users onto the network or changing their installation. The MAC process also includes the relocation of users and their systems.

Various studies have been conducted to measure the true cost of MAC efforts, directly related to both the network costs and the lost productivity of the workers affected. Given that employees may earn $50 an hour on average, a half-day move of even 20 employees will cost $4,000 in lost productivity, not including the impact on non-moved workers. Add the cost of wiring, configuring, installing, and relocating workstations and other systems, and the cost jumps significantly. With the average worker moving 1.1 times per year (according to some surveys from 1997), it is easy to see how this minor cost would quickly impact the finances of the company.

To address these costs, vendors have added features to simplify and accelerate the MAC process. These may include the use of VLAN/ELAN technology (Virtual LANs/Emulated LANs) and DHCP, for example. DHCP is a dynamic method for assigning IP addresses to workstations. The designer should consider these features in any new design and use any cost savings to help offset the initial costs against the recurring costs.

Protocol Scalability

Protocol scalability refers to a protocol's ability to service increasingly larger numbers of nodes and users. As an example, IP is capable of servicing millions of users with careful planning and design. AppleTalk, in contrast, does not scale well due to the chatty nature of the protocol and its use of broadcasts and announcements to inform all devices in the network about all other resources. IPX/Novell and NetBIOS share these limitations. Keep in mind that scalable protocols are frequently routable—they contain a Layer 3 address that routers can use for logical grouping. This address further groups and segments systems for efficiency.

Business Relationships

If there is one aspect of network design that overshadows all others, it would have to be the integration of the business objective with the implementation.

Consider these scenarios for a moment. A network is designed to carry data—data that is increasingly critical to a business. In addition, this business funds the network equipment and implementation. A similar scenario may involve a small home network. In preparing for a Cisco examination, an administrator creates a small lab with the objective of passing the test. Or the home user wishes to establish a LAN for sharing a printer and some files. On a grander scale, an international corporation uses networks to exchange data with business partners and workgroups alike. In each scenario, each of these groups is choosing to spend money on a network in the hope that the initial costs will be offset by the improvements in productivity or increased sales. Business types refer to this as "opportunity cost," and network designers should use this term as well.

There are really two types of business relationships that involve network designers. The first presents itself in the form of the requester. The requester may be the administrator—perhaps a technical benefit has been identified with respect to changing routing protocols. It is more likely that the request originates with the business itself, however. Such a request might appear in the form of a need to transfer billing information to a financial clearinghouse or configuring a system to permit salespeople to access their e-mail on the road. Whatever the request, the components of implementation remain fairly consistent. Cost, compatibility, security, supportability, and scalability all enter into the equation, and each of these will impact different business units differently.

There have been many incredible network designs presented to CIOs and presidents of large corporations. Of all these designs, only a handful are actually implemented. Only those network designs that reflect an understanding of a company's business needs and objectives are worthy of implementation—at least from a textbook perspective. For example, consider a simple request for a connection to the Internet. From a technical perspective, a design using OC-48 might be just as valid as a connection using ISDN (Integrated Services Digital Network) or ADSL (Asymmetric Digital Subscriber Line). Yet few would consider placing a 100,000-person company on a single ISDN BRI (Basic Rate Interface) or purchasing a SONET ring for a small school. Designing a network without an understanding of the objective(s) is folly at best.

So, what is a business relationship and how does it fit into the design of a network or the preparation for an examination? Well, the truth is that this is a hard question to prepare for, even though network designers are confronted with this challenge each and every day. This is why such a seemingly simple topic requires so much attention.

A business relationship ideally begins before a project is conceived and involves a bit of cooperation. Many companies place an information specialist in at least one departmental meeting each week to ask questions at the same time the business challenge is addressed. This also affords the opportunity to provide as much warning as possible to the network, server, and workstation groups (assuming that they are different). The relationship may take on an informal tone—there is nothing wrong with obtaining information about the Marketing department's newest effort during the company volleyball game, as an example. The objective remains the same: to provide as much assistance to the business as early in the process as possible.

Network Design Methodology

For the designer who is approaching the task of setting up a network for the first time, it would be nice to have an overview of the tasks that are frequently required. This design methodology is presented as a very high-level overview of the design process. Figure 1.13 provides a general outline of the steps necessary for a successful network design.

FIGURE 1.13 Basic network design methodology

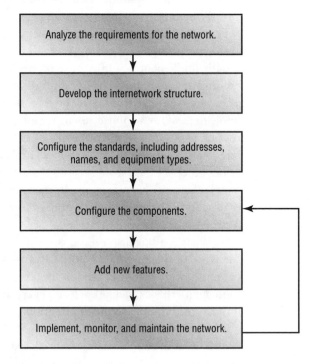

Note that Figure 1.13 is by no means comprehensive. For example, the role of facilities in obtaining power, cooling, and space has not been presented, nor has the process of locating vendors—and the roles that contracts and requests for proposals (RFPs) play in that process—been introduced. Also note that the ordering process has not been included. (This step could easily enter into the flow at any point following the requirements analysis; however, some installations may find that some components must be ordered well in advance.) This flow chart concentrates solely on the technical aspects. Keeping that in mind, let's examine each step in more detail.

1. Analyze the network requirements. The requirements analysis process should include a review of the technical (both technology and administrative) components, along with the business needs assessment.

2. Develop an internetwork structure. Composing a network structure will depend on a number of criteria. The designer will need to first determine if the installation is new or incorporates pre-existing features. It is always easier to build a new system than to add to an existing one. This chapter includes a number of models for designing networks, but for our purposes a simple three-tier model, as shown in Figure 1.14, will suffice.

FIGURE 1.14   The three-tier (hierarchal) network

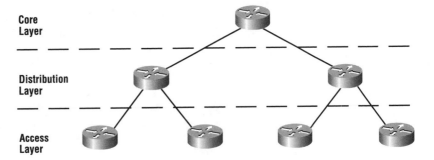

3. Configure standards. Once the topology of the network is drafted, an addressing and naming convention will need to be added. This is the phase where consideration must be given to route summarization, subnetting, security, and usability. Figure 1.15 illustrates a simple addressing and naming standard for the three-tier network structure.

FIGURE 1.15 The three-tier network with IP addressing and DNS names

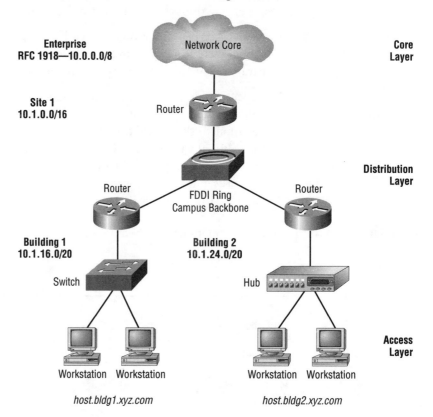

host.bldg1.xyz.com   host.bldg2.xyz.com

4. Configure components. This phase presumes that hardware and software have already been selected. For the project to move forward, an order would need to be placed at this phase. The selection and configuration of components should include cabling, backbone, vertical and horizontal wiring, routers, switches, DSU/CSUs (data service units/ channel service units), remote-access services, ISP/Internet providers, and private WAN telecommunication vendors.

5. Add new features. The flow chart classifies this fifth step as adding new features. This is a bit misleading, as it could include the addition of an entirely new network or of a single protocol. Additional services, including access lists and advanced features, could also be included.

6. Implement, monitor, and maintain the network. The final step is really a recurrent phase of the network design process. Whether the network is completely new or simply modified, a required step in the project is a review of the initial design requirements, a review of the health of the network, and general administration. Only by reviewing the project (including the nontechnical portions) can a team gain valuable information that will eventually simplify the next effort and identify future needs for the current project.

Designing with a Client

Let's walk through a simple network design process. Do not be concerned if you are unfamiliar with the specific technologies noted in this scenario—the actual details are unimportant. However, a good designer should always have a list of technologies to research and learn, and you may wish to add the unfamiliar components to your list.

The Sales department has requested a DSL-based solution for their team. One of the senior sales executives has read articles touting the benefits of DSL, which has led to this request. Users will want access to corporate data and the Internet at high speeds. In addition, users may be at home, at a client's site, or in a hotel. The budget for the project is undefined; however, you are told that there will be funding for whatever it takes.

Stop for a moment and consider the different factors and issues associated with this request. List some of the questions that should be answered.

Here is a short list of preliminary questions:

- How much data will actually be transferred?

- Does the data require security/encryption?

- How often will the user be at home? At a client's site? At a hotel?

- What protocols are to be used?

- How many users will there be?

Note that some of these questions will not have an answer, or the answer will be vague.

The designer will have to make some interesting decisions at this point. The requirement for high-speed access from client sites and hotels is one issue. DSL requires a pre-installed connection. It is not widely available, unlike POTS (plain old telephone service), and is either configured as private (similar to Frame Relay in which companies share switches and other components, while PVCs keep traffic isolated) or public, which usually connects to an ISP and the Internet. An immediate red flag would be the lack of DSL availability in remote locations. Note that the request specified DSL. Why? Is it because the technology is needed or because it is perceived as newer, better, and faster?

Depending on the answers, it may still make sense to use DSL for the home. However, the design will still fail to address the hotel and customer sites. Perhaps a VPN (Virtual Private Network) solution with POTS, ISDN, and DSL technologies would work. This solution may include outsourcing or partnering with an ISP (Internet Service Provider) in order to implement the design. Note that at no point in the process have routing protocols, hardware components, support, or actual costs been discussed. These factors should be considered once the objectives for the project have been defined.

Network Design in the Real World: Nontechnical Solutions

Network designers should not be afraid to suggest nontechnical solutions in response to requests. For example, consider a request to install a Frame Relay T1 for a connection to another company. There will be a large data transfer every month of approximately 100Mb. The data is not time sensitive, and no additional data is anticipated (i.e., neither the frequency of the data nor the volume of data is expected to increase.)

This problem begs a nontechnical solution, especially since the costs for a technical solution, even for Frame Relay, would be very high. As a variation on SneakerNet, why not propose FedExNet? (SneakerNet was one of the most popular network technologies ever used—users simply walked floppies and files to recipients.) It is important to consider the alternatives—in this case the requirements did not mandate a technical solution, just a solution. A CD-ROM or tape would easily contain the data, and, at current tariffs, the cost would be less than 1/20th the technical solution. It may not appear as glamorous, but it is secure and reliable. Note these last two points when considering an Internet-based solution, which would also be cheaper than private Frame Relay.

This chapter has already touched upon cost as a significant factor in network design, and the majority of these costs are associated with the telecommunications tariff. The tariff is the billing agreement used, and, like home phone service, most providers charge a higher tariff for long-distance and international calls than they do for local ones. Designers should always consider the distance sensitivity and costs associated with their solutions— Frame Relay is typically cheaper than a leased line, for example.

References and Other Sources

Rather than list a number of references in this section, the authors have decided to provide in Appendix C a listing of reference materials, RFCs (requests for comments), and books to augment the development of network design skills. However, even the material placed in Appendix C will quickly become dated. Therefore, it is recommended that readers use the appendix as a preliminary reference point and then continue on with research at the local library or bookstore or on the Internet.

Readers will find the following types of information in Appendix C.

- Development group Web sites
- Employment search Web sites
- Vendor Web sites
- Relevant RFC numbers

Summary

This chapter presented a great deal of material regarding the theories and models used in network design. This information will serve as the foundation for later chapters, which will introduce more technical material. While later chapters will focus less attention on the business relationships, always keep the importance of these nontechnical factors in mind when considering technical solutions.

Having completed this chapter, readers should:

- Understand that technology is only one portion of the network design process.

- Be able to describe the benefits of the three-tier model.

- Know the definitions of scalability and adaptability.

- Realize that costs in network design have different meanings and impacts on the business.

- Understand that most good network designs are a collaborative effort.

- Know the primary network design issues:

    - What is the problem?

    - What future needs are anticipated?

    - What is the network's projected lifespan?

- Be familiar with the considerations of a network design, including those listed below:

    - Excessive broadcasts

    - Media contention

    - Security

    - Addressing

    - Bandwidth

    - New payloads

    - Configuration simplification

- Protocol scalability
- Business relationships
- Know the network design methodology.
- Be able to define the role of each layer of the three-tier model.
- Understand the limitations of the three-tier model.

Review Questions

1. A small, four-location network might use which of the following network designs?

    A. A star topology

    B. A ring topology

    C. A full-mesh topology

    D. A star/mesh topology

    E. A mesh/ring topology

2. Which of the following are considerations of a good network design?

    A. Security

    B. Control of broadcasts

    C. Bandwidth

    D. Media contention

    E. All of the above

3. Place the following in chronological order:

    A. Develop an internetwork structure

    B. Analyze the network requirements

    C. Add new features

    D. Implement, monitor, and maintain the network

    E. Configure standards

4. Why do network designers use the three-tier model?

    A. It lends itself to scalable network designs.

    B. It costs less to implement three-tier networks.

    C. Without three tiers, networks cannot be secured.

    D. Business considerations are impossible to integrate without three tiers.

5. Which of the following are types of costs?

   A. Recurring

   B. Episodic

   C. Initial

   D. Dollar-cost-averaged

6. The network core is designed to:

   A. Provide a single point of failure.

   B. Provide a central, reliable, and secure area for the transfer of packets from one region to another.

   C. Use Layer 2 technology only.

   D. Use Layer 3 technology only.

7. Access lists should not be included in:

   A. The core.

   B. The distribution layer.

   C. The access layer.

   D. All of the above.

8. When designing DNS domains, which layer lends itself to being the root?

   A. The core

   B. The distribution layer

   C. The access layer

   D. DNS domains do not map to network layers.

9. Which of the following pieces of information would be important to a network designer at the beginning of the project?

   A. The number of users who will use the network

   B. The amount of data to be transferred and the types of applications that will be involved

   C. The budget for the project

   D. The expected lifespan of the network

   E. All of the above

10. To implement a full-mesh Frame Relay network for seven locations, the designer would need how many PVCs?

    A. 7

    B. 6

    C. 49

    D. 21

11. A designer is specifically addressing a high percentage of broadcasts as a problem in the network. Which of the following would serve as a solution to this problem?

    A. Switching

    B. Bridging

    C. Routing

    D. Removal of EIGRP

12. An audit of the network indicates that bandwidth utilization is high on a number of segments. The designer might use which of the following to resolve the problem?

    A. Switching

    B. Increase in bandwidth

    C. Reduction in the number of workstations per segment

    D. All of the above

13. Access lists might be found at which of the following three-tier model layers?

    A. The core layer

    B. The distribution layer

    C. The access layer

    D. The extranet layer

14. The 80/20 rule states which of the following?

    A. That 80 percent of the traffic should leave the local subnet.

    B. That 20 percent of the traffic should be in the form of broadcasts.

    C. That 20 percent of the traffic should remain local.

    D. That 20 percent of the traffic should leave the local subnet.

15. Which of the following would not be included as a good network design criteria?

    A. Low cost

    B. Adaptiveness

    C. VLSM

    D. Scalablility

16. The network design strives to simplify the move-add-change (MAC) process. Thus, the designer should consider which of the following?

    A. DHCP

    B. Dynamic VLANs

    C. EIGRP

    D. OSPF

17. Which of the following is the most common trade-off in network design?

   A. Size versus features

   B. Features versus redundancy

   C. Cost versus availability

   D. Future capabilities versus scalability

18. Please rate the following designs based on their inherent redundancy.

   A. Full mesh

   B. Partial mesh

   C. Hierarchical

   D. Star

19. Hierarchical networks do NOT include which of the following?

   A. Three tiers divided with Layer 3 devices

   B. Enhanced scalability

   C. Easier troubleshooting

   D. Fewest hops between end points

20. Based on the model and network characteristics specified in each answer, which would use the greatest number of circuits?

   A. Using the mesh model, the network is fully meshed and contains seven sites and a total of seven routers.

   B. Using the hierarchical model, there are two access layers per distribution layer with two distribution layer routers and one core and a total of seven routers.

   C. Using a ring topology, the network contains seven sites and a total of seven routers.

   D. Using a star (hub-and-spoke) topology, the network contains seven sites and a total of seven routers.

Answers to Review Questions

1. A, B, C.

2. E.

3. B, A, E, C, D.

4. A.

5. A, C.

   While expenses may appear suddenly, a good design and budget should plan for these as recurring costs.

6. B.

7. A.

   The core should be used only for the rapid transfer of data.

8. A.

   This question requires a bit of thought, and it is unlikely that it would appear on the exam. The context is that upper layers often can relate to lower layers. While the entire DNS domain could be in all points in the three-tier model, it is likely that the design would break these into subdomains at the distribution tier.

9. E.

10. D.

11. C.

    Designers should also consider server and workstation tuning as possible solutions. Recall that Layer 2 does not divide the broadcast domain.

12. D.

13. C.

14. D.

15. C.

VLSM is typically part of a good network design, but it is not a criteria for a design.

16. A, B.

17. C.

Cost is always a limiting factor for the network designer.

18. A, B, C, D.

19. D.

A simple hierarchical design would incorporate at least four hops between access layers. A full mesh might keep this number down to one.

20. A.

The math works as follows: A=21, B=6, C=7, and D=6.

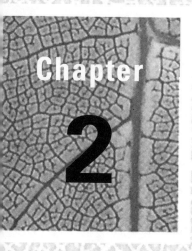

Chapter 2

Network Design Technologies

CISCO INTERNETWORK DESIGN EXAM OBJECTIVES COVERED IN THIS CHAPTER:

- ✓ List common reasons that customers invest in a campus LAN design project.

- ✓ Examine statements made by a client and distinguish the relevant issues that will affect the choice of campus LAN design solutions.

- ✓ Define switches, virtual LANs, and LAN emulation.

- ✓ Examine a client's requirements and construct an appropriate switched campus LAN solution.

- ✓ Define routing functions and benefits.

- ✓ Examine a client's requirements and construct an appropriate campus LAN design solution that includes switches and routers.

- ✓ Examine a client's requirements and construct an appropriate ATM design solution.

- ✓ Construct designs using ATM technology for high-performance workgroups and high-performance backbones.

- ✓ Upgrade internetwork designs as the role of ATM evolves.

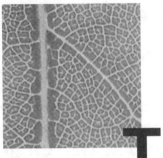

The first chapter of this book focused on the many nontechnical facets of network design. This chapter will depart from the nontechnical components and begin to develop the technical components.

The technical components of networking include many different elements. All of these elements require consideration by the network designer in virtually every design. Decisions made in one area can quickly force compromises in another area that may not be fully anticipated. While a full explanation of some of the common issues is beyond the scope of this text (and the exam), the text will take some steps to identify and address these issues.

The network design technologies include the components of the first three OSI model layers. Repeaters, hubs, switches, and routers all work in different ways to integrate within the infrastructure. Designers must understand the differences between these devices and their functions. They must also consider newer technologies and more complex systems. These may include ATM, ATM LANE, FastEtherChannel (FEC), GigEtherChannel (GEC), and VLAN (virtual LAN) trunking. Some vendors are beginning to deploy Layer 5 switching technology—a development that may alter design models in future years.

Network Technologies in Local Area Networks

As defined in Chapter 1, most networks are deployed to meet the needs of the business. Businesses that invest in campus LAN projects typically benefit from the collaborative advantages that result from these expenditures. Reduced costs also promote the deployment of a LAN—imagine if companies bought stand-alone printers for each desktop, for example. The net result would be substantial added expense and a single tactical solution that could not resolve subsequent issues.

At times it seems as if the technology that drives networks is constantly changing. However, it might be simpler to think of the process as more evolutionary. For example, switches are simply an extension from bridges and other technologies to their predecessors.

The importance of understanding the customer needs was presented in Chapter 1, along with a number of high-level criteria for integrating the business needs with the network design. The designer will need to take these criteria and apply technology appropriate to both the current requirements and to a logical growth path that works to preserve the investment.

In the first presentations of network design using switches, vendors advocated the transport of VLANs across the backbone. Recall that VLANs, or virtual LANs, are logical groupings of the broadcast domain. The logic was that workgroups could be physically isolated while retaining the benefits of operating at Layer 2. This design was primarily based on the fact that routers, or any Layer 3 processing, would be slower than switching packets from end to end. Given the evolution of the technologies, vendors now advocate the sole use of Layer 3 processing in the core.

Before dismissing the use of Layer 2 in the core, consider both the positives and negatives of such use. Layer 2 provides a secure environment wherein all traffic is local. Connections between nodes require neither processing by a router nor the conversions that are performed in routing. The number of router interfaces can be lower and the configuration of the network is simplified. All of these benefits gave administrators cause to pursue the design model in the mid-1990s.

However, as the technology advanced and Layer 3 processing moved closer to wire speeds, it became less advantageous from a performance perspective to avoid routers. The benefits of broadcast control and geographic isolation became more attractive to designers, and while it could still cost more to create additional VLANs, integration of Layer 3 into the switching fabric eroded this disadvantage as well.

Within the context of the current exam, switches are purely Layer 2 devices, and the integration of routing and other technologies is out of scope unless explicitly referenced.

Designers should also consider business needs when evaluating technologies and the subsequent changes in direction that occur. While vendors profit substantially from the purchase of new equipment, the business may not share in the benefits from the upgrade. The corporation is interested in reliable economic growth, and the network is typically the mechanism by which business is performed—it rarely is the business itself. Consider this in a different perspective. Corporation X makes hockey sticks. It doesn't matter whether the network is using EIGRP on FastEthernet with HSRP (Hot Standby Router Protocol). It does matter whether the network operates during the two shifts that manufacture the product and during the end-of-month financial reports. Upgrading to ATM may sound desirable, but if the network is stable on Ethernet and isn't growing, upgrading is unlikely to garner a return on investment.

In the same context, the designer should focus on the specific problem at hand and work to resolve it within any existing constraints. With new designs, it becomes more important to anticipate potential problems, which is the mark of an excellent designer. Cisco categorizes network problems into three specific areas: media, protocols, and transport. While these parameters may be oversimplified, they should help novice designers identify and resolve the issues that will confront them.

Media The media category relates to problems with available bandwidth. Typically, this refers to too high a demand on the network as opposed to a problem with the media itself. Designers would likely use switches and segmentation to address this category of problem, although links of greater bandwidth would also be practical.

Protocols Protocol issues include scalability problems. Many of the chapters in this text will discuss the problems with certain protocols due to their use of broadcasts. This usage may lead to congestion and performance problems, which would not be resolved with media modifications per se. Protocol issues are typically resolved with migrations to the Internet Protocol (IP), although some tuning within the original protocol can provide relief as well. IP is suggested primarily because of current trends in the market and advances that have increased its scalability.

Transport Transport problems typically involve the introduction of voice and video services in the network. These services require more consistent latency than traditional data services. As a result, transport problems are typically resolved with recent Ethernet QoS (quality of service) enhancements or ATM switches. Transport issues may seem similar to media problems, but there is a difference. The transport category incorporates new time-sensitive services, whereas the media category is targeted more toward increased demand.

LAN Technologies

In modern network design, there are five common technologies, as enumerated below. Each provides unique benefits and shortcomings in terms of scalability and cost. However, many corporations also consider user familiarity and supportability along with these factors.

Ethernet Includes FastEthernet, GigabitEthernet, and enhancements still under development to increase theoretical bandwidth. Ethernet is the most frequently deployed networking technology. Many network designs have included switched-to-the-desktop Ethernet, which increases available bandwidth without requiring a change at the workstation.

Token Ring Token Ring is a very powerful networking technology that was frequently deployed in large financial institutions that started with mainframe systems. However, it never met with the success of Ethernet—primarily because of the expense involved. Token Ring adapters were always significantly more expensive than Ethernet NICs (network interface cards), and many firms based their decisions on financial considerations. In later years, Ethernet was enhanced to FastEthernet and switching was added. This overcame many of Token Ring's positive attributes and placed it at a significant disadvantage in terms of performance (16MB early-release Token Ring versus 100MB full-duplex Ethernet).

FDDI Fiber Distributed Data Interface and its copper equivalent, CDDI, were very popular for campus backbones and high-speed server connections. Cost has prevented FDDI from migrating to the desktop, and advances in Ethernet technology have eroded a significant portion of the FDDI market share.

ATM Asynchronous Transfer Mode was the technology to kill all other technologies. It is listed here as ATM, as opposed to ATM LANE, discussed below. In this context it is not considered a LAN technology, but ATM is frequently considered along with ATM LANE in LAN designs. There is no question that ATM will expand as a powerful tool in wide area network design and that many companies will first accomplish the integration of voice, video, and data using this technology. However, vendors are beginning to map IP and other transports directly onto fiber—especially using the dense wavelength division multiplexing (DWDM) that has matured in the past few years. This technology may ultimately remove ATM from the landscape. Note that some large campus installations use ATM to replace FDDI rings—a design that does not include LANE.

ATM LANE LAN Emulation on ATM is listed separately from ATM because the two serve different functions. ATM LANE was designed to work with legacy LAN technologies while providing a migration path to desktop ATM. Thus far, most companies have used the technology in small deployments. These organizations have selected Ethernet-based technologies for enhanced services—a move that ultimately saves money. ATM LANE requires new equipment, training, support tools, and still-emerging standards that may not be sufficient to offset the benefits that are included with the technology. Quality of service and integration with video and voice were powerful motivators for companies to install ATM and ATM LANE, but the market has since moved many of these services to Ethernet.

Local Area Networks

Local area networks are found in the access layer of the hierarchical model. This coincides with their role of servicing user populations. Figure 2.1 illustrates the hierarchical model's relationship to the local area network. Note that this design is not redundant.

FIGURE 2.1 The hierarchical model and local area networks

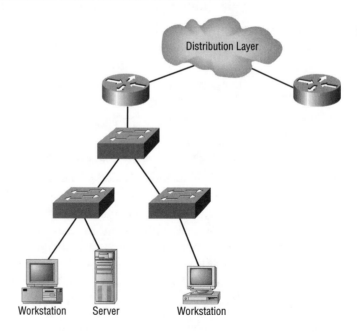

Designers require a number of components in the design and administration of the LAN. These include cabling, routers, and concentrators (hubs or switches).

Within this text, routers are considered to be the only Layer 3 devices, while switches operate at Layer 2. This is consistent with the current exam objectives; however, modern switching products now address Layers 3 and 4, while development is in progress to expand awareness to Layer 5. This will improve caching and QoS functionality. Some consider these new switches to be little more than marketing hype, but there is little doubt that increased knowledge regarding the content of data will augment security and prioritization of flows. This text will not enter the debate of switch versus router—it will simply define switching as a Layer 2 function and routing as a Layer 3 function. Note that some hierarchical models use Layer 2 switches as the access layer, with the first router at the distribution layer.

Cabling

Designers often ignore cabling in the network design process, although up to 70 percent of network problems can be attributed to cabling issues. Responsibility for infrastructure is left to facilities staff or other organizations, especially within large corporations. This is certainly not the best methodology for effective network deployments. The cable plant is the single most important factor in the proper maintenance of the network and, as noted in Chapter 1, the cable plant has the longest life cycle of any network component.

Most LAN infrastructures continue to use copper-based cable for the desktop and fiber for riser distribution. Placing fiber at the desktop is slowly becoming popular, and with the introduction of RJ-45-style (MT-RJ) connectors, the space required for these installations is not an issue. Designers should be familiar with the certified maximum distances that are permitted for the various media. The specifications incorporated into the physical media standard for each protocol virtually guarantee successful connectivity. While such values are more than rules of thumb, they are easy to incorporate into network designs and insulate the designer from having to understand the detailed electrical criteria involved in twisted-pair wiring and fiber optics. Table 2.1 notes the physical media distance limitations.

TABLE 2.1 Physical Media Distance Limitations

Media/Protocol	Distance
CDDI (CAT 5)	100 meters
FDDI (MM)	2,000 meters
FDDI (SM)	30,000 meters
ATM LANE (OC-3 MM)	2,000 meters
ATM LANE (OC-3 SM)	10,000 meters
Token Ring (UTP, 16 MB)	200 meters
Ethernet (CAT 3 or 5)	100 meters
Ethernet (MM)	2,000 meters
FastEthernet (CAT 5)	100 meters
FastEthernet (MM Full)	2,000 meters
FastEthernet (MM Half)	400 meters
FastEthernet (SM Full)	10,000 meters

FastEthernet and GigabitEthernet modules are available to span distances over 55 miles.

Cabling design considerations also include terminations and installation. For example, fiber connectors use SC, ST, FC, and other termination types. The choice will impact patch cables, future hardware purchases, and rack space—some connectors may be installed with greater density. For example, MT-RJ is similar to RJ-45 in scale, which requires half the space of ST, FC, or SC connectors.

The installation of the cables will also be an important factor and will affect future modifications to the cable plant and troubleshooting. Some companies require a "home run" from the panel to the station. This type of installation uses a single, continuous wire. In contrast, other organizations install riser cable that terminates to a frame in the closet. These terminations cross-connect to the stations. This type of installation is often cheaper and permits additional flexibility. In either configuration, punch-down work and other maintenance should occur at a single point whenever possible. It is also extremely important to document what is installed.

Professional cable installers should be used whenever possible. A good cable installer will have both the equipment and training required to adhere to the standards and to properly install and dress the cables. A good cable installation should be capable of service for up to 15 years and is a significant expense.

Network Design in the Real World: Cabling

A recent trend in data installations is to use Category 5E, 6, or 7 copper wire to the desktop. These installations operate on the premise that the greater electrical characteristics of this wire will provide a future-proof migration path as newer technologies and greater bandwidths to the desktop become commonplace. Given the upcoming 10Gbps Ethernet standard and the resulting 1000-fold increase in theoretical bandwidth (2000-fold with full-duplex technology), it is clear that higher capacity links to the desktop will be in networking's future.

On the other hand, fiber proponents will be quick to point out the advantages of augmenting copper installations with glass or forgoing copper altogether. Today, this method still adds a significant premium to the installation and material costs, but it may yield a less-expensive solution in the long term.

At this point, it is too difficult to provide a long-term recommendation—each installation is different and each company unique. Factors to consider include current applications and services, a lease versus ownership of the facility, and the company's budget.

One recommendation that is easily made, however, is that you personally interview all cable installers before hiring them. Make sure that a foreman is assigned to your project, in addition to a project manager. Ask for referrals and check them. Also, look for certifications—not only because they are required (by law or insurance policy), but also because they help to ensure a consistent installation.

Also, make certain that you have a qualified person review the installation before you sign off on it. That person should look for kinks in the cable that have been straightened, improper labeling, poor or missing documentation, compressed bundles (use Velcro tie-wraps, not nylon), and untwisted terminations. It does little good to buy Category 7 cable and find that the installer left an inch of space between the panel and the twists.

As previously noted, cable problems can be some of the most difficult to troubleshoot. While equipment and installations have improved, this caveat still holds true.

Routers

Routers are perhaps the most significant tool in the network designer's repertoire of dealing with broadcasts in the enterprise. As noted in Chapter 1, it would be ideal to reduce the number of broadcasts in the network at the source, but this is not an option under most circumstances.

Unlike Layer 2 devices, routers block broadcasts from leaving the network segment. In other words, routers define the broadcast domain. This is an important consideration, as few protocols will scale beyond 200 nodes per broadcast domain—thus, routers are usually needed in inefficient multiprotocol networks of over 200 nodes.

There are other benefits to routers as well. Routers convert between different media—for example, FDDI and Ethernet. The Catalyst switch (along with most other multiprotocol switches on the market) will also perform this function, but many designers still consider the use of a router to be superior when performing a media conversion. Routers also impose a logical structure on the network, which is frequently necessary when designing large environments. Lastly, routers are very useful for implementing policies regarding access. Access control lists (ACLs) may be used to block access to certain devices in the network or to filter informational packets regarding services (an IPX SAP access list, for example).

While the performance of routers has improved significantly in the past few years, any device at Layer 3 must perform additional processing on each packet in order to function. Therefore, the downside of routers is usually their latency and packets-per-second (PPS) performance. Newer routing technologies use network data-flow-based switching and other techniques to route only the first packets and then switch the remainder of the flow.

Network Design in the Real World: Routers

During the late 1990s, router technology changed substantially. This advancement is best seen in the Catalyst 6500 series (with the Multilayer Switch Feature Card), Catalyst 8500 series switches, and the 12000 GSR series router products from Cisco.

Each of these Layer 3 devices departs from the traditional bus technologies found in the 7500 series routers (which are still mainstream core products) and uses forms of a non-blocking "switch" fabric between the line cards. In addition, the 12000 GSR (Giga Switch Router) provides some insight into the future of network routing—all traffic on the backplane is converted into cells and each line card maintains its own processor and routing table. (Note that these cells are not ATM cells). The 12000 product is intended to terminate OC-12 and OC-48 connections in the core—predominately in ISP (Internet Service Provider) installations. However, it wasn't that long ago that ISPs were the only ones using BGP. Today, more and more large companies are moving to the Internet design model for their *private* networks. Predictably, the GSR and routers developed from this technology will find their way into the data center.

Bridges and Switches

Switches build upon the same technology as bridges, but during their evolution switches have added features to their offerings. In addition, switches frequently operate at "wire speed," i.e., any amount of data entering the port will be processed and forwarded without the need to discard the frame. This is a substantial improvement from the first generation of bridges, in which a burst of frames could quickly saturate the buffers.

One of the keys to obtaining performance from a switch is the proper design of the network. Resources, or those devices that service many users, should be provided with the fastest ports available on the switch. Stated another way, it would be poor design to put a file server on a 10MB interface servicing 100MB workstations. The greatest bandwidth should always be allocated to servers and trunk links.

Technically, switches are defined within Layer 2 of the OSI model, and Cisco continues to use this definition. However, as noted in the previous section, modern switches are greatly expanding upon the definition of their original role. For the purposes of this discussion, switches forward frames based only on the MAC layer address.

Switches are also responsible for maintaining VLAN information and may isolate ports based on the end-station MAC address, its Layer 3 address (although forwarding decisions are still based at Layer 2), or the physical port itself.

Most switches operate in one of two forwarding modes. Cut-through switches forward frames as soon as the destination address is seen. No CRC (cyclical redundancy check) is performed, and latency is consistent regardless of frame size. This configuration can permit the forwarding of corrupted frames. The second forwarding mode is called store-and-forward. The entire frame is read into memory, and the CRC is performed before the switch forwards the frame. This prevents corrupted frames from being forwarded, but latency is variable and greater than with cut-through switching.

Although switches are defined in the main text, designers should consider the "real-world" state of the technology. Layer 3 switching routers are capable of handling basic LAN-based Layer 3 functions, including routing and media conversion. Newer switching products are adding Layers 4 and 5 to their forwarding and processing lookups. This high-speed LAN-optimized routing technology is particularly important when considering load-balancing and queuing, because additional information regarding the packet flow can greatly increase the efficiency of the overall network capacity.

Summary of Routing and Switching

This overview of the LAN technologies provides the designer additional information about routing and switching technologies. This information is crucial to understanding the methods for designing scalable networks. Designers should consider the differences in broadcast and collision control and should also take note of loop prevention.

Hubs and repeaters   Hubs and repeaters work at Layer 1 of the OSI reference model. No filtering or blocking occurs, and they are used to extend cable length.

Bridges and switches   Bridges and switches limit the collision domain but not the broadcast domain. Bridges and switches control loops with the Spanning-Tree Protocol (STP). Switches are considered high-speed, multiport transparent bridges, with advanced features. These advanced features include broadcast suppression and VLAN trunking. Bridges and switches both operate at Layer 2 (the MAC layer). Switches also incorporate bandwidth flexibility—for example, a LAN using a hub shares all bandwidth among the stations. Thus, 10 stations must contend for a single 10Mbps network. Installation of a switch immediately provides each station with a dedicated 10Mbps, or a total theoretical bandwidth of 100Mbps. The limitation moves to the switch's backplane and buffers. In the same context, a shared FDDI ring operating at 100Mbps can be replaced with an ATM switch operating at OC-3 speeds (155Mbps). Each port has a dedicated link. Many designers divide shared media by the number of devices—thus, 10 stations on an FDDI ring will each receive 10Mbps. This is a simplified method for estimating performance increases.

Routers   Routers operate at Layer 3, limiting the collision and broadcast domains. Loops are handled within the routing protocol, using mechanisms such as split-horizon and time-to-live counters. Routers require logical addressing.

Nodes

Network design can be a precise exercise in which the designer knows exactly how much data will be sent across the network and when these transmissions will occur. Unfortunately, such accuracy would be short-lived and extremely time-consuming to obtain. General guidelines are actually just a means of simplifying the technical process while maintaining sufficient accuracy.

A number of factors combine to determine the number of nodes per network. For example, 10-Base-2 will support only 30 nodes according to the specification, but most installations surpass this threshold. Ignoring this limitation, most network designers today are concerned with Ethernets, broadcasts, and cable distances.

The 10-Base-T specification permits 1024 nodes per collision domain and has a variety of rules, such as the 5-4-3-2-1 rule that governs node placement and installation. However, broadcast traffic and protocol selection greatly erode those guidelines. Table 2.2 notes the recommended maximum number of nodes per broadcast domain for the various common protocols on Ethernet technologies. Other physical media may not support the number of nodes reflected in the table.

TABLE 2.2   Recommended Maximum Number of Nodes per Broadcast Domain (Figures Based on Broadcast and Protocol)

Protocol	Number of Nodes
AppleTalk	200 or less
NetBIOS	200 or less
IPX	500
IP (well designed)	1000

A number of companies have successfully designed networks well beyond these figures. These numbers are intended to provide a generic guideline that covers broadcasts and other limitations of the networking equipment.

Please note the "well-designed" IP guideline. This is consistent with a tuned non-broadcast-oriented installation. Windows (NetBIOS) installations typically show minor degradation at the 200-node level, although tuning will permit an increase in that number. Windows NT installations that utilize WINS as opposed to broadcast-based server discovery typically scale very well. When combining protocols, it is best to use the smaller number and include a factor for the added broadcasts and other traffic. For example, an installation with both Windows and Macintosh systems would best be kept to approximately 150 nodes. An installation with Novell and Unix might be capable of 400 nodes, although an analysis of RIP/SAP traffic and other criteria is likely warranted.

The 5-4-3-2-1 rule was used in the design of 10MB Ethernet networks with repeaters. It is not applicable with switches and faster Ethernet installations. The rule stated that Ethernet networks could have the following: five segments, four repeaters, three populated, two unpopulated, and one network. This rule was a guide to prevent collisions and contention problems that would pass through repeaters.

Trunking in Network Design

A powerful tool for the modern network designer is trunking technology, which combines multiple VLANs onto a single physical circuit. This design permits a single interface to support numerous networks—reducing costs and making more ports available for user connectivity. Trunks may be used between switches and routers, as shown in the following figures, or between switches. Switch-to-switch installations are more common, although this trend is changing. Designers should also note that trunking technology is available on network interface cards for server connections. This design may be used to provide a local presence from one server onto a number of subnets without using multiple NICs. Consider Figure 2.2, which illustrates a non-trunked VLAN installation.

FIGURE 2.2 Non-trunked VLAN installation

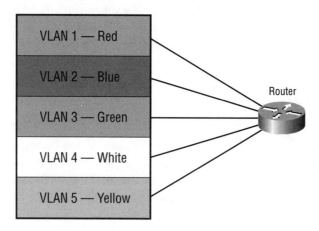

As the diagram shows, the designer must connect each VLAN to a separate router interface. Thus, for this five-VLAN model, the designer would
need to purchase and connect five different links.

Figure 2.3 displays a trunked installation, which provides a single,
100MB Ethernet interface for all five VLANs. This design is commonly
referred to as the "router on a stick" design. Were the non-trunked VLANs
connected with 10MB interfaces, this design would clearly provide as much
theoretical bandwidth.

FIGURE 2.3 Trunked VLAN installation

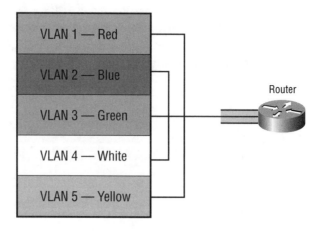

However, many administrators and designers would fret about taking five 100MB interfaces and reducing them to a single 100MB trunk. While their concern is clearly justified, each installation is different. Fortunately, there is a compromise solution that can provide ample bandwidth and retain some of the benefits found in trunking.

Cisco has introduced EtherChannel technologies into the switch and router platforms. This configuration disables the spanning tree and binds up to four links to provide four times the bandwidth to the trunk. This solution works well in practice for a number of reasons, including:

- It is rare for all VLANs to require bandwidth concurrently in production networks. This fact allows for substantial oversubscription of the trunk without providing underutilized bandwidth.

- EtherChannel links may continue to provide connectivity following a single link failure, which can be an additional benefit in fault-tolerant designs. Normally, this addresses potential port failures on the router.

- The creation of new VLANs frequently requires the designer to order hardware to support the VLAN. Extra hardware is not a factor when combining trunking with channeling.

- Newer network designs make use of multilayer switching—including Layer 3 path-selection switching. These technologies significantly reduce the number of packets requiring the router, as they are routed once and switched for subsequent packets.

EtherChannel technology is independent of trunking technology, and the two may be combined. The concept is that two or more channels may be used to provide additional bandwidth for a single VLAN or trunk—thus, the link between two switches could operate at up to 400Mbps full-duplex (bonding four 100Mbps full-duplex links). The following sections describe the various trunking protocols.

ISL

The Inter-Switch Link (ISL) protocol adds a 30-byte encapsulation header to each frame. This encapsulation tags the frame as belonging to a specific VLAN. ISL is proprietary to Cisco, and while other vendors (including Intel) have licensed the technology, it is slowly losing market share to the ratified IEEE 802.1q standard. ISL provides a great deal of information in its headers, including a second CRC in the encapsulation. ISL trunks can be deployed between routers and switches, switches and switches, and servers and switches or routers.

It is likely that Cisco will migrate away from the ISL protocol in favor of 802.1q. Designers should consider this factor when evaluating the protocol. Such a migration, should it occur, will likely take many years to come to fruition.

802.1q

The IEEE 802.1q standard provides a low-overhead method for tagging frames. Since it is an open standard, most designers select 802.1q when using non-Cisco equipment or to avoid committing to a single vendor. The 802.1q specification adds four octets of header to each frame. This header identifies the frame's VLAN membership, but it does not include a CRC checksum for validation of the header. This is not a significant issue in most reliable networks. The reduced header, compared to ISL, and lack of CRC greatly diminishes the overhead associated with this trunking technology.

Both ISL and 802.1q may cause incorrectly configured network devices to report *giants* (oversized frames). These "giant" frames are beyond the specified number of octets, as per the Ethernet standard. It is important to understand that both the ISL and 802.1q specifications increase the maximum number of bytes allowed—in contrast to traditional Ethernet.

802.10

FDDI may be used as a trunking medium in VLAN networks by incorporating the 802.10 protocol, which was originally developed to provide Layer 2 security. However, the use of the Security Association Identifier, or SAID, permits assignment of a VLAN ID. SAID provides for 4.29 billion VLANs.

The 802.10 encapsulation consists of a MAC header followed by a clear header. The clear header is not encrypted and consists of the 802.10 LSAP, or Link State Access Protocol (LSAPs are defined by the IEEE and occupy the LLC portion of the frame, comprising the destination service access point, source service access point, and control byte), the SAID, and an optional Management Defined Field, or MDF. The standard provides for a protected header to follow the MDF, with data and a checksum, referred to as the Integrity Check Value, or ICV. In VLAN trunking, only the IEEE 802.10 LSAP and the SAID value are used before the data block.

To configure 802.10, the administrator must define the relationship between the FDDI VLAN and the Ethernet VLAN. The first VLAN, or default VLAN, is defined automatically.

It is important to note that 802.10 VLAN packets are valid MAC frames and may cross non-802.10 devices within the network. Also, VLAN IDs and SAID values are independent of each other—except when related in the switch table.

LANE

LAN Emulation (LANE) will be described in greater detail later in this chapter. For the moment, note that LANE is also used as a trunking technology. LANE is often introduced as the first-phase migration step to ATM in the network.

Network Design and Problem Solving

As discussed in Chapter 1, most network design projects are conceived to address one or more problems within an existing network. Consider the list of network problems and the corresponding tools noted in Table 2.3.

TABLE 2.3 Network Design Solutions

Issue	Possible Solutions
Contention for the media	Migrating from shared to switched media is the best solution to this problem. However, it may be necessary to segment the network with routers to reduce the number of nodes per broadcast domain.
Excessive broadcasts	Network broadcast control is the responsibility of the router. The only other solution would be to reduce the number of broadcasts at the source.

TABLE 2.3 Network Design Solutions *(continued)*

Issue	Possible Solutions
Protocol issues	Typically, protocols on the network are defined by the application, although designers may use tunneling and encapsulation to maintain single-protocol segments. This solution is especially applicable in WAN designs.
Addressing issues	Given the logical structuring role of the address, addressing issues must include the involvement of a routing device.

Network Design in the Real World: Design Solutions

Most designers find that their solutions are the result of reactive efforts and not proactive ones. This is the nature of the beast in most large, fast-paced corporations.

Therefore, it is imperative that the designer continue to hone skills related to troubleshooting. In the largest organizations, staff in other departments may be responsible for actually connecting the protocol analyzer to the segment or generating the remote monitoring (RMON) reports, but the designer and architect will need to know what information to ask for. This arrangement can make the process more difficult—many troubleshooting efforts on very complex problems are actually solved by "That doesn't look right" observations.

One of the best ways to avoid this situation is to generate reports that a lay person can understand. A number of products are available—my favorite is Concord Network Health, although there are others, including Cisco's RMON tools. The designer can post the resulting reports on a Web site so that users can see the status of the network whenever they wish.

A fear that non-network designers will start to second-guess every issue in the reports is natural, and it will happen from some people. However, the reports can also provide the needed visibility to upper management to justify funding and resources. Most networks hide the problems, so they never get fixed. If you need to be convinced that disclosure is a positive step, take a look at Cisco's Web site, www.cisco.com. The vast majority of bugs in Cisco's software are documented and disclosed publicly. Granted, such problems can be embarrassing to the company, but the result over the past few years has been an incredible increase in market share and a vast improvement in the overall product line. Improved service should be the goal of every IT department.

Physical Topologies

The physical layout of the network is sometimes dissimilar to the logical and simple layout suggested by the hierarchical model. Consideration must be given to access, cabling, distances, shielding, and space.

Most installations use two distinct components for the intra-building configuration. These are defined as horizontal and vertical systems.

Vertical systems are typically backbone services and move up through the building. These services are usually run on fiber media, which is capable of greater bandwidth and is less susceptible to electromagnetic interference.

Horizontal systems are almost always copper, but this trend is changing as more desktops are wired for fiber. These installations usually start at a wiring closet and are fed under the floor or in plenum (ceiling). The wiring closet will typically contain a switch or hub that links the vertical connections.

The typical network installation will have a single main distribution point for the network. This location would terminate all the vertical runs and all the telecommunications services from outside the building.

Network Design in the Real World: Cabling

I inherited a network years ago that had chronic problems. User connections would degrade or fail at seemingly random intervals. The tools available to us showed huge jumps in error rates, although no new stations had been added to the network. Both Token Ring and Ethernet were affected.

Eventually, we learned that copper cables had been run next to the freight elevator shaft, and the elevator motor and systems played havoc with the data. When fiber was installed along with shielding (for copper-only services), the problem was resolved. A sharp electrician found the problem.

 The distribution room is typically in the basement or on the first floor of the building, although the designer should consider the risk of flooding and other disasters before allocating facilities. Usually, the room will need to align with the wiring closets on the other floors.

Figure 2.4 illustrates a typical building installation. This design is called a *distributed backbone*—routers on each floor connect to the backbone, typically via FDDI. No end stations are placed on the backbone.

The actual design shown in Figure 2.4 is uncommon in modern designs. This is primarily due to the expense of having routers on each floor. This design would likely have used hubs in the place of switches.

Figure 2.4 also has similarities with legacy Token-Ring installations. Consider Figure 2.5, which illustrates a common Token-Ring installation. All rings operate at 16Mbps. It should be clear that a bottleneck will appear at the backbone or on the server ring—four user rings at 25 percent utilization would equal the entire backbone capacity. The use of the 80/20 rule (where 80 percent of traffic remains local) would provide more growth room. However, many Token Ring installations were installed for mainframe (off-subnet) access. FastEthernet or FDDI was often used to resolve this oversubscription problem. Another popular technique was to create multiple backbone rings, typically divided on a per-protocol basis.

FIGURE 2.4 LAN intra-building installation

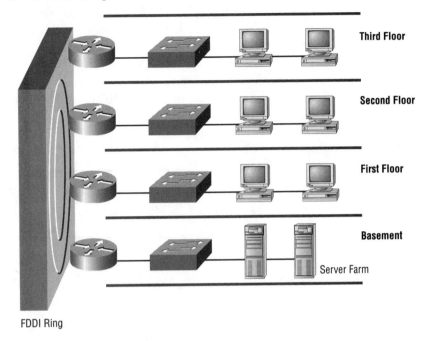

FDDI Ring

FIGURE 2.5 LAN intra-building installation with Token Ring

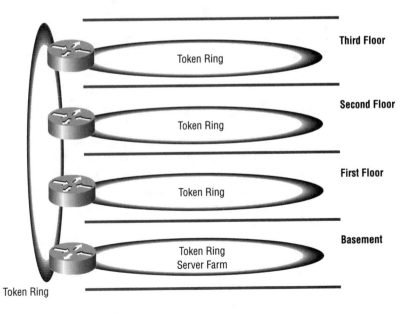

Token Ring

As routing technology advanced and port density increased, the LAN model migrated toward the collapsed backbone. This design would place a single router in the main telecommunications room and connect it to hubs in the wiring closets. This configuration would frequently incorporate switches. Figure 2.6 illustrates the collapsed backbone design. Note that the vertical links would likely use fiber connections. FDDI is still extremely popular today among many Fortune 500 companies due to its fully redundant design capability.

FIGURE 2.6 LAN intra-building installation with collapsed backbone

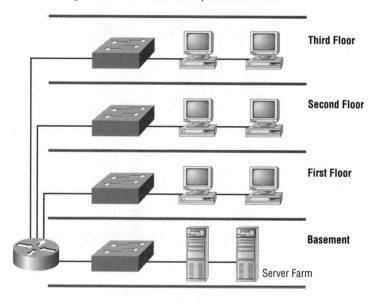

New Network Designs—Layer 2 versus Layer 3

Current network design models strive to eliminate spanning-tree issues. As a result, switches and routers must work together to create a redundant, loop-free topology without relying on the Spanning-Tree Protocol or Layer 2 redundancy. As switch technology has advanced, this option has been made more available.

Network Design in the Real World: The Future of Token Ring

While only time will tell, it appears fairly inevitable that Token Ring will depart from the landscape. As of this writing, the 802.5 committee (responsible for Token Ring standards) had diminished substantially and was discussing its options—including a hibernation phase for the group. Whatever happens, it seems clear that efforts to migrate to and install Ethernet will be more prevalent in the future.

Please note that this section is beyond the scope of the exam, but it is likely that Cisco will include this material in future exam revisions. A practical application of this material necessitates its inclusion here.

Consider the design illustrated in Figure 2.7. A complete loop has been created at Layer 2, but spanning tree is configured to block a port on the access-layer switch. Routers are not displayed in order to emphasize the Layer 2 facets of this installation.

FIGURE 2.7 Layer 2 switch design

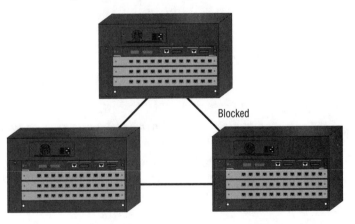

Consider the change to the network that is illustrated in Figure 2.8. The link between the two distribution layer switches has been removed for the VLAN that services the access layer. HSRP has also been deployed. While this design is shown in Figure 2.8 with external routers, the connections could also be provided by a route module in the switch.

FIGURE 2.8 Layer 3 switch design

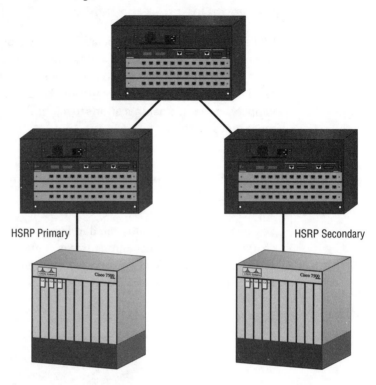

Figure 2.8 shows the use of external routers, which may lead to a split subnet or black hole problem, as discussed in Chapter 13. This design works best when using RSM or internal Layer 3 logic in the switch, as the link failure from the distribution switch to the access switch will down the router interface, preventing this problem.

In making this change, the designer has eliminated the slower spanning-tree process and potentially eliminated the need for BPDUs (Bridge Protocol Data Units) altogether—although there is still a risk of the users creating bridging loops. The design is redundant and quite scalable. In addition, with routers and switches working together in multilayer switching configurations, the latency often associated with routers is reduced as well. A typical installation using this design model would place a single transit VLAN between the switches. Such a design would still avoid a Layer 2 loop while maintaining a through switch connection. Designers should consider the expected network behavior during both normal and failed scenarios when architecting any configuration.

Designers should not disable the Spanning-Tree Protocol unless they can ensure a loop-free topology.

Network Design in the Real World: Spanning Tree

Spanning tree is perhaps one of the most difficult considerations in network design. This is not due to the protocol or function per se, but rather the need for designers to consider the Layer 2 topology when incorporating Layer 3 functions, including HSRP. It is easy to create an efficient Layer 2 architecture and a separate Layer 3 design, but the two ultimately must map together to be manageable and practical. One technique is to make the HSRP primary for the VLAN root bridge. However, there are other techniques, including defining multiple default gateways on each host or using proxy ARP.

As of this writing, a new committee was meeting to design a new, faster Spanning-Tree Protocol. This protocol will likely reduce the shortcomings of the original specification, which was never designed to support today's higher speed networks. However, as presented in the main text, the real issue is whether to design loops into the Layer 2 network at all.

At present, one school of thought on the subject is to avoid loops whenever possible and use Layer 3 routing to provide redundancy—technologies such as HSRP and MPLS (Multiprotocol Label Switching) allow fault tolerance and switching of Layer 3 packets. The other school of thought believes that spanning tree is still useful but that new features must be added to make it work in today's networks. Cisco has a number of features that work toward this option, including PortFast and UplinkFast.

PortFast is used on switch ports that connect to a single workstation. Under this scenario, the port cannot participate in a loop, so the port should not have to go through a listening-and-learning mode. The port should also not go into blocking—there is no loop potential at this point in the network. It is important to note that this does not disable spanning tree—it simply activates the port faster than the 30-second listening/learning process would require. This feature is recommended for workstations (some of which can fail authentication to the network while the port is blocked). However, a major caveat must be added—the port cannot be connected to a hub or switch. This rule will prevent the loop creation that spanning tree was designed to prevent.

The second feature, UplinkFast, was designed to activate the blocked link quickly in the event of primary failure. Again, there are drawbacks to this feature, but when properly implemented it can greatly extend the functionality of Layer 2 loops and loop protection.

The Role of ATM

Asynchronous Transfer Mode (ATM) has been the networking technology of the 1990s. Merging the historical divisions between data, voice, and video, ATM was designed and marketed to replace all other technologies in both local and wide area networks.

At the end of the 1990s, it appeared clear that replacement of existing networks would not occur. Rather, another evolution—merging ATM with legacy technologies such as Ethernet—will likely color network design theories into the next century.

However, even with the introduction of 10Gbps Ethernet, there are still situations in which ATM can and should be deployed. Such situations include both LAN and WAN environments.

ATM operates via fixed-length cells. This design contrasts with the variable-length frames found in Ethernet and other technologies. Fixed-length cells provide consistent buffering and latency—allowing integration between voice (constant bit rate) and data (variable bit rate). ATM operates over permanent virtual circuits and switched virtual circuits.

As noted previously, ATM uses a fixed-length cell transport mechanism. These cells, at 53 bytes, are substantially smaller than the frame sizes used by Ethernet, Token Ring, and FDDI. In order to migrate between frames and cells, ATM devices perform segmentation and reassembly (SAR). The SAR function frequently became a bottleneck in older switches; however, this overhead is a minor factor today. Designers should discuss SAR processing (cells/frames per second) with their vendors before selecting a product.

ATM is often used in modern network design for WAN links and the integration of voice and data circuits. This type of installation is similar to multiplexing. In the LAN environment, ATM and ATM LANE installations are frequently used for high-speed campus backbones. This design provides a migration path for pushing ATM toward the desktop. ATM is one option for designers wishing to replace aging FDDI rings.

ATM in the LAN with LANE

LAN deployments of ATM almost always take advantage of LANE, or LAN Emulation, to integrate legacy topologies with ATM. It is unlikely that any organization would allocate sufficient funds to replace their entire existing infrastructure without some migration phase.

LANE was covered in some detail in Sybex's *Cisco LAN Switching Course Study Guide*. This section will present an overview of that material for those preparing for the CID exam before the CLSC exam.

LANE makes use of at least three separate logical processes: the LAN Emulation Client (LEC), the LAN Emulation Server (LES), and the broadcast and unknown server (BUS). A fourth resource is optional but recommended. The use of the LAN Emulation Configuration Server (LECS) can greatly simplify the administrative effort needed to deploy LANE.

LAN Emulation Client

The LAN Emulation Client, or LEC, is responsible for data forwarding, address resolution, control functions, and the mapping of MAC addresses to ATM addresses.

LECs are devices that implement the LANE protocol; they may be ATM-equipped workstations, routers, or switches. It is common for an LEC to be a single element on a switch serving numerous Ethernet or Token-Ring ports. To the ATM network, it appears that the single ATM LEC is requesting data—in actuality, the LEC is simply a proxy for the individual requests from the legacy nodes.

LAN Emulation Server

The LAN Emulation Server, or LES, is unique to each ELAN (emulated LAN). The LES is responsible for managing the ELAN and providing transparency to the LECs.

Given the interdependency of the LES and BUS services, most references use the term LES/BUS pair to denote the server providing these services.

Broadcast and Unknown Server

Broadcasts and multicasts are quite common in the traditional LAN environment. Since all stations, even in Ethernet-switched installations, receive all frames destined for a MAC address containing all ones, this process works quite well and serves many upper-layer protocols, including the Address Resolution Protocol, for example.

However, ATM requires that a point-to-point virtual circuit serve all connections. This requirement precludes the traditional media-sharing capabilities of Ethernet and Token Ring. To resolve this function, the ATM Forum LAN Emulation committee included in the specification a broadcast and unknown server, or BUS. Each ELAN must have its own BUS, which is responsible for resolving all broadcasts and packets that are addressed for unknown, or unregistered, stations. Under the original LANE 1.0 specification with Cisco ATM devices, without SSRP (Simple Server Redundancy Protocol), only one BUS is permitted per ELAN. Other vendors invented their own redundancy options to augment the specification. SSRP is a proprietary method of allowing redundancy in ATM LANE by permitting dual LECS and LES/BUS pairs.

Cisco's implementation of LANE places the BUS on the same device as the LES. This design will likely change in the future, since it is inconsistent with other vendors' offerings.

LAN Emulation Configuration Server

While the LAN Emulation Configuration Server, or LECS, is not required in LANE, administrators frequently find that configuration is greatly simplified when it is employed.

The LECS is similar to Dynamic Host Configuration Protocol (DHCP) servers in the IP world. The workstation queries a server for all information that is needed to participate in the network. With DHCP, this is limited to IP address, default gateway, and DNS/WINS (Domain Name Service/Windows Internet Naming Service) servers, depending on implementation. In ATM, the LECS provides the address information for the LES and BUS to the LEC.

The Initial LANE Connection Sequence

The best way to understand the four components of ATM LANE is to visualize the initial startup sequence. This sequence is illustrated in Figure 2.9.

As shown, the client (LEC) must connect with the LES in order to join the ELAN. Most installations make use of the LECS; therefore, the LEC connects with the LECS to learn the address of the LES. Note that the LEC could also be configured with the address of the LES for its ELAN, or it could use the well-known address for the LECS. The well-known address is part of the LANE specification and is used when another method is unavailable.

Once the LEC connects with the LES and joins the ELAN, another connection is established with the BUS. Both of these VCs (virtual circuits) are maintained, but the LECS connection may be dropped. The LES typically maintains a connection to the LECS.

The *CLSC Study Guide* from Sybex provides more detail regarding ATM LANE and the Catalyst 5500 platform, including the LS1010.

FIGURE 2.9 The LANE connection sequence

Phase 1: The LEC queries the LECS.

Phase 2: The LEC joins the ELAN.

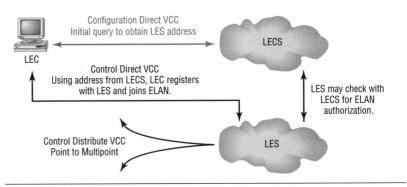

Phase 3: The LEC connects to the BUS.

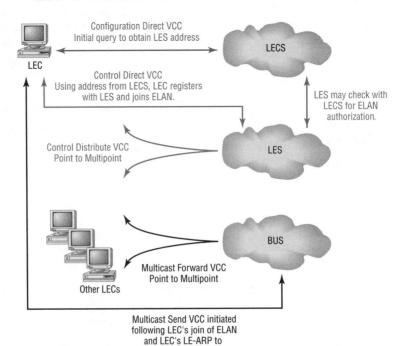

Network Design in the Real World: ATM LANE

Perhaps one of the greatest benefits of ATM LANE has been the enhancements to frame-based Ethernet. This is an ironic twist, but the complexities and expense of LANE frequently surpass the benefits afforded by many new technologies, including RSVP and GigabitEthernet.

One must consider two specific factors regarding the viability of LANE. LANE was designed to provide an emulation of frame-based broadcast networks. This technology typically provides a number of benefits and detriments, including consistent ATM fabric latency (cell-based traffic is consistent; variable-frame is not) and support for greater bandwidth and integration with voice and video. The negatives include the cell tax (the overhead added by ATM), the SAR function (where frames are sliced into cells and reassembled back into frames), and the added complexity and relatively immature nature of the technology. For example, the PNNI (Private Network-Network Interface) and MPOA (Multiprotocol over ATM) functions (dynamic routing and route once/switch many functions) were just becoming deployable in the late 1990s, and many more features, including PNNI hierarchy, are still unavailable. Vendor interoperability is also a concern.

The threat of ATM and ATM LANE was enough to make vendors add many features to the cheaper and more familiar Ethernet standards, including quality of service (QoS) and MPLS (Multiprotocol Label Switching) (another form of route once/switch many) technology.

I have designed, installed, and supported both ATM LANE and ATM networks and would recommend that new LANE deployments be approached with great care. There are certainly times when it is the right solution, but it may be appropriate to consider the alternatives. Some of these are discussed in Chapter 13 in greater detail, including DTP (Dynamic Transport Protocol) and Packet over SONET (POS). Designers leaning toward using LANE need to consider supportability, cost, and features before committing to this technology.

It is also important to note that the caveats regarding LANE do not necessarily include ATM—the two really need to be considered different technologies. ATM in the wide area network is virtually inevitable—most Frame-Relay cores use ATM, in addition to DSL (Digital Subscriber Line) and voice circuits. ATM does offer many advantages in this configuration. However, the features specific to LANE often do not offset the complexities of the protocol.

Summary

This chapter discussed many of the tools and technologies used in the local area network to address problems typically faced by network designers. Newer technologies, such as ATM LANE, were covered, in addition to more traditional tools and technologies, including Ethernet routers and switches. Specific attention was given to:

- LAN technologies
  - Ethernet
  - Token Ring
  - FDDI
  - ATM
  - ATM LANE
- Interconnectivity tools
  - Repeaters
  - Hubs
  - Switches
  - Routers
- Problem categories
  - Media
  - Transport
  - Protocols
- Trunking protocols
  - ISL
  - 802.1q
  - 802.10
  - LANE

The chapter defined key components in network design, including the interconnectivity tools in frame-based networks. It also presented the ATM components: LECS, LEC, LES, and BUS. Finally, it reviewed building topologies, including distributed and collapsed backbones.

Much of the text in the following chapters will focus more on Layers 2 and 3 of the OSI model, so readers will become comfortable with the various functions of hardware in the network and the limitations.

Review Questions

1. Broadcasts are controlled by which of the following devices?

    A. Bridges

    B. Repeaters

    C. Routers

    D. Switches

2. Routers perform which of the following functions?

    A. Access control

    B. Logical structure

    C. Media conversions

    D. None of the above

3. Which of the following devices operate at Layer 2 of the OSI model?

    A. Routers

    B. Gateways

    C. Switches

    D. Bridges

4. Which of the following is true regarding cut-through switching?

    A. The frame is forwarded following verification of the CRC.

    B. The frame is forwarded following verification of the HEC.

    C. The frame is forwarded upon receipt of the header destination address.

    D. The frame is forwarded out every port on the switch.

5. Which of the following is true regarding store-and-forward switching?

   A. The frame is forwarded following verification of the CRC.

   B. The frame is forwarded following verification of the HEC.

   C. The frame is forwarded upon receipt of the header destination address.

   D. The frame is forwarded out every port on the switch.

6. Negating overhead and conversions, the designer chooses to replace the legacy FDDI ring with an ATM switch attached via OC-3. Assuming a backbone of 10 devices, no overhead, and equal distributions, the increase in available bandwidth per device is:

   A. 55Mbps

   B. 100Mbps

   C. 145Mbps

   D. 1Gbps

   E. 1.54Gbps

7. An Ethernet switch:

   A. Defines the collision domain

   B. Defines the broadcast domain

   C. Defines both the broadcast and collision domains

   D. Sends all broadcasts to the BUS (broadcast and unknown server)

8. Which of the following would be a reason to not span a VLAN across the WAN?

   A. VLANs define broadcast domains, and all VLAN broadcasts would have to traverse the WAN, which typically uses slow links.

   B. Reduced costs, since fewer router interfaces are required.

   C. Easier addressing during moves.

   D. Non-routed workgroup traffic across geographically removed locations.

9. Which of the following are considered WAN design issues?

   A. Bandwidth

   B. Cost

   C. Service availability

   D. Protocol support

   E. Remote access

   F. All of the above

10. The Cisco IOS offers some benefits to designers regarding WAN deployments. These benefits do not include which of the following?

    A. Compression

    B. Filters

    C. HTTP proxy

    D. On-demand bandwidth

    E. Efficient routing protocols, including EIGRP, NLSP, and static routes

11. Which of the following reasons might influence a designer to use a single WAN protocol?

    A. Easier configuration

    B. More-difficult configuration

    C. More-difficult troubleshooting

    D. Increased traffic

12. Which of the following is not an open standard?

    A. 802.10

    B. 802.3

    C. 802.1q

    D. ISL

13. Which of the following would be valid technical reasons to readdress the IP network?

   A. Implementation of VLSM

   B. Implementation of HSRP

   C. Implementation of EIGRP

   D. Implementation of OSPF

14. A distributed backbone typically:

   A. Contains a single router in the data center

   B. Is completely flat within the building or campus

   C. Contains multiple routers, typically with one per floor or area

   D. Requires the use of ATM LANE, version 2.0

15. ATM uses:

   A. 53-byte cells

   B. 53-byte frames

   C. Variable-length cells

   D. Variable-length frames

16. Which of the following is optional in ATM LANE?

   A. LEC

   B. LES

   C. BUS

   D. LECS

17. Which function is used to convert frames to cells?

A. LES

B. LEC

C. LECS

D. SAR

18. Excessive broadcasts are typically resolved with (select three):

A. Switches

B. Tuning of the network protocol

C. Replacement of the network protocol

D. Routers

19. Transport issues differ from media issues in that:

A. Media issues relate to Layer 1, while transport issues relate to Layer 3.

B. Media issues involve voice and video, while transport issues are related to increased demand by existing services.

C. Transport issues incorporate voice and video services, while media issues are limited to the offered load on the network.

D. None of the above.

20. Addressing issues are the responsibility of:

A. Hubs

B. Servers

C. Switches

D. Routers

Answers to Review Questions

1. C.

2. A, B, C.

3. C, D.

4. C.

5. A.

6. C.

FDDI operates at 100Mbps. With 10 shared stations, each station receives 10Mbps. OC-3 switched offers 155Mbps per station.

7. A.

8. A.

9. F.

10. C.

11. A.

12. D.

13. A.

While not covered until Chapter 4, readdressing for OSPF and EIGRP is common, making C and D correct as well.

14. C.

15. A.

16. D.

17. D.

18. B, C, D.

Routers are a poor choice for resolving excessive broadcasts, although they can divide the broadcast domain. Switches may offer broadcast suppression, but this feature is more appropriate for broadcast storms than for normal broadcast traffic.

19. C.

20. D.

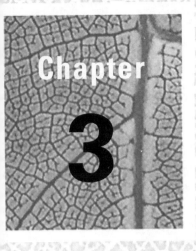

Chapter

3

TCP/IP Network Design

CISCO INTERNETWORK DESIGN EXAM OBJECTIVES COVERED IN THIS CHAPTER:

✓ Choose the appropriate IP addressing scheme based on technical requirements.

✓ Identify IP addressing issues and how to work around them.

Due in large part to the explosive growth of the Internet, the IP protocol has easily surpassed IPX, AppleTalk, DECNet, and all other desktop protocols in modern network design. The IP protocol has proven itself as a multivendor, scalable standard that supports mainframe, desktop, and server applications.

The roots of IP are well developed in the Unix arena. However, many consider its release into the Windows environment, with incorporated services like WINS (Windows Internet Naming Service) and DHCP (Dynamic Host Configuration Protocol), to be its actual migration to the desktop. Others believe that the Internet alone was responsible for its popularity and that Microsoft and other vendors caught up to the emerging standard.

There is little doubt that modern designers and administrators will have to develop and support networks that use IP, regardless of which theory is correct.

This chapter presents many of the issues in IP design that confront network designers, including:

- Address assignments

- Subnet masks

- Address summarization

In order to understand the design criteria for IP networks, let's define some of the terminology. The terms shown below are important not only from a vocabulary perspective, but also from a conceptual one. Most of these concepts incorporate repetitive themes in IP.

Classful   A classful routing protocol does not include subnet information in its updates. Therefore, routers will make decisions based on either the class of IP address or on the subnet mask applied to the receiving interface. In classful networks, the network mask for each major network should be the same throughout the network. Recall from previous explanations (presuming that readers have obtained CCNA-level experience, if not certification) that the subnet mask defines the bits in the IP address that are to be used for defining the subnet and host ranges. A binary 1 in the subnet mask defines the network portion of the address, while a binary 0 defines the host portion. Routing is based on the network portion of the address.

If concepts such as subnet masks and IP addresses are unfamiliar, you may wish to obtain and study the Sybex *CCNA Study Guide*.

Classless   Classless routing protocols include subnet mask information in their updates.

Major network   The concept of a major network is analogous to the concept of a natural mask and relates to the class of the address, which will be defined later in this chapter. For example, the major network for address 10.12.12.40 would be 10.0.0.0.

Subnet mask   A subnet is a logical division of addresses within a major network, defined by borrowing bits from the host portion of the address.

Variable-length subnet mask   Variable-length subnet masks (VLSM) provide the designer with address flexibility. For example, the designer could allocate two hosts to a point-to-point link, while expanding the mask to permit 500 hosts on a user subnet. VLSM support is provided by classless routing protocols, including EIGRP and OSPF. RIP and IGRP require all subnets to be equally sized and contiguous. As a general rule, link-state protocols and hybrid protocols (such as EIGRP) support VLSM. RIP v2 also supports variable subnets.

Discontiguous subnets   A discontiguous subnet is a major network that appears on two sides of another major network. Classful routing protocols cannot support this configuration, and the designer is well advised to avoid this situation whenever possible. Should another solution be necessary, the designer may employ secondary interfaces or tunnels to link the two parts of the disjoined networks, or convert to a classless routing protocol. It is important to note that each of these solutions comes with some costs, including greater overhead, more difficult troubleshooting, and more difficult administration.

The automatic summarization feature found in EIGRP can create problems with discontiguous subnets. Therefore, many sources recommend disabling this feature. It is included for easier integration and migration with IGRP.

Secondaries A secondary address permits two or more IP subnets to appear on the same physical interface. Secondaries may be used to link discontiguous subnets, as noted previously, or to support other objectives. These objectives include migration to larger subnet masks without converting to a classless routing protocol (support for VLSM) or instances where local routing is appropriate. It is important to note that local routing is no longer considered an acceptable practice—the use of switches and trunking technologies is recommended. Trunking is a concept that permits logical isolation of multiple subnets on a physical media by marking each frame with a tag. Examples of trunking include Inter Switch Link (ISL) and 802.1q.

IP Addresses

Unlike most other protocols, IP demands careful planning by the designer before address allocation. In subsequent chapters, the address formats of IPX and AppleTalk will be presented in greater detail; however, both of these protocols permit the designer to assign only the network portion of the address. IP places the responsibility for assigning the host portion of the address on the administrator. Please note that the host assignment must also be unique for each network.

It is easy to forget that the IP addressing scheme was originally developed for a handful of networks and hosts. Early adopters would have been hard-pressed to predict the millions of devices in use today. As written, the initial IP addressing model incorporated the concept of *class*, or a way to define the scope of a network based on a parameter defined within the address itself. This strategy made sense in the early days of the Internet because the routing protocols were very limited and address conservation was unnecessary. However, in the present time, it has led to a crisis and shortage of available addresses—particularly in the largest address class.

RFC 760, the original IP specification, did not refer to classes. RFC 791 incorporated the term *classful addressing*.

As reflected in Table 3.1, there are five IP address classes. The high-order bits in the first octet determine this arrangement—thus, any address with the first bits equal to 10 in the first octet belong to Class B. The bit value is significant in determining the major class of the network. Note that the high-order bits in Table 3.1 reflect the binary representation of the number—for example, 00000001 in binary equals 1 in decimal. Without changing the first bit from a 0 to a 1, the highest number that can be represented is 127; however, this is reserved and not part of the Class A space, shown in the first column. The decimal range of the numbers available with the shown high-order bits is presented in the third column.

TABLE 3.1 IP Address Classes

Class	High-Order Bits	First Byte in Decimal
A	0	1-126
B	10	128-191
C	110	192-223
D	1110	224-239
E	1111	240-254

As a result, the designer should be able to identify that the address 131.192.210.13 is in Class B and that, using the natural mask, the network portion of this address is 131.192.0.0. Notice that the address class is independent of the subnet mask—the mask modifies only the subnet (or supernet) parameters. A supernet is created by inverting the subnet mask to take bits from the natural network portion of the address. Thus, a supernet of 192.168.2.0 and 192.168.3.0 would be presented as 192.168.2.0 255.255.254.0, rather than the natural mask of 255.255.255.0.

IP Network Classes

The IP protocol, version 4, was designed around the concept of network classes in order to provide a natural boundary that all routers could use. This was slightly better than the flatter area-code model used by the telephone company, wherein each area may contain only 10 million numbers and each sub-area is limited to 10 thousand numbers.

Examples using phone numbers are based on the North American numbering plan. Countries based on other numbering plans typically share the characteristics of this model but may not provide the same number of available addresses.

The early designers of the Internet realized that some sites may need thousands of subnets, or prefix (sub) areas. Others, they reasoned, might need only one or two. This strategy evolved into the five address classes noted in Table 3.1, which have the following characteristics.

Class A Addresses

Class A addresses contain a 0 in the first bit of the first octet. These IP addresses are presented as 0-126 in the first octet. Designers like Class A address blocks because they allow the most flexibility and largest range of addresses, particularly when classful routing protocols are in use. However, assignments in Class A also waste a huge number of addresses—addresses that go unused. This single factor has led to the development of IP v6 and other techniques to extend the life of IP v4, including CIDR (Classless Internet Domain Routing), RFC 1918 addresses, and network address translation (NAT).

The network address 127.0.0.0 is reserved for the loopback function. This feature is used for diagnostic purposes and typically encompasses the single address of 127.0.0.1. However, any address in the range is reserved for the function.

Class B Addresses

Class B addresses contain a 1 in the first bit of the first octet and a 0 in the second bit of the first octet. These IP addresses are presented as 128-191 in the first octet. The benefit to Class B addresses becomes clear in larger organizations. These addresses provide a broad block of addresses for the organization while attempting to reduce the waste caused by Class A block sizes—few organizations need the volume of addresses provided by Class A blocks.

Class C Addresses

Class C addresses contain a 1 and a 1 in the first two bits of the first octet and a 0 in the third bit of the first octet and range from 192 to 223 in decimal notation. Up to 254 hosts may be assigned within the class, assuming that the entire subnet is equal to the major network. Under the current addressing allocations, Class C address blocks are easier to obtain than Class A or B allocations but are very limited for most organizations. Therefore, companies generally receive a block of contiguous Class C blocks, which are summarized as a *supernet*. This is also referred to as CIDR.

Class D Addresses

Class D addresses are reserved for IP multicast. Additional information regarding multicast is presented in Chapter 13.

Class E Addresses

Class E is reserved for future use and is currently undefined.

Subnetting in IP

The idea of *subnetting* in IP is perhaps the concept most misunderstood by new administrators and designers. Unlike AppleTalk and IPX, IP addresses are assigned at both the network and host levels. In AppleTalk and IPX, the administrator or designer need only assign the network-level address. An interesting twist on these protocol characteristics is that the control that IP offers designers can also be a hindrance in that more must be manually configured. This manual process requires decisions and sets limitations that are not present in AppleTalk or IPX.

As will be described in Chapter 6, IPX addresses are a combination of the MAC (Media Access Control) layer address (hardware address) and the IPX network number, which is assigned by the administrator on the router. A virtually unlimited number of hosts may become members of an IPX network.

AppleTalk is slightly more limited in that the administrator or designer assigns a cable range. Each range supports over 250 hosts, as described in Chapter 5. While this assignment requires additional planning, there is generally little need to conserve addresses in AppleTalk as there is with IP. Therefore, no penalty is associated with allocating cable ranges that will support thousands of hosts—the implementation of which is highly unadvised.

The IP protocol suffers from both the manual assignment noted previously and a shortage of legal addresses. Later in this chapter, one solution to this problem will be presented—the use of private addresses. However, conservation of address space can also become a concern with private addresses.

Network Design in the Real World: Addressing

It would be hard to believe that a corporation with only a few hundred routers could use all of its addresses in a three-year timeframe, but it does happen. The most significant contributor to the exhaustion of addresses is the lack of VLSM support. Being forced to use a consistent mask for all addresses quickly leads to hundreds of addresses being unallocated on point-to-point links and other small segments.

One such network used all of its upper two private address spaces (RFC 1918 is defined later in the chapter) and all of its public Class C address blocks. When each of the few hundred routers contained at least three interfaces, and many included 10 to 20, the addresses became exhausted. Secondaries and poor documentation further added to the problem.

Ultimately, a complete readdressing strategy was needed, and encompassed in this plan was a change of routing protocol to support VLSM. This required a great deal of resources and a large expense—ideally, having a VLSM-aware protocol would have prevented the problem.

You may point out that VLSM-aware protocols are relatively new and some of these networks are relatively old. That is true. And many of these networks needed additional addresses that were assigned via secondaries. This eventually led to bigger problems since troubleshooting and documentation were greatly affected. Today, no organization should continue to use secondaries and non-VLSM-aware protocols as a strategic direction. The penalties of not migrating in terms of hidden costs are too great to ignore in the long run.

Table 3.2 documents the common subnet divisions used by network designers. It is important to note that 24- and 30-bit subnets are used most commonly—LANs using 24 bits and point-to-point WAN links using 30 bits. The number of subnets referenced in Table 3.2 presumes a Class B network—other base classes will differ.

TABLE 3.2   Typical Subnet Configurations

Number of Network Bits	Subnet Mask	Number of Subnets	Number of Hosts Per Subnet
18	255.255.192.0	2	16,382
19	255.255.224.0	6	8,190
20	255.255.240.0	14	4,094
21	255.255.248.0	30	2,046
22	255.255.252.0	62	1,022
23	255.255.254.0	126	510
24	255.255.255.0	254	254
25	255.255.255.128	510	126
26	255.255.255.192	1,022	62
27	255.255.255.224	2,046	30
28	255.255.255.240	4,094	14
29	255.255.255.248	8,190	6
30	255.255.255.252	16,382	2

Designers should consider the following factors when allocating subnets:

- The total number of hosts
- The total number of major network numbers

- The allocation of hosts

- The number of point-to-point links

- The number of extranet and secure segments

- The availability of VLSM-aware protocols

- The need for non-VLSM subnets to remain contiguous

- The use of static routes and distribution lists to control routes

- The use of public and private address space

- The desire to summarize addresses at the distribution or access layers

Network masks may be written in various formats. The mask 255.255.255.0 may be written as /24, to reflect the number of ones in the mask.

Address Assignments

Today, network design requires a thorough understanding of TCP/IP addressing in order to be successful. Most of this requirement is facilitated by the explosive growth of the Internet (and its use of the IP protocol); however, the IP protocol also scales well, which generates benefits when it is used in the private network.

Unlike AppleTalk and IPX, IP addressing and routing benefits from summarization and other design criteria that are not available in the other protocols' addressing schemas. IP permits efficient and logical addressing based on various criteria—unfortunately, most current networks evolved, rather than planned, their addressing schemes, effectively negating any benefits that may have been available from the protocol itself.

The design of IP addresses in the network requires the organization to make a number of decisions. These decisions concern:

- The use of public or private address space

- The use of variable-length subnet masks

- The use of address summarization

- The use of automatic address assignment

- The existence of addresses already in the network

- The translation of addresses

Designers are also typically responsible for allocating addresses in DHCP pools—a mechanism that permits dynamic addressing in IP networks. This greatly simplifies the administration requirements at the workstation and is covered in greater detail in Chapter 7.

One of the keys to a strong network design is the use of consistent addresses in the network. For example, most designers allocate a block of addresses for network devices at the beginning or end of the address range. This arrangement accomplishes two goals: First, the identification of a device is greatly simplified, and second, access lists and other security mechanisms can be defined consistently.

Public and Private Addresses

The Internet connects a wide array of networks, with each requiring a methodology of uniquely identifying each device in the network. As such a methodology, IP addresses must be unique between devices.

Unlike the burned-in address (MAC) found on a network adapter, the IP address is assigned and is used to create a logical confederation of devices. These groupings are then used to distribute information to other devices in the network. This scenario is typically referred to as *routing*.

The IP address itself is likely familiar to most readers, so just consider the following as beneficial review. IP addresses, in version 4, are 32-bit values written in dotted decimal notation. For example, an IP address might appear as 10.100.100.9. This address must be unique within the network, and the address may be assigned either manually or dynamically via a process such as DHCP.

All devices contain an address (subnet) mask in addition to the IP address. This mask is applied to the address to identify the scope of the logical grouping. The mask is also 32 bits long.

Consider that the designer wishes to create a medium-sized IP network. The mask could be 255.255.255.0, which when applied to the address 10.100.100.9 yields a grouping of 256 addresses. The first address and the last are reserved, and the resulting mask permits 254 hosts. Note that the network portion of the address was defined by the ones portion of the mask—the 255 decimal notation. The zero notation signified eight zero bits, or the number of unique hosts within that network—equal to the same decimal number as two to the eighth power. In the same manner, the designer could select a mask of 255.255.255.252, which would permit a total of two hosts. These would be 10.100.100.9 and 10.100.100.10. The addresses 10.100.100.8 and 10.100.100.11 would fall into the reserved region.

It is also important to note that all IP addresses incorporate an implied mask. This will be discussed later in this chapter; however, it is important to note that 10.100.100.9 would contain a *natural* mask of 255.0.0.0.

Once the routers understand the mask information, it is possible to cluster these devices. Clustering is similar to the area-code function in phone numbers. (Clearly, it is easier to remember that 312 is located in Chicago and 213 is in Los Angeles. Each of these area codes represents millions of telephones.) This clustering function makes IP routing possible—otherwise, a forwarding table containing each individual host address would require extreme amounts of processing capacity to maintain the database.

The concept of *prefix routing* is also called *hierarchical addressing*. This process differs from summarization, but the basic concepts are similar. Again, the example of an area code and telephone number works well to illustrate the process, as shown in Figure 3.1.

FIGURE 3.1   Hierarchical addressing

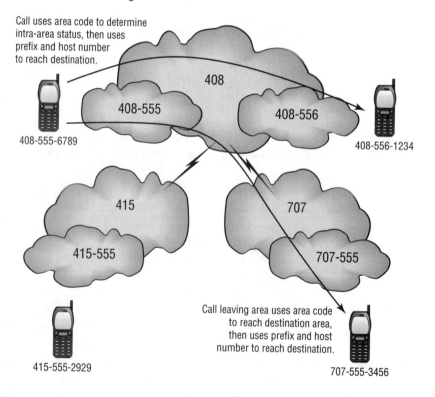

Call uses area code to determine intra-area status, then uses prefix and host number to reach destination.

408

408-555

408-556

408-555-6789

408-556-1234

415

707

415-555

707-555

415-555-2929

Call leaving area uses area code to reach destination area, then uses prefix and host number to reach destination.

707-555-3456

Designers should note that traditional classful routing would typically combine the area code and prefix numbers in route determination. Address assignments making use of summarization more closely mirror the telephone company model—using the area code to reach an area and then using the prefix, followed by the host number.

In addition to assigning an address and network, the designer must also choose which addresses to use. There are four possible methods for accomplishing this:

- Use legal, public addresses assigned to the Internet Service Provider (ISP).

- Use legal, public addresses assigned to the organization.

- Use legal, public addresses that belong to another organization—a choice that precludes full connectivity to the Internet.

- Use private addresses that do not propagate across the Internet.

Private Addresses—RFC 1918/RFC 1597

RFC 1918, one of the most-used RFCs (requests for comments), defines the private, reserved IP address space. Addresses in this space can be quite convenient, as the designer need not register with any authority. In addition, addresses assigned by the ISP belong to the ISP—should the corporation wish to change providers, it will also need to readdress all its devices.

RFC 1918 replaced RFC 1597; however, each basically defines the same policy. Under these RFCs, the public Internet will never assign or transport specific blocks of addresses, which are thus reserved for the private use of organizations. These addresses are shown in Table 3.3.

TABLE 3.3 RFC 1918 Addresses

Address	Available Allocation
10.0.0.0	1 Class A network
172.16.0.0 through 172.31.0.0	16 Class B networks
192.168.0.0 through 192.168.255.0	255 Class C networks

These address ranges provide the designer with an allocation in each of the IP classes—Classes A, B, and C, which will be defined in greater detail later in this chapter. The primary advantage to this approach is that the designer may assign addresses based on Class A or B address space. This option rarely exists for most small and medium-sized organizations.

Another advantage to RFC 1918 addresses is that they imply a degree of security. If the address cannot be routed on the Internet, it is very difficult for a remote attacker to reach the internal network. This is clearly oversimplified, as it would likewise be impossible for the internal devices to reach legal addresses on the Internet. Actually, designers use *proxies*, or devices that represent the internal network resources, in order to reach the public Internet. These proxies typically present themselves in firewalls; however, it is possible to translate only the address information or provide non-secure proxy services. The translation of address information is called NAT, or network address translation, which is presented in Chapter 11.

Public Addresses

Differing from the private addresses, public addresses are assigned and unique throughout the Internet. Unfortunately, under IP v4 and the methods used to assign addresses, there is a shortage of address space, especially in the larger network allocations—Classes A and B.

There should be little surprise that the advantages of RFC 1918 addresses are the disadvantages of public addresses, given the binary nature of selecting public or private address space. The corollary is also true.

The most significant negative of private addresses is that they are private. Anyone in any company can select any of them to use as they see fit. Some would argue that the benefits of returning IP addresses to the public pool to address the negatives are worth the complexities, including address translation and proxying Internet connections. However, consider the impact when two corporations not using RFC 1918 addresses merge in the context of the following:

- NAT and proxies are not needed.

- Protocols that do not support NAT, including NetBIOS, can traverse the network without difficulty.

- Designers are assured that their addresses are unique. This may become an issue following the merger of two companies that selected addresses under RFC 1918.

- Troubleshooting is simplified because Layer 3 addresses do not change during a host-to-host connection.

When corporations merge, they ultimately will merge data centers and resources to reduce operating costs. This will typically require readdressing for at least one of the two merged organizations if there is overlap. In addition, it is atypical for two design teams to allocate addresses exactly the same way. For example, architect one may place routers at the top of the address range, while architect two may prefer the bottom. Both ways are valid, but upon integration this minor difference may cause problems for support staffs and administrators.

The Function of the Router

The router is designed to isolate the broadcast domain and divide networks on logical boundaries—a function of the OSI model's Layer 3. This differs from switches and bridges, which operate at Layer 2, and repeaters and hubs, which operate at Layer 1.

Today's routers provide many additional features for the network architect, including security, encryption, and service quality. However, the role of the router remains unchanged—to forward packets based on logical addresses. In network design, this is considered routing.

Routing

The router provides two different functions in the network beyond the simple isolation of the broadcast domain. First, the router is responsible for determining paths for packets to traverse. This function is addressed by the routing protocol in use and is considered overhead. The dynamic updates between routers are part of this function.

The second function of the router is packet switching. This is the act of forwarding a packet based upon the path-determination process. Switching encompasses the following:

- Entry of the packet into the router.

- Obtaining the address information that will be needed for forwarding the packet. (In ATM, or Asynchronous Transfer Mode, it is the cell's VPI/VCI, or virtual path identifier/virtual channel identifier.)

- Determining the destination based on the address information.

- Modifying the header and checksum information as necessary.

- Transmitting the packet/frame/cell toward its destination.

While the router may also handle additional services, this list describes the functional steps required by the forwarding process. In addition to the forwarding of packets based on the Layer 3 logical address, the router is also required to determine the routes to those destinations—a process that relies on the administrative distance function described in the next section. However, routing, or more accurately, administration of the router, requires designers to consider many factors. Addressing, routing protocols, access lists, encryption, route maps (manipulation of the routing tables), and router security will only demand more attention in future years. Paths will also incorporate mobile IP and VPN (Virtual Private Network) technologies as the concept of an 80/20 rule migrates through 20/80 and toward 2/98. This means that virtually no traffic will remain local to the subnet, and as a result, the demands on administrators to work with other service providers will also increase.

If the router does not have a local interface in the major network and it receives a routing update with a classful protocol, the router will presume the natural mask. The natural mask for Class A is 255.0.0.0; for Class B it is 255.255.0.0; and for Class C it is 255.255.255.0. Readers should make sure that they understand how to identify an address' class and what the natural mask would be before continuing. This subject is covered in greater detail in the CCNA and ICRC preparation materials.

Administrative Distance

A router performs its function by determining the best method to reach a destination—a function that relies on the routing table and metrics. Metrics will be reviewed in greater detail in Chapter 4, but for now the metric of hops used in the IP RIP protocol will be our basis. You may recall that IP RIP adds a hop to each route when it passes through a router. Therefore, a source router can compare two or more routes to the same destination and typically presumes that the lowest hop count determined by the routing protocol will correspond with the best path through the network. Chapter 4 will discuss the limitations of the hop-based methodology; however, this system works reasonably well for links of similar bandwidth.

Cisco routers can also differentiate between IP routes based on the administrative distance. By adjusting the administrative distance, the administrator can implement a routing policy. This policy may be used during migration from one routing protocol to another or when multiple protocols exist in the network. Another use of the administrative distance is floating static routes, which are frequently used to supply a route when the routing protocol or link fails. Under these conditions, the static route is normally used with a DDR (dial-on-demand routing) circuit, and the administrator assigns a higher administrative distance to the static route than would be found with the dynamic protocols; once the dynamic routing protocols have exhausted all their routes, or the protocol has failed due to link failure, the highest administrative distance is the static route. Table 3.4 documents the administrative distances associated with various route sources. Note that by default a static route will supersede a dynamic routing protocol.

TABLE 3.4 The Default Administrative Distances

Route Type	Administrative Distance
Directly connected	0
Statically defined	1
BGP	20
BGP external	170
Internal EIGRP	90
External EIGRP	180
IGRP	100
OSPF	110

TABLE 3.4 The Default Administrative Distances *(continued)*

Route Type	Administrative Distance
RIP	120
Floating Static	Varies based on administrative preference; however, it is typically set above 130.

The administrative distance is set with the di stance command. The highest value is 255, and it is placed on each interface.

The router will select routes based on their administrative distance before considering the routing metric. This is an important consideration in both design and troubleshooting as the router may not act as expected—in actuality, it is doing exactly what it was told. This issue is particularly common in route redistribution. Designers employ route redistribution when a routing protocol's information must be propagated via another routing protocol. For example, the designer would use redistribution to transfer RIP routes into OSPF (Open Shortest Path First).

Selecting a Routing Protocol

One of the considerations novice network designers frequently forget is the selection of a routing protocol for IP. As a result, many networks begin with RIP version 1, and this installation remains in the network.

The following list presents some of the criteria for selecting a routing protocol:

- Support for variable-length subnet masks (VLSM)
- Network convergence time
- Support for discontiguous subnets
- Interoperability with existing hosts, servers, and routers
- Scalability to support existing and future needs
- Consideration for standards-based protocols

- Interoperability with autonomous systems and redistribution

- Usage of a small amount of bandwidth

- Adaptability to changes in the network as implemented

Routing protocols also incorporate characteristics that may require additional consideration. For example, connections likely fit into one of the following three types:

- Host-to-router

- Router-to-router

- Autonomous system-to-autonomous system

Host connections may obtain router information using a number of methods. These methods include:

- A preconfigured gateway address on the host.

- Use of the Proxy Address Resolution Protocol. Proxy ARP is also called the ARP hack, and it is enabled by default. It typically adds unnecessary broadcast traffic to the network. Proxy ARP routers will respond to ARPs for off-network resources and will make the original host believe that the remote host is local.

- Use of the ICMP (Internet Control Message Protocol) Router Discovery Protocol (IRDP).

- Use of the Gateway Discovery Protocol (GDP).

- The previous items in concert with Cisco's Hot Standby Router Protocol (HSRP).

- RIP on the host, preferably in passive mode.

Router-to-router connections are typically called *interior* routes and use interior routing protocols such as RIP, OSPF, IGRP, or EIGRP. The routes will all be contained within one autonomous system. Connections between autonomous systems are referred to as *exterior* routes and use exterior routing protocols. The most common exterior gateway protocol is eBGP. Note the small *e*, denoting the exterior implementation of the protocol. eBGP, also called BGP, is aptly defined as the routing protocol of the Internet.

It is important to note that classless routing protocols, such as EIGRP, look for the longest, or most specific, match when evaluating a route. This is also true for classful routing protocols. However, the designer must bear in mind that the mask for these routes must remain consistent. The router will assume the natural mask *or* the interface's mask.

Consider a router processing a packet destined for host 10.12.24.48. The following routes would be selected in order of appearance, as reflected in Table 3.5.

TABLE 3.5 Classless Routing Protocol Route Selection

Route	Mask	Device
10.12.24.48	/32	Host
10.12.24.0	/24	Subnet
10.0.0.0	/8	Network
0.0.0.0	/0	Default

Based on this example, it would be fair to say that the router has four routes to the host. And clearly, the best route is the most specific host route. However, as noted before, it is impractical for every router to maintain information regarding each host in the network. Referring to the area-code model, it would be just as valid for a remote router to maintain the subnet or network routes—the path, or next hop, remains the same. Taken to the extreme, networks at the far end of a hub-and-spoke design, shown in Figure 3.2, can provide connectivity with a single route. The default route is used when no other routes match the packet. Since Router A in Figure 3.2 sees everything except 192.168.2.0 as being outside the serial interface, it is easy for the designer to omit all other routes from this router and, in essence, fully summarize the routing table.

FIGURE 3.2   The use of the default route in hub-and-spoke designs

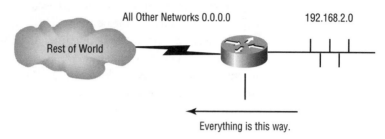

The ODR (on-demand routing) protocol, discussed in Chapter 4, will present this concept in greater detail. ODR uses a default route on the remote router to forward packets accordingly.

Discontiguous Subnets

One of the problems frequently encountered with classful routing protocols is the need to support discontiguous subnets. A discontiguous subnet is two or more portions of a major network that are divided by another major network. Figure 3.3 illustrates the concept.

FIGURE 3.3   Discontiguous subnets

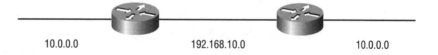

As shown, the major network 10.0.0.0 is split by the network 192.168.10.0. When running a classful routing protocol, RIP for example, each router believes that the major network is contained entirely outside its interface. Therefore, the router on the left believes that the entire 10.0.0.0 network is available outside the interface connected to the left. The same is true for the router on the right.

Administrators can resolve discontiguous subnet problems by using *tunnels*, or secondary interfaces, to link the two portions of the major network. This, in effect, makes the two networks contiguous. A better solution is to use a classless routing protocol that can summarize and accurately maintain information regarding the two halves of the network. This also avails VLSM and other features to the network and typically simplifies administration.

Discontiguous networks can be addressed with static mappings and other techniques; however, this can lead to *black holes*. This concept is presented in Chapter 13; briefly however, a black hole may leave a network unreachable under various failure scenarios.

Address Summarization

Address summarization provides a powerful function in IP networks. Under normal circumstances, each subnet would require a routing entry on every router in order to get packets to their destination. Thus, a collection of 32 subnets would require 32 routes on every router.

However, the router is concerned only with the path to the destination. As noted previously, a single default route could provide this path. While this configuration seriously limits redundancy and scalability in the network, it is a reasonable solution.

The compromise approach incorporates address summarization. Summarization can present hundreds of routes as a single entry in the routing table. This reduces memory demands and can prevent the need to recalculate a route should only a portion of the summarized network fail. For example, if 10.0.0.0 is available only via the FDDI (Fiber Distributed Date Interface) ring, it makes little difference if 10.12.24.0 is unavailable because the administrator shut down its interface.

Consider the following block of network addresses:

- 192.168.4.0

- 192.168.5.0

- 192.168.6.0

- 192.168.7.0

Each of these addresses would typically be deployed with the natural Class C mask—255.255.255.0. This would result in four route entries and four access-list entries. However, it would be much more efficient to use a single route entry and a single access list to represent all four address blocks.

Consider the binary representation of these addresses, as shown in Table 3.6.

TABLE 3.6   Binary Representation of IP Addresses

IP Address	Binary Representation
192.168.4.0	11000000.10101000.00000**100**.00000000
192.168.5.0	11000000.10101000.00000**101**.00000000
192.168.6.0	11000000.10101000.00000**110**.00000000
192.168.7.0	11000000.10101000.00000**111**.00000000

Notice how the only variance in the addresses is limited to two bits, off-set in bold? In order for the router to understand the range of addresses that is important, the administrator need only define the base address—192.168.4.0—and the number of bits that are significant—22. The 23rd and 24th bits don't matter, as whatever they equal still meets the range.

As a result of summarization, the network may be referenced as 192.168.4.0/22, or 255.255.252.0—the 23rd and 24th bits are moot. This summarization may be used in access lists (defined with a wildcard mask) or routing entries, although administrators should take care when using summarization and non-subnet-aware routing protocols. This topic will be discussed in detail in Chapter 4.

Summarization can be accomplished because the range of addresses meets two very important criteria. These are:

- The range of addresses is a power of two. In this example, there are four addresses in the range.

- The significant byte, which in this example is the third octet, is a multiple of the number of subnets in the range. Again, this number is four.

Consider summarization in a network's design along with addressing. An addressing plan that places three subnets in each remote office will likely not summarize at all—192.168.3.0 through 192.168.5.255, for example. This leads to inefficiencies that are too important to ignore if the network is to scale, and as a result it is generally preferable to skip addresses in the assignment process so that each range provides for growth and evenness. It is not uncommon to assign eight 254-host networks to a fairly small office, although it is practical to do so only when using RFC 1918 address space.

Beyond the academic presentation of summarization, designers will find in subsequent chapters and their designs that summarization is imperative to the configuration of a hierarchical network. Without effective summarization, the network cannot scale and becomes difficult to administer.

Load Balancing in IP

The router's physical design and its interfaces allow for a variety of switching processes on the router. This frees up the processor to focus on other tasks, instead of looking up the source and destination information for every packet that enters the router. Network designers should consider the options available to them in the processing of IP packets at Layer 3. This section will define and contrast the various methods Cisco routers use to handle forwarding.

Process Switching

Process switching is the slowest and most processor-intensive of the routing types. When a packet arrives on an interface to be forwarded, it is copied to the router's process buffer, and the router performs a lookup on the Layer 3 address. Using the route table, an exit interface is associated with the destination address. The processor encapsulates and forwards the packet with the new information to the exit interface. Subsequent packets bound for the same destination address follow the same path as the first packet.

The repeated lookups performed by the router's processor and the processor's relatively slow performance eventually create a bottleneck and greatly reduce the capacity of the router. This becomes even more significant as the bandwidth and number of interfaces increase and as the routing protocols demand more processor resources.

Fast Switching

Fast switching is an improvement over process switching. The first packet of a new session is copied to the interface processor buffer. The packet is then copied to the CxBus (or other backplane technology as appropriate to the platform) and sent to the switch processor. A check is made against other switching caches (for example, silicon or autonomous) for an existing entry.

Fast switching is then used because no entries exist within the more efficient caches. The packet header is copied and sent to the route processor, where the fast-switching cache resides. Assuming that an entry exists in the cache, the packet is encapsulated for fast switching and sent back to the switch processor. Then the packet is copied to the buffer on the outgoing interface processor, and ultimately it is sent out the destination interface.

Fast switching is on by default for lower-end routers like the 4000/2500 series and may be used on higher-end routers as well. It is important to note that diagnostic processes sometimes require reverting to process switching. Fast-switched packets will not traverse the route processor, which provides the method by which packets are displayed during debugging. Fast switching may also be inappropriate when bringing traffic from high-speed interfaces to slower ones—this is one area where designers must understand not only the bandwidth potential of their links, but also the actual flow of traffic.

Fast switching guarantees that packets will be processed within 16 processor cycles. Unlike process-switched packets, the router's processor will not be interrupted to facilitate forwarding.

Autonomous Switching

Autonomous switching is comparable to fast switching. When a packet arrives on the interface processor, it checks the switching cache closest to it—the caches that reside on other processor boards. The packet is encapsulated for autonomous switching and sent back to the interface processor. The packet header is not sent to the route processor. Autonomous switching is available only on AGS+ and Cisco 7000 series routers that have high-speed controller interface cards.

Silicon Switching

Silicon switching is available only on the Cisco 7000 with an SSP (Silicon Switch Processor). Silicon-switched packets are compared to the silicon-switching cache on the SSE (Silicon Switching Engine). The SSP is a dedicated switch processor that offloads the switching process from the route processor, providing a fast-switching solution. Designers should note that packets must still traverse the backplane of the router to get to the SSP, and then return to the exit interface. NetFlow switching (defined below) and multilayer switching are more efficient than silicon switching.

Optimum Switching

Optimum switching follows the same procedure as the other switching algorithms. When a new packet enters the interface, it is compared to the optimum-switching cache, rewritten, and sent to the chosen exit interface. Other packets associated with the same session then follow the same path. All processing is carried out on the interface processor, including the CRC (cyclical redundancy check). Optimum switching is faster than both fast switching and NetFlow switching, unless you have implemented several access lists.

Optimum switching replaces fast switching on high-end routers. As with fast switching, optimum switching must be turned off in order to view packets while troubleshooting a network problem. Optimum switching is the default on 7200 and 7500 routers.

Distributed Switching

Distributed switching occurs on the VIP (Versatile Interface Processor) cards, which have a switching processor onboard, so it's very efficient. All required processing is done right on the VIP processor, which maintains a copy of the router's routing cache. With this arrangement, even the first packet needn't be sent to the route processor to initialize the switching path, as it must with the other switching algorithms. Router efficiency increases as more VIP cards are added.

It is important to note that access lists cannot be accommodated with distributed switching.

NetFlow Switching

NetFlow switching is both an administrative tool and a performance-enhancement tool that provides support for access lists while increasing the volume of packets that can be forwarded per second. It collects detailed data for use with circuit accounting and application-utilization information. Because of all the additional data that NetFlow collects (and may export), expect an increase in router overhead—possibly as much as a five-percent increase in CPU utilization.

NetFlow switching can be configured on most interface types and can be used in a switched environment. ATM, LAN, and VLAN (virtual LAN) technologies all support NetFlow switching.

NetFlow switching does much more than just switching—it also gathers statistical data, including protocol, port, and user information. All of this is stored in the NetFlow switching cache, according to the individual flow that's defined by the packet information (destination address, source address, protocol, source and destination port, and incoming interface).

The data can be sent to a network management station to be stored and processed. The NetFlow switching process is very efficient: An incoming packet is processed by the fast- or optimum-switching process, and then all path and packet information is copied to the NetFlow cache. The remaining packets that belong to the flow are compared to the NetFlow cache and forwarded accordingly.

The first packet that's copied to the NetFlow cache contains all security and routing information, and if an access list is applied to an interface, the first packet is matched against it. If it matches the access-list criteria, the cache is flagged so that the remaining packets in the flow can be switched without being compared to the list. (This is very effective when a large amount of access-list processing is required.)

NetFlow switching can also be configured on VIP interfaces.

For each of these forwarding processes, designers should consider the impact of access lists. At present, NetFlow typically provides the best performance when access lists are needed. A recent study mentioned in an article by Peter Morrissey in *Network Computing* demonstrated a 700 percent performance benefit when using NetFlow and a 200-line access list. Performance benefits are lower with shorter lists; however, with anything beyond a single-line access list, NetFlow will yield better performance than optimal switching.

Cisco Express Forwarding

Cisco Express Forwarding (CEF) is a switching function, designed for high-end backbone routers. It functions on Layer 3 of the OSI model, and its biggest asset is the capability to remain stable in a large network. However, it's also more efficient than both the fast- and optimum-switching defaults. CEF is wonderfully stable in large environments because it doesn't rely on cached information. Instead of using a CEF cache, it refers to the Forwarding Information Base (FIB), which consists of information duplicated from the IP route table. Every time the routing information changes, the changes are propagated to the FIB. Thus, instead of comparing old cache information, a packet looks to the FIB for its forwarding information.

CEF stores the Layer 2 MAC addresses of connected routers (or next-hop) in the *adjacency table*. Even though CEF features advanced capabilities, you should consider several restrictions before implementing CEF on a router. According to the document "Cisco Express Forwarding," available from the Cisco Web page Cisco Connection Online, system requirements are quite high. The processor should have at least 128MB of RAM, and the line cards should have 32MB each. CEF takes the place of VIP distributed- and fast-switching on VIP interfaces. The following features aren't supported by CEF:

- ATM DXI

- Token Ring

- Multipoint PPP

- Access lists on the GSR (Giga Switch Router)

- Policy routing

- NAT

- SMDS

Nevertheless, CEF does many things—even load balancing is possible through the FIB. If there are multiple paths to the same destination, the IP route table knows about them all. This information is also copied to the FIB, which CEF consults for its switching decisions.

Load balancing can be configured in two different modes. The first mode is load balancing based on the destination (called *per-destination load balancing*); the second mode is based on the packet (called *per-packet load balancing*). Per-destination load balancing is on by default and must be turned off to enable per-packet load balancing.

Accounting may also be configured for CEF, which furnishes you with detailed statistics about CEF traffic. You can make two specifications when collecting CEF statistics:

- To collect information on traffic that's forwarded to a specific destination

- To collect statistics for traffic that's forwarded through a specific destination

CEF was designed for large networks—if reliable and redundant switching paths are necessary, CEF is certainly preferred. However, there are significant hardware requirements, and some Cisco IOS features may not be available.

Cisco routers may support concurrent load balancing when routing IP. However, this feature is dependent on the switching mechanism in use. Up to six paths may be balanced in the current releases of the IOS, dependent on the routing protocol in use.

Autonomous and silicon switching have been updated with optimum, distributed, and NetFlow. However, from a load-balancing perspective, they operate in the same manner as their replacements. Autonomous and silicon-switched packets will be load-balanced by destination.

Summary

This chapter presented a wide array of material on the IP protocol and on some of the criteria for selecting an IP routing protocol. The next chapter will build upon this material and provide greater depth regarding the options available to designers regarding IP routing protocols.

Readers should feel comfortable with the following concepts:

- IP address structures

- IP address classes

- IP address summarization

- The implications of RFC 1918/RFC 1597

- The methods used by the router to forward packets

- The role of the router and its additional features

- The problems associated with discontiguous subnets and the benefits of VLSM-aware protocols

Designers should also be prepared to integrate this material into the following chapter, which details the IP routing protocols, and subsequent ones, which address non-IP-based protocols and the issues that confront designers in typical networks.

Review Questions

1. Which of the following are methods used to assign IP addresses?

   A. Manual configuration

   B. WINS

   C. DHCP

   D. BootP

   E. NFS

2. The designer's major issues when designing for IP networks are:

   A. Routing

   B. Addressing

   C. Security

   D. Naming

   E. All of the above

3. When selecting a routing protocol, the designer would NOT consider which of the following?

   A. Convergence time

   B. Addressing flexibility

   C. CDP packets

   D. Support across vendors/platforms

   E. Resource utilization

   F. Topology of the network

4. Which of the following would be reasons to summarize routes?

   A. Reduction in the size of the routing table

   B. Increase in the size of the routing table

   C. Redundancy

   D. Load balancing

5. The designer configures the network to present the routes from the distribution layer to the core as 10.11.0.0/16. This is an example of:

   A. DHCP

   B. Route summarization

   C. BootP

   D. CDP

6. To support VLSM and route summarization, a routing protocol must be:

   A. Classful

   B. Classless

   C. Dynamic

   D. Enhanced

7. A classful routing protocol will:

   A. Not support VLSM

   B. Route on the first octet bits and their significance

   C. Not include subnet information in routing updates

   D. All of the above

   E. None of the above

8. A classless routing protocol will:

   A. Not support VLSM

   B. Route on the first octet bits and their significance

   C. Not include subnet information in routing updates

   D. All of the above

   E. None of the above

9. The natural mask for address 148.241.14.56 would be which of the following?

   A. 255.0.0.0

   B. 255.255.0.0

   C. 255.255.255.0

   D. Cannot be determined with the information provided

10. A routing update using a classful routing protocol (assuming no network member interfaces on the receiving router) for 10.11.1.0/24 would appear as which of the following?

   A. 10.0.0.0

   B. 10.11.0.0

   C. 10.11.1.0

   D. Cannot be determined with the information provided.

11. The summary address 192.168.8.0/22 represents:

   A. 192.168.0.0 to 192.168.7.255

   B. 192.168.0.0 to 192.168.255.255

   C. 192.168.8.0 to 192.168.11.255

   D. Class C address space cannot be summarized

12. Which summarization best covers 162.15.4.0 through 162.15.7.0?

    A. 162.15.7.0/24

    B. 162.15.7.0/22

    C. 162.15.0.0.22

    D. 162.15.4.0/22

13. To summarize the addresses from 162.110.84.0 to 162.110.87.255, the designer would best use:

    A. 162.110.87.0 255.255.252.0

    B. 162.110.84.0 255.255.255.0

    C. 162.110.87.255 255.255.255.255

    D. 162.110.84.0 255.255.252.0

14. The address 121.45.11.40 is:

    A. Class A

    B. Class B

    C. Class C

    D. Class D

15. The address 127.60.80.12 is:

    A. Class A

    B. Class B

    C. Class C

    D. None of the above

16. One disadvantage of classful routing protocols, including RIP and IGRP, is:

    A. All interfaces must be of the same type.

    B. All interfaces must use the same network mask.

    C. All interfaces must use the natural mask.

    D. All interfaces must be within the same subnet.

17. Secondary interfaces do not provide:

    A. A means to link discontiguous subnets

    B. A method for adding hosts to a physical media

    C. Trunking via ISL or 802.1q

    D. Support for local routing

18. Which of the following would be the best reason to use registered public address space?

    A. To avoid addressing problems should the corporation merge with another organization

    B. To obtain Class C address space

    C. To simplify NAT processes

    D. None of the above

19. Each Class C network could support:

    A. Two hosts

    B. 16 hosts

    C. 64 hosts

    D. 254 hosts

20. Which of the following routes would the router most likely use?

    A. A route to the subnet

    B. A route to the host

    C. A route to the network

    D. A default route

Answers to Review Questions

1. A, C, D.

   DHCP and BootP are dynamic assignment methods.

2. E.

3. C.

4. A.

5. B.

6. B.

7. D.

8. E.

9. B.

10. A.

11. C.

12. D.

13. D.

14. A.

15. D.

16. B.

17. C.

18. A.

19. D.

20. B.

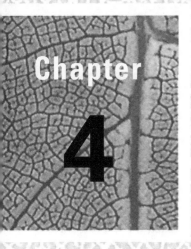

Chapter 4

The IP Routing Protocols

CISCO INTERNETWORK DESIGN EXAM OBJECTIVES COVERED IN THIS CHAPTER:

- ✓ Choose the appropriate IP routing protocol and features based on convergence, overhead, and topology.

- ✓ Identify IP routing pathologies and issues and how to avoid them.

- ✓ Use modular design and summarization features to design scalable Open Shortest Path First (OSPF) internetworks.

- ✓ Allocate IP addresses in contiguous blocks so that OSPF summarization can be used.

- ✓ Determine IGRP convergence time for various internetwork configurations.

- ✓ Use IGRP for path determination in IP internetworks.

- ✓ Use Enhanced IGRP for path determination in internetworks that support IP, IPX, and AppleTalk.

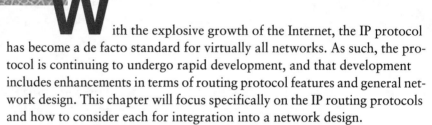

With the explosive growth of the Internet, the IP protocol has become a de facto standard for virtually all networks. As such, the protocol is continuing to undergo rapid development, and that development includes enhancements in terms of routing protocol features and general network design. This chapter will focus specifically on the IP routing protocols and how to consider each for integration into a network design.

Readers will likely note a number of recurrent themes in this presentation—the features of each protocol and the convergence time characteristics. Whenever a network topology changes, it is the job of the routing protocol to reroute traffic and determine the new best paths for data flow on the internetwork. (The amount of time required to complete this process in the event of any change is referred to as *convergence time*.) These are two of the most significant factors in selecting a routing protocol. Additional factors include familiarity, support, and availability.

IP Routing Protocols

In the previous chapter, the Internet Protocol (IP) and the criteria for designing networks using IP were addressed. This chapter will build upon those concepts by adding the dynamic IP routing protocols including RIP, RIP version 2, IGRP, EIGRP, OSPF, ODR, BGP, and IS-IS.

Dynamic routing protocols were developed to circumvent the deficits found in static routing. This chapter will present network design with static routes, in addition to the IP routing protocols listed in Table 4.1. Please note that each of these protocols will be presented in greater detail later in this chapter—Table 4.1 is primarily concerned with providing an overview of the routing protocols that will be discussed.

TABLE 4.1 Comparison of the IP Routing Protocols

Protocol	Characteristics
RIP	The Routing Information Protocol (RIP) supports IP and is still a reasonable choice for small networks that do not require variable-length subnets. It is supported by most vendors and is interoperable with servers and workstations. Unfortunately, RIP uses hops only to determine the path, and the hop count is limited to 15. In addition, updates are sent every 30 seconds and incorporate the entire routing table.
RIP v2	Version 2 of RIP builds upon the success of the original protocol. However, it is still limited by hop count, sends its complete routing table every 30 seconds, and is limited by a 15-hop network diameter. Version 2 also adds VLSM (variable-length subnet mask) support and authentication.
IGRP	Interior Gateway Routing Protocol (IGRP) is a Cisco proprietary, distance-vector, routing protocol. It uses a composite metric of 24 bits and offers faster convergence when compared to RIP. However, it does not support VLSM and sends its entire routing table every 90 seconds.
EIGRP	Enhanced IGRP (EIGRP) is built upon IGRP, and thus the protocol is also proprietary to Cisco. It was designed for easy migration from existing IGRP networks and adds a number of features to the routing process. These enhancements include support for VLSM, fast convergence, incremental updates, compound metrics, and additional support for IPX and AppleTalk, which are not supported in IGRP.

TABLE 4.1 Comparison of the IP Routing Protocols *(continued)*

Protocol	Characteristics
OSPF	The Open Shortest Path First (OSPF) routing protocol will typically be selected by designers looking for an open standards-based routing protocol that compares with EIGRP. Updates are based on a link-state database, which is shared by all routers in the network area.
IS-IS	The Intermediate System-to-Intermediate System (IS-IS) protocol is also an open standards-based routing process that provides fast convergence. In addition, updates contain only changes. IS-IS uses a hello-based system (hello-based systems confirm the operation of the adjacent router with hello packets) and supports variable-length subnet masks; however, it has a limited metric and some topology restrictions. Updates are based on links, not routes.
ODR	On-demand routing (ODR) makes use of data in the proprietary Cisco Discovery Protocol (CDP) function in the Cisco IOS (Internet Operating System). CDP packets typically provide diagnostic information only about other Cisco routers; however, the ODR process can use this information to develop a routing table. It is a very limited routing function, but it provides many of the benefits of static routes without incurring the overhead of a routing protocol.
BGP	The Border Gateway Protocol (BGP) is the de facto protocol of the Internet backbone. Technically a path-vector protocol, the external version (eBGP) is primarily concerned with the relationships between autonomous systems (AS). One benefit to BGP is its use of persistent TCP sessions for the exchange of routing information.

Chapter 3 defined path determination as an overhead activity for the router. This factor directly impacts the selection of a routing protocol.

Designers should consider the different resources that are needed to implement a routing protocol, including router CPU, router memory, link bandwidth, support staff familiarity, and protocol features, which include support for VLSM, summarization, and convergence.

Designers should ask themselves the following questions when selecting a routing protocol:

- Under what conditions are routing updates sent?

    - This relates to timers, events, or both.

- What is transmitted during a routing update?

    - Some protocols send only the changes to the routing table during an update. Other protocols send the entire routing table.

- How are routing updates propagated?

    - Some routing protocols send updates and information only to adjacent neighbors, while others send information to a cluster of routers (an area) or to an autonomous system.

- How long does the convergence process take?

    - The time required to converge all routing tables in the internetwork depends upon many factors. Re-convergence occurs when a path that is used suddenly becomes unavailable. Dynamic routing protocols make every effort to locate an alternative route to the destination. Some protocols, like EIGRP, calculate alternative paths before the failure, which facilitates rapid convergence. Other protocols require significant amounts of time to distribute information regarding the failure and calculate the alternative path.

Routers also combine various methods for learning routes. These methods should be designed to work together to establish the most efficient routing throughout the network. In addition to the technical considerations, designers should also consider cost in defining efficiency.

The router may obtain route information from any or all of the following sources:

- Connected interfaces

- Static routing entries

- Information learned from dynamic routing protocols

- Redistribution between routing protocols

- ARP, Inverse ARP, and ICMP redirects

- Manipulation of the previous methods via access lists and other filters

Designers should also consider what methods are available to trigger failure updates. Local interfaces can be detected via keepalives, including ATM OAM (operation, administration, and maintenance) cells, and the carrier-detect lead.

Network Design with Static Routing

Before presenting the dynamic routing protocols, it is appropriate to provide an overview of static routes. Static routes refer in the generic to those routes that are manually entered by the network administrator into the router's configuration file. These routes may be used in at least one of three typical situations.

- The administrator needs to define a default route for packets to leave the network.

- The administrator requires a route that takes effect upon failure of the dynamic routing process. This is called a *floating-static route*.

- A dynamic routing protocol is not available or desirable. This may be for security, bandwidth, or compatibility concerns. Frequently, static routes are used to reduce overhead on single-point, low-bandwidth circuits.

There are a couple of deficits with static routes, however. First, the routes are static—as the name suggests. This means that failures in the network topology cannot be detected and circumvented automatically. Second, the administrator must manually populate the routing table and maintain the entries whenever a change to the network is made.

Cisco routers automatically support proxy ARP on most interfaces. The proxy ARP function will spoof off-network resources with the router's MAC (Media Access Control) address, and the router will take the responsibility of forwarding packets to the final end node. This behavior permits the establishment of routes based on interfaces as opposed to the IP address. For example, the route may be through router 192.168.5.1, but the administrator can reference the route as being out interface Ethernet 0/0.

Because of security, diagnostic, and performance concerns, it is recommended that administrators not use the proxy ARP function and that it be disabled on all interfaces. While it is possible to find network administrators with little or no experience with one of the more advanced dynamic routing protocols, it is very unlikely that an administrator will not have experience with static routes. This static route experience may be to define a default route off the network or to define routes in areas where a dynamic routing protocol would be undesirable, including those in secure arenas and between companies.

Static routes offer the administrator a high degree of control over the network and consume no bandwidth for routing updates, making them advantageous on limited-bandwidth or low-reliability links. So, given the benefits of static routes—familiarity, controllability, and efficiency—why would a designer choose to not use static routes?

The answer typically is that designers do use static routes and, in fact, may use them quite often in the overall network design. However, the scalability of the network is greatly limited if the entire network is designed using static routes. This chapter will address the benefits of the dynamic routing protocols later, but for now will define these benefits as load balancing, redundancy, and scalability.

Network Design in the Real World: A Production Design Consideration

Before addressing the details of each routing protocol, it is important to establish a context that brings us back to design. The specifics of each routing protocol could easily consume an entire text on their own, and there are many solid treatments on each. However, for the exam objectives, it is only necessary to have a cursory understanding of each protocol—a level of detail that would be insufficient in production networks.

Therefore, this sidebar includes a scenario to illustrate a simple design challenge related to the selection of a routing protocol. The deployed solution is provided, so do not consider this to be a test. Rather, review this at a high level—the specific details of each protocol are provided only as a matrix for this solution set. In your network designs, you will likely add much more detail in terms of cost, complexity, supportability, and availability.

A large financial institution recently deployed a 70+-router network using all static routes. Clearly, it is possible to route a large number of networks using static routes; however, the design is severely limited, particularly in terms of administrative overhead. The network is a hub-and-spoke design with limited bandwidth and single routes throughout. The institution also desired that the network support different subnet masks, although the initial design was based on two hosts per subnet (a /30 mask). Given these conditions, consider the choices available to the designers and whether you would agree with the solution deployed. The routing options for a hub-and-spoke network are as follows:

RIP   No support for VLSM. Efficient, but consumes bandwidth.

RIP v2   Supports VLSM and is efficient, but is unfamiliar to this organization and consumes bandwidth.

OSPF   While a strong choice from a number of perspectives, the design team was concerned about router CPU utilization and potential design issues should the enterprise convert to OSPF. The protocol supports VLSM and is fairly efficient regarding bandwidth utilization. Guidelines vary, but most experts recommend fewer than 50 OSPF neighbors (contrasting with EIGRP's recommendation of 30—partly the result of memory requirements and partly the benefit of link-state protocols), so this design would be pushing that constraint.

EIGRP   While supported on the more advanced routers used for the pilot, EIGRP was not supported on the CBOS (Cisco Broadband Operating System) routers (600 series) that were preferred for cost reasons. In addition, EIGRP isn't well suited to hub-and-spoke designs and may have problems with low memory/CPU routers with as few as 12 neighbors. A good protocol overall, EIGRP is not well suited to this design.

IGRP   IGRP would not support VLSM, and it was not supported by the CBOS routers.

Static   Static routes consume no bandwidth and use a minimal amount of CPU. In addition, the use of static routes will support variable-length subnet masks (in a manner of speaking). The downside is that static routes must be configured by the administrator.

> Following a review of the above material, the only viable choices were RIP v2 and static routes. RIP v2 was considered, but the number of remote configuration steps and the bandwidth consumption issues were sufficient to put it in second place.
>
> Notice some of the themes used in selecting a routing protocol: link bandwidth, router CPU utilization, router memory, support for VLSM, redundant paths, load balancing, availability, and support staff familiarity. These will be important factors in your designs.

Network Design with RIP

The Routing Information Protocol (RIP) is an amazing protocol. Few things in computing have lasted as long—and with as few changes (not counting RIP v2). However, IP RIP is a very limited (by today's standards) distance-vector protocol capable of serving networks with up to 15 hops. It is classful, which means that the protocol does not include subnet mask information—therefore, route summarization and VLSM functions are not available.

In actuality, RIP and the other classful routing protocols do summarize—unfortunately, it is on the classful boundary, which was discussed in Chapter 3. Therefore, summarization with a classful protocol is typically a deterent.

RIP v2 builds upon the original RIP specification and adds a number of features, the most significant of which is the sharing of subnet mask information. Thus, RIP v2 supports VLSM. Figure 4.1 illustrates the packet formats for both RIP and RIP v2. Note that there are many similarities between the two in order to facilitate interoperability.

FIGURE 4.1   The RIP and RIP v2 packet formats

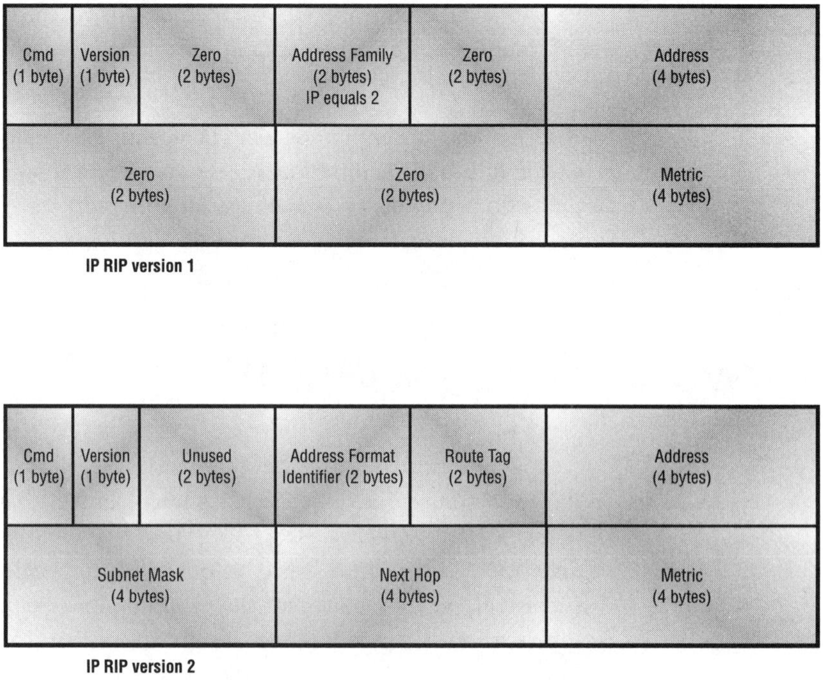

Cmd (1 byte)	Version (1 byte)	Zero (2 bytes)	Address Family (2 bytes) IP equals 2	Zero (2 bytes)	Address (4 bytes)
Zero (2 bytes)			Zero (2 bytes)		Metric (4 bytes)

IP RIP version 1

Cmd (1 byte)	Version (1 byte)	Unused (2 bytes)	Address Format Identifier (2 bytes)	Route Tag (2 bytes)	Address (4 bytes)
Subnet Mask (4 bytes)			Next Hop (4 bytes)		Metric (4 bytes)

IP RIP version 2

Consider the network illustrated in Figure 4.2. This network is a radical departure from the hierarchical model, but it is an excellent model from which to describe and understand RIP and hop count. Note that this topology would be considered a partial mesh or complex mesh, as opposed to a full mesh.

The numbers on each line reflect the hop count for each router hop. Therefore, the hop count from Router A to Router B is 3, while the hop count from Router A to Router C is 1. In this scenario, the designer has manipulated the hop counters to reflect policy, which was likely related to the bandwidth of the circuit. While this drawing does not so indicate, assume that a hop count of 1 is a full T1 circuit and higher numbers reflect proportionally lower bandwidth paths.

FIGURE 4.2   Complex mesh network with RIP

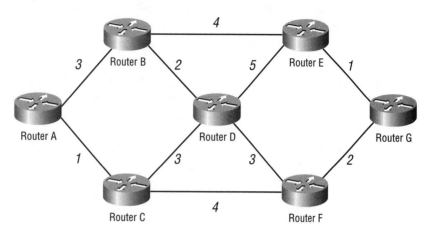

RIP uses hop count only to determine the path. Using Figure 4.2, determine the path that Router A would use to send packets to Router G. You will find that the path A-C-F-G, with a hop count of 7, would be used over the other routes. Note that the hop count values do not surpass 15—a hop count of 16 marks the route as unavailable in RIP.

It is important to note that RIP networks designed with the hierarchical model would have a maximum default hop count of 6—easily within the 15-hop limitation. Other designs, especially those that manipulate the hop metric, may exceed this limitation more easily.

Convergence time is an important consideration in selecting a routing protocol. RIP is one of the slower routing protocols in terms of convergence, although the hierarchical design model also works to facilitate the fastest possible convergence.

Network Design with IGRP

The Interior Gateway Routing Protocol (IGRP) is quite common in large, enterprise-scale, corporate networks. However, like EIGRP, the protocol is proprietary to Cisco and requires a commitment to the Cisco platform. Many companies are reluctant to make such a business decision, and designers will likely need to deploy an open-standard protocol, such as

OSPF. In addition, IGRP, and its successor, EIGRP, tolerate arbitrary topologies better than OSPF—however, designers should strive to follow the hierarchical model in order to improve convergence and troubleshooting.

It is unlikely that a designer would select IGRP for a completely new network design, but it might still be warranted for reasons that will be presented in this section. It is much more likely that the use of IGRP will be based on previous deployments of the protocol and the required integration that the network will demand. A recent Cisco survey found IGRP and EIGRP in over 50 percent of networks.

IGRP is a more advanced protocol than RIP, which it was designed to replace. It is a distance-vector protocol that uses a 24-bit metric value to determine the best route, with a maximum of 254 hops (default value of 100 hops). This is greatly enhanced over RIP's 15-hop-based metric. Other benefits include load balancing and path determination, where the protocol can select from multiple default networks. IGRP is also more tolerant of non-hierarchical topologies; unlike EIGRP, IGRP can support arbitrary topology configurations. However, both protocols operate better when deployed with a strong design. It is important to note that complex mesh configurations will impact convergence in both IGRP and EIGRP, but the redundancy benefits of these designs may offset the negatives.

As with RIP, IGRP transmits the entire routing table with each update, which by default occurs every 90 seconds (compared to RIP at every 30 seconds). These updates may contain 104 route entries (within a 1,500-byte packet), which is a clear improvement over IP RIP, which includes only 25 routes. Unfortunately, the entire routing table is sent each time. Of more importance in advanced networks, IGRP does not support VLSM and is classful. Finally, IGRP uses the concept of *split-horizon* to prevent routing loops. By default this feature is on. However, the architect may disable it to support point-to-multipoint installations.

Some texts state that split-horizon is disabled automatically with some topologies, such as SMDS. This is incorrect. You should use the show ip interface command to check the current status of an interface.

Split-horizon is used to prevent routing loops by blocking the advertisement of a route out the interface that it was learned from. *Poison reverse* is a variation on this concept that sends the route back to the source, but with an illegal metric.

IGRP Metrics

The IGRP metric is one of the most significant advantages for network designers using the protocol. Unlike RIP, which uses hop count as a single metric, IGRP uses two important factors, of six possible metrics, to determine routes. These are presented in Table 4.2.

TABLE 4.2   The IGRP Routing Metrics

Metric	Characteristics
Bandwidth	The bandwidth metric is based on the bandwidth statement on an interface in the routing path. It is used in the calculation of IGRP routing metrics. The value is cumulative and static. Unless configured with the bandwidth command, IGRP will presume the default of T1, or 1.544Mbps on standard serial interfaces (default for Ethernet is 10Mbps).
Delay	The delay metric is also static and is an accumulation of the entire path delay. It is inversely proportional to bandwidth.
Reliability	Calculated from keepalives, the reliability metric (if enabled) is dynamic and represents the reliability of the path over time. A link with lower reliability would become less desirable. Values range from 0 to 255, with the default 255 being 100 percent reliable.
Loading	Loading is a dynamic measure of the utilization of the link, expressed as a value from 0 to 255, with the default 0 being 0 percent load. It would make sense to use this value to avoid congestion. However, doing so could result in significant changes to the routing table—and these changes may occur too slowly to improve real-time data transfers. Note that loading is not enabled by default.

TABLE 4.2 The IGRP Routing Metrics *(continued)*

Metric	Characteristics
MTU	The maximum transmission unit (MTU) portion of the metric (if enabled) takes into account the fact that some media can support larger packet sizes. For example, Ethernet (ignoring jumbo frames and trunking) can support only 1500-byte packets, whereas FDDI, ATM, and Token Ring can all easily exceed that value. By the same measure, some serial interfaces cannot support MTUs greater than 576 bytes. Because fragmentation and header overhead are reduced with a larger MTU, these routes are preferable. MTU is not considered by IGRP. A well-designed network will typically configure all links for the same MTU in order to reduce overhead—the value of 1500 being most common to account for Ethernet.
Hops	The hop metric is the same basic function found in IP RIP. The protocol simply counts the number of routers between itself and the destination. In IGRP, the hop count is used to break ties.

By default, IGRP considers only two metrics in determining the best route through the network—bandwidth and delay. Under ideal conditions, IGRP will weight bandwidth more heavily for shorter routes (routes with fewer hops) and delay for longer routes. This can provide a more accurate representation of the network's capacity.

Load Balancing

As noted previously, IGRP supports the function of both equal- and unequal-cost load balancing (if configured), which provides multiple active routes through the network. This can both aid performance and improve convergence—when an alternate route is already in use, it can be used for additional traffic that was normally destined for the failed link.

Unequal-cost load balancing relies on an IGRP setting called *variance* to be set to a value other than the default of 1. The method in which packets are balanced differs based on the type of switching in use.

Recall that the router can forward packets based on process switching, in which each packet is processed by the processor, or fast switching, in which case forwarding is not reliant on the processor for each datagram. For this presentation, please consider fast switching to encompass all other forms of switching, including autonomous and distributed.

In process switching, load balancing is allocated based on the bandwidth of the link. As shown in Figure 4.3, this would yield one packet on a 64Kbps circuit to every two packets on a 128Kbps circuit. This also assumes that variance is configured at 2.

FIGURE 4.3   Process-switched load balancing

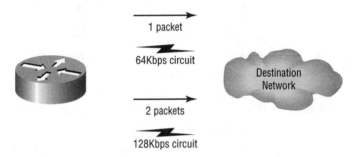

In fast switching, the overhead incurred for per-packet load balancing would be significant. As a result, the router forwards packets on a per-destination basis. As illustrated in Figure 4.4, this yields two destinations serviced by one router to every one destination serviced by the other router in the load-balanced installation. Variance should remain at 1 for fast-switched load balancing to avoid *pinhole congestion*. Pinhole congestion traps a higher demand connection to a slower link—an undesirable characteristic.

FIGURE 4.4   Fast-switched load balancing

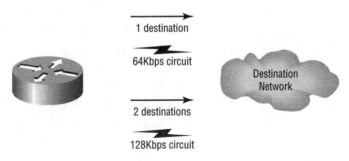

IGRP Convergence

The most significant test of a dynamic routing protocol is observed in its response to a network failure. Based on the characteristics of the routing protocol, the network may recover (assuming redundant paths) quickly or slowly. The amount of time required for the network to recover is called *convergence*.

IGRP was designed to reduce convergence time, and while it is not as fast as EIGRP, it can handle most outages in less than the 90-second update interval. This is made possible by the use of triggered updates.

Triggered updates will occur when the routing protocol is informed of a link failure. This is instantaneous for Fiber Distributed Data Interface (FDDI) and Token Ring, or when carrier detect is lost. For other network interfaces, failure is determined by keepalives, and failure is dependent on the keepalive timer interval. The following output provides an example of the keepalive timer as shown in the show interface command:

```
Router_A#show interface s0
Serial0 is up, line protocol is up
  Hardware is MK5025
  Description: Circuit
  Internet address is 10.1.5.181/24
  MTU 1500 bytes, BW 1544 Kbit, DLY 20000 usec, rely 255/255,
      load 2/255
  SMDS hardware address is c121.3555.7443
  Encapsulation SMDS, loopback not set,
   keepalive set (10 sec)
  ARP type: SMDS, ARP Timeout 04:00:00
  Mode(s):  D15 compatibility
  Last input 00:00:00, output 00:00:00, output hang never
  Last clearing of "show interface" counters 1w1d
  Queueing strategy: fifo
  Output queue 0/40, 0 drops; input queue 1/75, 0 drops
  5 minute input rate 41000 bits/sec, 18 packets/sec
  5 minute output rate 17000 bits/sec, 17 packets/sec
     12401968 packets input, 171211114 bytes, 0 no buffer
```

```
Received 0 broadcasts, 0 runts, 0 giants, 0 throttles
0 input errors, 0 CRC, 0 frame, 0 overrun, 0 ignored,
    0 abort
10583498 packets output, 1920074976 bytes, 0 underruns
0 output errors, 0 collisions, 0 interface resets
0 output buffer failures, 0 output buffers swapped out
0 carrier transitions
```

Upon failure, IGRP will transmit a triggered update to notify its neighbors of the unreachable networks. The neighbors, or adjacent routers, will then trigger updates to their neighbors, ultimately leading to the information reaching all routers in the network. Each of these triggered updates occurs independently from the regular update, although the triggered update and the regular update may coincide. Holddown timers are also used to assist in the convergence process. By default, the holddown timer is equal to three times the update interval of IGRP, plus 10 seconds. This results in a default holddown time of 280 seconds, during which time the router will not respond to routes that have been *poisoned*, or advertised as unreachable. It is important to note that some designers eliminate the holddown timer on links with high bandwidth. Without the holddown function, it is possible to generate a significant amount of traffic during the convergence process. The command to manipulate this function is `no metric holddown`. Normally, if a higher metric route to a destination appears, it is poisoned to prevent loops.

Triggered updates are invoked on link-state changes only.

Designers should also note that the holddown timer does not dictate convergence times when load balancing is configured and that routes are flushed based on the flush timer. The flush timer is seven times the update interval, or 630 seconds, by default.

> **Network Design in the Real World: IGRP**
>
> In the financial and insurance industries, it seems as if every Cisco shop migrated to IGRP and has been cursed ever since. It is unfortunate that the protocol has garnered this reputation, as it is an improvement over IP RIP.
>
> The majority of the problems associated with IGRP involve its lack of VLSM support. In addition, the proprietary nature of the protocol further limits its flexibility in the network.
>
> Today, few networks are being designed around IGRP, and most companies have committed to migrations away from the protocol. There is little doubt that it will remain in use for some time, but EIGRP, OSPF, RIP v2, and other protocols will certainly replace it in the long run.
>
> It is important to note that EIGRP configuration, discussed in the next section, is very similar to IGRP—an effort by Cisco to facilitate conversion.

Network Design with EIGRP

The Enhanced Interior Gateway Routing Protocol (EIGRP) is one of the more interesting protocols for the network designer to consider. First, the protocol is proprietary to Cisco, which will greatly limit the designer's options in incorporating other vendors' hardware. Second, the protocol offers many of the benefits found in OSPF without requiring a rigid design model. Unfortunately, it is this second item that frequently causes problems in EIGRP—designers and administrators use EIGRP without understanding it or planning for its use. This may be due to its position as a replacement for IGRP, which frequently adds the complexity of incorporating the legacy network into the design.

EIGRP is based on the distance-vector model, although it is quite advanced and shares components of link-state as well. The protocol supports variable-length subnet masks (VLSM), which can greatly assist the designer in IP address allocation. EIGRP works to prevent loops and speed convergence, both factors that assist the network architect. EIGRP also supports equal-cost load balancing, which can greatly augment the bandwidth and reliability of the network. Unequal-cost load balancing is also supported with the variance mechanism.

If there were a single negative factor with EIGRP, it would have to be its lack of documentation and use in the real world. This situation is quickly changing, but many companies have deployed IP EIGRP only to later remove it because of CPU, memory, and route-flapping issues. Once properly configured and designed, EIGRP quickly redeems itself, given its powerful features. One criterion towards this goal is to avoid using EIGRP in hub-and-spoke designs, as these configurations quickly demonstrate the protocol's inability to scale and converge. This presentation of EIGRP will focus solely on IP EIGRP; it is important to note that EIGRP will support AppleTalk and IPX routing. However, separate tables are maintained for each of the three supported protocols, and each protocol uses separate hello messages, timers, and metrics.

In addition to the separate routing, topology, and neighbor tables maintained on the router for each protocol, EIGRP uses reliable and unreliable transports to provide routing functions. The primary mechanism in EIGRP is the hello datagram, which is used to maintain verification that a router is still active. When a topology change event occurs in the network, the protocol will establish a connection-oriented communications channel for the updates.

Many of the EIGRP commands and default behaviors are similar to IGRP in order to augment migration efforts. For example, EIGRP performs an automatic classful summarization like IGRP, although EIGRP adds VLSM support.

EIGRP Neighbors

One of the most limiting factors regarding EIGRP is the lack of detailed information about the protocol. A significant component of this is the neighbor relationship. Neighbor relationships are established between two routers running in the same EIGRP autonomous system (AS).

While the "Network Design in the Real World: EIGRP" sidebar provides additional tips regarding EIGRP, most designers would be well advised to consult with others who have deployed the protocol. Although EIGRP is extremely powerful, the reality is that little information is available regarding actual deployments. This can be a significant factor in deployments with high numbers of neighbors, poor addressing and design, and low memory and CPU availability on the routers. Many problems with EIGRP involve the number of neighbors, especially with the Route Switch Module (RSM) in the Catalyst product line. Unlike a router, the RSM typically terminates multiple networks and has many neighbors—more than are found in a typical installation with routers. In addition, the RSM is relatively limited in terms of backplane connectivity (400Mbps) and processor (an RSP 2). Therefore, a high number of neighbors will affect an RSM before a comparable installation with RSP 4s and a 7513 router—a factor that has impacted many EIGRP conversions.

The Diffusing Update Algorithm

The Diffusing Update Algorithm, or DUAL, is the route-determination process in EIGRP. It permits the routing process to determine whether a path advertised is looped or loop-free. In addition, routers using EIGRP can determine alternative paths before receiving updates that link failure has occurred from other routers. The concept of always having a "second-best" route in memory greatly aids in reducing convergence time, which can increase the reliability of the network design.

The primary design criterion for EIGRP is the maintenance of a loop-free topology at all points in the route-calculation process. At the same time, EIGRP attempts to reduce the total amount of convergence time by maintaining alternate routes in memory, a factor that typically works against loop-free techniques. EIGRP maintains information about successors (the best possible route to a destination) and feasible successors (the second-best route to a destination) in order to reduce the amount of time involved in convergence.

Like OSPF, EIGRP uses a hello mechanism to monitor router availability. These messages are sent every five seconds and significantly differentiate EIGRP from other distance-vector protocols. Most distance-vector protocols rely on timers to detect route failure. The benefit of hello messages is the avoidance of *black holes*—routes that lead to nothing. It is also important to note that updates in EIGRP are sent only when necessary and only to those destinations that require them. This greatly reduces the overhead of the protocol from a bandwidth perspective. In addition, these updates are sent reliably, which means that all updates are sequenced and acknowledged. This works to guarantee convergence assuming that all other factors, including router memory and processor, are working properly. The protocol used for EIGRP is the Reliable Transport Protocol (RTP), but, contrary to its name, it may transport unreliable messages as well.

One of the misunderstood concepts in EIGRP is that of the *feasible successor*. The feasible successor is not selected from any adjacent router that can reach the destination—rather, the feasible successor *must* have a lower metric than the router calculating the feasible successor. Stated another way, the *reported distance*, a value determined by the adjacent router providing its cost to the destination, must be less than the *feasible distance*, or the second-lowest cost for the calculating router to the destination. The reported distance does not include the cost of the link between the adjacent router and the calculating router. Figure 4.5 illustrates this concept.

FIGURE 4.5   EIGRP feasible successors

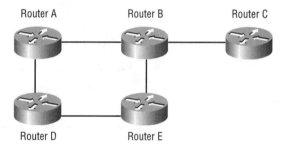

Router A   Router B   Router C

Router D   Router E

In this example, we will presume that the metric is simply based on hop count. As such, Router B is one hop from Router C, and Router D is three hops from Router C. The destination in this example is Router C, and the router we are concerned with is A, which is two hops away.

Router A, assuming all links are active, will place into the routing table a route through B to C—this is clearly the shortest path through the network. However, it will *not* place a feasible successor route in its table using the route A-D-E-B-C. In the event of link failure between A and B, the router must recalculate the path to C. The rationale is that in order for a route to be feasible, it must have a lower cost to the destination than the current routing metric on the router itself. For example, D would consider D-A-B-C to be feasible in the event of link failure—A's cost to C is one hop less than D's.

The behavior of feasible successors is related to the protocol's primary objective—no loops may exist in the topology at any time. By always selecting a router with a lower metric, the protocol avoids such scenarios, even though this may hinder convergence. Most EIGRP convergence scenarios complete within one second; however, in the worst case a properly working

EIGRP process will take 16 seconds. This convergence estimate is based on the detection of a link failure and the time necessary to respond with a new route calculation. In addition, EIGRP provides for multiple feasible successors, which are defined as a set, and up to four variant paths may be load-balanced if configured. Again, the rules defined in the IGRP section apply regarding the variance value and switching methodology, and the benefits are the same. The specific steps used in convergence are shown in Figure 4.6.

FIGURE 4.6 EIGRP convergence process

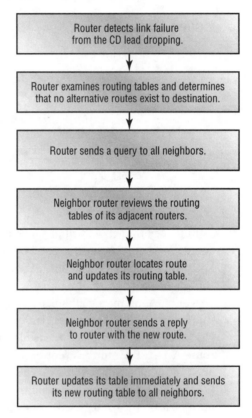

Router detects link failure from the CD lead dropping.

Router examines routing tables and determines that no alternative routes exist to destination.

Router sends a query to all neighbors.

Neighbor router reviews the routing tables of its adjacent routers.

Neighbor router locates route and updates its routing table.

Neighbor router sends a reply to router with the new route.

Router updates its table immediately and sends its new routing table to all neighbors.

Eventually, designers and administrators working with EIGRP will receive the following console message:

```
%DUAL-3-SIA: Route 192.168.12.0 stuck-in-active state in
IP-EIGRP 70.
```

This message may result from one of two problems—the first is simply a lack of available memory on the router to calculate the route. A route that is unparsed (undergoing recomputation) is considered active, whereas a stable route that has been placed in the tables is passive. The second possible cause is a lack of bandwidth on the link between the two routers—preventing communications between them for route update transmission. One method for addressing this problem is to augment the available bandwidth EIGRP is allocated. By default, EIGRP cannot consume more than 50 percent of the link. Another technique that can help is route summarization.

Designers should keep in mind that EIGRP maintains not only its routing table but also the routing table of each adjacent router. This fact is significant in understanding the importance of summarization, small neighbor relationships, and the routing update mechanism. DUAL uses this additional information to determine the feasible successor, and this data determines whether a computation is required.

Administrators may wish to adjust the amount of bandwidth available to EIGRP with the ip bandwidth-percent eigrp command. This permits modification of the default 50 percent utilization allowed, which may be necessary for slower links in order to speed convergence.

Route summarization in EIGRP is automatic across major network boundaries, but many administrators disable this feature in order to take advantage of manual summarization on all boundaries and gain more control. For discontiguous subnets, this feature must be disabled. This powerful feature not only reduces the size of the routing table but also provides a strong motivator for readdressing projects. The best EIGRP designs yield very small core routing tables—divided at a very high level based on summarization.

A number of companies have migrated to the reserved addresses specified in RFC 1918 in order to reduce the public Internet addressing shortage under IP v4. Designers should give careful consideration to both IP v6 and the use of public IP addresses—a number of service providers are finding it difficult to provide Layer 3 solutions with private addresses.

Designers should also note that EIGRP can maintain six routes to a destination—a characteristic that can reduce convergence time, as the router simply moves packets to the remaining paths.

Another feature of EIGRP that is often overlooked is *mobile hosting*. A mobile host is a host that is no longer on its natural subnet. The router will place an exception route to the host in the table—the more specific route superseding the subnet route. Clearly, this can reduce efficiency and greatly increase the size of the routing table. However, as wireless devices become more common in the enterprise, the demand for this feature will increase. This feature was added in IOS version 10.2.

Interrelationships with IGRP

EIGRP is built in part on the foundation laid by IGRP. Many designers migrate to EIGRP to add features to their networks while retaining some of the benefits of IGRP. Most conversions are promoted by the need for VLSM, although faster convergence and other benefits may also lead to the recommendation for conversion.

There are two methods for redistributing IGRP and EIGRP routes. The first is to assign the same autonomous system (AS) number to both the IGRP and EIGRP processes. The second method is similar to the technique used for other routing protocols—the administrator manually places a redistribution command into the routing process.

Of the two redistribution methods, most experienced designers lean toward the second, or manual redistribution. This solution affords a greater degree of control over the process, which frequently becomes desirable. For example, EIGRP, unlike IGRP, provides a method for identifying routes as internal or external. An external route is one that was learned from another routing process. IGRP contains no such mechanism, which may impact the administrative distance and other factors the router will use when selecting a route. Manual redistribution also affords the opportunity to use distribution lists, route maps, and other techniques to control the routing process.

Designers should use some care when converting from IGRP to EIGRP. Perhaps the most significant design criterion is to select only a few routers to handle the redistribution—ideally, routers in the core or distribution layers.

EIGRP designs tend to be most successful when using the three-tier, hierarchical model.

This section has noted that designers typically select EIGRP as a replacement for IGRP without describing some of the reasons a designer would do so. Here is a list of advantages provided by EIGRP:

Low bandwidth consumption (stable network)   When the network is stable, the protocol relies only on hello packets. This greatly reduces the amount of bandwidth needed for updates.

Efficient use of bandwidth during convergence   When a change is made to the routing topology, EIGRP will enter a period of active convergence. During this time, the routers will attempt to rebuild their routing tables to account for the change—typically the failure of an interface. To conserve bandwidth, EIGRP will communicate only changes in the topological database to other routers in that AS, as opposed to communication of the entire routing table, which consumes a great deal of bandwidth, especially in larger networks.

Support for VLSM   As noted previously, EIGRP supports variable-length subnet masks. This support, along with support for classless Internet domain routing (CIDR), can greatly assist the network designer by offering greater flexibility in IP addressing.

Designers should use some caution in deploying VLSM in the network. Ideally, there should be only two or three masks for the entire enterprise. These typically include /30 and /24. The reason for this is not specifically a routing protocol limitation, but rather a consideration for troubleshooting and other support issues. The concepts of VLSM and CIDR have been around for many years, but an understanding of both features, especially in the server and workstation arenas, is still wanting—network designers may find that their workstation support staffs are unfamiliar with these concepts and may find resistance to a readdressing effort. Remember that IP addressing affects not only the network, but also all other devices in the network, including Dynamic Host Configuration Protocol (DHCP), workstations, and servers. In well-administered networks, the use of VLSM is transparent to end users. However, the lack of familiarity by administrators and users can cause problems—consider the impact on the network if end users changed their subnet mask to the default value because they found it to be wrong. The problem is not technical but educational. Fortunately, these concerns and issues are being quickly eliminated from the landscape as VLSM gains in popularity and designers become more familiar with it. Recall from

Chapter 3 that VLSM helps designers construct efficient IP addressing schemes.

EIGRP and IGRP share the same composite routing metrics and mathematical weights; however, EIGRP supports metrics up to 32 bits. This differs from IGRP, which supports only 24 bits for the metric. EIGRP will automatically handle this issue, and after conversion metrics from either protocol are interchangeable.

Pay special attention to memory and CPU capacity on routers that will run EIGRP. The protocol can be very memory intensive, especially as the number of neighbors increases.

Network Design in the Real World: EIGRP

On the surface, it would appear that most Cisco-only networks should automatically use EIGRP. The protocol provides extremely fast convergence, relatively easy configuration, and variable-length subnetting.

Unfortunately, as with most things, it is not that simple to deploy EIGRP. The most significant problem frequently relates to memory and CPU; however, other factors can hinder deployment.

The simplest recommendations for designers thinking of deploying EIGRP fall into four basic areas, as follows:

- Maximize the amount of memory available on each router and increase the capacity of each router as the number of neighbors increases. There are formulas that predict the amount of memory that an EIGRP installation will require based on the number of neighbors and the number of routes, but these solutions are far from accurate. One installation I consulted on, after the deployment failed, had over 40MB of free router memory—the formula predicted that just over 1MB was sufficient. The deployment was ultimately removed, but it is important to note that the most critical issue involved the number of neighbors.

- Limit the number of neighbors. This is easier said than done, especially when the network has evolved over time. One technique is to use passive interfaces, although doing so significantly diminishes the overall benefits of EIGRP. Cisco recommends the use of ODR in hub-and-spoke designs, which can also reduce the number of neighbor relationships, but again, this reduces the overall benefits of EIGRP. The generic guidelines recommend that EIGRP neighbors be kept to fewer than 30; however, this is dependent on the amount of memory and the number of routes. Networks have failed with fewer neighbors, and a small number of networks have deployed over 70 neighbors successfully.

- Don't use the automatic redistribution feature unless the network is very simple. Automatic redistribution is a feature Cisco provides in order to make IGRP-to-EIGRP migration easier. You configure this feature by setting the AS number to the same value in the two protocols. The automatic feature works well, but many administrators find that it does not afford enough control over the redistribution process, which may be necessary for the migration.

- Administrators and designs should disable automatic route summarization and manually summarize routes whenever possible. Route summarization is an automatic process within the major network address, and it may require readdressing. However, summarization reduces the size of the routing table and can further enhance stability and convergence.

External EIGRP Routes

One of the most unique features in EIGRP is the concept of an external route, which is how IGRP routes are tagged in EIGRP upon redistribution. External routes are learned from one of the following:

- A static route injected into the protocol

- A route learned from redistribution from another EIGRP AS

- Routes learned from other protocols, including IGRP

All routes tagged as external are given a higher administrative distance than internal EIGRP routes. This effectively weights the internal routes for preference, which typically benefits the overall network. However, designers will wish to monitor this characteristic to ascertain the appropriateness of the routing table and to avoid asymmetric routing, if desired. Asymmetric routing is a situation wherein the outbound packets traverse a different path than the inbound packets. Such a design can make troubleshooting more difficult.

When EIGRP tags a route as external, it includes additional information about the route in the topology table. This information includes the following:

- The router ID of the router that redistributed the route (EIGRP redistribution) and the AS number of that router

- The protocol used in the external network

- The metric or cost received with the route

- An external route tag that the administrator can use for filtering

IGRP does not provide an external route mechanism. Therefore, the protocol cannot differentiate between internally and externally learned routes.

Network Design with OSPF

The Open Shortest Path First (OSPF) protocol is perhaps one of the most difficult routing protocols to configure correctly. This is due to the protocol's feature set, which includes route summarization and the ability to use areas to logically divide various elements in the network. OSPF is a nonproprietary, link-state routing protocol for IP. It was developed to resolve some of the problems found with the RIP, including slow convergence, susceptibility to routing loops, and limited scalability. Given its nonproprietary nature, OSPF may be better suited for network designs than IGRP and EIGRP when non-Cisco equipment is a design criterion. Many educational networks use OSPF.

OSPF supports various network types, including point-to-point and broadcast/nonbroadcast multiaccess networks. Hellos are used to establish neighbor relationships under most circumstances; however, manual configuration is needed for nonbroadcast multiaccess networks. The hello mechanism communicates with the *designated router* in each area and will be presented in greater detail later in this chapter. These occur at 10-second intervals and do not incorporate the entire routing table. Every 30 minutes, OSPF will send a summary link-state database, regardless of link failure; the rest of the time only hellos will traverse the link. Link failure will cause additional updates, and this process will be defined later as well.

OSPF uses the Dijkstra algorithm to calculate the shortest path for the network. In addition, OSPF supports VLSM and discontiguous subnets. Discontiguous subnets are subnets within a major network that are split by a different major network.

Apart from a VLSM-aware routing protocol, such as OSPF, discontiguous subnets are handled by the use of secondaries, or tunnels to link the two segments of the major network.

From a design perspective, OSPF relates well with the textbook three-tier model. Consider the following guidelines and limitations of the protocol as they relate to the three-tier model:

Keep workstations and other devices off the backbone.   In both models, the core/backbone is a critical resource that should never contain non-network devices. In designing a small network, the designer may use OSPF with a single area—the special backbone area zero. Under these circumstances, workstations and other devices will have to be included in this area. Under all other circumstances, designers will wish to keep the core as a secure transit area. This will reduce eavesdropping efforts and maintain a stable network. Note that OSPF backbones are best served when hosts are not placed in this backbone, a design criterion shared with the hierarchical model.

Maintain a simple backbone topology.   As with the previous guideline, both OSPF and the three-tier model benefit from stable, simple backbones.

Limit each area to less than 100 routers and incorporate no more than 28 areas in the network.   These Cisco recommendations for OSPF design match well with the demands of most networks designed under the three-tier model.

Assign network addresses in contiguous blocks and summarize where possible. Note that OSPF, like EIGRP, supports variable-length subnet masks (VLSM). This design, along with logical summarization aggregation points, lends itself well to small routing tables within the core.

Use totally stubby areas. This chapter will address stubby and totally stubby areas in greater detail, but for now include this guideline as an objective for good OSPF network design.

Types of Routers in OSPF

Each router in an OSPF network is defined as a type based on its function. Table 4.3 outlines the four common router functions in an OSPF hierarchy.

TABLE 4.3 OSPF Router Types

Type of Router	Description
Internal router	Internal routers have all interfaces in a single OSPF area. They are typically found in the access layer of the network.
Area border router	Area border routers (ABRs) interconnect multiple areas in the OSPF model. They are almost always used between the core and distribution layers. The three-tier design lends itself well to OSPF network designs.
Backbone router	A backbone router has at least one interface in area zero, which is also the backbone by design. This includes ABRs and internal routers in the core.
Autonomous system boundary router	Also referred to as autonomous system border routers, autonomous system boundary routers (ASBRs) exchange routes with routers in other autonomous systems. OSPF is an interior gateway protocol that defines a single autonomous system.

Some sources state that internal routers may contain the routers within area zero. This is not accurate—area zero backbone routers are usually not considered internal routers. Due to their role, they are backbone routers.

Autonomous systems (AS) are logically groupings of networks, typically associated with a single administrative group. Exterior gateway protocols, like eBGP, are used to route between these systems. OSPF is an IGP, or Interior Gateway Protocol, that assumes a single AS.

Figure 4.7 illustrates each of the four router types in OSPF. Note that a router belongs to more than one category if it is an area border router (ABR) or an autonomous system boundary router (ASBR).

FIGURE 4.7   The placement of each type of router in the OSPF model

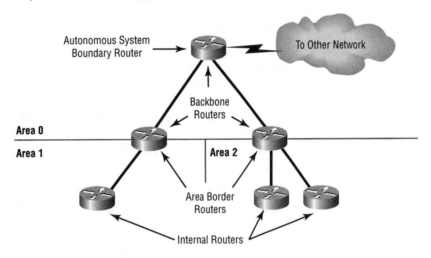

The OSPF Areas

Every OSPF network contains a single area zero, which is associated with the core layer of the network. All other areas must connect with area zero, which indicates the restrictive and logical nature of OSPF designs. However, these constraints are not necessarily bad—they simply require some discipline and collaborate well with a logical network design. In addition, each router in an area will have the same link-state database, which will incorporate information from all link-state advertisements (LSAs) for the area. Within the area, this information will incorporate specific links, and when learned from other areas and external (other AS) sources, this information will include specific links, summary links, and default links.

The concept of *areas* benefits the network greatly. For instance, convergence times can be greatly reduced by summarizing routes at the area border router. In addition, the requirement that all areas connect directly with area zero works to limit the depth of the entire network, which typically aids in the design and troubleshooting processes.

While it is preferable to keep all areas directly connected to area zero, it is possible to attach an area to area zero through another OSPF area. This is called a *virtual link*. Designers should avoid using virtual links whenever possible.

Route summarization is a manual process within OSPF, and it requires a bit of planning. For established networks, it may require a complete readdressing of the network. Summarization works best when a large allocation of contiguous subnets is availed to each area. The summary link advertisement represents the block to the adjacent areas. It is important to note that large allocations may lead to wasted addresses. Therefore, many designers opt to use the Internet-reserved private address space, RFC 1918, when readdressing for OSPF deployments. The technique used to divide the address space is called *bit splitting*. This is effectively the same process used in subnetting and supernetting—a number of bits are used to define the *significant bits*, the bits used in defining the summarization.

It can be preferable to make each summarization area equal; however, subnets within the area can take advantage of VLSM functionality. Remember that VLSM address allocations are best limited to two or three masks.

The biggest advantage to summarization is the impact it has on both the routing table and convergence. Summarized routes may take the place of hundreds of specific routes. In addition, summarization can shield routers from flapping link overhead in a different area. This greatly increases the stability of the network—areas outside of the flapping route do not recalculate via the shortest path first (SPF) algorithm, nor do the routing tables change inside the shielded area.

Within each area, a single router is elected to be the *designated router*. The designated router, or DR, is selected by an election process that uses the highest IP address on the router. Most administrators use the loopback interface to override the highest IP address and manually manage the election of the DR. A Priority-ID may also be used to determine DR during election. It is preferable to use a router with the most memory and CPU capacity for the DR. In addition to the DR, a backup designated router (BDR) is also selected to provide redundancy in the event the primary router fails. The designated router provides an aggregation point for OSPF LSAs. Note that the command `ip ospf priority` may be used to make a router the DR. Under these circumstances, the IP address is used in the event of a tie.

One last consideration for designers is the configuration of stubby areas and totally stubby areas. (Don't laugh, that's what they're called.)

A stubby area consolidates external links and forwards summary LSAs, specific LSAs, and the default external link, which is analogous to the default route of 0.0.0.0.

The concept of a totally stubby area is Cisco IOS-specific. Only the default link is forwarded into the area by the area border router. The command to configure this feature is `area {N} stub no-summary`. Because the totally stubby area receives only a default route, it is limited; however, it also works to control the total number of routes advertised into an area, which may benefit the designer in controlling routing propagation.

OSPF Link-State Advertisements

As a link-state protocol, OSPF relies on advertisements to announce information regarding the network. The link-state advertisements are given a sequence number and acknowledged, resulting in reliable information transfer. This feature aids in the fast convergence offered by the protocol. There are five primary types of OSPF link-state advertisements, as identified in Table 4.4.

TABLE 4.4 The OSPF Link-State Advertisements

Advertisement	LSA Type	Description
Router link advertisement	1	An intra-area information advertisement, the router link advertisement contains information regarding the sending router's links to neighbor routers.
Network link advertisement	2	Also an intra-area information advertisement, the network link advertisement contains a list of routers attached to a network segment. The designated router will send this update for all other routers on multiaccess networks.
Summary link advertisement	3 & 4	Summary link advertisements contain inter-area information and are used to present routes between OSPF network areas. Type 3 is used by an ABR router. LSA Type 4 is for ABR-to-ASBR information.
External link advertisement	5	External link advertisements present information about routes in other autonomous systems. Type 5 is used by the ASBR. These updates are allowed to flood all areas. There is a great deal of information regarding OSPF, including external link advertisements, that is beyond the scope of this text. It is recommended that readers interested in additional information on OSPF consult the RFCs and other texts on the subject, including the Cisco Web site.

There are two additional LSA types. Type 6 is for Multicast OSPF, or MOSPF. Type 7 is defined for NSSAs, or not-so-stubby areas. While both may gain popularity in the future, they are not commonly found in most networks.

OSPF Route Calculations

OSPF is an excellent protocol for calculating routes, and the actual process is quite simple. This process includes the incorporation of a calculated cost for each interface type. By default, cost is computed by taking 10^8 (100,000,000) and dividing by the manually configured bandwidth of the link. Table 4.5 presents some of the default OSPF calculated costs.

TABLE 4.5   OSPF Costs

Interface	Type	Cost
FDDI	(100Mbps)	1
Ethernet	(10Mbps)	10
Serial T1	(1.544Mbps)	64
Serial 56K	(56Kbps)	1728

As shown in Table 4.5, OSPF's default costs present a substantial negative for modern networks, as it fails to automatically account for bandwidths greater than 100Mbps. The lowest OSPF cost is a value of 1. By default, from the 100Mbps bandwidth point upwards, OSPF will regard any interface as being equal to any other interface of equal or *greater* bandwidth. Thus, by default, OSPF cannot consider the differences between an FDDI ring and a Gigabit Ethernet segment. The OSPF command OSPF AUTO-COST REFERENCE-BANDWIDTH <#> is commonly used to change the default computation of 10^8 (100,000,000) to a higher number (so the computed cost is a value other than 1 on high-speed networks). Care should be taken, however, to confirm that this setting has been applied to all routers that will be affected by this links cost. Network designers will need to consider this issue when selecting OSPF for their networks. Under such circumstances, designers will likely alter these costs to account for faster media.

Each router in an OSPF area maintains a link-state database. This database is identical on each router in the area and is populated via link-state advertisements. As previously noted, there are different types of advertisements, but the information will appear in the form of specific links, summary links, and default links.

Based on the LSA advertisements, the router will recalculate to determine the best route via the shortest path first (SPF) algorithm. This is also called Dijkstra's algorithm. The specifics of the algorithm are beyond the scope of the exam; however, the algorithm is interesting reading and is available in many distributions.

As with most network routing protocols, OSPF designers are frequently concerned with convergence time. OSPF is a very strong protocol in terms of convergence time—each router is aware of the entire topology in the area. This results in fast convergence. However, if a link *flaps*, or changes between up and down status quickly, a flood of LSAs may be generated. This may prevent the router from converging, and as a result, a command will be added to the IOS to limit the impact of flapping routes. Administrators may use the `spf holdtime` command to force OSPF into a waitstate before computing a new route.

OSPF convergence is determined by a number of factors and processes. The first step is link failure detection, which is dependent on each type of media. This may result from a carrier detect failure, the loss of keepalives, or a lack of OSPF hellos on the link. Depending on the detection method used, the delay may be negligible or significant—up to 40 seconds. Delay at this point will hinder the second step, which is the propagation of LSAs and the recalculation of the SPF algorithm. This process should take less than one second under most circumstances. In order to prevent flapping and other inappropriate fluctuations to the routing tables, OSPF adds an SPF hold timer of five seconds. Thus, convergence is fairly predictable—within a broad range. Link failures can take between six and 46 seconds to converge. The flow of this process is illustrated in Figure 4.8.

FIGURE 4.8 OSPF convergence

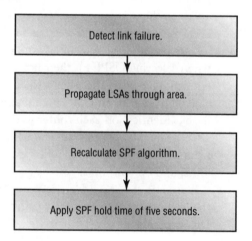

Convergence time factors may be negated somewhat by load balancing. OSPF supports up to four equal-cost paths per destination, which can maintain connectivity in the event of a single link failure. As with other routing protocols, designers should use the `bandwidth` command to accurately reflect the capacity of their links and optimize traffic flows.

Network Design in the Real World: OSPF

OSPF configuration, done properly, can be more difficult than other protocols, as noted in the main text. However, many of the design concepts mandated by OSPF are well suited for other routing protocols. This is especially true for route summarization.

There are two common issues with OSPF implementations. The first is the over-simplified model. The placement of all routers in area zero is affectionately called *the over-simplified model*. A surprising number of fairly large networks have deployed this model in the past, and many designers unfamiliar with OSPF may be tempted to do the same. The problem with this deployment is that it does not scale, and ultimately many of the benefits integrated into OSPF will be lost. It is better to complicate a small network design slightly by anticipating its growth than to take this shortcut.

The second common problem in OSPF design is redundancy and, more importantly, diversity. One large ATM network we were deploying was originally slated for OSPF; however, backup links frequently crossed local access and transport area (LATA) boundaries. Crossing a LATA typically increases the cost for a circuit—in our design this almost tripled the recurrent costs. As a result, to provide the needed redundancy, we had to consider virtual links or abandon the structure of OSPF in favor of a less-demanding protocol.

Clearly this was an unacceptable solution, and so our original design with symmetric distribution layers in different geographic locations was too difficult to implement with the area constraints mandated by OSPF. There were alternatives, including the use of virtual links; however, each was deemed suboptimal. The network was ultimately deployed with EIGRP, which still permitted summarization at the access layer, and many of the other features required by the project, including fast-convergence and VLSM support.

Network Design with ODR

On-demand routing, or ODR, is perhaps one of the most interesting routing protocols available on the Cisco platform—perhaps because it is not a routing protocol at all.

At present, ODR is not incorporated into the CID exam or its objectives. However, the protocol is very useful in simplifying small hub-and-spoke network routing, as it adds virtually no overhead.

It would be most accurate to describe ODR as a routing process. However, the process relies on the Cisco Discovery Protocol (CDP). The CDP packets are a proprietary method for exchanging information between two Cisco devices. The majority of this information is used in troubleshooting and administration. For example, CiscoWorks and other SNMP/RMON (remote monitoring) tools now use the CDP information to assist in the discovery and map-building processes.

ODR adds another function to CDP. By listening to CDP packets in a simple hub-and-spoke design, a master router (located at the hub) is able to learn about all the other routers in the network. The remote routers are configured with a single default route to the hub. This design does not provide many of the benefits of a formal routing protocol, but it will provide connectivity and status regarding the remote router interfaces without consuming additional bandwidth. Of course, CDP can be disabled—it is on by default. Figure 4.9 illustrates a typical ODR installation.

As of this writing, Cisco does not support CDP on ATM links. However, this feature and support for secondary interfaces are documented as available in IOS 12.0.

FIGURE 4.9   On-demand routing

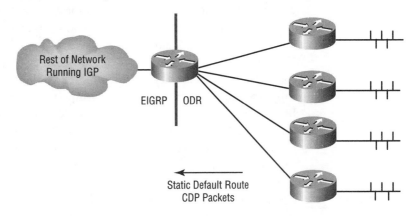

Network Design with BGP

The Border Gateway Protocol (BGP) could accurately be called the routing protocol of the Internet. It is virtually impossible to have an advanced (ISP or multi-homed, multi-ISP) connection within the Internet without having at least a few external BGP (eBGP) routes.

This section provides greater detail regarding the BGP protocol and process than required for the Cisco objectives. The extra information is provided because of the limited amount of information available on the protocol and the likely migration by Cisco toward greater use of BGP in enterprise deployments.

However, Cisco has recently advocated the use of BGP in the internal network when the network gets particularly large. Consider for a moment how you might design a network with 10,000 routers. Even OSPF with multiple areas will have difficulty handling that many devices, to say nothing about the introduction of new networks and, in some cases, acquired companies.

BGP is best described as a path-vector routing protocol. The protocol, in this context, is less concerned with the internal routes and more concerned with the relationships between autonomous systems. For this presentation, consider an AS to be synonymous with individual companies, although in actuality the term defines the administrative domain. BGP is also called an inter-autonomous system routing protocol.

Overall, BGP is a very powerful protocol—primarily due to two specific characteristics. First, the protocol removes the concept of network class and supports address summarization and supernetting like OSPF does. Second, BGP operates over TCP, which provides it with a more robust transport architecture than other routing protocols. Part of this function includes a graceful shutdown—errors and other messages are sent before the protocol shuts down whenever possible. BGP uses TCP port 179.

Another useful function in eBGP is the characteristic that governs its advertised routes. BGP will advertise to its peers only the routes that the BGP speaker uses, rather than routes only known from other announcements. Routes are further defined on a hop-by-hop basis.

There are three autonomous system types that designers considering BGP should understand:

Stub AS Provides a single exit point and is used for local traffic only. Local traffic is traffic that belongs to the AS.

Multi-homed AS A multi-homed AS provides multiple exit points for local traffic.

Transit AS A transit AS is used for both local and transit traffic. Transit traffic is traffic that is not destined for the autonomous system but uses that AS to reach another system. This type is typically used only in ISP environments.

BGP works by maintaining a direct transport layer connection between two systems and providing updates whenever changes occur. A full routing table is sent upon session establishment. Keepalive messages are sent periodically to validate the integrity of the connection. These are sent, by default, at one-third the hold-time interval.

As of this writing, there are over 65,000 networks in the Internet routing table. This information is shown in the `ip bgp summary` that follows:

```
Inet_Rtr#show ip bgp summary
BGP table version is 17453706, main routing table version
    17453706
65353 network entries and 101590 paths using 9735069 bytes
    of memory
```

```
14801 BGP path attribute entries using 1187400 bytes of
    memory
3143 BGP filter-list cache entries using 50288 bytes of
    memory
Dampening enabled. 57 history paths, 93 dampened paths
BGP activity 690913/625560 prefixes, 4454740/4353150 paths
4327988 prefixes revised.
```

Administrators are advised to use the loopback address on the router for all BGP traffic. Doing so can work to stabilize the routing process and maintain connectivity in the event of an interface failure. This stability is the result of the TCP session being established via the loopback interface—a link failure, given other paths, will not require re-establishment of the TCP session between BGP pairs.

Multi-homed BGP configurations can bias the exit point advertised by the eBGP peer. This is called the *multi-exit discriminator*, and it may be used to provide a fixed value—the lowest is preferred—or it may be based on the IGP metric, which is typically provided by OSPF. Note that this value does not propagate beyond the link.

Administrators may also use route maps to modify and influence the routing tables. Route maps operate on a match-and-set model where conditions may be checked before the router applies the set. For example, the administrator may wish to modify only routes from network 172.16.0.0. In this configuration, the route map would match 172.16.0.0 and then set the modified value. The administrator may wish to use this function to adjust the metric.

The following BGP configuration is provided as a sample of some of the commands used. In reality, BGP configurations can be very simple; however, most installations to the Internet require additional parameters that can cause difficulty. Notice how the specific IP address of each neighbor is provided in the configuration and that the update-source for AS 65342 is defined as Loopback0. The route-map Filter has also been applied.

```
router bgp 65470
 no synchronization
 bgp dampening
 network 10.9.14.0 mask 255.255.255.0
 neighbor 192.168.19.33 remote-as 65391
```

```
neighbor 192.168.19.33 soft-reconfiguration inbound
neighbor 192.168.19.33 route-map Filter out
neighbor 172.16.55.10 remote-as 65342
neighbor 172.16.55.10 update-source Loopback0

route-map Filter permit 10
match ip address 192
```

The BGP routing protocol selects routes based on information obtained from the Adjunct-RIB-In table. There are actually three tables according to the specifications, as shown in Table 4.6. RIB stands for Routing Information Base.

TABLE 4.6 The BGP Process Tables

Table	Function
Adjunct-RIB-In	Learned from inbound update messages. Contains routes that are unprocessed from inbound peer advertisements.
Adjunct-RIB-Out	Contains routes that the local BGP speaker will advertise to peers.
Local-RIB	Contains local routing information that the BGP speaker obtained from applying local policies to Adjunct-RIB-In routing information.

While these databases are presented as separate entities, they are not necessarily so.

There are three route-selection decision-process phases. These are described in Table 4.7.

TABLE 4.7 BGP Route Selection

Selection Phase	Function
Phase 1	Calculates the preference for each route received and advertises routes that have the highest preference.
Phase 2	Selects the best route for each destination and places that route into the appropriate Local-RIB.
Phase 3	Disseminates routes in the Local-RIB to each neighbor AS peer.

Typically a route will have a *best* path that the router can use, but it is possible to have a tie. In this scenario, the lowest multi-exit discriminator (MED) value is used to break the tie. If the MED is not provided, the route with the lowest interior distance cost will be used. BGP speakers with the lowest BGP identifier—the IP address—will win ties as well. This is another use of the loopback address in BGP installations.

Network Design with IS-IS

Like OSPF, IS-IS (Intermediate System-to-Intermediate System) is an interoperable, link-state, standards-based routing protocol that is supported by various vendors. However, it also can be difficult to configure due to topology restrictions, many of which are shared with OSPF. The sole metric—bandwidth—is also viewed as a limitation to the protocol and may account for its low acceptance in the market.

The benefits of IS-IS include fast convergence and support for VLSM. Hellos are sent at regular intervals and routing updates are sent only in response to a topology change—and then only include the changes themselves.

One of the concepts of IS-IS is that it is an interior routing protocol, like OSPF, RIP, and IGRP. Interior routing protocols are generally considered to be inappropriate for use between administrative entities—BGP being the de facto standard for these connections. As noted previously, BGP is both an internal and external (iBGP and eBGP) protocol, depending on the AS configuration.

The exterior routing protocol, ES-IS, is used for exterior routing.

IS-IS makes use of a two-area structure, with *area* defined as *layers*. Layer 1 is used for intra-domain routing, whereas Layer 2 is used for inter-domain routing—Layer 2 linking two routing domains (areas) in the IS-IS syntax. Hierarchies are established as Layer 1 routers need only find a Layer 2 router for forwarding—similar to a border router in OSPF.

Metrics in IS-IS, by default, are comprised of a single path value—the maximum value of which is 1024. Individual links are limited to a maximum setting of 64. IS-IS also provides a limited quality-of-service function in its CLNP header, which can account for other link costs. CLNP stands for Connectionless Network Protocol, which was originally developed for the routing of DECnet/OSI packets. The protocol has been modified to support IP. At the present time, there is little reason to select IS-IS—EIGRP and OSPF dominate the marketplace. The Cisco Web site provides additional information on the protocol, should you wish to study it further.

Summary

This chapter addressed the IP routing protocols and processes as they relate to network design. These protocols include the following:

- Static (actually not a protocol, but a process)
- RIP
- RIP v2
- OSPF
- IGRP
- EIGRP
- ODR (actually not a protocol, but a process)
- BGP

The chapter also identified some of the reasons IP routing might be better handled by one protocol than another. Incorporated into that decision were a number of criteria, including the following:

- Availability

- Scalability

- Ease of administration

- Bandwidth efficiency

- Router memory utilization

- Router CPU utilization

- Multi-vendor interoperability

- Adjacencies (number of neighbors)

- Support staff familiarity

In addition, the chapter addressed the proprietary IGRP routing protocol and presented features and options that the designer might wish to consider when deploying this routing protocol. Some of these issues included convergence and efficiency.

The presentation on OSPF discussed several of the advantages offered by this protocol, including its wide availability. In addition, designers should feel comfortable with a number of the implementation techniques used for successful OSPF designs, including the following:

- Route summarization, including address-allocation efficiencies

- Simple backbone designs with no hosts

- Fewer than 100 routers per area and fewer than 28 areas

The process by which convergence occurs was also described.

Review Questions

1. IS-IS defines areas:

   A. As Layer 1, which is intra-area, and Layer 2, which links two areas

   B. As a single AS linked by multiple ABSRs

   C. As multiple Layer 1 inter-area links

   D. As Layer 2 intra-areas and Layer 1 transit areas.

2. Under IGRP, split horizon would be off, by default, for which of the following?

   A. Token Ring

   B. Ethernet

   C. SMDS

   D. FastEthernet

   E. None of the above

3. IGRP will do which of the following?

   A. Send hellos every 10 seconds.

   B. Send hellos every two hours.

   C. Send the entire routing table every 90 seconds.

   D. Send only changes to the routing table every 90 seconds.

4. In IGRP, the default update timer is:

   A. 30 seconds

   B. 60 seconds

   C. 90 seconds

   D. 120 seconds

5. In IGRP, the default holddown timer is:

   A. 30 seconds

   B. 90 seconds

   C. 270 seconds

   D. 280 seconds

   E. 300 seconds

6. By default, IGRP will use only which of the following to determine a route's metric?

   A. Bandwidth

   B. Delay

   C. Reliability

   D. Loading

   E. MTU

   F. Hops

7. Which of the following would be a benefit in using static routes?

   A. Low bandwidth utilization

   B. 10-second updates

   C. Automatic configuration

   D. Load balancing

8. Which of the following routing protocols support VLSM?

   A. RIP

   B. RIP v2

   C. OSPF

   D. IGRP

   E. EIGRP

9. Which of the following is a benefit of VLSM?

   A. Faster convergence with RIP

   B. Faster convergence with OSPF

   C. Faster convergence with IGRP

   D. Efficient IP address assignment

10. Which of the following protocols uses a persistent TCP connection to communicate with neighbor routers?

    A. OSPF

    B. BGP

    C. RIP

    D. EIGRP

11. A virtual link is which of the following?

    A. A conduit through area zero

    B. A conduit through two EIGRP autonomous systems

    C. A connection between an EIGRP AS and an OSPF area

    D. A connection between a remote area and area zero via another area

12. True or false: IGRP uses triggered updates.

    A. True

    B. False

13. EIGRP can maintain how many routes per destination?

    A. 1

    B. 2

    C. 4

    D. 6

14. A discontiguous subnet is:

   A. Two or more subnets from a major network divided by a different major network

   B. A single summary route from a major network

   C. Not permitted in OSPF

   D. Permitted in OSPF, but not part of the link-state database

15. OSPF can load-balance, by default, how many routes?

   A. 2

   B. 4

   C. 6

   D. OSPF cannot load-balance.

16. The algorithm used by OSPF is called which of the following?

   A. DUAL

   B. SPF (Sequenced Packet Format)

   C. Dijkstra's

   D. Radia

17. The OSPF link-state summary table is sent under which of the following circumstances?

   A. Every 30 minutes

   B. Every 90 seconds

   C. Every 30 seconds

   D. Every time there is a change in topology

18. EIGRP will support discontiguous subnets; however, the administrator must:

    A. Disable auto-summary

    B. Use different AS numbers

    C. Manually summarize routes

    D. Use static routes, as EIGRP cannot support this function manually

19. Which of the following would not be considered an advantage of OSPF?

    A. An open standard supported by many vendors

    B. Quick convergence

    C. Support for discontiguous subnets

    D. Use of unicast frames for information exchange

    E. Support for VLSM

20. Which of the following would likely not be configured by a corporate WAN designer?

    A. Stub AS

    B. Transit AS

    C. Multi-homed AS

    D. All of the above

21. IS-IS is:

    A. A classless, distance-vector protocol suited to small networks

    B. A classful, link-state protocol that scales to support large networks

    C. An exterior routing protocol used in the Internet

    D. A classless, link-state protocol that supports large networks

    E. An interior routing protocol used to support small networks using ATM

22. Which of the following are link-state protocols?

A. RIP v2

B. OSPF

C. IS-IS

D. EIGRP

E. IGRP

23. Which best describes BGP?

A. Distance vector

B. Distance path

C. Link state

D. Path vector

E. Exterior link-state vectoring

24. While BGP was intended for Internet connectivity, many large networks are advised to consider it:

A. As an exclusive IGP routing protocol

B. As an interconnecting routing protocol between different IGPs

C. Only in concert with IS-IS

D. Only for extranet connections

25. The BGP multi-exit discriminator:

A. May be a fixed value

B. May be based on an IGP metric

C. May be either A or B

D. Works only with OSPF

Answers to Review Questions

1. A.

2. E.

3. C.

4. C.

5. D.

6. A, B.

7. A.

8. B, C, E.

9. D.

10. B.

11. D.

12. A.

13. D.

14. A.

15. B.

16. C.

17. A, D.

18. A.

19. D.

20. B.

21. D.

22. B, C.

23. D.

24. B.

25. C.

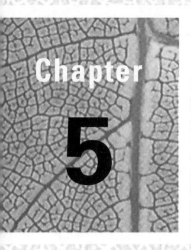

Chapter

5

Designing AppleTalk Networks

CISCO INTERNETWORK DESIGN EXAM OBJECTIVES COVERED IN THIS CHAPTER:

✓ Use Enhanced IGRP for path determination in internetworks that support IP, IPX, and AppleTalk.

✓ Examine a client's requirements and construct an appropriate AppleTalk design solution.

✓ Choose addressing and naming conventions to build manageable and scalable AppleTalk internetworks.

✓ Use Cisco IOS ™ features to design scalable AppleTalk internetworks.

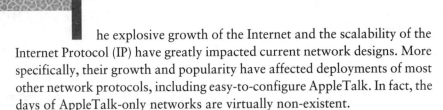

The explosive growth of the Internet and the scalability of the Internet Protocol (IP) have greatly impacted current network designs. More specifically, their growth and popularity have affected deployments of most other network protocols, including easy-to-configure AppleTalk. In fact, the days of AppleTalk-only networks are virtually non-existent.

AppleTalk became popular because of the many benefits its design afforded. It was designed to negate the need to configure addresses, network masks, and default gateways on individual workstations and to handle naming and service updates automatically. These features greatly reduced the number of administrative errors that could be introduced, and along with the early successes of the Macintosh, provided networks with many other advantages. Nonetheless, AppleTalk has become less popular because of its relatively poor scalability, which is due in large part to its reliance on broadcasts.

Recently, a number of relatively new services have been added to AppleTalk to counteract some of the scalability problems found in the original protocol. These new services, plus the many benefits of AppleTalk and the resurgence of the Macintosh platform in recent years, make it important to address the issues that frequently confront network designers working with the protocol.

Designing for AppleTalk Networks

The design goal of any network is typically the same: provide a scalable, logical platform from which users may complete tasks and other functions with a high degree of performance and reliability.

AppleTalk, as a protocol, can address many aspects of this goal in its native form. However, it falls short when it comes to scalability. This shortcoming combined with the rise in popularity of IP-only segments in lieu of multiprotocol networks has made AppleTalk fall out of favor. While some older applications may still rely on traditional AppleTalk services, the most recent versions of AppleTalk and MacOS do support the exclusive use of IP. It is important to note, though, that AppleTalk is a separate protocol from IP, and there are no dependencies between them. The current CID examination continues to focus on AppleTalk, and so readers preparing for the examination should focus on this chapter in that context. With the release of System 8 and later, however, more and more production networks that use Macintosh systems are forgoing the AppleTalk protocol completely. This chapter is irrelevant to those installations and will only be of interest from a historical perspective or for those designers migrating from AppleTalk to IP.

Before beginning to design an AppleTalk network, it is important to evaluate the validity of using AppleTalk in a new network installation. While the rest of this chapter is dedicated to designing and installing AppleTalk networks, a designer must first address the conventional wisdom in modern network design, which, as was just mentioned, is to use a single protocol on the network where possible. While not without its shortcomings, that protocol is IP.

Once an AppleTalk network design is chosen, the designer will wish to focus on creating a design that is easy to use and maintain. This is especially true when deploying a network in an environment without a full-time technical staff, such as would be found in smaller schools, for example. However, these objectives are always a good idea regardless of venue—remember the adage, "Keep it simple."

In addition, the designer will want to create an AppleTalk design that accomplishes as many of the following goals as possible:

- Reduce broadcast traffic.

- Maintain scalability.

- Make configuration easy, where possible.

- Use policy routing, where appropriate.

- Incorporate with non-AppleTalk protocols, where appropriate. This might include the use of AppleTalk tunnels or a numerically significant addressing scheme that conforms to IP, IPX, and AppleTalk.

The designer should also keep in mind that AppleTalk is not a single protocol, but rather a family of protocols that interoperate. These protocols include:

- AppleTalk Address Resolution Protocol (AARP)
- Routing Table Maintenance Protocol (RTMP)
- AppleTalk Echo Protocol (AEP)
- Name-Binding Protocol (NBP)
- AppleTalk Transaction Protocol (ATP)
- Zone Information Protocol (ZIP)
- Datagram Delivery Protocol (DDP)
- AppleTalk Data Stream Protocol (ADSP)

According to convention, this chapter will use the term AppleTalk. However, a protocol's definition is actually based on its underlying physical media. Thus, the correct terms are EtherTalk, FDDITalk, and so forth.

The most important protocols will be presented in subsequent sections, but the remainder will only be discussed here briefly and will not be referred to again in this chapter. These less important protocols include AEP and ADSP. AEP is useful in troubleshooting and operates similarly to IP Ping. ADSP is a connection-oriented protocol that provides reliable full-duplex byte-stream services.

Figure 5.1 illustrates the relationship between AppleTalk and the OSI model. As with most protocols, there are no direct mappings between the theoretical OSI model and the actual divisions of the protocols themselves. However, based on the function each protocol serves, it is appropriate to place DDP and AARP into the network layer (Layer 3) and ZIP and NBP into the session and transport layers, respectively.

FIGURE 5.1   AppleTalk and the OSI model

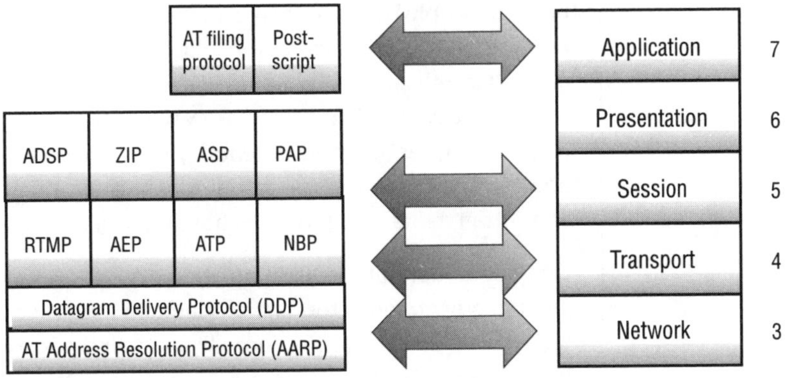

Network Design in the Real World: Theoretical Issues

One of the more enjoyable aspects of network design (or any dialog in more advanced networking) is the potential for disagreement. There are many ways to design a network. Consider secondary addresses versus super-netting, for example. Neither is necessarily the right answer every time, and the really talented members of this exclusive group will be able to adapt solutions to fit the relevant business needs and technical concerns at hand.

Recently, a group of people preparing for Cisco certifications entered a lively debate regarding IP ARP (Address Resolution Protocol). A participant commented that ARP is a Layer 3 protocol, and another participant disagreed, contending that it is actually a Layer 2 process. (For the record, many sources, including Cisco, cite ARP as a Layer 3 protocol.)

I believe that the debate is more important than the answer. Most people can remember facts, but knowing that ARP is Layer 3 or that ARP is Layer 2 does not really show that you understand the function of the protocol. In addition, the OSI model is exactly that—a model. So long as people can argue their position (one participant contended that ARP is a Layer 7 protocol, and he provided a solid argument), I contend that learning and expertise will result.

In the context of AppleTalk, Figure 5.1 illustrates the common relationship between AppleTalk protocols and the OSI model. Clearly, arguments could be raised that impact the actual placement of the protocols within the diagram. It is unlikely, though, that you will see a question worded on an exam as, "What Layer is X protocol?" However, you should be comfortable answering such a question and *defending your answer*. Although the Cisco answer, for our purposes, is the *right* answer, that may not provide much comfort in a late-night troubleshooting session.

One additional note—surround yourself with as much talent as you can. Technology changes too fast to maintain expertise in every area all of the time. If you do this, you're more likely to find a resource in your circle who is well-versed in the area in question. Today, for example, I discussed an Enhanced Interior Gateway Routing Protocol (EIGRP) migration for a large company with two colleagues. Everyone contributed, and all of us learned new things from the dialogue. Some of the lessons came from new ways to ask the questions rather than assuming the answer.

The following section provides additional information regarding the major AppleTalk protocols:

AppleTalk Address Resolution Protocol   AARP performs two different functions in AppleTalk. First, it is responsible for mapping AppleTalk addresses to hardware addresses. This Layer 3 to Layer 2 mapping is similar to the ARP process in IP. Second, AARP handles the dynamic assignment of node addresses.

Datagram Delivery Protocol   DDP provides unique addressing of all nodes on the AppleTalk internetwork and is responsible for connectionless delivery of datagrams between nodes. Also, DDP, in conjunction with AARP, provides the functions of Layer 3. DDP is responsible for connectivity to the upper-layer protocols, and AARP is tasked with connectivity to the lower layers.

Name-Binding Protocol   NBP provides name-to-address resolution that is similar to DNS in TCP/IP. It also handles additional functions, including the population of names in the Chooser for resources on the network.

Routing Table Maintenance Protocol   RTMP is AppleTalk's default routing protocol. Updates are sent every 10 seconds, and routes are aged out of the table after 20 seconds, which can result in route flapping on congested segments as the RTMP updates are dropped.

Zone Information Protocol   Zones are logical divisions of AppleTalk resources. ZIP maps zone names to network addresses. Although nodes belong to one zone, zones can span multiple physical networks.

When designing for the use of AppleTalk in most small- to medium-sized networks, the most significant issues will involve addressing and naming, which will be covered in this section. The next two sections will address those issues that frequently arise with larger networks—specifically, routing and scalability.

AppleTalk Addressing

The AppleTalk protocol was designed to limit the amount of technical expertise required to configure the workstation for operation on the network. As a result, the workstation has virtually no configuration options and obtains its address via a dynamic querying process.

In AppleTalk, the network administrator will assign a cable range, or block of addresses that the workstations will use. For our purposes, we will ignore the issues between AppleTalk phase one and phase two and assume the use of only phase two in this presentation. Recall that AppleTalk phase one does not permit cable ranges and allows for only 127 node addresses, as reflected in Table 5.1.

AppleTalk phase one is severely limited in scalability, and it is recommended that companies migrate to phase two if they have not already done so.

TABLE 5.1 Comparison of AppleTalk Phase One and AppleTalk Phase Two

	AppleTalk Phase One	**AppleTalk Phase Two**
Number of network addresses per segment	1	65,279
Number of host addresses per network	254 devices per network, however, only 127 hosts may be accommodated.	253 per network address. Virtually unlimited.
Number of zones per network	1	255

Table 5.1 presents AppleTalk phase two as being virtually unlimited in terms of host addresses. This is due to the theoretical capability of AppleTalk to consider cable range 1–65,279 as one network and 253 hosts per single cable range (cable range 1–1, for example). Thus, the true number of maximum nodes in an AppleTalk network is approximately 16 million. Although possible, this number is well beyond the broadcast and physical limitations of most networks, and most cable ranges do not span more than 10 digits (10–19, for example).

For additional information regarding AppleTalk phase one and phase two, please refer to *CCNP: Cisco Internetwork Troubleshooting Study Guide* (Sybex, 1999).

AppleTalk addresses are comprised of two parts: a network number and a node number. These are written in the format *network.node*.

The network number is defined by the cable range value for the segment and is configured on the router. Under AppleTalk phase two, multiple cable range values may be linked to a single AppleTalk network. For example, cable range 4–4 would service only 253 nodes; however, under AppleTalk phase two, the designer could define the cable range as 10–19, permitting hundreds of nodes. Note that these 10 cable ranges become a single logical network. This is comparable to expanding the mask in IP, but AppleTalk networks do not share the concept of a separate net mask. For example, nodes on cable range 10–19 might appear as 14.91 and 17.132. In this case, both nodes are on the same network.

Cisco recommends that AppleTalk cable ranges follow some numerically significant schema, and more importantly, that administrators and designers document these numbers. Remember that the ranges cannot overlap and must remain unique within the network.

Some administrators assign network numbers based on the geography of the environment. A campus with five buildings might have four-digit cable range numbers. The first digit could relate to the building, the second to the floor within that building, and so on. Since there are over 64,000 network numbers available, the designer should be able to develop a numbering plan that is easy to understand, which will simplify troubleshooting.

As noted previously, the node number is a unique identifier of the device on the network. As a Layer 3 protocol, the network number is the routable portion of the address space—the node number is insignificant until the packet arrives on the local segment.

In addition to the network number and node number, there is a third significant parameter to the AppleTalk address: the socket number. Socket numbers in AppleTalk are very similar to socket numbers in TCP and UDP. They provide a specific interface on the node for communications. Therefore, the network-visible entries (NVEs) are identified by three addressing parameters: the 16-bit network number, the 8-bit node number, and the 8-bit socket number. Network-visible entries are network devices—a fancy term to describe a host, server, printer, or other element that might appear to the user.

AppleTalk Naming

One of the conveniences of AppleTalk is its use of names to identify resources within the network, which is not unlike the DNS and WINS (Windows Internet Naming Service) services in the IP world. However, unlike the two IP naming techniques, AppleTalk included naming in the initial protocol.

In fact, there are actually two names in the AppleTalk arena: the zone name and the resource name. Consider the zone name in the same manner you might think of a sub-domain name in the IP DNS structure. The main difference between the two naming schemes is that AppleTalk does not incorporate the idea of sub-domains and hierarchical structures. Alternatively, for those more familiar with Windows, AppleTalk is similar to the workgroup model. Resources are members of a grouping, but the grouping is only one of many equals—names in AppleTalk are flat. The DNS structure allows for names to traverse multiple layers—for example, the file server in Marketing in the fifth building in Dallas. AppleTalk designers are limited to using names such as Marketing or Marketing_Dallas for their structures.

From a design standpoint, zone names in AppleTalk are usually implemented with two parallel viewpoints in mind. The names need to be used by both the user community and the network administrators, and fortunately, in this instance, the solution will please both groups.

AppleTalk zone names are case sensitive. Nonetheless, there are instances when connectivity may appear to function correctly even though the router has the incorrect form of the name. Such an installation will eventually experience some problem that will require resolution. Some designers use all lowercase names to avoid this issue.

Designers ideally will select zone names that reflect the departmental grouping related to each particular network, typically resulting in names like "Marketing" for the Marketing group and "Human Resources" for the Human Resources group. This naming scheme will help users locate the services provided by devices in each zone, and typically, these groups (departments, like Human Resources) will be physically located in the same general area. Such a scheme will also further assist administrators, because troubleshooting is simplified when the Marketing zone is no longer visible in the Chooser.

The Chooser is the service-selection tool in the Macintosh OS. It lists all zones in the network. Once the user selects a zone, all of the resources in that zone will be presented, and the user can select a resource within the zone.

One minor downside to the AppleTalk zone-naming scheme is that it relies on broadcasts to announce the presence of each zone. These names are propagated throughout the entire network, so a large network might have hundreds of broadcasts every minute to cover all of the zones. In addition, each router summarizes all of the zones it knows about and advertises this information to the rest of the network, quickly adding to the load imposed by the process. Another minor downside is the somewhat limited number of zone names permitted in an AppleTalk network. The specification permits only 255 names, which could be a factor for the network designer to consider. In practice, designers should limit the number of zones to less than 100.

Do not place all WAN networks into a single zone. While AppleTalk supports multiple cable ranges per zone, it is best to limit each zone to a single cable range. Designers may wish to span a select number of zones for some service clusters.

Since the Chooser lists zone names in alphabetical order, most designers use a prefix of at least one "Z" when they want to move these zones to the bottom of the list. This tactic is very appropriate for WAN segments and other non-user-related zones.

Machine names in AppleTalk are generally a more difficult design issue, and many times they are omitted from the network design layer. This omission is a double-edged sword, as a logical naming structure would greatly assist the inventory and troubleshooting processes. However, most Macintosh workstations are named for their users or another unique characteristic. For example, Apple names its routers for famous comedians and other figures rather than using the perhaps more boring names Router_A and Router_B.

The AppleTalk naming standard introduces a larger concept that has, as of yet, remained unaddressed in this text. The naming standard under any protocol should be an important consideration for all network designers. While Daffy and Mickey might be cute names for routers, they fail to communicate their function or location. At the opposite extreme, router RC7500-B-ORD might clearly refer to Cisco router type 7500 at the second location (location B) in Chicago, but the name doesn't exactly roll off the tongue, so to speak. Another danger with the more formal naming convention is that it might not scale as initially intended. For example, how would the designer name the router in the fifth Chicago location? ORD probably should not refer to routers in all five locations. (ORD stands for Orchard Field, the original name for Chicago O'Hare International airport.)

It is important for designers to compose naming conventions that provide unambiguous names for nodes. In AppleTalk, names are ultimately presented in the format *Node Name: Device Type@Zone*. This format relates directly to the address information of the node, i.e., the zone name is the logical grouping of devices and the node name relates to a specific machine. The device type provides the socket information referenced earlier in this chapter. The device type might appear as Server:AFPServer@Sybex Sales. Cisco recommends that user nodes be named for their user and that they be listed last name first to facilitate searching. Unlike some other platforms, Macintosh resources frequently serve as both client and server; therefore, there may be numerous device types for a particular resource.

The AppleTalk Chooser

The Chooser in Macintosh systems is similar to the Network Neighborhood in Windows networks. See Figure 5.2. Apple users utilize the Chooser to select files, print, and perform other services.

FIGURE 5.2   The Macintosh Chooser

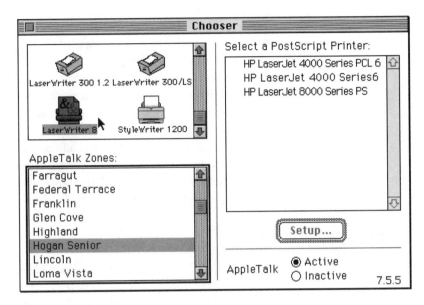

Under any version of MacOS, a Macintosh will send a GetZoneList (GZL) query to populate the resource list in the Chooser. This message is sent to every router that services a zone and to every server node in that zone. Each will then respond to the requester. Therefore, designers should limit the number of resources per zone so that each request returns a small number of responses. This rule is particularly important for zones that are frequently accessed, such as a server zone.

Most Macintosh computers have been upgraded to System 7 or greater. (System is the name of the Macintosh operating system.) When such is not the case, designers should stress the importance of this deployment. The AppleTalk Chooser uses NBP to locate resources on the network, resources that are organized based on the objects' type, zone, and name. Before System 7, the Chooser would send a broadcast every three seconds while the user had the Chooser window open, which obviously generated a great deal of traffic. And, because the message was transmitted as a broadcast, the network's performance could suffer. With the release of System 7, the Chooser began to use a delay between broadcasts that increases exponentially, which has reduced the rate at which broadcasts are sent.

AppleTalk Routing Protocols

Dynamic routing within the AppleTalk environment may use a number of protocols, which include AppleTalk RTMP, AppleTalk EIGRP (Enhanced Interior Gateway Routing Protocol), and AURP (AppleTalk Update-Based Routing Protocol). This section will introduce each of these along with information for designers to consider when selecting the appropriate protocol for their environment.

While floating static routes are typically not incorporated into most AppleTalk designs, Cisco introduced the concept of floating static routes for AppleTalk in IOS version 11. This feature may be useful for designers when incorporating backup routes into the network.

AppleTalk RTMP

The default AppleTalk routing protocol is RTMP, which is very similar to the Routing Information Protocol (RIP) found in IP. Both protocols are limited to a hop count of 15, and AppleTalk always incorporates a split-horizon update mechanism. Unlike IP RIP, though, RTMP sends updates every 10 seconds. Updating so frequently significantly adds to the chatty reputation of the overall protocol. Updates appear in the form of "tuples," which contain the cable range and hop count values.

The designer must consider a number of factors with RTMP. First, networks are limited to 15 hops due to the requirements of the routing protocol. This limitation may not be a large concern, as a well-designed network should rarely need 15 hops between networks, but the limitation remains and is a factor in the design. Second, RTMP is very chatty, as noted before, and so the designer may wish to use another protocol to conserve bandwidth and resources. However, this option is not always available because workstations and servers need to hear updates in order to operate on the network. Consequently, populated segments do not have RTMP disabled.

The designer should also consider the following with regard to AppleTalk RTMP packets:

- RTMP transmits every 10 seconds by default.

- An RTMP packet can contain up to 100 tuples.

- Each RTMP packet can be up to 600 bytes long (DDP).

- A tuple is created for each AppleTalk cable range.

By using this information, the designer may calculate the impact that routing updates have on the network. This impact is especially important on low-speed WAN links, where bandwidth may be severely limited. It is clear that a large routing table, transmitted every 10 seconds in its entirety, would quickly consume a substantial percentage of the bandwidth on a 56Kbps circuit.

Partial-mesh networks are also thwarted by the demands of split-horizon updates in RTMP. As a result, designers will need to use full-mesh topologies or consider the other two routing protocols, AT EIGRP or AURP. The EIGRP version of AppleTalk is perhaps best suited to address this problem.

AppleTalk EIGRP

As with all of the EIGRP routing protocols, the AppleTalk EIGRP (AT EIGRP) is proprietary to Cisco and requires the administrator to commit to an all-Cisco solution. For some environments, this restriction does not pose a significant shortcoming, and the use of AT EIGRP can greatly enhance the scalability of the AppleTalk protocol.

Unlike EIGRP for the IP and IPX protocols, AT EIGRP does not use the same autonomous system (AS) or process identifier for all routers in the network. In fact, the AT EIGRP identifier must be different for each router in the network that will participate in AT EIGRP. This requirement is an important design and documentation consideration that should be incorporated into the addressing and naming convention. In addition, the number following the AT EIGRP command, `appletalk routing eigrp router-number`, is not an AS number but a router-number, as shown.

As noted in the previous section, the default AppleTalk routing protocol, RTMP, does not scale well. This is due to its 15-hop-count limitation and its frequent broadcasts of the entire routing table. In addition, the required use of split-horizon updates can limit designs that use partial-mesh configurations. This limitation is negated with the use of AT EIGRP.

The exclusive use of AT EIGRP is most appropriate on WAN links. Nonetheless, it may also be used in the backbone and other transit segments that do not require RTMP updates. When enabling AT EIGRP, the router will automatically redistribute route information between AT EIGRP and RTMP. The most significant benefits to AT EIGRP are its conservation of bandwidth (updates occur only following a network change) and rapid convergence (under one second following a link failure). Of course, convergence times within the RTMP environment will be limited by that protocol.

It's important to keep in mind that Apple devices cannot be placed in AT EIGRP-only segments because they must receive RTMP updates.

To calculate the metric in AT EIGRP, the router employs a simple formula that makes each hop appear as a 9,600bps link. The RTMP hop count information is preserved.

The formula used is as follows:

AT EIGRP metric = number of hops × 25652400

As noted in the AppleTalk RTMP section, RTMP is limited in partial-mesh network designs because of the requirement that split-horizon must always be used. In AT EIGRP, this requirement no longer exists, and so RTMP may, therefore, be better suited for such designs as these. The command to remove split-horizon from AT EIGRP networks is `no appletalk eigrp-splithorizon`.

AURP

No, someone didn't just lose their lunch. AURP specifies a standard way of connecting AppleTalk networks over point-to-point lines, including dial-up modems and T1 lines. More importantly, it provides a specification for tunneling AppleTalk through foreign network systems, such as TCP/IP, X.25, OSI, and DECnet.

AURP also reduces routing update traffic. As opposed to the default 10-second update interval of RTMP, AURP updates routing tables only when a network change occurs. These updates include changes only to the topology and not the entire routing table, which further reduces the volume of traffic on the WAN link. Another benefit to the protocol is that it is an open standard under the Internet Engineering Task Force (IETF), which makes it well suited to multivendor environments. The same is not true with AT EIGRP.

Designers should remember the following when considering AURP:

- The protocol is standards based.

- AURP does not replace RTMP.

- AURP is a tunneling specification that typically operates over IP but is supported on other protocols.

- AURP sends routing updates only when needed, reducing routing traffic overhead.

- The standard provides for the remapping of addresses, similar to the Network Address Translation/Port Address Translation functions in IP.

- AURP allows for manipulation of the hop count, permitting potentially larger networks than would be available with RTMP. Designers using this technique can reduce the number of hops at the AURP tunnel—thus, a network eight hops away can appear to be only two hops away, based on the designer's configuration.

Figure 5.3 illustrates the AURP tunnel configuration.

FIGURE 5.3 The AURP tunnel over an IP-only WAN

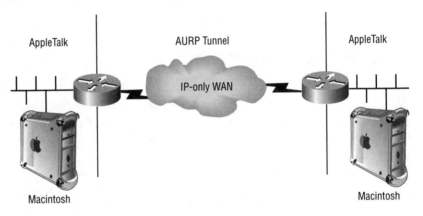

Cisco IOS Features for AppleTalk

As found in most protocols, Cisco has incorporated a number of platform-specific features that can enhance the functionality of the overall system. In AppleTalk, these features include the aforementioned AppleTalk EIGRP routing protocol and the AppleTalk access lists. In addition to the typical Cisco access list, a number of protocol-specific access lists are available to the designer, including ZIP filters and NBP filters. These will be presented in this section.

AppleTalk Access Lists

AppleTalk access lists operate in much the same way as they do in IP or other routing protocols. Therefore, the administrator or designer may use them to create distribute lists that control RTMP packets and block cable ranges. They may also be used as part of a security model.

It is important to note that there are additional filters in AppleTalk that are specifically designed to handle certain restrictions in AppleTalk networks. These are presented in this section, and the designer should use them when appropriate. For example, you should not use distribute lists to block zone information. Doing so may cause problems within the network. It is best to use the ZIP reply filter or the GetZoneList filter. All of these filters are based on AppleTalk access lists.

AppleTalk Zone Information

Zone Information Protocol (ZIP) packets advertise zone information to the network. This information must relate to the route, or routes, that corresponds to a particular zone. When ZIP advertises information about a route that does not have a corresponding zone, it can cause a ZIP storm. Cisco routers prevent ZIP storms by holding routing updates for networks that have not sent corresponding zone information. In so doing, the potential for ZIP storms is greatly reduced. Note that this feature greatly increases the stability of the network, but it may slow the propagation of route information.

AppleTalk ZIP Reply Filters

Available since Cisco IOS 10.2, AppleTalk ZIP reply filters can be an effective mechanism for blocking zone information at the router. This action may be warranted at a border router between two organizations, but AppleTalk is typically not shared between organizations. Rather, the function is used to control zone information between different divisions within the company—either on departmental or geographical boundaries. In all cases, this function is employed between administrative domains.

The ZIP reply filter does not affect RTMP updates between routers but does squelch the ZIP reply to the corresponding ZIP request, effectively hiding the zones from the opposing network. The network, or cable range, associated with that zone will also be removed from the routing table, since there is no associated zone name.

A separate function available to AppleTalk designers is the *free-trade zone*. This zone may be created between two organizations or two parts of the same domain. In both cases, networks on either side of the free-trade zone are blocked from the other.

The command that applies the ZIP reply filter is `appletalk zip-reply-filter`.

AppleTalk GetZoneList Filters and NBP Filters

It is possible to limit the zone information presented to a group of users with GetZoneList filters. This mechanism may be used to provide limited security or to simplify a portion of the network.

The administrator places the GetZoneList filter on the router that services the users. The filter must be placed on every cable range that user nodes use to access the network. This placement requirement limits the scalability of this function. The filter operates by responding to GetZoneList queries with a parsed version of the network zone list.

The NBP filters were introduced with version 11 of the IOS and are used to block specific services from hosts.

The commands that relate to GetZoneList and NBP filters as shown in Table 5.2.

TABLE 5.2 AppleTalk GetZoneList and NBP Filter Commands

Command	Function
`appletalk distribute-list in`	Applied in interface mode, this command filters routing updates coming in on the interface. It is used in concert with an access list.
`appletalk distribute-list out`	The `appletalk distribute-list out` command is applied on an interface and filters outbound routing updates. Neither the `in` nor the `out` version of the command should be used with AT EIGRP.
`appletalk getzonelist-filter`	The GetZoneList filter controls the router's replies to ZIP GZL requests from the Chooser.
`appletalk access-group`	Like IP access groups, the `appletalk access-group` command applies an access list to an interface.
`appletalk permit-partial-zones`	AppleTalk zones may span cable ranges. As a result, the router may learn of a zone from one of two or more cable ranges that service that zone, which results in a partial zone. By default, the router will drop the zone completely. The `permit-partial-zones` command alters this behavior and continues to advertise the zone even if one or more portions of the zone are unavailable. Spanned zones may be accommodated with this command; however, for diagnostic purposes it is better to maintain a one-to-one match whenever possible.

AppleTalk Tunnels with GRE

There are instances where the designer may wish to use a single protocol in the network backbone, and with increasing frequency that protocol is IP. However, if the corporation needs to connect two or more AppleTalk segments using the backbone, this problem is resolved with AppleTalk tunneling, wherein the AppleTalk packets are encapsulated in another protocol.

Tunneling is typically an encapsulation of one protocol inside another—in this specific instance, AppleTalk inside of IP. There are two tunneling encapsulations: Generic Routing Encapsulation (GRE) and Cayman. Cayman is used when connecting a Cisco router to a GatorBox, and GRE is used when connecting two Cisco routers. This section will focus only on GRE.

From a logical perspective, tunnels are point-to-point links. As such, each link requires the creation of a separate tunnel. Note that GRE tunnels are not AURP tunnels (although they are similar). GRE tunnels do not encompass a routing process like AURP, for example.

Designers should consider the negatives of using tunnels versus using two protocols on the backbone and configuring the AppleTalk protocol. The following list should assist in this evaluation:

- With tunnels, performance is decreased.

- Tunnels require additional configuration.

- Tunnels add overhead to both packets and processor utilization.

- Tunnels permit maintenance of a single protocol in the backbone, which may simplify configuration and troubleshooting within the core.

- AppleTalk tunnels should be deployed in star topologies to connect isolated LANs.

- If tunnels are not used, designers should evaluate AT EIGRP in the core along with the deployment of AppleTalk.

Network Design in the Real World: Tunnels

While tunnels are a possible way to solve many design problems, it seems as though most architects are migrating away from this solution. The primary reasons for this involve training and supportability. The installation of a tunnel is fairly straight-forward; however, it becomes substantially more complex as the number of tunnels increases. In addition, diagnostic processes no longer follow the intraprotocol methodologies that many technicians learned and employed. Rather than troubleshooting an AppleTalk problem, the administrator must add a diagnostic step to troubleshoot the IP portion and confirm that fragmentation and routing for the IP protocol is functioning correctly. As a result, it's best to consider the arguments for and against using tunnels and then establish a policy for your installation if you decide to go ahead with them—like potato chips, you can't have just one tunnel.

Some of the issues you should consider include:

Documentation—Will your team update and maintain a complete listing of all tunnels and their functions?

Troubleshooting—Does the expertise exist in all layers of the organization to troubleshoot tunnels and their problems? This answer requires knowledge of both protocols in use (the encapsulation and the native) and the hops between the end points of the tunnel.

Solvability—Unrelated to AppleTalk, one environment that I'm familiar with used tunnels to address subnets that are not contiguous with Interior Gateway Routing Protocol (IGRP). The ultimate solution was to migrate to EIGRP and complete an addressing project that seemed to extend forever. Most of the staff contended correctly that tunnels are a dirty patch to a chronic problem and that the company needed to invest in the resources to directly address the root cause. Ultimately, the scope grew to incorporate the original fixes *and* the removal of over fifty tunnels.

Scalability—This is included here because it is one of the bastions of network design; however, it really reverts back to solvability. Does the use of a tunnel solve a problem that *cannot* be resolved any other way?

Macintosh IP

Macintosh IP (MacIP) was an interesting protocol, albeit a short-lived one. Rather than providing an IP stack, MacIP acted, more accurately, as a proxy or gateway. While most modern installations use a fully compliant version of the IP stack for the Macintosh, MacIP software allowed IP connectivity over the lower-level DDP protocol and required the command `appletalk macip` for operability on Cisco routers.

MacIP was most frequently configured to support LocalTalk or AppleTalk Remote Access (ARA). These installations required MacIP in order to permit clients access to IP resources. LocalTalk was a low-bandwidth networking solution that preceded AppleTalk. ARA is still used in some installations, and it was an efficient means of connecting Macintosh devices to the network via a modem.

Configuration of MacIP required the following:

- Packets between Macintosh clients and IP hosts had to pass through the router if the client was configured to use it as a MacIP server. This design could add overhead and an extra hop when the two nodes resided on the same subnet.

- Router memory usage increased proportionally to the total number of active MacIP clients, consuming approximately 80 bytes per client.

- In addition, the router had to be configured as follows:

    - AppleTalk routing had to be enabled on at least one interface.

    - At least one interface had to be configured for IP routing.

    - The MacIP zone name configured had to be associated with a configured or *seeded* zone name.

    - The MacIP server had to reside within the AppleTalk zone.

    - An IP address specified to the MacIP server using the `appletalk macip` command had to be associated with a specific IP interface on the router. The IP address had to be one to which ARP could respond.

    - Any access list for IP had to apply to MacIP sessions.

AppleTalk Interoperability

This chapter has already addressed a number of AppleTalk interoperability issues, including tunneling and the AppleTalk version of EIGRP. However, there are a few other items to keep in mind.

First, while AppleTalk generates a significant number of broadcasts in the network, the impact of other protocols on AppleTalk-only nodes is greatly reduced. Stated another way, IP and IPX broadcasts are discarded by AppleTalk-only devices at an earlier point than broadcasts in other protocols. In fact, AppleTalk-only stacks will discard all packets from all other Layer 3 protocols.

Second, the number of broadcasts in AppleTalk will significantly impact other devices on the network. Both IP and IPX stacks will process AppleTalk broadcasts like any other broadcast. Therefore, adding IP to Macintosh systems or running IPX- and IP-based PCs on segments with AppleTalk devices will greatly magnify the impact of broadcasts.

In most current networks, designers have removed, or are in the process of removing, AppleTalk. Where AppleTalk segments remain, the general guideline is to use less than 200 nodes to populate a segment.

Summary

The AppleTalk protocol is perhaps one of the most user-friendly networking protocols ever developed. Unfortunately, the scalability limitations of the protocol and the impact of the Internet (with its implied dependence on IP) have restricted its usage.

In this context, this chapter addressed the issues that confront network designers using AppleTalk in both large and small networks and also suggested methods by which the designer might address the limitations of the RTMP protocol. This might include the use of AppleTalk EIGRP, access lists, and specific naming and addressing conventions.

In addition, this chapter addressed some of the enhancements to the AppleTalk protocol, including AURP and the efficiency of using MacOS version 7. Also, filters specific to AppleTalk were reviewed.

Readers should be fairly comfortable with the features and benefits of AURP and AT EIGRP as they relate to the default RTMP as well. The operations of the Chooser in AppleTalk networks are also important concepts to understand.

Review Questions

1. Which of the following are limitations of the AppleTalk protocol?

    A. No hierarchical addressing scheme

    B. No hierarchical naming scheme

    C. High dependence on broadcasts

    D. All of the above

2. When using the AppleTalk version of EIGRP, what unique convention must be followed?

    A. The same AS number must be used on all routers in the domain.

    B. Different process numbers must be used on each router in the domain.

    C. RTMP must have the same AS number as AT EIGRP.

    D. There is no version of AppleTalk EIGRP.

3. To connect two AppleTalk networks across an IP-only backbone, the designer must use which of the following?

    A. AppleTalk tunnels

    B. ZIP—Zone over IP

    C. AT CGMP

    D. AppleTalk cannot traverse IP-only segments.

4. Which of the following would be a valid AppleTalk cable range?

    A. 4–4

    B. Marketing_Zone

    C. 10.12

    D. 4–10

5. Which of the following might be used to block zone information from reaching another AppleTalk administration domain?

   A. AppleTalk EIGRP

   B. AppleTalk RTMP

   C. AppleTalk ZIP reply filters

   D. AURP

6. In order to reduce traffic on WAN links, designers should:

   A. Use AT EIGRP with route summarization enabled.

   B. Use AURP.

   C. Use RTMP.

   D. Use RTMP on the WAN and AURP on the LAN.

7. How many updates may be included in an RTMP packet?

   A. 25

   B. 50

   C. 100

   D. 256

8. In order to simplify troubleshooting AppleTalk networks, designers should:

   A. Design cable ranges that are numerically significant

   B. Use MacOS version 7 or greater

   C. Use RTMP

   D. Use AT EIGRP

9. Network designers should work with the workstation administrators to:

   A. Configure WINS servers for AppleTalk segments

   B. Disable the Chooser Scanning Protocol (CSP)

   C. Use MacIP whenever possible

   D. Upgrade all workstations to a minimum of System 7

10. True or false, AURP and AppleTalk GRE tunnels are the same.

    A. True

    B. False

11. Before System 7, the Chooser requested zone information how frequently?

    A. Every 3 seconds

    B. Every 5 seconds

    C. Every 10 seconds

    D. Every 60 seconds

12. Two devices are addressed as 4.5 and 7.9, respectively. Are they in the same network if the cable range is 1–9?

    A. Yes

    B. No

13. Which routing protocol sends updates only?

    A. ZIP

    B. RTMP

    C. AURP

    D. None of the above

14. Which of the following is true regarding MacIP?

    A. It is a compliant IP stack for interoperating with non-Macintosh systems.

    B. It provides TN3270 emulation.

    C. It is faster than TCP/IP for file transfers.

    D. It is similar to a proxy service.

15. Which of the following is a reason to use tunnels for AppleTalk?

    A. Additional overhead and processing

    B. Transport of AppleTalk over IP-only networks

    C. Additional security

    D. Compatibility with CDP

16. Node number 231 is on cable range 50–59. Which of the following is a possible AppleTalk address?

    A. 50.59

    B. 231.51

    C. 50–59

    D. 56.231

17. Cisco recommends that nodes follow which naming convention?

    A. User name, last name first

    B. User name, first name first

    C. Same as AppleTalk address

    D. Named for famous people

18. AppleTalk network numbers should:

    A. Be assigned sequentially

    B. Always start with a one

    C. Relate to a location, possibly using a site, building, and floor office model

    D. Be the same for all WAN segments

19. Which of the following is not true regarding MacIP?

    A. It requires at least one IP network.

    B. It requires at least one AppleTalk network.

    C. The MacIP server must be in the AppleTalk network.

    D. It operates only with AppleTalk Remote Access (ARA).

20. AppleTalk tunnels are best configured in:

    A. Star configurations

    B. Ring configurations

    C. Hierarchical configurations

    D. None of the above. Tunnels are available only on point-to-point serial links.

Answers to Review Questions

1. D.

2. B.

3. A.

4. A, D.

5. C.

6. B.

7. C.

8. A.

9. D.

10. B.

11. A.

12. A.

13. C.

14. D.

15. B.

    Some designers may note that tunnels can be encrypted, thus augmenting security. However, enhanced security is not a primary reason to use tunnels for AppleTalk in this context.

16. D.

17. A.

18. C.

19. D.

20. A.

Chapter 6

Designing Networks with Novell and IPX

CISCO INTERNETWORK DESIGN EXAM OBJECTIVES COVERED IN THIS CHAPTER:

- ✓ Use Enhanced IGRP for path determination in internetworks that support IP, IPX, and AppleTalk.

- ✓ Examine a client's requirements and construct an appropriate IPX design solution.

- ✓ Choose the appropriate routing protocol for an IPX internetwork.

- ✓ Design scalable and manageable IPX internetworks by controlling RIP and SAP traffic.

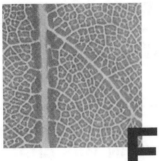

For many years, Novell's IPX protocol commanded a significant share of the networking market. However, like AppleTalk, Novell's IPX protocol is being replaced with TCP/IP in most modern networks.

As with AppleTalk, IPX was designed to simplify administrative functions and avoid some of the manual, complex tasks that were required by administrators and designers. For example, IPX does not incorporate the concept of subnets, which negates the need for calculating subnet masks or pre-limiting the number of hosts that will be supported by the network. This is both a positive and a negative—administrators need to configure the network address only once and all workstations will automatically learn this information. However, this automation adds to the total overhead.

This chapter will address many of the common issues that arise when designing IPX networks, and it will also provide some direction to creating a scalable design.

The IPX Protocol

As noted at the beginning of this chapter, Novell's IPX protocol was designed to simplify the configuration of the network. While this chapter will document some of the penalties that came from these features, it is important for designers to be aware of how these features differ from IP and how they may benefit from using IPX. Table 6.1 compares the IP and IPX protocols.

TABLE 6.1   Differences between IP and IPX

Service	IP	IPX
Automatic addressing	Automatic address assignment requires DHCP.	Automatic address assignment is built in. IPX routers assign a four-byte network number that is added to the MAC (Media Access Control) address to create a unique address.
Automatic naming	Resource names require WINS (Windows Internet Naming Service) or DNS (Domain Name System).	Server names and other resources are communicated via the SAP (Service Advertising Protocol) process. This feature is built in.
Route summarization	Available.	With NLSP (NetWare Link Services Protocol), IPX routes can be summarized.
Internet connectivity	IP is the protocol of the Internet; therefore, IP workstations can connect directly to the Internet.	IPX traffic cannot traverse the Internet, and IPX-only workstations require a gateway.
Subnet masks	The IP protocol is designed around the concept of subnet masks.	IPX does not include a subnet mask.
Scalability	Scales with minor effort.	Can scale to hundreds of networks, but typically requires filters and other techniques.

In modern network design, it is increasingly unlikely for designers to select IPX because of Novell's support for IP and the growth of the Internet. Many designers prefer to use a single network protocol when possible, and the most-supported protocol is IP. However, legacy networks may incorporate large installations of IPX, and there are still applications that may warrant its deployment.

This chapter will focus on the IPX protocol on Novell servers, but it is important to note that Novell also supports NFS (Network File System) for Unix systems and AFP (AppleTalk File Protocol) for Apple systems on the server. This is in addition to the native NCP (NetWare Core Protocol) running on IPX. Novell also supports gateway services for mainframes with its SAA (Systems Application Architecture) gateway product.

Cisco and Novell recommend that individual IPX networks contain no more than 500 nodes. This limitation results from the broadcast traffic inherent in IPX designs. In practice, this value is fairly high—most IPX environments experience degradation at the 200-to-300-node level.

In production networks, do not use the broadcast percentage to evaluate the health of the network. Broadcasts-per-second values provide a clearer indication of *how* the broadcasts are affecting the users.

Also, note that Cisco routers typically require the configuration of an IPX internal network number for NLSP and other services within the Novell environment. As with other network numbers, the internal network number must be unique within the internetwork.

IPX RIP and SAP

Novell IPX employs a routing protocol similar to IP RIP, which is transmitted every 60 seconds (as opposed to every 30 seconds) and may contain up to 50 different network entries per update packet. The network diameter is still limited to 15 hops when using IPX RIP, the same as with IP RIP.

While there are many similarities between IP RIP and IPX RIP, please note that they are different routing protocols.

In order to reduce the possibility of routing loops, IPX RIP must use split horizon—similar to the requirement with AppleTalk RTMP. In addition, IPX RIP employs a lost-route algorithm that helps prevent routing loops. This function also locates new routes upon failure.

IPX RIP Metrics

Unlike IP RIP, IPX RIP includes two mechanisms for determining the best route. In addition to a hop counter, IPX RIP incorporates delay into the protocol. By default, all LAN technologies are assessed a cost of one tick, or 1/18 of a second. WAN technologies, regardless of their actual bandwidth, are assessed by default a cost of six ticks (this value can be changed). Cisco routers augment these metrics by using the local interface delay to break ties in both hop count and ticks. However, Cisco supports multiple concurrent IPX paths, which the designer enables with the `ipx maximum-paths` command.

By default, Cisco routers support a single IPX route through the network. The `ipx maximum-paths` command allows the designer to permit up to four route entries. By establishing more than one IPX path, the designer can incorporate faster convergence and load balancing into the design.

It is important to note that there are differences between IP switching and IPX switching. These differences will also factor into a designer's implementation.

Table 6.2 describes the various types of switching and load balancing in Cisco routers.

TABLE 6.2 IPX Load Balancing

Switching Type	Similar to IP	Load Balancing
Process switching	Yes	Packet by packet
Fast switching	No	Packet by packet
Autonomous/silicon	Yes	Destination by destination

Designers can modify the default IPX RIP metrics by using the `ipx delay` command.

Do not infer from Table 6.2 that IPX cannot be fast-switched—it can. Its behavior is different from the characteristics of IP fast switching. Also note that some versions of the IOS, including 11.2(12), have problems with IPX fast switching, and administrators should upgrade their routers as applicable.

Controlling IPX SAP Traffic

The Service Advertising Protocol, or SAP, is responsible for the distribution of information regarding file, print, and other services provided by the network.

For the network designer, the SAP process can be both a help and a hindrance. The most significant problem with SAPs is their reliance on broadcasts, which in turn limits scalability.

However, it is not the broadcast update mechanism that hinders scalability with SAP. The issue is the method used to create the updates. Each router and server in the network recalculates SAP traffic. This information is then retransmitted as a complete SAP table, which should be consistent throughout the network. Rather than sending information about just the services that that server provides, the device sends information about all services that all devices provide. Also, separate SAP entries are created for each service, so a NetWare server with three printers, file sharing, and four database entries would create eight SAP entries—requiring two SAP packets.

Each SAP update is transmitted at 60-second intervals, and each update packet contains up to seven services. The designer can readily see how the addition of a single service on the network would add to the SAP traffic when repeated by 1,000 routers and servers, for example.

It is important for the network designer to consider filtering IPX SAP traffic even when the network is quite small—possibly as small as 20 networks. The use of IPX SAP access lists can provide security and scalability features to the network. As with most network policies, SAP access lists are best deployed at the distribution layer of the hierarchical model.

Table 6.3 shows the three different locations where administrators may employ SAP access lists.

TABLE 6.3 Available SAP Access Lists

Location	Command
Input	input-sap-filter
Output	output-sap-filter
Source	router-sap-filter

The IPX SAP access lists are numbered from 1000 to 1099 and are configured in a similar fashion to IP access lists. The syntax is as follows:

```
Access-list {number} [deny | permit] network[.node]
[service-type[server-name]]
```

A network number of –1 will match any network, and a service type of 0 will match all services. Like other access lists, SAP access lists are parsed in sequence and with an implicit deny at the end.

SAP update timers can also be controlled without filtering the contents. You accomplish this with the `ipx sap-incremental` command, which was introduced with Cisco IOS 10.0. This option is available to administrators without the IPX EIGRP protocol as well. The argument `rsup-only` is added to the command.

For use with non-Cisco equipment, it is possible to adjust the default update increment for SAP broadcasts; however, you must deploy this option with caution and consistency. The benefit of this option is the reduction of bandwidth consumed by SAP broadcasts. However, as with most options, the designer and administrator must accept a compromise. As the time between updates increases, the time for notification of a failed service also increases. This may not be a significant concern in most networks, but it is worth considering before selecting this SAP control option.

It is recommended that no nodes be placed on a segment that has a modified SAP timer; however, it is permitted so long as all nodes on the segment are modified to reflect the new configuration.

IPXWAN

While it is uncommon, there may be an instance when the designer or administrator would wish to connect a Novell server to a Cisco router via the Point-to-Point Protocol (PPP). Such installations are occasionally used for disaster recovery.

The IPXWAN protocol operates over PPP to provide accurate routing metrics on dial-up connections, which is accomplished via a handshake process. IPXWAN is an established standard, which permits interoperability between non-Cisco devices. Cisco has supported the protocol since IOS 10.0.

It was noted previously that IPXWAN links incorporate a cost of six ticks. This is automatically resolved when using IPXWAN over PPP. The command `ipx link-delay` is used to adjust the cost of each link. Table 6.4 provides suggested delay values based on formulas from Cisco and Novell. Note that these values were developed for IPXWAN 2.0.

TABLE 6.4 Suggested Delay Values with IPX WAN 2.0

Bandwidth	Ticks
9600 bps	108
19.2Kbps	60
38.4Kbps	24
56Kbps	18
128Kbps	12
256Kbps	6
1.544Mbps	6

IPX Frame Types

When Novell first released the IPX protocol, it included a specification for the two octets that immediately followed the source MAC address in the LAN frame. In the proprietary Novell Ethernet specification, this incorporated a length field immediately followed by the data (unlike the IEEE standard, which specified a length field followed by an LLC, or Logical Link Control, header). However, as standards evolved and multiprotocol and multitopology support was required, numerous frame encapsulations for IPX were ratified. These are defined in Table 6.5.

TABLE 6.5   The IPX Frame Types

Novell Frame Type	Cisco Frame Type	Encapsulation
Ethernet 802.3	novell-ether	802.3 with FFFF (length)
Ethernet 802.2	sap or iso1	802.2 with E0E0 SAPs
Ethernet SNAP	snap	802.2 SNAP with 8137
Ethernet II	arpa	ARPA with 8137
Token Ring	novell-tr	802.2 with E0E0 SAPs
Token Ring SNAP	snap	802.2 SNAP with 8137
FDDI SNAP	snap	802.2 SNAP with 8137
FDDI 802.2	sap or iso1	802.2 with E0E0 SAPs

It is important to note that each frame type is a separate network in IPX. This is true for multiple physical media running the same encapsulation or for multiple encapsulations on a single physical media.

Connecting Same-Interface Frame Types

There may be design requirements that mandate temporary support for multiple IPX frame types on the same media. This is frequently the case when migrating from one encapsulation to another. Older software programs may also require a specific encapsulation, necessitating the use of multiple frame types. Fortunately, few programmers would consider writing an application "down the stack" today, which negates this concern for most administrators.

When configuring to support multiple frame types, designers must keep in mind that all traffic destined for the other network on the wire must traverse the router. This is called *local router*, even when using subinterfaces. In this configuration, all broadcast traffic on the wire is doubled. Ideally, networks should be designed to use multiple frame types on the same segment as seldom as possible. Figure 6.1 illustrates the multiple frame-type installation.

FIGURE 6.1   Multiple frame types on an interface

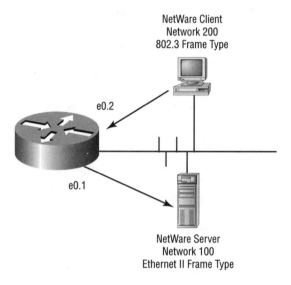

NetWare Client
Network 200
802.3 Frame Type

e0.2

e0.1

NetWare Server
Network 100
Ethernet II Frame Type

The administrator and designer can take a couple of steps to improve performance under multiple frame-type configurations: First, the command `ipx route-cache same-interface` will enable faster processing of packets between networks on the same local wire. Second, installations of Windows 95/98/NT should be configured for the specific frame type in use on the segment. The setting of auto, which is the default, can occasionally cause problems and loss of connectivity, and it may also generate additional network traffic. This is the result of a station requiring a router to transmit to another station running a different automatic frame type—depending on the software, auto may select the first or select all heard frame types, which can result in four packets being transmitted where one was necessary.

IPX Get Nearest Server

The Get Nearest Server (GNS) process provides a mechanism for clients to locate a server. The server will then provide the necessary information to the client so that the login and authentication process may continue.

Designers should be familiar with the overall GNS process and how these datagrams may affect users on the network. It is important not only to understand the process, but also to consider what impact the user might experience if the server is located on the remote end of a slow WAN link. There are instances when it is not appropriate to place servers in every remote location, but performance—specifically login performance—will likely suffer.

The GNS request is specified as part of the Service Advertising Protocol (SAP). GNS is a broadcast datagram that is answered by any IPX server on the network. If there are multiple servers on a network segment, the client receives a response from each one and accepts the first one for the rest of the initialization process. Note that the first server may not be the preferred server listed in the client's configuration file. When configured for a preferred server, the client will wait to hear from that server until a timeout occurs, and the next available server will be used. An example of the GNS broadcast, which is captured with an EtherPeek analyzer, follows. In this example, the workstation's MAC address is 00:60:08:9e:2e:44, and the first packet is the client's GNS request.

```
Flags: 0x80 802.3
Status: 0x00
Packet Length:64
Timestamp: 22:56:14.565643 10/07/1998
802.3 Header
```
Destination: ff:ff:ff:ff:ff:ff Ethernet Brdcast
Source: 00:60:08:9e:2e:44
LLC Length: 38
```
802.2 Logical Link Control (LLC) Header
```
Dest. SAP: 0xe0 NetWare
Source SAP: 0xe0 NetWare Individual LLC Sublayer Management Function
Command: 0x03 Unnumbered Information
```
IPX - NetWare Protocol
```
Checksum: 0xffff

Length: 34
Transport Control:
Reserved: %0000
Hop Count: %0000
Packet Type: 0 Novell
Destination Network: 0x00000000
Destination Node: ff:ff:ff:ff:ff:ff Ethernet Brdcast
Destination Socket: 0x0452 Service Advertising Protocol
Source Network: 0xf3df9b36
Source Node: 00:60:08:9e:2e:44
Source Socket: 0x4000 IPX Ephemeral
SAP - Service Advertising Protocol
Operation: 3 NetWare Nearest Service Query
Service Type: 4 File Server
Extra bytes (Padding):
.... 00 04 00 04 00 04 00 04 00
Frame Check Sequence: 0x00000000

Novell networking adheres to a client-server model in almost all cases. Therefore, servers are strictly servers and clients are resources that use the services provided by servers. This differs from AppleTalk and Microsoft peer-to-peer networking, where clients can be servers as well.

Note that the GNS request is a broadcast and is not forwarded by a router. Although this might lead an administrator to believe that an IPX server must be installed on each network segment, such is not the case. IPX places a GNS listener on each IPX network. The router also contains a SAP table and responds as necessary to GNS requests.

Cisco routers do not respond to a GNS request if a NetWare server is on the segment with current versions of the IOS.

Figure 6.2 provides a visual representation of the GNS process in an IPX network where the server is separated from the client by a router. The first two transmissions from the client are broadcasts, whereas the responses are unicasts. NCP is a connection-oriented protocol that is used for primary Novell functions. Once the client and server establish an NCP session, the client proceeds to the login phase. At this point, the designer may be involved to address slow login issues.

FIGURE 6.2 The Novell connection sequence with a remote server

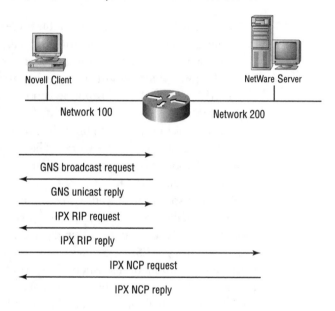

Designing Networks with NLSP

Most distance-vector routing protocols are inefficient when compared to link-state routing protocols. These inefficiencies include high bandwidth utilization, slow convergence, and limited route calculations. Link-state protocols improve upon distance-vector protocols; however, they typically consume substantial amounts of processor and memory resources.

In order to improve the scalability of the IPX protocol, Novell developed NLSP, or the NetWare Link Services Protocol. NLSP is an open standard that greatly improves upon the limitations found in IPX RIP. These benefits include faster convergence, lower bandwidth consumption, and a greater network diameter.

Networks that use both IPX RIP and NLSP are limited to the 15-hop diameter imposed by IPX RIP. It is possible to adjust the hop count during redistribution; however, this can be confusing in a troubleshooting scenario and should only be used with clear documentation and training.

Unlike IPX EIGRP, NLSP is available on servers, which can permit its use on populated segments. This factor can facilitate migration to an all-NLSP network, which would allow for a greater network diameter.

In addition, NLSP supports route aggregation, a service not supported by IPX EIGRP or IPX RIP. This option can greatly reduce the size of the IPX routing table.

Network architects should limit the number of routing nodes per NLSP area when designing their networks. The recommended limit is approximately 400 nodes; however, a more accurate impact definition may be found with the formula $n*\log(n)$.

NLSP is also best deployed with each area contained in a geographic region—a single campus, for example. Large, international IPX networks should not place all routers in a single area.

Incorporating NLSP into a network design is made easier by the automatic redistribution mechanism on Cisco routers. Routers running both IPX RIP and NLSP will automatically learn of the other process's routes, and the implementation will automatically limit the likelihood of routing loops. Note that this may lead to suboptimal routing, and designers should verify the routing table following implementation to confirm that the paths selected are, in fact, the most desirable.

Some administrators are leery of deploying NLSP because they believe that readdressing will be required. Readdressing is necessary only to create logical areas for summarization. If the network resides in a single area, readdressing will not be required.

This leads to a design consideration for new networks, of course. Designers should strive to create logical addressing schemes even when not designing for NLSP, for two reasons. First, a logical addressing scheme will greatly assist in address assignments and troubleshooting. Second, the use of logical addressing will avail route summarization options in the future should the network expand beyond the initially conceived boundaries.

Consider a network design where slow frame-relay links are used for the WAN. The designer would likely select NLSP over IPX RIP and IPX EIGRP for the following reasons:

- NLSP uses little bandwidth.

- NLSP can be configured for fault tolerance.

- NLSP is based on standards.

- NLSP is based on updates.

- NLSP can perform route summarization.

Typically, in link-state protocols a full-mesh topology is required. This would reduce the desirability of using NLSP, as the costs associated with the network would increase—additional PVCs (permanent virtual circuits) would be required to maintain the full mesh. This is not a fault of NLSP, but rather an outcome of the full-mesh requirement. In NLSP, the designated router creates a pseudonode, which is responsible for reporting the adjacencies to all other routers. Because of this, the number of PVCs in a five-router Frame Relay configuration can be reduced to four, as opposed to the ten that would be required with a full mesh. Note the formulas to calculate this:

- Full-Mesh Topology = $n*(n-1)/2$

- Partial-Mesh Topology = $n-1$

N is equal to the number of routers in the network. These formulas discount redundant links and other considerations.

Figures 6.3 and 6.4 illustrate the use of NLSP and the summarization of addresses within NLSP areas.

FIGURE 6.3   NLSP areas

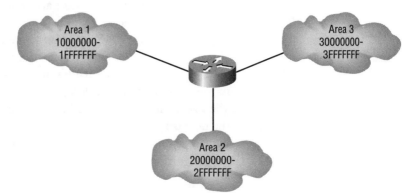

FIGURE 6.4 IPX addressing and summarization within NLSP areas

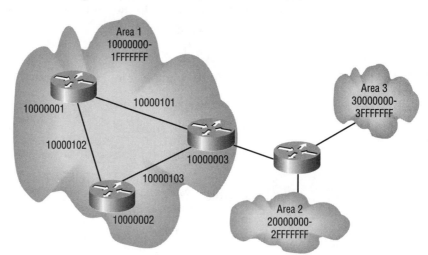

Designing Networks with IPX EIGRP

In order to augment support for the IPX protocol, Cisco developed a version of EIGRP to replace IPX RIP on WAN links and other transit media. IPX EIGRP is very similar to IP EIGRP in that the AS number must be the same on all routers in the autonomous system. This differs, as you may recall, from AppleTalk EIGRP, which uses different AS numbers on each router.

This chapter will later present the use of access lists to block SAP traffic from different portions of the network. However, one benefit of IPX EIGRP is that it can replace the normal SAP distribution method and control broadcasts so that they are transmitted only when there is a change in the SAP table. This can greatly conserve bandwidth on slower WAN links. Unfortunately, this may not resolve all of the designer's issues with SAP traffic in the network, as the size of the SAP table to be calculated and propagated throughout the network remains the same.

Cisco strongly recommends the use of IPX EIGRP when constructing scalable IPX networks.

The tick count is not incremented when converting from IPX RIP to IPX EIGRP. The hop count is incremented at each conversion; thus, two hops are added when going from IPX RIP to IPX EIGRP and on to another IPX RIP segment.

Designing for NetBIOS over IPX

Networks that rely on NetBIOS typically include those platforms that grew out of the LAN Manager environment. These include OS/2 and Windows. NetBIOS was originally developed to operate over the LLC2 protocol, or NetBEUI. This was an excellent solution for small, non-routed networks and afforded the administrator an easy-to-install-and-maintain environment. Unfortunately, small non-routed networks cannot support the large user populations typically needed in today's environments.

One of the NetBIOS negatives is its reliance on broadcasts. Given its original design for small, non-routed networks, NetBIOS doesn't scale particularly well. This is also true when the underlying protocol is IPX; however, it is important for designers to consider using IPX when their Novell networks also require NetBIOS. This solution may negate the need for IP or NetBEUI in the network, which facilitates a single-protocol architecture by placing all traffic on IPX.

In order to scale the protocol (increase the number of networks and users), most designers employ NetBIOS name filtering to control the scope of the broadcasts. This is available in both the IPX NetBIOS implementation and the NetBEUI/NetBIOS protocol.

In order to filter on NetBIOS names, the designer must create, in essence, a NetBIOS domain by establishing a naming scheme that is unique to each subnet. For example, the designer would likely prefix all machines in the marketing department with MKT. In so doing, the router can filter those broadcasts from leaving their local domain or from entering domains that would not contain any devices with that prefix. Consider Figure 6.5—there is no reason for the router's e0 interface to forward NetBIOS requests for devices with MKT* domain names. The same is true for e2 and SLS* domain names.

FIGURE 6.5 NetBIOS name filtering

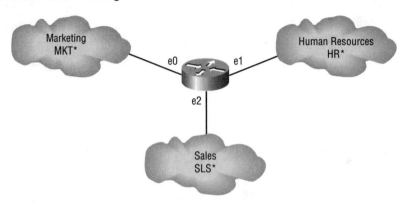

While Figure 6.5 shows varying-length prefixes for NetBIOS names, most administrators and designers use a convention that fixes the length at two or three characters. Some designs use geographic considerations for filtering as well.

IPX Type 20

As noted previously, NetBIOS was originally designed around flat networks that would support broadcasts. However, this solution cannot scale beyond a few hundred nodes, which mandated the use of an alternative lower protocol for NetBIOS traffic. In IP, this protocol is defined as NetBT. In Novell IPX it is called NWLink. By encapsulating NetBIOS in a routable protocol, the network can scale to greater dimensions.

Novell IPX can also support NetBIOS broadcasts in otherwise routed designs. This is serviced with the ipx type-20-propagation command. This command instructs the router to forward all NetBIOS broadcasts to all other interfaces. Remember that routers typically drop broadcasts by default, and the ipx type-20-propagation command does not affect those broadcasts.

The NetBIOS protocol is fundamental to Windows networking. It will be presented in greater detail, as it relates to Windows, in Chapter 7. Please note that Windows 2000 and Active Directory promise to remove the dependency on NetBIOS from the Windows environment.

IPX Access Lists

Cisco routers support filtering based on a number of protocols, including IPX. In the Novell environment, the designer may choose to employ access lists for security or scalability reasons.

One of the most common reasons for deploying IPX access lists concerns the propagation of SAP traffic. These service advertisements can quickly impact overall network performance, especially on slower WAN links. Consider for a moment the SAP traffic generated by servers in Tokyo. While the data center in Sydney may need to receive these updates, it is unlikely that the Chicago office will need access to files and printers in the Tokyo office. By employing SAP filters, the designer can reduce the size of the Chicago office's SAP table. Administrators should note that input filters will block SAPs from the local table, while output filters will block the transmission of the SAP entry—the local router will remain aware of the advertised service.

IP eXchange Gateway

The IP eXchange gateway product, now owned by Cisco, was designed to provide access to the Internet and other IP-based resources without installing an IP stack on every client workstation in the Novell environment.

Unfortunately, the simplified workstation administration was offset by the slower performance of gateway translation and the installation of client software for the IP eXchange product. In addition, a server running either Novell or Windows NT was required for the translation, which introduced a single point of failure and added administration.

One of the beneficial features of the IP eXchange gateway was its use of a single IP address to service all the clients in the network. This greatly simplified troubleshooting and administration.

Figure 6.6 illustrates the connectivity between devices in the IP eXchange environment.

FIGURE 6.6 The IP eXchange IPX-to-IP gateway product

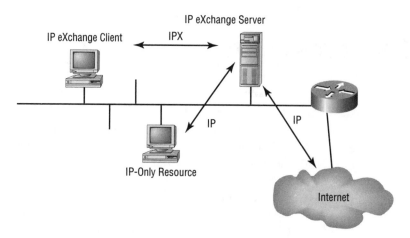

IPX Watchdog Spoof and SPX Spoofing

In Novell networking, the IPX server will transmit an IPX watchdog packet in order to verify that the client is still available. This process is used to clear connections to the server that were terminated incorrectly.

Unfortunately, this transmission can cause DDR (dial-on-demand routing) connections to activate. Many designers have forgotten or ignored this function in Novell networks and been surprised when the first telecommunications bill arrived. IPX watchdog packets are sent at five-minute intervals.

Fortunately, Cisco has developed a service to permit the use of IPX watchdog packets in DDR installations. The IPX watchdog spoof process will effectively proxy for the remote client and permit the router to acknowledge the watchdog packet from the server. This function prevents the DDR circuit from activating, so the server believes that it is still connected to the remote workstation.

SPX spoofing is another useful service in DDR environments. This service operates at the remote end of the DDR connection and acknowledges SPX keepalives transmitted by the client. This may be for an rconsole (a remote administration tool for Novell servers) session or connectivity to an SAA (Novell SNA or Systems Network Architecture) gateway. The use of SPX spoofing prevents the router from activating the circuit, which usually reduces costs in the DDR environment.

Figure 6.7 illustrates the IPX watchdog process. Figure 6.8 illustrates the SPX spoofing function. Note that watchdog spoofing was introduced in Cisco IOS version 9.1.9, and SPX spoofing was introduced in 11.0.

FIGURE 6.7 IPX watchdog

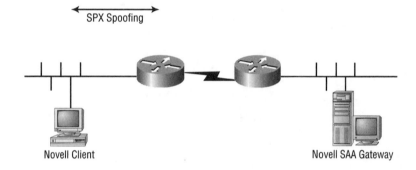

FIGURE 6.8 SPX spoofing

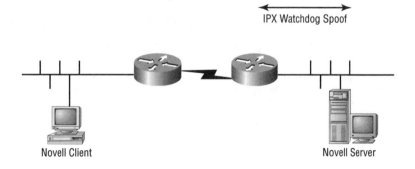

Summary

Novell's IPX remains one of the easier networking protocols in terms of configuration and support. However, it is limited in scalability, and, like AppleTalk, it has lost significant market share because of the success of IP. In fact, with the release of NetWare 5, Novell changed the default networking protocol to IP. Most network designers will choose to follow this trend, where appropriate, as it may lead to a single protocol for the enterprise. However, many networks continue to use and deploy IPX, and an understanding of this protocol is beneficial for both the exam and production networks.

This chapter presented the following:

- The Novell routing protocols, including:

    - IPX RIP

    - IPX NLSP

    - IPX EIGRP

- The Service Advertising Protocol (SAP)

- Design techniques for NetBIOS over IPX

- IPX access lists

- The IP eXchange product

- Methods to increase the scalability of IPX, including:

    - The `maximum paths` command to enable load balancing and faster convergence

    - The use of IPX EIGRP and NLSP to improve the routing process

    - The use of SAP filters and NetBIOS name filters

    - The use of IPXWAN to improve routing metric accuracy on WAN interfaces

Review Questions

1. Load balancing is available for IPX on Cisco routers with which of the following commands?

   A. `ipx load-balance`

   B. `ipx maximum-paths`

   C. `ipx fast-cache all-interfaces`

   D. Not available for IPX

2. The network diameter is limited to which of the following when using IPX RIP?

   A. 7 hops

   B. 15 hops

   C. 16 hops

   D. 224 hops

3. Cisco routers can support more than one IPX frame type on a major interface without the use of secondaries. True or false?

   A. True

   B. False

4. Which of the following are true regarding IPX RIP?

   A. Supports update-based routing updates

   B. Provides for 15 hops

   C. Supports subnetting

   D. Sends updates every 60 seconds

5. In order to limit the broadcasts inherent in NetBIOS, the designer should incorporate which of the following into the design?

   A. Select a naming convention that permits optimal filtering

   B. Configure an IPX WINS server on every network

   C. Avoid IPX and use IP only

   D. Provide no fewer than three equal-cost routes in the network

6. True or false: Cisco routers, by default, permit only one IPX route per destination.

   A. True

   B. False

7. The general rule of thumb regarding IPX limits the number of nodes per network to which of the following?

   A. 100

   B. 200

   C. 300

   D. 500

8. Which command is needed to configure a Cisco router for multiple IPX route support?

   A. `ipx load-balance`

   B. `ipx maximum-paths`

   C. `ipx fast-cache all-interfaces`

   D. Not available for IPX

9. IPX EIGRP requires which of the following?

    A. Cisco routers

    B. The same AS number for all routers in the domain

    C. Different AS numbers for all routers in the domain

    D. Point-to-point links

10. Which of the following are true regarding the SAP process?

    A. SAPs provide alternative routes.

    B. SAPs are sent every 10 seconds.

    C. SAP traffic provides a mechanism for advertising network services.

    D. Due to their broadcast-intensive nature, SAPs can limit the overall scalability of the network.

11. IPX type 20 traffic is responsible for which of the following?

    A. IPX RIP

    B. IPX NLSP

    C. IPX EIGRP

    D. NetBIOS

12. Why might a designer select IPX for a new network design?

    A. Ease of configuration and support for specific applications

    B. Permits the use of a single protocol for the Internet

    C. Scales to support over 20,000 routers and over 100,000 networks

    D. Permits routing table summarization with IPX RIP

13. The designer wants to deploy the most scalable, standards-based, IPX routing protocol. Which of the following would you recommend?

A. IPX EIGRP

B. NLSP

C. IPX RIP

D. IPXWAN

14. Which of the following was a benefit to the IP eXchange product?

A. Slower processing

B. Additional administration

C. The use of a dedicated client on each workstation

D. The use of a single IP address for each device in the network

15. IPX watchdog spoof is deployed:

A. At the workstation

B. At the router interface facing the workstation

C. At the router interface facing the server

D. At the server

16. The SPX spoof function is deployed:

A. At the workstation

B. At the router interface facing the workstation

C. At the router interface facing the server

D. At the server

17. Which of the following is not true regarding NLSP?

   A. NLSP supports summarization.

   B. NLSP is a link-state protocol.

   C. NLSP is a distance-vector protocol.

   D. NLSP is not a replacement for IPX RIP.

18. Why would a designer wish to use IPX watchdog spoofing and SPX spoofing?

   A. To prevent activation of DDR circuits

   B. To filter SAP broadcasts

   C. To make sure DDR circuits do not disconnect

   D. To encapsulate these packets across WAN links

19. The delay for GNS queries on a serverless segment is (assume version 11.2 of the IOS for this question)?

   A. 500 ms

   B. 1 second

   C. 0 ms

   D. Variable depending on the LAN media

20. The router may be configured to:

   A. Respond to GNS queries in a round-robin fashion.

   B. Respond to GNS queries when there is a server on the local segment.

   C. Encapsulate GNS queries for transport to a central server.

   D. The router does not respond to GNS queries. This is a server function.

Answers to Review Questions

1. B.

2. B.

3. B.

The administrator must use subinterfaces or secondaries.

4. B, D.

5. A.

6. A.

7. D.

8. B.

9. A, B.

10. C, D.

11. D.

12. A.

13. B.

This is one of the few times when the Cisco solution isn't the requested one. IPX EIGRP is not an open standard and requires the use of all Cisco routers.

14. D.

15. C.

16. B.

17. C.

18. A.

19. C.

20. A.

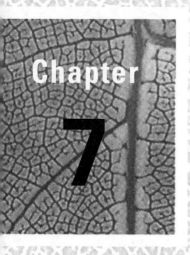

Chapter 7

Designing for Windows Networking

CISCO INTERNETWORK DESIGN EXAM OBJECTIVES COVERED IN THIS CHAPTER:

✓ Examine a client's requirements and construct an appropriate NetBIOS design solution.

✓ Design a source-route-bridged internetwork that provides connectivity for NetBIOS applications and controls NetBIOS explorer traffic.

As the most popular desktop operating environment, Windows holds a substantial position of prominence in modern network designs. Yet this chapter truly encompasses a great deal more than just networking with Windows-based systems and the design criteria for these environments. It also incorporates information regarding the other major desktop protocols—AppleTalk and IPX—as they relate to each other and as they compare to Windows-based systems.

This chapter also discusses the NetBIOS protocol, the foundation of the Windows-based operating systems. NetBIOS-based networks are found in the following operating systems/environments:

- Microsoft LAN Manager

- OS/2 LAN Manager

- MS-DOS with the LAN Manager Client

- Windows for Workgroups

- Windows 95/98

- Windows NT/2000

Also identified in this chapter is the importance of the interoperation of NetBIOS with other protocols. For example, NetBIOS, as a foundation for Windows-based networks, was originally designed to operate over NetBEUI, a non-routable protocol. Both IPX and TCP/IP have been enhanced to support NetBIOS encapsulation, greatly enhancing the protocol's incorporation into modern large-scale networks and providing designers with a means to support NetBIOS without NetBEUI.

Desktop Protocols

As mentioned in previous chapters, all of the desktop protocols were designed around the client/server model (although Macintosh and Windows platforms could service both functions). This design includes the use of LANs with multiple hosts and typically operates as a single broadcast domain. The client is responsible for locating the server—the GNS process in IPX, for example—and the protocols rely on broadcasts, which adds substantially to the network load.

Unlike NetBEUI, the original underlying protocol for NetBIOS, the other common desktop protocols use routable Layer 3 structures. In Novell networks, these are NCP and SPX packets on top of IPX packets; in Macintosh environments, these are the protocols that comprise AppleTalk. As such, desktop protocols are defined at Layer 3 and above in reference to the OSI model. Most designers work with the desktop protocols as suites rather than addressing the facets of each individual protocol in the stack. This works from an architecture standpoint, as the protocols were designed to operate together, and most desktop issues may be isolated to the access layer of the hierarchical model.

Broadcasts

The issue of *broadcasts* in designs has been raised throughout this book. This is predominately due to the client workstation impact of broadcasts and the overhead on the individual processors caused by receipt of those datagrams. This is not an issue with unicasts, where the destination station performs all processing required by the upper-layer protocols. However, in broadcasts, all nodes in the broadcast domain must process the packet, and the majority of the nodes will discard the information, resulting in waste.

Broadcasts may be measured using two methods: broadcasts per second and broadcasts as a percentage. A good metric is dependent on the number of broadcasts per second—100 being a recommended guideline. Unfortunately, most networkers learned a long time ago that 10 percent broadcast traffic was a threshold and that networks were healthy so long as traffic remained below that value. Yet in practice, using a percentage as a metric is too limited for a number of reasons:

- As theoretical data rates increase, the percentage method permits an increase in the number of broadcasts.

- The percentage method does not consider the true impact of broadcasts in the network. For example, bandwidth is not a concern until collisions, contention, buffering, and other factors are surpassed—none of which relates to broadcasts directly.

- Broadcasts require the host processor to parse the datagram before the packet can be discarded. Since most broadcasts are not destined for a specific host, this is unnecessary overhead.

- The processing of broadcasts can quickly consume processing cycles on the host. At approximately 100 broadcasts per second, a Pentium 90 host is using up to two percent of its processor. While faster processors will also affect this figure, the load from broadcasts does not remain linear. There may be sufficient processor capacity available, but why make it do unnecessary work?

Windows Networks

The NetBIOS protocol is traditionally mapped to the session layer of the OSI model. It relies on names and name queries to locate resources within the network. Thus, network designers should keep the following in mind when architecting Windows-based networks:

- NetBIOS can operate over three lower-layer transports: NetBEUI, NWLink (NetBIOS over IPX), and NetBT (NetBIOS over TCP/IP; commonly referred to as NBT). NetBEUI is not routable.

- Most scalable NetBIOS designs require the use of filters. This mandates a naming convention that lends itself to access lists.

- Cisco routers avail name caching and proxying as enhanced options in NetBIOS networks. Designers should consider these features.

Workgroups and Domains

Groups of computers in Windows-based networks may be organized in one of two logical clusters: workgroups and domains. These groupings are not unlike the zone function in AppleTalk, but there are a few differences.

The basic grouping of machines is a *workgroup*. Workgroups may be created by any set of workstations, and the cluster does not participate in any authentication or central administration process. Each machine in a workgroup may permit access to its resources, and any machine may join the workgroup. Thus the security level in workgroups is quite low, and the model is only suited to small organizations when administration is shared among all the users.

Domains, more formal groupings of computers than workgroups, significantly change the level of security offered to the organization. First, domains are administered via a Primary Domain Controller (PDC). There can be only one PDC for the domain, and it is authoritative for that domain. To provide redundancy, the PDC may be supported by any number of Backup Domain Controllers (BDCs). In practice, most organizations deploy only one or two BDCs in their configurations, although it may be warranted to deploy more. BDCs are typically installed in remote locations to speed local login and authentication while retaining a centralized administrative model.

Windows Domains

The domain concept establishes the authentication and security administration model for Windows-based networks. However, there are times when scalability or administrative concerns warrant the use of more than a single domain controller.

There are several domain models that are employed in modern Windows networks. They range from the relatively simple single domain, which is best suited to smaller organizations, to the multiple master domain model, which is typically used in large, multinational organizations.

Single domain   A single domain model is best used for small to medium-sized environments with a single administrative scope.

Global domain   The global domain model incorporates numerous domains that are administered by different organizations, typically within the same corporation. In this configuration, all domains trust all other domains.

Master domain   In the master domain model (see Figure 7.1), all other domains trust a single master domain. This model may be well suited to situations when authentication needs to be centralized but control of resources needs to be administered at the departmental level. The master domain trusts no other domain.

FIGURE 7.1   The master domain model

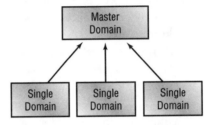

Multiple master domain   The multiple master domain model (see Figure 7.2) is simply a scaled-up version of the master domain model. In this configuration, multiple master domains trust each other, and each individual master domain is responsible for serving as the master domain for its single domains.

FIGURE 7.2   The multiple master domain model

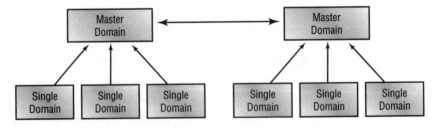

Name Resolution Services

Computers are quite comfortable operating with numerical values of significant length. Humans, on the other hand, typically appreciate text-based information and names. For example, we could certainly address everyone by a unique identification number—a Social Security number in the United States, for example. Thus, people would address me as 123-45-6789, and I would never turn around when someone said "Rob" at a party. Unfortunately, I have a difficult time remembering my own Social Security number, let alone those of my friends, family, and colleagues. (Of course, I sometimes forget names too, but I'd prefer not to dwell on that.)

In the computing environment, this idea holds true. I could certainly ask you to connect to the Web site at 10.62.70.133, but that would be harder to remember and would communicate no information regarding the content of the site. Yet if I were to say, "Connect to www.sybex.com," you would have an immediate trigger for remembering the site name and likely would associate it with this book.

All that said, a *name resolution service* provides users with a simple mechanism for names to associate with computer-related identification—typically an address operating at Layer 3 of the OSI model. As detailed in the next sections, the common name resolution services in Windows networking—LMHOSTS, WINS, and DNS—are each unique, though they provide similar functions.

LMHOSTS

The first generation of name resolution services for NetBIOS involved the LMHOSTS file. This file was manually maintained and static, and it resolved host names in the LAN Manager (LM) environment. The file could be maintained on each host and typically listed only a few critical resources, including off-subnet domain controllers.

The LMHOSTS file could also reside on the Primary Domain Controller. In this configuration, the clients would query the PDC for information. Unfortunately, this configuration required a great deal of manual effort, and maintenance of the file was only possible for small networks. Therefore, this configuration is not recommended as a modern solution.

WINS

Designers need to remember that Windows-based networking was originally designed for small, single-network environments. This meant that broadcasts were an acceptable method for registering and locating services. However, in modern routed networks, broadcasts are not permitted to cross Layer 3 boundaries. In addition, addressing of IP resources migrated from static assignments to dynamic ones, which simplified administration at the host and worked to prevent the waste of IP v4 addresses.

It became fairly clear that the LMHOSTS file would not scale to support significant networks. Each machine was tasked with maintaining its own file, and administrators either frequently scheduled downloads to keep the information on each workstation current or they had to maintain an LMHOSTS file on the PDC that was referenced by each workstation in the network.

To provide a dynamic method for registering NetBIOS names and associating them with IP addresses, Microsoft developed the Windows Internet Name Service (WINS). The service provides the following benefits:

- Clients on different subnets can register with a central repository for name resolution.

- Dynamic host address assignment (DHCP, or Dynamic Host Configuration Protocol) can be used while preserving name resolution services.

- Broadcasts can be reduced significantly.

- NetBIOS names can be mapped to IP addresses.

Though WINS allows for broadcasts to be reduced significantly, by default the clients will still broadcast name information for compatibility with older systems. Broadcasts should be disabled whenever possible. While beyond the scope of this book, interested readers should consult Microsoft's documentation regarding B-nodes, P-nodes, and H-nodes.

The WINS mechanism requires that the workstation know the address of the WINS server. This may be manually configured on the client, but it is typically provided in concert with DHCP. With the specific IP address of the WINS server, the client may communicate using unicast packets.

DHCP is described in greater detail later in this chapter.

The WINS server may also be accessed via a subnet broadcast mechanism, and designers may wish to consider using the WINS Relay function to forward WINS datagrams. This installation effectively proxies the WINS server onto the local subnet but, due to the extra administration and cost factors, is seldom used. Recall that proxies add additional overhead and latency

Finally, there may be multiple WINS servers on the network for redundancy and scalability. These servers interconnect via a replication process. Under this configuration, the client is configured (locally or via DHCP) with multiple WINS server addresses. Upon bootup, the client registers with a WINS server; if a server in the list is unavailable, the client attempts a connection with another in the list. This configuration is particularly common in international networks, as the latency and cost of sending name information across the WAN is quite high (albeit quickly becoming cheaper). However, performance for the end user is substantially greater with a local name resolution resource.

In a campus configuration, WINS servers may be deployed at the distribution layer in order to provide redundancy. The challenge for most designers is to limit the number of servers—and like most other things, simpler is better. Two or three WINS servers should not prove to be a significant problem regarding replication overhead and administration. However, some early deployments opted for a WINS server per domain or per department. Such a design quickly falls into the "bad thing" category.

DNS and Dynamic DNS

The Domain Name Service (DNS) was originally developed to provide name resolution for Unix hosts and their IP addresses. It was fundamentally easier to telnet to Cygnus, a server, than it was to telnet to 192.168.67.219. In BIND, or the DNS daemon process in Unix, administrators manually and statically entered name and IP address information. The static nature of DNS is also its most significant negative, as the administrator must manually establish and maintain each entry. This precludes the use of DNS in DHCP environments, where the address is assigned dynamically.

A fairly new enhancement to DNS has emerged within the past year—Dynamic DNS (DDNS). The DDNS specification is compatible with traditional DNS, but information regarding addresses and host names is learned dynamically. This makes DNS compatible with DHCP, which is a significant enhancement in the address assignment arena.

In Windows NT, it is also possible to configure the interchange of WINS information into the DNS structure. This permits non-Windows-based systems—Unix hosts, primarily—to use name references. Most large network designs create a sub-domain for names learned via this method. Thus, an existing Unix DNS structure is maintained for `company.com`, for example, while a sub-domain of `wins.company.com` is referenced for the dynamic entries. In addition, Windows clients may use DNS information for name resolution.

A number of third-party programs are available to integrate WINS, DHCP, and DNS/DDNS functions. Yet as the enterprise grows, many administrators find that the integrated applications are not powerful enough. Some applications worth considering include NetID and Meta IP from Nortel and Checkpoint, respectively.

DHCP

The Dynamic Host Configuration Protocol (DHCP) is actually an open standard that is used by Unix and Macintosh clients as well as Windows-based systems. However, the protocol attained mainstream, corporate recognition when the server module was incorporated into Windows NT.

DHCP allows a host to learn its IP address dynamically. This process is termed a *lease*, as the address assigned belongs to the host for an administratively defined time. By default, on Windows implementations this assignment is for 72 hours.

DHCP leases are discussed in the following section.

From a router perspective, DHCP requires one of two components—a DHCP server on the local subnet or a method for forwarding the broadcast across the router. DHCP requests are broadcasts, so the designer needs a DHCP server presence on each segment in the network. This clearly would not scale well and is impractical in most network designs; however, this would provide addressing information to the clients.

The alternative is to provide a little help to DHCP. This is accomplished with the *IP helper address*, a statically defined address on each router interface that is connected to the local segment requiring the help, which in turn points to the DHCP server. Broadcast requests for addresses are sent to the helper address as unicasts or directed broadcasts, significantly reducing overall broadcast traffic. Most DHCP implementations, including Microsoft's, can provide a great deal of information to the client as well, including time servers, default gateways, and other address-based services.

When designing for DHCP, most architects and administrators consider the following:

- DHCP lease length
- DHCP server redundancy
- Address assignments

Cisco routers can provide limited DHCP services; however, most installations make use of a dedicated server.

DHCP Lease Length

The length of the DHCP lease governs the amount of time a host "owns" the address. In order for the host to continue using the address, it must renew with the server before the lease expires. Designers must consider the overhead of this renewal traffic and the impact of failed or unavailable DHCP servers. In general, fixed configurations are appropriate venues for long leases, and short leases are applicable in more dynamic installations.

Consider a fully functioning network with a hundred workstations and a lease length of five minutes. This is an extreme example (DHCP typically sends a renewal request at an interval equal to one-half of the lease timer), but the overhead incurred would be 6000 requests per hour for just IP addresses. This is a high amount of overhead for information that should not change under normal circumstances. In addition, when a lease expires, the host must release its IP address. Without a DHCP server, it would be unable to communicate on the network for want of an address.

The alternative to a short lease is to make the lease very long. Consider the impact of a lease equal to 60 days. Should the hosts remain on a local subnet with very few changes, this would substantially reduce the volume of traffic. However, this would not be appropriate for a hotelling installation. *Hotelling* is a concept introduced years ago where notebook users would check into a cubicle for a day or even a week. DHCP is a great solution for such an installation as the MAC addresses are constantly changing, but a long lease time would be inappropriate here. Consider a scenario where each visitor connects once per quarter, or every 90 days. And, for this example, presume that there are 800 users of the service, and the pool is a standard Class C network of 254 host addresses. If the lease were long—90 days for this example—only the first 250 users would be able to obtain an address. Clearly, this is not appropriate to the type of installation—an important consideration for the designer.

As mentioned earlier, the default DHCP lease renewal interval is 72 hours. This results in renewal requests every 36 hours (typically, this process begins at 50 percent of the lease period). For reference, the mechanism by which DHCP obtains an address is illustrated in Figure 7.3. Note that DHCP uses a system of discovery to locate the DHCP server—a phase that makes use of the helper function. Once the DHCP server is found, the offer is returned to the workstation, and the request is acknowledged or declined.

FIGURE 7.3 The DHCP process

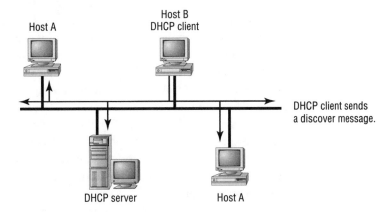

DHCP client sends
a discover message.

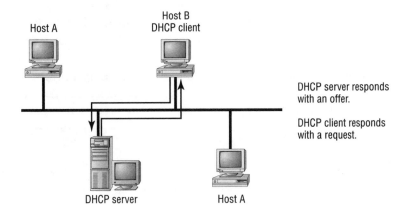

DHCP server responds
with an offer.

DHCP client responds
with a request.

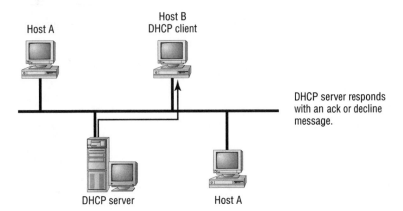

DHCP server responds
with an ack or decline
message.

DHCP Server Redundancy

Given the critical function of the DHCP server, most designers place at least two of them in a network, thus providing *DHCP server redundancy*. This design offers benefits similar to the redundant WINS servers discussed previously in this chapter. Depending on the implementation, these DHCP servers may or may not be able to share address assignment information. Multiple helper addresses may be placed on each interface on a Cisco router.

Many designers break the DHCP scope when working with DHCP servers that are not capable of automatic redundancy. Recall from the discussion on IP addressing that designers frequently reserve a small number of addresses at the beginning of the address range for routers, switches, and other network equipment. In a single DHCP server installation, the scope would expand from this initial address reservation, whereas dual DHCP servers would take this scope and divide it to provide two ranges of addresses for the same subnet. For example, Table 7.1 documents a single DHCP server scope definition, where the server does not support redundancy.

TABLE 7.1 An Example of a Non-Redundant, Single DHCP Server

Scope Function	Address Range
Administration	192.168.1.1 to 192.168.1.31
Users	192.168.1.32 to 192.168.1.254

All of the addresses in Table 7.1 are naturally subnetted.

In a redundant DHCP installation, many administrators will configure their servers as shown in the example in Table 7.2.

TABLE 7.2 An Example of Redundant, Non-Aware DHCP Servers

Scope Function	Address Range
Administration	192.168.1.1 to 192.168.1.31
Users, Server A	192.168.1.32 to 192.168.1.127
Users, Server B	192.168.1.128 to 192.168.1.254

The configuration shown in Table 7.2 would support 95 users under the worst-case single failure. Given this information, designers should consider the network mask in use, the number of users per subnet, expansion, VLSM, and other factors before selecting a DHCP redundancy method.

As presented earlier in this chapter, modifications to the lease renewal interval can be used to reduce the impact of a DHCP server failure.

Older DHCP clients required access to the DHCP server on each boot before they could use the address previously assigned, even if the lease interval was still valid. This behavior has been changed in newer releases of the client software, and the workstation can use the assigned address up to the end of the lease.

Address Assignments

Certain network devices do not lend themselves to dynamic address assignment. Routers, switches, managed hubs, servers, and printers all fall into this category. Many networks opt to define an address block for these devices at the beginning or end of the subnet. For example, possibly all host addresses from .1 to .31 are omitted from the DHCP scope for manual assignment. This assumes that no network mask on populated segments uses less than /24 (255.255.255.0), which is a consideration when composing a number scheme.

Designers may also choose to include servers and other devices in the network with permanent, dynamic assignments. The DHCP server may be configured with a static entry that includes the MAC address of the interface card.

Either of the two above methods permits an entry in the DHCP database that maintains a single address for the resource. However, the latter method raises the potential for the server to lose its lease for the address. While no other host may use the address, the server must renew its lease as if the address were truly dynamic.

NetBIOS Protocols

As noted in the introduction of this chapter, NetBIOS operates with a number of lower-layer protocols, including NetBEUI, IPX, and IP. The original mating of NetBEUI and NetBIOS was quite convenient when networks were very small and didn't need routers. However, as networks grew and became more complex, the need for routers quickly overrode the benefits afforded by the simple NetBEUI protocol.

In modern network designs, it is quite rare to need the non-routable NetBEUI protocol (which uses only the MAC address and does not have a network address). This is because most networks require the benefits of routing or the use of another protocol—frequently TCP/IP. Given these factors, many installations will forego NetBEUI as a transport and use NBT (NetBIOS over TCP/IP) or NWLink instead.

For reference purposes, Figures 7.4, 7.5, and 7.6 illustrate the relationships between NetBEUI/NetBIOS and NBT. Figure 7.4 shows the layers found in NetBEUI/NetBIOS, and Figure 7.5 reflects the browser function using NetBIOS over UDP. Figure 7.6 illustrates NetBIOS over TCP and the structure used when connecting to file systems (in this example, adding protocols to support Microsoft Exchange).

FIGURE 7.4 NetBIOS over NetBEUI

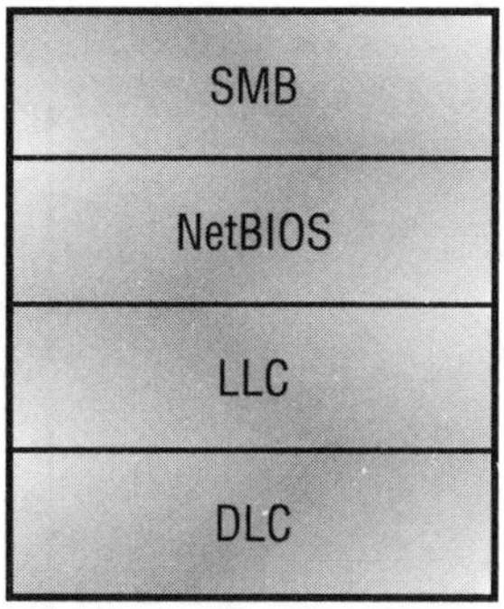

SMB
NetBIOS
LLC
DLC

FIGURE 7.5 NetBIOS over UDP

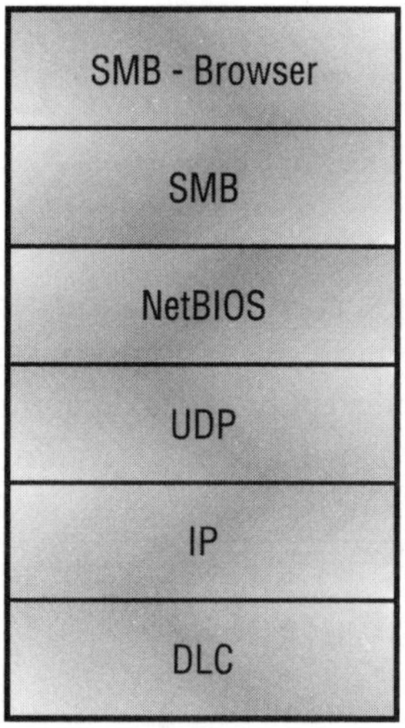

SMB - Browser
SMB
NetBIOS
UDP
IP
DLC

FIGURE 7.6 NetBIOS over TCP/IP

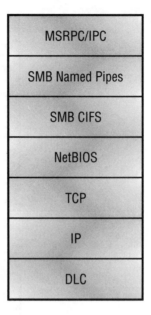

Pure NetBEUI/NetBIOS installations may instinctively seem sufficient for very small networks, and designers would be correct in pointing out that the overhead and administration of this design would be reduced. However, the implementation also requires substantial modifications if and when either the network expands or direct Internet (via a firewall, preferably) connectivity is desired.

Designs with NetBIOS

There are numerous methods for designing NetBIOS networks. However, this section encompasses only a few common configurations for reference.

NWLink in a Small Network

Figure 7.7 illustrates a small network designed to support NetBIOS using the IPX/NWLink protocol and includes both Novell servers and a PDC. This type of network design would be common in migrations from Novell NetWare to Windows NT, and it includes the use of the IP eXchange product from Cisco (now discontinued; this product is no longer used in most networks).

FIGURE 7.7   NWLink, NetBIOS, and IP eXchange

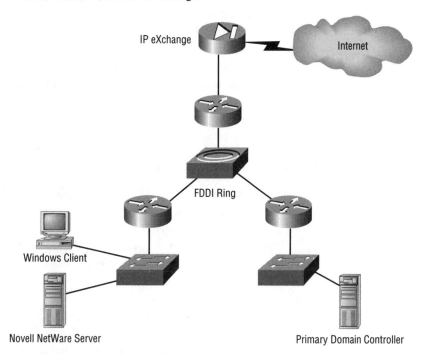

As shown in Figure 7.7, the center of the network is composed of an FDDI ring routing IPX only. The IP eXchange product permits the use of IPX-only clients when accessing the Internet and other IP-only resources. However, it requires a client software application; this prerequisite negates some of the advantages offered by IP eXchange. In addition, most network cores have migrated to IP only (in contrast to IPX only). As a result, the current and future trends will likely be to continue to use NBT in most installations. IPX/NWLink would still be preferred in large, legacy Novell installations, particularly when applications mandate the need to remain on IPX.

NetBEUI in a Small Network

The use of the NetBEUI protocol typically infers the use of a small network, as NetBEUI cannot be routed. Therefore, the network design is very limited, and the use of WINS servers is optional, as the NetBIOS protocol can operate only in broadcast mode. This type of installation is frequently found in schools and small offices, although basic home networks also may use only NetBEUI/NetBIOS.

In these networks, a single station is elected the Browse Master. All other stations advertise their presence on the network with a broadcast and use a broadcast to locate resources. The election of the Browse Master is also handled via broadcasts, and the network can support several backup Browse Masters. Remember that this type of network was deployed frequently in peer-to-peer environments, not in client/server installations (for which the broadcast model works well).

NBT in a Large Network

The IP protocol exploded onto the Windows networking scene with the growth of the Internet. However, the protocol offers benefits beyond access to the world's largest network.

The IP protocol is one of the most scalable. New features are being added to the protocol every month, and should the designer wish, it is possible to use IP with up to 1000 hosts on a subnet. However, this design requires specific attention to broadcasts and bandwidth.

Network designers frequently select the IP protocol for Windows installations in modern network design. The obvious benefit is standardization on a single protocol that is supported on all desktop platforms. With NBT, the circle is complete, and Windows-based systems can also operate.

Many of the other topics in this chapter relate to NBT, including WINS and DHCP. Figure 7.8 illustrates one possible example of an NBT network installation for a multinational firm. Note that most firms would include BDC installations and multiple WINS servers.

Designers should note that the SAMBA utility is available for Unix hosts to provide SMB (Server Message Block) services to Windows-based systems. This permits file and print sharing (functions that use the SMB protocol) without the need for the NFS and LPD Unix applications on Windows.

FIGURE 7.8 NBT, NetBIOS, and TCP/IP in a large network

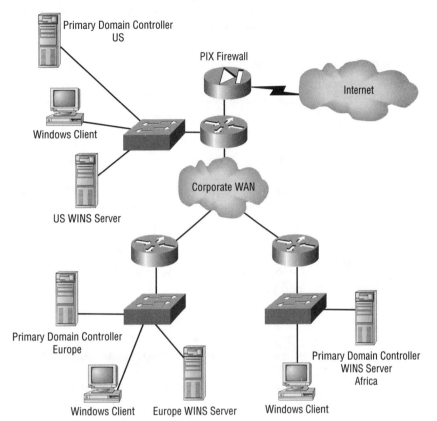

Remote Networking with Windows NT

Remote networking services are incorporated within Windows NT to service dial-up connectivity. Access to the Public Switched Telephone Network (PSTN) is universal and provides an easy method for users to access e-mail and files.

Microsoft's Windows NT Remote Access Server (RAS) is built upon the Point-to-Point Protocol (PPP), which provides support for multiple upper-layer protocols, including those identified in Table 7.3.

TABLE 7.3   PPP-Supported Protocols and Their RAS Names

Upper-Layer Protocol	RAS Notation
TCP/IP	IPCP
IPX	IPXCP
NetBEUI	NBFCP

Cisco products will also support these encapsulations when running IOS version 11.1 or greater.

Network Design in the Real World: Remote Access

From an administrative perspective, designers should discourage the use of a single server for RAS and traditional file and print functions. While Microsoft scaled RAS to 256 connections on the Alpha platform, it may be even better to consider a dedicated, hardware-based remote access solution, such as the Cisco AS5x00 product line. Security, manageability, and scalability should drive this decision process, yet many RAS installations begin with cost and rapid deployment as driving factors.

Summary

This chapter addressed a number of issues related to the common desktop protocols—NetBIOS, AppleTalk, and IPX—and introduced networking with Windows, the most common desktop environment.

Windows networking incorporates a number of standards and proprietary-based services, including WINS, DHCP, DNS, DDNS, NBT, NWLink, and domains, which are important for the designer to understand and consider when architecting the network.

This chapter discussed the following topics:

- The negatives of broadcasts in network designs

- The differences between workgroups and domains

- The use of the LMHOSTS file in NetBIOS networks

- The use of WINS servers in a network and their ability to reduce broadcast traffic in support of NetBIOS systems

- The integration of DNS and DDNS with WINS and NetBIOS networks

- The use of DHCP for address assignment

- The control of DHCP scopes to allocate permanent, manually assigned addresses to servers and routers

- Considerations for selecting a routable protocol for NetBIOS encapsulation

- The functionality of the Browse Master

- The RAS application and the underlying protocol support

In most modern networks, designers need to focus on the Windows environment more than Novell and AppleTalk. However, understanding the mechanisms by which each of the desktop protocols operates will greatly facilitate troubleshooting and support considerations. In addition, designers are frequently called upon to support multiple platform installations or to migrate from AppleTalk and IPX to IP.

While not addressed in this chapter, cost and history also are factors in NetBIOS/Windows network design. The battles between Novell and Microsoft have been effectively rendered moot, and the best outcome from this history is a realization that the best tool for the job makes the most sense.

The issue of thin Windows clients (terminals that display only applications served from a multiuser server) is also outside the scope of this chapter.

In short, much progress has been made in the technology of these tools in recent years. Designers should carefully measure the traffic loads generated by these devices, particularly during traditional peak traffic periods. Thin clients can greatly simplify administrative issues, but it is important to ensure that sufficient capacity to store all data on the server is available, and that all mouse/keyboard and video updates are transmitted efficiently across the network—such datagrams consume a surprising amount of bandwidth.

Review Questions

1. Designers planning to use WINS must:

   A. Plan to install a WINS server on every subnet

   B. Manually enter all IP and NetBIOS name information

   C. Also configure a DHCP server

   D. Consider the need for multiple WINS servers

2. The LMHOSTS process:

   A. Is suited to small networks only

   B. Is recommended for large networks only

   C. Requires the use of DHCP

   D. Dynamically learns PDC and BDC information

3. NetBIOS over IPX is called:

   A. NBT

   B. NetBEUI

   C. NWLink

   D. NetBIOS does not operate over IPX

4. Broadcasts:

   A. Are fine so long as they consume less than ten percent of bandwidth

   B. Are unnecessary with desktop protocols

   C. Should be reduced whenever possible to reduce unnecessary processing and conserve bandwidth

   D. Should be regarded the same as unicasts

5. Which of the following protocols may not be routed?

    A. NetBEUI

    B. IPX

    C. IP

    D. NWLink

6. The IP eXchange product provides designers of Windows-based networks:

    A. The ability to configure the PDC on NetWare servers

    B. The ability to configure up to three BDCs to run on three different NetWare servers

    C. The ability to provide IP connectivity without loading IP on each client

    D. IPX HRSP

7. Microsoft's RAS product:

    A. Provides DHCP services

    B. Uses the PPP protocol

    C. Supports IP only

    D. Cannot run on an NT server

8. Traditionally, DNS was unable:

    A. To dynamically interoperate with DHCP

    B. To translate names to IP addresses

    C. To operate in Unix environments

    D. To accept manual mappings

9. A designer needs to create a network with 2000 Windows workstations and servers while providing access to the Internet and Unix servers. The best solution would include:

A. IP eXchange and NWLink

B. NBT and IPX

C. NBT, WINS, DHCP, and TCP/IP

D. NetBEUI and Cisco GSR routers

10. Broadcasts are controlled:

A. With switches

B. With routers

C. With hubs

D. With repeaters

11. Designers attempt to reduce broadcasts for which of the following reasons?

A. Broadcasts require unnecessary processing by the workstations.

B. Broadcasts consume four times the bandwidth of data.

C. Broadcasts are not necessary in LAN protocols.

D. Broadcasts cannot operate in NBMA topologies.

12. In order to reduce bandwidth requirements on the WAN link, the designer might:

A. Place the DHCP server at the remote site and keep the lease timers short

B. Place the DHCP server at the remote site and lengthen the lease timers

C. Centralize the DHCP server and use the default DHCP timers

D. Use multiple DHCP servers with short timers

13. A network contains 27 subnets. How many DHCP servers are required for dynamic address assignment?

    A. One

    B. Two—one configured as a BDC

    C. 27

    D. Cannot answer from the information provided

14. How do hosts locate the WINS server?

    A. Using a multicast to 224.0.0.17

    B. Using a unicast to an administratively defined address

    C. Using the IP helper service

    D. Using the DHCP server as a relay

15. Which of the following is true?

    A. Cisco routers may function as WINS servers.

    B. Cisco routers may function as DHCP servers.

    C. Cisco routers may function as both WINS and DHCP servers.

    D. None of the above.

16. NetBIOS networks should be designed:

    A. Using only network masks of /24 (255.255.255.0)

    B. With naming conventions that reflect the owner of the workstation

    C. With numerical naming only

    D. With naming conventions that begin with an easily filtered prefix

17. Which of the following limitations exist in DHCP?

    A. DHCP cannot exist in WINS networks.

    B. DHCP can assign addresses only to Windows-based machines.

    C. Only one DHCP server can exist in the network.

    D. None of the above.

18. Servers should always have the same IP address for administrative purposes. Therefore:

    A. The DHCP scope should include a reservation block of addresses in the subnet for servers or should not include the address range.

    B. DHCP cannot be used in the subnet.

    C. Servers must all use the address 0.0.0.0 for all datagrams.

    D. WINS must be used.

19. The master domain:

    A. Trusts all single domains

    B. Is trusted by all single domains in the group

    C. Shares a bi-directional trust with all single domains

    D. Can be the only domain in the corporation

20. The LAN services browser mechanism is replaced by:

    A. DHCP

    B. DDNS

    C. WINS

    D. LMHOSTS

Answers to Review Questions

1. D.
2. A.
3. C.
4. C.
5. A.
6. C.
7. B.
8. A.
9. C.
10. B.
11. A.
12. B.
13. A.
14. B.
15. B.
16. D.
17. D.
18. A.
19. B.
20. C.

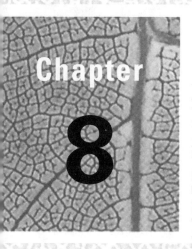

Chapter

8

Designing for the WAN

CISCO INTERNETWORK DESIGN EXAM OBJECTIVES COVERED IN THIS CHAPTER:

✓ List common concerns that customers have about WAN designs.

✓ Examine statements made by a customer and distinguish issues that affect the choice of WAN designs.

✓ Design core WAN connectivity to maximize availability and optimize utilization of resources.

✓ Design a full- or partial-mesh Frame Relay nonbroadcast multiaccess (NBMA) core for full or partial connectivity.

✓ Choose a scalable topology for NBMA Frame Relay.

✓ Use subinterface Frame Relay configurations to design robust core WANs.

Network designers frequently need to connect geographically distant locations with relatively high-speed links. Unfortunately, costs generally increase as the available bandwidth increases, and thus the designer is compelled to find the best solution in terms of cost, performance, scalability, and availability.

There are a number of ways to connect networks across large geographical areas. In the earliest networks, this required the use of expensive leased lines or slow dial-up connections—both of which were limited in terms of bandwidth compared to modern, cheaper solutions. Today's offerings, which are substantially cheaper on a per-megabyte basis, include Frame Relay, ATM (Asynchronous Transfer Mode), and SMDS (Switched Multimegabit Data Service). Each of these technologies relies on the reliability of modern fiber-optic and copper networks and scales to support at least DS-3 (45Mbps) bandwidth—ATM is currently available in OC-48 and OC-192 (optical carrier) offerings, yielding up to 10Gbps of bandwidth.

This chapter does not focus so much on the increasing performance of modern WAN technologies, such as DWDM (dense wavelength division multiplexing), which multiplies the number of signals that can traverse a fiber, or the issues surrounding OC-192 and OC-48 networks. Rather, each of these technologies (Frame Relay, ATM, and SMDS) is presented in detail, and the differences between frame-based and cell-based transports are discussed. Additionally, this chapter focuses on the general concepts of wide area networking technologies. Beyond nontechnical concerns such as cost, this chapter reviews more technological factors, including scalability, reliability, and latency.

> **NOTE** While SMDS is included in the CID exam objectives, its availability has waned in recent years. Standard ATM services have effectively replaced such installations, while Frame Relay has always held a substantial market share. SMDS did not fail due to technology—in fact, it was a very good protocol. Rather, it required additional expertise and expensive equipment compared to the alternatives. Many providers never offered the technology.

Wide Area Network Technologies

The design goals—and technologies—of a wide area network (WAN) are slightly different than those for local area network (LAN) installations. For example, it is fairly simple to add an extra connection in a LAN, while in a WAN this may take 90 days or more. Also, in a LAN, most designers are concerned with port density and broadcast control, while in a WAN, bandwidth and cost are frequently the foremost concern. Further, the interactions with outside vendors required in a WAN can alter significantly the issues involved in the design.

There are two categories of WAN design technology in use today: dedicated services and switched services. *Dedicated services* include the traditional leased T1 and T3 services. They are called dedicated services because only one connectionpoint, which follows a pre-determined path, exists within the circuit. This connection may be transported over shared media within the provider's network; however, the full amount of bandwidth will always be allocated (dedicated) for the specific connection.

Readers may notice a lack of emphasis on dedicated services in this chapter. This is primarily due to the text's focus on the Cisco exam objectives and the actual test. However, it is also presumed that most CCDP candidates are familiar with the basic concepts of these connections from their experience or the CCDA, CCNA, and CCNP materials. If the concepts of time division multiplexing, inverse multiplexing, and the serial protocols (HDLC, PPP) are unfamiliar, please make sure that you review this material before continuing your certification efforts. While the test does not ask questions outside the constraints of the objectives, it presumes a certain foundation.

Switched services include circuit, packet, and cell-switched connections; ISDN, telephone service (POTS), X.25, Frame Relay, ATM, and SMDS. Switched services typically incorporate charges for distance and bandwidth used, but this is dependent on the specific tariff in use. Most telecommunications services are charged based on a *tariff*— a set, regulated price structure that includes parameters for installation and administration processes.

There are two benefits of switched technologies. First, in the case of dynamic circuits, the designer can establish a connection to any other eligible recipient. For example, both POTS and ISDN connections can be established with a simple access number—the connection into the network is sufficient, and there is no requirement to define each possible link ahead of time. Second, switched services typically share bandwidth better within the cloud. As this chapter's discussion turns to committed information rates (CIR—Frame Relay) and SCR (Sustained Cell Rate—ATM), you will see that the network can logically adapt to the requirements of the users and allow bursts of traffic within the constraints of total capacity.

When reviewing the WAN technologies and designs presented in this chapter, it is important to consider the following issues: reliability, latency, cost, and traffic flows and traffic types. Most network designers focus ultimately on cost as the most important design consideration; however, reliability may require additional expense. Latency, various traffic flows, and traffic types are supported with most modern technologies and thus lose some importance in modern designs. Of course, this text ignores some of the older and more limited protocols in WAN design, such as BiSYNC and digital data system (DDS) circuits—two areas in which these issues deserve more prominence.

Network Design in the Real World: SONET

Private SONET rings (Synchronous Optical Networks), wireless, and certain point-to-point technologies are outside the scope of Cisco's exam objectives. However, these solutions are frequently selected for an array of reasons, including facilities, security, and cost. The most scalable installations, at the lowest cost, frequently use Frame Relay and, to an increasing degree, ATM. Wireless technologies are well suited to temporary installations and areas where wire-based services are unavailable, although this alternative has gained favor as a means to reduce dependency on the carriers. SONET offers high reliability and is a fundamental transport technology in the carrier world. Packet over SONET (PoS) and Dynamic Packet Transport (DPT) can both operate over these rings.

Reliability

Unlike LAN connections, WAN links tend to be a bit unstable and often are unreliable. This may be due to fiber cuts, equipment failure, or misconfiguration by the service provider. Unfortunately, it is difficult to add reliability to

WAN installations simply by selecting a different technology. For example, Frame Relay is just as susceptible to a fiber cut as ATM; in fact, ATM transports most Frame-Relay installations in the provider's core network.

Since reliability is a physical-layer concern, augmented by the higher layers, designers typically have to think of the physical layer first. For example, fiber cuts can be circumvented by wireless technologies, yet these are sometimes degraded by snow, rain, or fog. To augment reliability from a physical context, the designer needs to consider the available options, many of which are beyond the scope of this text. (Consult with your vendors for the most current information regarding WAN options.)

However, it is possible to add a degree of reliability to the network with the selection of a WAN technology. This chapter addresses some forms of redundancy for network designers to consider. Frame Relay and ATM, with their ability to service multiple connections from a single port, typically provide more reliability than point-to-point connections—should one virtual link fail, the other should still be available (presuming the lack of a port or local loop failure).

Latency

Latency, the delay introduced by network equipment, has become a minor concern in most designs as protocols have migrated toward delay tolerance in the data arena. However, with voice and video integration on data networks, even today's wire-speed offerings may require the attention once afforded time-sensitive protocols on slower links; this would include SNAP (Sub-Network Access Protocol), used in mainframe connectivity. Modern network designs can address these issues with queuing, low-latency hardware, cell-based technologies like ATM, and prioritization. One of the benefits afforded by ATM is a consistent latency within the network.

The latency category frequently incorporates throughput and delay factors. Compared to LANs, most wide area links are very slow, and performance suffers as a result. Designers should work with application developers and server administrators to tune the network to address this limitation. Possible solutions include compression and prioritization (queuing), yet these functions can degrade performance more than the link if not deployed correctly. Designers should also make use of static routes or *quiet* routing protocols and employ other techniques, such as IPX watchdog spoofing (discussed in Chapter 6), to control overhead traffic. Under the best circumstances, designers should focus on moving limited amounts of data between servers on very slow WAN links whenever possible.

Network Design in the Real World: WAN Technologies and Latency

Historically, WAN access was provided by telecommunications service providers on circuits originally provisioned for voice services. The system of T1 and E1 channels was mapped directly to the number of voice channel time slots afforded (24 for T1, 30 for E1). The technologies presented in this chapter are based upon these solutions.

Recently, however, advances in laser technology and the availability of fiber optics has provided designers with new solutions, including the option to use GigabitEthernet in some wide area solutions. While limited to approximately 55 miles, this connectivity works well in a metropolitan installation. Microwave and wireless laser solutions are also available to designers who wish to reduce the cost and installation time of traditional remote access.

In the context of latency, all of these options provide a more consistent transport infrastructure. Rather than converting from Ethernet to Frame Relay and back to Ethernet, the designer can install fairly long connections and maintain Ethernet throughout. This lack of conversion can substantially reduce the complexity of the installation and the latency.

Cost

WAN networking costs typically exceed those for a LAN. There are a number of reasons for this; the most significant factor is the recurring costs that exist in WAN networks. Unlike the LAN, where the company owns the connections between routers, the WAN infrastructure is owned by the telecommunications provider. As a result, the provider leases its fiber or copper cables. This differs from LAN installations, where the company purchases and installs its own cable. The initial cost of establishing a WAN may be greater, but the lack of recurring costs quickly reduces the amortized impact.

The technologies used to reduce WAN costs—Frame Relay, ATM, and SDMS—are presented throughout this chapter. Yet in short, Frame Relay provides the greatest savings per megabit. ATM is quickly providing savings in WAN costs, but this is based more on the integration of voice and data than on lower tariffs.

Though not discussed in this book, both MAN-based Ethernet and DSL, a shorter-range technology, appear to further reduce WAN costs.

Point-to-point circuits generally represent the highest cost in the WAN. This is because, unlike Frame Relay, the bandwidth is dedicated, which can oversubscribe and group users based on actual usage. *Oversubscribing* is the intentional configuration of more theoretical bandwidth on a circuit than it could accommodate. This is similar to providing 10 phones for 100 people—if, on average, only seven concurrent phone calls occur, there is sufficient capacity, even though the system is oversubscribed overall. The risk of 20 callers is very real, but the savings of not providing 100 lines is substantial.

Traffic Flows and Traffic Types

Compared to local area networks, some WANs provide limited protocol support. This may be for simplification, but in most cases this results from the desire to conserve the bandwidth that typically is needed to support additional protocols. The designer can consider encapsulation and other methodologies, including conversion and isolation, to remove or omit protocols from the WAN. Many designers are converting from AppleTalk and IPX to IP.

Previous chapters have addressed the concept of tunneling in the context of AppleTalk and other protocols. However, the general concepts and concerns regarding tunnels are universal. The most significant issue with tunnels is performance, though troubleshooting is also a major issue that can be complicated by encapsulation.

Like other networking technologies, serial connections require a protocol to transmit information from one side of a link to another. The selection of an encapsulation, in addition to the use of tunnels and the type of traffic traversing the link, can impact performance and manageability. The encapsulations for data over serial lines are:

- SDLC
- Cisco's HDLC

- PPP (Point-to-Point Protocol)

- LAPB (Link Access Procedure, Balanced)

The data frame for each of these protocols is derived from SDLC, which is used in SNA. As shown in the following illustration, there are five components to the frame, excluding the variable-length data portion. The beginning frame flag is one byte in length and contains a hexadecimal pattern of 0x7F. The ending frame flag is set to 0x7E. The address field is shown as one byte, but it can be expanded to a two-byte value. The control field marks the frame as informational, supervisory, or unnumbered. The frame check sequence (FCS) provides limited error checking. Cisco's HDLC encapsulation adds a type field between the control and data fields, and PPP places a protocol field in this location.

Flag (1 byte)	Address [1 or 2 byte(s)]	Control (1 byte)
Data (Variable)		
FCS (2 bytes)		Flag (1 byte)

HDLC

Cisco's implementation of the HDLC protocol is the default serial line encapsulation on the router. It supports the AutoInstall feature, which permits remote configuration of newly installed routers; however, it is also proprietary. Regardless of this limitation, most administrators use Cisco HDLC.

PPP

The Point-to-Point Protocol provides a number of benefits over the HDLC encapsulation; however, it also includes a slight amount of overhead by comparison. The fact that PPP is an RFC standard is its greatest advantage, but the protocol also offers authentication and link-control features. Authentication is typically provided by the Password Authentication Protocol (PAP) or by the more secure Challenge Handshake Authentication Protocol (CHAP).

LAPB

Link Access Procedure, Balanced is a reliable encapsulation for serial connections. It provides the data-link layer for X.25, but it may be used without that protocol. LAPB features link compression and excellent error correction, which makes it well suited to unreliable analog media. Because of this overhead, LAPB tends to be slower than other encapsulations.

One of the configuration options in LAPB is *modulo*, or the sequence number. Initial implementations of LAPB supported only eight sequence numbers—modulo 8, which quickly resulted in a windowing delay for higher speed connections. (Modulo 128 was developed to address this limitation.) Designers should make certain that the same value is used on both sides of the link.

Network Design with Frame Relay

Frame Relay networks offer the network designer many benefits that do not exist in point-to-point, leased-line transports. These include:

- Distance-insensitive billing

- Multiple destinations per physical interface

- The ability for data to burst above the tariffed data rate

Most vendors offer Frame Relay under a fairly simple tariff, or cost structure, based on the reserved capacity of the virtual circuit. Leased lines charge on a per-mile basis, and the bandwidth charge is equal to the total capacity of the circuit. As a result, Frame Relay connections can be significantly less expensive, especially when traversing hundreds of miles.

Circuit costs are recurring and thus can quickly overshadow any installation and capital expenditures.

Frame Relay is also considered a *burstable* technology. This refers to the difference between reserved bandwidth and total potential bandwidth available. Consider a point-to-point circuit—the network will transport only as much data as the circuit will provide, and unused bandwidth will remain unused because the connection is dedicated. Frame Relay circuits are typically provisioned with a bandwidth reservation lower than the capacity of the link—256Kbps on a T1, for example. Vendors combine virtual circuits so that the remaining bandwidth is utilized, but if the physical media has unused bandwidth, any of the virtual circuits can burst beyond their allocation and temporarily increase their available bandwidth.

Frame Relay circuits are typically provisioned with two distinct bandwidth parameters, unlike standard HDLC or switched-56 circuits, which are provisioned with the data rate equal to the port speed. In addition to the physical capacity of the circuit, Frame Relay incorporates a committed information rate, or CIR.

The CIR function varies with different telecommunications vendors, though most use the value to represent a guaranteed available bandwidth to the customer. This may be calculated on a per-second or per-minute basis, but the net result is that customers can reserve bandwidth at a lower level than the capacity of the local loop connection. For example, a CIR of 768Kbps on a T1 would offer at least 768Kbps to the customer and provide a burst up to 1.5Mbps for a short duration.

Different vendors implement bursting differently, including the concept of zero CIR, where no bandwidth is reserved. Designers should fully understand their vendor's implementation before provisioning circuits.

Frame Relay connections use *permanent virtual circuits* (PVCs) to specify connections from one node to another. These PVCs are identified by a DLCI, or *data link connection identifier*. Frame Relay switches forward frames based solely on the DLCI in the header of each frame.

Switched virtual circuits (SVCs) are available in Frame Relay, yet most vendors do not support this configuration. As a result, this chapter discusses PVC-based Frame Relay connections only. PVCs and SVCs are discussed in more detail later in this chapter.

The Frame Relay switch simply takes one port/DLCI connection and forwards it to another port/DLCI connection. In this context, the term "port" refers to the physical interface, and "DLCI" refers to the logical Frame Relay interface. DLCIs only have local significance, and while vendors typically assign a single DLCI for each link in the PVC, it is possible to have different ones.

Consider the connections shown in Table 8.1:

TABLE 8.1   DLCI Connections

San Francisco to Denver	
Port 1, DLCI 100	Port 7, DLCI 100
San Francisco to Chicago	
Port 1, DLCI 200	Port 12, DLCI 400
Denver to Chicago	
Port 7, DLCI 200	Port 12, DLCI 200

These connections are shown in Figure 8.1. Note that each physical connection in the diagram carries two user DLCIs, and that while a single Frame-Relay switch is shown for clarity, there would be more switches for such long connections. There are three PVCs in this full-mesh configuration.

FIGURE 8.1   A basic Frame Relay network

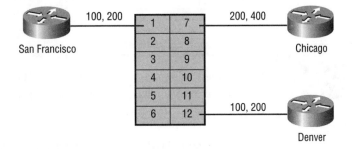

The Local Management Interface

The *Local Management Interface*, or LMI, provides signaling on Frame Relay connections. This process is responsible for the keepalive function, in addition to information about the PVC status.

There are three versions of LMI that designers should be familiar with:

- Frame Relay Forum LMI (Cisco)

- ITU-T Q.933 Annex A

- ANSI T1.617 Annex D

Cisco routers default to the Frame Relay Forum LMI specification, and many designers use that default. A number of vendors recommend Annex D because of its improved congestion handling. For reference, the LMI frame format is illustrated in Figure 8.2.

FIGURE 8.2 The LMI frame format

Flag (1 byte)	LMI DLCI (2 bytes)	Unnumbered Information Indicator (1 byte)	Protocol Discriminator (1 byte)	Call Reference (1 byte)
Message Type (1 byte)	Information (Variable)	FCS (2 bytes)		Flag (1 byte)

Cisco added an auto-sense function in IOS 11.2, which automatically detects the version of LMI in use. Administrators may manually set the LMI type with the `frame-relay lmi-type {ansi | cisco | q933a}` command.

The Frame Relay/Cisco LMI specification operates over DLCI 1023, whereas Annex A and Annex D use DLCI 0. Both of these DLCIs are reserved and cannot be used for non-management data.

The Frame Relay Standard—RFC 1490

The use of standards-based protocols and technology is recommended whenever vendor operability is a concern. Standards-based systems also tend to garner better diagnostic support, including documentation.

Frame Relay is described in RFC 1490, which documents its support for both bridged and routed traffic. The RFC also documents the *Inverse ARP* function. Inverse ARP provides a mechanism for dynamically mapping upper-layer protocols to the appropriate lower-layer address. This function is enabled by default and can greatly simplify router configuration.

Frame Relay Address Mapping

As with other Layer 3 protocols, Frame Relay requires a mechanism for associating the network address with the data link address. This appears in the form of an address mapping.

Many network designers manually enter the mapping statements into the router, which can facilitate troubleshooting. The commands, which are entered on an interface level, note the protocol, the remote address, the DLCI, and, in these examples, the broadcast keyword.

```
frame-relay map ipx 200.0000.30a0.831d 200 broadcast
frame-relay map ip 10.11.200.2 200 broadcast
```

Note that each Layer 3 protocol is mapped separately to a DLCI.

Nonbroadcast Multiaccess

One of the more advanced concepts in WAN design involves the concept of nonbroadcast multiaccess (NBMA) technologies. Unlike LAN protocols, WAN installations were originally designed around simple point-to-point connections. Addressing was unnecessary, and in the most basic installations, a connection required only one device to be DTE and the other DCE. Such connections are often used to link to routers together without the benefit of a DSU/CSU (data service unit/channel service unit).

Nonbroadcast multiaccess networks acknowledge the limitations of most WANs in comparison to local area networks. The typical wide area network does not lend itself well to broadcasts. This reflects the nonbroadcast portion of NBMA. The multiaccess portion acknowledges that some WAN technologies provide more than one destination—recall that the first WAN links were simple point-to-point configurations.

Frame Relay significantly changes this model, as the protocol becomes most efficient when a single port services multiple destinations. This reduces hardware costs and provides for efficient oversubscription of the network. However, this configuration is not without limitations. When a Frame Relay network is configured as a single subnet over multiple PVCs, the route processor must copy each broadcast and transmit it over each link. This adds a substantial amount of overhead to the router.

NBMA designs also impact the routing protocol, which leads to a recommendation that the network always be configured in a full mesh. However, this is not necessarily required. Split-horizon, or the configuration of a router such that an update never repeats back on the learned interface, can keep portions of the WAN from learning about the remainder of the network. This is shown in Figure 8.3, where subnet 192.168.1.0 will not learn of subnet 192.168.2.0, and vice versa. This is because split-horizon blocks the update about each network from transmitting out of the router on the left side of the diagram.

FIGURE 8.3 An NBMA partial-mesh configuration

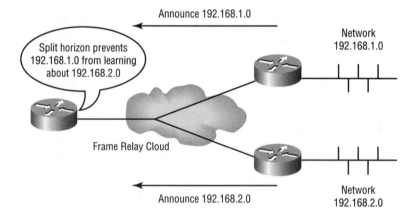

The two remote networks, 192.168.1.0 and 192.168.2.0, send routing updates about their Ethernet segments, but split-horizon prevents propagation out of the incoming interface. As a result, neither remote router learns of the other network. Clearly, this problem could be addressed by disabling split-horizon, or with static routes and other techniques. However, these solutions are not without shortcomings. Remember that split-horizon was designed to prevent routing loops; disabling this function will again subject the network to this possibility. The other solutions require a substantial amount of manual intervention and administration—steps that are unnecessary. The next section describes yet another alternative—a means to keep split-horizon enabled and provide full routing in a partial-mesh configuration.

Frame Relay with Point-to-Point Subinterfaces

The preferred method for designing large Frame Relay networks is to use point-to-point subinterfaces. This overcomes the limitations in split-horizon routing that cause problems in NBMA designs. However, each PVC becomes a separate subnet, which can require larger routing tables. Good Frame Relay designs will take advantage of VLSM and route summarization when deploying subinterface configurations.

Subinterface configurations can use either a full-mesh topology or a partial-mesh design. Most partial-mesh installations are designed around a hub-and-spoke topology.

Most administrators consider the number of PVCs, subnets, and hops required for their chosen topology. The formula for calculating the number of PVCs in a full-mesh design is $N^*(N-1)/2$, where N is equal to the number of nodes. Clearly, a partial-mesh point-to-point installation requires the fewest PVCs, yet it adds a hop in each spoke-to-spoke connection. Point-to-point designs also require the greatest number of subnets, which may be a concern in some networks.

Full-mesh designs are not recommended for OSPF (Open Shortest Path First). Hub-and-spoke topologies are not recommended for EIGRP (Enhanced Interior Gateway Routing Protocol), discussed in Chapter 4. These guidelines are based on the characteristics of each protocol.

Redundancy through Dial-on-Demand Routing

As with most WAN installations, network designers attempt to maintain connectivity options under all circumstances with remote locations. This serves two scenarios—the first is basic connectivity for the remote users, many of whom require access to corporate data in order to be productive.

The second goal is one of support; many remote locations lack the technical staff to provide troubleshooting and other diagnostic services.

In order to provide users with the most connectivity options, designers often incorporate dial-on-demand routing (DDR) services on the router. This configuration makes use of another design concept—*floating static routes*.

Recall the presentation on IP routing and the administrative distance (AD) parameter. Each route could be provided by one or more routing protocols, and the router maintained an administrative distance that it used to select routing information. Floating static builds upon this concept of administrative distance. Normally, a static route has an administrative distance of one, making it one of the best routes from the protocol's perspective. This would tend to override dynamic routing information, which is undesirable in many instances.

However, if the administrator informed the router that the static route had an AD of 240 (the highest number is 254), then the dynamic protocols would have lower ADs and would be used instead. As shown in Figure 8.4, the IGRP route through the Frame Relay cloud is used under normal circumstances. However, the floating static route between the two modems on the dial-on-demand connection is used when the Frame Relay link fails.

FIGURE 8.4 Floating static routes

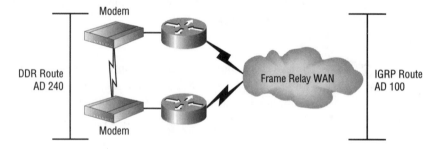

Note that floating static routes may be used on any link and are not dependent on DDR connections.

Backup Interfaces

An alternative to floating static routes is the *backup interface*. Under this configuration, the router is instructed to bring up a link if the interface goes down. The backup interface is associated with the primary interface. While this configuration has merits, the use of floating static routes typically works better in Frame Relay configurations. This addresses the concern of failed PVCs—the link may remain up/up (interface is up/line protocol is up); however, a switch failure in the cloud will collapse the PVC.

The Local Management Interface was designed to prevent this type of failure, yet there are specific scenarios that LMI cannot detect.

Since the router has no method for detecting this failure (unlike ATM OAM cells, discussed later in this chapter), it continues to believe that the interface is valid. The routing protocol may eventually record the fact that the link is unavailable, but this requires the use of a routing protocol, which adds overhead.

Network Design with ATM

Asynchronous Transfer Mode technology was developed to combine video, voice, and data in the network. The ATM Forum, a working group of vendors, developed a cell-based system for transporting these types of information. Cells are fixed in length, and therefore latency and delay can be determined and controlled accurately.

ATM provides many services for the network designer and should be considered in any wide area network design. This is especially true when considering the integration of voice and data. An emerging trend in networking is to focus on the *services* that are provided by the network and not the methodology employed. This technique simplifies the business-to-technology modeling process. Business-to-technology modeling is a process that incorporates the concepts presented in Chapter 1, where the business demands and needs are integrated into the technology and its abilities.

When selecting ATM as a WAN technology, there are two interesting issues that warrant careful consideration. First, every conversion from cell to frame requires processing and adds a small amount of latency. This is an important factor to consider when choosing a partial-mesh topology. The second consideration is vendor availability, especially with new features. For example, vendors deployed only IMA technology in mid-1999. Inverse multiplexing for ATM (IMA) is a major feature for network designers to consider since it provides a middle ground between T1 and DS-3 circuits. In many locations, IMA is the only way to provide greater than T1 bandwidth in remote locations—IMA bonds multiple T1s into a single data conduit.

Network Design in the Real-World: The Benefits of ATM

As networks have advanced, the lines between voice and data have blurred significantly. From a historical perspective, voice services and data have operated over separate circuits. When the two were integrated, it was via time division multiplexing (TDM), which maintained distinct channels for each service. Asynchronous Transfer Mode (ATM) allows for the true integration of these services, in addition to video, so Cisco recommends that designers use ATM whenever possible. Thus far the marketplace has continued to use Frame Relay and other technologies, yet providers are developing better tariffs and offerings to make ATM more attractive. Vendors are also providing ATM in more regions and with more equipment options.

Virtual Path and Virtual Circuit Identifiers

Every ATM cell contains a *virtual path identifier* (VPI) and a *virtual circuit identifier* (VCI). These values are combined, depending on the switch configuration, to create unique conduit information for the cell. This is very similar to the DLCI in Frame Relay, although the difference between path and circuit does not apply in ATM. Frame Relay understands only the equivalent concept of circuit.

The virtual path identifier encompasses a large number of virtual circuit identifiers. A four-line roadway tunnel is one way to visualize this. Each lane is analogous to the VCI, and the tunnel itself is the VPI. The lanes can diverge at either end of the tunnel, but within the tunnel they are fixed to the single path.

The terms "virtual path" and "virtual circuit" do not relate to permanence or switched characteristics. Both PVCs and SVCs require a VPI/VCI pair.

Figure 8.5 illustrates the flow of data through the ATM switches. As with the DLCI in Frame Relay, the VPI/VCI pair is used by the ATM switch to forward cells.

FIGURE 8.5 ATM data flow

While Figure 8.5 presents only a single VPI/VCI for both data directions, ATM considers each direction independently. In addition, each value has local significance from the port only—thus the VPI/VCI of 0/67 could be used for the entire definition. This usage is highly recommended since it facilitates troubleshooting.

In Figure 8.5, the terms "client" and "server" relate to Layer 7 functions, not ATM services.

The incorporation of a virtual path is illustrated in Figure 8.6. Virtual path switching considers only the path (VPI) for switching decisions; the VCI value is ignored. This permits the creation of a single PVC to transport multiple VP/VC transfers.

FIGURE 8.6 ATM virtual path switching

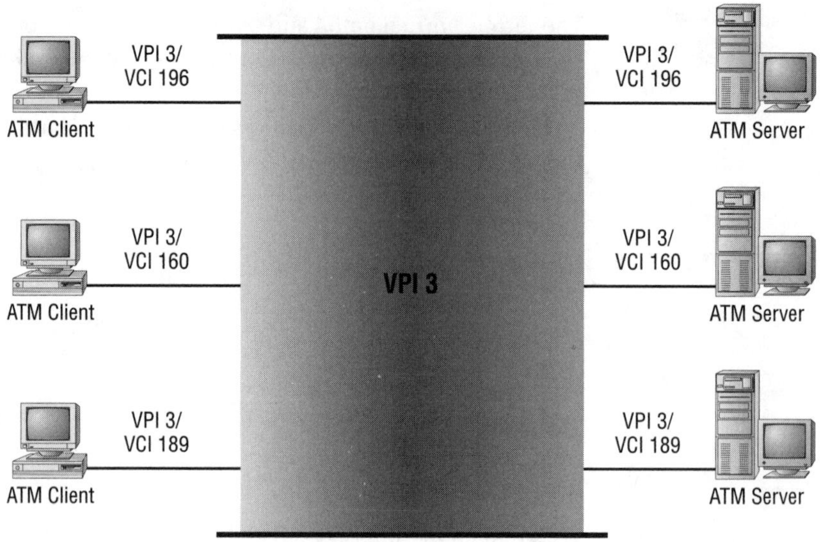

ATM Adaptation Layer 5

The most common ATM adaptation layer in use for data services is AAL 5 (ATM adaptation layer 5). This adaptation layer defines the methodology used by ATM equipment for the transmission of data cells. The use of a SNAP (Sub-Network Access Protocol) header in the encapsulation is also specified.

There are two different ATM cell formats in use for all adaptation layers, including AAL 5. Connections between end nodes and switches are carried via UNI, or *User-to-Network Interface*; UNI defines the way that ATM devices communicate with each other. There are three current versions of the UNI specification—3.0, 3.1, and 4.0. Version 3.1 is found in most implementations at present. The UNI header and cell format is illustrated in Figure 8.7.

FIGURE 8.7   The ATM cell format (AAL 5, UNI)

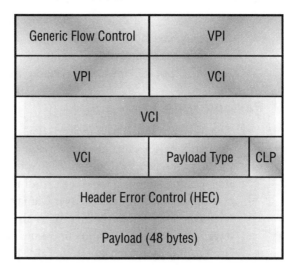

For switch-to-switch links, the ATM specification calls for the use of the *Network-to-Network Interface* (NNI). It omits the GFC (Generic Flow Control) field, as shown in Figure 8.8. The following sections describe each of the fields found in the UNI and NNI specifications, which should provide a better overview of how these protocols operate in the ATM environment.

FIGURE 8.8   The ATM cell format (AAL 5, NNI)

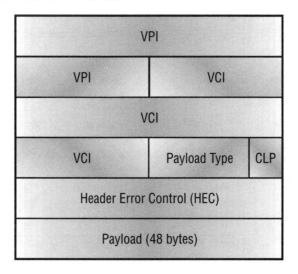

Generic Flow Control

The Generic Flow Control (GFC) bits are found only in the UNI specification; they have not been implemented in an open standard. As a result, most switches set them to all zeros and ignore them on receipt. Flow control has been incorporated into the payload type field, described below.

Payload Type

The three bits of the payload type (PT) are used to differentiate between user data and maintenance data, although the VPI/VCI effectively directs this traffic to the proper destination. In addition, the PT field may be used for flow control, and it is used for end of message markers in AAL 5.

Connection Associated Layer Management information is referred to as F5 flow. Congestion information is also incorporated into this section, depending on the PTI coding bit values. The PTI coding (most significant bit first) is interpreted as shown in Table 8.2.

TABLE 8.2 PTI Coding

PTI Coding	Definition
000	User data cell with no experienced congestion. The SDU (Service Data Unit) type is 0.
001	User data cell with no experienced congestion. The SDU type is 1.
010	User data cell with congestion experienced. The SDU type is 0.
011	User data cell with congestion experienced. The SDU type is 1.
100	Segment OAM F5 flow-related cell.
101	End-to-end OAM F5 flow-related cell.
110	Reserved.
111	Reserved.

Segment OAM cells are limited to switch-to-switch connections; the end-to-end OAM cells include the router interfaces or end station. F4 type cells are used for virtual paths and use a VCI of 3; F5 type cells are used for virtual circuits and use a VCI of 4.

OAM is a powerful tool for the designer, as it provides visibility to the entire PVC. Unlike LMI in Frame Relay, this tool allows the router (or other ATM device) to detect faults in the ATM cloud—an area that typically remains veiled from the administrator. As a result, OAM-managed PVCs can detect a failure within seconds and immediately trigger failover to an alternate circuit. Without OAM, the network may appear to be functioning properly while discarding all cells.

Cell Loss Priority

The Cell Loss Priority (CLP) bit identifies the cell as eligible to be discarded when the bit rate is not reserved. There are a number of bit rates, including:

- Unspecified bit rate

- Available bit rate

- Variable bit rate—real-time

- Variable bit rate—non-real-time

- Constant bit rate

These bit rate settings correspond to the type of data in the cell. For example, voice traffic is considered constant bit rate (CBR), while data typically uses unspecified, available, or variable bit rates—UBR, ABR, and VBR, respectively.

Header Error Control

The Header Error Control (HEC) is responsible for validating the ATM header of the cell only. It does not provide CRC for the payload data. The HEC can handle most single-bit errors without requiring additional data or retransmission. However, the medium used in ATM and the error-free nature of the medium significantly reduce the potential for an error.

Payload

The payload portion of an AAL 5 cell is 48 bytes. Therefore, a 64-byte frame in Ethernet would require two cells in ATM, and since each cell must equal

53 bytes, the ATM cell is padded. This leads to some concerns in the networking arena that there is too much overhead in ATM when linking frame-based networks.

Designers should note that ATM does not provide error checking on the payload section of the cell; it leaves that responsibility to the upper-layer protocols.

Network Design in the Real World: Other ATM Adaptation Layers

There are five adaptation layers in the ATM specifications, although layers 3 and 4 are generally regarded as a single layer. AAL 1 is typically used for voice traffic, while AAL 2 is rarely used at all.

Due to their similarities, AAL 3 and 4 are frequently listed as AAL 3/4. Unlike AAL 5, AAL 3/4 incorporates a message identifier, a sequence number, and a cyclical redundancy check in each cell. This reduces the payload portion of the cell to 44 bytes.

Because of this overhead, there are some advantages to AAL 3/4. Receivers can reassemble cells based on the message identifier and the sequence number, which permits reconciliation of out-of-sequence frames. While this overhead is beneficial for connectionless configurations, it also results in a significant performance penalty. In addition to the added *cell tax*, or the overhead per cell, the segmentation and reassembly process is substantially more involved, which can lead to further delay. As a result, AAL 3/4 is not as popular as AAL 5.

Permanent Virtual Circuits

The simplest ATM designs make use of permanent virtual circuits (PVCs). In advance of the anticipated need, an administrator defines these virtual connections. This is identical to PVCs in Frame Relay.

The advantage to PVCs is that there is no signaling required for call setup, and all circuits are available for data at all times. Unfortunately, this also requires manual configuration of the circuits—a step that can become cumbersome as the network increases in size. Traditionally, the administrator must manually configure each VPI/VCI path statement at each switch in the

PVC. However, vendors have created tools that can graphically define the PVC and automatically establish the path.

Most data network encapsulation using ATM is defined in RFC 1497. This RFC outlines the requirements and methods used to transport multiple protocols over ATM using SNAP. This differs from another RFC-defined methodology, RFC 1577, which defines encapsulation for IP only.

Figure 8.9 illustrates the use of RFC 1483 with a permanent virtual circuit. Note that RFC 1483 does not require the use of PVCs—SVCs are valid also.

In Figure 8.9, the PVC is defined as an end-to-end connection that does not terminate at the switch with the physical layer. In addition, the network layer is the same as frame-based, network-layer traffic—IP, for example, would start at this point. All of the traditional rules regarding subnets and routing apply. The previous layer, RFC 1483, effectively establishes the data-link layer.

FIGURE 8.9   Permanent virtual circuits

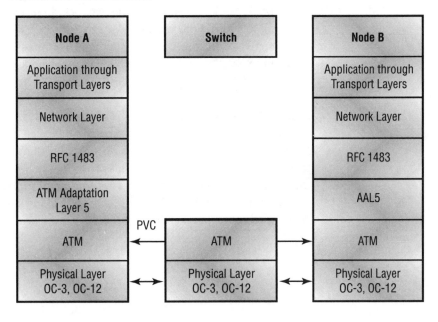

NOTE

On Cisco routers, the network is associated with the PVC on a subinterface level, and designs are point-to-point.

As with Frame Relay, ATM PVCs are typically configured with two bandwidth parameters. The maximum cell rate is referred to as the *Peak Cell Rate* (PCR), while the amount of bandwidth available for data is called the *Sustained Cell Rate* (SCR). The SCR is analogous to the CIR in Frame Relay (discussed earlier in this chapter), and under the FRF.8 specifications, the two are somewhat interchangeable. (The FRF.8 and FRF.5 specifications define the methods by which ATM and Frame Relay traffic are interchanged.)

Switched Virtual Circuits

Unlike permanent virtual circuits, switched virtual circuits (SVCs) are not established in advance. Rather, the switches are responsible for dynamically establishing the circuit through the network. In most other ways, SVCs are identical to PVCs. For example, SVCs may be used for nonbroadcast multi-access network designs (point-to-multipoint) or point-to-point configurations.

Figure 8.10 illustrates the components involved in establishing a switched virtual circuit. The Q.2931 standard is used for signaling information between the switch and ATM clients, which are labeled NSAP (Network Service Access Point) A and NSAP B. The signaling between single end nodes is called UNI; switches signal each other with NNI, as described previously.

The illustration in Figure 8.10 also includes the SSCOP layer, or Service-Specific Convergence Protocol. This protocol is responsible for reassembling the cells on the signaling channel. This is different from the segmentation and reassembly process in AAL 5—the cells serviced by SSCOP are usually messages used in the management of the ATM network and not user data.

FIGURE 8.10   Switched virtual circuits

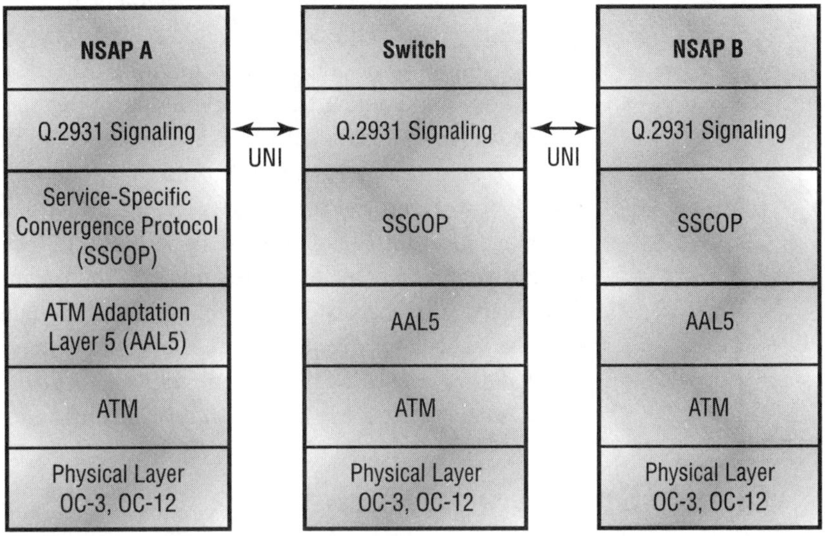

NSAP A		Switch		NSAP B
Q.2931 Signaling	←→ UNI	Q.2931 Signaling	←→ UNI	Q.2931 Signaling
Service-Specific Convergence Protocol (SSCOP)		SSCOP		SSCOP
ATM Adaptation Layer 5 (AAL5)		AAL5		AAL5
ATM		ATM		ATM
Physical Layer OC-3, OC-12		Physical Layer OC-3, OC-12		Physical Layer OC-3, OC-12

ATM Routing

There are two common methods for routing cells across ATM switches: *Interim Inter-Switch Signaling Protocol* (IISP) and *Private Network-Network Interface* (PNNI).

IISP is a static routing model that provides for a backup path in the event of primary link failure. This is somewhat limited compared to a dynamic routing protocol—IISP cannot take advantage of multiple backup paths. Designers need to remember that ATM is still a fairly new technology with many interpretations of the standards, and as a result, IISP was one of the best routing methods available.

The dynamic routing protocol, PNNI, is an improvement on the manual and static IISP. However, it is still limited in that the current standard does not support hierarchical routing and is limited in scalability as a result. PNNI provides for prefix-based routing and route aggregation while also supporting multiple alternative paths. As ATM network complexity increases, it becomes more imperative to use PNNI.

Both routing protocols support e.164 addresses, which are used in public ATM networks, and NSAP addresses, which are used in private installations. NSAP addressing is the 20-octet addressing format, while e.164 is a 10-digit number similar to phone numbers in North America. Some e.164 addresses have additional bits/digits, as shown later in the SMDS section.

The design models for ATM are very similar to those used in traditional networks. For example, configurations may follow the hierarchical model or operate in a start topology. Most ATM tariffs are quite expensive at present; however, substantial discounts may be found in local installations. Unlike most other network technologies, it is very important to avoid congestion in ATM networks. This is due to the impact of a single lost cell on the data flow—a lost cell may require 20 cells to repeat the frame. All 20 cells will be retransmitted even though only one cell was lost to congestion. This adds to the original congestion problem and results in greater data loss.

Cisco's StrataCom Switches

In the years following the acquisition of StrataCom, Cisco struggled with developing and marketing this powerful product. As of this writing, pundits continue to criticize the product and the strategic direction presented by the company regarding this system. Nonetheless, the platform is still competing with alternative offerings, including Nortel's Passport. The criticisms of the past may return should Cisco falter in its current efforts to link the product with the rest of the company's offerings or should Cisco fail to add additional features to bring it in line with the competition.

However, in recent months the product has successfully competed against rivals and, more important in this context, the CID exam contains a number of questions regarding this platform. It is very important to note that the current exam objectives do not explicitly note the StrataCom product line.

The StrataCom product line provides a number of network services. These include the following:

- Cell-based trunk links are provided with either standard 53-byte ATM cells or the 24-byte FastPacket cell configurations. FastPacket cells are proprietary.

- Dial-up services are provided with the Intelligent Network Server (INS). This independent processing system supports dial-up Frame Relay, voice-switched circuits, and ATM SVCs.

- Frame Relay frame forwarding is supported. In addition, the system supports the UNI and NNI specifications.

- StrataCom switches also provide voice connections, point-to-point connections, and bandwidth control.

It is important to understand the limitations and functions of the Strata-Com product. Table 8.3 describes the differences in the various switches.

TABLE 8.3 StrataCom Product Features

StrataCom Product	Features
BPX/AXIS switches	The BPX/AXIS product is targeted toward the larger, higher-demand networks and is a broadband switch. The BPX uses a redundant, 9.6Gbps cross-point switch matrix for interconnection services, and the AXIS shelf provides termination for Frame Relay, T1, E1, ATM, CES, and FUNI services. BPX nodes are interconnected via OC-3 or DS-3 links.
IGX switches	The IGX product is offered in 8-, 16-, or 32-slot configurations and uses a redundant, 1.2Gbps cell-switching bus for backplane interconnections. It is important to note that the switch can operate in stand-alone mode, which allows it to both provide access functions and act as a multiservice switch. It interoperates with the BPX and IPX platforms.
IPX switches	Similar to IGX switches, the IPX switch products also provide 8-, 16-, or 32-slot configurations, but they provide cell switching at only 32Mbps. Typically, they are deployed around a central BPX, and the IPX terminates narrowband applications including voice, fax, data, video, and Frame Relay.

StrataCom switches are usually administered with the StrataSphere Network Management software. These applications provide planning tools including StrataSphere Modeler and StrataSphere Optimizer. The Statistics agent and BILLder applications are more targeted toward management and operations functions.

Many changes have occurred with the StrataCom product line and Cisco's positioning of this platform. Please consult the technical and sales information available online.

StrataCom Network Design Models

Network design with StrataCom switches is similar to generic network design; however, there are important differences in terminology and deployment. Table 8.4 documents the three general classifications of StrataCom network designs—flat, tiered, and structured.

TABLE 8.4 The StrataCom Network Design Models

Design Model	Characteristics
Flat	Flat StrataCom networks regard all nodes as equal partners. There are no hierarchical characteristics under this design. The flat design can support 48 nodes; however, processing and addressing limitations can impact the overall success of this deployment. Under the flat design model, all nodes must maintain information about all other nodes in the network.
Tiered	StrataCom's tiered design model adds hierarchical characteristics to the network and is substantially more scalable than the flat model. Under the tiered model, IPX, IGX, and AXIS platforms are connected to a backbone consisting of BPX nodes.
Structured	The structured model permits expansion to 384 nodes in the network. Various StrataCom switches are linked under a loose domain model that groups switches. These groupings typically mirror other domain models—devices are grouped on geographic or administrative boundaries.

Network Design with SMDS

Switched Multimegabit Data Service (SMDS) was designed to provide the performance characteristics and connectivity features of local area networks in the WAN. This was accomplished by using a connectionless, on-demand transport based on the 802.6 MAN standard. However, the underlying structure of SMDS is cell-based ATM, and it uses ATM AAL 3/4. Recall that data ATM networks use AAL 5 in most installations.

It is unfortunate that SMDS technology did not succeed. The protocol offered network designers many benefits. For example, changes were very simple, and additional nodes could be added quickly. In addition, all interfaces in the same SMDS region were addressed in the same subnet, and all stations had direct, connectionless access to every other node. However, SMDS never received widespread adoption, and many carriers avoided the technology in favor of Frame Relay or ATM. Customers also avoided the technology, though this was primarily due to the high cost of equipment and low availability. Today it is virtually impossible to order SMDS—vendors will direct you to ATM or Frame Relay.

While configured as a connectionless topology, SMDS offered a reasonable degree of security for corporations. Addresses were entered into screening and validation tables to permit connectivity between nodes. This isolated each company logically within the switch, yet inter-company SMDS communications could be enabled with a minor table modification.

Broadcasts from the source router would reach all other routers—the packet automatically being forwarded by the SMDS switch to all routers in the network. This was accomplished with group addressing. SMDS addresses in North America were assigned like traditional analog phone numbers; however, they were prefixed with a C or an E. C addresses are for individual nodes, and E addresses are used within a group for the group address. The group address for an SMDS network in Chicago might appear as e131.2555.1212, for example. Packets sent to the group address are forwarded to all nodes in the subnet (as defined in the SMDS switch). This simplified processing on the source router—recall that in Frame Relay, the router repeated the broadcast for each PVC.

The router sends only one copy of the packet to the group address. The network/switch is responsible for distributing and repeating that packet to all members of the group. The network/switch will not transmit the packet back to the sender, even though the sender is a member of the group.

SMDS required the use of an SMDSU (SMDS Unit) or SDSU (SMDS Data Service Unit). Since SMDS never attained the volume found with Frame Relay and other WAN technologies, it is understandable that these DSUs would have a higher cost.

SMDS supports a number of upper-layer protocols, including:

- IP
- IPX
- AppleTalk
- CLNS
- XNS
- DECNet
- Vines
- Transparent bridging

This wide array of protocol support was one of the advantages of SMDS. For example, IP could use the multicast function in SMDS to perform ARPs, which saved a great deal of time normally required for manual configuration.

The following output demonstrates a typical SMDS interface configuration. Note that both static and multicast entries are present—the administrator could rely on multicasts to the group address for all traffic, yet in this instance static entries for each element were chosen to reduce queries and to facilitate troubleshooting. Also note that both IP and IPX are configured for this SMDS group.

```
interface Serial1/1
  description SMDS Interface
  ip address 10.1.2.1 255.255.255.0
  encapsulation smds
```

```
smds address c141.5555.1234
no smds dxi-mode
smds static-map ip 10.1.2.11 c141.5555.1111
smds static-map ip 10.1.2.20 c141.5555.1120
smds static-map ipx 100.0000.3048.e909 c141.5555.1120
smds multicast IP e141.5555.0001 10.1.2.0 255.255.255.0
smds multicast ARP e141.5555.0001 10.1.2.0 255.255.255.0
smds multicast NOVELL e141.5555.0001
smds enable-arp
ipx network 100
ipx output-sap-filter 1000
```

As with other WAN technologies, SMDS should be evaluated on availability, equipment, and cost factors. Note that many vendors, including Pacific Bell/Southwest Bell, will no longer provision SMDS for new installations.

Summary

This chapter provided a substantial background into three different WAN technologies: Frame Relay, ATM, and SMDS. It also provided an overview of dedicated leased lines, which are also common in WAN design. As with most factors in network design, architects need to be familiar with the scalability and costs associated with their designs while considering the business factors and services that are required.

Specifically, readers should come away from this chapter with a comfortable understanding of the following:

- The WAN design factors
- Serial line encapsulations
- Frame Relay
  - LMI
  - Frame Relay PVCs

- Inverse ARP

- Nonbroadcast multiaccess networks

- ATM

  - Cisco's StrataCom product line

  - Switched virtual circuits

  - Permanent virtual circuits

  - The AAL 5 specification

  - The ATM cell format

- SMDS

The next chapter builds upon some of these concepts as it addresses the remote access technologies, including ISDN and X.25. Generally, these services are of lower bandwidth than ATM and Frame Relay.

Review Questions

1. In a flat configuration, the StrataCom switch can support how many ports?

   A. 12

   B. 24

   C. 48

   D. 192

2. Which product would be most appropriate for terminating low-bandwidth user services?

   A. IPX

   B. IGX

   C. BPX

   D. eIPX

3. Which WAN technology is best suited for integrating voice, video, and data?

   A. Frame Relay

   B. SMDS

   C. ATM

   D. ISDN

4. Which of the following WAN technologies is being phased out?

   A. ATM

   B. SMDS

   C. Frame Relay

   D. T1

5. A cell in ATM AAL 5 is:

    A. 48 bytes long

    B. 53 bytes long

    C. Variable in length, but never more than 48 bytes long

    D. Variable in length, up to a maximum of 1514 bytes

6. The payload section of an AAL 3/4 cell is:

    A. 5 bytes

    B. 44 bytes

    C. 48 bytes

    D. 53 bytes

7. The header in AAL 5 is:

    A. 5 bytes

    B. 9 bytes

    C. 48 bytes

    D. 53 bytes

8. Which of the following is not true of an ATM cell formatted within the AAL 5 specification?

    A. It operates with PVC and SVC circuits.

    B. It provides 48 bytes per cell for payload.

    C. It provides 5 bytes per cell for header.

    D. It provides a checksum for the cell payload.

9. In AAL 5, error checking includes:

A. The ATM header

B. The ATM payload

C. Both the ATM header and the ATM payload

D. Neither the ATM header nor the ATM payload

10. Frame Relay provides a better pricing model for designers because of which features?

A. Single destination per physical interface and per-mile charges

B. Multiple destinations per physical interface and per-mile charges

C. Multiple destinations per physical interface and distance-insensitive charges

D. Single destination per physical interface and distance-insensitive charges

11. The BPX switch employs which of the following?

A. A 1.2Gbps frame-based backplane

B. A 3.6Gbps backplane link via the Phoenix ASIC

C. A redundant 1.2Gbps cell-switching bus

D. A redundant 9.6Gbps crosspoint switch matrix

12. StrataCom switches do not provide which of the following services?

A. ATM

B. Video

C. FDDI

D. Voice

13. Rather than disabling split-horizon, the designer of a Frame Relay network could design:

 A. A full mesh with separate subnets for each PVC

 B. A partial mesh with separate subnets for each PVC

 C. A full mesh with a single subnet

 D. A partial mesh with a single subnet

14. Which of the following is not an encapsulation for Frame Relay?

 A. AAL5SNAP

 B. Frame Relay Forum LMI

 C. ITU-T Q.933 Annex A

 D. ANSI T1.617 Annex D

15. Inverse ARP performs which function?

 A. Dynamic addressing of router interfaces

 B. Dynamic mapping of Layer 3 addresses

 C. Frame Relay control signaling

 D. ATM LANE address mapping

16. NNI cells do not contain which of the following?

 A. VPI

 B. VCI

 C. GFC

 D. HEC

17. The AAL 3/4 specification provides more user bandwidth than AAL 5. True or false?

 A. True

 B. False

18. The structured design model for StrataCom switches employs which concept?

   A. Hierarchical domain model that supports up to 384 nodes

   B. Full-mesh model that supports up to 384 nodes

   C. Hierarchical domain model that supports up to 64 nodes

   D. Partial-mesh model that supports up to 64 nodes

19. DLCIs must be the same throughout the entire PVC. True or false?

   A. True

   B. False

20. Generic Flow Control provides which of the following features?

   A. Congestion control

   B. Buffering control

   C. Path determination for congestion control

   D. None of the above

Answers to Review Questions

1. C.
2. A.
3. C.
4. B.
5. B.
6. B.
7. A.
8. D.
9. A.
10. C.
11. D.
12. C.
13. B.
14. A.
15. B.
16. C.
17. B.
18. A.
19. B.
20. D.

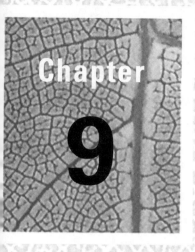

Chapter 9

Remote Access Network Design

CISCO INTERNETWORK DESIGN EXAM
OBJECTIVES COVERED IN THIS CHAPTER:

- ✓ Design scalable internetwork WAN nonbroadcast multi-access X.25.

- ✓ Design scalable, robust internetwork WAN with X.25 subinterface configuration.

- ✓ Use X.25 switching to provide X.25 service over an integrated IP backbone.

- ✓ Explain ISDN services.

- ✓ Examine a customer's requirements and recommend appropriate ISDN solutions.

- ✓ Construct an ISDN design that conserves bandwidth and is cost effective.

- ✓ Examine a client's requirements and recommend appropriate point-to-point and asynchronous WAN solutions.

- ✓ Choose appropriate link encapsulation for point-to-point circuits.

While the technologies presented in this chapter are different from the WAN systems discussed in Chapter 8, readers should find some similarities between them. All WAN systems ultimately introduce factors that are not present in LAN designs—sometimes these factors are significant. Consider the fact that most WAN solutions reduce the amount of control availed to the administrator. This loss of control may be due to a partnership with a telecommunications provider or to end-user activity. Either factor can greatly complicate troubleshooting and support.

Another common factor in remote access and WAN solutions is performance. While it is possible to obtain OC-48 SONET (Synchronous Optical Network) rings (yielding over 2Gbps) for WAN connectivity, these solutions are also very costly (up to and exceeding $30,000 a month, depending on distance). Remote-access solutions typically utilize significantly slower connection methods, including X.25, ISDN, and standard telephone services (PSTN/POTS or Public Switched Telephone Network/plain old telephone service). Therefore, designers should work with users and application support staff to minimize the demands on the remote access solution, thereby providing the greatest performance for users.

This chapter will address X.25 and ISDN technologies in detail. It will also present the various ways remote users access the corporate network, including remote gateways, remote control, and remote nodes.

This chapter will include a section on xDSL technologies as well. While xDSL is not on the current CID examination, the quick growth of this transport technology will certainly play a role in future network designs.

Network Design with X.25

The X.25 protocol was intended to address the connectivity demands of low-bandwidth, poor-quality connections. As a result, the protocol contains a significant amount of overhead related to error-checking that is typically unnecessary in modern networks. However, it is also a widely available protocol, so network designers may likely need to integrate legacy X.25 into more modern network designs. The protocol remains quite prevalent in some countries and in the telecommunications industry as well. Companies with networks outside the US and Japan should consider X.25 for lower cost, lower bandwidth connections, especially as a transport for IP traffic—however, X.25 will transport most protocols.

The basic tenet of X.25 is that the protocol should be reliable. Therefore, the protocol is based on LAPB (Link Access Procedure, Balanced), which provides flow control and reliable transport at the data-link layer. One feature in X.25 is the use of channels, which are effectively logical virtual circuits. As indicated previously, compared to other protocols, including Frame Relay, X.25 has very low throughput and high latency—a characteristic of packet-relay transports. While most X.25 implementations connect to a public network, a significant number of private systems exist. These are frequently found in telecommunications and financial environments, although ISDN, xDSL, and low-bandwidth Frame Relay are slowly eroding this market share.

In a Cisco-based network design, the X.25 protocol is used to create WAN links where the carrier provides the DCE (data circuit-terminating equipment) and the router takes on the role of the DTE (data terminal equipment). However, the router can be configured as the DCE when necessary. Connections are established by defining an X.121 address in the router. X.121 addresses are comprised of a four-digit Data Network Identification Code (DNIC) and a National Terminal Number (NTN), which may be up to 10 digits in length. It is important to note that most X.25 services are billed on a per-packet basis, so most designers use static routes and filters to limit the traffic on the network.

Most designers without X.25 experience typically have some Frame Relay expertise. This expertise is beneficial, as Frame Relay compares with X.25 from an overall topology perspective. The network core can be configured via X.25, but it is generally recommended that a full-mesh design be implemented. In addition, careful consideration should be given to over-subscription, as bandwidth is limited. Designers also need to consider X.25 under the same guidelines as any NBMA (nonbroadcast multiaccess) configuration, which was covered in the Frame Relay section of the previous chapter.

Cisco introduced subinterface support for X.25 in IOS version 10.0. This eliminated the NBMA factors of partial-mesh connectivity and split-horizon, so the designer can provide full connectivity with a partial-mesh configuration. As with other subinterfaces, each link is a different network.

The router can also provide the functions of an X.25 switch via its serial ports. This allows connectivity between two packet assembler/disassembler (PAD) devices. Unfortunately, X.25 and LAPB are the only protocols supported on the link, which precludes other encapsulations. Both PVC (permanent virtual circuit) and SVC (switched virtual circuit) links are supported.

Network Design with ISDN

Integrated Services Digital Network (ISDN) technology was developed in large part from the conversion to digital networks from analog switches by the telephone companies in North America, which at the time was AT&T for the United States. This conversion, which started in the 1960s, resulted in the following features:

- Clearer, cleaner signals.

- Compressible voice, resulting in better trunking utilization.

- Longer distances between switching devices.

- Value-added features, including caller ID and three-way calling.

- Greater bandwidth—a single connection to the telephone company can service more than one phone number.

- Elimination of load coils and amplifiers in the network.

ISDN was originally conceived as a means to move the digital network into the home, where a single ISDN connection would provide two standard phone lines and digital services for data. This migration from the analog phone would continue to use the existing copper wire plant while adding services that would ultimately increase revenues.

Unfortunately, users failed to accept ISDN in the numbers desired. This was especially true in the United States, where installation problems, service availability, and pricing all combined to hinder acceptance.

Standard ISDN service is popular for videoconferencing and as a residential connection to the Internet. Cable modems and xDSL technologies will probably replace this market in the 21st century, however.

Most ISDN installations in remote locations use the Basic Rate Interface (BRI), offering users two B channels for user data and a single D channel (16Kbps) for signaling. This provides a total bandwidth of 144Kbps; however, each B channel is only 64Kbps, for a total user bandwidth of 128Kbps.

ISDN BRI is really a 192Kbps circuit; the remaining bandwidth of 48Kbps is overhead. The physical frame in ISDN BRI is 48 bits, and the circuit sends 4,000 frames per second.

Host connections typically terminate with ISDN PRI (Primary Rate Interface) services, which use T1 circuits. This provides 23 B channels, and all signaling occurs on the D channel. Each channel is 64Kbps, for a total data rate of 1.535Mbps. The remaining bandwidth is overhead.

Designers should carefully review the costs associated with ISDN before committing to the technology. Since most tariffs are based on per-minute billing, bills in the thousands of dollars per month are not uncommon when improper configurations are deployed. This factor is the largest negative regarding ISDN for telecommuting. Users will also notice that connections require a few seconds to be established—ISDN is not an always-on technology.

A D-channel-based service, called *always-on ISDN*, is available from some vendors. This provides up to 9.6Kbps for user data and can be used as a replacement for X.25 networks.

Communications over ISDN may use the Point-to-Point Protocol (PPP) where desired. PPP provides many additional services, including security via the Challenge Handshake Authentication Protocol (CHAP). PPP is an open standard defined in RFC 1661, and the PPP protocol, through the Link Control Protocol (LCP), performs initial configuration. Multilink PPP may be used for B channel aggregation as well.

Multilink PPP (MP) performs a number of functions, but it primarily is responsible for the segmentation and sequencing of packets across multiple channels. This bonds the two B channels for a total of 128Kbps of user data, but it does not allow each channel to cross multiple chassis. The protocol is defined in RFC 1717, and it adds four bytes of overhead to each packet on the link. Network designers may find this function useful in videoconferencing applications; however, it is also applicable for remote data connectivity.

The Multilink Multichassis PPP protocol (MMP) is another protocol that combines B channels. MMP operates across multiple routers and access servers and is more scalable than the standard Multilink Protocol. Various B channels can span numerous chassis, allowing for larger, more scalable access farms and better redundancy options, since the failure of a single switch may not result in the loss of a session. When additional capacity is needed for a cluster, an administrator need add only another peer access device.

MMP relies on an MMP process server to reassemble the calls. One possible implementation of this would include a 4700 router fronted with multiple AS5200s. The AS5200s combine to create a logical federation called *stackgroup peers*, and these peers use the Stackgroup Bidding Protocol (SGBP) to elect a process server. SGBP is a proprietary protocol. Although MMP may be used similarly to MP, the multichassis nature of the protocol allows for greater scalability and aggregate bandwidth. The SGBP process selects resources based on previously existing sessions and processor load.

ISDN may also be used for L2F (Layer 2 Forwarding Protocol), PPTP (Point-to-Point Tunneling Protocol), and L2TP (Layer 2 Tunneling Protocol) tunnels, which are described in Chapter 11. These secure conduits are ideal for Internet connectivity; however, they may also be used in private networks. One application for tunnels includes telecommuting—rather than having all users call a central, long-distance number, they can call a local point-of-presence and pay for a local call. The point-of-presence may be private and be maintained by the corporation or an ISP on the Internet. This concept is used for Virtual Private Network (VPN) solutions.

Remote Access

Over the years, users have demanded access to corporate LANs from their homes, hotel rooms, and customer sites. These requirements depart significantly from the fairly comfortable and controlled structure of the local area network.

In fact, many companies have decided to address remote connectivity with VPNs or with a combination of services that are outsourced to a provider. Outsourcing is a good way to control costs, although the costs are generally higher than with internally administered remote access solutions. This setup works in most corporations because hiring full-time personnel is very costly. Frequently, outsourced solutions can also decrease communications costs, which are recurring and can quickly overrun the best budgets, as the major telecommunications providers maintain points-of-presence in virtually all calling areas. For the corporate user, the call into the remote-access system is a local one rather than a long-distance or 800 call, each of which costs the corporation substantially more.

Network designers need a thorough understanding of the remote connectivity options for either outsourcing or corporate-provided solutions. These solutions incorporate remote nodes, remote gateways, and remote control. However, this text will also incorporate remote users and their requirements into the mix.

It is important to note that most of these solutions are still deployed on standard telephone services, although some deployments use ISDN. Within the first few years of the 21st century, it is likely that cable modem and xDSL solutions will also be incorporated into remote-access deployments, and these technologies will likely replace ISDN and POTS.

Designers need to realize the limitations that come with any of these transport technologies. For example, standard telephone services are slow, but they are also universally available. Solutions based on DSL are fast and comparatively cheap compared to ISDN and analog dial-up (based on bandwidth), but they must be pre-installed and are fixed in location at the remote end. While this makes the higher speed solution less attractive to remote users who travel, it would be an ideal solution for an at-home telecommuter.

Remote Gateway

Remote gateways are designed to solve a single remote access need, and as a result they can be fairly inexpensive. The most common remote gateways are used for e-mail, but they can be configured to provide other services as well. A remote gateway is a remote-access device that services a single application.

The key to remote gateway solutions is that they generally do not scale because the remote gateway device typically processes the application in addition to the remote session. Therefore, the designer may address a single need quickly without building in scalability. As a result, the designer selecting remote gateway technology would likely purchase separate modems and phone lines for each gateway deployment—resulting in an expensive long-term solution as more and more gateway services are added.

Remote Control

The concept of remote control has been a powerful tool for diagnostics and troubleshooting for years. Under remote control, a machine is operated from a remote location. Everything that can be done locally on the machine is available to the remote user via the application. (PCAnyWhere is one popular remote-control solution.) As a result, technical support staff have been able to use this resource to fix workstation problems—a solution much more efficient than the "please click on the button and tell me what it says" approach, which requires training in addition to research and troubleshooting.

For the network designer deploying a remote access solution, the process is reversed. The host machine is located in the data center and typically contains a fixed configuration that provides access to most of the applications that would be available to local users on a local workstation. This configuration is sometimes used with thin-client deployments as well. A thin-client is a workstation that relies on a server for most processing; applications on a thin-client are typically very small as well. A fat-client maintains more of the processing and servicing on the workstation.

For remote users, this solution offers some powerful advantages. First, the configuration and support issues are virtually limited to the server system. The remote user need only be concerned with the remote-control client. Second, the remote user can access all of the applications that are available on the host without installing the application. Third, performance for some applications is increased with remote control. For example, consider a large database query. This might require the transfer of 10 megabytes of data across the phone line. Remote-control solutions would limit the data flow to a screenful of data at a time—a fraction of that figure.

All of these advantages cannot be without disadvantages. The most significant is that users must be connected to the remote-control host to access applications and data. So a worker using remote control for eight hours a day pays for a connection for the full eight-hour day. The modem and other equipment at the hosting site are also reserved for that user. In addition, performance is limited to the speed of the connection and the compression provided by the hosting application. The host computer's memory and CPU capacity will also limit the performance of remote-control sessions.

Another consideration for remote-control solutions is the lack of offline availability. Many workers need to work while traveling on airplanes or busses, and while wireless solutions exist, they are expensive and unreliable. If the remote-access user will be mobile part of the time, the remote-control solution requires greater scrutiny.

Remote Node

It would be nice to allow remote users the same on-LAN service that they have in the office, and remote-node technology allows exactly that. Although remote-node technology is slower, remote users must connect as a remote node only when transferring data. Under all other circumstances, they can operate with the applications and data stored on their local workstation. This situation introduces support issues that did not exist with remote-control and remote-gateway solutions, but it also makes the service scalable.

Under remote control, a user would need to connect to the server for eight hours a day to be productive. With a remote node connecting only for data transfer, this time could be cut to perhaps less than 15 minutes per day—long enough to transfer a few files and capture e-mail five or six times. In theory, then, the single connection could support 32 users. To illustrate, consider Table 9.1. Designers can make use of the fact that users are not concurrent (a measure of simultaneous users) to oversubscribe the modem pool. As shown, 32 users at 15 minutes can be serviced with four circuits, or 640 users can be supported with 80 circuits at an oversubscription rate of 8:1, which is still double the average concurrent usage figure.

TABLE 9.1 Remote Node Utilization

Users	Duration	Circuits	Concurrent Usage
32	8 hours	32	32
32	15 minutes	4	2
640	15 minutes	80	40

This clearly reduces the costs associated with remote access. Because the LAN connection is slow—the workstation thinks that the modem is a LAN adapter—applications and other static data should be stored locally.

Remote-node solutions are sometimes considered more secure than other remote-access methods, and Cisco supports this position. However, once a node connects, it is capable of running any software on the client workstation, including hacking tools and other applications that may not adhere to corporate policy. Remote gateways, by serving a single function, and remote-control hosts, by placing applications under administrative control, may be more secure solutions.

Given the flexibility of remote-node solutions and the scalability afforded by them, most designers in modern remote solutions will opt for this solution first. If remote control is necessary, it can be combined with remote node by simply attaching to the remote-control host over the network session established as a node. This hybrid solution can provide the bandwidth savings sometimes available with remote control without making it the only connection method.

Remote Users

So far, this chapter has merely touched upon remote users and their needs. However, it is important to expand upon their requirements. After all, the entire reason to deploy remote access is to provide services to users.

Remote users typically fall into one of three general categories:

- Occasional users, who may telecommute or need mobile access infrequently.

- Telecommuters, frequent users who telecommute from a fixed location. This would include small office/home office (SOHO) users with small LANs in their home.

- Mobile users, frequent users who travel a significant amount of time. This usage pattern often applies to the corporate sales force, sometimes called "road warriors."

Cisco recommends different hardware solutions for each of these categories; however, all are predicated on the deployment of remote-node solutions. Let's look at the various hardware solutions.

Low-Density Solutions

Cisco recommends the use of its 2509/2511 series routers for small user pools. This solution would address the needs of eight to 16 users and use external modems to provide a modem bank. Note that this solution is analog, which means that v.90/56k is not supported. This will limit users to 28.8 or 33.6Kbps.

Fixed-Location Solutions

Cisco positions its 760/770 ISDN router platform for the remote user operating from a fixed location. This solution incorporates ISDN, which may significantly add to the access costs; however, it also provides greater bandwidth than a dial-up solution. As of this writing, it appears that Cisco is departing from the 760/770 platform in favor of newer 800 series systems. For actual deployments, designers should consult with their local Cisco representative.

One of the benefits to an ISDN-based SOHO solution is the use of a single line for voice and data. The installation may be configured to use both B channels (ISDN BRI) for data-only transmissions. A voice call can use either of the two channels, and this configuration will still provide data connectivity.

On the hosting side of ISDN connections, the designer has a number of options. Multiple ISDN BRI circuits may be terminated to Cisco's 4000 series router. However, this solution would service only a few connections. Deployment of the 4000 or 7000 series routers with ISDN PRI connections could support a larger population of users. An alternative Cisco solution is the 3600 platform; however, this platform was unavailable when the current exam was developed.

Some recommendations in this book suggest using end-of-life or discontinued equipment. This is due to the age of the examination objectives and is reflective of the current examination. Please consult Cisco's Web site for the most recent information.

High-Density Solutions

Cisco also offers the AS5200, which may be used for termination of ISDN and analog phone connections and can provide service for fixed-location users. This platform yields the greatest flexibility of these solutions. Both the AS5100 (discontinued) and AS5200/AS5300/AS5800 products offer integrated modems, which may benefit administrators concerned with rack space. Integrated solutions typically benefit from lower total costs as well.

High-density solutions may also benefit large pools of mobile users. The smallest AS5200 configuration is typically 24 digital modems. Mobile user pools would not be served well with the 4000 or 7000 platform.

Both the 4000/4000M and 7000/7010 models are classified end-of-life at this writing. Please check the Cisco Web site for current information.

Network Design with DSL Technologies

Digital Subscriber Line (DSL) technologies were developed to be the "magic bullet" of the telecommunications industry. Primarily designed to add bandwidth to the home without installing fiber optics, the xDSL protocols have the potential to provide 52Mbps over already installed copper wire—a marked increase in performance. This feat is accomplished with special encoding of the digital signal. At present, DSL technologies are being used as a replacement for ISDN and analog ISP connections. However, as DSL technologies are accepted into the home and office, it is likely that they will be used for primary and backup data transfer and for high-demand services such as live video.

DSL technologies and cable modems are not included as an exam objective at present. This section is provided only as optional material for those readers interested in this technology.

The various DSL technologies, referred to in the generic as xDSL, provide for varying amounts of upstream and downstream bandwidth based on the equipment in use and the distances between that equipment. As a result of its distance sensitivity, xDSL typically must terminate within three miles of the central office, but access technologies may be employed to extend the range. Access products connect a remote termination device to the central office via fiber optics, which greatly extends the reach of xDSL. Figure 9.1 illustrates a typical installation of DSL with and without an access product. As shown, a home four miles away cannot obtain xDSL access without an access product. Please note that most xDSL technologies support distances between 1,800 and 18,000 feet.

As of this writing, vendors are deploying DSL at fairly low speeds and as an Internet connectivity solution. Most vendors provide 1.544Mbps downstream bandwidth, as viewed from the central office side, and 128Kbps to 384Kbps upstream. These bandwidths greatly surpass ISDN and analog offerings, but they cannot provide the multi-service goals of xDSL—primarily MPEG-2 video streaming. Table 9.2 shows the various xDSL technologies available.

FIGURE 9.1 xDSL installations

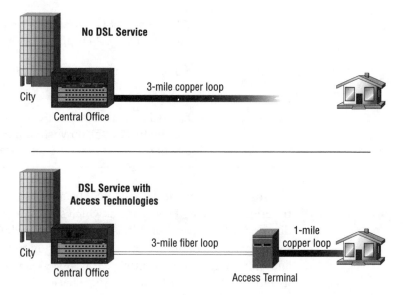

TABLE 9.2 The Various xDSL Technologies

Standard	Characteristics
ADSL	There are a number of flavors to Asymmetric DSL; the two most popular are G.dmt (discrete multi-tone) and G.lite. The G.lite specification provides 1.5/384 bandwidth and typically invokes lower capital costs. The G.dmt specification can provide 8Mbps downstream and 1.5Mbps upstream.
HDSL	HDSL is similar to Symmetric DSL, but it makes use of dual and triple pairs of copper wire. Most other DSL technologies operate over a single pair. HDSL typically provides distances reaching 15,000 feet.
IDSL	ISDN-based DSL typically allows the greatest distances but is limited to 144Kbps.
SDSL	SDSL provides 2Mbps bi-directional bandwidth over a single pair. Distances are typically limited to 10,000 feet.
VDSL	Limited to distances less than 4,500 feet, VDSL can provide up to 52Mbps downstream bandwidth. This is usually the shortest range DSL service.

Most vendors are deploying xDSL from two perspectives. The first is the traditional ISP-based installation, which simply substitutes ISDN or analog dial-up for DSL. Because DSL is an always-on technology, there is no call setup or teardown process, and the connection to the DSLAM, or Digital Subscriber Line Access Multiplexer, is always active. The second connectivity model is RLAN, or Remote LAN. This model places the DSL connection on par with Frame Relay or point-to-point links in the WAN; however, the solution is being deployed for telecommuters as opposed to interoffice connections. Ultimately, designers may find that the consumer level of support currently offered in DSL will be augmented and the lower price will encourage replacement of frame and lease-line installations for interoffice traffic as well.

Both of these implementation methods can assist a modern network design. However, some caveats should be considered.

At present, most DSL vendors offer a single PVC with DSL installations. This limits connectivity options and makes redundancy difficult. A second PVC could provide a link to another head-end (distribution layer aggregation point), and most vendors have multiple DSLAMs in the central office. An SVC-based solution would also assist in designing fault-tolerance.

Another concern with current DSL installations is that most products do not offer security solutions. The RLAN model greatly reduces this risk because the links are isolated at Layer 2, but all connectivity must be provided by the head-end. This includes Internet connectivity. For Internet connections to an ISP, the risk is significantly greater, especially when considering the bandwidth available for an attack and the use of static IP addresses or address pools. A number of significant attacks have already occurred as a result of these issues, and while they should not deter the use of the technology, the risks should be addressed with firewall technology.

A third consideration in DSL is the installation delay compared to other technologies. Vendors are moving towards *splitterless* hardware so that the telephone company does not have to install a splitter in the home. The splitter divides the traditional phone signals from the data stream and provides a jack for standard telephones—DSL transports data and voice over the same twisted-pair wiring used for standard analog phone service. At present, installations require weeks to complete in order to validate the circuit to the home and install the splitter.

Cable Modems

It would be unfair to present the DSL technologies without providing some space for cable modems. Cable modems operate over the same cable system that provides television services using the same coax cable that is already used in the home. Most installations will provide two cables, one for the television and one for the data converter, but the signaling and system are the same. This is accomplished by allocating a television channel to data services. Bandwidth varies with the installation; however, 2Mbps in each direction is not uncommon.

Detractors of cable modem technology are quick to point out that these installations are shared bandwidth, similar to Ethernet, which results in contention for the wire among neighbors. This design also introduces a security risk in that network analysis is possible, although vendors are working to address this concern. This issue does not exist in DSL, as the local loop connection to the home is switched. Traffic is not integrated until it reaches the central office, and the switch will only forward traffic destined for the end station based on the MAC address. Cable modems are a shared technology—similar to 802.2 Ethernet versus 10-Base-T. Along the same lines, a cable modem is really a broadband Ethernet bridge.

Network designers may wish to consider cable modems as part of a VPN deployment, as the technology will not lend itself to the RLAN-type (Remote LAN-type) designs availed in DSL. Recall that an RLAN requires Layer 2 isolation—a service not offered by cable modem providers at present. This may change in the future if channels can be isolated to specific users. This may be especially true in very remote rural areas, where cable is available and DSL is not.

Summary

Remote connectivity has become increasingly important in modern networks as various organizations expand their requirements. These requirements frequently include the need for data to be available at locations outside of the traditional corporate office. Such sites may include retail sales outlets, employee homes, hotel rooms, and customer locations.

This chapter presented two of the more traditional remote-access technologies—ISDN and X.25. Both have been used heavily to provide point-of-sale access to corporate data, including credit card verification and inventory systems. While deployments are waning in the shadow of low-speed, low-cost Frame Relay and xDSL solutions, designers and administrators will have to work with these older technologies for the foreseeable future.

In addition to the specific remote-access technologies incorporated into the exam objectives, this chapter also addressed the various design models for providing remote connectivity to telecommuters and other remote staff. These included:

- Remote gateway

- Remote control

- Remote node

The chapter also discussed some of the needs frequently addressed in remote access solutions and the technology Cisco recommends to meet these challenges.

Review Questions

1. A remote gateway:

   A. Provides access to a single application or service

   B. Provides access to a display-only connection

   C. Places the remote workstation on a slower extension of the LAN

   D. None of the above

2. Remote-control solutions:

   A. Are very limited because they allow access to only one application

   B. Are very limited because there must be a connection in order to access applications and data

   C. Cannot be used for remote access

   D. Always consume more bandwidth than other remote-access solutions

3. Deployment of remote node systems:

   A. Is extremely costly and serves a single function, which impacts scalability

   B. Allows administrators to control all applications at a central source

   C. Requires the use of fixed locations for remote users

   D. Provides an effective connection to the LAN, although it is usually slower

4. The designer needs to provide 10 remote users with dial-in access. Cisco recommends that this design use:

   A. The 2500 series platform with internal modems

   B. The 2500 series platform with external modems

   C. The 760 series router

   D. The 7000 series router with the AS5200 modem bank

5. Because of billing and low-bandwidth factors, designers should incorporate which of the following into their X.25 designs?

   A. Full-mesh configurations

   B. PVC installations only

   C. Traffic filters and static routes

   D. Traffic filters only, as static routes are not available in Cisco's X.25 implementation

6. Which of the following is not true regarding X.25?

   A. Provides high reliability

   B. Provides high bandwidth

   C. Cannot provide DCE functionality

   D. Cannot provide DTE functionality

7. The X.25 protocol relates to which layer of the OSI model?

   A. Application

   B. Session

   C. Data link

   D. Network

8. True or false: A Cisco router cannot provide X.25 switching services.

   A. True

   B. False

9. Which of the following is not an encryption technology for tunnels on ISDN?

   A. L2F

   B. CDP

   C. PPTP

   D. L2TP

10. ISDN PRI provides which of the following?

    A. Two B channels and one D channel for a total of 144Kbps

    B. 23 B channels and one D channel on a T1

    C. 24 B channels on a T1

    D. 12 B channels for data and 12 B channels for voice on a T1

11. A service that provides a LAN-equivalent, albeit slower, connection to the corporate network is called:

    A. Remote gateway

    B. Remote control

    C. Remote network

    D. Remote node

12. The network architect does not wish to deploy a full-mesh X.25 network. The best solution would be to do which of the following?

    A. Select another protocol, as X.25 must be configured in a full mesh.

    B. Use subinterfaces.

    C. Use the X.121 specification.

    D. Use the LAPB protocol and tunnel X.25 in PPP.

13. Cable modems are most similar to which of the following technologies?

    A. X.25

    B. Frame Relay

    C. ATM

    D. Ethernet

14. True or false: MMP is an open standard.

    A. True

    B. False

15. A benefit of ISDN in the home office is:

A. Greater bandwidth than any other technology

B. Low cost

C. Data and voice services on the same BRI

D. Always-on service

16. A dial-in server that provides access to the company's e-mail system is typically part of:

A. A remote-node solution

B. A remote-control solution

C. A remote-gateway solution

17. Multilink Multichassis PPP operates:

A. Between two devices, connecting a single BRI circuit between them

B. Between a single remote device and two local devices, terminating a data channel on one server and a control channel on the other

C. Across multiple routers and access servers

D. With ISDN PRI only

18. Compared to Frame Relay, X.25 has:

A. Higher latency

B. Higher bandwidth

C. Less overhead

D. Less international support

19. True or false: Both Frame Relay and X.25 support subinterfaces.

A. True

B. False

20. ISDN BRI provides how much B channel bandwidth for the user?

    A. 64Kbps

    B. 128Kbps

    C. 144Kbps

    D. 1.544Mbps

Answers to Review Questions

1. A.
2. B.
3. D.
4. B.
5. C.
6. B.
7. D.
8. B.
9. B.
10. B.
11. D.
12. B.
13. D.
14. B.
15. C.
16. C.
17. C.
18. A.
19. A.
20. B.

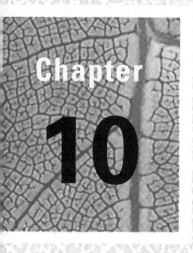

Chapter 10

Designing for Mainframe Connectivity

CISCO INTERNETWORK DESIGN EXAM OBJECTIVES COVERED IN THIS CHAPTER:

- ✓ Discuss the hierarchical and connection-oriented nature of SNA.

- ✓ Describe the use of gateways to attach Token Ring devices to an SNA network.

- ✓ Explain how LLC2 and SDLC sessions are established.

- ✓ Describe reasons for integrating SNA technology with internetworking technology.

- ✓ Examine a client's requirements and recommend SNA internetworking solutions.

- ✓ Construct SNA designs that replace legacy communications equipment with multiprotocol routers.

- ✓ Build redundancy into SNA internetworks.

- ✓ Design remote source-route bridged SNA internetworks in full- and partial-mesh configurations.

- ✓ Choose the appropriate place to do priority queuing or custom queuing for SNA.

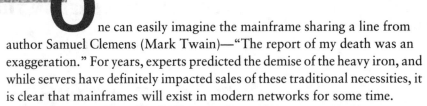

One can easily imagine the mainframe sharing a line from author Samuel Clemens (Mark Twain)—"The report of my death was an exaggeration." For years, experts predicted the demise of the heavy iron, and while servers have definitely impacted sales of these traditional necessities, it is clear that mainframes will exist in modern networks for some time.

The mainframe was initially designed to be a central processing point in the corporation, sharing resources with hundreds of users on dumb terminals—workstations that could not function without a host. This chapter will focus more on SNA and the evolution from front-end processors and cluster controllers to 3270 terminal emulators than on the mechanics of dumb terminals and the intricacies of the protocol itself. This includes the integration of the mainframe into the modern network design.

Mainframe Overview

It's best to begin at the beginning, and in mainframe networks that requires an understanding of the traditional dumb-terminal configuration and the protocols that were, and still are, used.

As shown in Figure 10.1, traditional mainframe networks typically incorporate four basic components. These include the host, a front-end processor (FEP), a cluster controller, and dumb terminals. Such installations communicate using SNA. The FEP is responsible for handling all user communications, which frees the host for processing. Under this configuration, the FEP runs the Network Control Program (NCP) and the host typically runs the Virtual Telecommunications Access Method (VTAM) program.

FIGURE 10.1   The traditional mainframe installation

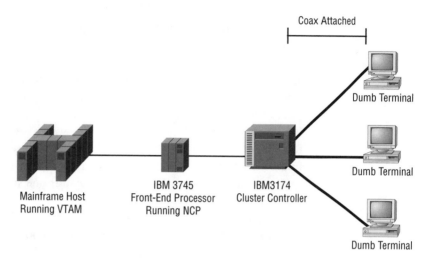

SNA divides each component in the network into one of three logical elements, called Network Addressable Units, or NAUs. These are:

- Logical units (LU)

- Physical units (PU)

- System services control points (SSCP)

These components interact with the data-flow control, transmission control, path control, and data-link control layers of the SNA protocol. Designers must keep in mind that SNA was never designed to operate on the reliable high-speed, variable-delay links found in modern networks. Rather, the protocol was designed for consistent, low-latency, low-delay connections, and sessions can be lost with only the slightest variation. A recurrent theme in SNA is the fact that longer, more complex paths through the network demand greater attention to timers and latency than other protocols, such as IP.

The LUs are further divided into two subcategories. Primary LUs (PLUs) are associated with host applications, while secondary LUs are associated with the end user.

PUs are the actual devices used in communications. However, this component of SNA is responsible for communication with the SSCP as well as the control and monitoring of the physical systems.

The SSCP is part of the VTAM program on the host system. It is responsible for controlling all sessions with the mainframe. These sessions may be divided into domains, creating logical groupings of devices.

SNA is generally considered a hierarchical networking technology. This is more due to the control placed on the domain by the host than the physical and logical design of the topology. The host computer, which is usually the mainframe, groups PLUs and the various host systems. These systems are usually referred to by their individual names, including CICS (Customer Information Control System) and TSO—which are both applications that run in regions on the mainframe. VTAM and SSCP are found at a lower layer of the hierarchy—VTAM and SSCP map closer to an operating system than to applications. One of the benefits of mainframe systems is the isolation between different operations in the machine.

The physical layer of the mainframe is called the *channel*. This is typically an ESCON (Enterprise System Connect) connection; however, bus and tag is also used. ESCON connections operate at 17MBps (megabytes per second), which is greater than Fast Ethernet in the non-mainframe environment. While they are not as fast as the SuperHPPI (High Performance Parallel Interface, capable of 800 MBps) standard and other high-bandwidth technologies, designers must keep in mind that ESCON connections are very efficient and that mainframe data typically involves very small, 2-thousand-byte transfers. While large file transfers do occur, they usually use tape and other high-capacity media.

The FEP is a Type 4 node in SNA, contrasted with the Type 5 designation given the host. This function is typically provided with a 3745 communication controller, which can connect to the network via a Token Ring adapter, or TIC (Token Ring interface coupler). The Type 4 device connects to cluster controllers (devices that provide sessions to dumb terminals) or logical units via SDLC or Token Ring. Ultimately, connections are established between two logical units, which require connections to be established between the SSCP-LU and SSCP-PU. The LU is a logical unit, whereas the PU is a physical unit.

Over its evolution, mainframe access has changed substantially from the dumb terminal (3270) and cluster controller days. Gateways once provided the connections between PCs and the mainframe, allowing corporations to remove the dumb terminals from the desktop. As this technology evolved, companies began providing gateway services through Web browsers to reduce the costs and maintenance associated with client installations. The mainframe administrator would create a sysgen, or system generation macro. This defined the Token Ring gateway as a switched major node. Depending on the configuration, the gateway could be configured as a PU Type 2 device or as an LU.

In addition, software and hardware for the PC also allowed the elimination of the gateway—the PC could *directly* connect to the host. While this added administration tasks for the administrator, it also improved the performance of the 3270 connection—the gateway and the necessary conversions were no longer a bottleneck. This solution was better suited for advanced users with a demand for more complex services than the gateway and thin-client approach. Many companies (who have not converted to TCP/IP-based hosts) still provide gateway services, which are a suitable compromise for the majority of users, providing reasonable performance with simplified client administration.

As SNA evolved, numerous protocols have been developed to transport it across modern networks. These technologies include SDLC tunneling (STUN, or serial tunneling), remote source-route bridging, data-link switching, and SDLC-to-LLC2 conversions. LLC2 stands for Logical Link Control, version 2, and is a common framing transport. In addition, Cisco has announced a new technology—SNASw (Systems Network Architecture Switching Services). This continuing development toward support for SNA is a likely indication that the protocol will remain significant in the near term.

It is important to remember that SNA is not a routable protocol (OSI definition), even though the term "SNA routing" is scattered throughout this text and the IBM documentation. Through the use of the Routing Information Field and other techniques, the source station can control the bridged paths used by Token Ring.

The Routing Information Field

The Routing Information Field, or RIF, is a Token Ring-specific function that allows the workstation to find a single path through the bridged network. You may recall from previous texts that there are numerous types of bridging, the most common of which is transparent bridging. Transparent bridging relies on each bridge to maintain a table showing which MAC addresses are available for each interface.

Token Ring frames provide for a field to store the path information—removing the need for the bridges in the network to store this information. Workstations (or other source devices) begin sessions by sending an explorer packet into the network. This packet is flooded throughout the network, and each bridge will append routing information to the RIF of the packet. The first packet received by the destination will be returned with the populated RIF—providing step-by-step instructions for future packets. This mechanism not only provides for routing in a bridged environment, but also can provide limited load balancing because the first packet received likely took the shortest path with the least delay.

One of the negatives of source-route bridging is the mechanism that populates the RIF. This is provided by the explorer packet, which is the flood referred to in the previous paragraph. This packet is replicated to traverse every ring in the network for each new connection between two stations. On a large network, this may result in a substantial amount of multicast traffic, and many designers rely on proxy services to populate the RIF without the need to flood the network. Proxy explorer functions are provided on Cisco routers and operate by remembering previous RIF information—the first connection to a station still floods, but all subsequent connections from that ring can use the proxy information to provide the route.

The RIF is stored in the format ring-bridge-ring, where each ring and bridge is assigned a unique number. These numbers can augment troubleshooting since the administrator can look at the RIF to help find the troublesome component.

It is important to note that Ethernet and other protocols do not support the concept of a RIF. When transiting these topologies, the network will either encapsulate the frame or rely on transparent bridging.

Network Design with SDLC Tunneling

SDLC tunneling (STUN) provides for the encapsulation of SNA traffic in three different configurations. The first is called *serial direct*, wherein the serial ports on the router are directly connected to local controllers. The controllers then connect to terminals. The other two configurations, HDLC and TCP/IP, are considerably more advanced than serial direct.

HDLC (High-Level Data Link Control) encapsulation is used between routers and offers the best performance for traffic over a serial connection.

The third encapsulation method uses TCP/IP to provide a reliable connection between two routers. However, this requires a substantial amount of overhead in comparison. The trade-off is that local acknowledgements are available to the designer, when so configured. Local acknowledgements effectively trick the SNA connection into thinking that the destination is on the same ring—at least in terms of performance. This prevents session time-outs and disconnects due to congested or slow WAN links, and performance is increased because the end station can transmit before the destination receives and acknowledges the frame.

A common theme in the design of SNA networks is delay and latency. At a high level, SNA cannot tolerate substantial amounts of delay—delay that poses little difficulty for other protocols. The next sections of this chapter describe ways to merge complex networks with SNA.

Network Design with RSRB

Remote Source Route Bridging (RSRB) establishes tunnels between routers in the internetwork for connections. This permits source route bridging across non-Token Ring links and greatly increases the functionality within networks. Additional features, including local acknowledgement, work to improve response time and reliability. Figure 10.2 illustrates a simple RSRB installation across a serial connection.

FIGURE 10.2   Remote Source Route Bridging

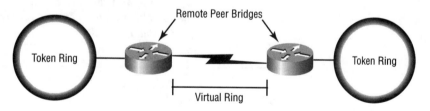

There are five encapsulation protocols for use in RSRB configurations. These are outlined in Table 10.1.

TABLE 10.1 RSRB Encapsulation Protocols

Protocol	Characteristics
Local SRB	Available on end-to-end Token Ring networks. Requires little overhead, as no encapsulation is needed. LLC2 frames cross routers.
Direct	Also requires little overhead, but encapsulation takes place in the data-link header. Useful for point-to-point links. Encapsulations may use HDLC, for example.
Frame Relay	Using the specifications in RFC 1490, this transport encapsulates SNA into LLC2 frames on Frame Relay networks.
IP FST	Fast Sequenced Transport over IP encapsulates LLC2 frames in IP datagrams. It involves more overhead than the previous methods, but it demands less overhead than TCP encapsulations. Designers must ensure that packets will arrive in sequence and without fragmentation.
TCP	The TCP encapsulation wraps the LLC2 frame with a TCP packet. The trade-off for the obvious overhead is greater reliability and local acknowledgement. Packets may be fragmented and can arrive in any sequence—this encapsulation also reconstructs the packets. Most network designers will find TCP encapsulation the most consistent solution for their networks.

RSRB is not without limitations, and many new network designs will opt to use the DLSw (Data Link Switching) option, given its superior handling. DLSw is discussed in the following section. However, the long history of RSRB certainly requires designers of modern mainframe networks to understand the protocol—many organizations have been slow to adopt newer methodologies because of the lack of perceived benefits that come with upgrading and the required training and support demands. In the context of most organizations, which appear to be moving away from SNA, the strategic benefits of changing are dubious at best.

The steps to configure RSRB differ slightly for each encapsulation type; however, the primary steps are similar. A sample configuration for TCP encapsulation is shown in the following output. Note that the virtual ring is given the number 406 and has two remote peers and that the Marketing Segment on Token Ring 4/0 is linked to the virtual ring via the source-bridge command.

```
source-bridge ring-group 406
source-bridge remote-peer 406 tcp 10.100.105.254
source-bridge remote-peer 406 tcp 10.1.1.1

interface TokenRing4/0
 description Marketing Segment
 ip address 192.168.19.1 255.255.255.0
 no ip directed-broadcast
 no keepalive
 early-token-release
 ring-speed 16
 source-bridge 226 3 406
 source-bridge spanning
 source-bridge proxy-explorer
```

Network Design with DLSw

DLSw was developed to address some of the shortcomings in RSRB, and it is gaining popularity, but many organizations are resisting a changeover. This was likely the result of Year 2000 preparations and other new deployments that demand resources from organizations. In the context of network design, an entire chapter could be written regarding the proper installation and configuration of DLSw. However, for the purposes of the exam objectives, readers should be concerned only with a high-level understanding of the protocol itself. Consult RFC 1795 for additional information.

DLSw provides many features to the network designer. These include:

- Supports LLC2 termination, which eliminates the need for keepalives to cross WAN links. This feature provides functionality similar to local acknowledgement and also avoids timeouts, which are a significant concern to designers with the time-sensitive SNA protocol. The local router acknowledges frames.

- Supports SNA traffic over TCP, which adds reliability to the transport across WAN links.

- Supports NetBIOS over TCP; however, few implementations use this function.

- Provides for termination of the RIF (Routing Information Field). In RSRB, the RIF is incorporated into the WAN cloud. This feature limits SRB to seven hops. In DLSw, the RIF field is terminated in a virtual ring, which is the connection between two DLSw peer routers. This permits 13-hop installations; however, administrators should be cautioned that the RIF will be incomplete for troubleshooting. The greatest benefit to this feature is that explorer packets are contained on each side of the cloud, reducing traffic and preserving bandwidth.

- Permits load balancing and allows for backup peer routers.

- Is an open standard, and as such, it allows designers to interconnect different router brands.

In addition, Cisco offers enhanced DLSw features (referred to as DLSw+), including:

- Peer groups

- Border and on-demand peers

- Backward compatibility with STUN and RSRB

Of these enhanced features, designers may find backward compatibility useful in migrations from STUN or RSRB to DLSw, which is generally regarded as the superior methodology. Peer groups can also assist the design. Routers within a peer group work to permit "any-to-any" connectivity, but peer groups also can simplify configuration and optimize explorer packet processing.

Peer routers also can provide the designer with load balancing. When configured, the router will use a round-robin method to balance sessions on a connection basis. This requires equal-cost paths. If load balancing is not enabled, the router will use a single preferred path for all explorer packets.

The following output provides a sample DLSw configuration, where the ring group has been defined and the router has been configured as a local peer in the group. This configuration uses its loopback address in order to circumvent interface failures.

```
source-bridge ring-group 9
dlsw local-peer peer-id 10.12.24.1 (loopback)
dlsw remote-peer 0 tcp 10.14.10.1
dlsw remote-peer 0 tcp 10.10.18.1
dlsw bridge-group 9
```

It is very unlikely that the loopback interface will fail—unlike the physical interfaces. (Cisco defines the loopback as never failing, but sometimes an administrator will inadvertently delete the interface or remove its address.) Use of the loopback can greatly enhance the reliability and supportability of the router. The loopback notation in the previous output reflects the IP address of the router's loopback interface—LO0. This is administratively assigned, as opposed to the traditional IP loopback of 127.0.0.1.

Redundancy as a Design Consideration

The critical nature of mainframes in modern networks mandates the use of redundant links for connectivity. In IP-based mainframe installations, this function frequently incorporates the use of VIPA, or virtual IP addressing. In SNA environments, other techniques are used.

One of the most fundamental redundancy techniques in SNA designs is to install dual front-end processors (FEP). Given the critical nature of the FEP in the network, this is a reasonable precaution.

When dual FEPs are configured, they use the *same* locally administered address (LAA). The client, when sending an explorer packet, will connect to the first FEP that responds via the RIF.

NOTE
The RIF provides a hop-by-hop path through the Layer 2 network. This path is comprised of ring numbers and bridge numbers.

The SNA session will not recover automatically from a failure of the host FEP. However, clients can reattach to the other FEP with a simple explorer packet and reconnect. These types of installations work best if each FEP has at least two TICs (Token Ring interface couplers) and two routers. Each TIC is configured with a presence on each ring serviced by the routers. This configuration is illustrated in Figure 10.3. Ring 100 is shown in the thicker lines, whereas ring 200 is shown with thinner lines. The connections to the mainframe are omitted for clarity. Note that routers are shown in the diagram, but SNA is not routable and the frames are truly bridged.

Redundant SNA designs may also make use of dual backbone rings. Under this design, the connections to the FEPs are available with partial ring failures. Bridge failures are also addressed. This design is illustrated at a high level in Figure 10.4.

FIGURE 10.3 Redundant dual front-end processors

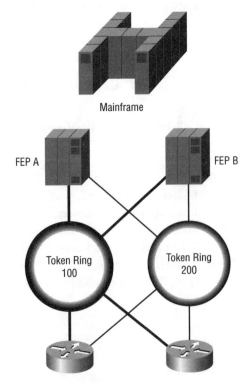

FIGURE 10.4 Redundant dual backbones

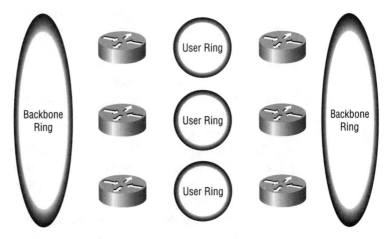

Experienced designers should be quick to note that explorer packets could be problematic under this design. This problem would be best controlled with a restriction on the hop count for explorer packets. Presuming that the FEPs and servers are connected directly to the backbones (a common, albeit suboptimal, configuration), the maximum hop explorer count could be set at one. Connectivity between all user rings and the backbone would be available, but connectivity between clients would be blocked if it attempted to leave the ring. These installations typically place servers directly on the user rings.

A variation on the dual backbone design is the dual, collapsed-backbone design. This configuration establishes a virtual ring within each router to bridge the physical user rings and the rings that connect to the FEPs. The failure of either router, or its virtual ring, is covered by the other router and its connections.

Queuing as a Design Consideration

Many designers find that the time-sensitive nature of SNA is problematic when merging the protocol to interoperate with other protocols. This is one of the reasons that local acknowledgement and encapsulation are beneficial to the designer.

There are times and installations when the designer does not wish to use these techniques to control SNA traffic. For these instances, the designer may wish to employ queuing to provide a higher priority to SNA traffic—reducing the delay experienced in the router's buffer. Both queuing types are best suited for lower bandwidth serial connections.

Priority queuing is a process-switched solution to queuing. Four output interface queues are established, and the processor removes frames from the queue with the highest priority. The queues are named and sequenced as high, medium, normal, and low.

This type of queuing is best suited to installations where SNA traffic is of the greatest importance to the company, as other traffic will be discarded in order to accommodate the higher priority queue. Should the designer find that packets are consistently dropped, the solution would be to install more bandwidth. The benefit may still remain, however. SNA traffic would, all things being equal, have less latency than other protocols.

It is important to note that priority queuing is very CPU-intensive and requires frames to be process-switched. This is the slowest switching method available on the router. It is also possible that protocols in the lower priority queues will not be serviced and the frames will be dropped.

Figure 10.5 illustrates priority queuing. Note that SNA traffic has been given high priority and, as a result, sends all packets into the queue before IP and IPX.

FIGURE 10.5 Priority queuing

Custom queuing is also available to prioritize SNA traffic and is processor-intensive. However, it is less likely to completely block traffic from lower priority protocols. Rather than allocate all of the available bandwidth to a single high-priority queue, custom queuing defines up to 16 output interface queues that are accessed in sequence. The number of bytes permitted per sequence provides the prioritization. For example, the administrator wishes to provide roughly 75 percent of the circuit to SNA (RSRB) and the remainder to IP.

Under these objectives, the queue for SNA could be defined as 4,500 bytes, while 1,500 are allocated to IP. Individual installations and experience will help to develop the final parameters, but the installation makes certain that SNA receives service, as a function of bandwidth, 75 percent of the time.

Figure 10.6 demonstrates custom queuing. Note that SNA has been allocated 50 percent of the queue priority, while IP and IPX each have 25 percent of the queue. As a result, the last SNA packet must wait until the IP and IPX packets in the queue have been processed. Note that the right side of Figure 10.6 is read from right to left—the rightmost side shows the first packet exiting the router. Assuming full queues, this results in an SNA packet, an SNA packet, an IP packet, and an IPX packet, given the percentages above. This process will continue so long as all queues are filled.

FIGURE 10.6 Custom queuing

Designers are apt to place queuing at the access layer of the network. This placement typically results in the least performance degradation and is consistent with the hierarchical model. However, in practice, queuing is configured when and where it makes the most sense to do so—perhaps ahead of a slow serial link or at an aggregation point. Because queuing is not a zero-sum gain, i.e., there is a significant cost associated with it, most designers and administers avoid using either type of queue unless there is a specific reason to do so.

It is also noteworthy that priority queuing should be regarded as a last-resort option and that queuing impacts only outbound traffic. High volumes of high-priority traffic in priority queuing will block all other traffic—it is better to use custom queuing so that all traffic is serviced.

Advanced Peer-to-Peer Networking

Advanced Peer-to-Peer Networking (APPN) was developed to provide a mechanism for routing SNA traffic along with other protocols. It was typically implemented in order to link two end stations—the benefit being that the mainframe was no longer required as an intermediary. IBM developed the protocol so that administrators wouldn't need to spend as much time predefining paths and systems, although some configurations could quickly lead to problems and quickly become more complex. The protocol also offered enhanced classes of service and mechanisms for clustering traffic into sub-areas.

While APPN is being presented in the past tense, designers should make no mistake in presuming that it is a dead protocol. Many large organizations with their roots in mainframe-based systems continue to use APPN today, although new applications are typically written for IP. Therefore, designers should be familiar with a few of the concepts behind APPN. Table 10.2 defines the more common components of APPN.

TABLE 10.2 APPN Concepts

Service	Function
CP	The control point (CP) activates nodes or resources between nodes. The CP is also responsible for handling deactivations and the exchange of information between nodes, including topology information.
NN	The network node (NN) is an APPN router. It is responsible for locating and connecting sessions and resources. The NN is a PU 2.1 control point.
EN	The end node (EN) is effectively the application host, and it accesses the network via the NN. The EN does not participate in topology maintenance functions, including rerouting; however, it contains other APPN functionality. The EN is also a PU 2.1 control point.

TABLE 10.2 APPN Concepts *(continued)*

Service	Function
LEN	The low-entry networking (LEN) node allows connectivity between two stations. It is a peer node that does not rely on VTAM, such as the AS/400 and the System 36. It is somewhat limited in functionality—for example, it cannot provide routing services, nor can it use an NN server without a predefined resource.
CNN	The Composite Network Node (CNN) defines APPN functionality in VTAM. A combined NCP and CNN can operate as an NN.

SNASw

For years, application developers and network designers used advanced peer-to-peer networking (APPN) to link mainframe resources and other devices in the network. These solutions worked reasonably well, but they were generally difficult to configure and troubleshoot. Cisco recently announced SNASw, or Systems Network Architecture Switching Services. It transports SNA packets across IP networks and promises to simplify many of the negative aspects of APPN. Cisco also views SNASw as a possible migration path toward complete IP connectivity on the mainframe. SNASw was developed in concert with IBM.

Network Design in the Real World: SNA

While the predicted demise of the mainframe was quite premature, it is apparent that the predicted departure of SNA from the network horizon is well under way. Many shops continue to use the protocol in order to support legacy applications, but the clear majority of firms have migrated to IP.

One of the critical features in IP-based mainframe connectivity is redundancy. One option in this vein is VIPA, or virtual IP addressing. In a VIPA installation, a subnet is created within the host itself, and two distinct subnets are attached to the virtual subnet—typically via the Cisco Channel Interface Processor (CIP) and ESCON connections, which greatly improve the performance of the connection between the routed network and the mainframe. However, there are other options. VIPA provides for router, CIP, ESCON interface, and ESCON connection failures, as the virtual subnet is available via the alternative path. Note that the alternative path is not used just for backup—VIPA can facilitate load balancing as well.

Designers should plan for these implementations with care, noting that the mainframe IP stack typically does not support advanced or proprietary routing protocols. Therefore, it is likely that static routes or RIP redistribution will be necessary on the router.

The router may also front-end TN3270 connections to the mainframe. This removes some of the processing overhead required for terminal access.

Summary

This chapter addressed many of the issues that involve mainframe connectivity in modern network design. These issues included an overview of the encapsulation methods available for SNA traffic and the frequent need for redundancy in these installations.

This chapter also addressed the common design criteria and options associated with mainframe installations and the SNA protocol, including:

- RSRB

- DLSw

- APPN

- Redundancy

- Queuing

Due to both the history of RSRB and its foundation in the other protocols, designers are encouraged to make certain that they feel comfortable with RSRB from a practical perspective as well as an exam perspective. Even in organizations that have migrated to newer protocols, the concepts embedded in RSRB offer a strong foundation for the designer and administrator.

Review Questions

1. The designer is concerned about reliability and is interested in local acknowledgement. Which of the following encapsulations would be the best choice?

   A. IP FST

   B. Direct

   C. TCP

   D. Local SRB

2. Which of the following is true regarding custom queuing?

   A. Bandwidth is guaranteed to SNA only.

   B. Bandwidth is guaranteed to Layer 3 protocols only.

   C. Four queues prioritize traffic.

   D. Bandwidth is allocated more fairly than with priority queuing.

3. In a dual FEP design, which of the following is true?

   A. Routers must use HSRP.

   B. The LAA is the same on both FEPs.

   C. The LAA must be different on both FEPs.

   D. Both FEPs must be running VTAM.

4. A risk in priority queuing is:

   A. Protocols in the lower priority queues will not be serviced and the frames will be dropped.

   B. Bandwidth will be consumed to maintain information regarding the queue.

   C. Compression, required on priority queues, will consume too much processor.

   D. The fast switching table will be corrupted.

5. When designing a redundant network using dual backbones, designers are cautioned:

   A. Against using dual FEPs

   B. Against using SNA

   C. Against leaving explorer packet forwarding at its defaults

   D. Against leaving the LU forwarding metric at its defaults

6. All packets in priority queuing are:

   A. Fast switched

   B. Process switched

   C. Switched via NetFlow on T1 or greater links

   D. Distributed switched on VIP-2 40 modules

7. DLSw+ peer groups provide which of the following benefits?

   A. Any-to-any connectivity

   B. Easier configuration

   C. Optimized explorer packet processing

   D. All of the above

8. Peer group DLSw configurations provide for:

   A. Unequal-cost load balancing

   B. Equal-cost load balancing

   C. Per-packet forwarding

   D. Per-packet forwarding over unequal-cost paths

9. STUN local acknowledgement provides which of the following benefits?

A. Prevention of application timeouts

B. Packet conversion

C. Compression

D. Encryption

10. An LAA is:

A. An SNA DLSw address

B. A locally administered IP address

C. A locally administered MAC address

D. Stored on the TIC only

11. True or false: Dual FEPs can use the same LAA.

A. True

B. False

12. True or false: The odds of packet loss are greater for lower priority packets with priority queuing than with custom queuing.

A. True

B. False

13. The RIF field:

A. Marks a frame as modified by DLSw

B. Marks a frame as discard eligible

C. Provides a hop-by-hop path through the bridged network

D. Provides a hop-by-hop path through the routed network

14. Local acknowledgement is available with which of the following encapsulations?

   A. STUN

   B. RSRB

   C. DLSw

   D. All of the above

15. Which of the following techniques may be used to provide redundancy in mainframe installations?

   A. Dual front-end processors

   B. Dual backbone rings

   C. Dual Token Ring interface cards

   D. All of the above

16. SSCP is part of which of the following?

   A. TIC

   B. FEP

   C. VTAM

   D. PU

17. APPN provides which function?

   A. End station-to-end station connectivity, sans host

   B. SNA routing

   C. SNA encapsulation

   D. A and B

   E. A and C

18. A Cisco router can terminate physical mainframe connections:

  A. Via the channel interface processor

  B. Via the PA FE-ISL adapter

  C. Only via TCP/IP

  D. By forcing DTR high on all serial connections, including ESCON

19. True or false: Ethernet contains a RIF.

  A. True

  B. False

20. Priority queuing might be used by the network designer:

  A. To provide basic service quality to SNA packets

  B. To compress data in order to conserve bandwidth

  C. To add an encryption algorithm to the packet flow

  D. To intentionally discard packets based on packet type

Answers to Review Questions

1. C.
2. D.
3. B.
4. A.
5. C.
6. B.
7. D.
8. B.
9. A.
10. C.
11. A.
12. A.
13. C.
14. D.
15. D.
16. C.
17. D.
18. A.
19. B.
20. A.

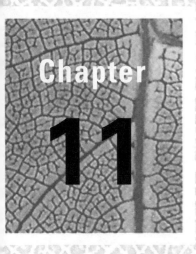

Chapter 11

Designing Secure Networks

CISCO INTERNETWORK DESIGN EXAM OBJECTIVES COVERED IN THIS CHAPTER:

- ✓ Examine a client's security requirements and recommend firewalls and gateways.

- ✓ Design a firewall system using packet-filtered routers and bastion hosts.

- ✓ Choose protocols to be filtered on routers in the firewall.

As touched upon in Chapter 1, security is a component of network design that overshadows every other facet of the network. Thus, it is imperative to consider data security from the onset of any design. While it is possible to add security to a strong network design, this tactic typically incorporates compromises. These compromises start with the security model itself and ultimately lead to significant changes in the overall network design.

Since every network is different, it is up to each designer to evaluate the security needs of their own networks. Also important to consider are the network's interrelationships with other components, including routing protocols, operating systems, and physical security. Physical security is as important as the logical components designers typically consider—the best access list is void if the hacker can physically access the router, for example.

Primarily, this chapter focuses on the generic, conceptual level of network security. Don't make the mistake of considering this chapter a comprehensive dissertation on the subject. It would be easy to compose a complete text on network security, and many authors have. Yet for the exam, this presentation provides sufficient information and yields some additional elements to help apply this material in a production network. For example, one specific area that warrants more treatment than is required for the CID exam is interoperability between firewalls and Cisco routers. Readers may wish to explore the issues surrounding this topic and consider how it applies to the Cisco-centric view. For instance, most firewalls do not support EIGRP. This automatically results in a requirement to use static routes or a redistribution of EIGRP into a more universally supported routing protocol—typically RIP or OSPF. This fact could significantly alter a security design.

The majority of this text addresses the concept of TCP/IP security, which clearly does not present a complete security solution. However, many of the ideas presented herein are applicable to the broader demands of data protection.

Understanding Security Threats

In order to understand the data security component of networking, it is important to view threats to the network as internal or external. An *internal threat* is one that uses privileged information to gain access from the outside or an attack that starts from an internal, trusted network. An *external threat* is one that uses an untrusted access point, such as the Internet, to gain access to the corporate network.

Some attacks may use a combination of internal and external means to gain access to data. For example, a fired employee may use his internal knowledge of the network to gain access via an outside connection. According to security experts, most attacks involve at least some inside information or access.

Corporations must realize that data security is an interesting legal problem. Many countries have not developed adequate regulations to make hacking a crime. Unfortunately, this results in little recourse when an attack is successful. While the legal system is catching up to the incredible pace of change, it is preferable to prevent as many attacks as possible and to capture as much information as possible.

This text uses "hacking" in a generic context to encompass all types of unauthorized entry into computer systems, including phreaking (phone hacking) and cracking.

Designing for Network Security

All security models must start with a policy—a statement of what will and will not be permitted within the network. The best way to approach this is with a security document that clearly spells out the terms of the policy. This may be very detailed, spelling out each and every element of the policy, or it may be intentionally vague, simply framing the general authorizations. Unfortunately, few organizations actually take the time to compose such a document, and when it is written, it remains fairly static—meaning that it outlines a historical policy, rather than one that keeps up with the ever-changing landscape.

As if the lack of documentation wasn't discouraging enough, many architects and managers find that the senior business management will not sign even the most basic of security documents. This typically results from fear—either a lack of understanding or the desire to not take responsibility should the network be compromised. This places any and all technical solutions at grave risk.

When the business has not predefined the expectations of the security solution, it cannot succeed. In addition, each time a specific business desires to add new services, there will need to be a new evaluation of the request and risk—a time-consuming and politically charged proposition.

Rather than dwell on the importance of good company politics in security designs, this section addresses other single points in perimeter protection, including:

- Firewalls
- The Cisco PIX (Packet Internetwork Exchange)
- Access lists

In addition to physical security, complete security models must also include server and workstation operating system security. This chapter approaches this with discussions of encryption, host security, and authentication and authorization.

Perimeter security, establishing a border around the trusted network, typically uses a *firewall* to thwart attacks. The purpose of the firewall is to implement policy and provide the administrator with a single point from which to control access. An important consideration for the designer is to not make this a single point-of-failure in the installation. Figure 11.1

illustrates a typical, single-system firewall deployment. In this case, the firewall actually uses two components—the router and a distinct firewall device (the Cisco PIX, which is discussed in detail later in this chapter).

FIGURE 11.1 A simple firewall deployment

Internal Network   Cisco PIX   Cisco Router with Access List   Internet

While the perimeter devices shown in Figure 11.1 include only a router and a firewall, production installations generally include some or all of the following:

- Firewalls

- Bastion hosts or public servers

- Routers with access lists

- Demilitarized zones (DMZs)

- Isolation LANs

- Proxy servers

- Middleware servers

- Load balancers

In order to contrast the potential complexity of a firewall deployment, refer to Figure 11.2. In this diagram, the firewall policy is distributed across a wide array of devices and includes dual ISP connections, dual DMZs (demilitarized zones—a concept of no man's land taken from the warfare arena), connections to internal resources, Web server redirection and redistribution, and internal connectivity.

FIGURE 11.2 A complex firewall deployment

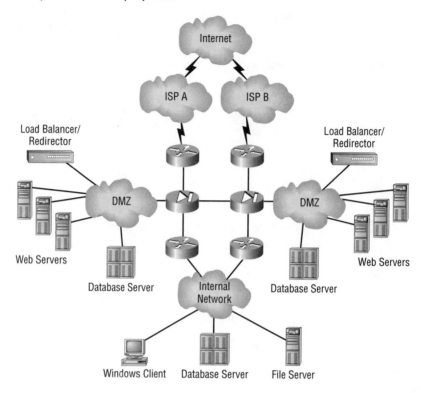

In their purest sense, DMZs do not have implied trust for any organization—all resources are suspect. A bastion host would be found in the DMZ. You may note that Figure 11.2 includes redirectors and redistribution resources, devices that help scale the Web server farm to support millions of connections. Most designers today must consider the inclusion of these resources in their designs, although this information is beyond the scope of the exam. Redirectors serve a single uniform resource locator (URL) and redirect users to one of many servers. This provides a simple load-balancing mechanism.

It may not be readily apparent, but the security offered by the network in Figure 11.2 is poor at best. The illustration is not intended to show a good design, but rather one that uses various components.

Implementing a Security Policy

There is more to implementing a security policy than purchasing and installing a firewall, even if the deployment is limited to this single mechanism. The implementation needs to include the policy itself, the acquisition and configuration of the various components, and installation, testing, and auditing.

An effective security policy, which provides a road map for the actual security deployment, should include the following elements:

A simple, fault-tolerant design   This design does not necessarily require redundant systems, but should include solid hardware components and battery backup systems. In addition, if the staff is familiar with Unix, it makes little sense to implement an NT-based firewall. The reverse is also true. The exception to this rule is performance and inherent security; many NT firewalls lag behind their Unix counterparts in terms of performance. Note that dedicated hardware platforms, including Cisco's PIX, are also an option. However, new hardware often requires additional training.

Expense relative to the required security   It makes little sense to spend $500,000 to secure $40,000 worth of information. However, designers must include the cost of downtime and lost productivity in their calculations. In addition, it is hard to quantify raw data costs; sometimes planners need to use another determination metric, such as market capitalization, to bolster their case. This guideline also relates to the amount of security required—most expensive solutions provide many features that would go unused in smaller organizations.

Understanding what data should be accessible by outsiders   This step should be part of the initial security document described in the beginning of this chapter, though a more thorough understanding will be required. In addition, it is appropriate to consider access methodologies including private circuits, encryption, and single-use authentication.

Strong monitoring and logging features   The best firewall solutions are worthless if the administrator is not warned of an attack or breach. This part of the security policy may directly relate to the cost of the solution, though not necessarily. Available to the administrator are several affordable options, which may consist of little more than syslog (system log) output. More expensive solutions typically provide filtering and other features to reduce the volume of messages requiring the administrator's attention.

It may be appropriate to hire a dedicated specialist to address your firm's security needs. This person may be an employee reassigned from another position, a new hire, or a consultant. Consultants may yield the cheapest deployment given their experience with different organizations and equipment. If you hire a consultant, make sure that they warrant the trust that your firm will be placing in them and that everything they do is documented. It is always a good idea to conduct a thorough background review, as well as to check references. Non-disclosure agreements are also helpful, though it may be difficult to provide sufficient legal proof of breach for this to fully protect the organization.

Always have a second person trained on the security systems and technology. People leave jobs and fall ill—either way, there will be a lack of support.

Detecting and Addressing Attacks

The best security plans include an auditable and verifiable component. It is one thing to prevent the attack in the first place, but if the administrator cannot ascertain that all attacks have been unsuccessful, there is a significant risk to the corporation.

Logging is one of the best methods for capturing the techniques used in an attack and for determining which resources were compromised. However, administrators must realize that truly skilled hackers can easily hide their activity or purge the logs if they are improperly stored. Thus, logs should *always* be written to a separate system with another layer of security between devices.

Logs should always be written to a secure server other than to the firewall itself. Once the firewall is compromised, a hacker can easily purge the log files, which are the best form of documentation for criminal prosecution.

Honey Pots

Remember Winnie-the-Pooh? He was a stuffed bear that came to life and, like most bears, loved honey. One of many themes in the Pooh stories was Winnie getting stuck because of his love of honey; one tale had his arm trapped in a honey pot, a vessel with a small opening used for storing honey.

Well, in the network security arena, honey pots build upon this very idea: Attackers want the honey, and they may get trapped if they try to obtain it.

Basically, the *honey pot* is a special fictional system designed to appear like the corporate data being sought—and designed to be hacked. Once an attack is detected by the firewall, the system redirects the session to the fictional data and invokes additional logging to capture information regarding the attack and the hacker.

This recent trend in data security provides two benefits. First, the hacker thinks he's successful when in fact the live data is still protected. Second, detailed information regarding the attack hacker is obtained for authorities. This information may include:

- Traceroute and ping information regarding the attacker

- DNS information regarding the attacker's host

- Detailed logs of every command and application used in the attack

- Time and date of the attack

- Real-time notification of the attack

- Finger, whois, and other information regarding the attacker

Unfortunately, for the average designer/administrator, little may come from documenting an attack, especially if the attack is launched from another country. The U.S. legal system is just now starting to discover the limitations of local laws in international events, and the majority of the written laws fail to address computing and networking at all. In fact, a California district attorney recently used a horse-trading law from over 100 years ago to charge a man who allegedly ran fraudulent auctions on the Internet—no other regulation was relevant.

Another problem that honey pots do not address is that some software still focuses on port scans from a single IP address to trigger an attack warning. Many hackers have gotten together to launch large-scale attacks with scans originating from hundreds of machines, fooling the software into thinking that there are a lot of "dumb users" out there. This type of attack should be considered in feature evaluations when selecting a firewall vendor.

Network Design in the Real World: Social Engineering Attacks

If it wasn't clear from the first chapter, I will state here and now that I enjoy the humanistic side of business and computing as much as the technical. In fact, I think that I'd be bored if I only built networks and couldn't deal with the human issues.

So now you're saying, "Who cares?" Fine, but let me explain anyway. I note the dual-faceted nature of my career as an introduction to the *social engineering attack*—an attack methodology that can defeat even the best firewalls. I love it because it is simple and proves once again that mice can become smarter than the mousetrap. Different social engineering attacks work in different ways, but my two favorites are the fake circuit and the CEO support attacks.

The *fake circuit attack* actually occurs with the installation of a real circuit (despite its misleading name); it typically hits small, remote offices with little or no on-site support. The attack succeeds because most corporations fail to work with the staff in these locations when it comes to networking. Generally, attackers using this technique pose as telephone company employees and pretend to install a new T1 for an "upgrade project." In reality, the circuit is simply a short connection that connects to a cheap piece of hardware installed by the hacker. Wireless technology has made this technique even easier, but the net gain from the attack is internal access to the corporate data system.

The *CEO support attack* is a work of wonder. As with the fake circuit attack, it operates on the premise that most people want to be helpful. The attacker selects a victim and calls the secretary of the CEO or other executive who likely has a high level of access to the company systems. The cover story is that the CEO reported a problem with an application on their machine, and the attacker, posing as a member of technical support, wishes to test the modifications on the server to make sure the problem was resolved correctly. Once given the password, the hacker can then use another access method, perhaps a dial-in line, to gain access to the company's information. This attack works best if the attacker appears to be calling from an internal number. However, it works in many cases because the secretary wants to help and the administrator could always get to the files anyway—the presumption being that server administrators can access all files on the server, regardless of ownership or rights.

You may be asking what good a system password is if the hacker does not have access to the system. Good point. Ask yourself what happens if the remote access system uses the bindery/NDS or NT directory for authentication—the attacker gets in through the same system designed to prevent such an attack. Again, even the best firewalls will fail to flag this type of scenario, and ultimately some data may be compromised.

Security Design Failures

In general, most security designs fail for at least one of the following reasons:

- The solution or issue is misunderstood.
- Securing against the threat is too complex.
- Securing against the threat is too costly.
- The design poses a threat to other corporate structures.
- Data security is superseded by other objectives within the organization.

Most corporations have very detailed security plans that are signed by every employee under threats of termination and prosecution for violators. Unfortunately, more often than not, these documents are unenforced. Note that these documents are different from a security policy statement.

Consider the following corporate security issues as they relate to three specific categories.

- Corruption of data, typically in the form of introducing erroneous information

  - Viruses

  - Destruction of data, typically in the form of deleting files

- Theft of data

  - Leakage of proprietary information

  - Theft/destruction of computing resources

- Abuse of data/access

  - Employee access abuse

  - Unauthorized access by outsiders

  - Access abuse by non-employee authorized users

  - Hacking of phone/PBX/VM. The PBX, or public branch exchange, and the voice mail (VM) system can provide the attacker with free phone access or a means to tarnish the corporate image—consider the impact if everyone's voice mail announced to callers that the company went bankrupt.

At first glance, there would appear to be little a network designer could do to thwart all of the above items other than understand the corporate culture and assist in the education of both management and workers. In fact, most network administrators and designers hold to the premise that the network is not a security device, and to a certain degree an argument in favor of this position can be made. However, as with most other problems, a solution that involves various components can frequently address the issue better than a single option. In this vein, designs may incorporate services or options that each address a part of the problem.

For example, consider the first security issue—corruption of data. Clearly, a good backup strategy is the best solution to this problem, because an off-site, near real-time copy of the data counteracts the damage done by fires, floods, and user errors (including the inevitable deletion of that critical sales file). However, this solution does not offer a prevention phase—a chance to prevent the problem from occurring. The network designer may choose a firewall/proxy product that incorporates virus scanning of all files that are accessed from the Internet, yet this solution will fail to address *all* virus infections—a floppy brought in by an employee could quickly circumvent all detection efforts at the firewall.

Network Design in the Real World: Network Attacks

A recent ZDNet publication provided hackers with the opportunity to attack a specially established network with a typical security model. The site provided Linux- and NT-based Web servers and used general firewall software, in addition to application-level security, on each server.

The first successful attack made on this network did not defeat the front-end firewall or any of the access lists on the routers—two typical security methods used by network designers and administrators. These devices blocked the failed attempts and permitted only the approved traffic to access the site.

The attackers ultimately created a suidroot shell (a means to gain root, or super-user access) in a directory accessible by the hacker. While this required a fairly detailed level of CGI, C, and Linux knowledge, the attack showed how easy it is to defeat the network designer's primary tools. Few network architects concern themselves with server security, but a partnership with the groups that do can significantly improve the overall security model.

There are a number of ways to reduce the likelihood of a successful network attack. First, most servers provide information to all systems regarding their operating system version and applications. A hacker may use this information to find bugs and opportunities specific to that software. Designers and server administrators should work together to block all unnecessary identification information from being sent to clients.

Second, many of the techniques used in this case study were published and/or patched mere days before the attack. While such monitoring is impractical, a technician constantly monitoring the various hacking Web sites may discover a technique to defeat the attack in time to implement a solution. Many companies rely on their vendors to perform this task, though restrictive permissions on the server and firewall can greatly diminish the number of techniques that can be used. To provide the best security for the corporation, security technicians and designers must become hackers themselves—similar to the way law enforcement officers profile criminals—although this activity must be balanced with the other tasks required by the organization.

A colleague at Cisco likes to cite the quote "The question isn't if you're paranoid. The question is, 'Are you paranoid enough?'" Well-placed paranoia can be a very useful tool so long as it does not result in paralysis.

Network Security Solutions

A wide array of tools and methods are available to the network designer for providing protection against attacks. This section presents a number of solutions for the network designer to consider and use as part of an overall security model. Firewalls, the Cisco PIX, caching, access lists, address translation, and encryption can all work together to provide a strong security presence.

Firewalls

Firewalls have been regarded as the sole critical protection from the evils of the Internet. While firewalls are helpful, this position is inaccurate. Firewalls do not provide complete protection from external threats. They offer a single point of attack, and, according to the latest surveys (1998), most attacks avoid the firewall as a contention point altogether. These attacks may be accomplished via dial-up, social engineering, or backdoor tactics, but the net result is the same.

In addition, most firewalls are deployed without concern to internal threats. Designers should always consider the possibility of internally sourced attacks, including those that exploit internal systems from the out-side—an attack scenario that starts with an external host compromising an internal, trusted host and then using that trusted host to attack another inter-nal resource.

The best firewalls offer the designer solid security options with easy administration and configuration. Application-level firewalls go far beyond the basic protocol-based selection process available from a router. For exam-ple, many firewalls can block Java applets within HTTP streams—the router could only permit or deny HTTP. A router cannot block Java or ActiveX applets, nor can it provide virus-scanning functions. Many firewalls can pro-vide these services.

Protecting the Router-Based Firewall

There are many arguments in favor of using firewalls as opposed to routers for protecting the perimeter of a network. For our purposes, a firewall has awareness beyond Layer 4, while also performing a routing function.

Cisco has introduced the IOS Firewall Feature Set, which adds some firewall functionality to the basic port filtering available in access lists. Designers will have to evaluate the appropriateness of this solution against other systems, including Gauntlet, Sidewinder, the Cisco PIX, and Checkpoint.

However, even with these systems it is important to provide whatever protection you can for the firewall itself. This frequently warrants some con-figuration of the router for basic, front-line security. Your efforts should include the following:

- Use static routes. This protects against route spoofing, where the attacker redirects data to resources they control. Route spoofing is one of the top techniques used by internal hackers.

- Do not configure the router for additional services, including TFTP.

- Disable Telnet access to the router and use a locally attached console. If this is not practical, use an access list to permit a handful of addresses to the VTY interfaces, and then allow only data flowing into the internal interface from an authorized source.

- Disable *small servers* on the router. Cisco considers a number of services to be part of the small servers keyword, including the echo and finger services.

- Use the password-encryption features, ideally using TACACS+ for authentication.

- Disable proxy ARP.

- Disable or strengthen security on SNMP services. Deny these services on the external interface.

- Block Telnet access to internal resources from external hosts and the firewall. Blocking firewall-sourced Telnet sessions requires placing a router inside the firewall; once compromised, the firewall can no longer be trusted to provide this protection.

In addition, administrators should invoke interface-level access lists on the front-line router. These access lists should protect both the front-line router and the firewall. The only drawback to this method is reduced router performance, though placing a short list on a reasonable routing platform should add only negligible delay. NetFlow and other technologies can reduce the impact of access lists on router performance and should be evaluated against the specific hardware in use. Inbound access lists can impact performance more than outbound ones; however, it is more secure to block on the inbound interface, and doing so negates the need for a routing lookup. The specific placement of access lists in your network will depend on the type of router, the type of IOS, and the level of security required.

Network Design in the Real World: SNMP Security

When working for a fairly small company, I had a small router connected to an Internet Service Provider—a router that also functioned as a limited firewall. The ISP recommended that they monitor our router for us, since we had no 24-hour staffing and no remote monitoring services at the time. I recommended that we allow only pings for monitoring, but I was outvoted and soon enabled SNMP using the ISP's default passwords.

Needless to say, the access list rules were disabled within three months, and we were unfiltered to the Internet. We caught the problem as part of a weekly, manually initiated audit process—the syslog feature on the router was unreliable. (Note that this was not a Cisco router, although the same problems could exist on a Cisco-based platform.) The router was compromised because it was protected from SNMP attacks only by a simple, unencrypted password (clear-text) and an IP address restriction. Further, while the ISP never admitted that it had been hacked, there is little doubt that someone (either inside or outside the ISP) compromised the machine (or spoofed the IP address) that was given access and used it to attack us.

The immediate response to this attack was to disable the SNMP mechanism and re-enable the filters. A full audit of all systems did not detect any further compromises.

Designers should take a few lessons away from this story. First, don't trust an ISP or any outside source to be secure. This is *very* hard to implement in practice—I worked on one network where the ISP *was* the maintainer of the firewall, and the IS staff was completely blocked from any involvement. This is a very poor practice, though many companies lack the internal staff resources necessary to properly maintain a firewall. In my opinion, when this function gets outsourced, the mindset shifts to one of blame distribution rather than security, which is never good.

The second lesson is to always push for another solution. I didn't do this once management had made their decision, though I knew that SNMP was not secure (since version 2 uses clear-text passwords), and neither was a single-firewall router design. Unfortunately, I was unsuccessful in getting the budget for an internal firewall or the proper resources to manage and monitor the router.

The Cisco PIX

Cisco provides a *stateful-inspection* firewall with its Packet Internetwork Exchange (PIX) product line. Stateful-inspection firewalls do not examine each packet through the application layer—rather, they analyze the beginning of the data flow and then maintain information about that flow's state. *State* is comprised of IP addresses, sequence numbers, and ports used. The benefit of the stateful-inspection firewall is that it is typically much faster than application-level firewalls; however, any additional features, including caching and virus checking, have to be provided by external devices.

The PIX's features provide many benefits for the network designer. It is important to note that it is possible to install the PIX with only two IP addresses—one on the internal interface and one on the external. In addition, the administrator can interconnect PIX boxes for fail-over (which provides redundancy) and the integrated *Network Address Translation* (NAT) function (see Figure 11.3). NAT permits addresses to be changed and remapped at the translation device—a handy feature that allows the use of RFC 1918 (InterNIC-registered) addresses on the internal network while retaining Internet connectivity, although this requires a larger pool of IP addresses. Figure 11.3 illustrates the conversion process undertaken by a packet traversing the translation device.

FIGURE 11.3 Network Address Translation

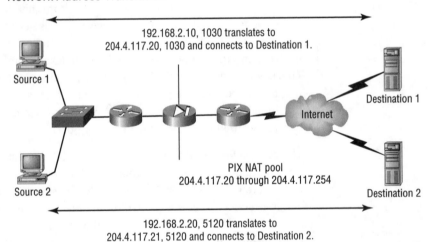

The PIX also supports PAT, or *Port Address Translation* (see Figure 11.4). This feature is interesting in that a single IP address on the firewall can service all of the external connections, yielding a significant savings in total IP address allocations. PAT works by assigning each session a unique port number that maps to the IP address on the internal interface. Note that Figure 11.4 differs from 11.3 in that only the TCP port number is changed—the same IP address is used on the external interface. This duplication conserves addresses on the public network.

FIGURE 11.4 Port Address Translation

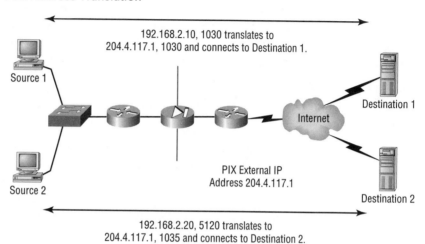

192.168.2.10, 1030 translates to
204.4.117.1, 1030 and connects to Destination 1.

Source 1

Destination 1

Internet

PIX External IP
Address 204.4.117.1

Source 2

Destination 2

192.168.2.20, 5120 translates to
204.4.117.1, 1035 and connects to Destination 2.

Destination 2 believes it is speaking only
to 204.4.117.1, 1035—it is completely
unaware of the PAT process.

It is important to consider the types of traffic that will traverse a device providing PAT and NAT services. FTP, HTTP, and Telnet all operate well in this configuration; however, NetBIOS-based services, including Windows naming services, will not function properly. It is likely that this problem will be addressed as corporations migrate to Active Directory and Windows 2000.

As noted previously, the PIX also provides for failure of the firewall in redundant configurations. This is accomplished with an interconnect cable and is somewhat limited in that both PIX boxes must be in close proximity. Thus, this solution addresses hardware and most software failures, yet it provides no protection from site and facilities failures.

Caching

While bandwidth is becoming cheaper and more widely available, there are still many benefits to *caching*. When data is cached, the data elements are copied and provided from sources closer to the requestor. The *cache* is the collection of data elements that are provided.

Consider a Web page with three large graphics. It takes 10 seconds to download those graphics across the Internet with a T1. If a company cached Web traffic, the first employee would take 10 seconds to load the page, but each subsequent employee would receive it in a fraction of that time—perhaps a single second. The cache serves the data from a local resource, rather than requiring another transfer from a remote location. This results in more efficient use of the T1, the Internet, and the Web server, while providing the user a better response time.

Internet Service Providers have begun to place caches in their networks to further accelerate the distribution of data. This method again improves performance and yields a cheaper solution. Consider caches as you would commuting options. Adding lanes for more cars is significantly less efficient than using a train, bus, or ferry. While there are times when bigger pipes are required, it is best to evaluate the actual need. There are also instances where it's best to take another tack—personally, I look at adding extra lanes for cars like I do combating obesity by getting larger pants. The same is true in networking—more bandwidth will not decrease the performance bottleneck caused by large, uncompressed graphics.

From a security perspective, caching can be problematic, although this problem is diminishing as the technology advances. The original issue was that pages viewed were stored on the caching server and could be viewed without authentication. As more sites employ Secure Hypertext Transfer Protocol (HTTPS) and non-caching flags, this problem should subside. Administrators can reduce this risk by securing the caching server as they would any other corporate resource.

Access Lists

An *access list* provides the ability to block or permit traffic based on address, port number, and/or the concept of established communications. There is no awareness of upper-layer protocols, and thus protection against application-layer attacks is not available. A significant number of companies continue to use router access lists as the sole means of securing their networks. Yet, while such lists certainly belong in most security deployments, the access list itself is fairly limited.

One of the misunderstood components in an access list is the established keyword—there is no bona fide established bit or validation of sequence numbers. Rather, the established keyword requires packets to have the ACK (acknowledgment) bit set. The acknowledgment bit is set on the second packet in the TCP three-way handshake that starts all sessions, as well as on all subsequent packets. The router presumes that any inbound packet with an ACK bit is in response to a datagram sent by the trusted station. One denial-of-service (DOS) attack made use of this characteristic—the SYN-ACK flood operated by sending a large number of packets to the target with both the SYN and ACK bits set. Most systems would overflow their buffers in servicing the traffic.

The established keyword is used in a different context on the PIX firewall and should not be confused with the description in this section.

The FIN (finished) bit will also pass the established filter.

Thwarting address spoofing is another common use of access lists. This technique prevents IP addresses outside the network from entering and possibly taking advantage of permissions granted to internal resources. To configure this solution, the administrator blocks all internal addresses from being the source address on the external interface.

Time-Based and Reflexive Access Lists

Two new kinds of access lists have been added to the most recent versions of the IOS. *Time-based access lists* provide designers with the ability to activate security policies based on the time of day or the day of the week. This is an interesting conflict in traditional security policies—normally anything that is not permitted is never permitted. Time-based lists alter this situation by allowing specific functions to traverse the router at certain times. These lists might be used to allow backups to run in the middle of the night from servers in the DMZ, for example. Unfortunately, this would also permit hackers to exploit the increased permissions in order to launch an attack.

There is little doubt that administrators will use time-based access lists. However, to do so without fully incorporating the feature with a security policy would be irresponsible.

Reflexive access lists go beyond the traditional "permit all established" access lists by incorporating reflexive technology. A reflexive list permits traffic only in response to a prior event—an originating packet from the internal network, for example.

Perhaps the best way to understand the operation of a reflexive access list is to consider the configuration used, which is shown in the following output:

```
interface hssi 3/0
description Interface to Inet
ip access-group in-filter in
ip access-group out-filter out

ip reflexive-list timeout 120

ip access-list extended in-filter
permit tcp any 10.11.2.0 0.0.0.255 reflect allowed
(Note the implicit deny)

ip address-list extended out-filter
deny icmp any any
deny udp any any
evaluate allowed
```

In this example, the serial 0 interface is configured with inbound- and outbound-named access lists. The outbound filter denies ICMP and UDP traffic and then references the reflexive tcp traffic filter—a filter that permits the return of any TCP traffic that originates inside the network. This is similar to the established bit, but the advantage is that this permission exists only for 120 seconds or for the duration of the TCP session—a significant reduction in the amount of time a hacker might have to exploit the permission. Note that the default timeout value is 300 seconds, which applies to lost TCP sessions and connectionless UDP sessions. Reflexive access lists work with UDP traffic; however, the termination of the reflexive access list permission is based only on the timer.

Encryption

The concept of *encryption* is best exemplified by the childhood code games that most pre-teens play. These games send secret messages composed of offsets—for example, each letter may be three characters removed from the actual letter. Thus, the letter D might represent the letter A, and the letter Z would be represented with the letter C.

Obviously, such a simple code would be fairly easy to crack. In wartime, such codes incorporated garbage characters, floating offsets, and other techniques to provide additional protection. By World War II, these ciphers had become quite advanced and made use of simple computers that added additional randomness to the sequence. A famous Allied victory incorporated the cracking of a German code—a victory made possible only because a German officer transmitted the same message twice. By dissecting the pattern, the Americans and the British were able to build their own computer for decoding the secret messages.

With today's computational power, the ability to encode and decode data streams is fairly simple, and a wide variety of methods may be employed. The majority of these methods incorporate the concept of a *key*, or password, and the number of bits used for the key directly relates to the potential security afforded by the encryption. A key is the base code used to calculate the encryption code. For example, the formula for my encryption code might be to add two and subtract one, but if I allow the user to define the initial number, the result should be different from those of other users (clearly this is a very simple example).

Recently, the United States government took steps to authorize the export of higher-security encryption keys to 128 bits. Prior to this time, export keys were restricted to 56 bits, and munitions laws governed the use of higher encryption key values.

This text does not address specific technologies for encryption given the ever-changing landscape of the encryption marketplace. However, it is clear that a standard will emerge and that at least 128-bit keys will be required to provide the required level of protection.

An educational and military effort is currently working on a chaos encryption system. This system would operate on the premise that background noise can be used to filter the underlying data stream and that such a technique could thwart hackers even if they knew the data was present. This concept carries over to existing encryption challenges as well.

To Encrypt or Not to Encrypt

One prevalent debate in encryption is whether to encrypt all data or only the important datagrams. In the days of slower encryption engines and processors, this issue was of more importance than it is today.

Also at issue is the concept of marking important data for the hacker—it is much easier for the attacker to locate important data when it is labeled (encrypted). The same argument could be made in a file-cabinet-based system—is it prudent to label the drawer "Top Secret"? The alternative is to encrypt everything from lunch plans to financial statements. Hackers can still try to decrypt the data, but they have an equal chance of getting an order for a pastrami sandwich as they do the blueprint for a new product. Thus, designers and corporations alike have to decide if the performance hit is worth this level of subterfuge.

Another debate in encryption is the security of private media cables. Clearly, a private fiber-optic link is more secure that a copper connection to the Internet, but would a company benefit significantly from encrypting the private fiber? Note Table 11.1, which describes the security risks of private and public fiber-optic and copper cables in descending order.

TABLE 11.1 Security Risks of Private and Public Fiber-Optic and Copper Links

Link	Risk
Private fiber-optic	Being difficult to tap and monitor given the characteristics of glass, encryption may not be warranted for this media.
Public fiber-optic	Again, the medium is difficult to tap, but the cloud affords the opportunity to mirror data. Frame Relay and other switched technologies can be easily mirrored and redirected; however, the vendors typically provide a small degree of protection.

TABLE 11.1   Security Risks of Private and Public Fiber-Optic and Copper Links *(continued)*

Link	Risk
Private copper	Depending on the run, this medium could be hacked without intrusion, again given the characteristics of the medium.
Public copper	The risks are the same as for public fiber; however, the tap point now includes the local loop.

Table 11.1 is based on the electrical characteristics of the media. Electrical signals carried on copper cables can be monitored from an external detector, whereas fiber prevents such eavesdropping. Fiber connections can be tapped with an optical splitter, though this requires disrupting the circuit.

Host Security

The majority of host-based security solutions employ the basic tenet of physical isolation. Typically, this places the server in a locked room with limited access.

Unfortunately, many companies augment this security model only with simple passwords and don't use the network devices—primarily routers—to enhance the security model. This leads to two interesting schools of thought regarding whether the network is a security device. (Ignore firewalls and other applications on the network that provide security; we're focusing only on the infrastructure in the network, including switches, routers, and hubs.)

One school claims that the network is not a security device. Proponents of this view argue that the network is for the transport of packets and that security is the responsibility of the end station. Conversely, the other school contends that the network is a security device and that routers are to be used as instruments of that policy.

In practice, the real answer to this question generally requires a hybrid of these two schools. This is where most host security models fail—the ideal is to have the host and network work together to provide the most secure solution, but many companies enter into security focused solely on the network and firewalls. From a security perspective, using simple access lists and strong passwords along with giving much consideration to performance will likely yield the best solution.

Of course, one of the risks in data security is developing a solution that impedes productivity. A perfect example of this in the workstation world is the analog modem. Many companies approve the installation of a measured business phone line, not realizing that the employee can use it with remote-control software. The user unintentionally thwarts the security policy by installing a program that can provide a connection via the phone line. Once the attacker controls the machine connected to both the modem and the LAN, they can access corporate resources on the network. This circumvents any protections installed by the network designer or administrator.

Authentication and Authorization

The security triad is composed of three distinct functions: authentication, authorization, and accounting. (The accounting function will be described in the following section.) Authentication and authorization work hand-in-hand to provide the proper parties with the access permitted. *Authentication* typically includes a user identification and password, though some systems use tokens (something you have and something you know). Token systems are similar to bank ATM cards—I have the card, and I know my PIN. *Authorization* operates once an individual has been authenticated, and this process defines what may or may not be allowed. For example, you may know the enable password, but your user account will not authorize the use of the enable command.

Together, these methods provide better protection than either one on its own. Newer systems are using voice-print technology and fingerprinting, in addition to optical scanners that image the face or retina. Programs that record the cadence of keystrokes have been around for years—they operate on the premise that everyone types a bit differently than others. So you may know my password is "secret," but unless you pause between the c and r, the system will not let you in.

It is possible to maintain databases on these devices in order to provide authentication and authorization, but it should be clear that this solution is very limited and will not scale. Two of the more popular centralization systems/protocols used are TACACS+ (Enhanced Terminal Access Controller Access Control System) and RADIUS (Remote Access Dial-In User Service).

Both of these services can provide authentication services with a centralized repository of passwords and permissions. The following output is from a TACACS+ configuration file—note how two groups, operator and operator_plus (members of the default service, permit, are given all commands) are established to restrict the commands available to the user:

```
#TACACS+ V2.1 configuration file
#created 5/14/96
#edited 8/20/99
#
#If user doesn't appear in the config file user/etc/
password
default authentication = file /etc/passwd
accounting file = /home1/logs/tacacs+.accounting
#Must be same as router IOS "tacacs-server key"
key = C1sc0
#
user=netops {
   member=operator
   login=cleartext dilbert
}
user=rpadjen {
   # Robert Padjen
   default service=permit
   login=cleartext yummy
}
group=operator {
   name="Network Operator"
   cmd=debug {
      permit .*
   }
   cmd=write {
      permit terminal
   }
   cmd=clear {
      permit .*
```

```
            }
        cmd=show {
        #permit show commands
        permit .*
        }
    }


    user=tlammle {
        # Todd Lammle
        member=operator_plus
        login=cleartext flatshoe
    }
    group=operator_plus {
        name="Network Operator Plus"
        cmd=debug {
            permit .*
        }
        cmd=write {
            permit terminal
        }
        cmd=clear {
            permit .*
        }
            #permit show commands
        cmd=show {
            permit .*
        }
        cmd=configure {
            permit terminal
        }
        cmd=interface {
            permit .*
        }
        cmd=shutdown {
            permit .*
```

```
    }
    cmd=no {
        permit shutdown
    }
}
```

Numerous texts provide the details of these protocols and the features, including port numbers and encryption, available to the designer. Yet at this point, designers should be concerned only with the availability of both protocols and the knowledge that both freeware and licensed versions exist. Cisco offers their CiscoSecure product as one possible solution, and each product (including freeware, alternative vendors, and Cisco) has advantages and disadvantages. The benefit of each is that a single system can provide access control for all network devices, and the password information is not stored on the network components themselves. This design provides a slight degree of added security for the architect and greatly simplifies ongoing administration.

Accounting

It is beyond the scope of this book to address all of the components necessary for designing a secure network, even if the scope is limited to the network systems themselves. Various controls on the workstation, server, databases, and other systems are all required to make a system more secure.

However, all security solutions require the presence of an *accounting* function. This may be part of a TACACS+ or RADIUS solution, or it may appear in the form of log files and audit trails.

The general security guidelines for accounting must include at least two components—sufficient information to reconstruct the events during the period and, ideally, a method for quickly parsing out significant events. It is extremely inefficient for administrators to manually examine the log files looking for problems. This is one of the areas in which firewalls are strong— the good ones provide real-time alerts of suspicious activity and highlight and summarize general activity.

Accounting also has a benefit outside of the security arena. Designers may be asked to look at accounting to provide charge-back mechanisms and other revenue-generating services. In fact, it is likely that vendors will migrate to usage-based billing for Internet connections before 2005—a move that may yield greater revenue than the current flat-rate contracts.

Virtual Private Networks

At present, *virtual private networks* (VPNs) are not included in the CID exam objectives. However, this relatively new functionality can greatly reduce costs and management issues in the network and should be considered with care by designers. Most VPN deployments build upon the basic concepts of tunneling and add security to the offering. At its simplest definition, a VPN is a tunnel between two points across an untrusted or public network. The contents of the tunnel are typically encrypted, reducing the risk that a session would be intercepted and the data compromised.

The biggest benefit of VPNs, their low cost, is the result of local points-of-presence—users dial a local number rather than an 800 number or a long-distance one. There is little doubt that low access costs will make VPNs a common service in the network. However, many corporations are having difficulty deploying the service for technical and political reasons. Most frequently, the political reasons involve a lack of trust regarding the security of VPNs and the reliability of using the public network for business-critical data. Many vendors now offer guaranteed service levels for VPN traffic that remains within their network.

Another advantage to VPN technology is the flexibility afforded the designer. The typical remote-access solution, which VPN is designed to replace, requires the designer and administrator to order circuits at both the local and remote ends. These circuits are usually user-specific—user A might use ISDN and user B might use analog dial-up. Even with discounts and 800 numbers, the costs for these services quickly grow and significantly add to the burdens of the support organization. It is not unheard of for users to generate monthly ISDN charges of thousands of dollars. In addition, users are limited to the remote technology deployed for them.

VPN technology simplifies this model substantially as a single point (foregoing redundancy) that can provide connectivity for an array of access methods, including cable modems, DSL, dial-up, ISDN, and Frame Relay. A wide array of protocols and methods, including the Point-to-Point Tunneling Protocol (PPTP), L2F (Layer 2 Forwarding), L2TP (Layer 2 Tunneling Protocol), and IPSec (IP Security), are available to encrypt data and provide secure "virtual" connections between the access points. Each technology provides different standards and benefits, including support for multiple protocols, NAT, and multicasts.

However, the landscape is changing very quickly, and readers are advised to examine vendor materials and standards documents before selecting a technology. Note that at present, though IPSec appears to be the likely VPN solution, Cisco strongly supports L2TP or a combination of L2TP and IPSec, which can provide most services except NAT. Microsoft's Windows 2000 product will also support these specifications. It is important to note that IPSec supports only IP and was initially designed to provide only encryption, authentication, and key-management services.

One challenge with most of these connection technologies is key distribution. For example, a remote user wishes to activate the VPN client on his home computer and connect to the corporate VPN server. This requires a key on the client that authenticates to the server. How does that key get transmitted securely? To answer this question, designers looking at VPN technologies need to ask a few preliminary questions, including:

- Is administration of the authentication database insourced or outsourced? (Many companies are looking to outsourcing even with the security risks.)

- How many points-of-presence are available on the ISP's network?

- What service levels are available?

- How scalable is the solution?

- Which encryption technology is used? Is the client built into the remote operating system, or must a disk/CD go to each user?

- How are keys managed?

Once the designer obtains answers to these questions, they can use the information to compare and select vendors and applications. For example, key management is a critical issue that may be best handled via outsourcing. However, it also requires trusting another party to control security—a direct security risk that most companies are unwilling to accept. Many companies manage their own keys on a certificate server maintained by the vendor, but this option is not universally available. As a result, the security requirements will need to match the services offered by the vendor, or another vendor will be required.

Summary

This chapter addressed a number of issues related to data security and network design. While the design of the network can certainly augment an overall security policy, the reality is that the network may or may not be an appropriate security device. Network designers need to consider both internal and external threats to the network, in addition to the different access methods that an attack may use—modems, networks, Internet connectivity, VPNs, and other conduits.

Incorporating the security needs of the enterprise into the overall design can certainly benefit the designer by centralizing resources, reducing costs, and maintaining a consistent plan. Designers should also consider the physical requirements of designing a secure network, including locked equipment rooms and fiber connections.

Review Questions

1. A firewall is aware of packets beyond which Layer?

   A. 3

   B. 4

   C. 5

   D. 6

   E. 7

2. A router acting as a firewall should:

   A. Deny Telnet on all interfaces

   B. Deny Telnet destined for the router itself on all interfaces and employ a directly connected console

   C. Permit Telnet on the external interface only

   D. Permit Telnet on the internal interface only

3. Most corporate security issues encompass which of the following three categories?

   A. Corruption, theft, and abuse of data

   B. TCP, UDP, and ICMP

   C. Audit, cracking, and phreaking

   D. Denial of service, SYN-ACK, and IP spoofing

4. Which of the following access methods operates with VPN technologies?

   A. ISDN

   B. Frame Relay

   C. Dial-up (POTS)

   D. Cable modems

   E. All of the above

5. Which of the following best defines a firewall?

A. A router with an access list on each interface

B. A specific device that blocks or permits traffic based on policy at all layers of the OSI model

C. Any router with an access list

D. Any access list that uses the established bit

6. The PIX firewall requires a minimum of:

A. One IP address

B. Two IP addresses

C. One IP subnet

D. Two IP subnets

7. IP address spoofing is best defined as:

A. An internal host using the IP address of an external host

B. An internal proxy

C. An external host using the IP address of an internal host

D. Mapping of IPX addresses to IP addresses

8. A well-configured firewall should:

A. Provide TFTP services

B. Use proxy ARP for security

C. Deny encrypted passwords

D. Implement the security policy

9. A security plan need not consider host security. True or false?

A. True

B. False

10. What do L2TP, L2F, and IPSec have in common?

    A. All are authentication protocols.

    B. All are virtual private networking protocols.

    C. All are Cisco proprietary protocols.

    D. They have nothing in common.

11. Corporations should:

    A. Hire a dedicated specialist for data security

    B. Outsource all security functions

    C. Incorporate data security into server administration

    D. All of the above

12. The PIX firewall is capable of providing NAT functions. True or false?

    A. True

    B. False

13. IP access lists can provide:

    A. Filtering through Layer 2

    B. Filtering at Layers 3 and 4

    C. Filtering at Layer 5

    D. Filtering through Layer 7

14. Implementation choices are determined by:

    A. Product availability

    B. Product price

    C. Product features

    D. Policy

15. Devices found in the DMZ might include:

A. An anonymous FTP server

B. A Web server

C. A DNS server

D. All of the above

E. None of the above

16. An InterNIC-registered address (rather than an address defined in RFC 1918) is required:

A. On all interfaces in the network

B. On all internal interfaces in the network

C. On all external interfaces in the network

D. Only when using stateful inspection

17. In addition to a honey pot, what other security mechanism provides the best information to the administrator regarding attacks?

A. Syslog entries

B. Packet filters

C. Proxy files

D. DNS cache entries

18. Which service is responsible for maintaining a trail regarding system access?

A. Authentication

B. Authorization

C. Accounting

D. None of the above

19. Which of the following best describes Port Address Translation?

   A. A unique IP address is used for each session traversing the firewall.

   B. A unique IP address and port address is used for each session traversing the firewall.

   C. A non-unique IP address is used for each session traversing the firewall.

   D. A non-unique IP address is used for each session traversing the firewall, but the port address is unique.

20. Which of the following statements would most likely be part of a security policy?

   A. Telnet is permitted to the firewall from external hosts.

   B. Telnet is permitted to internal hosts from external hosts.

   C. Telnet is not permitted from the firewall to internal hosts.

   D. Telnet is not permitted from internal hosts to external hosts.

Answers to Review Questions

1. B.

2. B.

3. A.

4. E.

5. B.

6. B.

7. C.

8. D.

9. B.

10. B.

11. A.

12. A.

13. B.

14. D.

15. D.

16. C.

17. A.

18. C.

19. D.

20. C.

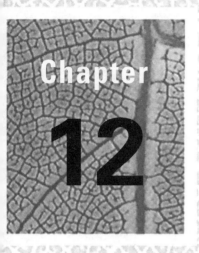

Chapter

12

Network Design Review

✓ Summarize the major concepts covered in this class.

✓ Recall the steps for internetwork design.

✓ Describe methods for monitoring your internetwork design.

✓ Return to your environment with fresh ideas and plans for internetwork designs.

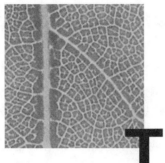

The other day I came across an e-mail thread that discussed a 10-year-old boy who has passed a number of the Cisco exams and attained CCNP certification. While I certainly applaud his efforts and initiative (though I do question the authenticity of the report), it compelled me to think about this chapter specifically. The authors, editors, and publishers of these Study Guides and related books strive to provide readers with the information needed to pass more than a certification exam. While all of the material in this book is geared toward the CID exam objectives, it is not our intent to provide the answers. To do so would diminish the certification process. Quite frankly, the exams cover only a small fraction of the material that you need to succeed in this field.

In the majority of books related to exams and certification, it is stressed that *real world* experience is a must. This is very true, although the topic of design does migrate toward the theoretical. However, it helps to have the practical knowledge to apply and understand the concepts. Having said that, I encourage readers who don't work on production networks daily to seek out a mentor who can share configurations and diagrams before they attempt the exam. Frequently, the mentoring process is educational for both participants; the effort helps to fill in gaps in the learning process.

You will find that the majority of the items discussed in this chapter are familiar—hopefully because you have experience in your own network. This chapter is significantly less formal than the previous chapters and reflects upon the material in this book much in the same way that the objectives reflect the classroom experience. In fact, it is likely that you are using this book as part of a formal lecture, which should aid in integrating this material.

Back to the young man who became certified. If permitted the soapbox for a moment, I'd like to stress to all readers the importance of knowing the nontechnical in addition to the technical aspects of internetwork design. It took years before I learned this important lesson. The best designers are not those who *only* pass the test. They are usually not the ones who know every nuance of the IOS. They are the ones who think *outside the box* or, as a friend once corrected me, *outside the circle*. He was right.

It is also important to hone skills unrelated to your field or desired field. For example, the chief of the Seminole tribe in Florida brought in casino gambling a few years ago, and with this came new jobs and added income. The money was used to diversify into non-gambling markets, and recently the tribe purchased an aircraft manufacturer. The plane will be called the Micco, after the chief's son.

How does this relate to network design? It doesn't. It relates to skills and diversity. The chief knows that he and his family will have enough money and that their son will learn the business skills used by his father—skills that will help make his son successful, too. However, in a 1999 interview, the chief noted that when his son is old enough he will teach him alligator wrestling, a dangerous sport, to say the least. The chief's rationale: "I'll catch a 'gator for him to wrestle at some point, so he'll have a skill he can keep in his hip pocket. So, when all else goes wrong, he can find a 'gator and make a few dollars off of it." In network design, that hip pocket may include marketing, sales, or any other business or non-business focus. Communication and interaction skills will be increasingly important in the future as well. My final point: Some headhunter and career-planning studies report that workers will have up to eight different *careers* in their lifetime. Thus, flexibility is important in both career planning and in the singular career of network design and administration.

So, as you read this chapter and reflect on the material presented throughout this book, take a moment and think about the application of it all. Consider taking a moment to go to lunch with the sales folks to learn about their business and how they use the network. Better yet, learn how they *don't* use the network. Understanding why the network doesn't meet the needs of the user community is critical to addressing those needs.

Major Concepts of the CID

Obviously, Cisco wrote their objectives in the context of the Internetworking course materials, and the applicability of a review is questionable in a static text. In the Cisco materials, the summary of the course typically receives a quick gloss-over and provides the instructor with the opportunity to address a running list of issues that have been identified during instruction. When this book is used as a training aid in a classroom setting, I recommend that you spend some time now to review the materials covered in the course.

In a static setting, such as when you are working by yourself, it would be opportune to flip through and look over any highlighting or other marks. It would be difficult to repeat all the material that might be needed at this phase. However, following is a list of those areas that are significant because they are either difficult or important. Do not view this list as comprehensive for passing the exam—it is not intended to be and it is not constructed based on the live exams. Simply use this list as a foundation for asking yourself if you understood this material.

- Know the various network design models, especially the hierarchical model.

- Feel comfortable with applying the material in this book in real-world situations. It might be beneficial to have a study buddy or group—ask each other how to apply this material.

- Understand VLSM and IP addressing.

- Be familiar with the capabilities of the IP routing protocols.

- Understand the benefits of AURP.

- Understand the benefits of NLSP.

- Know the characteristics of EIGRP in its three flavors.

- Know the components of ATM LANE.

- Understand the differences between ATM LANE and ATM PVCs.

- Understand remote connections, including control, node, and gateway.

- Understand Frame Relay, ISDN, and X.25.

- Understand the mainframe technologies, including RSRB and DLSW+.

- Know the characteristics of desktop protocols.

- Be familiar with the issues regarding Windows networking.

- Know the ways to secure a network.

- Review the CID exam objectives.

Overview of Network Design

Network design is many things. Typically, it accomplishes the following:

Implements cost-effective solutions.   This requires that the design include both initial and recurring cost analysis. Designers need to consider scalability and adaptability in determining the cost effectiveness of their solutions as well.

Utilizes the best technologies.   It's difficult to know what the best technologies will be in the future, yet at present the industry appears committed to IP, Ethernet, Frame Relay, and ATM. Future technologies will undoubtedly include wireless, DSL, Packet over SONET, Dynamic Packet Transport, and DWDM (dense wavelength division multiplexing). These technologies are here today. Soon, vendors will champion cutting-edge concepts based on current research, including the use of jellyfish for data storage and carrying IP packets on photons.

Consists of scalable designs.   Scalable designs are a must when considering resource and capital costs—if the network does not scale, it cannot support growth or new features. This will require replacement costs when the company's needs grow.

Utilizes an easy-to-administer hierarchical model.   The hierarchical model simplifies the incorporation of scalability in the design. It also improves diagnostic processes.

Provides redundancy and integrates other methods to reduce downtime.
Depending on the business demands, the network may require redundancy and fault tolerance, especially in financial and other real-time environments. However, the costs associated with downtime (based on per minute, per salary, per person) can become very high, even without a direct customer interface. Since some redundancy can be incorporated at low or no cost, it should be included in any design.

Meets or exceeds the customer's business and technical requirements.
It is hard to fail when you surpass expectations. This goal should include anticipating needs, meeting the predefined objectives, and completing the project on time.

The best network designs result from a thorough planning phase in which all of these elements are addressed. This stage should result in a list of objectives that will be compared to the final result—refrain from determining the success of the project until you've met the initial objectives or improved upon them.

Designers should also note that sometimes these objectives will be mutually exclusive in the eyes of the business. For example, a redundant, hierarchical model may require more than double the funds compared to a sufficient design. A remote office with 20 workers and its own file and print services may not need redundant links—it depends on the business.

Applying Network Design Theory

Perhaps the best way to understand the application of network design theory is to review the recommended steps for a network design project. By no means are these lists exhaustive; however, they do provide a good template for designers on a wide variety of projects.

The Network Design Methodology Model

The first list is the textbook CID model that was presented in Chapter 1. It is presented again in Figure 12.1.

FIGURE 12.1   The network design methodology

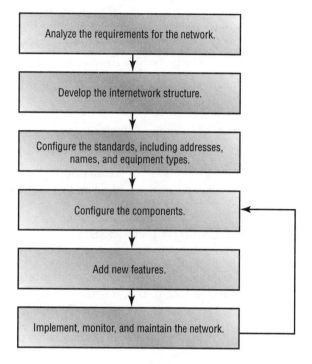

Though Cisco expects this flow for the exam, many experienced designers would take some issue with the order used and the omissions, including vendor evaluations, pricing, and user testing, for example. However, this flow does incorporate some very positive elements. For example, the use of a review and continuous process is frequently omitted from most projects—everyone completes the first project and moves to the second. Remember, there are four phases to a project or, at least, a well-run project:

- Conception

- Provision

- Implementation

- Review

It would be easier to remember the order of these steps if all four ended in 'tion, yet perhaps it's easier to remember *because* the steps don't exactly flow together. Another memory aid is to skip the implementation step and think CPR. Many projects require first aid soon after implementation because the review step was dismissed.

The CID model illustrated in Figure 12.1 accomplishes a number of things. The key points to remember are:

- The sequence follows a logical flow from project conception to review.

- The methodology incorporates the critical task of obtaining customer requirements and expectations.

- The concept of standardization is incorporated. This occurs most visibly at the naming and addressing phase.

The Network Design Process

The following recommended network design process incorporates more detail than the model above, but it stops before the implementation and review phases. In fact, it is specifically targeted to the conception and provisioning steps, which frequently determine the success of the project.

1. Identify any business constraints on the project or design.

   - Document the budget and resources available for this project and establish a time line. Gantt charts, which show the relationships between each task over time and per resource, are very helpful in this phase. All participants in the project should be able to identify the dependencies with other efforts and tasks.

   - Identify the staffing requirements, including hiring, training, and contracting. Vendor requirements should also be identified. This step is sometimes appropriate before the equipment is selected; a few thousand dollars spent on a class to see that the equipment is not appropriate for the company is cheap compared to the purchase price. If the company uses the equipment, the expenditure is not wasted.

2. Identify the security requirements for the network.

   - Assess the security risks and determine what security will be needed and of what type. As presented in Chapter 11, this process should include physical and logical security against internal and external threats.

- Determine outside access requirements for data. This may include Web transaction servers and database access; attention should be given to vendor support connectivity as well. Many vendors need remote control or remote node connectivity in order to provide support.

- Identify any requirements for authenticating routes received from access routers or other routers. This task rarely evolves into a significant issue, but route spoofing and other attacks, such as DNS spoofing, should be considered.

- Determine the authorization and authentication requirements for users, including those in corporate branch offices, mobile users, and telecommuters. VPN technologies and services, including TACACS+ and RADIUS, are important to consider in this phase.

- Identify the requirements for host security, including the physical security of hosts and user accounts. Again, physical security is a foundation to all other protection mechanisms. Consideration should be given to user acceptance of the security model to make certain that they don't proactively circumvent it.

3. Identify manageability requirements.

- Identify the requirements for fault management, accounting management, configuration management, performance management, and security management. It may also be appropriate to consider change management at this phase. This is an area where many companies falter. Placing a circuit in the network is relatively easy, but failure to consider the support of that circuit can harm even the best design.

4. Extract application requirements.

- Obtain and document the names and types of new applications and the protocols that will be used. Include port numbers where applicable. This phase typically requires repeated efforts, as many applications use administratively defined ports or internally defined ones that are unknown to the system administrators.

- Document the projected number of users who will use the new applications and protocols. This is a key component of scalability and capacity planning.

- Diagram the flow of information through the network for new applications. This should be compared to current data-flow diagrams. Again, this is a key component of capacity planning.

- Identify the peak hours of usage of new applications. This information should be stored in a central location outside of the project so that other groups can anticipate future demands.

5. Characterize new network traffic.

- Characterize the traffic load. This includes many components from the application requirements; however, it needs to include dependencies on other servers and resources.

- Characterize the new application's traffic behaviors, including broadcast/multicast, supported frame size(s), windowing and flow control, and the error-recovery mechanisms available.

6. Identify any performance requirements and define preliminary design goals. This may include service-level projections such as:

- Application and network response time—two factors in the user experience.

- Network and application availability. If there are high-availability needs, it is likely that redundancy and fault-tolerance efforts will require funding.

- Threshold for network utilization. This may include historical projections and failure scenarios. For example, a network failure (single event) may not affect the application performance by more than a certain amount. Consider two load-balancing circuits and a service level that precludes user impact during a single circuit failure. The user should not see a reduction in response time or throughput when only one circuit is busy. A threshold of no more than 50 percent would be required in order to ensure that packets will be accommodated on the single circuit. Ideally, this number would be reduced to a comfortable level—perhaps 35 to 40 percent when both circuits are operational—that doesn't saturate the circuit.

- Data throughput, measured between nodes per unit of time, usually seconds. This accounts for bursts in the network. Most designers will not design for bursts, opting for a five-minute to one-hour average utilization instead. However, if the user saturates the link for five minutes and the link is idle for the remaining 55 minutes, this will lead to poor performance as observed by the user.

- Network latency, which is a minor concern in most networks today. However, carriers should be held to a maximum service-acceptable latency—somewhere between 50 and 85 ms for a cross-country (US) circuit. The routing of the circuit can impact not only latency, but also reliability—it is usually better to have the straightest path as opposed to a circuitous one.

7. Create a customer needs specification document (optional).

- Record the customer's requirements and constraints and the characteristics of the existing network. This type of document is critical to providing a clear review process—did the project meet the objectives?

Some argue that this step is not optional and that it should appear earlier in the process. Experience should provide a guide in your individual environment.

Of course, this list is somewhat utopic. The sad reality is that many of these steps are skipped in the mad rush to deploy new systems. Nonetheless, this is a good list to know for the exam and a wonderful target to strive for in production networks.

Select those items that are most beneficial to your environment and create a form that addresses them. It doesn't have to be bureaucratic. Rather, use it for your own reference and augment it as necessary.

Network Monitoring and Management

As networks grow, it becomes increasingly difficult to monitor and maintain each individual component. At the same time, it's likely that the critical nature of each component increases to the point where outages can cost millions of dollars.

Network monitoring tools were designed to alert operations staff to real-time problems. Most of these solutions use polling, SNMP (Simple Network Management Protocol), and RMON (Remote Monitoring) to detect changes in the environment, and most incorporate a graphical interface that interconnects the various devices. Network management expands upon the basic monitoring tools and typically adds configuration and enhanced monitoring capabilities. This may incorporate extended RMON functions, including embedded protocol capture.

For obvious reasons, Cisco champions their CiscoWorks network management suite. This product can work with other platforms, including HP's OpenView and Sun's Domain Manager. Like most network management tools, CiscoWorks uses a database to maintain information regarding the network elements. It also provides a number of features, including the following:

- Router and switch configuration tools

- Monitoring of the current network state

- Real-time network analysis

- Historical data collection for trend analysis

Network management tools can also aid in the configuration of the network. Programs are available to simplify the establishment of VLANs and other parameters that would otherwise require manual input with the command-line interface. Tools can not only speed up the configuration process, but they can allow less-trained workers to perform these tasks—they will not have to learn the intricacies of the command-line interface (CLI).

While the network-management tools like CiscoWorks can greatly assist the network administrator, there are other methods that can be used to obtain information regarding the network's health. These include:

- The command-line interface (CLI)
  - The Cisco show and debug commands
  - The Cisco ping, telnet, and traceroute commands

- Protocol analyzers

- Logging, including syslog

Baselining is the act of measuring normal network characteristics under typical conditions. This information is invaluable for capacity planning and can assist in troubleshooting. During configuration or baselining, there are additional resources and tools to consider during a network outage. These resources include:

- DNS and WINS

- TFTP and FTP

- DHCP and BOOTP

- RADIUS and TACACS+

When deploying network-monitoring tools, designers should evaluate the importance of each tier and segment. For example, the core layer likely requires a substantial amount of monitoring in real time, while elements at the access layer will likely have less impact on the overall network than will a problem in the core. Thus, a designer may place RMON probes in the core but use the command line to diagnose problems in remote locations.

In addition, the designer should consider implementing technologies in a manner that augments troubleshooting. This may include:

- An out-of-band management VLAN for switches. Out-of-band connections do not traverse the same connections as user data paths, called in-band connections.

- Out-of-band connections to the console or auxiliary port on network devices.

- Terminal servers to connect to all network devices out-of-band.

- The use of hot standby router protocols and other technologies.

- The use of redundant Supervisor engines and power supplies.

- Placement of the network management tool in the core of the network.

- Training of nontechnical staff to provide minimal support in remote locations.

- Documentation of the network, IP addresses, configuration files, and design objectives.

- Configuration of backup servers.

Summary

This chapter incorporated a number of concepts regarding the overall network design process and the tools that administrators and designers may use to gain more control over increasingly complex environments. In addition, it highlighted the concepts that are most common in network design as well as the material that typically causes students the most difficulty. Finally, this chapter detailed two design templates that can assist designers new to the network design process.

At this point, readers should feel comfortable with the importance of considering nontechnical aspects of network design as well as the technical. The benefits of project-management methodologies and experience should also be clear.

Review Questions

1. Following the implementation phase of a project, the network designers should:

   A. Review the original project goals against the existing implementation

   B. Move on to the next project

   C. Take a vacation

   D. Run down the hall screaming, "Bad thing!" when the network crashes

2. Which of the following is not true regarding network-management tools?

   A. They assist administrators by alerting them to potential network problems.

   B. They provide an efficient means of configuring network devices.

   C. They replace the need for a good network design.

   D. In most cases, they use SNMP and RMON.

3. Following the development of an internetwork structure, the designer should:

   A. Configure the network equipment

   B. Determine the business needs

   C. Configure the network standards, including naming and addressing

   D. None of the above

4. The first step in a network design project should be:

   A. Order the equipment

   B. Develop a naming convention

   C. Select a vendor

   D. Consult with the business

5. The last step in a well-run network design is:

   A. Documentation

   B. Benchmarking

   C. Configuration backup

   D. There is no last step. Good network design should incorporate continuous review, although the other three answers are part of this process.

6. Which of the following is a tool that can assist the administrator in monitoring the network?

   A. CiscoWorks

   B. HP OpenView

   C. Sun Domain Manager

   D. All of the above

7. In a dual-circuit load-balancing configuration, at what point should the capacity of a single circuit be increased so that a single circuit failure does not impact the user?

   A. 10 percent

   B. 40 percent

   C. 80 percent

   D. 100 percent

8. Manageability is a step in the network-design process. True or false?

   A. True

   B. False

9. The cost of one hour's downtime, based on 100 employees impacted at an average rate of $60 per hour, would be roughly how much, presuming a 100 percent reliance on computer systems and a noncustomer-facing environment?

   A. Nothing

   B. Less than $1000

   C. Around $6000

   D. More than $500,000

10. A well-run project should have which of the following?

    A. Conception, Implementation, and Diagnostic phases

    B. Weekly status meetings and monthly parties

    C. Conception, Provision, Implementation, and Review phases

    D. None of the above

Answers to Review Questions

1. A.
2. C.
3. C.
4. D.
5. D.
6. D.
7. B.
8. A.
9. C.
10. C.

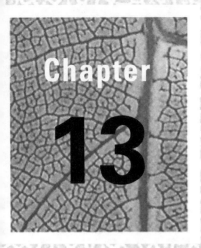

Chapter

13

Advanced Network Design

A number of modern network design concepts do not fit within the framework of the CID exam objectives. While this book has incorporated some of these issues in the main text—Digital Subscriber Line (DSL) and on-demand routing (ODR), for example—there are other subjects that are best covered in an isolated chapter.

Therefore, this chapter will cover some of these other issues that confront modern network designers, including:

- IP multicast

- Redundancy

- Layer 2 and Layer 3 design

- Troubleshooting

- The Internet

- Wireless

- Case management

- Trend analysis and capacity planning

- Encryption

- The future of networking

The bulk of this chapter incorporates concepts that are not part of the Cisco exam objectives, and so readers are encouraged only to review this material. Some specific attention should be given to IP multicast, however.

IP Multicast

As the need for one-to-many communications increased, developers realized that the traditional unicast and broadcast would be unable to scale and accommodate the demand. A method to transmit a single packet and forward that packet to multiple receivers on a dynamic basis was needed.

IP multicast accomplishes precisely this function. Clients inform the network that they wish to receive a data stream. This is analogous to tuning a television. However, the multicast does not specify a certain channel. Rather, it sends a datagram with a specific IP address from the Class D block, which ranges from 224.0.0.0 to 239.255.255.255. Note that there are well-known multicast addresses that are used by some protocols, including HSRP and EIGRP—this section is more concerned with multicasts that traverse routers. All stations in the multicast group will use an address from this block to join and receive the data flow. It is interesting to note that the MAC address for these IP addresses is also defined in the protocol (RFC 1112). The first three octets are 01:00:5E, and the last 23 bits are defined from the last three octets of the multicast IP address. For example, multicast group 227.4.5.6 will use MAC address 01:00:5E:04:05:06, with the remaining bit (high order in the fourth octet) always set to 0.

Designers should refer to RFC 1469 for information regarding Token Ring multicast.

Once the client joins the multicast, the routers are responsible for permitting the data flow to move from the server to the end station. This prevents the multicast from forwarding onto segments that do not wish to participate. In addition, the workstation can use the multicast address to determine whether it wishes to receive the multicast at Layer 2. For non-recipient stations on the same segment, this eliminates unnecessary interrupts. Figure 13.1 illustrates a typical multicast network. Only those routers that need to forward the multicast out an interface receive the data stream. The thicker lines and black serial connection indicate this arrangement. The white serial connections and the thin lines denote a pruned connection—the multicast is not forwarded on these links, which ultimately conserves bandwidth. Pruning, like trimming the branches on a tree, infers that the path from the trunk to the leaves has been cut.

Note that this diagram implies the use of CGMP, or Cisco Group Messaging Protocol. CGMP further parses the multicast flow by limiting it to specific switch ports. Without this function, all members of the VLAN would be flooded with the multicast—the switch would have no mechanism to block the multicast packets from non-recipient ports. CGMP differs from IGMP (Internet Group Management Protocol), described later in this chapter. CGMP is responsible for blocking multicast traffic from individual ports on a Cisco switch; IGMP is a workstation-to-router process that instructs the router to forward the multicast on a segment basis.

FIGURE 13.1 IP multicast in the network

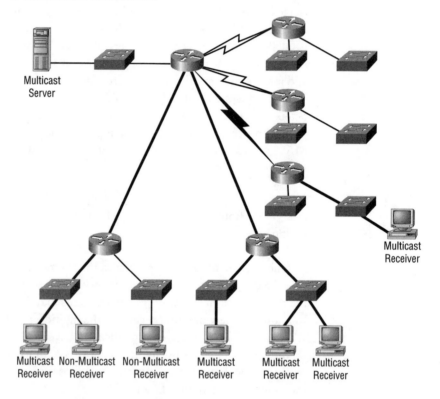

Network designers should consider the various implementations of IP multicast in their installations. However, there are some general guidelines that are common to most installations.

First, multicast clients request to join the multicast via an IGMP request to their local router. The primary rational behind this mechanism is to keep multicast traffic from forwarding onto a segment—allowing the segment to be pruned. Note that IGMP is a Layer 3 protocol, operating at the same layer as IP or ICMP.

Second, designers will need to select a multicast protocol that operates between the routers in the network. PIM (Protocol Independent Multicast) is typically found in many deployments. However, DVMRP (Distance Vector Multicast Routing Protocol) is also available. DVMRP is usually found in installations that connect the MBONE, or the Internet's multicast backbone. Cisco's implementation of DVMRP is incomplete, depending on the IOS (Internet Operating System) version, and so most installations use PIM.

PIM operates in three modes on Cisco routers: dense mode, sparse mode, and sparse-dense mode. Functionally, each of these modes works to control the multicast tree; however, sparse mode uses a rendezvous point (RP). Dense mode is very similar to DVMRP—both protocols assume that bandwidth is not a factor and that all routers wish to join the multicast. Sparse mode indicates that the routers are farther apart (sparsely populated) and that bandwidth is typically constrained. This situation is common in WAN environments; however, sparse mode may be used in LANs as well.

Sparse-mode protocols operate under the premise that each router must explicitly join the multicast. In this design, each source transmits its multicast along the shortest path to the RP, which distributes the packet to registered receivers.

It is important to note that PIM relies on an underlying unicast routing protocol regardless of configuration for sparse or dense mode. In addition, each multicast group should contain a single rendezvous point. Sparse mode uses a process called *shortest path switchover* to join and leave the multicast tree, which conserves bandwidth.

As noted previously, PIM also operates in sparse-dense mode on Cisco routers. In this configuration, the router will first operate in sparse mode and will then convert to dense-mode operation if a problem arises. Such a problem typically involves failure of the RP. Therefore, Cisco recommends the use of sparse-dense mode for all large-scale multicast deployments. These types of installation typically involve low-bandwidth or geographically distant links and require some degree of redundancy. Designers should note that the RP can be located via two dynamic methods—auto-RP and candidate-RP announcements. In addition, every router in the multicast group can be configured with a static entry for the RP.

The multicast routing protocols are designed primarily to avoid forwarding loops. Consider a generic rule that states that all multicasts are forwarded out all interfaces except the source interface. This method works fine for simple linear topologies. However, it is easy to understand that a loop would occur if the topology provided additional paths. For example, router A forwards to B, which forwards to C, which returns the packet to A.

DVMRP and PIM both operate to prevent looping from occurring by understanding the network topology and using Reverse Path Forwarding (RPF). This mechanism uses the distance back to the multicast source and effectively creates a spanning tree to control the flow of the multicast packets. RPF is not part of the 802.1d specification but operates as part of a Layer 3 process on the routers participating in the multicast.

Catalyst switches offer the ability to squelch broadcasts and multicasts at a predefined threshold based on per-second monitoring. Designers should use this feature with care as the deployment of multicasts may exceed this setting.

Multicast will be an important component in the deployment of voice, video, and data services. As part of its Architecture of Voice, Video and Integrated Data (AVVID) initiative, Cisco announced new multimedia applications that will provide video services to the desktop. In addition to the IP/TV offering, Cisco will release IP/VC in early 2000. These products build upon H.323 and other standards to provide compression of the data stream and encoding. Administrators may wish to evaluate the IP/VC product, which promises to operate with the Windows Media Player—a benefit that may preclude the installation of new software at every workstation.

Design Considerations for Quality of Service

Most vendors champion their QoS, or quality of service, offerings as a value added into the network. This set of features was a primary motivator for the migration to ATM in the mid-1990s. A second method, RSVP, or the Resource Reservation Protocol, was also developed to provide guaranteed bandwidth.

At present, QoS simply refers to the ability of the network to reserve bandwidth for the application data stream. For example, a program may query the network to obtain 1Mbps of available bandwidth that cannot be impacted. Doing so provides the application with quality service—performance is not degraded for the requesting application because it has reserved all the bandwidth it should need. All other applications are left to contend for the remaining bandwidth.

Under most circumstances, QoS is a factor only when bandwidth is limited. Most designers opt to provide additional bandwidth under the premise that no single application warrants more access to the network than another. Of course, in some instances, it is appropriate to reserve bandwidth. A typical situation would be for real-time data, including voice and video.

It is important for designers to note that RSVP is not a routing protocol. Rather, RSVP operates at the transport layer and is used to establish QoS over an existing routed path.

Designers planning to implement enterprise-wide multicast services or real-time data services should review and evaluate the QoS features available to them.

Redundancy and Load Balancing

One of the simplest redundancy options available to network designers is the Cisco proprietary HSRP, or Hot Standby Router Protocol. HSRP configurations establish two router interfaces on the local subnet and duplicate the MAC address and the IP address on each router. This duplication is permitted because only one HSRP interface is active at any time. Each interface also has its original IP address and MAC address. This configuration is illustrated in Figure 13.2, which shows the left router as the HSRP primary and the right router as the HSRP secondary.

FIGURE 13.2 The Hot Standby Router Protocol

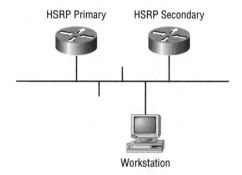

 The non-proprietary HSRP flavor, VRRP, is discussed later in this section.

One of the keys to a redundant design is the use of monitoring tools and automatic failover. The term "failover" defines the actions necessary to provide comparable service in the event of a failure—the network fails over to another router, for example. In ATM installations, many designers opt to configure OAM (operation, administration and management) cells. These cells work to provide connectivity information regarding the entire virtual circuit, as opposed to the physical connection. Because OAM cells can detect a failure faster than the routing protocol can, they are used to trigger an update.

Some network configurations use the backup interface function in the IOS to activate a standby link in the event of primary failure. This is an excellent solution for low-bandwidth requirements where circuit costs are high.

Perhaps the most redundant solution is to install multiple paths through the network. The majority of this book focused on single paths through the network, in part because this concept is easier to understand. In fact, most examples in Cisco's extensive library of information and configurations fail to consider redundant paths through the network unless the specific topic demands this level of detail.

The best counsel regarding multiple circuit designs is to use a high-end routing protocol and the hierarchical model. In addition, it is advisable to consider more than just link failure when mapping circuits.

From a physical layer perspective, the network can fail at one of three points. These are illustrated in Figure 13.3.

FIGURE 13.3 Physical layer failure points

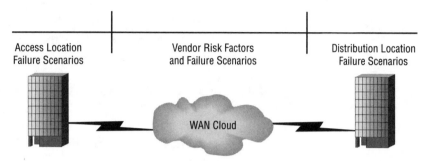

As shown in Figure 13.3, the middle failure point incorporates the WAN cloud. This encompasses failures in switching equipment and provider networks. Unfortunately, the only viable method for addressing this failure scenario is to select diverse providers. This solution can add to the cost of the network and become a factor when corporate mergers (between telecommunication vendors) occur.

The two end failure points actually encompass two different solution sets. The first is the physical entry into the building. For critical locations, designers should consider diverse entry paths into the building—possibly terminating in two different demarks, or demarcation points. A *demarcation point* is the point at which the telephone company turns over the cabling to the business. While this solution adds significantly to the costs, it can prevent a multitude of failures.

The second solution set incorporates the distribution layer destination. Consider an access layer site with two circuits from different providers that terminate into the same distribution layer building. Perhaps the designer improved on this design by terminating each circuit on a different router. While this design may be the only one available, the scenario of complete building failure quickly ruins such a design. Building failure may occur from an earthquake, a hurricane, a flood, a tornado, or non-nature-driven events, including civil unrest and power failure. Whenever possible, designers should opt for two physically separate termination points.

Virtual Router Redundancy Protocol

Cisco released its proprietary HSRP in 1994, which greatly enhanced the options available to designers in regards to redundancy. With the added tracking feature, which adjusts the HSRP priorities based on the status of another interface, HSRP was capable of addressing router and link failures in specific scenarios. While HSRP was not without limitations—not the least of which was its proprietary nature—many Cisco-centric designs made use of this service.

As of this writing, a number of vendors are adding the non-proprietary Virtual Router Redundancy Protocol, or VRRP, to their products. Cisco has agreed to support this protocol alongside HSRP, which should provide many options for the network architect. As defined in RFC 2338, VRRP provides similar functions to HSRP.

One of the primary benefits availed by VRRP, in addition to its multi-vendor support, is ICMP (Internet Control Message Protocol) redirect. The ICMP redirect feature allows a default gateway to teach a workstation about an alternative router that is better suited to send packets to the destination. While Cisco has announced that this feature will be added to HSRP, its absence has led to a number of limitations for designers in asymmetric routing configurations—instances where the two routers servicing the segment have widely diverse remote paths.

Layer 2 versus Layer 3 Design

The issue of Layer 2 versus Layer 3 design appeared in a few sections of this text; however, the majority of the CID material and exam objectives view Layer 2 solutions as the only ones available. This attitude will be changed with the next revision of the course materials and exam.

For years, vendors pushed customers to leave the slow, difficult-to-configure, routed world in favor of flat, switched networks. This trend has effectively reversed itself—primarily as a result of "wire–speed" Layer 3 awareness.

As a result, switches with Layer 3, 4, and 5 awareness are becoming quite functional and necessary in order to facilitate the designs that are now in vogue. Typically, networks are required to address a high volume of off-network traffic. Specialty segments for databases, Web servers, and e-mail delivery demand an understanding of the session, presentation, and application layers of the OSI model.

The availability of Layer 3 awareness in a switch has also permitted a migration from the old, flat model. This migration addresses some of the limitations that resulted from the vendor and Layer 2 industry push—shared media control and spanning-tree control both failed to scale beyond a few hundred devices in most networks due to the lack of broadcast control. The general guideline still holds for fewer than 1,000 devices to be placed in a single broadcast domain, and all of those devices should be well-tuned, IP-only workstations without a reliance on NetBIOS.

Black Holes

One of the dangers poised by the removal of Layer 2 connections is defined by the concept of a *black hole*. A black hole in space is a former star that has collapsed upon itself and become so dense that its gravity consumes most matter, including light. The theory is that nothing can escape this attraction, although Professor Hawking and others have shown that some matter does escape. The simplified image of a black hole is that all things entering the black hole are lost.

A black hole in networking is substantially simpler, but the net impact on a data packet is the same—the packet will be lost forever. Figure 13.4 illustrates the typical Layer 2 design model. As shown, any single physical layer failure can be resolved at Layer 2—no black hole exists.

FIGURE 13.4   Layer 2 network with HSRP

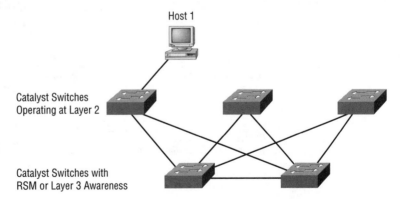

At Layer 2, a single link failure will require a recalculation of the spanning tree. However, since all connectivity at Layer 2 remains, the impact of this failure is nominal.

The argument could be made that since Layer 2 is so simple, it should be used under all circumstances. The reason that another solution is desirable is that the spanning tree was never intended to address the complex bridging environments of modern networks. As a result, many administrators have found the need to use additional features, including portfast, to accommodate their systems—even so, the ability for the Spanning-Tree Protocol to protect against loops in the topology is limited. In the case of a spanning-tree failure, a single broadcast packet in a looped Layer 2 topology can saturate a 100Mbps link and consume over 10 percent of the Supervisor II's processor. The Supervisor II is a processing engine on the Catalyst 5000/5500 product line. Portfast is a Cisco feature that eliminates the normal listening and learning phases of a port in a spanning tree—the port will enter forwarding immediately. This feature requires that the port be terminated with a single connection—portfast ports cannot be connected to another switch, for example.

While disabling the Spanning-Tree Protocol altogether is probably not a good idea, it may be prudent to remove any physical layer loops. The immediate concern with this idea is that a layer of redundancy will be removed. An example of this topology is shown in Figure 13.5.

FIGURE 13.5 Layer 3 network with HSRP

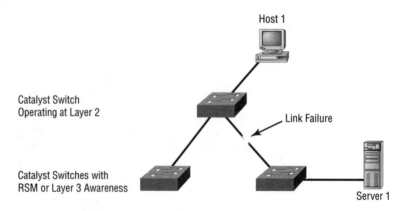

In Figure 13.5, the link between the two core switches shown in Figure 13.4 has been removed. Ignoring the link failure for a moment, note that a physical loop is impossible with this configuration. Host 1 has only one path to each of the routers on its subnet (via HSRP). Server 1 is the problem—its traffic must traverse the access-layer switch (shown at the top of the diagram) in order to reach the core switch on the left side. This lack of an alternate physical layer path leads to the black-hole scenario—the packet destined for the server has a 50-50 chance of getting there. The packet may be forwarded to the workstation segment never received by the server. The packet ultimately goes nowhere from a data-flow perspective. This scenario is shown in Figures 13.5 and 13.6; however, the flow of the packets is omitted. Note that there are a number of variations on black holes in terms of data flow, but the context is the same.

Another difference between Figures 13.5 and 13.6 is the lack of multiple access-layer switches. This lack leads to one of the disadvantages of the Layer 3 design. As noted before, this configuration creates the potential for a black-holed segment with the loss of a single link. This potential is shown in Figure 13.6.

FIGURE 13.6   Black-holed Layer 3 network with HSRP

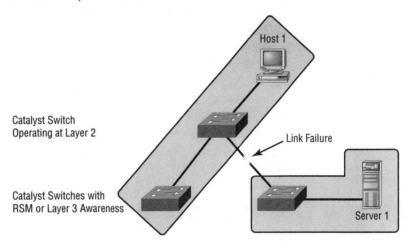

The solution for the designer is somewhat limiting, although implementation is simplified and the negatives of the Spanning-Tree Protocol in large-scale switched networks are negated. By not allowing any intra-VLAN connections except the feed links and the access-layer switch, the designer may use HSRP or VRRP to provide redundancy and a loop-free configuration. This design admittedly removes some of the advantages of VLANs—the network is again highly reliant upon Layer 3, but that is acceptable in modern design. With Layer 3 awareness at wire speeds, any performance disadvantages are virtually negated and the benefits of broadcast control are added.

Troubleshooting as a Design Consideration

Previous chapters touched upon the concept of troubleshooting as a design consideration, but it certainly warrants additional space. Many designers omit this crucial step in developing their designs.

Consider a fairly simple need in the operation of a network—change windows and outages. These concepts address the fact that changes will be needed in the network in order to meet evolving business needs. However, these changes may conflict with uptime requirements of another business application.

The network architect can plan for these issues with a thorough understanding of the business and a well-planned outage schedule. Perhaps the backup system requires connectivity to the mainframe in order to operate. The designer can use this information to isolate this system from the rest of the installation. When the mainframe technicians schedule an IPL (Initial Program Load), the backup system and the network can be repaired and upgraded as well—users cannot access the down system, making this a logical window for troubleshooting. Using this tactic, the entire network can be mapped to provide the best upgrade schedule with the minimum overlap.

Internet Network Design

No computing book today would be complete without a section on the Internet. Perhaps no other single event has so quickly combined the technical and nontechnical worlds, and as presented in Chapter 11 and embellished here, perhaps nothing is more important to the successful use of the Internet than security.

The importance of linking business needs to the technology available has been presented throughout this text. This is especially true for the Internet, although unique issues arise when planning for this medium.

The scope of Internet connectivity in companies today ranges from basic e-mail services through multi-homed, e-commerce solutions. Each of these connections requires different levels of security, access, performance, and technical skill to operate successfully.

Designers typically focus on the security aspects of Internet connectivity, and while this is a significant area of concern, it is an incomplete attitude. Installing a firewall does not encompass a security solution.

A recent successful hacking event, an event made possible by a ZDNet publication using a specially established network, made use of a minor CGI (Common Gateway Interface) bug and knowledge of Unix to completely bypass the company's firewall and the front-end access lists. The attack was really performed at the application layer—the routers and firewalls were not attacked or disabled in order to grant the hacker access to the server. This attack resulted in only a modified home page on a Web server; however, in other installations, the damage could have easily included corrupted database files and the loss of market share resulting from the bad publicity. The issue, as a Cisco employee states, is not whether you're paranoid, but rather whether you're paranoid enough. It is easy to take this attitude to an extreme—the reality is that attacks on corporate data can occur even without access to the Internet. Consider the impact on the company when the CFO's notebook containing all the financial data and strategic plans for the corporation is stolen. It happens.

For the network designer, it is impractical to think that the network can provide all the security necessary for a corporation, including its Internet connectivity. Too many additional factors must work together in order to achieve security. However, the network design can work to augment an overall security plan. Consider the following factors in your designs:

- Every security mechanism must be auditable by a third party.

- Access lists can provide a good front-line defense, but attention should also be given to network performance.

- Firewalls and bastion hosts certainly help to provide data security, but they must be well understood by administrators.

- Depending on the reference cited, up to 90 percent of attacks originate from *inside* the network, effectively bypassing most firewall installations.

- Auditing is perhaps the single most important function of a network security solution.

- Designers and administrators *should* attack their own networks with the knowledge of management. It is even better to have cooperative tests with another organization or with a third party.

- Network administrators must stay informed on the latest patches, programs, and attack methodologies.

- Designers must secure SNMP on every device in the network.

In addition to the network processes, designers should work with administration and other departments to provide the best security solution. This will frequently include scanning for viruses, controlling passwords, and using diskless workstations and encryption.

Companies frequently rush to deploy new services for customers that may compromise the best security models. One of these services is the self-service kiosk, a terminal that is available to customers in a business office or remote location. These devices frequently compare with automated teller machines, although their functionality is often much greater. They can pose a substantial security threat when placed on the same network as the corporate workers—an event that occurs regularly. Most companies rely on physical security to protect their computer systems—it should be difficult to walk into an organization and start entering data on a networked computer. Consider the impact of a hacker using a locally connected machine to launch an attack or placing a protocol analyzer on the segment—passwords and other data could easily be compromised. Another risk is the potential for questionable material to be loaded onto the kiosk machine—an adult Web site, for example. The public relations impact of this prank alone could be very damaging to the company.

The kiosk concept makes such attacks even simpler. Many companies have rushed to deploy these solutions and have used the standard workstation software image (software configuration loaded to all machines in the enterprise)—the one with the populated hosts file—in deployment. As noted previously, some companies have even placed these stations on the same network segment as regular production traffic with no security whatsoever.

Fortunately, the majority of readers already realize just how dangerous this design can be. It thus becomes the job of the designer to understand the business needs and then educate the business on the risks that it is facing.

Wireless Network Design

A number of wireless solutions are available to the network designer, including those based on the 802.11 standard. These solutions range from infrared links with handheld devices and notebooks all the way to OC-3-capable laser and microwave solutions.

At the low end, the network designer typically does not consider infrared links and other low-bandwidth solutions as part of the design. Usually, these services are deployed at the workgroup level.

At mid-tier, the network designer may use wireless solutions that include PCS (personal communications system—similar to but different than cellular), cellular, and radio. The network architect will frequently need to provide connectivity and security in these installations. In many corporations, these solutions are deployed in isolated networks that do not involve the production network. However, administrators are well advised to get involved early in these projects—ultimately these networks may connect to the primary network.

At the high end of wireless services are satellite, laser, and microwave. These solutions frequently connect entire networks and require the involvement of the network designer.

Satellite services are typically deployed to address two possible needs. The first involves the availability of cable-based installations—many countries are cursed with the theft of copper cables. Stories are rampant about circuits that have mysteriously failed. Upon dispatch, the vendors have learned that miles of copper cable have been cut and removed from the poles.

The second satellite installation usually involves mobile stations, including ships. These networks link shipboard computers with monitoring stations that use real-time data to schedule maintenance and provide communications. While the biggest negative to satellite communications is cost, the designer should also consider link delay.

Laser and microwave installations are excellent short-range solutions. Each avoids the need to trench or pull cable in order to connect two networks, and the reliability of these solutions has increased substantially.

Designers should consider reliability and distance when evaluating these options. The cost savings can be substantial, as there is only a one-time charge for the initial hardware purchase and there are no ongoing leased-line fees to pay.

Advances in wireless technology will likely improve wireless coverage and reduce the costs of these solutions.

Case Management

Most network managers and directors will point to documentation of the network as a key concern and trouble area. Another concern is case management.

Case management is a concept similar to trouble-ticket tracking, but it incorporates a broader scope. Many companies use trouble tickets to record problems called into the help desk or service center. Trouble-ticket tracking is the act of reviewing these tickets to improve customer service. Cisco provides an excellent example of case management that starts with the Cisco Connection Online Web site (CCO), located at www.cisco.com. Customers may reference trouble tickets and manually locate patch files and software images without the intervention of the TAC, or Cisco's technical assistance center. Should the customer find it necessary to speak to a staff member for problem resolution, the Web-based trouble ticket can automatically generate the request.

It is important to note that case management is more than just a ticket-tracking system. It is a philosophy that must incorporate ownership of the problems and, as Cisco has proven, admission of problems to customers in a timely fashion. Few other companies have been as brave in documenting their bugs and other problems as Cisco—few have been as successful in resolving them as well. In addition, Cisco surveys every customer and expects each technician to earn the highest satisfaction scores on every case. This acceptance of nothing less than the best has earned the company numerous distinctions.

Network design can augment the case-management process. As noted in Chapter 7, the use of naming conventions can greatly simplify the trouble-shooting process. By linking machine names, IP addresses, and other network information to the ticketing system, a single call could generate a note to all other call takers (and ultimately an automated system) that documents the possibility of a larger failure. This can easily shorten the diagnostic process since administrators are focused on a single problem instead of looking at each call as an isolated issue.

Many organizations are also providing real-time network data to end users, or at least small groups of end users. This preemptive measure can greatly reduce the number of calls reporting a network capacity problem (described in the next section) because the user can see that a link is operating at only five percent—thus showing that the problem is likely not caused by excessive utilization. While this does not exonerate the network, it does squelch the call to immediately upgrade the circuit. By providing this information, the designers and architect can initiate a stronger dialog with their users.

Trend Analysis and Capacity Planning

I was recently asked during an interview how I do trend analysis and capacity planning. I answered respectfully that I could provide two answers—the textbook response or the "real-world" truth. I passed over the question without further comment and accepted the position.

The sad truth is that many organizations haven't the time or expertise to perform an accurate analysis of their network resources. Numerous products, including CiscoWorks and Concord Network Health, can greatly simplify the data-collection process, but at some point the designer needs to understand the specific utilization on a circuit in order to determine if additional capacity is warranted.

You may wonder what could possibly be analyzed when the circuit is running at 100 percent capacity. However, as an architect, you need to understand why traffic rates are so high and to ascertain if this growth was part of the original analysis. Frequently, designers will learn with research that a 256Kbps circuit is supporting unnecessary Web browsing or another optional traffic flow—sometime these unnecessary data flows can consume 75 percent or more of a circuit.

While each organization is different, the last three audits performed by my team (for two different organizations) showed that over 80 percent of the utilization was for stock quotes, sports scores, and other non-business-related material on the circuit. Each company must define acceptable business use, but when utilization is unrelated to the business, it becomes difficult to ignore the associated expense.

Designers must become increasingly vigilant for the bandwidth trap—the addition of more and more bandwidth. This consideration will become increasingly important as the associated costs increase. Increasing costs are due to the fundamental limitations of WAN technology—high recurring costs and high latency (compared to local data stores and cached data). Of course, some organizations, including the government and the sciences, must transfer huge amounts of data daily. Business also may need to send large databases and other files, but compression and other techniques may provide a solution. Recently, a number of financial institutions audited their Web sites and reduced the size of their graphics files to accommodate their customers. Users of low-speed links immediately appreciated the effort, and little content was lost. Most important, however, the change extended the length of time that the current bandwidth capacity will continue to meet their needs. Historically, bandwidth demands have required a doubling of capacity every 6 to 12 months in this market.

Capacity planning is possible, and there are general easily implemented rules. For example, a redundant serial connection would likely require attention and expansion once the individual link utilization reaches 35 percent—allowing for sufficient bandwidth upon a single link failure.

Encryption

For the network designer, the issue of encryption has taken on greater importance in the late 1990s. Virtual private networks and business-to-business transactions, both of which may use the Internet for transport, can greatly benefit from encryption services. As discussed in Chapters 9 and 11, encryption is the act of scrambling data between the two endpoints in an effort to prevent interception of the data. Encryption may also be used to guarantee the authenticity of the data.

In addition to the wide area networking benefits of encryption, there may be instances when it is desirable to protect data flows in the internal network. Telnet, by its very nature, is completely insecure. Data is carried in clear text, resulting in flows that can be intercepted and read with ease. This is of particular concern when you consider the information commonly sent by administrators via Telnet—router logins and configuration files. Even with the benefits of switching, which can hide some of the data flows by only forwarding packets to genuine destinations, it is remarkably easy for an internal source to monitor the traffic destined for a router. The risk increases when Telnet is used for servers and other data-storage devices.

SNMP is another directly related protocol where the network components are placed at risk within the internal network. Like Telnet, SNMP (disregarding Version 3) has a very simple password mechanism, and it sends data in clear text. These two areas should be of some concern to the network administrator, as these security holes could be exploited to initiate a denial-of-service attack or cause other problems that impede the proper flow of business data through the network.

One solution to this problem is SSH, or secure shell. Using SSH coupled with a terminal server, the designer could augment a security model by denying Telnet via the network and providing access only via the console port. This adds some expense, but again, the expense may be justified.

Cisco recently added secure shell services to the IOS, which provides another solution.

Another tool at the designer's disposal outside the context of encryption is providing access lists to block the IP addresses permitted to access the SNMP ports on the network devices. This makes hacking of the password somewhat moot, as the attacker would also need to hijack the IP address—a more detectible event.

Why include Telnet and SNMP in a section regarding encryption? As noted before, SSH is one alternative to Telnet that uses encryption, and SNMP Version 3 supports a slightly higher level of security than Version 2.

However, the real connection between these seemingly non-related issues is two-fold.

First, designers need to realize that encryption is not the magic bullet of a security solution. Configuring a router (or front-end device) to provide encryption services does precisely that—it provides encryption services. Failure to secure non-encryption services like Telnet will allow simple attacks that ultimately could thwart the encryption stream.

The second factor in encryption is the selection of an encryption protocol. Rather than describe and define all the current solutions, of which there are many, it is easier to leave this topic to other texts and, more importantly, to vendor relationships. Corporations, like people, make many decisions based on nontechnical factors, which is natural and somewhat unavoidable. As a result, the selection of an encryption provider may be determined through familiarity with a certain vendor or previous solutions. For example, Nortel may provide a better VPN solution, but previous experience with Cisco's routers and the PIX may lead to a decision to use a Cisco device. Of course, the converse may also be true—Cisco may have a better solution for the organization, but having a shop full of Bay/Nortel routers may make the organization want to stay with such a solution.

Therefore, the best recommendations will likely result from a focus on asking the right questions and looking for standards-based support. Different protocols encrypt different portions of the packet, which may impact interoperability or diagnostic characteristics. Of course, greater encryption may augment security.

The Future of Network Design

The majority of this text addressed some of the more basic concerns in network design. In reality, future designs will prove to be much more difficult for designers to implement, relative to today, depending on whom you ask. Today, most designers are concerned with connecting workstations to servers and mainframes, and while remote access, wireless, and video-conferencing are all portions of the modern network, the current focus is on a fairly simple model wherein a relatively small number of devices communicate over clusters of networks that loosely interconnect.

In the future, the network will substantially increase in complexity. For example, not only will data require secure connections, but it will also demand true location transparency. In addition, automated data gathering, storage, and manipulation will become increasingly important, according to most futurists.

Consider the evolution of the computer. In a fairly small amount of time, computers have been deployed in many U.S. classrooms with Internet connectivity. When considered against the fact that most U.S. schools do not have per-room telephone service, this accomplishment is even more amazing.

Throughout this text, the term "Internet" has been used to mean the Internet that evolved from ARPANET—also called Internet One (I One). No dialog on the future of networking would be complete without noting the efforts in place to establish better networks dedicated to specific tasks, including academic research. However, the use of the term "Internet" does not encompass the Internet Two (I2) project or any of the other new networks.

In the academic arena, engineers and technologists are using systems that may ultimately drive the need for a capacity of over 5Gbps per user. These systems include components beyond virtual reality, wherein individuals relate with each other via sensors and feedback pressure suits. It is conceivable, according to some futurists, that the holodeck from Star Trek will be a reality within 50 years—the technology of today already mimics significant components of science fiction.

It will be interesting to see exactly what network services become commonplace in society. Today, many people carry cellular phones, PDAs (personal digital assistants), pagers, and watches; there is little reason not to combine all of these devices into a single unit. At present, most users continue to carry multiple devices for historical, user-interface, power, or availability reasons.

Consider the following scenario: What would happen if all such devices automatically communicated with each other? The demands on the network become fairly clear. For this example, consider that no fundamental changes have occurred from a business or humanistic perspective.

Let's say I received an e-mail message informing me that a friend is flying into the local airport at noon. I received the message at 10 a.m., and I've just gone to a meeting.

What if the network allowed a parser (a program that scans text) in my e-mail application to identify this message as being important—beyond the scope of *urgent* used today. The application could connect to my PDA over a wireless link and determine that I had just entered a meeting. Rather than disturbing me, the application could also determine that I had no plans for lunch. The application could send a response to my friend noting that I was unavailable to confirm, but that I would tentatively agree to lunch. Another application could propose three restaurants in the area.

My friend would respond to the e-mail and note that the $100-hamburger place at the airport was fine (ask a pilot if you don't get the reference). My calendar (possibly as part of my PDA) would automatically receive the update and, when my meeting was over, pop up a confirmation. An application could also automatically make a reservation at the restaurant, again over the network.

Notice how much of this exchange relied on the application layer and not the network. However, the applications required complete interconnectivity between devices—wireline and wireless—in order to complete the process.

It is likely that the majority of the hurdles in the foreseeable future will be based in Layer 8—politics. Even the end-user financial issues will pale in comparison, according to many researchers. As the model migrates toward services rather than transport, network designers will likely need to concern themselves less with the minutiae of packet flows and more with the interoperability of the services themselves. Stated another way, the challenge will be to explain and address corporate needs in nontechnical ways while also understanding the interoperability of the applications and their individual links. Billing for packets, for example, may become one of many new areas that require attention from the designer.

Few would argue that the computer revolution has just begun. There are legitimate concerns regarding the ability of the marketplace to continue support of such rapid and massive change. However, it appears probable that change will continue at a rapid pace.

Summary

This chapter dealt with some of the issues that confront network designers but that are not part of the Cisco exam objectives. In reality, this chapter could continue for quite some length, as the release of new products requires an ever-increasing dialog regarding the functionality that can be exploited from network technology.

I hope that you've enjoyed this text and wish you luck on both your exam and future endeavors. I sincerely believe that this text, coupled with some real-world experience, will easily prepare you for the CID exam. I also hope that this text will also become part of your permanent library for reference and reflection—Todd and I have both worked to add value that will transcend the short-term goal of certification.

Review Questions

1. IP multicast uses which class of IP address?

   A. Class A

   B. Class B

   C. Class C

   D. Class D

2. Which proprietary protocol is used by Cisco switches to control multicasts at Layer 2?

   A. PIM

   B. EIGRP

   C. CGMP

   D. IGMP

3. Which protocol is used by a workstation to inform the router that it wishes to participate in a multicast?

   A. CGMP

   B. IGMP

   C. PIM

   D. RIP

4. Sparse mode makes use of which of the following?

   A. CGMP

   B. A rendezvous point

   C. VLSM

   D. DVMRP

5. Cisco's initiative to integrate voice, video, and data is called:

   A. IP/VC

   B. VOIP

   C. AVVID

   D. IOS

6. Protocols including RSVP provide which of the following services?

   A. Quality of service

   B. Encryption

   C. Compression

   D. None of the above

7. Which two protocols provide router redundancy?

   A. CGMP and IGRP

   B. HSRP and VRRP

   C. HSRP and CGMP

   D. VRRP and PIM

8. HSRP tracking:

   A. Alters the HSRP priority based on the status of another, tracked interface

   B. Allows the administrator to see which packets traversed which router in HSRP configurations

   C. Allows for load balancing in HSRP installations

   D. Allows for ICMP redirect

9. A black hole network:

   A. Has no default gateway.

   B. Relies on Proxy ARP

   C. Has two routers connected to isolated sections of the same network

   D. Can occur only with token-passing topologies

10. One reason to create networks based on Layer 3 is:

    A. To avoid spanning-tree reliance

    B. To avoid the need for routers

    C. To allow for HSRP

    D. To support multicast sparse-mode operations

11. Designing the network with troubleshooting in mind can:

    A. Simplify outage scheduling and isolate systems

    B. Lead to problems

    C. Compel the designer to use VLSM

    D. Negate the use of OSPF

12. True or false: Most network attacks can be thwarted with a perimeter firewall.

    A. True

    B. False

13. What is the process of recording customer or user problems, owning the problem, and analyzing that data to improve customer service called?

A. Auditing

B. Bug tracking

C. Case management

D. None of the above

14. A designer wants to know at which point additional bandwidth might be required to provide a consistent user experience even during a circuit failure. This problem is answered within the context of which of the following?

A. Trend analysis

B. Capacity planning

C. Case management

D. Case planning

15. Virtual private networks require:

A. Encryption

B. Compression

C. Both A and B

D. None of the above

16. True or false: Telnet is a secure protocol.

A. True

B. False

17. Networks in the future will likely require:

A. Bandwidth

B. Security

C. Wireless solutions

D. Intelligent applications

E. Standards-based protocols

F. All of the above

18. The multicast address of 226.6.2.1 would be similar to which of the following MAC addresses?

A. FF:FF:FF:FF:FF:FF

B. FF:FF:FF:06:02:01

C. 01:00:5E:FF:FF:FF

D. 01:00:5E:06:02:01

19. True or false: More than one IP multicast address can use the same MAC address.

A. True

B. False

20. The first three octets of a multicast MAC address start with:

A. FF:FF:FF

B. 01:00:5E

C. Depends on the IP address

D. Is equal to the MAC address of the source

Answers to Review Questions

1. D.
2. C.
3. B.
4. B.
5. C.
6. A.
7. B.
8. A.
9. C.
10. A.
11. A.
12. B.
13. C.
14. B.
15. A.
16. B.
17. F.
18. D.
19. A.
20. B.

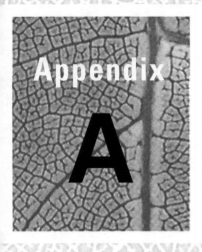

Appendix A

Practice Exam

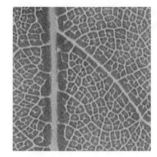

1. ESCON operates at:

   A. 10Mbps

   B. 17Mbps

   C. 100Mbps

   D. 17MBps

2. Without regard to the hierarchical model, queues are typically placed at which of the following points in the network?

   A. Access-layer routers

   B. Distribution-layer routers

   C. At the transmitting interface of a router connected to a slow link

   D. Only in the core

3. Which of the following is not an encapsulation method of serial tunneling?

   A. Direct

   B. HDLC

   C. RSRB

   D. TCP/IP

4. SNA connections between two nodes are typically provided by which of the following?

A. RSRB

B. APPN

C. DLSw+

D. None of the above

5. The RIF includes:

A. Ring numbers and SNA addresses

B. Ring numbers and IP addresses

C. Ring numbers and bridge numbers

D. Bridge numbers and SNA addresses

6. Each FEP must maintain a different LAA. True or false?

A. True

B. False

7. Traditional source-route bridging would be most efficient in which environment? (Forgo SR/TLB as a consideration.)

A. The entire link must be serial in nature.

B. The entire link must be Ethernet in nature.

C. The entire link must be Token Ring in nature.

D. At least two different topologies must be used.

8. DLSw differs from RSRB in that:

A. With DLSw, the RIF is not terminated in the WAN cloud.

B. With RSRB, the RIF is terminated at the edge of the WAN cloud.

C. With RSRB, the RIF does not exist.

D. With DSLw, the RIF is terminated at the edge of the WAN cloud.

9. By default, how often are hellos sent in EIGRP?

    A. Every 3 seconds

    B. Every 5 seconds

    C. Every 10 seconds

    D. Every 60 seconds

10. The best EIGRP designs are:

    A. Hierarchical

    B. Hub-and-spoke

    C. Partial-mesh

    D. Full-mesh

11. Following a link failure in EIGRP, without a feasible successor, the router will:

    A. Flood the entire AS for a new route

    B. Flood the entire network, including redistributed protocols, for a route

    C. Wait for the next update window and listen for an announcement from the missing network

    D. Query neighbor routers for a new route

12. Which best defines mobile hosts in EIGRP?

    A. A wireless host

    B. A host that is not located on its natural subnet

    C. Workstations that use DHCP

    D. None of the above. Only OSPF v2 supports mobile hosts.

13. To support discontiguous subnets in EIGRP, the designer must:

    A. Disable auto-summarization

    B. Enable auto-summarization

    C. Enable auto-discontiguous network services

    D. Take no action

14. Which of the following protocols use hellos?

    A. EIGRP

    B. IGRP

    C. OSPF

    D. ODR

    E. RIP v2

    F. All of the above

    G. None of the above

15. SAP access lists should be deployed:

    A. At the access layer

    B. At the distribution layer

    C. At the core layer

    D. All of the above

16. Which of the following sets of names would lend itself best to a NetBIOS name filter?

    A. MKT-FS1, MKT-FS2, MKT-PTR1

    B. MKT-FS1, MarketingFileSvr, Printer-MKT

    C. FS-MKT, PR-MKT, FS2-MKT

    D. 01FS, 02FS, 01PS

17. Configuring the router for IPX type 20:

   A. Blocks all NetBIOS packets

   B. Automatically requires the use of NLSP

   C. Permits the flooding of NetBIOS broadcasts throughout the network

   D. Disables IPX routing and enables bridging

18. IP eXchange:

   A. Requires a Unix server

   B. Needs a single IP address for all clients

   C. Tunnels IPX packets in IP datagrams

   D. Is a high-speed file transfer protocol

19. An NLSP area should be limited to:

   A. 100 nodes

   B. 200 nodes

   C. 400 nodes

   D. 800 nodes

20. Assuming a Cisco router is in an environment that has six IPX routes of equal cost, how many routes will the router use by default?

   A. One IPX route

   B. Two IPX routes

   C. Four IPX routes

   D. All IPX routes of equal cost

21. IPX process switching:

A. Provides no load balancing

B. Load balances packet by packet

C. Load balances by destination

D. Load balances based on the underlying routing protocol

22. How many Ethernet encapsulations are there?

A. One

B. Two

C. Three

D. Four

23. NetBIOS over AppleTalk is called:

A. NWLink

B. NetBEUI

C. NBT

D. None of the above. NetBIOS does not operate over AppleTalk.

24. The administrator elects to not use DHCP. Thus, the administrator:

A. Must use WINS

B. Cannot use WINS

C. Must assign addresses manually at the host

D. Cannot use NBT

25. NetBIOS operates:

A. At the network layer

B. At the transport layer

C. At the session layer

D. At the data link layer

26. A workgroup:

    A. Requires the use of a domain controller

    B. Requires membership in a domain

    C. Requires the use of WINS and DHCP

    D. Can be created by any two nodes

27. A network requires redundancy whenever possible. Which of the following cannot be configured for redundancy?

    A. WINS

    B. DHCP

    C. The domain controller

    D. None of the above

28. Which of the following cannot be used for name resolution in Windows networks?

    A. Broadcasts

    B. DHCP

    C. DNS

    D. WINS

29. Well-designed IP networks with broadcast controls can support up to:

    A. 100 hosts

    B. 200 hosts

    C. 500 hosts

    D. 1000 hosts

30. NetBIOS cannot run on Unix systems. True or false?

    A. True

    B. False

31. Which of the following is true regarding AAL 3/4?

    A. It provides for 44 bytes of payload.

    B. It includes a sequence number.

    C. It includes a message identifier.

    D. All of the above.

32. ATM headers provide which of the following?

    A. VPI and DLCI

    B. VCI and DLCI

    C. DLCI and CIR

    D. VPI and VCI

33. A network design must incorporate voice services. The designer should look to which technology as part of the solution?

    A. Frame Relay

    B. ATM

    C. SMDS

    D. Leased line

34. The default Frame Relay LMI encapsulation is which of the following?

    A. Annex D

    B. Annex A

    C. Frame Relay Forum LMI

    D. AAL 5 LMI

35. OAM F5 cells provide which of the following?

    A. Switch-to-switch management

    B. End-station-to-switch management

    C. End-station-to-end-station switch management

    D. End-station-to-end-station switch management for virtual circuits

36. Which of the following typically generates the greatest long-term costs in WAN design?

    A. Termination equipment

    B. Routers

    C. Switches

    D. Circuits

37. Compared to LANs, are wide area networks generally more or less reliable?

    A. WANs are more reliable.

    B. WANs are less reliable.

38. Which of the following provides the best reason to use VPN technology?

    A. Lower access charges

    B. Higher security

    C. Fault tolerance

    D. None of the above

39. For security, which provides the best protection from hackers?

    A. Private copper

    B. Private fiber

    C. Public copper

    D. Public fiber

40. The router dynamically permits access into the network based on outbound traffic. This likely uses which of the following?

   A. The established bit

   B. The SYN-ACK bit

   C. Reflexive access lists

   D. Time-based access lists

41. Which of the following is not true regarding AURP?

   A. It is an open standard.

   B. It converts AppleTalk packets to IP.

   C. It sends routing updates only on changes.

   D. It does not replace RTMP.

42. AppleTalk networks frequently:

   A. Fail to scale because of broadcasts

   B. Are difficult to configure

   C. Require manual configuration of addresses on each node

   D. Require DHCP servers

43. The GetZoneList filter:

   A. Blocks ZIP information from the local router to the node

   B. Blocks zone information from leaving the local zone

   C. Is used to proxy zone information

   D. Also blocks RTMP updates

44. What should the designer do when designing a tunnel for AppleTalk across IP? (Choose two.)

    A. Use a star topology.

    B. Remember that performance may degrade.

    C. Note that only RTMP is permitted.

    D. Use only AppleTalk phase one.

45. Which of the following would be the best zone name for a point-to-point WAN link between San Francisco and Chicago?

    A. ZZZ-WAN-SFO-ORD

    B. 3.4

    C. WAN-SFO-ORD

    D. Wan SFO ORD

46. Which of the following is not recommended in AppleTalk networks?

    A. Use filtering where possible.

    B. Do not use RTMP on WAN links.

    C. Permit more than 500 nodes per segment.

    D. Limit the number of resources per zone.

47. Vertical cable runs typically employ which of the following?

    A. Copper wires

    B. Fiber-optic cables

    C. SONET

    D. ATM

48. Cisco switches (Catalyst 5000 series) can connect to which of the following via ISL?

A. Other Cisco switches

B. Other Cisco routers

C. ISL-aware NICs for servers

D. All of the above

49. A single router connects multiple switches in the building. This design is best described as:

A. A distributed backbone

B. A flat network

C. A collapsed backbone

D. A hybrid backbone

50. The designer installs a simple 10Mbps switch to replace a shared 10Mbps Ethernet hub. The theoretical increase in available bandwidth for 12 stations is:

A. The same

B. Doubled

C. Increased by a factor of 12

D. Not enough information provided

Answers to Practice Exam

1. D.
2. C.
3. C.
4. B.
5. C.
6. B.
7. C.
8. D.
9. B.
10. A.
11. D.
12. B.
13. A.
14. A, C.
15. A.
16. A.
17. C.
18. B.
19. C.
20. A.
21. B.
22. D.
23. D.
24. C.

25. C.

26. D.

27. D.

28. B.

29. D.

30. B.

31. D.

32. D.

33. B.

34. C.

35. D.

36. D.

37. B.

38. A.

39. B.

40. C.

41. B.

42. A.

43. A.

44. A, B.

45. A.

46. C.

47. B.

48. D.

49. C.

50. C.

This is the best answer to the question; however, many designers would expand upon this by incorporating collisions, full versus half duplex, and number of nodes per segment. For example, half duplex yields a total of 10Mbps, while full duplex connections can double this. Also, many designers would consider the 10Mbps and divide this figure by 12 on a shared hub, yielding the bandwidth available per station.

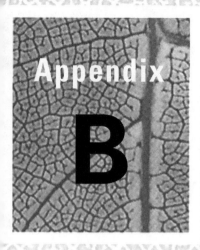

Appendix

B

Bonus Exam

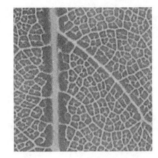

1. True or false: SNA is a routable protocol.

   A. True

   B. False

2. In SRB, the routing information field is created by:

   A. A proprietary protocol on Cisco routers

   B. The end station only

   C. The source station, by using explorer packets to discover each bridge in the network

   D. Each Ethernet switch in the network

3. A router may learn of routes from which of the following? (Select two.)

   A. Connected interfaces

   B. BootP packets

   C. Information learned from dynamic routing protocols

   D. DHCP packets

4. Ideally, an OSPF design should incorporate which of the following?

   A. A large area zero

   B. Virtual links

   C. Discontiguous subnets

   D. All areas adjacent to area zero

5. True or false: An EIGRP router maintains the routing tables for all routers in the AS.

   A. True

   B. False

6. Which protocol uses feasible successors?

   A. RIP

   B. IGRP

   C. OSPF

   D. ODR

   E. EIGRP

7. Which of the following is true regarding SAP updates?

   A. They are sent every 30 seconds.

   B. They are sent on updates only.

   C. They are sent every 60 seconds.

   D. They include 50 services per packet.

8. By default, IPX RIP packets are sent:

   A. Every 10 seconds

   B. Every 30 seconds

   C. Every 60 seconds

   D. On updates only

9. NetBEUI may not be routed because:

   A. It contains an 8-bit RIF field.

   B. It uses a network address that contains the MAC layer address.

   C. It does not contain a network address.

   D. NetBEUI can be routed over IP.

10. The WINS function:

    A. Provides enhanced NetBIOS routing

    B. Provides dynamic name resolution for NetBIOS and IP

    C. Is static by default

    D. Cannot scale beyond the subnet

11. The FastPacket cell supports which of the following?

    A. 24 bytes of user data per cell

    B. Variable-length cells

    C. Compression of cell data between switches

    D. Header compression between packet buffers

12. ATM SCR is analogous to which of the following?

    A. Frame Relay PVC

    B. SMDS e.164

    C. Frame Relay CIR

    D. Frame Relay DLCI

13. A risk with restrictive security policies is:

    A. Acceptance of the policy's restrictions

    B. Circumvention of the policy's restrictions

    C. Poor security implementations

    D. None of the above

14. A designer wishes to provide a central authentication resource for network devices. She might use which of the following? (Choose all that apply.)

   A. CDP

   B. TACACS+

   C. RADIUS

   D. Telnet

15. ZIP storms occur when:

   A. There is a bad NIC in a workstation

   B. Zone information does not sync with routes

   C. The Chooser is left open for more than three minutes

   D. Broadcasts reach 20 percent on a WAN link

16. Which of the following is not a benefit of AT EIGRP?

   A. It maintains hop count information throughout the network.

   B. Under most circumstances, it converges within one second.

   C. RTMP hops appear to be 9600bps serial links in AT EIGRP.

   D. It runs on Cisco routers and Apple routers.

17. When using X.25 in the network core, Cisco recommends:

   A. That partial-mesh topologies be used

   B. That full-mesh topologies be used

   C. That start topologies be used

   D. The hub-and-spoke topologies be used

18. When connecting to public X.25 networks, the router is typically configured as which of the following?

   A. DTE

   B. DCE

   C. Either DTE or DCE

   D. Neither DTE or DCE

19. The use of subinterfaces in X.25 can avoid problems typically found in which types of WANs?

A. Non-multi-access

B. Broadcast multi-access

C. Unicast-broadcast

D. Non-broadcast multi-access

20. A router has received a packet destined for 172.17.90.2. Which route will most likely be used?

A. 10.0.0.0/8

B. 172.16.29.0/24

C. 0.0.0.0/0

D. 172.18.0.0/16

21. Which of the following may be used to support discontiguous subnets?

A. Secondaries

B. Tunnels

C. Classless routing protocols

D. All of the above

E. None of the above

22. Routers operate:

A. At Layer 2 and are slower than switches

B. At Layer 2 and are faster than switches

C. At Layer 3 and are faster than switches

D. At Layer 3 and are slower than switches

23. The LEC is:

    A. Responsible for representing non-ATM devices in LANE

    B. Responsible for forwarding broadcasts

    C. Used for initial ELAN configuration information

    D. Used for spanning-tree control in ATM LANE

24. The assignment of 126 class A address blocks and the large number of Internet connected networks likely caused:

    A. An available address shortage

    B. Development of IP v6, CIDR, and NAT technologies

    C. The widespread usage of RFC 1918 address space

    D. All of the above

25. One possible advantage of using RFC 1918 addresses in the enterprise is:

    A. The return of public addresses

    B. Direct connectivity to the Internet

    C. Faster assignment of addresses from the ISP—the numbering authority for RFC 1918 addresses

    D. None of the above

26. Which of the following WAN technologies is connectionless and uses a group address?

    A. ATM

    B. SMDS

    C. Frame Relay

    D. ISDN

27. The greatest bandwidth permitted with DSL technologies typically uses which of the following?

    A. VDSL

    B. ADSL

    C. SDSL

    D. IDSL

28. The SGBP process performs which of the following? (Select two.)

    A. Snapshot routing

    B. Selection of resources based on processor load

    C. Static Gateway Border Processing, a method for detecting last-resort routes

    D. Selection of resources based on previously existing connections

29. In order to obtain the most scalability, designers should use:

    A. AppleTalk phase one

    B. AppleTalk phase two

    C. AppleTalk phase three

    D. MacIP

30. Which of the following are true regarding AppleTalk?

    A. All of its routing protocols on Cisco routers require the use of split-horizon.

    B. Its default routing protocol is NLSP.

    C. Its default routing protocol is AURP.

    D. With its default routing protocol, the network diameter is limited to 15 hops.

31. Which of the following is not a trunking protocol?

   A. ISL

   B. 802.1d

   C. 802.1q

   D. 802.10

32. LAN Emulation:

   A. Requires the use of ATM

   B. Requires the use of FDDI

   C. Requires the use of both ATM and FDDI

   D. Is independent of both ATM and FDDI

33. FDDI operates at:

   A. 10Mbps

   B. 20Mbps

   C. 100Mbps

   D. 155Mbps

34. The network designer is asked for a preliminary recommendation to merge voice and data in the WAN. The best preliminary solution would be to:

   A. Deploy FastEthernet

   B. Deploy ATM LANE

   C. Deploy ATM

   D. Deploy FDDI

35. Which RFC defines the private address space in IP? (Select two.)

   A. RFC 1597

   B. RFC 1009

   C. RFC 1918

   D. RFC 1819

36. The administrative distance for RIP, version 1, is:

A. 0

B. 1

C. 110

D. 115

E. 120

F. RIP, version 1, does not have an administrative distance.

37. Summarize 10.0.13.0 through 10.0.15.255.

A. 10.0.13.0/22

B. 10.0.13.0/24

C. 10.0.13.0/20

D. This address range cannot be summarized with a single entry.

38. Which answer best defines the primary purpose of a router?

A. Access control

B. Logical forwarding

C. Encryption

D. Media conversion

39. Network Address Translation is available: (Choose all that apply.)

A. With the PIX firewall

B. With any router running IOS 10.0 or higher

C. With any router running IOS 11.2 PLUS or higher

D. With any router running IOS 12.0 or higher

E. None of the above

40. xDSL technologies typically permit connections of up to how many feet?

   A. 328

   B. 1800

   C. 18,000

   D. 36,400

41. ISDN BRI provides how much total bandwidth?

   A. 64Kbps

   B. 128Kbps

   C. 144Kbps

   D. 1.544Kbps

42. The greatest distances permitted with DSL technologies typically use which of the following?

   A. VDSL

   B. ADSL

   C. SDSL

   D. IDSL

43. ISDN B channels provide:

   A. 48 bytes of bandwidth per cell

   B. 64Kbps

   C. 128Kbps

   D. 1.535Mbps

44. X.25 uses which protocol at Layer 2?

   A. LAPD

   B. LAPB

   C. HDLC

   D. None of the above

45. In addition to split-horizon, what two items work to prevent routing loops?

   A. Holddown timers

   B. VLSM

   C. Poison reverse

   D. Route summarization

46. Link failure is detected with carrier loss or which of the following?

   A. Redistribution

   B. Keepalive timers

   C. CDP packets

   D. None of the above

47. True or false: OSPF is classful.

   A. A. True

   B. B. False

48. NAT, as opposed to NAT overload or PAT, supports which of the following?

   A. A single IP address

   B. A pool of IP addresses

   C. A pool of IP networks

   D. Any of the above

49. The designer has four DLCIs in the Frame Relay network terminating on the same router. How many physical interfaces are needed?

A. One

B. Two

C. Three

D. Four

50. LMI is carried on which DLCI?

A. Zero or 1023

B. Any

C. All

D. 31

51. Static ATM routes are defined with which of the following?

A. PNNI

B. EIGRP

C. IISP

D. UNI or NNI

52. Is that your final answer?

A. Yes, Regis, that is my final answer.

B. No, I want to ask the audience.

C. No, I want to phone a friend.

D. No, I want an IPO.

Answers to Bonus Exam

1. B.
2. C.
3. A, C.
4. D.
5. B.
6. E.
7. C.
8. C.
9. C.
10. B.
11. A.
12. C.
13. B.
14. B, C.
15. B.
16. D.
17. B.
18. B.
19. D.
20. C.
21. D.
22. D.
23. A.
24. D.

25. A.

26. B.

27. A.

28. B, D

29. B.

30. D.

31. B.

32. A.

33. C.

34. C.

35. A, C.

36. E.

37. D.

38. B.

39. A, C, D.

40. C.

41. C.

42. D.

43. B.

44. B.

45. A, C.

46. B.

47. B.

48. B.

49. A.

50. A.

51. C.

52. Good luck on the exam!

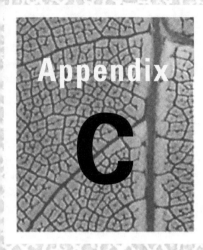

Appendix

C

References

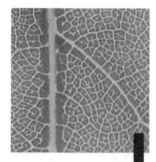

It is impossible for anyone to keep track of all the developments in network design, especially when including the nuances introduced by different software versions and hardware platforms. Good network designers are usually better off not trying to learn everything. Rather, the best designers know how to locate and obtain the information they require. The ability to research is a powerful skill in the designer's repertoire.

This appendix includes various references that should assist network designers. Note that not all of these sources were used in researching material for this book.

Web-Based Resources

This section lists some of the resources available on the Internet. By no means is it intended to be exhaustive.

While every effort has been made to provide an accurate list, the dynamic nature of the Internet and the static nature of this text will likely result in invalid references over time.

WAN Technologies

Organization	URL
ADSL Forum	`www.adsl.com`
DSL Life	`www.dsllife.com`
Frame Relay Forum	`www.frforum.com`
The ATM Forum	`www.atmforum.com/index.html`
Commercial Communications Standards	`www-comm.itsi.disa.mil/isdn/index.html`
The North American ISDN Users' Forum	`www.niuf.nist.gov/`

Operating Systems

Organization	URL
Apple	`www.apple.com`
Novell	`www.novell.com`
Microsoft	`www.microsoft.com`
CNET: WinFiles	`www.winfiles.com`
Linux	`www.linux.org`

RFCs and Standards

Organization	URL
The Internet Engineering Task Force	`www.ietf.cnri.reston.va.us/home.html`
Ohio State University Computer and Information Science Department	`www.cis.ohio-state.edu/hypertext/information/rfc.html`
IEEE	`www.ieee.org`

Other

Organization	URL
3Com	www.3com.com
Business 2.0	www.business2.com
Cisco Systems	www.cisco.com
CMP Tech Web	teledotcom.com
Consortium for School Networking	www.cosn.org
Distributed Management Task Force	www.dmtf.org
ENS Trends Web Page	www.ens.net/trends.htm
Globalnet System Solutions	www.lammle.com
GTE Internetworking	www.bbn.com/securitymatters
IBM	www.networking.ibm.com
International Telecommunication Union	www.itu.org
Internet Traffic Statistics	whatis.com/itraffic.htm
L0PHT Heavy Industries	www.l0pht.com
MCI WorldCom MAE(sm) Information	www.mae.net
Network World Fusion	www.nwfusion.com
NewBridge	www.newbridge.com
Nortel Networks	www.nortelnetworks.com
OpenView Forum International	www.ovforum.org
PC Week	www.pcweek.com
Pittsburgh Supercomputing Center	www.psc.edu/networking

Organization	URL
Securitywatch.com	`www.securitywatch.com`
Slashdot	`www.slashdot.org`
Sun Microsystems	`docs.sun.com`
Telecom Research	`www.telecomresearch.com`
Wireless Ethernet Compatibility Alliance (WECA)	`www.wirelessethernet.org`
Ziff-Davis	`www.zdnet.com`

Study Groups

Organization	URL
NetCerts	`www.netcerts.com`
Cisco Professional Association Worldwide (CPAW)	`www.ciscopaw.com`
Boson Software—Practice Tests	`www.boson.com`
Groupstudy.com	`www.groupstudy.com`
Network Study Guides	`www.networkstudyguides.com`

Job Search Web Sites

```
jobs.statestreet.com
talentmarket.monster.com
www.1-jobs.com
www.brainpower.com
www.brilliantpeople.com
www.careercast.com
www.computerjobs.com
www.dice.com
www.guru.com
www.headhunter.net
www.hotjobs.com
www.incpad.com
www.joboptions.com
```

```
www.modisit.com
www.monster.com
www.realrates.com
www.skillsvillage.com
www.techies.com
www.vault.com
```

Humor

```
www.userfriendly.org
www.dilbert.com
```

RFCs

It would be inappropriate to reprint the entire RFC index in this text. A number of Web sites provide this information in a continually updated manner. This list is intended to highlight some of the more important and frequently referred to RFCs.

1055—SLIP
1483—ATM AAL5, Multiprotocol Encapsulation
1487—LDAP
1490—Multiprotocol Connect over Frame Relay
1492—TACACS
1577—ATM ARP
1586—OSPF on Frame Relay
1631—NAT
1661—PPP
1700—IP Assigned Numbers
1918—Private IP v.4 Address Space
1925—The 12 Networking Truths (the most important RFC?)
1990—PPP Multilink Protocol
2002—IP Mobility
2132—DHCP Options
2281—HSRP
2324—Hyper Text Coffee Pot Control Protocol (really)
2328—OSPF v.2
2338—VRRP
2676—OSPF QoS
2740—OSPF IP v.6

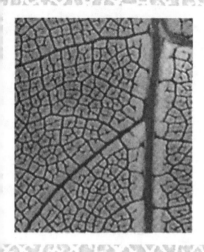

Glossary

A&B bit signaling   Used in T1 transmission facilities and sometimes called 24th channel signaling. Each of the 24 T1 subchannels in this procedure uses one bit of every sixth frame to send supervisory signaling information.

AAL   ATM Adaptation Layer: A service-dependent sublayer of the data-link layer, which accepts data from other applications and brings it to the ATM layer in 48-byte ATM payload segments. CS and SAR are the two sub-layers that form AALs. Currently, the four types of AAL recommended by the ITU-T are AAL1, AAL2, AAL3/4, and AAL5. AALs are differentiated by the source-destination timing they use, whether they are CBR or VBR, and whether they are used for connection-oriented or connectionless mode data transmission. *See also: AAL1, AAL2, AAL3/4, AAL5, CS, and SAR, ATM, and ATM layer.*

AAL1   ATM Adaptation Layer 1: One of four AALs recommended by the ITU-T, it is used for connection-oriented, time-sensitive services that need constant bit rates, such as isochronous traffic and uncompressed video. *See also: AAL.*

AAL2   ATM Adaptation Layer 2: One of four AALs recommended by the ITU-T, it is used for connection-oriented services that support a variable bit rate, such as voice traffic. *See also: AAL.*

AAL3/4   ATM Adaptation Layer 3/4: One of four AALs (a product of two initially distinct layers) recommended by the ITU-T, supporting both con-nectionless and connection-oriented links. Its primary use is in sending SMDS packets over ATM networks. *See also: AAL.*

AAL5 ATM Adaptation Layer 5: One of four AALs recommended by the ITU-T, it is used to support connection-oriented VBR services primarily to transfer classical IP over ATM and LANE traffic. This least complex of the AAL recommendations uses SEAL, offering lower bandwidth costs and simpler processing requirements but also providing reduced bandwidth and error-recovery capacities. *See also: AAL.*

AARP AppleTalk Address Resolution Protocol: The protocol in an Apple-Talk stack that maps data-link addresses to network addresses.

AARP probe packets Packets sent by the AARP to determine whether a given node ID is being used by another node in a nonextended AppleTalk network. If the node ID is not in use, the sending node appropriates that node's ID. If the node ID is in use, the sending node will select a different ID and then send out more AARP probe packets. *See also: AARP.*

ABM Asynchronous Balanced Mode: When two stations can initiate a transmission, ABM is an HDLC (or one of its derived protocols) communication technology that supports peer-oriented, point-to-point communications between both stations.

ABR Area Border Router: An OSPF router that is located on the border of one or more OSPF areas. ABRs are used to connect OSPF areas to the OSPF backbone area.

access list A set of test conditions kept by routers that determines "interesting traffic" to and from the router for various services on the network.

access method The manner in which network devices approach gaining access to the network itself.

access server Also known as a network access server, it is a communications process connecting asynchronous devices to a LAN or WAN through network and terminal emulation software, providing synchronous or asynchronous routing of supported protocols.

acknowledgement Verification sent from one network device to another signifying that an event has occurred. May be abbreviated as ACK. *Contrast with: NAK.*

ACR   allowed cell rate: A designation defined by the ATM Forum for managing ATM traffic. Dynamically controlled using congestion control measures, the ACR varies between the minimum cell rate (MCR) and the peak cell rate (PCR). *See also: MCR and PCR.*

active monitor   The mechanism used to manage a Token Ring. The network node with the highest MAC address on the ring becomes the active monitor and is responsible for management tasks such as preventing loops and ensuring tokens are not lost.

address mapping   By translating network addresses from one format to another, this methodology permits different protocols to operate interchangeably.

address mask   A bit combination descriptor identifying which portion of an address refers to the network or subnet and which part refers to the host. Sometimes simply called the mask. *See also: subnet mask.*

address resolution   The process used for resolving differences between computer addressing schemes. Address resolution typically defines a method for tracing network layer (Layer 3) addresses to data-link layer (Layer 2) addresses. *See also: address mapping.*

adjacency   The relationship made between defined neighboring routers and end nodes, using a common media segment, to exchange routing information.

administrative distance   A number between 0 and 225 that expresses the value of trustworthiness of a routing information source. The lower the number, the higher the integrity rating.

administrative weight   A value designated by a network administrator to rate the preference given to a network link. It is one of four link metrics exchanged by PTSPs to test ATM network resource availability.

ADSU   ATM Data Service Unit: The terminal adapter used to connect to an ATM network through an HSSI-compatible mechanism. *See also: DSU.*

advertising   The process whereby routing or service updates are transmitted at given intervals, allowing other routers on the network to maintain a record of viable routes.

AEP AppleTalk Echo Protocol: A test for connectivity between two Apple-Talk nodes where one node sends a packet to another and receives an echo, or copy, in response.

AFI Authority and Format Identifier: The part of an NSAP ATM address that delineates the type and format of the IDI section of an ATM address. *See also: IDI and NSAP.*

AFP AppleTalk Filing Protocol: A presentation-layer protocol, supporting AppleShare and Mac OS File Sharing, that permits users to share files and applications on a server.

AIP ATM Interface Processor: Supporting AAL3/4 and AAL5, this interface for Cisco 7000 series routers minimizes performance bottlenecks at the UNI. *See also: AAL3/4 and AAL5.*

algorithm A set of rules or process used to solve a problem. In networking, algorithms are typically used for finding the best route for traffic from a source to its destination.

alignment error An error occurring in Ethernet networks, in which a received frame has extra bits; that is, a number not divisible by eight. Alignment errors are generally the result of frame damage caused by collisions.

all-routes explorer packet An explorer packet that can move across an entire SRB network, tracing all possible paths to a given destination. Also known as an all-rings explorer packet. *See also: explorer packet, local explorer packet, and spanning explorer packet.*

AM Amplitude Modulation: A modulation method that represents information by varying the amplitude of the carrier signal. *See also: modulation.*

AMI Alternate Mark Inversion: A line-code type on T1 and E1 circuits that shows zeros as "01" during each bit cell, and ones as "11" or "00," alternately, during each bit cell. The sending device must maintain ones density in AMI but not independently of the data stream. Also known as binary-coded, alternate mark inversion. *Contrast with: B8ZS. See also: ones density.*

amplitude An analog or digital waveform's highest value.

analog transmission Signal messaging whereby information is represented by various combinations of signal amplitude, frequency, and phase.

ANSI American National Standards Institute: The organization of corporate, government, and other volunteer members that coordinates standards-related activities, approves U.S. national standards, and develops U.S. positions in international standards organizations. ANSI assists in the creation of international and U.S. standards in disciplines such as communications, networking, and a variety of technical fields. It publishes over 13,000 standards, for engineered products and technologies ranging from screw threads to networking protocols. ANSI is a member of the IEC and ISO. *See also: IEC and ISO.*

anycast An ATM address that can be shared by more than one end system, allowing requests to be routed to a node that provides a particular service.

AppleTalk Currently in two versions, the group of communication protocols designed by Apple Computer for use in Macintosh environments. The earlier Phase 1 protocols support one physical network with only one network number that resides in one zone. The later Phase 2 protocols support more than one logical network on a single physical network, allowing networks to exist in more than one zone. *See also: zone.*

application layer Layer 7 of the OSI reference network model, supplying services to application procedures (such as electronic mail or file transfer) that are outside the OSI model. This layer chooses and determines the availability of communicating partners along with the resources necessary to make the connection, coordinates partnering applications, and forms a consensus on procedures for controlling data integrity and error recovery. *See also: data-link layer, network layer, physical layer, presentation layer, session layer, and transport layer.*

ARA AppleTalk Remote Access: A protocol for Macintosh users establishing their access to resources and data from a remote AppleTalk location.

area A logical, rather than physical, set of segments (based on either CLNS, DECnet, or OSPF) along with their attached devices. Areas are commonly connected to others using routers to create a single autonomous system. *See also: autonomous system.*

ARM Asynchronous Response Mode: An HDLC communication mode using one primary station and at least one additional station, in which transmission can be initiated from either the primary or one of the secondary units.

ARP Address Resolution Protocol: Defined in RFC 826, the protocol that traces IP addresses to MAC addresses. *See also: RARP.*

ASBR Autonomous System Boundary Router: An area border router placed between an OSPF autonomous system and a non-OSPF network that operates both OSPF and an additional routing protocol, such as RIP. ASBRs must be located in a non-stub OSPF area. *See also: ABR, non-stub area, and OSPF.*

ASCII American Standard Code for Information Interchange: An eight-bit code for representing characters, consisting of seven data bits plus one parity bit.

ASN.1 Abstract Syntax Notation One: An OSI language used to describe types of data that is independent of computer structures and depicting methods. Described by ISO International Standard 8824.

ASP AppleTalk Session Protocol: A protocol employing ATP to establish, maintain, and tear down sessions, as well as sequence requests. *See also: ATP.*

AST Automatic Spanning Tree: A function that supplies one path for spanning explorer frames traveling from one node in the network to another, supporting the automatic resolution of spanning trees in SRB networks. AST is based on the IEEE 802.1 standard. *See also: IEEE 802.1 and SRB.*

asynchronous transmission Digital signals sent without precise timing, usually with different frequencies and phase relationships. Asynchronous transmissions generally enclose individual characters in control bits (called start and stop bits) that show the beginning and end of each character. *Contrast with: isochronous transmission and synchronous transmission.*

ATCP AppleTalk Control Program: The protocol for establishing and configuring AppleTalk over PPP, defined in RFC 1378. *See also: PPP.*

ATDM Asynchronous Time-Division Multiplexing: A technique for sending information, it differs from normal TDM in that the time slots are assigned when necessary rather than preassigned to certain transmitters. *Contrast with: FDM, statistical multiplexing, and TDM.*

ATG Address Translation Gateway: The mechanism within Cisco DECnet routing software that enables routers to route multiple, independent DECnet networks and to establish a user-designated address translation for chosen nodes between networks.

ATM   Asynchronous Transfer Mode: The international standard, identified by fixed-length 53-byte cells, for transmitting cells in multiple service systems, such as voice, video, or data. Transit delays are reduced because the fixed-length cells permit processing to occur in the hardware. ATM is designed to maximize the benefits of high-speed transmission media, such as SONET, E3, and T3.

ATM ARP server   A device that supplies logical subnets running classical IP over ATM with address-resolution services.

ATM endpoint   The initiating or terminating connection in an ATM network. ATM endpoints include servers, workstations, ATM-to-LAN switches, and ATM routers.

ATM Forum   The international organization founded jointly by Northern Telecom, Sprint, Cisco Systems, and NET/ADAPTIVE in 1991 to develop and promote standards-based implementation agreements for ATM technology. The ATM Forum broadens official standards developed by ANSI and ITU-T and creates implementation agreements before official standards are published.

ATM layer   A sublayer of the data-link layer in an ATM network that is service independent. To create standard 53-byte ATM cells, the ATM layer receives 48-byte segments from the AAL and attaches a 5-byte header to each. These cells are then sent to the physical layer for transmission across the physical medium. *See also: AAL.*

ATMM   ATM Management: A procedure that runs on ATM switches, managing rate enforcement and VCI translation. *See also: ATM and VCI.*

ATM user-user connection   A connection made by the ATM layer to supply communication between at least two ATM service users, such as ATMM processes. These communications can be uni- or bidirectional, using one or two VCCs, respectively. *See also: ATM layer and ATMM.*

ATP   AppleTalk Transaction Protocol: A transport-level protocol that enables reliable transactions between two sockets, where one requests the other to perform a given task and to report the results. ATP fastens the request and response together, assuring a loss-free exchange of request-response pairs.

attenuation   In communication, weakening or loss of signal energy, typically caused by distance.

AURP   AppleTalk Update-based Routing Protocol: A technique for encapsulating AppleTalk traffic in the header of a foreign protocol that allows the connection of at least two noncontiguous AppleTalk internetworks through a foreign network (such as TCP/IP) to create an AppleTalk WAN. The connection made is called an AURP tunnel. By exchanging routing information between exterior routers, the AURP maintains routing tables for the complete AppleTalk WAN. *See also: AURP tunnel and exterior router.*

AURP tunnel   A connection made in an AURP WAN that acts as a single, virtual link between AppleTalk internetworks separated physically by a foreign network such as a TCP/IP network. *See also: AURP.*

authority zone   A portion of the domain-name tree associated with DNS for which one name server is the authority. *See also: DNS.*

automatic call reconnect   A function that enables automatic call rerouting away from a failed trunk line.

autonomous confederation   A collection of self-governed systems that depend more on their own network accessibility and routing information than on information received from other systems or groups.

autonomous switching   The ability of Cisco routers to process packets more quickly by using the ciscoBus to switch packets independently of the system processor.

autonomous system (AS)   A group of networks under mutual administration that share the same routing methodology. Autonomous systems are subdivided by areas and must be assigned an individual 16-bit number by the IANA. *See also: area and IANA.*

autoreconfiguration   A procedure executed by nodes within the failure domain of a Token Ring, wherein nodes automatically perform diagnostics, trying to reconfigure the network around failed areas.

B8ZS   Binary 8-Zero Substitution: A line-code type, interpreted at the remote end of the connection, that uses a special code substitution whenever eight consecutive zeros are transmitted over the link on T1 and E1 circuits. This technique assures ones density independent of the data stream. Also known as bipolar 8-zero substitution. *Contrast with: AMI. See also: ones density.*

backbone   The basic portion of the network that provides the primary path for traffic sent to and initiated from other networks.

back end   A node or software program supplying services to a front end. *See also: client, front end, and server.*

bandwidth   The gap between the highest and lowest frequencies employed by network signals. More commonly, it refers to the rated throughput capacity of a network protocol or medium.

baseband   A feature of a network technology that uses only one carrier frequency, for example Ethernet. Also named narrowband. *Compare with: broadband.*

baud   Synonymous with bits per second (bps), if each signal element represents one bit. It is a unit of signaling speed equivalent to the number of separate signal elements transmitted per second.

B channel   Bearer channel: A full-duplex, 64Kbps channel in ISDN that transmits user data. *Compare with: D channel, E channel, and H channel.*

beacon   An FDDI device or Token Ring frame that points to a serious problem with the ring, such as a broken cable. The beacon frame carries the address of the station thought to be down. *See also: failure domain.*

BECN   Backward Explicit Congestion Notification: BECN is the bit set by a Frame Relay network in frames moving away from frames headed into a congested path. A DTE that receives frames with the BECN may ask higher-level protocols to take necessary flow-control measures. *Compare with: FECN.*

BGP4   BGP Version 4: Version 4 of the interdomain routing protocol most commonly used on the Internet. BGP4 supports CIDR and uses route-counting mechanisms to decrease the size of routing tables. *See also: CIDR.*

binary   A two-character numbering method that uses ones and zeros. The binary numbering system underlies all digital representation of information.

BIP   Bit Interleaved Parity: A method used in ATM to monitor errors on a link, sending a check bit or word in the link overhead for the previous block or frame. This allows bit errors in transmissions to be found and delivered as maintenance information.

BISDN Broadband ISDN: ITU-T standards created to manage high-bandwidth technologies such as video. BISDN presently employs ATM technology along SONET-based transmission circuits, supplying data rates between 155Mbps and 622Mbps and beyond. Contrast with N-ISDN. *See also: BRI, ISDN, and PRI.*

bit-oriented protocol Regardless of frame content, the class of data-link layer communication protocols that transmits frames. Bit-oriented protocols, as compared with byte-oriented, supply more efficient and trustworthy, full-duplex operation. *Compare with: byte-oriented protocol.*

border gateway A router that facilitates communication with routers in different autonomous systems.

BPDU Bridge Protocol Data Unit: A Spanning-Tree Protocol initializing packet that is sent at definable intervals for the purpose of exchanging information among bridges in networks.

BRI Basic Rate Interface: The ISDN interface that facilitates circuit-switched communication between video, data, and voice; it is made up of two B channels (64Kbps each) and one D channel (16Kbps). *Compare with: PRI. See also: BISDN, ISN.*

bridge A device for connecting two segments of a network and transmitting packets between them. Both segments must use identical protocols to communicate. Bridges function at the data-link layer, Layer 2 of the OSI reference model. The purpose of a bridge is to filter, send, or flood any incoming frame, based on the MAC address of that particular frame.

broadband A transmission methodology for multiplexing several independent signals onto one cable. In telecommunications, broadband is classified as any channel with bandwidth greater than 4kHz (typical voice grade). In LAN terminology, it is classified as a coaxial cable on which analog signaling is employed. Also known as wideband. *Contrast with: baseband.*

broadcast A data frame or packet that is transmitted to every node on the local network segment (as defined by the broadcast domain). Broadcasts are known by their broadcast address, which is a destination network and host address with all the bits turned on. Also called local broadcast. *Compare with: directed broadcasts.*

broadcast domain   A group of devices receiving broadcast frames initiating from any device within the group. Because they do not forward broadcast frames, broadcast domains are generally surrounded by routers.

broadcast storm   An undesired event on the network caused by the simultaneous transmission of any number of broadcasts across the network segment. Such an occurrence can overwhelm network bandwidth, resulting in time-outs.

buffer   A storage area dedicated to handling data while in transit. Buffers are used to receive/store sporadic deliveries of data bursts, usually received from faster devices, compensating for the variations in processing speed. Incoming information is stored until everything is received prior to sending data on. Also known as an information buffer.

bus topology   A linear LAN architecture in which transmissions from various stations on the network are reproduced over the length of the medium and are accepted by all other stations. *Compare with: ring, star, and tree topologies.*

bus   Any physical path, typically wires or copper, through which a digital signal can be used to send data from one part of a computer to another.

BUS   broadcast and unknown server: In LAN emulation, the hardware or software responsible for resolving all broadcasts and packets with unknown (unregistered) addresses into the point-to-point virtual circuits required by ATM. *See also: LEC, LECS, LES, and LANE.*

BX.25   AT&T's use of X.25. *See also: X.25.*

bypass mode   An FDDI and Token Ring network operation that deletes an interface.

bypass relay   A device that enables a particular interface in the Token Ring to be closed down and effectively taken off the ring.

byte-oriented protocol   Any type of data-link communication protocol that, in order to mark the boundaries of frames, uses a specific character from the user character set. These protocols have generally been superseded by bit-oriented protocols. *Compare with: bit-oriented protocol.*

cable range   In an extended AppleTalk network, the range of numbers allotted for use by existing nodes on the network. The value of the cable range can be anywhere from a single to a sequence of several touching network numbers. Node addresses are determined by their cable range value.

CAC   Connection Admission Control: The sequence of actions executed by every ATM switch while connection setup is performed in order to determine if a request for connection is violating the guarantees of QoS for established connections. Also, CAC is used to route a connection request through an ATM network.

call admission control   A device for managing of traffic in ATM networks, determining the possibility of a path containing adequate bandwidth for a requested VCC.

call priority   In circuit-switched systems, the defining priority given to each originating port; it specifies in which order calls will be reconnected. Additionally, call priority identifies which calls are allowed during a bandwidth reservation.

call set-up time   The length of time necessary to effect a switched call between DTE devices.

CBR   Constant Bit Rate: An ATM Forum QoS class created for use in ATM networks. CBR is used for connections that rely on precision clocking to guarantee trustworthy delivery. *Compare with: ABR and VBR.*

CD   Carrier Detect: A signal indicating that an interface is active or that a connection generated by a modem has been established.

CDP   Cisco Discovery Protocol: Cisco's proprietary protocol that is used to tell a neighbor Cisco device about the type of hardware, software version, and active interfaces that the Cisco device is using. It uses a SNAP frame between devices and is not routable.

CDVT   Cell Delay Variation Tolerance: A QoS parameter for traffic management in ATM networks specified when a connection is established. The allowable fluctuation levels for data samples taken by the PCR in CBR transmissions are determined by the CDVT. *See also: CBR and PCR.*

cell In ATM networking, the basic unit of data for switching and multi-plexing. Cells have a defined length of 53 bytes, including a 5-byte header that identifies the cell's data stream and 48 bytes of payload. *See also: cell relay.*

cell payload scrambling The method by which an ATM switch maintains framing on some medium-speed edge and trunk interfaces (T3 or E3 circuits). Cell payload scrambling rearranges the data portion of a cell to maintain the line synchronization with certain common bit patterns.

cell relay A technology that uses small packets of fixed size, known as cells. Their fixed length enables cells to be processed and switched in hardware at high speeds, making this technology the foundation for ATM and other high-speed network protocols. *See also: cell.*

Centrex A local exchange carrier service, providing local switching that resembles that of an on-site PBX. Centrex has no on-site switching capability. Therefore, all customer connections return to the CO. *See also: CO.*

CER Cell Error Ratio: The ratio in ATM of transmitted cells having errors to the total number of cells sent in a transmission within a certain span of time.

channelized E1 Operating at 2.048Mpbs, an access link that is sectioned into 29 B channels and one D channel, supporting DDR, Frame Relay, and X.25. *Compare with: channelized T1.*

channelized T1 Operating at 1.544Mbps, an access link that is sectioned into 23 B channels and one D channel of 64Kbps each, where individual channels or groups of channels connect to various destinations, supporting DDR, Frame Relay, and X.25. *Compare with: channelized E1.*

CHAP Challenge Handshake Authentication Protocol: Supported on lines using PPP encapsulation, it is a security feature that identifies the remote end, helping keep out unauthorized users. After CHAP is performed, the router or access server determines whether a given user is permitted access. It is a newer, more secure protocol than PAP. *Compare with: PAP.*

checksum A test for ensuring the integrity of sent data. It is a number calculated from a series of values taken through a sequence of mathematical functions, typically placed at the end of the data from which it is calculated, and then recalculated at the receiving end for verification. *Compare with: CRC.*

choke packet   When congestion exists, it is a packet sent to inform a transmitter that it should decrease its sending rate.

CIDR   Classless Interdomain Routing: A method supported by classless routing protocols, such as OSPF and BGP4, based on the concept of ignoring the IP class of address, permitting route aggregation and VLSM that enable routers to combine routes in order to minimize the routing information that needs to be conveyed by the primary routers. It allows a group of IP networks to appear to other networks as a unified, larger entity. In CIDR, IP addresses and their subnet masks are written as four dotted octets, followed by a forward slash and the numbering of masking bits (a form of subnet notation shorthand). *See also: BGP4.*

CIP   Channel Interface Processor: A channel attachment interface for use in Cisco 7000 series routers that connects a host mainframe to a control unit. This device eliminates the need for an FBP to attach channels.

CIR   Committed Information Rate: Averaged over a minimum span of time and measured in bps, a Frame Relay network's agreed-upon minimum rate of transferring information.

Cisco FRAD   Cisco Frame Relay access device: A Cisco product that supports Cisco IPS Frame Relay SNA services, connecting SDLC devices to Frame Relay without requiring an existing LAN. May be upgraded to a fully functioning multiprotocol router. Can activate conversion from SDLC to Ethernet and Token Ring, but does not support attached LANs. *See also: FRAD.*

CiscoFusion   Cisco's name for the internetworking architecture under which its Cisco IOS operates. It is designed to "fuse" together the capabilities of its disparate collection of acquired routers and switches.

Cisco IOS software   Cisco Internet Operating System software. The kernel of the Cisco line of routers and switches that supplies shared functionality, scalability, and security for all products under its CiscoFusion architecture. *See also: CiscoFusion.*

CiscoView   GUI-based management software for Cisco networking devices, enabling dynamic status, statistics, and comprehensive configuration information. Displays a physical view of the Cisco device chassis and provides device-monitoring functions and fundamental troubleshooting capabilities. May be integrated with a number of SNMP-based network management platforms.

classical IP over ATM   Defined in RFC 1577, the specification for running IP over ATM that maximizes ATM features. Also known as CIA.

CLP   Cell Loss Priority: The area in the ATM cell header that determines the likelihood of a cell being dropped during network congestion. Cells with CLP = 0 are considered insured traffic and are not apt to be dropped. Cells with CLP = 1 are considered best-effort traffic that may be dropped during congested episodes, delivering more resources to handle insured traffic.

CLR   Cell Loss Ratio: The ratio of discarded cells to successfully delivered cells in ATM. CLR can be designated a QoS parameter when establishing a connection.

CO   Central Office: The local telephone company office where all loops in a certain area connect and where circuit switching of subscriber lines occurs.

collapsed backbone   A nondistributed backbone where all network segments are connected to each other through an internetworking device. A collapsed backbone can be a virtual network segment at work in a device such as a router, hub, or switch.

collision   The effect of two nodes sending transmissions simultaneously in Ethernet. When they meet on the physical media, the frames from each node collide and are damaged. *See also: collision domain.*

collision domain   The network area in Ethernet over which frames that have collided will spread. Collisions are propagated by hubs and repeaters, but not by LAN switches, routers, or bridges. *See also: collision.*

configuration register   A 16-bit configurable value stored in hardware or software that determines how Cisco routers function during initialization. In hardware, the bit position is set using a jumper. In software, it is set by specifying specific bit patterns used to set startup options, configured using a hexadecimal value with configuration commands.

congestion   Traffic that exceeds the network's ability to handle it.

congestion avoidance   To minimize delays, the method an ATM network uses to control traffic entering the system. Lower-priority traffic is discarded at the edge of the network when indicators signal it cannot be delivered, thus using resources efficiently.

congestion collapse The situation that results from the retransmission of packets in ATM networks where little or no traffic successfully arrives at destination points. It usually happens in networks made of switches with ineffective or inadequate buffering capabilities combined with poor packet discard or ABR congestion feedback mechanisms.

connectionless Data transfer that occurs without the creating of a virtual circuit. No overhead, best-effort delivery, not reliable. *Contrast with: connection-oriented. See also: virtual circuit.*

connection-oriented Data transfer method that sets up a virtual circuit before any data is transferred. Uses acknowledgments and flow control for reliable data transfer. *Contrast with: connectionless. See also: virtual circuit.*

control direct VCC One of three control connections defined by Phase I LAN Emulation; a bi-directional virtual control connection (VCC) established in ATM by an LEC to an LES. *See also: control distribute VCC.*

control distribute VCC One of three control connections defined by Phase 1 LAN Emulation; a unidirectional virtual control connection (VCC) set up in ATM from an LES to an LEC. Usually, the VCC is a point-to-multipoint connection. *See also: control direct VCC.*

convergence The process required for all routers in an internetwork to update their routing tables and create a consistent view of the network, using the best possible paths. No user data is passed during a convergence time.

cost Also known as path cost, an arbitrary value, based on hop count, bandwidth, or other calculation, that is typically assigned by a network administrator and used by the routing protocol to compare different routes through an internetwork. Routing protocols use cost values to select the best path to a certain destination: the lowest cost identifies the best path. *See also: routing metric.*

count to infinity A problem occurring in routing algorithms that are slow to converge where routers keep increasing the hop count to particular networks. To avoid this problem, various solutions have been implemented into each of the different routing protocols. Some of those solutions include defining a maximum hop count (defining infinity), route poisoning, poison reverse, and split-horizon.

CPCS   Common Part Convergence Sublayer: One of two AAL sublayers that is service-dependent, it is further segmented into the CS and SAR sublayers. The CPCS prepares data for transmission across the ATM network; it creates the 48-byte payload cells that are sent to the ATM layer. *See also: AAL and ATM layer.*

CPE   Customer Premises Equipment: Items such as telephones, modems, and terminals installed at customer locations and connected to the telephone company network.

crankback   In ATM, a correction technique used when a node somewhere on a chosen path cannot accept a connection setup request, blocking the request. The path is rolled back to an intermediate node, which then uses GCAC to attempt to find an alternate path to the final destination.

CRC   Cyclical Redundancy Check: A methodology that detects errors, whereby the frame recipient makes a calculation by dividing frame contents with a prime binary divisor and compares the remainder to a value stored in the frame by the sending node. *Contrast with: checksum.*

CSMA/CD   Carrier Sense Multiple Access Collision Detect: A technology defined by the Ethernet IEEE 802.3 committee. Each device senses the cable for a digital signal before transmitting. Also, CSMA/CD allows all devices on the network to share the same cable, but one at a time. If two devices transmit at the same time, a frame collision will occur and a jamming pattern will be sent; the devices will stop transmitting, wait a predetermined amount of time, and then try to transmit again.

CSU   Channel Service Unit: A digital mechanism that connects end-user equipment to the local digital telephone loop. Frequently referred to along with the data service unit as CSU/DSU. *See also: DSU.*

CTD   Cell Transfer Delay: For a given connection in ATM, the time period between a cell exit event at the source user-network interface (UNI) and the corresponding cell entry event at the destination. The CTD between these points is the sum of the total inter-ATM transmission delay and the total ATM processing delay.

cut-through frame switching   A frame-switching technique that flows data through a switch so that the leading edge exits the switch at the output port before the packet finishes entering the input port. Frames will be read, processed, and forwarded by devices that use cut-through switching as soon as the destination address of the frame is confirmed and the outgoing port is identified.

data direct VCC   A bidirectional point-to-point virtual control connection (VCC) set up between two LECs in ATM and one of three data connections defined by Phase 1 LAN Emulation. Because data direct VCCs do not guarantee QoS, they are generally reserved for UBR and ABR connections. *Compare with: control distribute VCC and control direct VCC.*

datagram   A logical collection of information transmitted as a network layer unit over a medium without a previously established virtual circuit. IP datagrams have become the primary information unit of the Internet. At various layers of the OSI reference model, the terms *cell, frame, message, packet,* and *segment* also define these logical information groupings.

data-link control layer   Layer 2 of the SNA architectural model, it is responsible for the transmission of data over a given physical link and compares somewhat to the data-link layer of the OSI model.

data-link layer   Layer 2 of the OSI reference model, it ensures the trustworthy transmission of data across a physical link and is primarily concerned with physical addressing, line discipline, network topology, error notification, ordered delivery of frames, and flow control. The IEEE has further segmented this layer into the MAC sublayer and the LLC sublayer. Also known as the link layer. Can be compared somewhat to the data-link control layer of the SNA model. *See also: application layer, LLC, MAC, network layer, physical layer, presentation layer, session layer, and transport layer.*

DCC   Data Country Code: Developed by the ATM Forum, one of two ATM address formats designed for use by private networks. *Compare with: ICD.*

DCE   data communications equipment (as defined by the EIA) or data circuit-terminating equipment (as defined by the ITU-T): The mechanisms and links of a communications network that make up the network portion of the user-to-network interface, such as modems. The DCE supplies the physical connection to the network, forwards traffic, and provides a clocking signal to synchronize data transmission between DTE and DCE devices. *Compare with: DTE.*

D channel   1. Data channel: A full-duplex, 16Kbps (BRI) or 64Kbps (PRI) ISDN channel. *Compare with: B channel, E channel, and H channel.* 2. In SNA, anything that provides a connection between the processor and main storage with any peripherals.

DDP Datagram Delivery Protocol : Used in the AppleTalk suite of protocols as a connectionless protocol that is responsible for sending datagrams through an internetwork.

DDR dial-on-demand routing: A technique that allows a router to automatically initiate and end a circuit-switched session per the requirements of the sending station. By mimicking keepalives, the router fools the end station into treating the session as active. DDR permits routing over ISDN or telephone lines via a modem or external ISDN terminal adapter.

default route The static routing table entry used to direct frames whose next hop is not spelled out in the dynamic routing table.

delay The time elapsed between a sender's initiation of a transaction and the first response they receive. Also, the time needed to move a packet from its source to its destination over a path. *See also: latency.*

demarc The demarcation point between the customer premises equipment (CPE) and the telco's carrier equipment.

demodulation A series of steps that return a modulated signal to its original form. When receiving, a modem demodulates an analog signal to its original digital form (and, conversely, modulates the digital data it sends into an analog signal). *See also: modulation.*

demultiplexing The process of converting a single multiplex signal, comprising more than one input stream, back into separate output streams. *See also: multiplexing.*

designated bridge In the process of forwarding a frame from a segment to the route bridge, the bridge with the lowest path cost.

designated router An OSPF router that creates LSAs for a multiaccess network and is required to perform other special tasks in OSPF operations. Multiaccess OSPF networks that maintain a minimum of two attached routers identify one router that is chosen by the OSPF Hello protocol, which makes possible a decrease in the number of adjacencies necessary on a multiaccess network. This in turn reduces the quantity of routing protocol traffic and the physical size of the database.

destination address   The address for the network devices that will receive a packet.

directed broadcast   A data frame or packet that is transmitted to a specific group of nodes on a remote network segment. Directed broadcasts are known by their broadcast address, which is a destination subnet address with all the bits turned on. *Compare with: local broadcasts.*

discovery mode   Also known as dynamic configuration, this technique is used by an AppleTalk interface to gain information from a working node about an attached network. The information is subsequently used by the interface for self-configuration.

distance-vector routing algorithm   In order to find the shortest path, this group of routing algorithms repeats on the number of hops in a given route, requiring each router to send its complete routing table with each update, but only to its neighbors. Routing algorithms of this type tend to generate loops, but they are fundamentally simpler than their link-state counterparts. *See also: link-state routing algorithm and SPF.*

DLCI   Data-Link Connection Identifier: Used to identify virtual circuits in a Frame Relay network.

DNS   Domain Name System: Used to resolve host names to IP addresses.

DSAP   Destination Service Access Point: The service access point of a network node, specified in the destination field of a packet. *See also: SSAP and SAP.*

DSR   Data Set Ready: When a DCE is powered up and ready to run, this EIA/TIA-232 interface circuit is also engaged.

DSU   Data Service Unit: This device is used to adapt the physical interface on a data terminal equipment (DTE) mechanism to a transmission facility such as T1 or E1 and is also responsible for signal timing. It is commonly grouped with the channel service unit and referred to as the CSU/DSU. *See also: CSU.*

DTE   data terminal equipment: Any device located at the user end of a user-network interface serving as a destination, a source, or both. DTE includes devices such as multiplexers, protocol translators, and computers. The connection to a data network is made through data channel equipment (DCE) such as a modem, using the clocking signals generated by that device. *See also: DCE.*

DTR data terminal ready: An activated EIA/TIA-232 circuit communicating to the DCE the state of preparedness of the DTE to transmit or receive data.

DUAL Diffusing Update Algorithm: Used in Enhanced IGRP, this convergence algorithm provides loop-free operation throughout an entire route's computation. DUAL grants routers involved in a topology revision the ability to synchronize simultaneously, while routers unaffected by this change are not involved. *See also: Enhanced IGRP.*

DVMRP Distance Vector Multicast Routing Protocol: Based primarily on the Routing Information Protocol (RIP), this Internet gateway protocol implements a common, condensed-mode IP multicast scheme, using IGMP to transfer routing datagrams between its neighbors. *See also: IGMP.*

DXI Data Exchange Interface: Described in RFC 1482, DXI defines the effectiveness of a network device such as a router, bridge, or hub to act as an FEP to an ATM network by using a special DSU that accomplishes packet encapsulation.

dynamic routing Also known as adaptive routing, this technique automatically adapts to traffic or physical network revisions.

E1 Generally used in Europe, a wide-area digital transmission scheme carrying data at 2.048Mbps. E1 transmission lines are available for lease from common carriers for private use.

E.164 1. Evolved from standard telephone numbering system, the standard recommended by ITU-T for international telecommunication numbering, particularly in ISDN, SMDS, and BISDN. 2. Label of field in an ATM address containing numbers in E.164 format.

E channel Echo channel: A 64Kbps ISDN control channel used for circuit switching. Specific description of this channel can be found in the 1984 ITU-T ISDN specification, but was dropped from the 1988 version. *See also: B, D, and H channels.*

edge device A device that enables packets to be forwarded between legacy interfaces (such as Ethernet and Token Ring) and ATM interfaces based on information in the data-link and network layers. An edge device does not take part in the running of any network layer routing protocol; it merely uses the route description protocol in order to get the forwarding information required.

EEPROM   Electronically Erasable Programmable Read-Only Memory: Programmed after their manufacture, these nonvolatile memory chips can be erased if necessary using electric power and reprogrammed. *See also: EPROM, PROM.*

EFCI   Explicit Forward Congestion Indication: A congestion feedback mode permitted by ABR service in an ATM network. The EFCI may be set by any network element that is in a state of immediate or certain congestion. The destination end system is able to carry out a protocol that adjusts and lowers the cell rate of the connection based on value of the EFCI. *See also: ABR.*

EIGRP   *See: Enhanced IGRP.*

EIP   Ethernet Interface Processor: A Cisco 7000 series router interface processor card, supplying 10Mbps AUI ports to support Ethernet Version 1 and Ethernet Version 2 or IEEE 802.3 interfaces with a high-speed data path to other interface processors.

ELAN   Emulated LAN: An ATM network configured using a client/server model in order to emulate either an Ethernet or Token Ring LAN. Multiple ELANs can exist at the same time on a single ATM network and are made up of an LAN Emulation Client (LEC), an LAN Emulation Server (LES), a broadcast and unknown server (BUS), and an LAN Emulation Configuration Server (LECS). ELANs are defined by the LANE specification. *See also: LANE, LEC, LECS, and LES.*

ELAP   EtherTalk Link Access Protocol: In an EtherTalk network, the link-access protocol constructed above the standard Ethernet data-link layer.

encapsulation   The technique used by layered protocols in which a layer adds header information to the protocol data unit (PDU) from the layer above. As an example, in Internet terminology, a packet would contain a header from the physical layer, followed by a header from the network layer (IP), followed by a header from the transport layer (TCP), followed by the application protocol data.

encryption   The conversion of information into a scrambled form that effectively disguises it to prevent unauthorized access. Every encryption scheme uses some well-defined algorithm, which is reversed at the receiving end by an opposite algorithm in a process known as decryption.

Enhanced IGRP Enhanced Interior Gateway Routing Protocol: An advanced routing protocol created by Cisco, combining the advantages of link-state and distance-vector protocols. Enhanced IGRP has superior convergence attributes, including high operating efficiency. *See also: IGP, OSPF, and RIP.*

enterprise network A privately owned and operated network that joins most major locations in a large company or organization.

EPROM Erasable Programmable Read-Only Memory: Programmed after their manufacture, these nonvolatile memory chips can be erased if necessary using high-power light and reprogrammed. *See also: EEPROM, PROM.*

ESF Extended Superframe: Made up of 24 frames with 192 bits each, with the 193rd bit providing other functions including timing. This is an enhanced version of SF. *See also: SF.*

Ethernet A baseband LAN specification created by the Xerox Corporation and then improved through joint efforts of Xerox, Digital Equipment Corporation, and Intel. Ethernet is similar to the IEEE 802.3 series standard and, using CSMA/CD, operates over various types of cables at 10Mbps. Also called DIX (Digital/Intel/Xerox) Ethernet. *See also: 10BaseT, Fast Ethernet, and IEEE.*

EtherTalk A data-link product from Apple Computer that permits Apple-Talk networks to be connected by Ethernet.

excess rate In ATM networking, traffic exceeding a connection's insured rate. The excess rate is the maximum rate less the insured rate. Depending on the availability of network resources, excess traffic can be discarded during congestion episodes. *Compare with: maximum rate.*

expansion The procedure of directing compressed data through an algorithm, restoring information to its original size.

expedited delivery An option that can be specified by one protocol layer, communicating either with other layers or with the identical protocol layer in a different network device, requiring that identified data be processed faster.

explorer packet An SNA packet transmitted by a source Token Ring device to find the path through a source-route-bridged network.

failure domain The region in which a failure has occurred in a Token Ring. When a station gains information that a serious problem, such as a cable break, has occurred with the network, it sends a beacon frame that includes the station reporting the failure, its NAUN, and everything between. This defines the failure domain. Beaconing then initiates the procedure known as autoreconfiguration. *See also: autoreconfiguration and beacon.*

fallback In ATM networks, this mechanism is used for scouting a path if it isn't possible to locate one using customary methods. The device relaxes requirements for certain characteristics, such as delay, in an attempt to find a path that meets a certain set of the most important requirements.

FastEthernet Any Ethernet specification with a speed of 100Mbps. FastEthernet is ten times faster than 10BaseT, while retaining qualities like MAC mechanisms, MTU, and frame format. These similarities make it possible for existing 10BaseT applications and management tools to be used on FastEthernet networks. FastEthernet is based on an extension of IEEE 802.3 specification (IEEE 802.3u). *Compare with: Ethernet. See also: 100BaseT, 100BaseTX, and IEEE.*

fast switching A Cisco feature that uses a route cache to speed packet switching through a router. *Contrast with: process switching.*

FDM Frequency-Division Multiplexing: A technique that permits information from several channels to be assigned bandwidth on one wire based on frequency. *See also: TDM, ATDM, and statistical multiplexing.*

FDDI Fiber Distributed Data Interface: A LAN standard, defined by ANSI X3T9.5, that can run at speeds up to 200Mbps and uses token-passing media access on fiber-optic cable. For redundancy, FDDI can use a dual-ring architecture.

FECN Forward Explicit Congestion Notification: A bit set by a Frame Relay network that informs the DTE receptor that congestion was encountered along the path from source to destination. A device receiving frames with the FECN bit set can ask higher-priority protocols to take flow-control action as needed. *See also: BECN.*

FEIP FastEthernet Interface Processor: An interface processor employed on Cisco 7000 series routers, supporting up to two 100Mbps 100BaseT ports.

firewall A barrier purposefully erected between any connected public networks and a private network, made up of a router or access server or several routers or access servers, that uses access lists and other methods to ensure the security of the private network.

flash memory Developed by Intel and licensed to other semiconductor manufacturers, it is nonvolatile storage that can be erased electronically and reprogrammed, physically located on an EEPROM chip. Flash memory permits software images to be stored, booted, and rewritten as needed. Cisco routers and switches use flash memory to hold the IOS by default. *See also: EPROM, EEPROM.*

flooding When traffic is received on an interface, it is then transmitted to every interface connected to that device with exception of the interface from which the traffic originated. This technique can be used for traffic transfer by bridges and switches throughout the network.

flow control A methodology used to ensure that receiving units are not overwhelmed with data from sending devices. Pacing, as it is called in IBM networks, means that when buffers at a receiving unit are full, a message is transmitted to the sending unit to temporarily halt transmissions until all the data in the receiving buffer has been processed and the buffer is again ready for action.

FRAD Frame Relay access device: Any device affording a connection between a LAN and a Frame Relay WAN. *See also: Cisco FRAD, FRAS.*

fragment Any portion of a larger packet that has been intentionally segmented into smaller pieces. A packet fragment does not necessarily indicate an error and can be intentional. *See also: fragmentation.*

fragmentation The process of intentionally segmenting a packet into smaller pieces when sending data over an intermediate network medium that cannot support the larger packet size.

frame A logical unit of information sent by the data-link layer over a transmission medium. The term often refers to the header and trailer, employed for synchronization and error control, that surround the data contained in the unit.

Frame Relay   A more efficient replacement of the X.25 protocol (an unrelated packet relay technology that guarantees data delivery). Frame Relay is an industry-standard, shared-access, best-effort, switched data-link layer encapsulation that services multiple virtual circuits and protocols between connected mechanisms.

Frame Relay bridging   Defined in RFC 1490, this bridging method uses the identical spanning-tree algorithm as other bridging operations but permits packets to be encapsulated for transmission across a Frame Relay network.

FRAS   Frame Relay access support: A feature of Cisco IOS software that enables SDLC, Ethernet, Token Ring, and Frame Relay-attached IBM devices to be linked with other IBM mechanisms on a Frame Relay network. *See also: FRAD.*

frequency   The number of cycles of an alternating current signal per time unit, measured in Hertz (cycles per second).

FSIP   Fast Serial Interface Processor: The Cisco 7000 routers' default serial interface processor, it provides four or eight high-speed serial ports.

FTP   File Transfer Protocol: The TCP/IP protocol used for transmitting files between network nodes, it supports a broad range of file types and is defined in RFC 959. *See also: TFTP.*

full duplex   The capacity to transmit information between a sending station and a receiving unit at the same time. *See also: half duplex.*

full mesh   A type of network topology where every node has either a physical or a virtual circuit linking it to every other network node. A full mesh supplies a great deal of redundancy but is typically reserved for network backbones because of its expense. *See also: partial mesh.*

GNS   Get Nearest Server: On an IPX network, a request packet sent by a customer for determining the location of the nearest active server of a given type. An IPX network client launches a GNS request to get either a direct answer from a connected server or a response from a router disclosing the location of the service on the internetwork to the GNS. GNS is part of IPX and SAP. *See also: IPX and SAP.*

GRE Generic Routing Encapsulation: A tunneling protocol created by Cisco with the capacity for encapsulating a wide variety of protocol packet types inside IP tunnels, thereby generating a virtual point-to-point connection to Cisco routers across an IP network at remote points. IP tunneling using GRE permits network expansion across a single-protocol backbone environment by linking multiprotocol subnetworks in a single-protocol backbone environment.

guard band The unused frequency area found between two communications channels, furnishing the space necessary to avoid interference between the two.

half duplex The capacity to transfer data in only one direction at a time between a sending unit and receiving unit. *See also: full duplex.*

handshake Any series of transmissions exchanged between two or more devices on a network to ensure synchronized operations.

H channel High-speed channel: A full-duplex, ISDN primary rate channel operating at a speed of 384Kbps. *See also: B, D, and E channels.*

HDLC High-Level Data-Link Control: Using frame characters, including checksums, HDLC designates a method for data encapsulation on synchronous serial links and is the default encapsulation for Cisco routers. HDLC is a bit-oriented synchronous data-link layer protocol created by ISO and derived from SDLC. However, most HDLC vendor implementations (including Cisco's) are proprietary. *See also: SDLC.*

helper address The unicast address specified, which instructs the Cisco router to change the client's local broadcast request for a service into a directed unicast to the server.

hierarchical addressing Any addressing plan employing a logical chain of commands to determine location. IP addresses are made up of a hierarchy of network numbers, subnet numbers, and host numbers to direct packets to the appropriate destination.

HIP HSSI Interface Processor: An interface processor used on Cisco 7000 series routers, providing one HSSI port that supports connections to ATM, SMDS, Frame Relay, or private lines at speeds up to T3 or E3.

holddown   The state a route is placed in so that routers can neither advertise the route nor accept advertisements about it for a defined time period. Holddown is used to surface bad information about a route from all routers in the network. A route is generally placed in holddown when one of its links fails.

hop   The movement of a packet between any two network nodes. *See also: hop count.*

hop count   A routing metric that calculates the distance between a source and a destination. RIP employs hop count as its sole metric. *See also: hop and RIP.*

HSCI   High-Speed Communication Interface: Developed by Cisco, a single-port interface that provides full-duplex synchronous serial communications capability at speeds up to 52Mbps.

HSRP   Hot Standby Router Protocol: A protocol that provides high network availability and provides nearly instantaneous hardware failover without administrator intervention. It generates a Hot Standby router group, including a lead router that lends its services to any packet being transferred to the Hot Standby address. If the lead router fails, it will be replaced by any of the other routers—the standby routers—that monitor it.

HSSI   High-Speed Serial Interface: A network standard physical connector for high-speed serial linking over a WAN at speeds of up to 52Mbps.

ICD   International Code Designator: Adapted from the subnetwork model of addressing, this assigns the mapping of network layer addresses to ATM addresses. HSSI is one of two ATM formats for addressing created by the ATM Forum to be utilized with private networks. *See also: DCC.*

ICMP   Internet Control Message Protocol: Documented in RFC 792, it is a network layer Internet protocol for the purpose of reporting errors and providing information pertinent to IP packet procedures.

IEEE   Institute of Electrical and Electronics Engineers: A professional organization that, among other activities, defines standards in a number of fields within computing and electronics, including networking and communications. IEEE standards are the predominant LAN standards used today throughout the industry. Many protocols are commonly known by the reference number of the corresponding IEEE standard.

IEEE 802.1   The IEEE committee specification that defines the bridging group. The specification for STP (Spanning-Tree Protocol) is IEEE 802.1d. The STP uses SPA (spanning-tree algorithm) to find and prevent network loops in bridged networks. The specification for VLAN trunking is IEEE 802.1q. *Compare to: ISL.*

IEEE 802.3   The IEEE committee specification that defines the Ethernet group, specifically the original 10Mbps standard. Ethernet is a LAN protocol that specifies physical layer and MAC sublayer media access. IEEE 802.3 uses CSMA/CD to provide access for many devices on the same network. FastEthernet is defined as 802.3u, and Gigabit Ethernet is defined as 802.3q. *See also: CSMA/CD.*

IEEE 802.5   IEEE committee that defines Token Ring media access.

IGMP   Internet Group Management Protocol: Employed by IP hosts, the protocol that reports their multicast group memberships to an adjacent multicast router.

IGP   Interior Gateway Protocol: Any protocol used by the Internet to exchange routing data within an independent system. Examples include RIP, IGRP, and OSPF.

ILMI   Integrated (or Interim) Local Management Interface. A specification created by the ATM Forum, designated for the incorporation of network-management capability into the ATM UNI. Integrated Local Management Interface cells provide for automatic configuration between ATM systems. In LAN emulation, ILMI can provide sufficient information for the ATM end station to find an LECS. In addition, ILMI provides the ATM NSAP (Network Service Access Point) prefix information to the end station.

in-band management   In-band management is the management of a network device "through" the network. Examples include using Simple Network Management Protocol (SNMP) or Telnet directly via the local LAN. *Compare with: out-of-band management.*

insured burst   In an ATM network, it is the largest, temporarily permitted data burst exceeding the insured rate on a PVC and not tagged by the traffic policing function for being dropped if network congestion occurs. This insured burst is designated in bytes or cells.

interarea routing   Routing between two or more logical areas. *Contrast with: intra-area routing. See also: area.*

interface processor   Any of several processor modules used with Cisco 7000 series routers. *See also: AIP, CIP, EIP, FEIP, HIP, MIP, and TRIP.*

Internet   The global "network of networks," whose popularity has exploded in the last few years. Originally a tool for collaborative academic research, it has become a medium for exchanging and distributing information of all kinds. The Internet's need to link disparate computer platforms and technologies has led to the development of uniform protocols and standards that have also found widespread use within corporate LANs. *See also: TCP/IP and MBONE.*

internet   Before the rise of the Internet, this lowercase form was shorthand for "internetwork" in the generic sense. Now rarely used. *See also: internetwork.*

Internet protocol   Any protocol belonging to the TCP/IP protocol stack. *See also: TCP/IP.*

internetwork   Any group of private networks interconnected by routers and other mechanisms, typically operating as a single entity.

internetworking   Broadly, anything associated with the general task of linking networks to each other. The term encompasses technologies, procedures, and products. When you connect networks to a router, you are creating an internetwork.

intra-area routing   Routing that occurs within a logical area. *Contrast with: interarea routing.*

Inverse ARP   Inverse Address Resolution Protocol: A technique by which dynamic mappings are constructed in a network, allowing a device such as a router to locate the logical network address and associate it with a permanent virtual circuit (PVC). Commonly used in Frame Relay to determine the far-end node's TCP/IP address by sending the Inverse ARP request to the local DLCI.

IP   Internet Protocol: Defined in RFC 791, it is a network layer protocol that is part of the TCP/IP stack and allows connectionless service. IP furnishes an array of features for addressing, type-of-service specification, fragmentation and reassembly, and security.

IP address   Often called an Internet address, this is an address uniquely identifying any device (host) on the Internet (or any TCP/IP network). Each address consists of four octets (32 bits), represented as decimal numbers separated by periods (a format known as "dotted-decimal"). Every address is made up of a network number, an optional subnetwork number, and a host number. The network and subnetwork numbers together are used for routing, while the host number addresses an individual host within the network or subnetwork. The network and subnetwork information is extracted from the IP address using the subnet mask. There are five classes of IP addresses (A–E), which allocate different numbers of bits to the network, subnetwork, and host portions of the address. *See also: CIDR, IP, and subnet mask.*

IPCP   IP Control Program: The protocol used to establish and configure IP over PPP. *See also: IP and PPP.*

IP multicast   A technique for routing that enables IP traffic to be reproduced from one source to several endpoints or from multiple sources to many destinations. Instead of transmitting only one packet to each individual point of destination, one packet is sent to a multicast group specified by only one IP endpoint address for the group.

IPX   Internetwork Packet Exchange: Network layer protocol (Layer 3) used in Novell NetWare networks for transferring information from servers to workstations. Similar to IP and XNS.

IPXCP   IPX Control Program: The protocol used to establish and configure IPX over PPP. *See also: IPX and PPP.*

IPXWAN   Protocol used for new WAN links to provide and negotiate line options on the link using IPX. After the link is up and the options have been agreed upon by the two end-to-end links, normal IPX transmission begins.

ISDN   Integrated Services Digital Network: Offered as a service by telephone companies, a communication protocol that allows telephone networks to carry data, voice, and other digital traffic. *See also: BISDN, BRI, and PRI.*

isochronous transmission   Asynchronous data transfer over a synchronous data-link, requiring a constant bit rate for reliable transport. *Compare with: asynchronous transmission and synchronous transmission.*

ITU-T   International Telecommunication Union Telecommunication Standardization Sector: This is a group of engineers that develops worldwide standards for telecommunications technologies.

LAN   Local Area Network: Broadly, any network linking two or more computers and related devices within a limited geographical area (up to a few kilometers). LANs are typically high-speed, low-error networks within a company. Cabling and signaling at the physical and data-link layers of the OSI are dictated by LAN standards. Ethernet, FDDI, and Token Ring are among the most popular LAN technologies. *Compare with: MAN and WAN.*

LANE   LAN emulation: The technology that allows an ATM network to operate as a LAN backbone. To do so, the ATM network is required to provide multicast and broadcast support, address mapping (MAC-to-ATM), SVC management, in addition to an operable packet format. Additionally, LANE defines Ethernet and Token Ring ELANs. *See also: ELAN.*

LAN switch   A high-speed, multiple-interface transparent bridging mechanism, transmitting packets between segments of data-links, usually referred to specifically as an Ethernet switch. LAN switches transfer traffic based on MAC addresses. Multilayer switches are a type of high-speed, special-purpose, hardware-based router. *See also: multilayer switch, cut-through packet switching, and store-and-forward packet switching.*

LAPB   Link Accessed Procedure, Balanced: A bit-oriented data-link layer protocol that is part of the X.25 stack and has its origin in SDLC. *See also: SDLC and X.25.*

LAPD   Link Access Procedure on the D channel. The ISDN data-link layer protocol used specifically for the D channel and defined by ITU-T Recommendations Q.920 and Q.921. LAPD evolved from LAPB and is created to comply with the signaling requirements of ISDN basic access.

latency   Broadly, the time it takes a data packet to get from one location to another. In specific networking contexts, it can mean either 1) the time elapsed (delay) between the execution of a request for access to a network by a device and the time the mechanism actually is permitted transmission, or 2) the time elapsed between when a mechanism receives a frame and the time that frame is forwarded out of the destination port.

Layer-3 switch   See also: multilayer switch.

LCP   Link Control Protocol: The protocol designed to establish, configure, and test data-link connections for use by PPP. *See also: PPP.*

leaky bucket   An analogy for the basic cell rate algorithm (GCRA) used in ATM networks for checking the conformance of cell flows from a user or network. The bucket's "hole" is understood to be the prolonged rate at which cells can be accommodated, and the "depth" is the tolerance for cell bursts over a certain time period. *See also: GCRA.*

learning bridge   A bridge that transparently builds a dynamic database of MAC addresses and the interfaces associated with each address. Transparent bridges help to reduce traffic congestion on the network.

LE ARP   LAN Emulation Address Resolution Protocol: The protocol providing the ATM address that corresponds to a MAC address.

LEC   LAN Emulation Client: Software providing the emulation of the link layer interface that allows the operation and communication of all higher-level protocols and applications to continue. The LEC client runs in all ATM devices, which include hosts, servers, bridges, and routers. The LANE client is responsible for address resolution, data transfer, address caching, interfacing to the emulated LAN, and driver support for higher-level services. *See also: ELAN and LES.*

LECS   LAN Emulation Configuration Server: An important part of emulated LAN services, providing the configuration data that is furnished upon request from the LES. These services include address registration for Integrated Local Management Interface (ILMI) support, configuration support for the LES addresses and their corresponding emulated LAN identifiers, and an interface to the emulated LAN. *See also: LES and ELAN.*

LES   LAN Emulation Server: The central LANE component that provides the initial configuration data for each connecting LEC. The LES typically is located on either an ATM-integrated router or a switch. Responsibilities of the LES include configuration and support for the LEC, address registration for the LEC, database storage and response concerning ATM addresses, and interfacing to the emulated LAN *See also: ELAN, LEC, and LECS.*

link-state routing algorithm   A routing algorithm that allows each router to broadcast or multicast information regarding the cost of reaching all its neighbors to every node in the internetwork. Link-state algorithms provide a consistent view of the network and are therefore not vulnerable to routing loops. However, this is achieved at the cost of somewhat greater difficulty in computation and more widespread traffic (compared with distance-vector routing algorithms). *See also: distance-vector routing algorithm.*

LLAP   LocalTalk Link Access Protocol: In a LocalTalk environment, the data-link-level protocol that manages node-to-node delivery of data. This protocol provides node addressing and management of bus access, and it also controls data sending and receiving to assure packet length and integrity.

LLC   Logical Link Control: Defined by the IEEE, the higher of two data-link layer sublayers. LLC is responsible for error detection (but not correction), flow control, framing, and software-sublayer addressing. The predominant LLC protocol, IEEE 802.2, defines both connectionless and connection-oriented operations. *See also: data-link layer and MAC.*

LMI   An enhancement to the original Frame Relay specification. Among the features it provides are a keepalive mechanism, a multicast mechanism, global addressing, and a status mechanism.

LNNI   LAN Emulation Network-to-Network Interface: In the Phase 2 LANE specification, an interface that supports communication between the server components within one ELAN.

local explorer packet   In a Token Ring SRB network, a packet generated by an end system to find a host linked to the local ring. If no local host can be found, the end system will produce one of two solutions: a spanning explorer packet or an all-routes explorer packet.

LocalTalk   Utilizing CSMA/CD, in addition to supporting data transmission at speeds of 230.4Kbps, LocalTalk is Apple Computer's proprietary baseband protocol, operating at the data-link and physical layers of the OSI reference model.

LSA   link-state advertisement: Contained inside of link-state packets (LSPs), these advertisements are usually multicast packets, containing information about neighbors and path costs, that are employed by link-state protocols. Receiving routers use LSAs to maintain their link-state databases and, ultimately, routing tables.

LUNI LAN Emulation User-to-Network Interface: Defining the interface between the LAN Emulation Client (LEC) and the LAN Emulation Server, LUNI is the ATM Forum's standard for LAN Emulation on ATM networks. *See also: LES and LECS.*

MAC Media Access Control: The lower sublayer in the data-link layer, it is responsible for hardware addressing, media access, and error detection of frames. *See also: data-link layer and LLC.*

MAC address A data-link layer hardware address that every port or device needs in order to connect to a LAN segment. These addresses are used by various devices in the network for accurate location of logical addresses. MAC addresses are defined by the IEEE standard and their length is six characters, typically using the burned-in address (BIA) of the local LAN interface. Variously called hardware address, physical address, burned-in address, or MAC-layer address.

MacIP In AppleTalk, the network layer protocol encapsulating IP packets in Datagram Delivery Protocol (DDP) packets. MacIP also supplies substitute ARP services.

MAN Metropolitan-Area Network: Any network that encompasses a metropolitan area; that is, an area typically larger than a LAN but smaller than a WAN. *See also: LAN and WAN.*

Manchester encoding A method for digital coding in which a mid-bit-time transition is employed for clocking, and a 1 (one) is denoted by a high voltage level during the first half of the bit time. This scheme is used by Ethernet and IEEE 802.3.

maximum burst Specified in bytes or cells, the largest burst of information exceeding the insured rate that will be permitted on an ATM permanent virtual connection for a short time and will not be dropped even if it goes over the specified maximum rate. *Compare with: insured burst. See also: maximum rate.*

maximum rate The maximum permitted data throughput on a particular virtual circuit, equal to the total of insured and uninsured traffic from the traffic source. Should traffic congestion occur, uninsured information may be deleted from the path. Measured in bits or cells per second, the maximum rate represents the highest throughput of data the virtual circuit is ever able to deliver and cannot exceed the media rate. *Compare with: excess rate. See also: maximum burst.*

MBS Maximum Burst Size: In an ATM signaling message, this metric, coded as a number of cells, is used to convey the burst tolerance.

MBONE multicast backbone: The multicast backbone of the Internet, it is a virtual multicast network made up of multicast LANs, including point-to-point tunnels interconnecting them.

MCDV Maximum Cell Delay Variation: The maximum two-point CDV objective across a link or node for the identified service category in an ATM network. The MCDV is one of four link metrics that are exchanged using PTSPs to verify the available resources of an ATM network. Only one MCDV value is assigned to each traffic class.

MCLR Maximum Cell Loss Ratio: The maximum ratio of cells in an ATM network that fail to transit a link or node compared with the total number of cells that arrive at the link or node. MCDV is one of four link metrics that are exchanged using PTSPs to verify the available resources of an ATM network. The MCLR applies to cells in VBR and CBR traffic classes whose CLP bit is set to zero. *See also: CBR, CLP, and VBR.*

MCR Minimum Cell Rate: A parameter determined by the ATM Forum for traffic management of the ATM networks. MCR is specifically defined for ABR transmissions and specifies the minimum value for the allowed cell rate (ACR). *See also: ACR and PCR.*

MCTD Maximum Cell Transfer Delay: In an ATM network, the total of the maximum cell delay variation and the fixed delay across the link or node. MCTD is one of four link metrics that are exchanged using PNNI topology state packets to verify the available resources of an ATM network. There is one MCTD value assigned to each traffic class. *See also: MCDV.*

MIB Management Information Base: Used with SNMP management software to gather information from remote devices. The management station can poll the remote device for information, or the MIB running on the remote station can be programmed to send information on a regular basis.

MIP Multichannel Interface Processor: The resident interface processor on Cisco 7000 series routers, providing up to two channelized T1 or E1 connections by serial cables connected to a CSU. The two controllers are capable of providing 24 T1 or 30 E1 channel groups, with each group being introduced to the system as a serial interface that can be configured individually.

mips   millions of instructions per second: A measure of processor speed.

MLP   Multilink PPP: A technique used to split, recombine, and sequence datagrams across numerous logical data-links.

MMP   Multichassis Multilink PPP: A protocol that supplies MLP support across multiple routers and access servers. MMP enables several routers and access servers to work as a single, large dial-up pool with one network address and ISDN access number. MMP successfully supports packet fragmenting and reassembly when the user connection is split between two physical access devices.

modem   modulator-demodulator: A device that converts digital signals to analog and vice-versa so that digital information can be transmitted over analog communication facilities, such as voice-grade telephone lines. This is achieved by converting digital signals at the source to analog for transmission and reconverting the analog signals back into digital form at the destination. *See also: modulation and demodulation.*

modem eliminator   A mechanism that makes possible a connection between two DTE devices without modems by simulating the commands and physical signaling required.

modulation   The process of modifying some characteristic of an electrical signal, such as amplitude (AM) or frequency (FM), in order to represent digital or analog information. *See also: AM.*

MOSPF   Multicast OSPF: An extension of the OSPF unicast protocol that enables IP multicast routing within the domain. *See also: OSPF.*

MPOA   Multiprotocol over ATM: An effort by the ATM Forum to standardize how existing and future network-layer protocols such as IP, Ipv6, AppleTalk, and IPX run over an ATM network with directly attached hosts, routers, and multilayer LAN switches.

MTU   maximum transmission unit: The largest packet size, measured in bytes, that an interface can handle.

multicast   Broadly, any communication between a single sender and multiple receivers. Unlike broadcast messages, which are sent to all addresses on a network, multicast messages are sent to a defined subset of the network addresses; this subset has a group multicast address, which is specified in the packet's destination address field. *See also: broadcast, directed broadcast.*

multicast address   A single address that points to more than one device on the network by specifying a special non-existent MAC address specified in that particular multicast protocol. Identical to group address. *See also: multicast.*

multicast send VCC   A two-directional point-to-point virtual control connection (VCC) arranged by an LEC to a BUS, it is one of the three types of informational link specified by phase 1 LANE. *See also: control distribute VCC and control direct VCC.*

multilayer switch   A highly specialized, high-speed, hardware-based type of LAN router, the device filters and forwards packets based on their Layer 2 MAC addresses and Layer 3 network addresses. It's possible that even Layer 4 can be read. Sometimes called a Layer 3 switch. *See also: LAN switch.*

multiplexing   The process of converting several logical signals into a single physical signal for transmission across one physical channel. *Contrast with: demultiplexing.*

NAK   negative acknowledgment: A response sent from a receiver, telling the sender that the information was not received or contained errors. *Compare with: acknowledgment.*

NAT   Network Address Translation: An algorithm instrumental in minimizing the requirement for globally unique IP addresses, permitting an organization whose addresses are not all globally unique to connect to the Internet, regardless, by translating those addresses into globally routable address space.

NBP   Name Binding Protocol: In AppleTalk, the transport-level protocol that interprets a socket client's name, entered as a character string, into the corresponding DDP address. NBP gives AppleTalk protocols the capacity to discern user-defined zones and names of mechanisms by showing and keeping translation tables that map names to their corresponding socket addresses.

neighboring routers   Two routers in OSPF that have interfaces to a common network. On networks with multiaccess, these neighboring routers are dynamically discovered using the Hello protocol of OSPF.

NetBEUI NetBIOS Extended User Interface: An improved version of the NetBIOS protocol used in a number of network operating systems including LAN Manager, Windows NT, LAN Server, and Windows for Workgroups, implementing the OSI LLC2 protocol. NetBEUI formalizes the transport frame not standardized in NetBIOS and adds more functions. *See also: OSI.*

NetBIOS Network Basic Input/Output System: The API employed by applications residing on an IBM LAN to ask for services, such as session termination or information transfer, from lower-level network processes.

NetView A mainframe network product from IBM, used for monitoring SNA (Systems Network Architecture) networks. It runs as a VTAM (Virtual Telecommunications Access Method) application.

NetWare A widely used NOS created by Novell, providing a number of distributed network services and remote file access.

network layer In the OSI reference model, it is Layer 3—the layer in which routing is implemented, enabling connections and path selection between two end systems. *See also: application layer, data-link layer, physical layer, presentation layer, session layer, and transport layer.*

NFS Network File System: One of the protocols in Sun Microsystems' widely used file system protocol suite, allowing remote file access across a network. The name is loosely used to refer to the entire Sun protocol suite, which also includes RPC, XDR (External Data Representation), and other protocols.

NHRP Next Hop Resolution Protocol: In a nonbroadcast multiaccess (NBMA) network, the protocol employed by routers in order to dynamically locate MAC addresses of various hosts and routers. It enables systems to communicate directly without requiring an intermediate hop, thus facilitating increased performance in ATM, Frame Relay, X.25, and SMDS systems.

NHS Next Hop Server: Defined by the NHRP protocol, this server maintains the next-hop resolution cache tables, listing IP-to-ATM address maps of related nodes and nodes that can be reached through routers served by the NHS.

NIC network interface card: An electronic circuit board placed in a computer. The NIC provides network communication to a LAN.

NLSP NetWare Link Services Protocol: Novell's link-state routing protocol, based on the IS-IS model.

NMP Network Management Processor: A Catalyst 5000 switch processor module used to control and monitor the switch.

non-stub area In OSPF, a resource-consuming area carrying a default route, intra-area routes, interarea routes, static routes, and external routes. Non-stub areas are the only areas that can have virtual links configured across them and exclusively contain an anonymous system boundary router (ASBR). *Compare with: stub area. See also: ASBR and OSPF.*

NRZ Nonreturn to Zero: One of several encoding schemes for transmitting digital data. NRZ signals sustain constant levels of voltage with no signal shifting (no return to zero-voltage level) during a bit interval. If there is a series of bits with the same value (1 or 0), there will be no state change. The signal is not self-clocking. *See also: NRZI.*

NRZI Nonreturn to Zero Inverted: One of several encoding schemes for transmitting digital data. A transition in voltage level (either from high to low or vice-versa) at the beginning of a bit interval is interpreted as a value of 1; the absence of a transition is interpreted as a 0. Thus, the voltage assigned to each value is continually inverted. NRZI signals are not self-clocking. *See also: NRZ.*

NVRAM Non-Volatile RAM: Random-access memory that keeps its contents intact while power is turned off.

OC Optical Carrier: A series of physical protocols, designated as OC-1, OC-2, OC-3, and so on, for SONET optical signal transmissions. OC signal levels place STS frames on a multimode fiber-optic line at various speeds, of which 51.84Mbps is the lowest (OC-1). Each subsequent protocol runs at a speed divisible by 51.84. *See also: SONET.*

100BaseT Based on the IEEE 802.3u standard, 100BaseT is the Fast-Ethernet specification of 100Mbps baseband that uses UTP wiring. 100BaseT sends link pulses (containing more information than those used in 10BaseT) over the network when no traffic is present. *See also: 10BaseT, FastEthernet, and IEEE 802.3.*

100BaseTX Based on the IEEE 802.3u standard, 100BaseTX is the 100Mbps baseband FastEthernet specification that uses two pairs of UTP or STP wiring. The first pair of wires receives data; the second pair sends data. To ensure correct signal timing, a 100BaseTX segment cannot be longer than 100 meters.

ones density Also known as pulse density, this is a method of signal clocking. The CSU/DSU retrieves the clocking information from data that passes through it. For this scheme to work, the data needs to be encoded to contain at least one binary 1 for each eight bits transmitted. *See also CSU and DSU.*

OSI Open System Interconnection: International standardization program designed by ISO and ITU-T for the development of data networking standards that make multivendor equipment interoperability a reality.

OSI reference model Open System Interconnection reference model: A conceptual model defined by the International Organization for Standardization (ISO), describing how any combination of devices can be connected for the purpose of communication. The OSI model divides the task into seven functional layers, forming a hierarchy with the applications at the top and the physical medium at the bottom, and it defines the functions each layer must provide. *See also: application layer, data-link layer, network layer, physical layer, presentation layer, session layer, and transport layer.*

OSPF Open Shortest Path First: A link-state, hierarchical IGP routing algorithm derived from an earlier version of the IS-IS protocol, whose features include multipath routing, load balancing, and least-cost routing. OSPF is the suggested successor to RIP in the Internet environment. *See also: enhanced IGRP, IGP, and IP.*

out-of-band management Management "outside" of the network's physical channels. For example, using a console connection not directly interfaced through the local LAN or WAN or a dial-in modem. *Compare to: in-band management.*

out-of-band signaling Within a network, any transmission that uses physical channels or frequencies separate from those ordinarily used for data transfer. For example, the initial configuration of a Cisco Catalyst switch requires an out-of-band connection via a console port.

packet   In data communications, the basic logical unit of information transferred. A packet consists of a certain number of data bytes, wrapped or encapsulated in headers and/or trailers that contain information about where the packet came from, where it's going, and so on. The various protocols involved in sending a transmission add their own layers of header information, which the corresponding protocols in receiving devices then interpret.

packet switch   A physical device that makes it possible for a communication channel to share several connections, its functions include finding the most efficient transmission path for packets.

packet switching   A networking technology based on the transmission of data in packets. Dividing a continuous stream of data into small units—packets—enables data from multiple devices on a network to share the same communication channel simultaneously but also requires the use of precise routing information. *Contrast with: circuit switching.*

PAP   Password Authentication Protocol: In Point-to-Point Protocol (PPP) networks, a method of validating connection requests. The requesting (remote) device must send an authentication request, containing a password and ID, to the local router when attempting to connect. Unlike the more secure CHAP (Challenge Handshake Authentication Protocol), PAP sends the password unencrypted and does not attempt to verify whether the user is authorized to access the requested resource; it merely identifies the remote end. *See also: CHAP.*

parity checking   A method of error-checking in data transmissions. An extra bit (the parity bit) is added to each character or data word so that the sum of the bits will be either an odd number (in odd parity) or an even number (even parity).

partial mesh   A type of network topology in which some network nodes form a full mesh (where every node has either a physical or a virtual circuit linking it to every other network node), but others are attached to only one or two nodes in the network. A typical use of partial-mesh topology is in peripheral networks linked to a fully meshed backbone. *See also: full mesh.*

PCR   Peak Cell Rate: As defined by the ATM Forum, the parameter specifying, in cells per second, the maximum rate at which a source may transmit.

PDN Public Data Network: Generally for a fee, a PDN offers the public access to computer communication network operated by private concerns or government agencies. Small organizations can take advantage of PDNs, aiding them in creating WANs without investing in long-distance equipment and circuitry.

PGP Pretty Good Privacy: A popular public-key/private-key encryption application offering protected transfer of files and messages.

physical layer The lowest layer—Layer 1—in the OSI reference model, it is responsible for converting data packets from the data-link layer (Layer 2) into electrical signals. Physical-layer protocols and standards define, for example, the type of cable and connectors to be used, including their pin assignments and the encoding scheme for signaling 0 and 1 values. *See also: application layer, data-link layer, network layer, presentation layer, session layer, and transport layer.*

ping packet Internet groper: A Unix-based Internet diagnostic tool, consisting of a message sent to test the accessibility of a particular device on the IP network. The acronym (from which the "full name" was formed) reflects the underlying metaphor of submarine sonar. Just as the sonar operator sends out a signal and waits to hear it echo ("ping") back from a submerged object, the network user can ping another node on the network and wait to see if it responds.

pleisochronous Nearly synchronous, except that clocking comes from an outside source instead of being embedded within the signal as in synchronous transmissions.

PLP Packet Level Protocol: Occasionally called X.25 Level 3 or X.25 Protocol, a network-layer protocol that is part of the X.25 stack.

PNNI Private Network-Network Interface: An ATM Forum specification for offering topology data used for the calculation of paths through the network, among switches and groups of switches. It is based on well-known link-state routing procedures and allows for automatic configuration in networks whose addressing scheme is determined by the topology.

point-to-multipoint connection In ATM, a communication path going only one way, connecting a single system at the starting point, called the "root node," to systems at multiple points of destination, called "leaves." *See also: point-to-point connection.*

point-to-point connection   In ATM, a channel of communication that can be directed either one way or two ways between two ATM end systems. *See also: point-to-multipoint connection.*

poison reverse updates   These update messages are transmitted by a router back to the originator (thus ignoring the split-horizon rule) after route poisoning has occurred. Typically used with DV routing protocols in order to overcome large routing loops and offer explicit information when a subnet or network is not accessible (instead of merely suggesting that the network is unreachable by not including it in updates). *See also: route poisoning.*

polling   The procedure of orderly inquiry, used by a primary network mechanism, to determine if secondary devices have data to transmit. A message is sent to each secondary, granting the secondary the right to transmit.

POP   1. Point Of Presence: The physical location where an interexchange carrier has placed equipment to interconnect with a local exchange carrier. 2. Post Office Protocol (currently at version 3): A protocol used by client e-mail applications for recovery of mail from a mail server.

PPP   Point-to-Point Protocol: The protocol most commonly used for dial-up Internet access, superseding the earlier SLIP. Its features include address notification, authentication via CHAP or PAP, support for multiple protocols, and link monitoring. PPP has two layers: the Link Control Protocol (LCP) establishes, configures, and tests a link; and then any of various Network Control Programs (NCPs) transport traffic for a specific protocol suite, such as IPX. *See also: CHAP, PAP, and SLIP.*

presentation layer   Layer 6 of the OSI reference model, it defines how data is formatted, presented, encoded, and converted for use by software at the application layer. *See also: application layer, data-link layer, network layer, physical layer, session layer, and transport layer.*

PRI   Primary Rate Interface: A type of ISDN connection between a PBX and a long-distance carrier, which is made up of a single 64Kbps D channel in addition to 23 (T1) or 30 (E1) B channels. *See also: ISDN.*

priority queueing   A routing function in which frames temporarily placed in an interface output queue are assigned priorities based on traits such as packet size or type of interface.

process switching　As a packet arrives on a router to be forwarded, it's copied to the router's process buffer, and the router performs a lookup on the Layer 3 address. Using the route table, an exit interface is associated with the destination address. The processor forwards the packet with the added new information to the exit interface, while the router initializes the fast-switching cache. Subsequent packets bound for the same destination address follow the same path as the first packet.

PROM　programmable read-only memory: ROM that is programmable only once, using special equipment. *Compare with: EPROM.*

propagation delay　The time it takes data to traverse a network from its source to its destination.

protocol　In networking, the specification of a set of rules for a particular type of communication. The term is also used to refer to the software that implements a protocol.

protocol stack　A collection of related protocols.

PSE　Packet Switch Exchange: The X.25 term for a switch.

PSN　packet-switched network: Any network that uses packet-switching technology. Also known as packet-switched data network (PSDN). *See also: packet switching.*

PSTN　Public Switched Telephone Network: Colloquially referred to as "plain old telephone service" (POTS). A term that describes the assortment of telephone networks and services available globally.

PVC　permanent virtual circuit: In a Frame Relay network, a logical connection, defined in software, that is maintained permanently. *Compare with: SVC. See also: virtual circuit.*

PVP　permanent virtual path: A virtual path made up of PVCs. *See also: PVC.*

PVP tunneling　permanent virtual path tunneling: A technique that links two private ATM networks across a public network using a virtual path; wherein the public network transparently trunks the complete collection of virtual channels in the virtual path between the two private networks.

QoS   Quality of Service: A set of metrics used to measure the quality of transmission and service availability of any given transmission system.

queue   Broadly, any list of elements arranged in an orderly fashion and ready for processing, such as a line of people waiting to enter a movie theater. In routing, it refers to a backlog of information packets waiting in line to be transmitted over a router interface.

RARP   Reverse Address Resolution Protocol: The protocol within the TCP/IP stack that maps MAC addresses to IP addresses. *See also: ARP.*

rate queue   A value, assigned to one or more virtual circuits, that specifies the speed at which an individual virtual circuit will transmit data to the remote end. Every rate queue identifies a segment of the total bandwidth available on an ATM link. The sum of all rate queues should not exceed the total available bandwidth.

RCP   Remote Copy Protocol: A protocol for copying files to or from a file system that resides on a remote server on a network, using TCP to guarantee reliable data delivery.

redistribution   Command used in Cisco routers to inject the paths found from one type of routing protocol into another type of routing protocol. For example, networks found by RIP can be inserted into an IGRP network.

redundancy   In internetworking, the duplication of connections, devices, or services that can be used as a backup in the event that the primary connections, devices, or services fail.

reload   An event or command that causes Cisco routers to reboot.

RIF   Routing Information Field: In source-route bridging, a header field that defines the path direction of the frame or token. If the Route Information Indicator (RII) bit is not set, the RIF is read from source to destination (left to right). If the RII bit is set, the RIF is read from the destination back to the source, so the RIF is read right to left. It is defined as part of the Token Ring frame header for source-routed frames, which contains path information.

ring   Two or more stations connected in a logical circular topology. In this topology, which is the basis for Token Ring, FDDI, and CDDI, information is transferred from station to station in sequence.

ring topology   A network logical topology comprising a series of repeaters that form one closed loop by connecting unidirectional transmission links. Individual stations on the network are connected to the network at a repeater. Physically, ring topologies are generally organized in a closed-loop star. *Compare with: bus topology and star topology.*

RIP   Routing Information Protocol: The most commonly used interior gateway protocol in the Internet. RIP employs hop count as a routing metric. *See also: Enhanced IGRP, IGP, OSPF, and hop count.*

routed protocol   Routed protocols (such as IP and IPX) are used to transmit user data through an internetwork. By contrast, routing protocols (such as RIP, IGRP, and OSPF) are used to update routing tables between routers.

route poisoning   Used by various DV routing protocols in order to overcome large routing loops and offer explicit information about when a subnet or network is not accessible (instead of merely suggesting that the network is unreachable by not including it in updates). Typically, this is accomplished by setting the hop count to one more than maximum. *See also: poison reverse.*

route summarization   In various routing protocols, such as OSPF, EIGRP, and IS-IS, the consolidation of publicized subnetwork addresses so that a single summary route is advertised to other areas by an area border router.

router   A network-layer mechanism, either software or hardware, using one or more metrics to decide on the best path to use for transmission of network traffic. Sending packets between networks by routers is based on the information provided on network layers. Historically, this device has sometimes been called a gateway.

routing   The process of forwarding logically addressed packets from their local subnetwork toward their ultimate destination. In large networks, the numerous intermediary destinations a packet might travel before reaching its destination can make routing very complex.

routing domain   Any collection of end systems and intermediate systems that operate under an identical set of administrative rules. Every routing domain contains one or several areas, all individually given a certain area address.

routing metric   Any value that is used by routing algorithms to determine whether one route is superior to another. Metrics include such information as bandwidth, delay, hop count, path cost, load, MTU, reliability, and communication cost. Only the best possible routes are stored in the routing table, while all other information may be stored in link-state or topological databases. *See also: cost.*

routing protocol   Any protocol that defines algorithms to be used for updating routing tables between routers. Examples include IGRP, RIP, and OSPF.

routing table   A table kept in a router or other internetworking mechanism that maintains a record of only the best possible routes to certain network destinations and the metrics associated with those routes.

RP   Route Processor: Also known as a supervisory processor, a module on Cisco 7000 series routers that holds the CPU, system software, and most of the memory components used in the router.

RSP   Route/Switch Processor: A processor module combining the functions of RP and SP used in Cisco 7500 series routers. *See also: RP and SP.*

RTS   Request To Send: An EIA/TIA-232 control signal requesting permission to transmit data on a communication line.

sampling rate   The rate at which samples of a specific waveform amplitude are collected within a specified period of time.

SAP   1. Service Access Point: A field specified by IEEE 802.2 that is part of an address specification. 2. Service Advertising Protocol: The Novell NetWare protocol that supplies a way to inform network clients of resources and services availability on network, using routers and servers. *See also: IPX.*

SCR   Sustainable Cell Rate: An ATM Forum parameter used for traffic management, it is the long-term average cell rate for VBR connections that can be transmitted.

SDLC   Synchronous Data-Link Control: A protocol used in SNA data-link layer communications. SDLC is a bit-oriented, full-duplex serial protocol that is the basis for several similar protocols, including HDLC and LAPB. *See also: HDLC and LAPB.*

seed router   In an AppleTalk network, the router that is equipped with the network number or cable range in its port descriptor. The seed router specifies the network number or cable range for other routers in that network section and answers to configuration requests from nonseed routers on its connected AppleTalk network, permitting those routers to affirm or modify their configurations accordingly. Every AppleTalk network needs at least one seed router physically connected to each network segment.

server   Hardware and software that provide network services to clients.

session layer   Layer 5 of the OSI reference model, responsible for creating, managing, and terminating sessions between applications and overseeing data exchange between presentation layer entities. *See also: application layer, data-link layer, network layer, physical layer, presentation layer, and transport layer.*

SF   super frame: A super frame (also called a D4 frame) consists of 12 frames with 192 bits each, and the 193rd bit providing other functions including error checking. SF is frequently used on T1 circuits. A newer version of the technology is Extended Super Frame (ESF), which uses 24 frames. *See also: ESF.*

signaling packet   An informational packet created by an ATM-connected mechanism that wants to establish connection with another such mechanism. The packet contains the QoS parameters needed for connection and the ATM NSAP address of the endpoint. The endpoint responds with a message of acceptance if it is able to support the desired QoS, and the connection is established. *See also: QoS.*

silicon switching   A type of high-speed switching used in Cisco 7000 series routers, based on the use of a separate processor (the Silicon Switch Processor, or SSP). *See also: SSE.*

sliding window   The method of flow control used by TCP, as well as several data-link layer protocols. This method places a buffer between the receiving application and the network data flow. The "window" available for accepting data is the size of the buffer minus the amount of data already there. This window increases in size as the application reads data from it and decreases as new data is sent. The receiver sends the transmitter announcements of the current window size, and it may stop accepting data until the window increases above a certain threshold.

SLIP   Serial Line Internet Protocol: An industry standard serial encapsulation for point-to-point connections that supports only a single routed protocol, TCP/IP. SLIP is the predecessor to PPP. *See also: PPP.*

SMDS   Switched Multimegabit Data Service: A packet-switched, datagram-based WAN networking technology offered by telephone companies that provides high speed.

SMTP   Simple Mail Transfer Protocol: A protocol used on the Internet to provide electronic mail services.

SNA   System Network Architecture: A complex, feature-rich, network architecture similar to the OSI reference model but with several variations; created by IBM in the 1970s and essentially composed of seven layers.

SNAP   Subnetwork Access Protocol: SNAP is a frame used in Ethernet, Token Ring, and FDDI LANs. Data transfer, connection management, and QoS selection are three primary functions executed by the SNAP frame.

socket   1. A software structure that operates within a network device as a destination point for communications. 2. In AppleTalk networks, an entity at a specific location within a node; AppleTalk sockets are conceptually similar to TCP/IP ports.

SONET   Synchronous Optical Network: The ANSI standard for synchronous transmission on fiber-optic media, developed at Bell Labs. It specifies a base signal rate of 51.84Mbps and a set of multiples of that rate, known as Optical Carrier levels, up to 2.5Gbps.

SP   Switch Processor: Also known as a ciscoBus controller, it is a Cisco 7000 series processor module acting as governing agent for all CxBus activities.

span   A full-duplex digital transmission line connecting two facilities.

SPAN   Switched Port Analyzer: A feature of the Catalyst 5000 switch, offering freedom to manipulate within a switched Ethernet environment by extending the monitoring ability of the existing network analyzers into the environment. At one switched segment, the SPAN mirrors traffic onto a pre-determined SPAN port, while a network analyzer connected to the SPAN port is able to monitor traffic from any other Catalyst switched port.

spanning explorer packet   Sometimes called limited-route or single-route explorer packet, it pursues a statically configured spanning tree when searching for paths in a source-route bridging network. *See also: all-routes explorer packet, explorer packet, and local explorer packet.*

spanning tree   A subset of a network topology, within which no loops exist. When bridges are interconnected into a loop, the bridge, or switch, cannot identify a frame that has been forwarded previously, so there is no mechanism for removing a frame as it passes the interface numerous times. Without a method of removing these frames, the bridges continuously forward them—consuming bandwidth and adding overhead to the network. Spanning trees prune the network to provide only one path for any packet. *See also: Spanning-Tree Protocol and spanning-tree algorithm.*

spanning-tree algorithm (STA)   An algorithm that creates a spanning tree using the Spanning-Tree Protocol (STP). *See also: spanning tree and Spanning-Tree Protocol.*

Spanning-Tree Protocol (STP)   The bridge protocol (IEEE 802.1d) that enables a learning bridge to dynamically avoid loops in the network topology by creating a spanning tree using the spanning-tree algorithm. Spanning-tree frames called bridge protocol data units (BPDUs) are sent and received by all switches in the network at regular intervals. The switches participating in the spanning tree don't forward the frames; instead, they're processed to determine the spanning-tree topology itself. Cisco Catalyst series switches use STP 802.1d to perform this function. *See also: BPDU, learning bridge, MAC address, spanning tree, and spanning-tree algorithm.*

SPF   shortest path first algorithm: A routing algorithm used to decide on the shortest-path spanning tree. Sometimes called Dijkstra's algorithm and frequently used in link-state routing algorithms. *See also: link-state routing algorithm.*

SPID Service Profile Identifier: A number assigned by service providers or local telephone companies and assigned by administrators to a BRI port. SPIDs are used to determine subscription services of a device connected via ISDN. ISDN devices use SPID when accessing the telephone company switch that initializes the link to a service provider.

split horizon Useful for preventing routing loops, a type of distance-vector routing rule where information about routes is prevented from leaving the router interface through which that information was received.

spoofing 1. In dial-on-demand routing (DDR), where a circuit-switched link is taken down to save toll charges when there is no traffic to be sent, spoofing is a scheme used by routers that causes a host to treat an interface as if it were functioning and supporting a session. The router pretends to send "spoof" replies to keepalive messages from the host in an effort to convince the host that the session is up and running. *See also: DDR.* 2. The illegal act of sending a packet labeled with a false address, in order to deceive network security mechanisms such as filters and access lists.

spooler A management application that processes requests submitted to it for execution in a sequential fashion from a queue. A good example is a print spooler.

SPX Sequenced Packet Exchange: A Novell NetWare transport protocol that augments the datagram service provided by network layer (Layer 3) protocols, it was derived from the Switch-to-Switch Protocol of the XNS protocol suite.

SQE Signal Quality Error: In an Ethernet network, a message sent from a transceiver to an attached machine that the collision-detection circuitry is working.

SRB Source-Route Bridging: Created by IBM, the bridging method used in Token-Ring networks. The source determines the entire route to a destination before sending the data and includes that information in route information fields (RIF) within each packet. *Contrast with: transparent bridging.*

SRT source-route transparent bridging: A bridging scheme developed by IBM, merging source-route and transparent bridging. SRT takes advantage of both technologies in one device, fulfilling the needs of all end nodes. Translation between bridging protocols is not necessary. *Compare with: SR/TLB.*

SR/TLB   source-route translational bridging: A bridging method that allows source-route stations to communicate with transparent bridge stations aided by an intermediate bridge that translates between the two bridge protocols. Used for bridging between Token Ring and Ethernet. *Compare with: SRT.*

SSAP   Source Service Access Point: The SAP of the network node identified in the Source field of the packet. *See also: DSAP and SAP.*

SSE   Silicon Switching Engine: The software component of Cisco's silicon switching technology, hard-coded into the Silicon Switch Processor (SSP). Silicon switching is available only on the Cisco 7000 with an SSP. Silicon-switched packets are compared to the silicon-switching cache on the SSE. The SSP is a dedicated switch processor that offloads the switching process from the route processor, providing a fast-switching solution, but packets must still traverse the backplane of the router to get to the SSP and then back to the exit interface.

star topology   A LAN physical topology with endpoints on the network converging at a common central switch (known as a hub) using point-to-point links. A logical ring topology can be configured as a physical star topology using a unidirectional closed-loop star rather than point-to-point links. That is, connections within the hub are arranged in an internal ring. *See also: bus topology and ring topology.*

startup range   If an AppleTalk node does not have a number saved from the last time it was booted, then the node selects from the range of values from 65280 to 65534.

static route   A route whose information is purposefully entered into the routing table and takes priority over those chosen by dynamic routing protocols.

statistical multiplexing   Multiplexing in general is a technique that allows data from multiple logical channels to be sent across a single physical channel. Statistical multiplexing dynamically assigns bandwidth only to input channels that are active, optimizing available bandwidth so that more devices can be connected than with other multiplexing techniques. Also known as statistical time-division multiplexing or stat mux.

STM-1 Synchronous Transport Module Level 1. In the European SDH standard, one of many formats identifying the frame structure for the 155.52Mbps lines that are used to carry ATM cells.

store-and-forward packet switching A technique in which the switch first copies each packet into its buffer and performs a cyclical redundancy check (CRC). If the packet is error-free, the switch then looks up the destination address in its filter table, determines the appropriate exit port, and sends the packet.

STP 1. Shielded Twisted Pair: A two-pair wiring scheme, used in many network implementations, that has a layer of shielded insulation to reduce EMI. 2. Spanning-Tree Protocol.

stub area An OSPF area carrying a default route, intra-area routes, and interarea routes, but no external routes. Configuration of virtual links cannot be achieved across a stub area, and stub areas are not allowed to contain an ASBR. *See also: non-stub area, ASBR, and OSPF.*

stub network A network having only one connection to a router.

STUN Serial Tunnel: A technology used to connect an HDLC link to an SDLC link over a serial link.

subarea A portion of an SNA network made up of a subarea node and its attached links and peripheral nodes.

subarea node An SNA communications host or controller that handles entire network addresses.

subchannel A frequency-based subdivision that creates a separate broadband communications channel.

subinterface One of many virtual interfaces available on a single physical interface.

subnet *See: subnetwork.*

subnet address The portion of an IP address that is specifically identified by the subnet mask as the subnetwork. *See also: IP address, subnetwork, and subnet mask.*

subnet mask   Also simply known as mask, a 32-bit address mask used in IP to identify the bits of an IP address that are used for the subnet address. Using a mask, the router does not need to examine all 32 bits, only those selected by the mask. *See also: address mask and IP address.*

subnetwork   1. Any network that is part of a larger IP network and is identified by a subnet address. A network administrator segments a network into subnetworks in order to provide a hierarchical, multilevel routing structure, and at the same time protect the subnetwork from the addressing complexity of networks that are attached. Also known as a subnet. *See also: IP address, subnet mask, and subnet address.* 2. In OSI networks, the term specifically refers to a collection of ESs and ISs controlled by only one administrative domain, using a solitary network connection protocol.

SVC   switched virtual circuit: A dynamically established virtual circuit, created on demand and dissolved as soon as transmission is over and the circuit is no longer needed. In ATM terminology, it is referred to as a switched virtual connection. *See also: PVC.*

switch   1. In networking, a device responsible for multiple functions such as filtering, flooding, and sending frames. It works using the destination address of individual frames. Switches operate at the data-link layer of the OSI model. 2. Broadly, any electronic/mechanical device allowing connections to be established as needed and terminated if no longer necessary.

switched LAN   Any LAN implemented using LAN switches. *See also: LAN switch.*

synchronous transmission   Signals transmitted digitally with precision clocking. These signals have identical frequencies and contain individual characters encapsulated in control bits (called start/stop bits) that designate the beginning and ending of each character. *See also: asynchronous transmission and isochronous transmission.*

T1   Digital WAN that uses 24 DS0s at 64K each to create a bandwidth of 1.536Mbps, minus clocking overhead, providing 1.544Mbps of usable bandwidth.

T3   Digital WAN that can provide bandwidth of 44.763Mbps.

tag switching   Based on the concept of label swapping, where packets or cells are designated to defined-length labels that control the manner in which data is to be sent, tag switching is a high-performance technology used for forwarding packets. It incorporates data-link layer (Layer 2) switching and network layer (Layer 3) routing and supplies scalable, high-speed switching in the network core.

tagged traffic   ATM cells with their cell loss priority (CLP) bit set to 1. Also referred to as discard-eligible (DE) traffic. Tagged traffic can be eliminated in order to ensure trouble-free delivery of higher priority traffic, if the network is congested. *See also: CLP.*

TCP   Transmission Control Protocol: A connection-oriented protocol that is defined at the transport layer of the OSI reference model. Provides reliable delivery of data.

TCP/IP   Transmission Control Protocol/Internet Protocol. The suite of protocols underlying the Internet. TCP and IP are the most widely known protocols in that suite. *See also: IP and TCP.*

TDM   time division multiplexing: A technique for assigning bandwidth on a single wire, based on preassigned time slots, to data from several channels. Bandwidth is allotted to each channel regardless of a station's ability to send data. *See also: ATDM, FDM, and multiplexing.*

TE1   A device with a four-wire, twisted-pair digital interface is referred to as terminal equipment type one. Most modern ISDN devices are of this type.

TE   terminal equipment: Any peripheral device that is ISDN-compatible and attached to a network, such as a telephone or computer.

telco   A common abbreviation for the telephone company.

Telnet   The standard terminal emulation protocol within the TCP/IP protocol stack. Method of remote terminal connection, enabling users to log in on remote networks and use those resources as if they were locally connected. Telnet is defined in RFC 854.

10BaseT   Part of the original IEEE 802.3 standard, 10BaseT is the Ethernet specification of 10Mbps baseband that uses two pairs of twisted-pair, Category 3, 4, or 5 cabling—using one pair to send data and the other to receive. 10BaseT has a distance limit of about 100 meters per segment. *See also: Ethernet and IEEE 802.3.*

terminal adapter   A hardware interface between a computer without a native ISDN interface and an ISDN line. In effect, a device to connect a standard async interface to a non-native ISDN device, emulating a modem.

terminal emulation   The use of software, installed on a PC or LAN server, that allows the PC to function as if it were a "dumb" terminal directly attached to a particular type of mainframe.

TFTP   Conceptually, a stripped-down version of FTP, it's the protocol of choice if you know exactly what you want and where it's to be found. TFTP doesn't provide the abundance of functions that FTP does. In particular, it has no directory-browsing abilities; it can do nothing but send and receive files.

token   A frame containing only control information. Possessing this control information gives a network device permission to transmit data onto the network. *See also: token passing.*

token bus   LAN architecture that is the basis for the IEEE 802.4 LAN specification and employs token passing access over a bus topology. *See also: IEEE.*

token passing   A method used by network devices to access the physical medium in a systematic way based on possession of a small frame called a token. *Contrast with: circuit switching. See also: token.*

Token Ring   IBM's token-passing LAN technology. It runs at 4Mbps or 16Mbps over a ring topology. Defined formally by IEEE 802.5. *See also: ring topology and token passing.*

transparent bridging   The bridging scheme used in Ethernet and IEEE 802.3 networks, it passes frames along one hop at a time, using bridging information stored in tables that associate end-node MAC addresses within bridge ports. This type of bridging is considered transparent because the source node does not know it has been bridged, because the destination frames are sent directly to the end node. *Contrast with: SRB.*

transport layer   Layer 4 of the OSI reference model, used for reliable communication between end nodes over the network. The transport layer provides mechanisms used for establishing, maintaining, and terminating virtual circuits, transport fault detection and recovery, and controlling the flow of information. *See also: application layer, data-link layer, network layer, physical layer, presentation layer, and session layer.*

TRIP   Token Ring Interface Processor: A high-speed interface processor used on Cisco 7000 series routers. The TRIP provides two or four ports for interconnection with IEEE 802.5 and IBM media with ports set to speeds of either 4Mbps or 16Mbps set independently of each other.

TTL   Time To Live: A field in an IP header, indicating the length of time a packet is valid.

TUD   Trunk Up-Down: A protocol used in ATM networks for the monitoring of trunks. Should a trunk miss a given number of test messages being sent by ATM switches to ensure trunk line quality, TUD declares the trunk down. When a trunk reverses direction and comes back up, TUD recognizes that the trunk is up and returns the trunk to service.

tunneling   A method of avoiding protocol restrictions by wrapping packets from one protocol in another protocol's packet and transmitting this encapsulated packet over a network that supports the wrapper protocol. *See also: encapsulation.*

UDP   User Datagram Protocol: A connectionless transport layer protocol in the TCP/IP protocol stack that simply allows datagrams to be exchanged without acknowledgements or delivery guarantees, requiring other protocols to handle error processing and retransmission. UDP is defined in RFC 768.

unnumbered frames   HDLC frames used for control-management purposes, such as link startup and shutdown or mode specification.

VBR   Variable Bit Rate: A QoS class, as defined by the ATM Forum, for use in ATM networks that is subdivided into real time (RT) class and non-real time (NRT) class. RT is employed when connections have a fixed-time relationship between samples. Conversely, NRT is employed when connections do not have a fixed-time relationship between samples, but still need an assured QoS.

VCC   Virtual Channel Connection: A logical circuit that is created by VCLs. VCCs carry data between two endpoints in an ATM network. Sometimes called a virtual circuit connection.

VIP 1. Versatile Interface Processor: An interface card for Cisco 7000 and 7500 series routers, providing multilayer switching and running the Cisco IOS software. The most recent version of VIP is VIP2. 2. Virtual IP: A function making it possible for logically separated switched IP workgroups to run Virtual Networking Services across the switch ports of a Catalyst 5000.

virtual circuit Abbreviated VC, a logical circuit devised to assure reliable communication between two devices on a network. Defined by a virtual path connection (VPC)/virtual path identifier (VCI) pair, a virtual circuit can be permanent (PVC) or switched (SVC). Virtual circuits are used in Frame Relay and X.25. Known as virtual channel in ATM. *See also: PVC and SVC.*

virtual ring In an SRB network, a logical connection between physical rings, either local or remote.

VLAN Virtual LAN: A group of devices on one or more logically segmented LANs (configured by use of management software), enabling devices to communicate as if attached to the same physical medium, when they are actually located on numerous different LAN segments. VLANs are based on logical instead of physical connections and thus are tremendously flexible.

VLSM variable-length subnet mask: Helps optimize available address space and specify a different subnet mask for the same network number on various subnets. Also commonly referred to as "subnetting a subnet."

WinSock Windows Socket Interface: A software interface that makes it possible for an assortment of applications to use and share an Internet connection. The WinSock software consists of a Dynamic Link Library (DLL) with supporting programs such as a dialer program that initiates the connection.

workgroup switching A switching method that supplies high-speed (100Mbps) transparent bridging between Ethernet networks as well as high-speed translational bridging between Ethernet and CDDI or FDDI.

X.25 An ITU-T packet-relay standard that defines communication between DTE and DCE network devices. X.25 uses a reliable data-link layer protocol called LAPB. X.25 also uses PLP at the network layer. X.25 has mostly been replaced by Frame Relay.

ZIP   Zone Information Protocol: A session-layer protocol used by Apple-Talk to map network numbers to zone names. NBP uses ZIP in the determination of networks containing nodes that belong to a zone. *See also: ZIP storm and zone.*

ZIP storm   A broadcast storm occurring when a router running AppleTalk reproduces or transmits a route for which there is no corresponding zone name at the time of execution. The route is then forwarded by other routers downstream, thus causing a ZIP storm. *See also: broadcast storm and ZIP.*

zone   A logical grouping of network devices in AppleTalk. *See also: ZIP.*

Index

Note to the Reader: Throughout this index **boldfaced** page numbers indicate primary discussions of a topic. *Italicized* page numbers indicate illustrations.

LocalTalk protocol
  defined, 517
  MacIP for, 205
location transparency, 435
logging
  in CiscoWorks, 407
  in security, 364–365
Logical Link Control (LLC)
  defined, 517
  in IPX, 221
logical units (LUs), 335
loopback functions, 100
loopback interfaces, 343
lost productivity costs, 363
lost-route algorithm, 217
low-density solutions for remote access networks, **321**
low-entry networking (LEN) service, 349
LSA (link-state advertisement) types
  defined, 517
  in OSPF, **163–164**
LUNI (LAN Emulation User-to-Network Interface), 518
LUs (logical units), 335

M

MAC addresses, 518
MAC (Media Access Control) sublayer, 518
MAC (move, add, and change) process, 35–36
machine names in AppleTalk networks, 193
Macintosh IP, **205**, 518
mainframes, **334–337**, *335*
  with APPN, **348–350**
  with DLSw, **341–343**
  queuing in, **345–347**, *346–347*
  redundancy in, **343–345**, *344–345*

review questions, **351–356**
Routing Information Field for, **337–338**
with RSRB, **339–341**, *339*
with SDLC tunneling, **338–339**
summary, **350**
maintenance in network design, 41
major networks, 97
manageability
  in network design, 9, 403, **406–407**
  in three-tier network model, **20**
Management Information Base (MIB), 519
Manchester encoding, 518
MANs (metropolitan-area networks), 518
masks, 106
master domain organizations, 246, *246*
Maximum Burst Size (MBS), 519
maximum bursts, 518
Maximum Cell Delay Variation (MCDV), 519
Maximum Cell Loss Ratio (MCLR), 519
Maximum Cell Transfer Delay (MCTD), 519
maximum rate, 518
maximum transfer units (MTUs)
  defined, 520
  in IGRP, **144**
MBONE backbones, 417, 519
MBS (Maximum Burst Size), 519
MCDV (Maximum Cell Delay Variation), 519
MCLR (Maximum Cell Loss Ratio), 519
MCR (Minimum Cell Rate), 519
MCTD (Maximum Cell Transfer Delay), 519
Media Access Control (MAC) sublayer, 518
media contention
  in LANs, 71
  as network design issue, 31

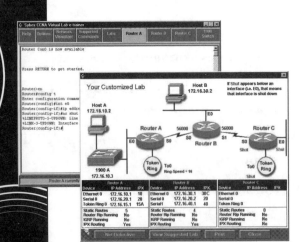

MAKE SURE YOU'RE READY

FOR CISCO® CERTIFICATION WITH EXAM NOTES™ FROM

SYBEX™

**CCNA Exam Notes:
Cisco Certified
Network Associate**

ISBN: 0-7821-2535-2

**CCNP Exam Notes:
Advanced Cisco Routing
Configuration**

ISBN: 0-7821-2540-9

**CCNP Exam Notes:
Cisco Internetwork
Troubleshooting**

ISBN: 0-7821-2541-7

**CCNP Exam Notes:
Cisco LAN Switching
Configuration**

ISBN: 0-7821-2542-5

**CCDP Exam Notes:
Cisco Internetwork
Design**

ISBN: 0-7821-2640-5

THE MOST EFFECTIVE REVIEW GUIDES AVAILABLE!

▲ Innovative *Exam Notes* approach reinforces knowledge of key points and identifies your weak spots

▲ Objective-by-objective coverage of the Cisco exams

▲ Essential information arranged for quick learning and review

▲ Exam tips and advice from expert trainers

▲ Perfect complement to Sybex Study Guides

Get the inside information on preparing for the Cisco exams!

SYBEX®
www.sybex.com

Furnishing the City

Furnishing the City

Harold Lewis Malt

McGraw-Hill Book Company

New York
St. Louis
San Francisco
Dusseldorf
London
Mexico
Panama
Sydney
Toronto

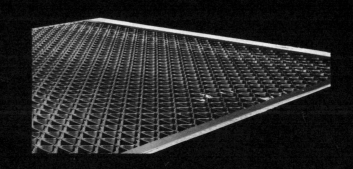

Sponsoring Editor William G. Salo
Director of Production Stephen J. Boldish
Designer Naomi Auerbach
Editing Supervisor Barbara Church
Editing and Production Staff Gretlyn Blau,
    Carol Ferrari, Teresa F. Leaden, George E. Oechsner

FURNISHING THE CITY

39845

1234567890 HDBP 7543210

Preface

Industrial designers are concerned with consumer use and acceptance of industrialized processes and products. At Carnegie-Mellon University we students of Kostellow, Lepper, Müller-Munk, were trained as generalists. We made design studies of communications, transportation, and even street furniture—traffic signals, fire hydrants, street lights—all the products that are supposed to make our cities habitable.

Later, at Syracuse with Arthur Pulos, we enlarged our studies to consider user needs in the complete public environment.

Since then much has changed. Standard of living. Technology. Man has gone to the moon while on earth your home is furnished with many amenities, labor-saving, comfort-producing devices such as TV, garbage disposal, automatic furnace or air conditioner. Yet outside, American cities are far uglier than they need be. The American street is still furnished with the same old junk and cities are buying more of the same. How is this possible?

This book looks at the problems and suggests modes of action for those concerned or responsible for renewing the older city and furnishing the new. Although much has been written recently about urban design, the point of view expressed here is not the excessively romantic, worshipful attitude toward nature, shaped and colored by European ideals and training.

The fact is, the streetscape now is synthetic not natural. No longer do grass and trees make the connection between man and his environment. Urban design has become the art of dealing with the artificial. Nine out of ten Americans will soon be contained within a totally manufactured envelope. For better or for worse, streets, sidewalks, traffic signs, mailboxes, light poles, and hundreds of products yet undesigned will make up the urban fabric which must be assembled from the consumer point-of-view. The task is to use technology in a more socially successful way.

While serving as design consultant to aerospace industries and federal agencies, I was exposed to the systems design and management approach. Here was a problem-solving technique proven successful in accommodating large numbers of complex interdependent variables in sophisticated outer-

v

space design. I was anxious to try it on earth-bound environmental design. Fortunately the opportunity came to apply a few of these ideas on campuses being built for the State University Construction Fund of New York. Some of the concepts developed here were first suggested to Dr. Anthony Adinolfi and appeared in *Site Products,* a manual of performance criteria written for the Fund.

But the big need is in the cities and these ideas were shaped in discussions with many people concerned with the quality of the urban environment. Howard Cayton, George Karas, Robert McCabe, Dorn McGrath, Jr., and Ralph Warburton particularly encouraged my attempt to introduce technical innovation.

Theories became reality with a U.S. Department of Housing and Urban Development Demonstration Grant. The city of Cincinnati was enabled to retain me as consultant for the application of the systems approach to the streetscape design of a specific urban renewal project.

For this book, the system becomes the ordering device as well as the content. Part One defines the urban product environment: problems, goals, and systems design approach. Part Two is about the man in the street— the guy who pays the bills and deserves better. Part Three develops performance and evaluation criteria for each component in the manufactured environment.

Like any designer, I have been tempted to do some blue-sky sketching, but this book does not attempt a quantum jump. It really isn't necessary. Nobody has to guess about the year 2000 when exciting, significant, and innovative results can be achieved within the state-of-the-art and the tools available now.

Harold Lewis Malt

Contents

Part One

Systems

Chapter One

Our Hand-me-down
Street Furniture

*During a time of increasing population and wealth the American city
has deteriorated—decayed and grown dull and deadly. An
important but little-recognized force in this ongoing process is the
sleazy, shoddy furnishings in the public streets and places.*

*What are these man-made elements that collectively connect people
to the urban visual and functional scene? Do these artifacts have
a common heritage? Did their form and manner of use evolve
from the needs and technical capabilities of other eras? What was
their importance in other times, and how meaningful can these
earlier solutions be in contemporary America?*

*Before setting off to explore new dimensions, let us for a moment
look backward from the point of view of the urban designer and
the user. Let us mark some of the milestones which may help
us determine future goals and evaluate various design approaches.*

SOME EARLY CONCEPTS
The Marketplace Marks Downtown

From the very beginning, people came together in a place and by their use made it a public space. They came together for elemental reasons: security, trade, social relationships. The life or death of primitive communities was quickly decided by basic facts: the economic, physical, and emotional needs of their people and how well they were satisfied. And as the people became less nomadic and more stabilized, the settlements evolved into communities with varying patterns of land division, all of which reserved by common agreement certain spaces for public access and use.

Much is made of the geometry of cities and the question of which physical layout may be best. The fact is that over the ages most Old World cities grew by happenstance, and many of these formless organisms endured and became rich in urban imagery. The street became not only a way to go but a place to be.

The more ordered forms of circulation and shelter usually shaped themselves into one of two classic patterns. The more simple is that of the hunter, which is still in use today in Africa, where primitive bush tribes surround the chief's compound with *circles* of huts and cattle pens. The important people are in the center where they want to be. The ring of huts of the others helps keep the livestock in and the enemy out. The soundness of this defensive planning has been thoroughly documented on TV, where regularly the wagon train forms a circle and the encircling redskins are picked off one by one. Serving the social purposes of primitive people most of the year, the central public space was equipped for a more important function. There campfire or religious rites provided the psychological warmth that helped meld the tribe. From the time of Stonehenge this kind of civic "theater-in-the-round" gave meaning to the tribes' existence. Altar benches or braziers were the most significant pieces of public furniture, and their design and use enhanced the tribes' position in a primitive world.

The *grid* pattern, which came later, was developed by the farmer, who plowed and sowed and divided land in a more geometric rectilinear manner. His settlements straggled along linear paths leading to the farming areas.

Regardless of form and almost simultaneously, these agricultural communities grew into populous cities of civilized permanence in many parts of the world. The cities of Mesopotamia, Peru, Mesoamerica, and China are all rich in examples of enriched or monumental urban design. But we start with Europe as the birthplace of Western ideals.

Antiquity is rich in examples of pedestrian malls such as Trajan's Forum, but the democratic way of life found expression in the development of the linear street. In Athens the road from the agora, or marketplace, led not only out to the country but back up to the Acropolis. It became not only a highway but a city street and a sacred way. Here was where the activity was. Stores and shops followed the people; banking and politics were not far behind. Soon came the golden age of Greece, when the rising standard of living created disposable income which the Athenians used to create a magnificent urban setting—spectacular and thrilling yet warm and comfortable. It was a place not only to visit but to live in.

The Athenian citizen, rich or poor, had a variety of places to go and things to enjoy. He could walk around the bottom of the hill, where the modest commercial buildings of the agora were grouped around a large open space near the business and civic center. The facades of these low buildings changed from time to time, as in any modern city, but were always in human scale and related to the square. Sculpture was abundant, the principal form of esthetic expression. It matters not that in retrospect art historians prefer the archaic sculpture to the later Hellenistic period, whose techniques mass-produced perfect torsos. This was an art for the people, and the city dweller could enjoy this urban space lavishly decorated with public art in the Greek humanistic and sensuous style of nude representation.

Nearby and built into the side of the hill was the Council House, where people sat on semicircular stepped seats. Or they went further along the base of the hill to the theater to hear the dramatic works of Sophocles, Euripides, or Aeschylus. And there was the broad flight of steps that led up the slopes of the Acropolis. These provided a clear view of the temple as well as serving as spectator seats for observing agora activities or just girl-watching.

Today the temple complex with Parthenon high on the sacred Acropolis surely is one of the most memorable urban landmarks in all the world. The emotional impact of this clearly defined cityscape must have been even more effective during the ancient ceremonies. Such an occasion was the Panathenaic procession along the Panathenaic Way.

Edmund Bacon tells us that the Panathenaic Way was far more than a city street. It was part of a regional way that linked some of the most sacred places in Greece. By 600 B.C. the road led from mystic graves through a pass to the Dipylon gate of the walled city of Athens and on up the slopes of the Acropolis. It was an important traffic artery used constantly by the people for many purposes. But the street had still another spectacular use.

Once a year a procession went through the city and up the hill to the gold and ivory statue of Athena in the Parthenon. This parade of horses and people was exceptionally stirring because everyone could become involved. Sculptors dramatically recorded its fervor on the Parthenon frieze.

Macy's Thanksgiving Day Parade.

And this event clearly was the organizing force providing the theme for the design and furnishing of this Athenian Main Street, whose every detail was planned to give *pleasure* to the people. The procession was the forerunner of the American institutionalized parade, whose bands and floats stimulate sales by attracting attention, bringing pedestrian traffic downtown, and contributing imagery and zest to city living.

People Want Public Works

The shape and quality of the public right-of-way has almost always symbolized the attitude of the government to the governed. The emotional value of parade streets and public places surely was known to the theocracy governing the cities of the Maya. Although little has been documented, their skill in the planning, programming, and building of vast urban complexes is self-evident. Working apart from the mainstream of Western civilization, these priests and nobles created many splendid environments of engineering substance and pleasing imagery.

Without wheel or horse, the Mayan central city was a huge pedestrian mall. The *streetscape* was deliberately designed with many levels and pedestrian concourses to contrast with the surrounding flat plain and achieve a three-dimensional quality. Chichén Itza, founded in A.D. 432 near the Yucatan coast, was such a city.

The designers first defined and walled a huge space 1,600 feet square. Within, the floor was thrust upward and modeled into an exciting mixture of functional forms. The focal point was the lofty Pyramid of Kukulcan. Nearby was the tall cylindrical Caracol—the observatory. A vast rectangular pit lined with stone contained a ball court. Berms and platforms became theatrical stages. And the marketplace was defined by the still-standing Colonnade of a Thousand Columns. Today, walking the steps, ramps, and different levels of Chichén Itza, one achieves a kinesthetic experience of involvement with the environment. In the previous era this sensation was intensified through the staging of many annual events during April and May, when special furnishings, copal incense, and lighting were provided. One event filled with pageantry was the sacrificial rite. Elaborately costumed priests led a muffled-drum procession 900 feet along the ceremonial road to the sacred cenote. Here, from the brink of the huge natural well, a blue-painted maiden was thrown into the green water 80 feet below.

Why human sacrifice? How could the Maya build their magnificent monumental stone structures working without metal and with only stone axes? What motivated the production of so profuse a public art? It all stemmed from corn.

Corn was the preoccupation of the world of the Maya, and Chac-Mool was their benevolent rain god. When it rained, the corn grew, so fast that the farmer labored only forty-eight days to produce his yearly needs. He was grateful to Chac-Mool, and he had nine to ten months leisure time during which he built the city. He would not support an army or warfare, but he did give freely for public facilities. But when there was a long drought, the Maya toppled their idols, abandoned their cities, went into the jungles, and were reduced to eating bark. In this "boom or bust" existence there evolved a public sculpture of harsh esthetic which depicted in bas-relief not only trade and sports but the skull and crossbones and human sacrifice.

Even greater than Chichén Itza was the three-dimensional city of Tikal. The site, a limestone outcropping between two ravines in the rain forest of what is now Guatemala, is spectacular. With visionary planning and immense effort the stone was hewed level, the ravines were made into reservoirs, and public buildings were begun. Soon five groups of buildings covered a square mile. By the middle of the ninth century eight pyramids had been built, four of which were as high as twenty-story buildings. The Great Plaza, at the base of the pyramids, was studded with texture and interest. Although highly ordered and disciplined and containing huge buildings, this plaza seems comfortable and human-scale even today, perhaps

Colonnade of a Thousand Columns, Chichén Itza, Yucatan.

Working without mortar, unskilled labor built the walls of Kabah and Uxmal of interlocked standardized stone shapes.

because of the stepped-back shape of the pyramids, which opens up the space. This ziggurat form invites and challenges climbing. And in the act of climbing the changing elevation constantly creates new perspectives of exciting visual scenes of smaller plazas and pedestrian concourses which were meant to be enjoyed from all views and approaches as a total experience. All this was the Downtown, with a high density of permanent population.

While the Maya had no need for city streets to channel conveyances, they did connect their many cities by sacebob, a road system of ceremonial as well as trading use. Frequently its public roads for runners and litter carriers became causeways elevated above swamps and were paved with crushed limestone packed smooth.

Another important Mayan city, noted for the quality of its urban design and sculpture, was Uxmal. Uxmal was a smaller city built without pyramids; it was not a capital city. Yet its designers evolved a way of building large structures without mortar through the interlocking of standardized, sculptured stones. The mosaic of thousands of these mass-produced stones cast an extravagant pattern of shadow detail that somehow unified the space. The most noted urban structure that achieved this effect was the House of the Governors, sometimes called the single most magnificent building ever erected in the Americas. This palace, 320 feet long, was built on a 5-acre podium 50 feet high. And positioned before the main axis, much like the obelisks with which Renaissance popes marked their plazas, was an enormous stone phallus.

The streetscapes of these Mayan cities, with their varied levels, terraces, and platforms, show the skill of Mayan designers, who, working without the slave manpower or metal of ancient Rome, were still able to model public spaces of intensified imagery. These monumental public works were made possible by a bureaucracy of priests and nobles able to devote a considerable portion of the public wealth to meeting the psychological as well as physiological needs of society.

Public Art Must Be Mass-produced

In medieval times ideas parallel to those of ancient Greece found new expression in Europe. After centuries of transition from castle stronghold to guild and burgher mentality, more humane ideas took hold. While the castle remained aloof, the square and surrounding streets filled with houses and shops of tradesmen and craftsmen. The town became the focus of an agricultural area, and its growth and material success created the need for marketplaces, which became the equivalent of the agora.

But the medieval town remained small, kept within the limits of its ability to defend and support itself. At the peak of the towns' growth in the fourteenth century only Milan and Venice exceeded 100,000 population. Paris, the largest northern town, boasted 80,000 people, while England only had one great town of 40,000 people—London.

All these towns grew without plan or order. Residential streets were added haphazardly, following the terrain up and down. They were narrow, crooked, confusing, and often dead ends. Garbage was dumped from windows; sewage flowed along the rutted lanes. The scale and effect on the senses were personal, human, and immediate.

The commercial street from city gate to marketplace was usually wider, but even here, because of close viewing conditions, the backs of important

"Nunnery" (Government Building), Uxmal, Yucatan circa A.D. *900. An immense Mayan quadrangle whose various steps, levels, setbacks, and wall mosaics create an exciting public space of human scale.*

Laundry hanging over narrow pedestrian lanes in old Barcelona still contributes to medieval personal scale.

buildings were ignored and the square was a two-dimensional space. Urban design consisted of making the facades of facing buildings interesting. The accessible front of the church had to develop into a vertical expression to be seen. And as the most dramatic feature of the town, a thirteenth-century Gothic cathedral such as Chartres or the duomo of Florence became not only a house of worship but the town landmark symbol and a work of public art.

How did the power structure of the community accomplish this within the financial resources of the people? How were the services of so many gifted artists secured? Where were they found? Who trained them? If lacking in sophisticated tools and technology, the master builder of a great cathedral had a powerful force going for him—communications. He could meet with the craftsmen and discuss their production problems as part of his conception of new design ideas. Problem solving was cooperative; action was immediate.

Moreover, on closer look we see that most cathedral stones are square standardized blocks. Their shapes are formalized, and they are as repetitively carved as the stones of Mayan Uxmal. They were literally the mass-produced components of a building system and could be assembled with a maximum amount of systematic labor and a minimum of spontaneity.

Although this public art had a technical side involving calculation, the designer and artisan were given the chance to make utilitarian forms into symbolic ones. This came about as medieval society attained new capabilities that led to the growth of powerful political states. Certain towns in these states enjoyed advantages because of strategic location or the favor of a ruler. In the guildhall of the town a spirit developed among the merchants and townspeople that led to the development of a cohesive and powerful bourgeoisie. This class had the organization and drive that evolved the livable community. The guilds spent lavishly on public shows. They encouraged creative work, and shrewdly they were willing to pay for it. The average guildsman was both entrepreneur and artisan. As Giedion pointed out, that extra effort had no technical value—water doesn't drain better out of a gargoyle's mouth than a weep hole in a wall. But the burghers found the contribution of the designer as well as the developer, the sculptor as well as the mason, of public value in adding passion and ecstasy to a city which otherwise offered only toil and existence.

Talent Needs a Patron

Not all towns had benevolent rulers or a cohesive bourgeoisie. Many communities founded in middle Europe in the twelfth or thirteenth century had dogged struggles with feudal lords that laid the foundations for modern

democracy. By the dawn of the Renaissance the economic center had shifted from town to court. But the city republics of Italy—Venice, Siena, and above all Florence—had achieved an independence of spirit that fostered great public works and public art for the enjoyment of the people.

In the Florence of the early Renaissance everyone was involved in an urban renewal program sponsored by the local governing families, whose money grants gave opportunity to talent and supported innovation. In some cities the stately open squares took hundreds of years to complete. The noblest of them all, the Piazza San Marco in Venice, remained unfinished for five hundred years. But in Florence, Brunelleschi added the dome to the duomo in 1420, Giotto and Pisano shortly afterward added the campanile, and other architects and sculptors quickly contributed buildings, statues, and squares. Many major talents helped plan the town. Leonardo da Vinci, for example, drew designs by means of which the Arno River was straightened as it flowed through Florence. He also proposed a scheme for separation of wheeled from pedestrian traffic by means of different levels. As in any urban renewal or public art project, there was controversy. Michelangelo's heroic statue of David was stoned because of the conspicuous genitalia. But there was interest; there was action.

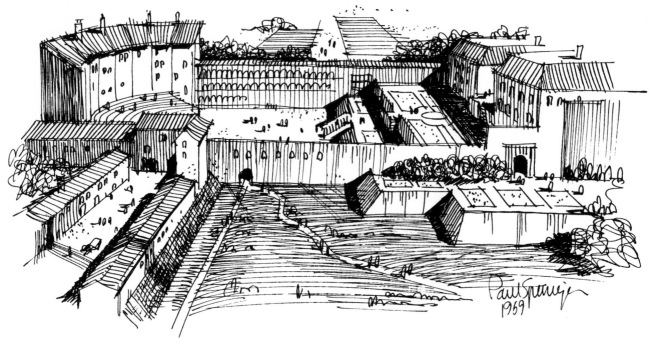

Multilevel gardens at the Vatican create new sensory experience for pedestrians.

Rome, however, was a different place, a city with an indifferent theocracy and a spiritless populace. At the close of the thirteenth century the population had shrunk to 17,000 people crowded into a fold of the Tiber River. The city was a polluted, pestilent place whose dominant visual component was the fortress Castel Sant'Angelo—a place of refuge for the Pope when the Vatican was attacked.

Not until the 1500s, when popes from mercantile families established a business center on the other side of the Ponte Sant'Angelo, was revitalization possible. With the arrival of merchants and bankers—and the reestablishment of the church, newly returned from the sanctuary of the Palais des Papes in Avignon, France—a physical transformation took place.

These new urban popes sponsored many innovative schemes to create order and grandeur from decay and chaos. They accepted large design solutions which flowed from physical needs. One problem was the mixture of blighted buildings and streets left over from many previous epochs plus the terrain, whose Roman hills made large-scale imposition of formal grid layouts impossible. The solution came from designer Donato Bramante, who modeled the three-dimensional floor as a unifying element to the varied streetscape. With levels and turns on different planes, his monumental stairways, terraces, and ramps of the Garden Court of Belvedere at the Vatican became a new element for urban design. The widespread adoption of this technique made Rome a kinesthetic as well as esthetic experience.

14

Sixtus V was the greatest planner and administrator of the time. Assuming the papacy in 1585 at the age of sixty-four, in the just five years before he died of malaria he planned and executed a public works program that brought urban order to what was still a sprawling, disorderly medieval city. He did it by going out to the neighborhoods. He did not neglect the religious core of Rome; he sponsored the addition of the cupola to St. Peter's dome and placed Caligula's obelisk in the center of the facing plaza. But most importantly Sixtus saw the city in its entirety and knew that public works of social benefit were essential to future growth.

First he changed a random group of roads into an urban transport system. Then he located future squares and plazas and marked them with obelisks. The brilliant use of Egyptian obelisks left over from the Roman days established nodes in the movement system and marked the focal points. Some of the roads and great squares were not completed for decades afterward, but the concept was indisputably established: the sheer presence of these permanent massive landmarks made the land-use decision irreversible.

In the short time Sixtus was Pope Rome rapidly grew, with more shops and houses accommodating an increased population. Then a water supply for the expanding city was urgently needed. His imaginative solution was to restore the old Roman aqueducts, which could conduct water to the highest elevations of the Roman hills, where the system terminated in important microarchitecture and street furniture—twenty-seven fountains in all. Many are in use now. The lion heads of the Moses Fountain still spit water to the passerby. But in Sixtus's time the fountain was also a cluster of street facilities: basins for horses and cattle, a public washing place for dirty laundry, a nearby community bath.

Providing *street furnishings* in public places quickly changed the character of the city, so much so that after some absence a priest returning to Rome wrote that he could hardly recognize the place: "Everything seemed so new—edifices, streets, squares, fountains, aqueducts, obelisks."

Plazas were essential to the needs of the Renaissance cities because they provided an ordered oasis amidst urban squalor. Sixteenth-century designers experimented with all sizes and shapes of plazas in all the major cities of Europe. But there was still one unsolved problem in urban design: tying the whole city together. This technique came from the park designers.

"L'état, c'est moi." The personal life of the monarch became the center of all state activity in the seventeenth century. The rise of the egoistic and ruthless despot began to supersede communal action. Rule changed from a public function to a private gesture. The baroque rulers of Europe such as Louis XIV hated large cities, narrow streets, and common people. Also during this time the feminine influence on court life grew. There was a demand for greater comfort and delicacy. Painting, sculpture, and interior

Der Stadt, Vienna, 1858. Designed for a figure on horseback (Franz Josef I), the Renaissance-inspired plaza has been conquered by the Volkswagen.

furnishings became mannered. The time was ripe for a change in the form and exterior furnishing of the royal residence, and Louis XIV boldly built his new residential and administrative complex in the country instead of in Paris.

Never before had so large a community (court society) been housed under such a roof (2,000 feet long). Started in 1661, the Chateau of Versailles was almost a half century in the making. Deliberately creating an environment for the aggrandizement of the royal ego and the pleasure of the court, the park designer, André Lenôtre, produced a palace that dominated the town behind it and nature before it. The doing required the development of a total landscape system of geometric design which, like later town planning, related a great number of components in a carefully ordered natural environment.

Versailles was conceived as a setting for the pedestrian activity of court society. It was also to be a royal extravaganza. Lenôtre therefore furnished the landscape with every imaginable feature, including lakes and a grand canal with gondolas; adult and children playgrounds; terraces, pools, and fountains; a zoo; and formal gardens. New standards of elegance were achieved for public furniture such as pavings, benches, balustrades, and lanterns. But the outstanding innovation was in the ordering device for so many parts. Lenôtre used a radial design that organized town and parks like spokes about the hub of the palace and aligned principal axes with main landscape features. The central and most important viewing axis was the highway from Paris, which led straight into the royal stables, penetrated the thin, long palace, and continued with clean vista over foreground gardens to the distant horizon. This system for ordering a complex of monumental buildings and vast parks produced so majestically simple a visual scene that it was reproduced in Vienna for the Austrian royal palace Schönbrunn and similarly adapted and applied around the world.

HANDMADE TO MACHINE-MADE

Engineering the Environment

The eighteenth century was a time of change, and the industrial revolution altered the appearance of cities far more than the social revolution. It was time for product innovation, and the urge to invent swept England in the 1760s like a national fever. Investors put money into new gadgets, schemes, products, and processes conceived by hundreds of unlikely persons. Farmers and a new breed of entrepreneurs contributed ideas as well as craftsmen. This excitement and acceleration in product development was given weight and substance by radical improvement in an old process—the making of iron.

Iron was hated and distrusted by classical architects, with much reason: although there had been ironworks since the fourteenth century and skilled armorers had forged the metal into useful and handsome lanterns, grilles, and railings, iron was expensive to work. Outdoor use in towns demonstrated other deficiencies, such as poor resistance to corrosion. But new qualities were given to the old metal by a succession of refinements. Abraham Darby invented the mechanical process of wet-sand casting in 1708. Now unskilled labor could make molten metal flow over the artisan's pattern and repetitively reproduce intricate designs at low cost. Other ideas quickly came from Darby and others. By the middle of the century the blast furnace was improved, making possible higher heats, improved metallurgy, and a new product—structural iron.

Many building tasks formerly reserved for stone could now be performed better by cast or wrought-iron beams and posts. Large lacy-looking bridges, aviaries, pavilions, and previously unheard-of structures were soon engineered to make daring use of this new exotic material. On Main Street, building technique and facade appearance were completely transformed within one hundred years. The framing of great halls with open ironwork, supported on thin cast columns and enclosed with glass, was quickly accepted. In the same period, because of this bounty of new mechanical products and processes to show and sell, the regional fair exploded into the international exhibition. And what more fitting a promotional technique than to house new factory-made iron-age products in an iron prefabricated structure? So the London 1851 International Exhibition of Machines was held in a Crystal Palace more dreamlike than any Renaissance palace. Joseph Paxton's systems design of small, serially repeated shop-made units was as dramatic in impact and import as Buckminster Fuller's geodesic dome of steel and acrylic units of Expo 67. The massive, traditional, Renaissance stone structure had disappeared, and in its place was a light tracery against the sky.

The machine esthetic was here, as the people realized if the academy did not. When the Parisian public protested about the unsuitability of a new group of market buildings made of stone, Baron Georges Eugène Haussmann, prefect of Paris under Louis Napoleon, made the architect tear them down and turn to iron and glass. Now this concept was expanded and revitalized, in Les Halles Centrales, the meat, fruit, and vegetable market of Paris, begun in 1853. It was a vast covered marketplace with a high transparent ceiling—so huge a place that it contained groups of pavilions, cobbled streets, and streetlamps on columns. Its utilitarian structures, stark and simple, with lacy iron vaults overhead that optically disappeared in the pouring sunlight, created a new esthetic feeling. "It looked like some great outsize modern machine, a great boiler for a people's digestion, a gigantic metal stomach

Crystal Palace, London, 1851.

with iron, glass and wood, riveted, bolted together, so elegant, so powerful. . . ." Such was Émile Zola's description of Les Halles.

These mechanical-looking marvels had such fascination for people that, like today's huge domed sports stadium, they established another function: *landmark*. In some instances this function became preeminent. The Eiffel Tower is one example. What an exuberant gesture, this 1,000-foot structure with no function except to afford people the pleasure of ascending and enjoying the view! The lesson of the emotional content achievable through the penetration of space by means of daring engineering sparked fanciful constructions such as the huge ferris wheel in the Prater, visible over much of Vienna, and continues to modern times with Saarinen's stainless-steel arch of St. Louis.

By definition these landmarks were novelties and unique. But businessmen and developers quickly grasped the central point. Iron was economical. Its use eliminated thick load-bearing walls and permitted longer spans with fewer supports, which meant more net usable space. Iron structures could be prefabricated in a factory and more quickly assembled on site. Businessmen recognized that the resultant imagery was valuable, but it was a byproduct, a bonus.

The interest of the business community provided the incentive for further experimentation. New techniques were developed for the factory manufacture of precisely dimensioned parts whose rivet holes would align during field assembly. New York took the highroad in 1868 with the erection of the first elevated railroad, the West Side and Yonkers Patented Railroad. While back in Paris, bridge designer Gustave Eiffel in 1876, thirteen years before his famous tower, built the Bon Marché department store and proved the commercial feasibility of iron and glass.

The use of natural light and air as a design element made possible a new shopping environment. The pleasurable atmosphere changed the design not only of the individual store but of the business street itself. The street frequently became an arcaded open space, as in Milan with the Galleria Vittorio Emanuele or as in Naples with the Galleria Umberto—both still in use. In America arcades were built in most major cities. The Cleveland Arcade—a complex of two nine-story office buildings linked by a central skylighted mall surrounded by four stories of shops and offices—is still functioning. These galleries were patronized by elegant society and became instant commercial successes. Their social as well as commercial values became the prototype for the contemporary regional covered shopping center, whose entertainment value as an all-day experience may be as important to the shopper as the location, convenience, and mass display of goods.

The Prater, Vienna.

Furnishing the Environment

Until the industrial revolution, street furniture in most cities consisted of the lantern, hitching post, and occasional bench. When used, street identification consisted of handmade plaques frequently of great artistry appliquéd to the walls of buildings at street intersections.

Lighting was a spotty practice, and oil-burning lanterns required the lamplighter to tend the wick. The flickering dim light was almost always cast too close to the supporting building. Only rarely did a handsome wrought-iron bracket cantilever the lantern far enough out over the street.

Then came the gas lamp, whose greenish yellow light brightened the nighttime scene of the nineteenth-century city. Frederick Albert Winsor patented his process for manufacturing gas from coal and staged the first public street lighting in 1807 along Pall Mall in London. But acceptance did not come easily in Europe; progress was delayed by prejudice and fear. Tastemakers such as Sir Walter Scott in England and Napoleon in France scoffed at the idea of lighting cities with smoke. While it was possible to install new utilities below ground, out of sight and mind, above ground these new engineered products were disparaged and resisted by academicians trained in the static viewpoint of the Renaissance. So that in Europe the appearance of street furniture and the visual scene remained unchanged for some time. In America, however, gas-lamp street lighting was gaining acceptance as early as 1815, when Baltimore became the first city to light most of its streets with gas, manufactured by a company founded by Rembrandt Peale.

The invention of the cast-iron hollow column eliminated all remaining resistance to street lighting. Although it was invented for other structural purposes, the advantages for street lighting of this English product of about 1790 were readily apparent. Now light could be evenly distributed in a linear pattern from lanterns put where needed and independent of building facades for support. This new kind of street furniture also could be put to other use. So while England and the Continent continued the custom of placing street names on building facades, in America, where developers were building streets before houses existed, street signs appeared on lampposts. Additional signs have been added since, until the support has become more signpost than lamppost in function.

While new in concept, these mass-produced components followed traditional styles in appearance. Street furniture became period pieces to complement city architecture. Burgeoning cities in America sought "instant tradition" and bought large monumental light columns in elaborate historical dress for Downtown. And a variety of revivals took place in cast-iron columns: Grecian, Gothic (bishop's crook of New York), all the classical styles.

Mechanical to Electrical

In the waning years of the nineteenth century the world was on the threshold of much that was new. Freud was exploring unconscious impulses, the impressionist Monet was painting shifting light, and new "things" were being invented that were energized. Edison turned on the world when he switched from gas flame to electric lamp.

Boston, Massachusetts.

San Francisco, California.

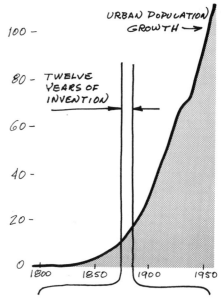

URBAN POPULATION GROWTH →

TWELVE YEARS OF INVENTION

The generation of electric power at a building site for lighting was quickly adopted and became common by the turn of the century; many new buildings produced their own direct current. Perhaps more important than his carbon glow lamp of 1879 was Edison's development in 1882 of the central electric power station and distribution system. Alternating current facilitated long-distance distribution of power with low power loss. Now brighter illumination of urban America was possible, and new utility lines were soon laid along streets to convert existing gas systems and hardware to electricity.

Power that made lamps hot and glowing could also energize the many new devices required to meet urban needs. Large-scale immigration turned towns quickly into cities which needed more communications. In 1884 telephone wires were strung from New York to Boston.

Simultaneously, in Madrid, Don Arturo Soria y Mata created not only a telephone system but also the first electric streetcar system. Suddenly the trolley ceased to be horse-drawn. Power could move more people about faster and more economically. Speculators and investors saw other opportunities and created many new utilities. Jungles of wire were added to

1877 TELEPHONE Alexander Graham Bell speaks from Salem to his assistant in Boston, 12 miles away.

1880 SKYSCRAPER William LeBaron Jenney builds the first skyscraper, ten stories tall, for the Home Insurance Co. in Chicago.

1880 INCANDESCENT LAMP The first filaments, made of carbonized sewing threads, burn for 40 hours in Edison's laboratory!

1885 ELECTRONIC TROLLEY CAR Baltimore replaces the horse—the first American city to do so.

1886 SUBWAY London is the first city to transport people underground, in an electric-powered system designed by Greathead.

1889 AUTOMOBILE The Daimler is whizzing along the roads at eleven mph!

1889 ELEVATOR Otis brothers install first electric elevator in Demarest building in New York.

Inventions that shaped the cities.

Main Street, Buffalo, New York, 1888. A boomtown and place of hullabaloo. Its affluence could be measured by the number of telephone wires draped from poles. Pedestrians were afforded the luxury of crosswalks set in the cobbled streets.

Main Street, Buffalo, New York, 1897. Affluence encourages more sophisticated standards. All utility wires are underground, new electric streetlights installed, the street repaved.

existing wire systems. Poles were planted thicker and higher. Soon the look of the American streetscape was established.

Engineers and draftsmen copied the architectural styles of the past to cloak and provide acceptance to their new inventions. Fire hydrants were fluted like Grecian columns, and fire-alarm mechanisms were housed in cast-iron Cape Cod cottages. In the mechanical age, pre-1900, it was quite easy and proper to use familiar imagery in coping with the new mechanical technology and use it as the design vocabulary for the townscape. That is why cast-iron hydrants and ornate gas lamps look right in early photographs of the city. On the other hand, just as the horseless carriage was the product of buggy manufacturers, so was the traffic signal made by railroad-equipment manufacturers; and although their engineers achieved high reliability standards, the ponderous traffic-control equipment imposed standards of weight and mass more suited to a product squatting beside a train track than suspended in space or pinned to a pole along the street.

MAKING THE CITY GREEN

Beauty and the Bureaucracy

The technical age had dawned, and in Europe Baron Haussmann understood the city as a technical problem. Louis XIV spent a lifetime building Versailles, with all the resources of France at his disposal. Starting in 1853, in just seventeen years Haussmann, as city administrator for Louis Napoleon, transformed Paris at a cost of 2.5 billion francs in the greatest public works programs of all time.

Haussman had to face all the problems of urban renewal, especially the social and political. He saw overall problems of traffic, transportation, and communications, and rather than merely enlarge existing streets, he quickly cut a new street system connecting railroad stations and key points by means of axial boulevards providing exciting vistas. Blocks of buildings were torn down in order to expedite his solutions to long-range problems. But in buying private property for public good, Haussmann made enemies. While some of the corrupt bourgeosie made profits, others called him a ruthless autocrat. And he was forced to leave before implementing his concept of a wide greenbelt around the city utilizing the old girdle of fortifications.

But Haussmann's unique administrative procedures and people remained at work. He had turned from artists and put together a staff of technicians to accommodate the city to the industrial changes involved in the design, installation, and maintenance of public works. For the first time anywhere administrative responsibilities were organized within three departments: water and sanitation, streets and parks, and planning.

Put in charge were engineering graduates of the École Polytechnique. Belgrand constructed the enormous sewer system of Paris and the aqueducts which for the first time provided an adequate water supply. Haussmann put Jean Alphand, a highway engineer, in charge of all landscape work. It was he who laid out the Champs-Élysées and the leisure grounds of Paris, including the kidney-shaped systems of walks used in the parks such as the Bois de Boulogne. He also invented tree-lifting machines that could transplant thirty-year-old trees in full leaf. But most importantly, Deschamps, head of the new municipal planning service, plotted the new street lines that contributed to the unique look of Paris. His boulevards were not only high-speed traffic lanes to the suburbs but also strolling areas for the common man where before had been only packed tenements.

The American Park Movement

More than sixty years before Haussmann started to transform Paris, the Versailles design concept of the grand geometric plan had been adapted by Charles L'Enfant to Washington, D.C. But the impressive boulevards of Paris were highly regarded and copied in most of Europe's capital cities, whereas in America most cities rapidly grew in size and industrial ugliness without relief of boulevard, open space, or greenery (until Frederick Law Olmsted was supported by visionaries).

Olmsted, a well-known social reformer, was also a farmer concerned about improper use of land. He saw the effect of rising urban population on ill-prepared cities and knew it was damaging to democracy. Fortunately, at the same time a few New York City businessmen had a vision of the future needs and growth of their city and in 1856 sponsored a competition to design a city park uptown, forty blocks from where the action was.

Olmsted won the Central Park competition and quickly implemented the self-evident beauty of his park plans and landscape designs there and in many other cities throughout the United States. His designs featured the urban park as an essential part of the city's fabric. Although he learned much from the English park system, Olmsted's contribution was unique. He established the notion that greenery for relaxation with nature must be made available for all.

City-beautiful Era

Around the turn of the century the American economy was booming, waves of immigration were doubling population, America was becoming a world power, and still-young cities were expanding and new ones being born. And until the Great Depression of the thirties, the nation experienced almost continuous urban growth.

Seeking symbols of newfound wealth and status, cities turned away from the machine and returned to classicism. Lacking an acceptable native image, the new cities copied the proved art of ancient Rome and lavished it upon monumental civic centers. As early as 1893, while Europe was still experimenting with the great iron landmarks housing the machine exhibitions, the World's Columbian Exposition at Chicago went back to the Renaissance for inspiration. But in its new adaptation at Chicago and elsewhere, the Renaissance style tended to become a wedding-cake style.

First mechanical traffic signal, illuminated at night with colored lantern, London, 1868.

POLICE NOTICE.

STREET CROSSING SIGNALS.
BRIDGE STREET, NEW PALACE YARD.

CAUTION.

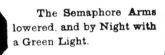

The Semaphore Arms lowered, and by Night with a Green Light.

STOP.

The Semaphore Arms extended, and by Night with a Red Light.

By the Signal "CAUTION," all persons in charge of Vehicles and Horses are warned to pass over the Crossing with care, and due regard to the safety of Foot Passengers.

The Signal "STOP," will only be displayed when it is necessary that Vehicles and Horses shall be actually stopped on each side of the Crossing, to allow the passage of Persons on Foot; notice being thus given to all persons in charge of Vehicles and Horses to stop clear of the Crossing.

RICHARD MAYNE,

Commissioner of Police of the Metropolis

December 10th 1868.

Louis Sullivan predicted that "the damage wrought to this country by the Chicago World's Fair will last half a century"; and true enough, the impact of this wedding-cake style struck the entire country. The Pan American Exposition of 1901 in Buffalo echoed the Chicago pattern of plaster palazzos on a grand canal filled with gondolas. Soon smaller towns emulated these examples and built vulgarized gates, arches, and fountains and even disguised water tanks as battlements or temples of love.

In the years that followed a few planners, such as Daniel Burnham, worked at developing the city in its entirety as a balanced system of parks and streets. Burnham considered the city in terms of essential relationships of systems of circulation arteries, parks, and public spaces. His followers established the urban planning profession and helped develop tools and techniques for control of the environment, such as zoning ordinances.

But in the main this was a period when there was more concern with the external shape of the city—buildings, esplanades, elegant neighborhoods. Few understood or examined the growing environmental problems of Downtown, the slums, and the growing use of motor cars.

The City as a Machine

Meanwhile a few urban designers were fascinated with the potential of practical inventions for solving functional problems. For example, just before the turn of the century Soria y Mata proposed "Linear City" in which utility lines would become the linear basis for city layout, so that houses and buildings could be plugged into water, communications, and power networks. He actually built such a linear city near Madrid, and the Russians used a similar concept in the building of Stalingrad.

France, with such illustrious examples as the Gallerie des Machines, Les Halles, and the Eiffel Tower, produced several visionaries who saw that the machine esthetic could be applied not only to shelter but to the complete environment. Eugène Hénard, architect for the city of Paris between 1900 and 1914, was such a man. His seminal ideas, reported in his book *Les Villes de l'Avenir,* were influential in shaping the directions of others, such as Le Corbusier and Antonio Sant'Elia.

Hénard had many startling ideas. Even before the Wright brothers came to France, he saw the need for an airport available to the city. In 1904, thinking in the then familiar terms of the dirigible, he proposed the first in-city landing field anywhere in the world. He envisioned an airdrome at the Champ de Mars in which the Eiffel Tower would be used as a signal tower and the Gallerie des Machines would become the hangar. As early as 1910 Hénard, clearly seeing that the rising demand for municipal services was creating a jungle of products, recommended the use of *multilevel* streets

Temple of Music, Pan American Exposition, 1901.

in high-density parts of the city. The historian Peter Wolf has reported on Hénard's comments to the Town Planning Conference in London that year. Hénard said that the ordinary street was still a country lane bordered with footpaths, but whose subsurface was layered with sewers and telegraph, electric, and telephone wires all without order or system. "When repair is necessary," Hénard said, "each system, whether it belongs to a private company or to one of the city departments, has to be dealt with separately." And he demonstrated how these services could be integrated. One of his proposals used various levels to accommodate mechanical functions, including ash and garbage collection, and featured vertical circulation to rooftop helicopter pads. All in 1910!

But in America there was little interest in such ideas. Periodically proposals were made for the "city of the future," featuring elevated transporta-

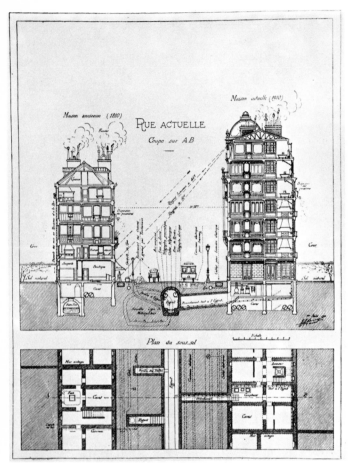

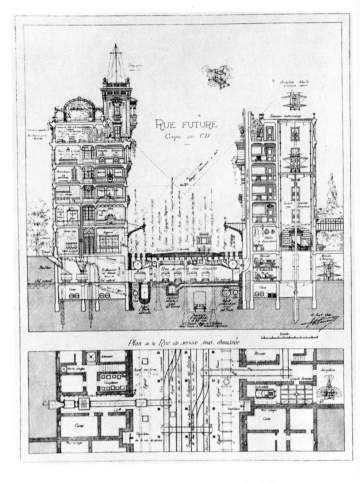

Hénard forecast multilevel use of public space by means of improved technology.

tion schemes in which vehicles ran over rooftops of continuous buildings or, sometimes, over lattice or grid. These variations of "motopia" usually appeared too mechanistic, offered little technological advancement, and received no public support. Most planning emphasis through the twenties and thirties was based on community social values to be achieved by greenbelts and nature rather than mass production and industry. With the passing of the Great Depression, New Deal interest in, and public support of, social change and massive public works waned, and the much-heralded change from bombs to building systems by sophisticated armament industries never developed after World War II.

Meanwhile the population of the country had multiplied from approximately 20 million at the turn of the century to 200 million, and was still soaring. The number of cars on the road had jumped from zero to 90 million and was straining toward double that by the end of the century. A tidal wave of people and products was sweeping over the green land, making it barren and ugly.

Crow's nest, adapted from railroad signal tower, installed on Woodward Avenue, Detroit, circa 1915.

More elegant crow's nest installed on Fifth Avenue New York. Motorists now watch signals rather than policeman inside.

Chapter Two

The Problem

The city has become a jungle of posts and products. Weedlike these dense growths sprout from barren asphalt and concrete and flourish without systematic planting, cultivation, or pruning. The public right-of-way has become encumbered by the thicket of products from building line to center of the street. Community appearance lacks visual as well as functional order.

Not only does the imagery of Downtown suffer; the very quality of the living experience in the neighborhoods or even suburbs is affected. The need to improve the quality and utility of the public environment is important to all. But the greatest difficulty we face in environmental design is the lack of understanding—agreement as to what the actual problems are and what can be done about them.

In order to develop an approach to problem solving, we must first determine what went wrong.

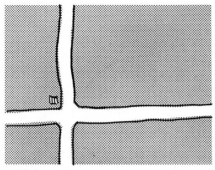

Fork in mud road with milestone

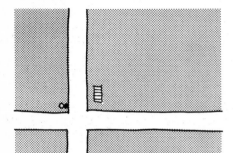

Paved street with gas lamp, street name, and horse trough

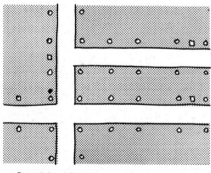

Street lighting, fire hydrant, and fire alarm

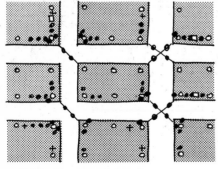

High density products with low-order control

THE HIGH COST OF VISUAL POLLUTION

Product Proliferation

Like a science-fiction story the American love affair with the automobile spawns increasing litters of cars, until the machines displace people from streets and houses, and concrete, not grass, covers the cityscape. The time is rapidly coming when the use of the private automobile on the public street will be curtailed. Cars will be subject to curfew, and their use will be prohibited in some areas. The advantage of the motor vehicle will have been lost through its very abundance. Already, according to testimony before the Senate Roads Subcommittee, the average speed of motor vehicles through the streets of New York has been reduced, in 1966, to 8.5 miles per hour, as compared with 11.5 miles per hour of horse-drawn vehicles in 1907.

This problem is not unique to larger cities or even to America. Europe, whose Renaissance cities are so appealing to American tourists, offers no design guidelines for the automobile age. In fact the elegant plazas and charming side streets of European cities are snarled almost beyond hope. In a typical day, according to London's first traffic commissioner, Peter Scott, "500,000 cars, 8,000 buses and 6,000 taxis jam the streets with the pace reduced to 2 mph during the peak period in, say, Old Kent Road."

While traffic congestion is acknowledged as a problem and highway design forms the basis for many urban studies, another dimension must be added: the number of public products required to sustain and control the private automobile. As will be discussed in a later chapter, the high cost of visual pollution is significant in psychological as well as economic terms; traffic-control devices are masters of people as well as public spaces.

A visual survey of any urban street reveals the extent to which many different products are repetitively required for communication with, and control of, the pedestrian and motorist. And great numbers of other devices are required for lighting, security, and amenity. Up to this time no American city has ever compiled and made available a complete inventory of its street furniture, equipments, and appliances. But some indication of the economic and visual importance of these items can be seen from a 1967 study made for the city of Cincinnati, with a population of 500,000. In just the downtown area of approximately seventy city blocks were contained:

50,000	linear feet roadway paving
90,000	linear feet sidewalk paving
14,000	linear feet crosswalk paving
300	pedestrian signals
250	traffic signals
70	emergency vehicle signals
1,000	traffic-regulation signs

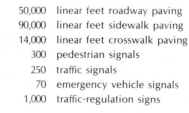

2,000 parking-regulation signs
935 light fixtures

There were other uncounted publicly owned furnishings, such as mail-boxes, trash receptacles, benches, clocks, phone booths, fire hydrants, signal controllers and detectors, police call boxes, fire-alarm boxes, gratings, parking meters, and landscaping. Peter Kory of the Urban Development Agency of Cincinnati initiated one of the first street-furniture analysis and design programs. But for most other cities the magnitude of the problem remains unrecognized.

And more is yet to come. Lacking study or design programs, the cities will have, as Patrick Geddes put it, "more and more of worse and worse." The size of the public investment in street furniture will increase in response to several forces at work. First, there is the demand spurred by population growth; second, the political and social need to rebuild much of our cities by the end of the century; third, the affluence to support the effort as expressed by voter approval of increased expenditures in the public works segment of national, state, and local budgets. School bond issues are sometimes defeated at the polls, but public works line-items are seldom questioned. However, as the investment in public environment increases, the quality will decrease unless solutions are found to such problems as street-furniture *styling*.

In architecture the monuments are single monuments; in urban design the furnishings are in multiples. A city can be and has been built around a Parthenon. What would be the effect of a thousand Parthenons scattered about the city? A city has light poles and fire hydrants. What is the effect of a thousand monumental light poles or Grecian fire hydrants on the observer? Does this styling approach contribute to an object's efficiency? Presently, most products on the public right-of-way are highly specialized, and each one is allowed to perform only one function. This single-function product-oriented design approach inevitably makes for vast overlapping and duplication of materials and costs. These inefficiencies must be paid for one way or another. If the city and its population were static, it might be possible to reduce the clutter and inefficiency by redesigning individual items. But in a dynamic situation there is urgent need for systematic review of all furnishings.

The real problem is not density of products per se; significantly it is *the way in which density is organized*. But urban areas that require a high order of product density unfortunately have a low order of management control.

Fragmented Bureaucracy

Visualize the result if the average American home were furnished in the following manner: each appliance, lamp, floor covering, article of furniture,

Products fill the public space and leave little room for people.

garbage can, picture, telephone, and so on, was selected and purchased by a different member of the family without regard for the needs of others, installed by a different person without regard for whatever already existed nearby, and maintained by still someone else without regard for other housekeeping needs. This approximates the procedure employed by municipal departments in many communities. *Uncoordinated procurement, installation, and maintenance is the rule.*

"The fact is," Lawrence Halprin wrote, "that attention to the detail and design of objects in its streets is as important to the qualities of a city's aesthetics as its buildings themselves—the modern city is a kaleidoscope of overlapping activities and people in motion. As the people eddy and move in a multifaceted series of actions, the furniture in the street becomes the fixed point which can guide and enrich their movements."

This is the need, but what is the reality? Referring to one item, parking meters, the *Buffalo Courier-Express* (Buffalo, New York, population 500,000) editorially complained, "The Board of Parking has no jurisdiction over them, but the Board of Safety decides where they should go; the Common Council decides what kind to buy; the Purchase Division buys them; the Police

Erratic, overlapping jurisdictions.

Buffalo, New York. Columbus on his pedestal discovers America to be a forest of poles.

Department installs and maintains them; and the Treasury Department collects the money."

With this kind of fragmented authority the ablest urban renewal or public works administration has difficulty in programming and getting a more efficient or esthetically satisfactory environment.

Design innovation is further hampered by the lack of research or test facilities to service the various departmental needs. A bureaucracy of fragmented technical departments lacks corporate muscle in competing for available funds. America is considered an affluent society. Yet when more than 60 percent of most municipal budgets is channeled to education, little is left for other activities such as maintaining the environment. Consequently the planning research of local government is often limited to traffic and land-use studies. Unless there is professional staff manpower or consultants are employed, reliance is placed on suppliers for the preparation of purchase specifications for street furnishings. This common practice leads to quantity rather than quality solutions—wider streets, more traffic signals, bigger signs—more "things," as industrial designer Arthur Pulos calls them.

Then too, codes and manuals of state or federal agencies frequently freeze the furnishings design of the city. Specification-type codes hamper innovation and protect obsolete practices and products. Only partially serving the purpose of protecting the public, regulatory codes do not in themselves create order. Established by yesterday's reform, they are today's fences against progress. However, if existing codes and other forms of minimum design requirements are to be set aside, what will be used for design guidelines? Performance criteria based on *user* requirements. More and more, federal and state aid, which considerably supplements local resources, is used as the leverage to secure the inclusion of generalized design objectives and performance criteria into renewal, housing, and public works programs. A document including these, once approved by funding agencies and the governing body, such as a city council, can become a legal ordinance. The program manager can then use this instrument to supersede narrow-focus codes and to secure the cooperation of all city departments.

Now consider the problem of the bureaucrat faced with the need to procure beauty. By whose standards is beauty defined? How much public money is she worth? How do you describe esthetics in a purchase requisition? *Quality* of environment does not enter into the cost/benefit formula which is the basis for evaluation and selection among public works projects competing for public money. Quality of environment is immediately disadvantaged vis-à-vis more quantifiable factors. It is essential, therefore, that a new design approach be employed which by the nature of its process produces a total environment of quality.

There has already been encouraging experimentation in some centralized

The result of product-oriented specification-type codes and regulations.

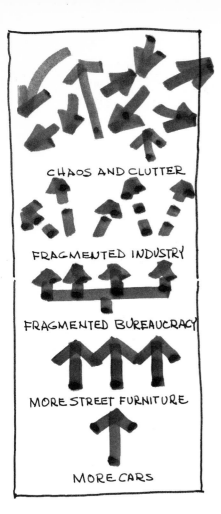

CHAOS AND CLUTTER

FRAGMENTED INDUSTRY

FRAGMENTED BUREAUCRACY

MORE STREET FURNITURE

MORE CARS

(Above, right) *Pollution of the public environment.* (Right) *San Francisco signal replacement. Is the new better than the old?*

administrative situations. Supported by strong mayors, the City Planning Commission of Philadelphia has been able to introduce *élan* into parts of Philadelphia. Planning departments of Minneapolis, Baltimore, and New Haven and a few other cities have received enough support from strong leadership to permit the coordinated process to work. Where the private developer is design-oriented, as the James Rouse organization is, a Columbia (Maryland) can result. Where a public authority directs its planners and designers to produce a complete environment (including parking, graphics, and lighting), a Toronto Airport, a Montreal Metro, or a Fresno Mall can result. When a state recognizes the limitations of splintered public works procedures and creates and finances a separate action organization (State University Construction Fund of New York), then dozens of large complexes of unique environmental character can be built in a few years (the campuses built for the fund). However, the magnitude of the problem is such and these solutions are so few that they project as oases in the urban desert of America.

Municipal mystique blocks consumer feedback and marketplace rejection of absurdity.

Fragmented Industry

Consider a suit of clothes in which the pants were made by one firm, the jacket by another, and the vest by a third—all without reference to each other. In what field of manufacturing and merchandising would such a bizarre practice be tolerated? In street furniture!

Nowhere in America is there available an interrelated line of municipal equipments for furnishing the city. No manufacturer produces more than a narrow segment of the broad spectrum of municipal, campus, airport, or shopping-center needs. Few manufacturers produce all important parts of their own product line. And it is notorious that the component elements comprising a common streetlight—the post, lamp, refractor, and luminaire, for example—are all made by different manufacturers and never meet until married on the sidewalk by the city fathers.

Perhaps these marriages of necessity will work better when the mating is arranged by computer. But this is not likely, and there remains as little contribution to the public good or the enrichment of the environment as there is commonality between equipments.

Why does this condition persist? Because almost all street furniture is still handmade by small nonintegrated producers with older plant and without sophisticated engineering or tooling. Because these handcraft products are installed by conventional construction-trade techniques with reliance on manual labor. Because the fragmentation of the municipal purchasing procedure prevents mass production of a complete environmental "package" and thereby results in higher unitized costs to the public.

Why, more than one hundred years after the industrial revolution, is industry still not convinced of the need to turn to mass production for high-volume distribution of better urban furnishings? Prevailing practice had its roots at the turn of the century, when many small companies began to supply the burgeoning cities' needs. Expertise was not a significant factor in producing nontechnological products; tooling and investment required was nominal; the use of heavy materials such as cast iron in lampposts and fire hydrants favored regional producers.

Now these same producers of street equipment—who were quick to adapt from the mechanical to the electrical age—are slow to advance into electronics. Research money has not been spent for more compact, less obtrusive, better-engineered and -appearing products of improved technology. Consequently industry has not offered products that offset the gap between construction-labor annual productivity and cost increase. The producers' present position remains archaic in a world rapidly moving toward a more rational use of its resources—in the construction industries toward modular control and preferred dimensions, international standards and *industrialized* systems.

THERE OUGHTA BE A LAW!   By Harry Shorten

As yet, few catalog selections of more compact, less obtrusive, and better-engineered products of improved technology can be made. Therefore the city must presently opt to design its own furnishings if it does not wish to add additional inefficient handcrafted articles to those already in the townscape. Some more sophisticated city agencies have sponsored new product designs of greater utility and development. The East Bay Water Works of Sacramento has its own proprietary fire hydrant; the New York Bureau of Gas, Water and Electricity sponsored a unique light standard; the urban renewal and redevelopment agencies of various cities, such as New Haven and Cincinnati, have sought more esthetic furnishings to unify their urban spaces. The number of cities recognizing the need to coordinate the design and siting of furnishings grows as professional planners and others seek to attack the total problem. Their interest will attract enterprises of more sophisticated management into the manufacture and distribution of the necessary environmental components.

Missing link (feedback).

Fragmented Consumer

Lack of feedback from consumer to manufacturer contributes to the perpetuation of inadequate street furniture on the public right-of-way. The manufacturer has contact with only the middleman (bureaucracy). The consumer, literally the man in the street, never sees a variety of shelf goods for comparison shopping. He cannot exercise the traditional veto of the marketplace.

Does not the motorist notice that eleven traffic signals instead of one at an intersection are confusing and dangerous? Of course! Does not a householder know that a glaring bright mercury streetlamp shining in his bedroom window is disturbing and destructive to neighborhood residential values? Of course! Does not the bus rider waiting in the rain without protection question the lack of shelter? Of course! Is not this public passivity in the face of environmental stupidity symptomatic of the emperor's-clothes syndrome, in which no one wants to be first to acknowledge the situation's absurdity? Perhaps. Or it may be that the consumer has not seen any other ways. He may be the victim of *municipal mystique*. He may assume there are no ways to make his environment look better and to provide him with more safety, amenity, and comfort.

We start with names for certain problems—"fire hydrant," "traffic light," "street sign." These names have already done our designing before we start. Because of municipal mystique the public is accustomed to think about these objects as fixed and static *things* rather than look for *solutions to needs* which can take new and different forms at different times depending on local conditions. Therefore people have not questioned the quality and

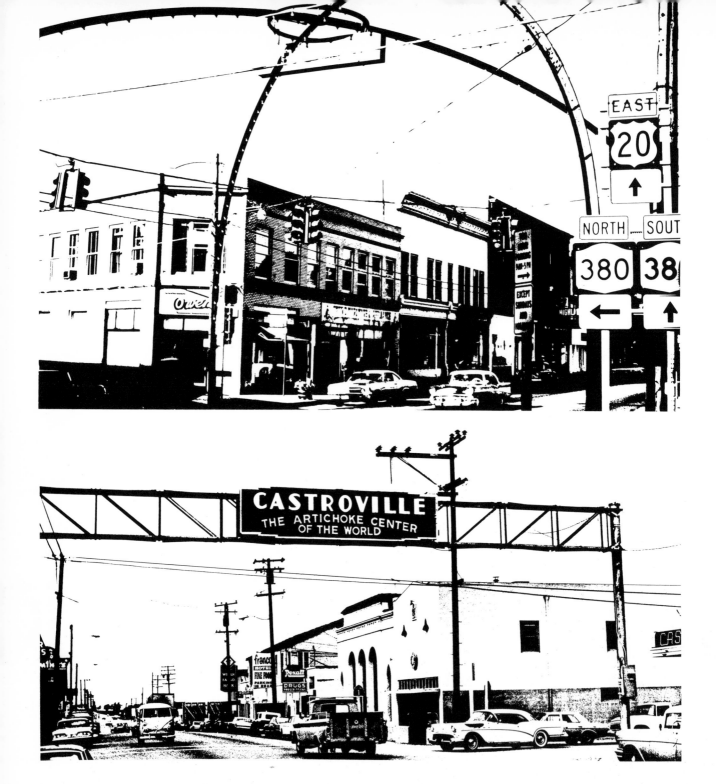

utility of their public furniture. And street clutter and ugliness have not been improved because there has not been the political need to acknowledge that the public street belongs to the people and is not the bailiwick of highway or other departments to use as they will. Conscientious planners and administrators have had little incentive to disrupt existing practice and face the rigors of innovation. Approving pats on the back come hard-earned for even low-level efforts such as removal of nonproductive or obsolete equipment from the streets.

This condition is in transition. Now the consumer is becoming more attuned to the confusion and ugliness of the environment through the public-opinion-molding mass media—TV documentaries, press editorials and reporting, cartoons and comic strips. The consumer has begun to realize that it is his money that is being spent for public improvements. Soon he will learn to articulate his needs. The city dweller will force purchasing changes by demonstration of his voting power.

Welcome! (Opposite, above) *Brocton, New York.* (Opposite below) *Castroville, California.* (Left) *Town of Amherst, New York.*

Chinatown, San Francisco.

"What place is this?"

A quick visual survey of almost every community discloses not only chaos and clutter but also an enormous sameness, a tedious dullness that deadens the civic senses and *joie de vivre*. And this condition will worsen. As towns become cities and cities merge into 600-mile-long megalopolises, local community imagery will become more essential in order to provide a sense of place that the city dweller can cling to. But there is more here too: the need for imagery translates into an economic need because imagery means selling, and cities must always be aware of the need for selling. Buying and selling are basic to our lives. Cities compete for favor (talent, loyalty, money) even as do corporations and individuals.

The need to create a favorable urban image has always existed. Kings built huge monuments to make visual their power. City-states erected extravagant symbols to attract trade and commerce. The bronze statue the "Colossus of Rhodes" was one of the Seven Wonders of the World until destroyed by earthquake in 227 B.C. It could only have been built by a city seeking to express the grandeur of its harbor and thereby attract more commerce. The romantic bridges and quais in Paris reflect a royal demand for beauty. The Ponte Vecchio over the Arno in Italy is now picture-postcard stuff; but the idea of shops on a bridge grew out of the merchants' need to go where the activity was. Venice made its defensive canal system into priceless imagery despite staggering costs of maintenance and preservation. All these costly projects were designed to bring the city glory or profit or, usually, both.

Now, with statistics showing that the average member of our mobile population changes residence every four years, our cities—and our neighborhoods too—must face a struggle for distinction in order to retain and attract consumers (shoppers, industry, taxpayers). Many older, more conservative cities, particularly in the East, seem unaware of the intensity of this competition, their complacency being visually manifested by the deterioration of their "brand image" and their overall unattractiveness. For those who are aware of the economic value of a favorable image, the problem is not *whether* to have an image but rather *what* kind and *how* is it to be achieved.

A few cities have been blessed with natural features of exclusive character that endure and can be enhanced through purposeful urban design. San Antonio, for example, is blessed with a river softly flowing at lower level through the town. The warm Spanish welcome to visitor and tourist is here

Powell Street cable car, San Francisco.

Carmel, California.

expressed by esplanades and restaurants and the river banked with red-blooming flowers. Pittsburgh, on the other hand, is a dynamic manufacturing center at the conflux of three rivers coursing between rugged hills. Many tunnels and great bridges as early as the Point Bridge of 1825 have created an awesome geometry in the spirit of the Gothic cathedral, and this image of industrial power is reinforced today by the Golden Triangle, a cluster of metallic skyscrapers at river point. San Francisco, built on seven hills like Lisbon, has splendid views of its own and the surrounding hills and the bay. And in the heart of the city the picturesque prevails. The city fathers have seen the commercial value to tourism of appropriate urban furniture in Chinatown; characteristic Oriental shapes have been applied to telephone booths and streetlights. The San Francisco cable cars, thought to be the country's oldest regularly operating transit system, are world-famous. There are thirty-nine of these quaint cars, which operate as a separate municipal railroad division and annually carry 10 million passengers. Each car cost $38,000 but is obviously priceless in terms of contribution to imagery.

Maintaining an image, even an image based on natural assets, is as important as creating one, and as difficult. The importance of Atlantic City and its boardwalk has declined because it has not been reinforced and enhanced. But Carmel, California, has for decades been building and protecting a consistent harmony of natural and man-made scenery. Its incom-

Magdalen Street, Norwich, England. Before rehabilitation, 1959.

Magdalen Street, Norwich, England. After rehabilitation, 1959.

parable cliffs and beaches along the Pacific have been complemented by the rustic character of all urban furnishings—sidewalks, parking areas, benches, telephone booths, litter baskets. Private developments and shopping centers are in a carefully controlled matching idiom.

When natural endowments are lacking, historical heritage can provide an auspicious approach to unique, time-honored identity, and consumer acceptance. Using as a guide the well-documented Norwich Plan of Norwich, England, several American neighborhoods and shopping streets are being rehabilitated with emphasis on the Victorian character of the streets and houses. Hampton, Virginia, whose renewal program was prepared by Doxiadis Associates, capitalized on a tradition that goes back to the time of the Pilgrims. The imagery of this project has been reinforced by replacing street lighting with antique posts and lanterns imported from England. Similarly, Chicago Old Town, once a decaying cluster of Victorian row houses centered around Wells Street, now presents to the romance-seeking tourist a potpourri of restaurants, pubs, galleries, and shops.

But there isn't enough of the real thing to go around. What of the city that grew up about a fork of the road, hard by a railroad junction, or just by happenstance? The majority of American cities lack natural or historical distinction and in fact are known only by place names and conjure no images to sight or mind. And what of all the new towns and cities still to be built this century? What will be their form and unique identity? With the design talent, technology, and financial resources available today it is possible to construct an "instant tradition" or a "happening environment" in any desired mode where before there was nothing. For example, a city could elect to emulate Disneyland, which may be the greatest piece of urban design in America in terms of commercial performance. But other values are necessary and important to permanent city dwellers, and it is through appraisal and exploitation of these values that every city can and should create its own unique identity.

Cosmetics

The cult of the body is only one manifestation of an American emphasis on personal appearance and youth. Cosmetic products that promise everything to everybody are successfully developed, marketed, and bought. Rapidly changing styles and fashions become more bold and venturesome. And as with men and women, aging cities resort to the use of cosmetics to enhance their public appearance.

The civic consumer is discovering every imaginable gewgaw and nostalgic knickknack of the Victorian era. Gas lamps are in. Redwood planter boxes on Main Street are in. Artificial asters and pansies in baskets hanging over

Main Street, Milpitas, California. Cosmetic planters do not hide overhead wires.

Rockport, Massachusetts. Cosmetic flower baskets do not beautify parking meters.

parking meters are in. Baroque is back. Why? The consumer is unhappy with the ugliness of the old Downtown and the sterility of the new housing developments, and he first turns to cosmetics to blur harsh lines and render fresher-looking the old public face. This popular approach to improvement of community appearance seems quick, easy, and not costly, and many local public-spirited private groups participate in the ritual. A church group will sponsor the boy scouts' cleanup around the neighborhood. The Main Street Merchants Association or local bank or utility will put planter boxes with colorful flowers in the parking lots.

No doubt, in many of these applications the public body, like the human body, profits from cleanliness and some artful enhancement. A canopy of well-cared-for trees, like a bouffant hairdo, can add much charm to a shopping street. But the urban appearance problem usually is more than skin-deep, so that more than cosmetics is needed. These are not a cure, but a palliative, and in that sense deprive the people of the opportunity to achieve a significant and permanent improvement. Indeed, such superficial "medication" may be deadly to civic economic and psychological health if it results in civic self-delusion which delays more painful but effective surgery.

In essence, urban ugliness is likely to be symptomatic of decay, and decay may be malignant, spreading and blighting adjacent healthy areas. Such organic malfunction or disease cannot be arrested or removed by cosmetics. Early diagnosis and basic treatment of the whole organism by professionals is required.

Montreal, Canada. Cosmetic fences conceal slum. Right, they became symbol for protest.

Chapter Three

The Systems Approach

"No single element in a city is, in truth, the kingpin or the key. The mixture itself is kingpin and its mutual support is the order."

JANE JACOBS

"Most complex systems such as weaponry or space exploration systems are univalent, unipurpose compared to the society that lives in cities. Urban society is indeed a multicomponent, multiinput, multioutput, multipurpose set of structures." WALTER ROSENBLITH, MIT

"Systems . . . are a way of approaching the environment as a total complex organism, of discovering an order which, once established, would preserve those aspects of the environment which we consider essential." MOSHE SAFDIE

"The systems concept is nothing more than formalized common sense tied to new tools and management methods."

HERBERT H. SWINBRUNE, FAIA

Growth of Systems Analysis

Man-machine systems exist to do work, and they are worth developing only if the work they do cannot easily or correctly be done by man alone. Consequently the machines or equipment in such systems are usually designed to extend man's capabilities or improve his relationship to the environment. Examples are many and obvious. The automobile moves faster than man can run. The hearing aid, first mechanical and now electronic, extends man's ability to hear. Traffic-control devices convey right-of-way data to many people simultaneously. These kinds of man-machine relationships are relatively recent, and their development has largely been trial and error and piecemeal. Street-lighting systems, for example, evolved through many inventions and devices, such as tungsten filaments and transformers. The concept of systems planning, however, is as old as civilization.

The earliest systems engineers were the successful military leaders of legendary campaigns. These aggressive leaders not only had the courage to invade hostile territory but also had the foresight to reconnoitre the size and disposition of opposing forces and use these data to determine the deployment and supply of their own troops. They were military decision makers who considered the complete problem in terms of the total environment.

This commonsense approach remained a nonformalized deductive process through millennia to World War I, which was fought in a static equilibrium of man in trench equalizing man in trench.

But the planning considerations of World War II of necessity changed in response to the altered dimensions and dynamics of opposing forces. Nowadays it is commonplace for planners and designers to start from the outset with a stated desired purpose, or task mission, and create a new totally organized system unlike any other. But the historical literature generally calls the British development of radar the first organized application of systems analysis and design. The accuracy of gunnery had to be improved by as yet unknown machines that would enable the beleaguered British to "see" enemy aircraft far away in the air or submarines deep underwater. Here was a need so desperate the establishment tolerated drastic management measures. Machines called radar resulted from the organized process, in which goals were defined, human needs were expressed, and a technological breakthrough was achieved to make the machines to man's measure. Out of this innovative process a new discipline quickly evolved, complete with vocabulary, modus operandi, and practitioners.

The use of these systems techniques rapidly spread throughout the technical community. Program managers eagerly accepted them because of their usefulness in helping control the increasing number and complexity of variables to be accommodated in reaching viable solutions. Beyond being a means to this end, systems became a design tool as well, a way of getting at problems originally and creatively, disregarding old shibboleths and seeking fresh solutions. Many startling configurations suddenly appeared that successfully accommodated fantastic tasks in weaponry, transportation, and communications. The Bell Aircraft Company's P-39 fighter plane was such a configuration.

The problem at the time was how to get more firepower into the air without sticking more machine guns all along the leading edge of the wings and engine cowling of the fighter plane. Robert Woods, designer of the P-39, achieved an astonishing success using a simple personal procedure of systems analysis.

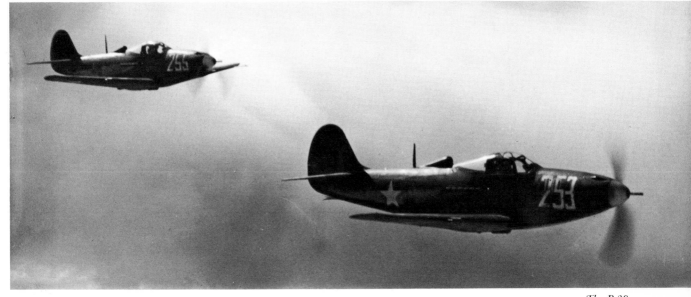

The P-39.

Since the goal was firepower, not aircraft, Woods first sketched a 39-millimeter cannon, the largest armament yet put into the air. Then he went through systems synthesis, in which the advantages and disadvantages of different possible configurations are swapped back and forth in order to assemble the optimum package. For example, in order not to complicate the rate of fire through the propeller blades, he designed the propeller hub to revolve about the barrel! This advantage, however, had the disadvantage that the cannon was now where the engine normally should be. The designer accepted this, moved the engine further back—behind the cockpit—and created additional space forward into which a nosewheel could be folded, making possible the first military tricycle landing gear. In the process, the designer put the pilot astride the drive shaft, making him interdependent with the systems of armament, propulsion, airframe, and control.

Would man be overwhelmed in the midst of all the machinery? I still vividly recall, from my several hundred hours in the P-39, the oneness I felt with the aircraft when the throbbing crankshaft immediately and closely responded to my touch. There must be, I think, the same sort of rapport between man and motorcycle or man and rocket belt.

Having met wartime challenges, government gave the aerospace industry and its satellite technical suppliers, unfettered by traditional technology, new horizons to conquer. Literally, "Get us to the moon" became the task. The goal was expressed by performance criteria rather than by hardware specifications. Once again faced with the competitive need to produce fantastically complex space-vehicle projects within compressed time schedules, industry turned to systems management and design to meet the performance criteria.

New depersonalized design techniques such as environmental simulation were developed in order to dry-run possible solutions to hazardous or incompletely defined missions. Because of lack of precedence new management procedures were encouraged. Some solved previously insoluble problems; spectacular performance achieved by technical breakthroughs became commonplace. This new know-how found other applications. Consider the V/STOL aircraft.

X-22A Tri-Service V/STOL.

Omnidirection aircraft resulted from a new approach to goals previously unattainable. Here the goal was a machine capable not only of vertical takeoff and landing, hovering, and turning 360 degrees but also the forward speed of conventional aircraft. Rather than rehash existing configurations such as rotary wing (helicopter) into unlikely or uneconomical designs, the systems planners devised a new arrangement which imaginatively used fans for both lift and, when rotated, forward thrust. Starting without preconceived notions of what such an airplane should look like, systems analysis produced a wingless four-engine aircraft whose propellers (four fans) point up!

But aircraft and space vehicles are only the beginning. The systems methodology is now affecting millions of people in more immediate and personal ways. It has become vital to the American way of life—in flow of goods to supermarket and to consumer, in the intensive-care systems used in hospitals, in entertainment and communications media such as TV, and in other, still-developing applications to the environment in which we live and work.

Uncommon Use of Common Components

The prevailing practice under which a fragmented bureaucracy specified the styled products of a fragmented industry tended to perpetuate visual pollution. Public products proliferated. Performance criteria were not established for street furniture. User needs were not considered. And producers left to their own devices had little incentive to improve obsolete products; they continued to produce according to the dictates of existing plant and tooling. The cityscape became a junkyard for primitive public equipments.

Meanwhile, in the private building sector, the performance and availability of architectural components improved enormously. Investors wanted bigger buildings cheaper and faster. Industry invested in research and tooling to meet enlarged marketing opportunities. Thousands of new mass-produced systems components offering economy and visual order were produced in the last decade.

The direction of much of this progress was determined by architectural designers. Designers such as Eames and Nelson and design-oriented architectural firms such as Skidmore, Owings & Merrill changed the reproduction approach to furniture and hardware design to an innovative approach which made the article more related to its intended use. Their development of completely new architectural products met the environmental conditions. Sometimes new manufacturing or assembly techniques were required by industry; these had to be developed to produce the design. Often these new components were of such obvious merit they became part of the manufacturer's regular line. These successes spurred similar efforts by other designers. And manufacturers continued to push out the frontiers of machine technology to meet the designers' demand.

In a short time selections of machine-made components that could be imaginatively assembled into a variety of needed building systems became available to all. Storefronts could be assembled at low cost from mass-produced off-the-shelf extrusions produced by several manufacturers. Movable metal office partitions offered new utility and appearance and became an important product line to large building-materials suppliers. The partitions' utility in shaping the interior environment depended largely on the infinite applications made possible through a great number of interrelated factory-made parts such as panels, moldings, clips, etc. Ceiling systems too became a particularly spectacular technical breakthrough. In addition to a selection of texture and form, manufacturers rapidly evolved greater values of flexibility and economy by new relationships to subsystems of illumination, acoustics, and ventilation.

Similar success accrued in storage walls with interchangeable panels, display systems with universal connectors and most importantly with exterior wall systems. Curtain walls could now package larger and larger building spaces. Using metal or synthetic factory-made materials, these components promoted flexibility of arrangement and size, allowable tolerance for field assembly, and a precise geometric configuration which facilitated self-positioning and locking. Their obvious esthetic and technical merit and their prefabricated economy promoted quick consumer acceptance by developers as well as designers.

The market for these building components was swiftly enlarged by the simplicity of use and the implied low level of skill or small amount of time necessary to arrive at serviceable and economical applications. These well-designed components could be assembled by almost everyone in an appropriate manner. And in the hands of a talented designer who sometimes arranged the standard parts in unexpected ways, the unexpected effect could be unique and intriguing.

Now other dramatic ideas are being proposed for all aspects of building technology, so that today most visually exciting developments seem to be those structures designed as a system of standardized parts whose arrangement does the job better and also creates novel spatial and visual relationships. Housing is undergoing an industrialized change, from site construction by hand labor to volume production by machine and unskilled factory labor. Innovators are now conceiving even more sophisticated systems which have in common the use of repetitive load-bearing or functional modules and components to achieve simplified site installation unobtainable by conventional building design.

Williamsville Pool Club, Amherst, New York. Prefabricated dressing rooms. Several hundred plugged into concrete floor in varying arrangements.

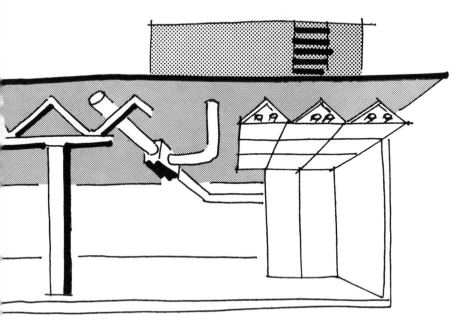

School Construction Systems Development (SCSD) was the definitive study in the field of systems building.

United States Pavilion, Expo 67, Montreal.

Habitat, Expo 67, Montreal.

The City as a System

The industrial revolution resulted in the machine's replacing muscle as a way of life. It became commonplace to think of machines as aids to perceiving and manipulating and making more enjoyable the environment. These new devices helped man to see in the dark, to make himself heard at great distance, to speed over great distances.

Rapidly the production of light evolved from lamp to lighting system, then became a power-distribution system. The telephone changed from voice-transmitting tool to conceptually sophisticated communication system. The airplane changed from a marginal-performance novelty to a utilitarian transportation system complete with terminals and controlled air routes. The accelerated development and acceptance of beneficial systems is probably the most spectacular technical accomplishment of our age. All these examples are man-made synthetic organisms. And just as the factory has become a system, so also is the city a system.

Each of course contains subsystems. The automated factory may have production lines. It also may be structured and framed with systems components; its interior spaces are analyzed and ordered; its environment is controlled by networks of communications, air conditioning, snow removal, fire control, and smoke warning.

The city, shopping center, or campus may contain similar subsystems. These environments must have systems of lighting, fire protection, and traffic control in order to be considered secure, healthful, and economically viable. Street-highway, pedestrian-sidewalk, and automobile-parking systems must be considered. No one system is independent of the others.

To make the city appreciably more useful and desirable, not one but all systems with significant relationships must be considered and upgraded. In truth, the urban community can be looked upon as a complex system of related functional activities directed toward meeting all the needs of its people. The functional areas of importance to every individual are the standard of living, housing, well-being and recreation, and support for the first three.

The importance of public facilities as support for these private, personal needs lies far beyond the obviously necessary environmental services such as sewers and water supply, power and transportation, and lighting and guidance. There are other values. As instrumentalities for community identity and appearance, urban furnishings are without peer. Since street furnishings include all visible physical surfaces, textures, and equipments in the public space, from the private building line to the center of the street, they *are* the public environment. Since they are largely machine-made, the urban fabric *is* synthetic.

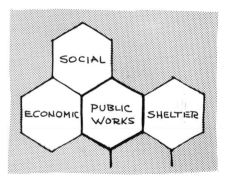

The interface of site improvements and community factors.

At less cost, this fabric can be designed and produced with imagination and artistry. Or it can remain dull, unimaginative, and inadequate in representing the best in a city's character.

In most cities of America, unlike Europe, there is little concern for how urban furnishings determine community appearance. Presently there is no office or agency charged with a design function and authority to coordinate the various fragmented jurisdictions and interests. The few attempts to cope with city imagery have been piecemeal solutions to nonbasic problems. Most attempts at furnishing the city are more tried than true. For example, if Downtown looks gray and dingy, then more lampposts are installed; if traffic is congested, then the streets are widened at the expense of the sidewalks; if neighborhood streets are shabby, then they are covered with fresh asphalt.

But furnishing the city and creating a unique environment are not that simple. For now the important thing is not to have more of the same kind of hardware, but to adopt an approach oriented toward broader objectives. Then the most immediate benefits will accrue from an analysis of all community appearance factors in their relationships with each other. Street paving, for example, is now to be considered not only in relation to vehicular traffic but also in context with graphics and markings and pedestrian crossways and as a floor for other furniture.

A basic problem in very many American cities is the lack of community identity and values sufficient to induce a sense of belonging or caring. The problem is not so much the shabbiness of the city as its lack of vitality and dilution of enjoyment. The old ethnic neighborhoods have had their distinctions diluted and destroyed without replacement by other characteristics of equal flavor. This basic problem will not be solved with new architectural monuments, whether bland and sterile or aggressive and dynamic. The nature of the problem requires people-oriented goals, which tend to require a completely new or rehabilitated product (environment) of such unique and desirable character as to stimulate public desire for ownership or participation. People must want to work for, to treasure, to enjoy a piece of the city—*their* city.

Another need is to put a "price" on the space allotted to competing city-department users. Generally the public space is regarded as a free "good;" thus it is used by city departments at will without regard for productivity. To establish goals and tasks for the space and "charge" for the space would provide an incentive for comparing the efficiency of various city departments. It might then become necessary for departments to justify use of space and therefore optimize the size and efficiency of their equipments within the space. It has even been suggested that the bureaucracy within each department should "pay rent" from the department budget for each unit of public space it uses.

THE METHODOLOGY

How It Works

In systems design for industry there are as many variations in procedure as practitioners. Various requirements of different applications such as construction planning or communications design mandate flexibility of approach. In environmental design the methodology is even less well defined, since the number of purposeful applications has been extremely limited.

This is all right, because the essential thing about systems thinking is that it is freewheeling. In systems thinking, unlike the mechanistic Bauhaus or the international "ism" schools of design, there is no cookbook of forms or dogmatic attitude toward design. There are no preconceived notions about what is and what is not good design. The designer can be more genuinely and freely experimental. He is free to move and develop with social as well as technical changes.

The systems approach is fundamentally a decision-making process. It considers alternative approaches to overall design to provide optimum performance. It is best suited to dynamic problems where inputs or conditions vary. The systems approach does start, however, with the proposition that in order for a highly complex arrangement of objects, people, and space to be optimally designed, the process of decision making must be placed on a rational and objective basis. Any successful methodology for getting at solutions to the problems of human needs that are involved must be an organized procedure.

The accompanying chart depicts such a procedure, including the principal phases and flow of a typical work program. For the sake of clarity of applica-

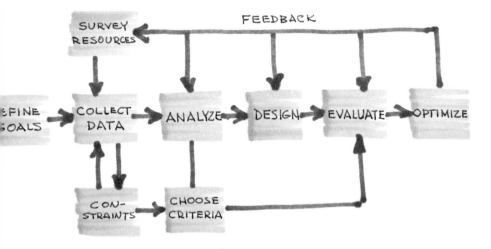

tion the procedure may be considered in the context of a hypothetical problem: how to furnish and unify a neighborhood renewal project containing 50 percent older structures, 50 percent new housing, new open spaces, and old streets and stores.

Definition of Problem, Establishment of Goals   First decide what needs to be done in general terms. The objectives must be broad enough so as not to predetermine solutions. Only the crucial issues should be formalized. These should be expressed in terms of user requirements so that the statement of goals is one which clearly considers the human values of the society in which the new system will perform. Example: for nighttime, the best way to unify the project is through a programmed lighting sequence, not just through deciding how many lampposts to install.

This statement of goals becomes the mandate, the charter, authorizing and approving the scope of effort, and should be approved and adopted as law by the community legislative body. With this authority the design guidelines can be activated and take precedence when existing building codes or minimum-specification guides come into conflict.

Data Collection   Program implementation starts with the collection of raw data by means of a systematic survey. The condition of things is recorded. City engineering and public works departments are a source of data on quantity and condition of existing public improvements in the area. This material can be tabulated. Information should also be collected on both the positive and the negative factors that may affect the program. Example: *Constraints* may include state codes, marginal bond capacity, inadequate public works budget, adverse features of climate or of street shape and size. *Resources* may include state or local funds that can be marshaled, new technology, interested private developers, community or businessmen's associations.

An important part of this input is the visual survey, which establishes the existing quality of the environment. The purpose of the survey is to note elements which can be capitalized and other elements which should be written off. These assets and liabilities are noted in terms of *consumer acceptance,* not architectural context. The analyst must say in his mind, "I am standing waiting for a bus. How do I feel? I am sitting in my car waiting for the traffic light to change. What do I see? I am walking on the sidewalk. What are its width, color, and condition?"

Every section of a city differs from any other and creates its own atmosphere, or local color. This may be either positive or negative, by attracting or repelling people. Sometimes commonplace features such as bridges, water towers, and street patterns which are different from those in other areas of the city can be accentuated and made to be beneficial landmarks orienting pedestrian and motorist as well as providing character.

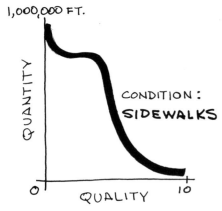

Site-improvements profile.

Among the several references on visual-survey techniques Paul Spreiregen presents the most rounded summary. He stresses that the survey should disclose where the area needs reshaping, and he mentions that a visual survey can be made of any town and at different scales, such as the neighborhood. Other writers, planners, and landscape architects have presented various techniques of observation, notation, and image mapping. Many of these tend to be highly abstract and arcane. As Spreiregen points out, the results ought to be presented in maps and photographs and in everyday terms easily understood by everyone.

Actually the fieldwork can be recorded in any shorthand form. The difficulty with visual-survey technique is the lack of understanding or definition of what is a common visual language. Once what has been seen has been recorded by whatever notation, the problem remains of how the personal, subjective views are to be interpreted and applied.

Analysis   The third step is really a process ongoing with data collection. Questions and curiosity stimulate thinking; good ideas may occur during the visual survey. As a conscious procedure in this phase the subproblems of the environmental system are identified and analyzed. The design parameters and relationships of components one to the other are established. Example: Decide how people of this neighborhood use the public right-of-way and spaces. Consider what kinds of facilities and imagery are required. Establish what interrelationships of form, color, materials, scale, and graphics are desired. Prepare new standards and performance criteria for each subsystem (floor, lighting, litter control) and information for evaluation of possible solutions.

Synthesis   This design phase develops specific solutions, which should deal in an innovative way with all the forces discovered to be relevant in the previous phases. Esthetics should not be consciously contrived. In order to meet the initial goals, they should result from the manipulation of existing forms, shapes, and products and all environmental features that interrelate. A number of specific concepts can be proposed that resolve the initially stated objectives of unification. Example: unify the neighborhood by means of a strong identifiable floor pattern with a collector strip between curb and sidewalk, gathering and organizing the street-furniture subsystems.

Optimization   In this process we select pieces of possible solutions and give up others in order to put together the most economical harmonious whole. Trade-offs are made; in a process of bargaining or compromising among subsystems with a view to enhancing the overall conglomerate performance. Various ideas are culled; the alternatives are weighed against evaluation criteria. The fundamental value consideration in choosing a design option is ratio of performance to cost of design chosen. But performance may have to be measured by a sizable variety of criteria, which will not necessarily be compatible with each other. Furthermore emphasis changes. For example, Ian McHarg and others stress the increasing importance of social benefit as a significant value factor in evaluating alternate highway routes.

In light of new national aspirations and social goals, livability joins and must be traded off against other "ilities"—maintainability, reliability, and so on. The weight of livability in the cost/benefit formula will vary among various environmental systems, such as traffic control, lighting, and fire protection, but its inclusion to some degree is now essential.

During optimization a model of the overall system is used to clarify and test the proposed solutions. Systems engineering and operations research makes much use of *mathematical models* as a relatively inexpensive way to dry-run expensive configurations. The more variables and possible choices, the more useful are computer techniques. The computer has been used by highway designers in cut-and-fill calculations for many years. And its structural-design potential was dramatically demonstrated at Expo 67 when the huge Gyrotron space structure was calculated in two days of computer time instead of four million man-hours. This imitation reality is a quick way to identify what needs to be measured and then measure it.

Mathematical models are organized logically. Their language and structure are those of symbolic logic, which simplifies reality and eliminates unessential considerations. The organization is rigorous, and assumptions are clearly stated. These basic principles can be applied well to the creative field of urban design. Planners have not yet made much use of mathematical models, probably because they have not had on hand the information needed to make them useful. In fact, automated information systems and mathematical models will develop together, as pointed out in a recent study on urban planning data systems by Campbell and LeBlanc. As more data, including graphic material on aperture cards, are captured in automated data processing systems, planners will be able to construct mathematical models and use them to better advantage.

Meanwhile much use is made of *visual models,* which are organized spatially. Whether three-dimensional, a map, or a photograph, the model has scale, and scale tends to simplify subsystem relationships for visualization. Things can be left out, or they can be overstated. The visual model can also be used to test out the design economically by altering features or substituting new features for old.

Many leading architectural firms use *illustrative site plans* to articulate major public improvements and demonstrate unifying elements. The interplay of public areas and facilities can be graphically shown by detailing, for example, pedestrian-channelization features such as walks, ramps, platforms, concourses, and arcades. The relationships of these elements to open-space

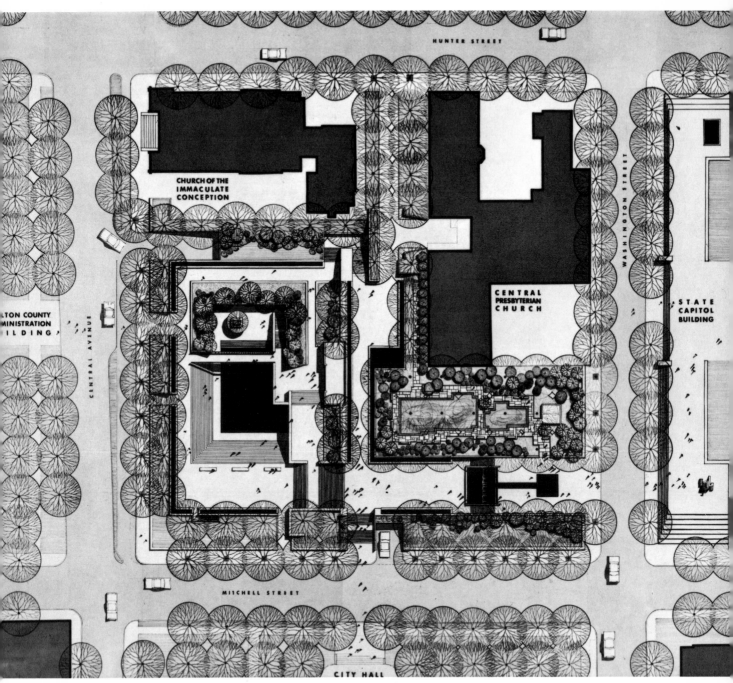

Illustrative site plan for Georgia Plaza.
Atlanta, Georgia.

Study model for Georgia Plaza (scale: ⅛″ 1′0′). Model helps develop design, working drawings, full-size mock-up.

features such as plazas, pools, and landscaping as well as to service parking systems can be illustrated. Areas planned for social and community activities such as happenings, parades, and concerts can be visualized in proper relationships.

But frequently the feel of the street furnishings in relationship with urban spaces can be better worked out in three-dimensional models. The models used are similar to models of industrial complexes, such as chemical plants with intricate piping crossovers and configurations. An environmental model need not represent each component in such expensive literal fashion but should facilitate plug-in of design changes rather than be merely a static presentation medium. Further, environmental simulation by means of enclosures into which the observer looks through low-elevation human-scale peepholes will be more meaningful than tabletop models which are viewed from above with Olympian detachment.

In addition, when street-furniture components are to be mass-produced, the cost of full-size mock-ups is warranted in order to optimize design, consider environmental scale, and anticipate production problems.

Whichever mode is selected, the model may be used to perform several functions: to clarify solutions, demonstrate cost/benefit relationships, test alternate combinations, and pick up interface or side-effect problems.

The resulting flow of information is distributed into the design process by means of "feedback." This term defines an important part of the design process whereby part of the output (information on solutions) is returned as input (design data) to the continuing systems development. As various parts of the project progress, these communications help ensure that the overall design is in balance.

The final step in systems methodology is to put the optimum configuration into action. This too is a systematic procedure and is discussed later in greater detail.

SYSTEMS DEVELOPMENT

Project Planning and Control

Sound project management is essential to any complex enterprise. It is perhaps most critical to the orderly progression of urban systems work, in consideration of the complexity of relationships between local city departments, outside agencies, consultants, and contractors. Because of the public nature of the work, a constant dialogue must be maintained between the urban planner, designer, and city administration. Communication between designer and contractor, lost since the days of direct feedback between master builder and craftsman, must be restored. When problems arise, there must be a means for presentation of alternates for reaching previously established goals. In short, the project manager must control the project through a number of phases of design, estimating, purchasing, contracting, quality control, installation, and support.

In the past decade three things have drastically increased the work burden of the project manager:

More Projects   Definite unique goals must be met by specific target dates.

Increased Size and Complexity   More technical problems involve more services and agencies and require more reports.

Increased Time Pressure   Target dates imposed by others require the manager to optimize resources of men, money, and machines.

Thus more and more the manager has to think in generalities. He cannot always be aware of all details; he cannot even be aware of all activities which are critical. Clearly, what is needed is a master model which shows the overall planning picture. The systems methodology inherently offers not only this but also an orderly procedure for the organized management and control of the project: configuration management can maintain the integrity of the system as it is shaped by many hands.

Several techniques derived from the needs of, and compatible with, systems design have evolved very recently. These replace the conventional master plan featuring a bar chart which listed milestones and required subjective estimates of percentage of work completed. The newer project planning systems tend to be self-maintaining and provide uniform display and interpretation while in concurrent use by city, consultant, and contractor or vendor.

Network planning provides the discipline within which design activities can be organized and the development process controlled. According to the AIA publication *Emerging Techniques of Architectural Practice,* most formats presently favored are adaptations or combinations of one of two network planning systems, program evaluation and review technique and the critical-path method.

Program evaluation and review technique (PERT) evolved through military systems needs; the first large-scale application was the Polaris missile program for the Navy in the late 1950s, when the efforts of some thirty-eight hundred participating groups were coordinated. The program was event-oriented; that is, certain milestones were set up as events that had to take place at certain times. The activities were compressed as required between events.

Now many models are activity-oriented; that is, the activities are diagramed so that no activity begins until the preceding jobs have been completed. Only after the project has been planned with this logic is time associated with activities, connecting nodes, or events.

The critical-path method (CPM) is simple in concept—a graphic presentation in which everything gets a label. Complete projects are reduced to diagrams in which arrows show the flow of work, one arrow representing a single activity or task. Several methods may be used to indicate the time consumed by each activity on the diagram. One way is to start the arrow with a beginning number, indicating that the project has to be that far along before that activity may begin, and an ending number to show at what point in the project's time the activity will conclude. Another number is assigned to show the duration in time of the particular task.

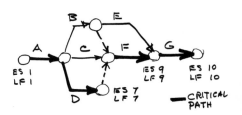

Two questions to ask in creating a critical-path diagram are these: "When must this particular activity be started?" and "When must it be completed to allow the next activity to begin?" Often one task will be preceded by several arrows, all of which must be completed before beginning the new job.

The critical path through the arrow network is the one which takes the longest time sequence to complete. It shows the shortest possible time in which the project may be completed. Paths can move up, down, and sideways. Paths of shorter duration have slack time available along the way since none is as time-consuming as the critical path. This slack time is called "float." Total float is the amount of time that any activity can be delayed without delaying the entire project. It is computed by subtracting the time required for the activity from the time available to accomplish it. Float time can be borrowed from noncritical activities and used as job conditions dictate to cut project time and control manpower.

Because the relationship of one activity to another is known, the CPM permits all participants to see trouble immediately and know how the overall project is affected by slippage in any particular activity. And the CPM can be updated periodically, thus presenting a constantly accurate model.

Project Development

The essence of systems design of public improvements is the concurrent design and procurement of all anticipated components necessary to satisfy the project goals. Conventional previous practice required public facilities to be developed in a piecemeal manner. First the street pattern would be planned; subsequently a lighting pattern would be drawn; traffic controls would be considered after the street was in use; and possibly at some time in the future parking controls, trash collection, and amenities like landscaping might be considered. This procedure cannot achieve proper interface of all major subsystems required for a simplified and less costly community appearance.

The State University Construction Fund of New York, recently faced with

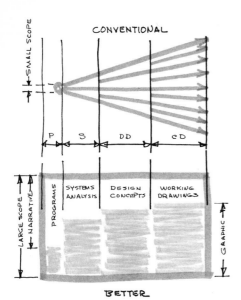

Parallel pattern development.

the task of planning and constructing some 1.5 billion dollars worth of new and rehabilitated campuses in the decade ending in 1970, evolved a number of design and management techniques under the direction of Anthony G. Adinolfi. This was possibly the first civilian bureaucracy oriented toward using contemporary management techniques to achieve massive public works of contemporary design. One campus alone (Buffalo), when completed in the mid-1970s, will be a 700-million-dollar planned community second in scope to none except possibly Brasilia. The program management techniques developed here have broad application in other areas of community improvement, even those of much lesser scope. One of the most useful techniques is parallel pattern development.

The principle has been established that to secure a balanced project design, all elements of the design must be considered initially and at each subsequent phase of the development. A gradual increase in detail of development across the board is desired even though emphasis changes from phase to phase. This requires that the initial scope be complete and a broad design concept be pursued from the onset.

The accompanying diagrams compare project development techniques. The upper chart describes the conventional process, starting with a narrow scope and developing the design by trial and error. The lower chart describes the parallel process, in which the initial scope, goals, program, functional requirements, and site and spatial requirements are complete and do not change. An orderly progression can thus be made through the schematic design and detailed drawing stages.

Prior to conceptualizing, the designer must receive from the administration (developer, management) all programs. In the case of a specific campus these could be presented in a document containing topics such as "Education Plan" and "Enrollment Plan." The former would list goals, policies, and assumptions—for example, philosophy and purpose of campus, programs offered, evening and community use. The latter might contain statements on present enrollment, anticipated enrollments by target dates, and student/faculty ratios.

The designer could then analyze these in terms of physical need for academic, dining, housing, circulation, and sports spaces and facilities, for instance. Facilities could in turn be analyzed in relationship to the site and the community and region. And finally, before actual design an economic analysis should be made to determine a meaningful budget estimate for the complete program through its target date.

Parallel development applies also to all stages subsequent to planning and design, including manufacturing. Once the overall configuration has been fixed, the system can be fractured into each major subsystem, or component, for development and production. However, each component would be in a controlled parallel path so as to be available for reintegration at the necessary time.

PUTTING THE TECHNIQUES TO WORK

Example: Campus Information System

Task: A completely new academic community with a projected full-time student population of 30,000 plus faculty, staff, and visitors requires parking regulation, motorist and pedestrian guidance, and building and space identification. The site is a 400-acre tract in Albany, New York. The designer is consultant to the architect, Edward Durell Stone and Associates; the client is the State University Construction Fund of New York.

Problem: The architectural complex is very homogeneous. The dormitory and academic buildings are not identifiable by shape, scale, or color. They are nearly identical structures positioned uniformly on vast podia. Therefore, on one hand, a great need exists for signage of visibility, legibility, and identity. But on the other hand, it is desired that the street furniture be minimal, neutral, and nonobtrusive. The problem is to organize an information system that communicates in a manner that satisfies both criteria.

Solution: Phase 1: Collect data on campus circulation, proposed location of facilities, and their uses. Make a visual survey. Simulate activity of a stranger in the environment. Enter the campus, park car, walk grounds (buildings and site work incomplete). Visualize needs of motorist and pedestrian for information. Determine needs of administration for control and regulation. Compile list of anticipated messages for signage.

Phase 2: Analyze information needs in context of use of spaces and architectural environment. Determine degree of visibility required, which in turn will establish scale of letter forms and panels. Consider suitability of materials. Determine tentative locations of graphic elements on site plan.

Concurrently establish performance criteria for evaluation of future designs. Typical criteria are:

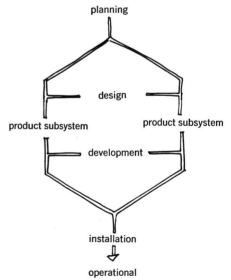

planning

design

product subsystem   product subsystem

development

installation

operational

Parallel development of project.

- a Greatest utility with fewest number of components.
- b Compatibility in color and symmetry of form to the very ordered architecture.
- c Minimum size consistent with legibility.
- d Resistance to vandalism.

Phase 3: Design a conceptual model containing the following interrelated subsystems in order of visitor need:

- a Traffic-control system (signals, signs, pavement markings) for safe exit from two major and five minor highway intersections into the campus road network and to parking lots (STOP, GO).
- b Campus directories which graphically provide position orientation to motorists at each of six entrances to campus (YOU ARE HERE).

Precast Wall System

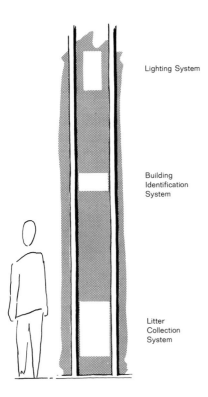
Lighting System

Building
Identification
System

Litter
Collection
System

c   Motorist-guidance system alongside roadways which directs motorists to parking lots (PARK THERE).
d   Pedestrian-guidance system alongside walks which graphically directs pedestrian to each of several architectural complexes.
e   Building-identification system that relates to the architecture (as hardware). This subsystem interfaces with the building curtain-wall subsystem in scale and mounting position and also to the overhead wall-mounted lighting system for illumination.
f   Campus-activity identification system (portable guidance).

Phase 4: Develop the designs after approval of concept. Fracture into manageable parts. Process the various subassemblies and components under parallel development, in which the design of each is refined and detailed to the procurement and installation stage, where they reunite. Standardize sign framing for all systems. Standardize sign-panel sizes and materials. Standardize color codes (reverse white letters on umber background for motorist signs, black and white on umber for pedestrian and motorist campus directories). Standardize size of letters. Design and adapt house-style alphabets (Standard Medium alphabet for motorist, Caslon for pedestrian signs). Standardize placement of signs and prepare location diagrams.

Phase 5: Optimize through trade-offs and realignment. Evaluate against selection and performance criteria. Make composite site plan of all subsystems. Simplify and reduce number of mounting and installation variations. Eliminate marginal units. Check for side-effect problems such as competition with nearby lampposts or reduced visibility of signs because of landscaping.

Phase 6: Become operational. Select vendors and proceed through bidding process. Monitor subsystems through fabrication period. Install and test

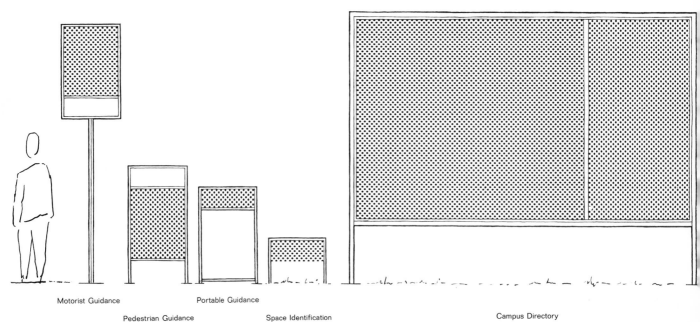

Motorist Guidance

Pedestrian Guidance

Portable Guidance

Space Identification

Campus Directory

components. Prepare *Campus Graphics Manual* that describes systems purposes, procedurizes and standardizes operations for administrative personnel, and specifies maintenance procedures for use by shop personnel.

SOME SYSTEMS LAWS FOR DESIGNERS

Let the Problem Program the Solution

Most public works programs, Downtown remodeling projects, airport programs, housing developments in the ghetto, and so on start with too limited and detailed a proposal. The larger the area to which programs and goals pertain, the greater the chances for implementation. Big beautiful plans capture the imagination and help get the needed support for execution. In the thirteenth century Kublai Khan inspired (or admonished, as was a custom with potentates) his boldest men to great efforts. "To build a beautiful city," he said, "we must start with a beautiful concept." Wisely, he did not specify an architectural form in the program for the city of Peking that he advanced to his philosophers and artists. The form evolved from the broad mandate to create a beautiful way of life in a new city. In the more contemporary towns of Europe and in the new American towns of Columbia and Reston, by contrast, the forms have evolved from uncompromised considerations of how shopping might be best done, how close people should live to each other and to the civic centers, etc.

A conceptual model is sometimes made in the systems analysis phase as an aid to defining the problem. Consider the realignment of a street system connecting three nodes equidistant from each other, as shown in the illustration on page 75. If the primary objective of the network is to provide a minimum of travel between points, the street system (B) will result. If the primary objective is to provide a minimal total street mileage at reduced cost, the network (A) will prevail. If the main objective is to preserve a historic monument or landmark, then the street pattern (C) will be followed. Thus the conceptual model must reflect the characteristics of the real systems which are to be investigated.

Environmental design, then, is not valid unless it has relationship to the complete basic problem. Example: A strip shopping plaza begins to have store vacancies and is unwanted by tenants on any terms. The developer might go to a designer and say, "Look, we are losing too much business. Do something about this. Put a bigger and more rustic-looking sign on the parking lot, and color all the facades green." The designer's problem then would not be how to make the strip plaza more acceptable to people, but how to design a more rustic sign. Obviously this is incorrect, because it is not a sign or the color of storefronts that is keeping people away, and it

73

may be the layout of the parking areas or the inconvenience of going from store to store in the rain and snow. The solution to those major problems might better be said to be to create a new circulation pattern or some means of climate control.

Or should the solution to the problems of the shopping area be expressed as follows:

1. Put in parking meters to open up more spaces to bring more visitors in cars?

2. Increase nighttime brilliance with more footcandles of light?

3. Widen the street to reduce traffic congestion? Not a very good approach. These are all possible solutions, but not broad enough objectives. They are all commonly used and frequently ineffective. The basic problem was not adequately assessed, and therefore the solutions are inadequate. Creative thinking is forestalled and frozen.

Making everyone in the community want to shop there should be the basic goal. This kind of problem formulation requires broader conceptual thinking and tolerates the expression of more innovative proposals and alternatives. Many interlocked areas of planning must then be considered. Some design goals might be:

1. Generate more pedestrian-shopper activity with exciting entertainment, recreational, cultural, or civic facilities.

2. Create a new landmark symbol (or restore a historical heritage) to provide a sense of place and identifying trademark.

3. Create a new environmental package or reinforce an indigenous neighborhood character by redesigning the street, using a comprehensive concept that emphasizes its distinction.

This approach is deductive; in it the designer works from the general to the specific. The viewpoint is wide and not focused on narrow objectives which lead to small solutions. The design concepts are based on the broadest possible terms that can be conceived and presented.

To consider another case, the design of a neighborhood housing project should relate to metropolitan or regional programs and possibilities. The concepts should be independent of existing boundaries, thinking, codes, practices. The definition of the scope of design should be as broad as possible, though the definition of the area of action will be limited to the area of jurisdiction.

If such a task seems difficult because as many as five different city agencies may be involved in the physical and administrative considerations of community appearance, then perhaps *this* is the problem. The goal then lies not in avoiding the problem or temporizing or accepting a weak design. The desirability for change of city administrative codes and procedures to permit the adoption and use of a desirable design becomes self-evident.

Components Should Complement
the Big Concept

Designers know that many forces are always chipping away at big visions, frequently cutting them down from heroic to less than life size. Systems design in which all components move forward concurrently and are interdependent tend to resist this abrasive action more strongly. To weaken one element means the degradation of all systems performance.

To ensure that all components are properly developing during the design process, the original program statement of requirements should be periodically reviewed and updated if necessary. Checkpoints should be built into the planning process and component designs constantly reviewed and evaluated against the overall environmental systems program.

The following criteria apply:

1. Good systems design works for and pleases people. Products or urban furnishings should not overwhelm the user.

2. The various components should do a better job collectively than separately. Example: a graphics system should be more effective than uncoordinated random signs.

3. Products should be related in scale, materials, and form to each other and the larger environmental expression.

4. Products must also have self-identifying characteristics. Components should have an exciting quality that helps build the total image. Each can have individuality yet serve to unify the environment.

5. Components should be planned more for flexibility than exactitude. Exterior spaces change and serve many uses. No public improvements are inviolate or permanent. Streets get resurfaced. Lighting needs increase.

Nonsense Input Produces Shrdlu

When the operator of a linotype machine fingers incomprehensible data into the machine, he gets back a type slug which says "shrdlu." Urban designers are not that fortunate. They have no fail-safe device to signal faulty input.

Basically, the ultimate goal of all decisions in community appearance design is to maximize the desired outcome. Since many real decision situations have many nonquantitive (esthetic) variables, they are too complex to be treated mathematically. It is often necessary to introduce simplifying assumptions by considering only the variables, relationships, and objectives that are deemed to be important by the decision maker.

System synthesis is the initial conception of a street-furniture system the purpose of which is to satisfy certain human needs. In order to make an intelligent selection of alternatives, designers are often required to specify design and operation criteria, study system properties, propose alternative schemes, and assess technological and economic feasibility.

In setting up the task, it is important to select a conceptual model which expresses the appropriate relationship of public facilities to the environmental needs. Therefore, identifying proper variables to feed into the conceptual model is one of the most important phases of the entire creative process. The importance of correct judgment in assessing this input to a proposed design project cannot be overemphasized. If an incorrect premise is assumed, no amount of creative discipline or elegance of design can save the resulting system from the error of misjudgment.

At present, urban data collection, processing, and evaluation do not constitute a rigorous procedure with a rigorous set of terms or definitions. There is no common language, no standard methodology, no uniform format for information gathering and processing. Controls are lacking to ensure the accuracy and validity of assumptions used to construct esthetic and visual systems in the cityscape.

Obviously, the assessment of project parameters depends largely on the sensitivity of the designer to critical features. Techniques need to be developed which assist in the evaluation by others of these conditions as both a fail-safe device and a model of existing or proposed conditions.

Evaluation criteria used to compare alternatives in design development.

	least									most
	1	2	3	4	5	6	7	8	9	10
1. Flexibility to site conditions										
2. Structural Efficiency										
3. Other Component Compatibility										
4. Simplicity										
5. Technological Feasibility										
6. Maintainability										
7. Life-Cost Benefit										
8. Community Identity										
9. User Efficiency/Convenience										
10. Public Safety/Street Utilization										

Total Score _____

One recent successful experiment along these lines was the Metropolitan Data Center Project, funded under a 1966 demonstration grant of the Renewal Assistance Administration (RAA). The purpose was to apply the capabilities of data processing equipment and techniques to planning problems. The project was concerned with the storage and analysis of information concerning land use, housing, and environmental factors. One cooperating agency, the Wichita-Sedgwick County Metropolitan Area Planning Commission, Wichita, Kansas, used a computer program which analyzed the capital-improvement programming alternatives. This developed methods for establishing priorities and balancing subjective judgments as to the proper course of action. Essential to the success of the project was the format of the document used to capture input data for the computer.

PROJECT FACTORS
PRIORITY DETERMINANTS
PARK PROJECTS

1. Evaluate the recreational value of the project in terms of its tendency to serve the citizenry with respect to each of the following

	Minor	Major
• physical well being	1 2 3 4 5 6 7 8 9	10
• mental and emotional health	1 2 3 4 5 6 7 8 9	10
• intellectual development	1 2 3 4 5 6 7 8 9	10
• ability to organize and carry responsibility	1 2 3 4 5 6 7 8 9	10
• character development	1 2 3 4 5 6 7 8 9	10
• social adjustment	1 2 3 4 5 6 7 8 9	10
• aesthetic and spiritual values	1 2 3 4 5 6 7 8 9	10
• values to society	1 2 3 4 5 6 7 8 9	10
• community attractiveness	1 2 3 4 5 6 7 8 9	10
• civic spirit	1 2 3 4 5 6 7 8 9	10
• education for democracy	1 2 3 4 5 6 7 8 9	10
• safety	1 2 3 4 5 6 7 8 9	10
• economy	1 2 3 4 5 6 7 8 9	10

2. Extent of value of proposed project as aesthetic improvement for a major part of the city.
1 2 3 4 5 6 7 8 9 10
None   Very Great

3. Special value of proposed project as deterrent to crime or delinquency.
1 2 3 4 5 6 7 8 9 10
None   Very Great

4. If proposed improvement is made, by what extent (%) will the facility/population ratio be above the accepted minimum?
1 2 3 4 5 6 7 8 9 10
0-10%   90-100%

5. If proposed improvement is made, by what extent (%) will the facility/population ratio be below the accepted minimum?
1 2 3 4 5 6 7 8 9 10
0-10%   90-100%

6. To what extent is this project a creation of new park-recreation facilities as opposed to improvement of existing facilities?
1 2 3 4 5 6 7 8 9 10
None   Very Great

7. To what extent is this project essential to preserve natural resources for public use and to prevent its early development for private use?
1 2 3 4 5 6 7 8 9 10
None   Very Great

Uncoordinated chaos

Modular coordination

Systems-sharing matrix

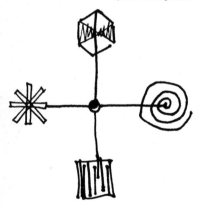

Various coordinating methods compared.

One Plus One Equals Three

The functional purpose of systems design is to make the whole greater than the sum of the parts. This synergism has value in urban design as in any other design situation of complexity involving many bits and pieces. No one doubts the existence of the terrible clutter of signs, products, and other "things" in the cityscape. Architects have always been sensitive to this kind of esthetic horror. Yet the vast synergetic benefit possible through consolidating these environmental components is hardly recognized.

This synergetic benefit will be secured through systems sharing—support, energy, form, envelope. Instead of self-contained relationships, an interdependence must be created between elements that constitute the product environment. When it is created, the resultant coalition structure not only is stronger and accommodates greater tasks than a competitive structure but also is less costly. The result is a higher payoff per element; we get higher performance per pound. Examples: several electrically actuated subsystems can be fed from one power-supply system; more passengers can be transported in a mass-transit vehicle than in private cars; many equipments can utilize the same post on a street corner; a large church congregation can share the parking lot of an adjacent plaza or department store on Sundays or during nonconflicting hours.

Frequently this increased value is achieved through systematic reduction in the number of discrete elements. Example: A mass-transit vehicle replaces forty cars. The reduced expenditure of resources (cost of highway construction, loss of private-property tax base) results in lower cost per unit (passenger-miles). With the constantly increasing competition for funds to furnish the city, coalition planning and design of street furnishings provide a way to make available money go further.

Moreover, products are not cheapened, but simplified and improved. In this sense the approach has similarities to value engineering, in which proposed or existing designs are evaluated for possible simplification and cost reduction in manufacture. The advantage in applying this to systems analysis is that the benefits are built in beforehand. They accrue before the fact rather than as belabored separate actions later.

By lessening competition of products for street space, product density is reduced. By reducing stimuli competing for man's attention, urban chaos is lessened. Although Mies van der Rohe's dictum "Less is more" applies, the resultant cityscape need not be visually sparse or "Miesianlooking" unless the designer wishes it so. Very likely the application of one plus one equals three will yield a completely new visual third dimension which will be an exciting quality in the urban cityscape.

Part Two

Man

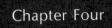

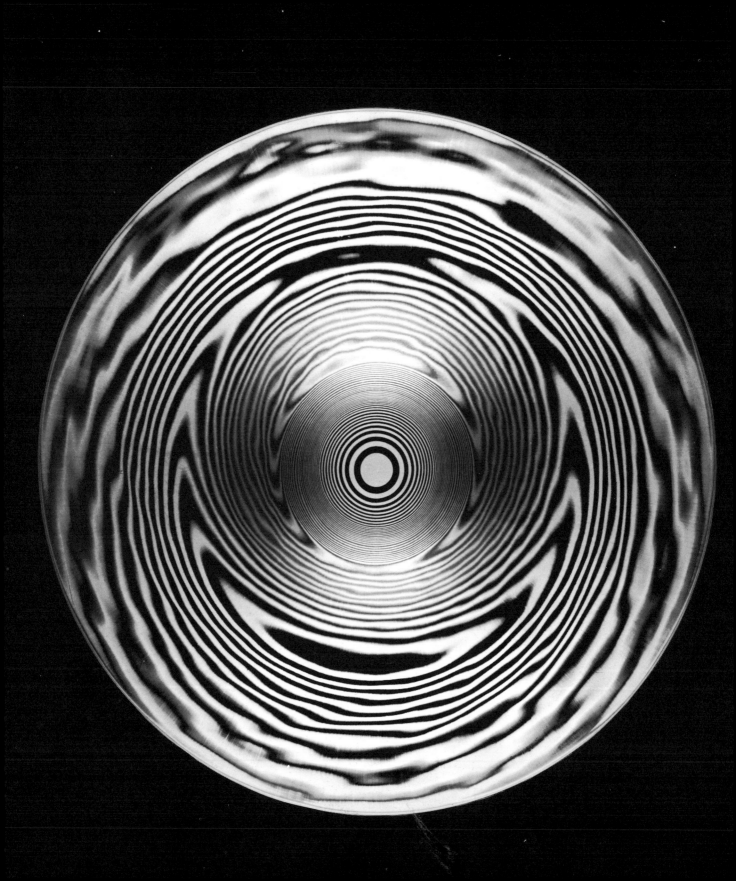

Consumer Is King

Meeting the environmental needs of man is the purpose of urban design; furnishing and equipping the city in the way people want is what this book is about. In a democratic society this should mean the seeking of the greatest good for the greatest number, rather than conferring a private vision on a selected few. However, as soon as we try to create the environment of universal appeal, we realize little is known about the most basic questions of all: What do people want from their surroundings? How are they affected by their environment?

If man is proposed as the all-important factor in the environmental man-machine systems equation, an understanding of his unique sensory capabilities and limitations is required.

The thoughtful designer has always worked along the lines of the social and behavioral scientist. He is sensitized to human feeling and behavior, and he uses a precise procession of procedures to order the environment so as to appeal to the human senses of hearing and smell as well as sight. Clearly, systems development can only be made effective by applying psychological principles.

MAN IS THE MEASURE

They Aren't Buying That Brand Anymore

A close relationship between client and designer during programming and design development helps ensure acceptability of the end product. But who is the client? In the design of the public right-of-way and its equipments the ultimate relationships are not always clearly evident. For although the line of contractual responsibility stretches between designer and bureaucracy, final approval rests not only with government but also with the business community and/or the public at large. And as consumers, the public will base acceptance on criteria of the marketplace rather than technical factors —cost of maintenance, for example. Therefore the need for great visual appeal and user satisfaction should be specified in the systems goals and evaluation criteria at the outset.

Presently, products in the public space seldom offer security, comfort, status, pleasure—the most elementary agreeable sensations that contribute to a good life. The term "street improvements" usually means structural, legal, or financial alterations or additions. Rarely does it mean betterment of emotional or social conditions.

Because of lack of progress in areas of significance, people reject their cities. The individual's refusal to buy the product is demonstrated countless times a day by his actions (or avoidance of action).

Examples: Talented or dynamic people leave a city for lack of interesting activities as much as for lack of economic opportunity. Middle-class employees refuse to work in the slums, so business moves to the suburbs. Businessmen reject a potential plant site because of a poor impression received at an inadequate airport terminal. Parents take children on a college shopping tour and choose the most attractive campus. Shoppers drive past dowdy neighborhood plazas to a far-off enclosed shopping center.

This consumer selectivity is accelerating today because our more affluent population has less community identification and more mobility. The grass is greener somewhere else even if it is synthetic, and fewer people, young or old, are locked into position. People are shifting from one end of the continent to the other seeking what they want where they think it is.

But the intent here is not to dwell on these well-known facts; rather, it is to emphasize the universal competitive effects. Every community, unless it is to lose the flow of profits and power, must compete with every other community for jobs from industry, school support from the state, and more money to rebuild with from the federal government.

This competition can be beneficial to the public if as a consequence city agencies offer a product of greater value. City administrators *can* assign greater priority to human needs relative to purely technical considerations in evaluating future community facilities, and a few are already doing just this thing. For example, in computerizing the capital-improvement system for the Wichita, Kansas portion of the 1966 RAA demonstration grant mentioned earlier, priority determinants were established for each possible project. Many possible public works programs were competing for available funds, and selection criteria were required. Noteworthy is the realistic appraisal of major factors in the decision-making process, with assigned weights reflecting their relative importance:

Factor	Weight
Citizen desires	4
Protection of life and property	2
Community promotion	2
Traffic movement	1
Drainage improvement	1

Certainly there can be little doubt that the administrator who satisfies citizen desires will have popular support for the execution of a project, and the people have power. But they have little knowledge and are not organized so as to have a decision-making capability or authority. Therefore the designer needs to serve the administrator in the useful role of people-oriented problem solver. He must be evaluator as much as anything else, researching the needs of the community.

The designer must also analyze the market needs and synthesize these human wants into design concepts which can be produced by industry with economy through the mass-production process. He will achieve his greatest success in improving the urban environment by paying attention to the ordinary details of daily life.

Criteria for Consumer Appeal

Presently we are in a period of great social change; never before have we had change at today's pace. Consider the increase in knowledge. It is said that the first doubling of knowledge since the birth of Christ took place about 1750, the second doubling in 1900, the third about 1950, and the fourth only ten years later in 1960. This means that daring as the most innovative physical change in the public environment may seem today, it is predictable that in a few years improved technology will permit far more revolutionary ones.

Technological change is highly desirable. We should admit that our cities grew by happenstance, without plan or order, in a frantic rush to meet the commercial and residential demand as rural America exploded into a mighty manufacturing nation. But these facilities cannot serve the changed needs of this half of the century. A replacement program is required. And the replacements themselves should not be considered inviolate or sacrosanct.

Yet many prominent figures still say the most important feature of an urban atmosphere should be "enduring values." This raises questions like "What and whose values?" The term "enduring" is seldom defined, and its worth young people constantly question. Nonetheless, as with corporate identity, change in order to improve community identity does not require rejection of continuity. Connection to the past and a sense of perspective sharpen our sensibility when we set out to approve or reject the new. Change must be purposeful, with new values substituted only when shown to be superior to the old. We now know that through conservation and heritage the city can be made more meaningful. The bulldozer blitz of the cityscape has been thoroughly discredited.

But the professional does not accept existing features or established criteria and concepts simply because they are there. To do so delimits creative scope and positions the designer behind the consumer, who subconsciously performs a dynamic evaluation. This questioning of society's values by the public transcends the usual alienation of younger generation from older. At this time in the history of cities a disaffection with the environment exists among most age groups, as well as racial and economic strata. The very young and the blacks may be more perceptive, and impatient, and their reflexes may be quicker, but in any event in much of society there is a growing attack on values based on materialism which results in "things." This has been expressed by Robert C. Wood as the "growing disinclination among the less powerful, the poor and the young, for example, to accept passively the judgements of those accustomed to running things."

What are the most valid criteria for consumer appeal in this dynamic social context?

Change of some unique, outstanding, and favorable kind should be a deliberate part of the process of making one particular place differ from every other dot on the dot-studded map.

Disposability offers far greater design possibilities in changing to immaterialism than does adherence to enduring values. For today the value of an object is not in the object, but in how people think about it. Mass-produced products are seldom considered valuable things anymore. In the public environment this means quality can be achieved by products being common and available, not exclusive and restricted. When common things are expendable, then planners can more freely use the medium of change. Disposability permits industry to improve the standard of city living through techniques similar to those employed in furnishing the home with synthetic products a generation ago. Then the housewife knew she was receiving little utility or gratification from a coal-burning stove, laundry hand-wringer, or

"Be-in," Buffalo, New York.

Washington, D. C. The ghetto consumer rejects the product (environment).

gramophone. Little persuasion was required to induce her to discard obsolescent appliances for the readily apparent benefits of cooktop, washer-drier, and self-wound record player. Given the choice and shown articles of new technology promoting greater comfort and amenity, the city dweller will not hesitate to approve junking of antiquated public facilities.

Mass production of components is essential to the goal of providing a better public environment for an expanding population. The transformation of our cities within tolerable economic limits can only be achieved by means of the massive resources and production capability of industry. Therefore the unlimited possibilities inherent in serial production processes must immediately replace handcraft and building-trades practices as the source for design concepts.

This does not mean that quantification is the goal in itself or that a decline in quality need result. In fact, new products yet to come in surveillance, sensing, lighting, and control will be made possible by the rigorous quality standards, sophisticated tooling, and precision capability of the industrial process. Because of both quantity and quality, industry will inevitably assume a more dominant role in shaping our environment than at present. And here designers can be useful. An overview of community goals must be maintained. The designer can be instrumental in relating industrial capability to user needs. But he can do this only if he couches his creations in machine language.

Miniaturization means *minimal* design. The fewer intrusions into our urban living space, by housekeeping items, the better. In the private sector, outhouses and exposed plumbing are symbols of inadequate sanitary facilities and poverty, and few people tolerate them. In the public sector, telephone and utility wires dangling from wooden poles, once a symbol of municipal affluence, now advertise urban poverty and cannot any longer be accepted. Primitive facilities of gross size must be removed. In the process of furnishing the city anew, the design direction should be size reduction and/or concealment of urban utilities and hardware.

Bigger is not necessarily better. A more effective systems relationship can be achieved through more appropriate scaling of components to each other and to the environment. Product proliferation requires us to reduce component size and conserve space. Every product can be redesigned by this criterion. Lighting transformers can be reduced in bulk or buried in vaults; fire hydrants can be put beneath the floor or relocated to the building fascia; traffic information can be more effectively displayed by means of electronic message-generating media than sign letter forms; traffic-control apparatus can be minimized through solid-state design.

Products of minimal design are not yet available from catalogs. The proportions and size of present-day street furniture are not based on human measurements or capabilities. Even for neighborhood use all available prod-

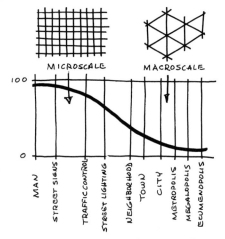

Design relationship of man, furniture, and environment.

ucts are scaled to automobile size and speed. Admittedly, the expressway or corridor is an environment unto itself. There man travels like a space voyager cocooned in a steel and plastic capsule and sealed from contact with earthly things. But in the pedestrian environment of neighborhood, campus, and shopping center, community furnishings of new design are required to stimulate a sense of contact, involvement, and personal relationships.

In order to achieve components of minimal dimension, it is necessary to shift to consumer scale. The point of view of the traditional architect has been omniscient, from on high, grandiose, productive of monumental squares and plazas. The future needs of the megalopolises may result in megastructures that dwarf man. But today's designer needs to see the city from the viewpoint of the man in the street—eyeball height, 5 feet 6 inches from the floor—and to think small.

Imagery of wide consumer appeal is essential if a community is to retain the support of the populace and attract favorable attention. Such imagery can be inherent in the natural environment in features of climate or terrain that are striking and unique. But few cities are so blessed, fewer grasp the nature of the blessing, and almost none reinforce natural wonders or capitalize them by upgrading the surrounding urban areas. Niagara Falls, New York, for example, has been slow to remove the shoddy stores and blight surrounding America's greatest natural attraction. The fact is, however, that imagery need not be based on a natural wonder. In a synthetic age identity can be man-made and can be more precisely made. Ideas are what distinguish one community from another. If the objective of imagery is to appeal to the observer's emotions, then the generation of community design parameters must revolve about consumer preferences. The possibilities are limitless. And the variety of imaginative proposals that have found favor in the past is astounding.

Abroad, notable community identity has been achieved by crowd-pleasing cathedrals, gardens, plazas, funiculars, amusement parks—all the various public places that induce active consumer involvement. Their success has erroneously been interpreted in the United States as calling for efforts to achieve a traditional appearance here. The result has been an aping of style mannerisms described as "classical." At the time of the city-beautiful era, designers could succeed with this approach, as in the Charles River development at Boston. But now it is no longer acceptable or desirable for the serious designer to polish the patina of tradition, even though the means exist for the mass production of "instant tradition": witness the rapidity with which new slums emblazoned YE OLDE VILLAGE are built, or the overnight appearance of ubiquitous gas lanterns for gasoline stations as symbols of beautification.

Two mother lodes rich in the stuff of environmental design can be mined for raw materials of intrinsic worth. The first area of design resources is the American idiom of showmanship and merchandising, that agreeable and exciting exaggeration of scale that sells something.

This quality of urban dynamics is missing in most depersonalized corporate and public construction projects. The environmental designer can restore or sharpen a sense of involvement and concern by utilizing combinations of materials, lighting, and color in variations of scale that touch and move the observer. The road to romance and adventure is lined with banners waving, bands playing, and lights splashing across the sky.

The second source of design concepts lies in the manifestations of our technological age to which the younger consumer best relates. As McLuhan points out, the message is in the media; and the media of kinesthetic sculpture and luminal art convey a more timely message than Grecian columns and Victorian lanterns. The systems designer, unfettered by past precedent, is free to create imagery of new dimensions by evolving new components and relationships to satisfy system performance criteria. A new design vocabulary is being developed featuring the plug-in, add-a-part, discard-a-part processes of the computer age.

These contemporary solutions will be useful solutions and not contrived, just as the San Francisco cable car was a working solution to the transportation needs of the mechanical age contrived with flair and daring in mechanical-age terms. A comparable creation was the Eiffel Tower, an innovative product of late-nineteenth-century technology which we still recognize to be valid and useful. However, what other cities need to express this age are obviously not more cable cars and towers of ironmongery, but transportation modes and street furniture of utility whose expressiveness will produce popular appeal and acquire a renown of their own.

Space to move in is a vital need for the city dweller. With 80 percent of the nation's population soon living on 1 percent of the land, a pileup of people is taking place. The time seems to be coming when a person moving 2 feet in either direction will bump into someone or something.

Many signs and signals are competing for attention, yet when viewed comprehensively, they produce more visual congestion than signal. The human organism has had to adapt to these contaminants polluting visual space as well as the more readily evident hazards of air and water pollution. The problem becomes apparent when one considers the brain as an enormously complex instrument that classifies and interprets all the sense data an individual is exposed to. The brain apparently has a filtering system in the feedback loop that stops transmission of many of the stimuli. But too much gets through, the social scientists are telling us. The observer is subject to communication overload and responds by withdrawal, by ignoring even the essential messages. It becomes a vital question of safety. As Lewis

American Folk Art. Squaw and papoose.

Expo 67, Montreal.

Ghirardelli Square, San Francisco.

The new design vocabulary.

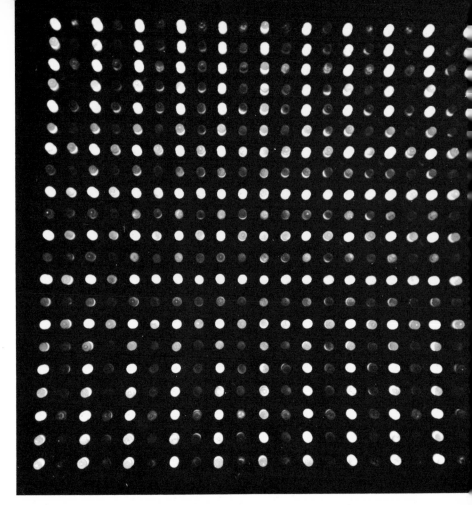

Form-making process which meets the variable environmental needs of man.

Mumford said, "We are overwhelmed by our symbol-creating capacity. [In order to survive] we have learned to achieve a certain opacity, a thickening of the hide."

Another critical problem which the environmental designer must face is the increasingly aggressive behavior of man. As the population increases, so does interpersonal aggression. An aggression explosion chain-reacts from the population explosion. Therefore increasing attention has been devoted to the man-environment relationship so that the urban designer can help defuse an aggression explosion. According to microbiologist Rene Dubos, "an impoverished environment results almost inevitably in biological and mental deficiency." Research indicates space is a determinate variable in man's behavior. Spatial settings trigger responses so deeply hidden that the individual is not even consciously aware of them. When space is inadequate, stress is built up, making possible disruptive and even lethal effects.

"Density" is a word often used in discussions of crowding. But "density" is no longer adequate to describe what is happening to great numbers of people living in overcrowded cities. "Intensity" best describes what faces the urban-pressure-cooker dweller struggling to reach home, office, or food market. Intensity, caused not only by congestion of human bodies but also by the accumulation of "foreign" bodies, by the clutter found in crowded streets and shopping-plaza parking lots, finally gets to people, creating a sense of hostile space.

Research is now establishing human levels of tolerance for crowding, visual congestion, noise, odors, and other sensory factors. Spatial arrangements that can complement man's needs vary from culture to culture. The problem facing us in rebuilding and equipping our cities is understanding the needs of large numbers of people. Particularly people in slums. It is less useful to measure the land-density needs of an affluent suburban commuter. His spatial experience is extended by travel and vacations. What of the ghetto dweller who has no place to go to recharge his senses and who needs a safety valve?

The environmental designer does not plan social actions, but he can provide man the refreshment he needs on the city streets.

MEASURING MAN

Why should anyone but a psychologist or physiologist want to know how we perceive the environment? The question has especial validity, since many concerned with improving the environment still believe science to be in-compatible with imagination. The answer lies in the fact that designers are traditionally preoccupied with visual patterns of structures—what one sees. They think, design, and render in a manner that is primarily visual. But the environmental experience is a multisensory one, and designers have to de-sign to exploit man's multisensory capabilities. Above all, for the designer the human material is the most interesting of all. The sensorial equipment of man includes visual, auditory, and other sense receptors, and today he is surrounded by a crowded, demanding world. Sounds, lights, and other attention-seeking stimuli constantly bombard the consumer. We know that people are more sensitive to, and react more strongly to, certain ones (light waves). Why and how the consumer discriminates one from the other is important. As designers, we are continually tickling these senses.

Consider the visual modality. Too much is demanded of our eyes when driving. It is estimated that 80 percent of all impressions are received through the eyes. It is not desirable or necessary to send all information through one sensory system. However, the American way of life encourages this phenomenon. There is picture talk all around us. We are visual. People respond to pictures, not talk.

SOCIOPETAL SPACE (alien to man)

SOCIOFUGAL SPACE (suitable to man)

Psychology of spatial arrangements.

Almost everyone is familiar with the description of the eye as an instrument for measurement. This organ measures light by means of sensitive cell structures called rods and cones. These visual cells are of two types comparable to fast and slow film. The rods mediate vision in starlight, like fast film. The slower cones activate at an illumination level one thousand times greater than the rods. There are considerably fewer cones than rods, and they are all packed together in the fovea, which is the center of the retina.

The designer of visual systems such as communications, traffic control, and lighting should consider the extent to which these receptors determine visual acuity. This human ability to distinguish fine detail depends upon this physical structure. Urban product systems that require levels of sensory discrimination exceeding this ability are dangerous. Example: lighting patterns at superhighway interchanges that appear confusing during night driving. To achieve more effective system performance, the designer might help increase observer visual acuity by:

1. Sharpening contrast between object and background
2. Providing greater nighttime light intensity

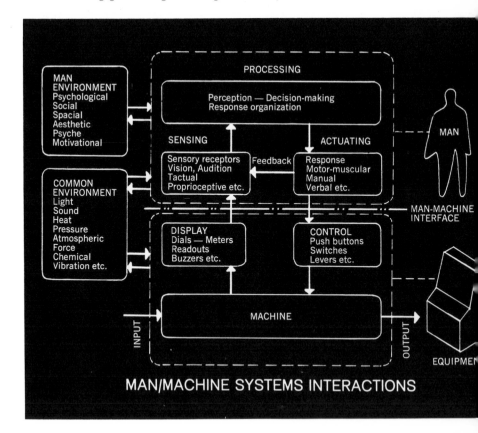

MAN/MACHINE SYSTEMS INTERACTIONS

Hazardous roadway lighting, the result of disregard for user needs and capabilities.

3. Arranging for more observance time

4. Simplifying display

Visual acuity, moreover, decreases with the distance of the object from the eye and with the angle of retinal stimulation. The eye does not see well at angles other than perpendicular to the fovea. An object only 20 degrees off center can be acquired by the fovea only one-tenth as well as an object that is straight ahead. This should influence the siting of various components. Obviously it is physiologically impossible to look straight ahead while driving and simultaneously read a sign mounted at the side of the road or on a building wall.

Seeing Is Believing

The psychology of perception is concerned with the organization and arrangement of complex forms of stimulation. One of the most vital psychological phenomena is the ability of the human being to perceive a world of three dimensions: height, width, and depth. Man can even achieve visual space perception generated by images on a two-dimensional surface.

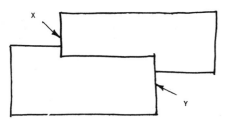

Interposition: the relative position (in space) of the two rectangles changes as vision shifts from X *to* Y.

Principle of similarity.

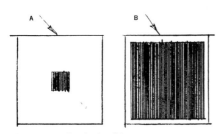

Figure-ground relationship.

The retina has but two dimensions. There is no depth. The retinal image of one object can only be to the left or right of, and/or above or below, the retinal image of another object. How the consumer records, interprets, and organizes these constantly shifting light patterns on the retina affects what he sees. Perception of three-dimensional space is initiated by two different sets of cues: environmental cues and physiological mechanisms, such as visual receptors. The designer is interested mainly in the manipulation of environmental cues for greater sensory gratification.

Environmental, or stimulus, cues initiate or reinforce three-dimensional perception. Some of the principal modes by which we perceive space and objects are:

Linear perspective
Light and shadow
Clearness (near objects defined, far objects hazy)
Movement (near objects faster)
Gradient (texture flattened with distance)
Interposition

Interposition can be especially useful to the product designer in creating depth and solidity or in giving special emphasis to certain features of the product. How the observer spontaneously perceives the figure is of critical importance to the designer, as in the matter of framing buildings or products.

Perceptual organization usually relates behavior to complex patterns of stimuli rather than an individual stimulus element. This "principle of similarity" is observed in the adjacent-stimulus pattern of twenty-five symbols, where the observer tends to perceive the pattern as a ground of columns, not rows of space. This is a function of how he sees *things,* not the spaces between. This is important to the designer evaluating a product in the environment, since like objects tend to be perceived together and, conversely, unlike objects appear separate. When shapes are constructed, the square will appear more like any other square than a circle. If a designer's primary concern were to create an attention-getting unique identity for a fire-alarm box in a sequence of other square shapes, he might differentiate by making it round.

There are many of these kinds of gestalt perceptual organizations. One of the best known is the "figure-ground relationship," in which perceptions vary so that a shape silhouetted in the foreground may alternately be seen as background. In the example, each shape may be seen as a hole or as a thing on a surround.

Illusions are false perceptions. The perceptual process organizes physical stimulation. Sometimes it organizes erroneously. When the designer permits this to happen, the physical environment is perceived in a way that does not correspond to reality. There are innumerable examples, only a few of which are mentioned.

Illusions of shape occur frequently. In the example shown the square is distorted due to its relationship to the circle. This poses obvious architectural and product design implications.

Illusions of size can be useful or harmful to design, as in the famous Müller-Lyer illusion, in which both vertical lines are equal in length but not perceived as such.

Illusions of brightness are achieved by strong contrast between figure and ground. A dark line or spot will appear darker in general as the brightness of its environment is increased; conversely, a white spot surrounded by a dark environment will appear brighter as the latter is darkened. In other words, black and white juxtaposed reinforce each other. The importance of contrasts in brightness or in color cannot be overemphasized; many practical demonstrations are visible at night under various light conditions. White traffic markings, for example, appear whiter on black asphalt than on concrete.

Illusions of movement are typified by the psychotechnical consideration know as "Phi phenomenon," an apparent movement where in fact none occurs. This is the design basis for many of those flashing, moving arrows that advertise the presence of roadside businesses. They are meant to be obviously, violently garish. They are, in fact, irresistible as attention getters.

These stationary signs that appear to move are successful because the designer has utilized a 1912 discovery of Max Wertheimer, founder of the

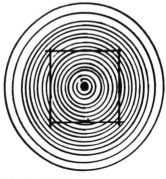

Illusion of shape.

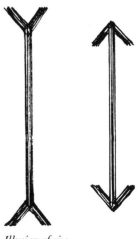

Illusion of size.

Two equal gray patterns which appear lighter or darker depending on background.

Concentric circles behind convex plastic lens. Observer himself becomes kinetic element by looking into lens and creating movement effect when in fact none exists.

gestalt school of psychology. Wertheimer projected two short parallel lines, 1 centimeter apart, at reading distance from the subject. The lines were flashed on a screen one after the other. The length of the time interval between the successive flashes determined what the subject perceived. When the interval between the exposure of each line was longer than 0.03 seconds, the subject perceived only what actually existed: two stationary lines, first one and then the other. When the interval was shorter than 0.002 seconds, the two lines appeared to be projected simultaneously. When the time interval was from 0.03 to 0.002 seconds, the observer perceived a flashing movement, with the first line seeming to jump from its own position to the second position.

The psychology of perception is being stressed because the designer should recognize that perception is synthetic rather than analytic. Man tends to put things together in wholes. This is perhaps most evident in reading, where we perceive shapes in words and phrases rather than individual letters. But while the basic quality of perception is the relating of one thing to another, any form of design language or coding depends upon distinguishing one thing from another. A thing usually carries information and is meaningful only to the degree that it is separable.

An awareness of the synthesizing nature of perception will help the designer achieve urban equipment solutions within the psychological capabilities of man. Simplicity of product design through invoking more effective modes of controlling human behavior will have to come because of the increased demands made on the psychological and physiological apparatus of perception. Indeed, the safety of the streets may depend upon the extent to which the designer utilizes available data on human sensory capabilities.

Thus psychological consideration of the consumer is necessary in all typical environmental system development activities such as:

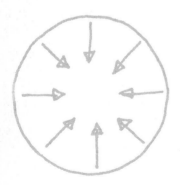

Establishing the design problem

Determining the systems package that will meet human needs

Establishing relationships between man and machines

Designing the product environment

Installing the systems and evaluating them in terms of human usage

Previously it was suggested that scaling the forms of the street furniture to fit man and make him comfortable enhances consumer appeal in that people can touch and feel, enjoy or ignore, as they choose. But clearly it is not good enough to be merely functional or even handsome. Furnishing the city requires meeting psychological and social needs.

Part Three

Environment

Chapter Five

Shaping the City Floor

Certainly most basic to the socioeconomic life of the urban environment are appropriate roads and streets and public places. In any but the most narrow definition, the creation of an acceptable public environment must include many considerations beyond paving materials.

No longer can cities install or repave streets using codes and criteria of minimum performance as the purchasing specification. To compete with the suburbs, as well as to meet the needs of urban developers and neighborhood residents, each with specific wants, the bureaucracy must plan and rebuild according to design standards of maximum performance that provide consumer satisfaction, comfort, and pleasure, as well as according to engineering considerations of maintainability and efficiency.

How will this be done? How will Downtown and the neighborhood street be restored to the people as places for enjoyable experiences? The first step is reevaluation of the function of the street in terms of contemporary social goals and economic pressures. Only then can the full resources of industry be applied and the benefits of the multidisciplinary approach to design be achieved.

PEOPLE ON WHEELS

Establishing Goals and Priorities

The street has always performed a number of communal functions. More than a way of movement, it has been a space for human activity—buying and selling, socializing, providing visual orientation to the visitor, symbolizing community character. Above all, through history, the street has been the road to romance.

A thousand years ago the Mayan trod the sacred sacebob of crushed white limestone threading through cedar and mahogany. Fragrant plants bloomed while brilliantly plumaged birds swooped and chattered. Ahead appeared the plazas, their platforms and pyramids white against the green lianas and palms. The Mayan became emotionally involved. He had reason to support this city and contribute to its splendor. He received from it benefits that contributed to his well-being and pride of association.

Little more than a hundred years ago the western settler rode horse and wagon through vast dry spaces until he reached the dusty track leading into the frontier town. Ahead he saw wooden sidewalks above the muddy manure-covered road. His spurs jangled when he strode the springy boards. False fronts and large signs promised full meals and drink. Main Street was a package whose delights were clearly defined to the traveler by sight, smell, and sound.

Then the auto roared into town, and the pedestrian experience has never been the same. The American Downtown has become dull and boring. Neighborhood streets have evolved into a place to drive through to get someplace else. Automobile movement has suppressed all other functions. Millions of miles of standardized black asphalt and hundreds of thousands of uniform traffic signs have obliterated the visual cues to where you are and where you've been.

It has been estimated that with the advent of expressways and belt loops *two-thirds* of downtown land has been given to moving and storing automobiles! Compare the area devoted to public right-of-way (not counting off-street parking) with that available for all other possible uses in the following typical urban renewal projects:

Example: Louisville, Kentucky, West Downtown

Total acres	290.0
Streets, alleys, etc.	99.0

Example: Buffalo, New York, Waterfront

Total acres	292.8
Streets, alleys, etc.	104.2

Pedestrian bridge erected across Broadway at Fulton, New York City, 1867. Removed 1868 because consumers preferred traffic hazards to climbing stairs.

Example: San Francisco, California, Western Addition

Total Area	276.0
Streets, Alleys, etc.	107.0

These and similar statistics suggest not only the possibility of wasteful overdesign as a general practice but also the opportunities at hand by virtue of public ownership for more efficient use of the vast amounts of expensive urban land.

Detailed discussion of transportation planning and land-use criteria is not within the scope of this book. But it must be noted that the shape of the urban fabric results from the selection of route and mode of circulation and the integration of transportation systems.

As Ian McHarg has pointed out in *Landscape Architecture,* qualitative factors are now considered only *after* the conclusion of cost/benefit analysis.

Present procedure by federal and state agencies involves calculating savings from, and costs of, the proposed urban highway. Savings are computed in time, operating costs, and reduction of accidents. Costs are those of construction and maintenance. Savings must exceed costs by a factor of 1 to 1.2.

This formula is no longer adequate. Future projects should from the outset be programmed to include social benefits as well as physiographic and traffic-engineering criteria. More emphasis should be placed on designs that favor least loss of taxable land. A formula based on least social cost and maximum social benefit will result in maximum social utility.

This poses difficulties. Novel considerations are interjected into the cost/benefit formula (though present methods of highway engineering allocate money values to convenience, a commodity as difficult to quantify as esthetics). Moreover, evaluation of new proposals must always be in terms relevant to contemporary goals. Everyone says we are going to rebuild America in the next thirty years. It will be the same old piece of merchandise unless we develop a new physical expression derived from a change in technology that satisfies goals of improved efficiency, added safety, greater public comfort, and less destruction of the urban fabric.

SEPARATING WHEELS FROM PEOPLE
Three-dimensional Design

One of the most critical urban design problems is the increasing transformation of city street into corridor or limited-access highway. Each city has its examples. In Chicago the Pershing Road Corridor will cut back private property along the roadway and expand from 66 feet to 150 feet in width. Many city comprehensive plans anticipate that major streets will have variable standards of width and other characteristics, depending upon traffic volume and the nature of the areas through which they pass. Where previous linear-city proposals utilized utility lines or railroads as the spine, current thinking uses the expressway as the spine. Such plans also suggest that multidisciplinary design be done by a task force whose members are drawn from the design professions as well as highway engineering. In practice, however, this seldom effectively happens.

Jane Jacobs's reaction was to write, "Most cities widen roadbeds. Far better to widen sidewalks." Perhaps other alternatives exist. In order to more efficiently separate incompatible traffic—pedestrian, auto, truck, mass transit—cities could be redesigned utilizing available air rights as well as the surface and subsurface. Many older solutions still apply as well as newer techniques. Their viability has been proved. The engineering know-how exists.

We could look to the New York or the Chicago "el" as a proved way

Midtown Plaza, Rochester, New York. Prototype protected mall is surrounded by stores, offices, hotel; there is even parking below and natural daylight above.

to increase the carrying capacity of existing streets. Subways are another example; those of Montreal are a particularly pleasant public experience. Monorails are back in vogue. We could note how the UN Park sits on a platform cantilevered over the East River Drive to create usable space where none existed before. We see the trend to put public parking underground in cities with hills such as San Francisco (Union Square) or Pittsburgh (Mellon Park). Something besides a park can be put on top of the parking. On a campus it might be tennis courts; downtown it might be a shopping plaza and hotel, such as Victor Gruen's Midtown Plaza in Rochester, New York. Or parking may be underneath the downtown office-building complex, as popularized by Rogers, Taliaferro, Kostritsky and Lamb at Charles Center, Baltimore, and Fountain Square, Cincinnati. Now even sports stadiums are elevated with parking under the podia, so direct enclosed access is provided from mobile seat to sports seat. In Washington, D.C., Nathaniel Owings was able to make L'Enfant's baroque patte d'oie, or goose-foot intersection, at the foot of Capitol Hill finally work by putting much of the traffic underground.

In the more successful large-scale spatial solutions to roadway congestion or circulation problems, separation has been achieved by use of two or more horizontal planes, one carrier level precisely over another, much as on a double-decker bridge. But a quantum jump will occur when we exploit the full potential of omnidirectional air rights. Then all activities, pedestrian and motorist as well as commercial, can be enhanced through interwoven ar-

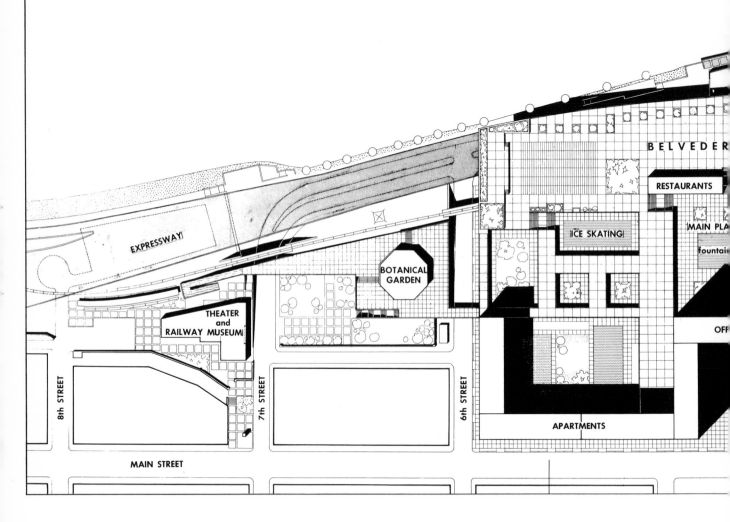

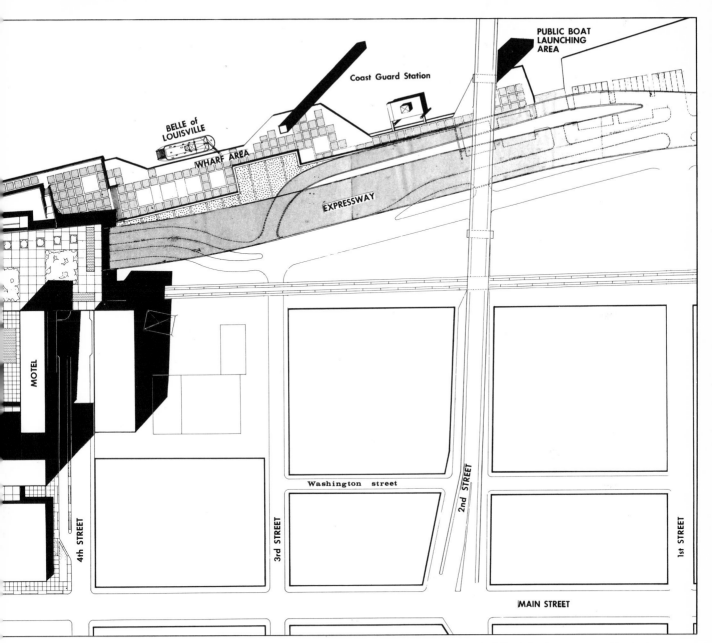

Multilevel development on public land brings new vitality to abandoned Louisville waterfront.

Fountain Square, Cincinnati.

rangements of spaces, uses, and access paths. Existing available public land can become a multidimensional linkage to private spaces.

Some such projects already exist. An elementary but pioneer installation has been made in Morristown, Tennessee. Its 1967 Skymart, believed to be the first double-deck sidewalk in the United States, runs 1,000 feet down each side of Main Street, provides access to second stories of commercial buildings, and carries power and telephone lines, eliminating overhead wires.

A more sophisticated pedestrian passageway is that of Cincinnati, based on a plan by Rogers, Taliaferro, Kostritsky and Lamb. This linkage moves irregularly through much of the downtown core at a 15-foot-high level and connects by spines and spurs many stores, hotels, and garages. This project demonstrates that linkage need not be linear, "hard-edge," or axial in the European tradition, but can be amorphous, encouraging pedestrian movement in appropriate directions. But its major significance lies in the fact that it takes the city as it is and becomes an additional public right-of-way,

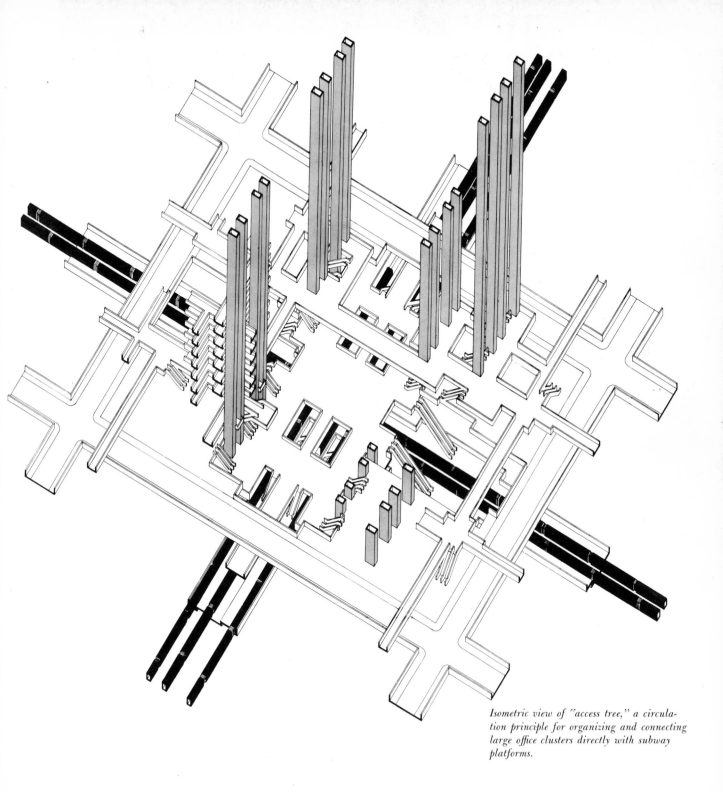

Isometric view of "access tree," a circulation principle for organizing and connecting large office clusters directly with subway platforms.

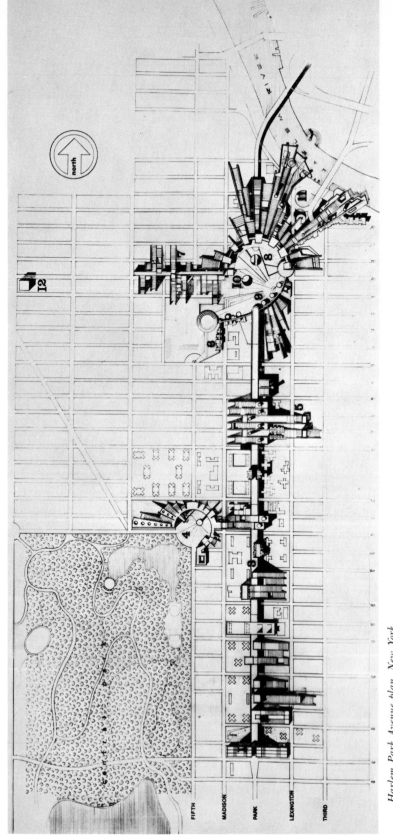

Harlem Park Avenue plan, New York.
1968.

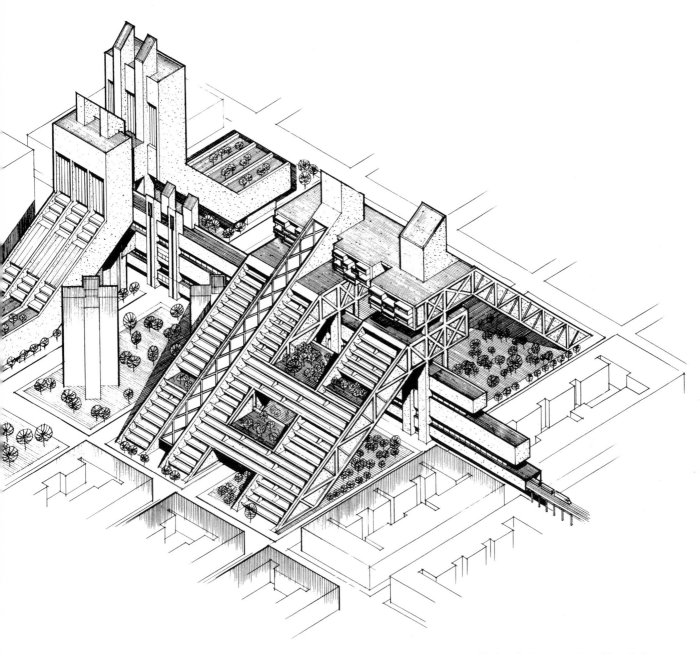

Harlem Park Avenue plan, New York, 1968. Enlarged view showing multilevel use of air rights over Grand Central tracks.

penetrating old as well as new buildings, and only occasionally in register with the streets below.

In the metropolis, the sensibility of the Cincinnati approach is as self-evident to businessmen, developers, and bureaucracy as it is to designers. Since Americans will not give up their love affair with the automobile and in fact want to give it custody of the street, then the pedestrian has to be put above or below the automobile. In the megalopolis, the problems are more intense and the solutions more drastic. Once the people are elevated, the economics suggest, they might as well be transported at the fifteen-story level as at 15 feet. When that happens, the true value of three-dimensional design of public space will be not only separation of wheels from people but people from people.

The success of all these mechanistic concepts will depend not only on the economics of land use but also on whether the proposed transportation system offers people greater enjoyment of the movement experience.

Middle two lanes decoratively converted but seldom used by pedestrians. Predominant street use remains vehicular.

Two-dimensional Design

Meanwhile keeping our two feet on the ground, we need to face immediate problems of separating wheels from people and use the sort of roadway design that still relies on two-dimensional grids: open this street to wheels not people; make this block a mall for people and close it to wheels; make this street an expressway for wheels and close it to people.

Pedestrianism, one mode of transportation which exists in conjunction with all other modes, is nonetheless the most neglected of all modes in current transport analysis and design. Yet walking under proper conditions, is delightful, healthful, and likely to remain important in three areas: in such concentrations as the center city, shopping centers, and campuses, where it is the primary mode of travel; in mode-interchange terminals such as airports; and in the home neighborhood, for school trips, visiting, and local shopping.

Because of their importance to commercial interests, most pedestrian design focus has been placed on malls. These have proliferated throughout America. In its simplest form, a mall can be the identification of a few blocks, usually in an important shopping district, by certain embellishments to the roadway which will attract more shoppers. Very frequently automobile traffic is not restricted from these blocks, because of timidity, cost, or lack of planning. In a more advanced form of mall, the street may be narrowed or configured to hamper vehicles (make them use some other route) or to provide more walking space. Or a large center median may be installed and furnished with decorative lights or plantings.

Sometimes halfway measures only halfway meet expectations. People on wheels will go where they can and not somewhere else. People on foot will not cross dangerous roadways midblock either to shop the other side or to sit on benches in the median in isolated grandeur. Regardless of any superficial appearance of having been inspired by H. G. Wells and Edward Bellamy or the more recent science fiction of movies and TV, the halfway type of urban mall is pale, insipid stuff at best.

An increasingly popular mall design, first developed by Victor Gruen, is one in which existing stores and facilities are not disturbed but wheels are excluded by rerouting. Commonly the street is filled to grade between curbs and enhanced in the central areas to encourage foot traffic and free movement. This design may or may not be successful, depending upon which of two approaches is used in the design treatment of the roadbed.

The unsuccessful approach is that of the hard-edge school of landscape design which evolved from the classic geometry of Beaux-Arts. Decorative linear patterns are used which frequently work at cross-purposes with function. Shopping centers must stimulate spontaneity which encourages com-

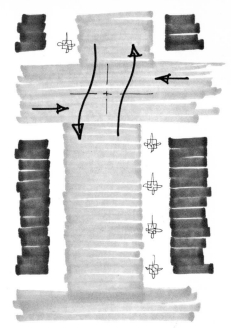

Washington Street Mall, Oakland, California. Pedestrian spaces created by widening alternate sidewalks.

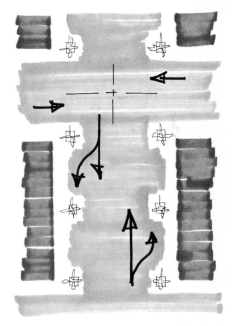

Alvarado Street Mall, Monterey, California. Pedestrian and parking spaces created by widening opposing sidewalks.

*Fresno Mall, California. Conversion of
street to all-pedestrian use. Casual pattern
is conducive to crisscross shopping.*

Prudential Center, Boston.

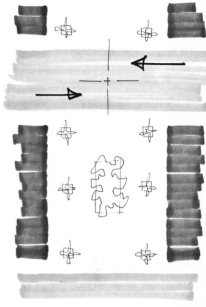

Santa Monica Mall, California. Conversion of street to all-pedestrian use. Formal repetition of sidewalk pattern inhibits crisscross shopping.

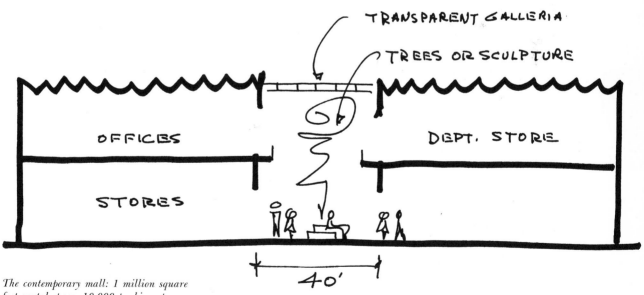

TRANSPARENT GALLERIA

TREES OR SCULPTURE

OFFICES

DEPT. STORE

STORES

40'

The contemporary mall: 1 million square feet rental space, 10,000 parking spaces. The convenience and imagery attracts 300,000 people.

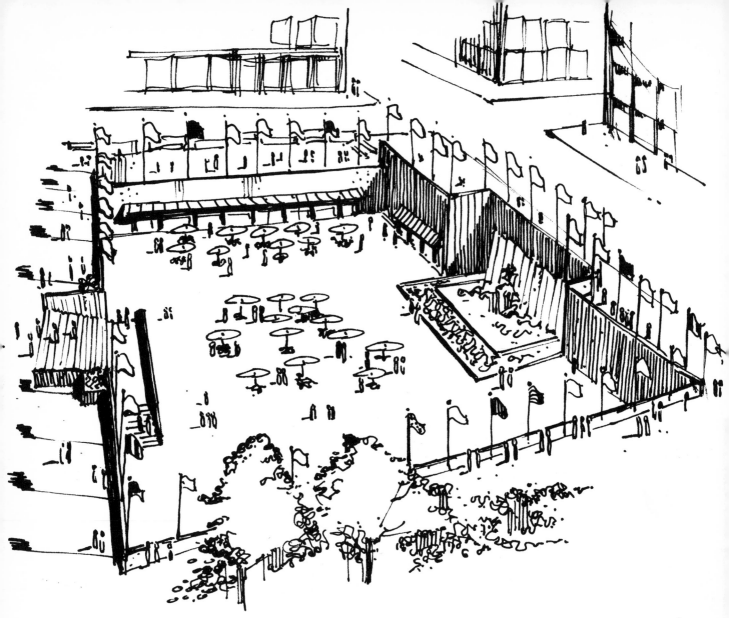

Rockefeller Center, New York.

parison shopping; crossover from side to side is essential. When streets are closed to vehicles and resurfaced as pedestrian malls, the hard-edge approach is to install new paving patterns which conform to the old pedestrian path. The old curbline (now without step) is restated by new decorative patterns that inhibit crossover. In an extreme of architectural vanity, even moats have been used; incredibly filled with water, they obviously perform the age-old function of keeping people away.

Clearly, if we eliminate the need to accommodate automobiles on the roadway, designs more meaningful and relevant than decorative sidewalk patterns can be employed. Developers of the suburban enclosed shopping center have proved that the successful mall is one which denigrates the storefront in relation to the environment and whose public space is made not much more than 40 feet wide to encourage crossover. Because the city right-of-way (storefront to storefront) is usually much wider, it is even more urgent to employ a functional design approach, as typified by several of Victor Gruen's solutions. The essence of this approach is spontaneity rather than Renaissance formality. Store and sight lines are blurred. The middle space is packed with attractions and a focal point; enticing changes in vista are offered to pull people from side to side. The central plaza becomes a place for sunning, sitting, lunching, or watching the girls go by in style.

Perhaps the most important development in the pedestrian space (aside from the enclosed and climate-controlled mall) is the trend to use of multi-level space. Rockefeller Center is usually cited as the early and classic example whose accommodation of varied activities on different levels contributes to an ever-changing vista of interest and excitement. New examples abound of multilevel spaces, such as the shopping promenade under Place Ville Marie in Montreal or L'Enfant Plaza in Washington, both by I. M. Pei.

Place Ville Marie, Montreal.

Circle Campus of the University of Illinois at Chicago.

Of course malls and plazas are built for purposes other than commercial. Take the plaza at the Circle Campus of the University of Illinois at Chicago, which the architects, Skidmore, Owings & Merrill, call a social plaza, a crossroads where young people meet and compare and barter ideas in an intellectual environment. It works in that fashion because it also serves as an elevated pathway, crossing train tracks and continuing at raised level into second-floor building entrances.

But even more plastic pathways will be evolved as a solution to the challenge of confrontation of vehicle and pedestrian. Paved surfaces can be shaped and modeled in swelling shapes whose constantly changing volumes give a sense of excitement and variety to the pedestrian participant.

Microscale metal cubes make sculpture and also suggest macroscale future floor.

(Left and above) *Civic Center, San Francisco.*

Auditorium, MIT

INTEGRAL SITE IMPROVEMENTS
Paving

Present practice in new construction or rehabilitation of old streets requires specification and bid by the square yard of paving and by the linear foot of curbing. Lowest first cost prevails, with side effects discounted. Environmental design in terms of human needs or neighborhood social factors is not performed. The potentiality of flooring to convey urbanity, elegance, or distinctive character is unexploited. The design of paving to achieve a neighborhood image has been neglected for the easy and routine, the dull and unimaginative. However, much of today's urban design places emphasis on open space—civic centers, shopping malls, campus podia, office buildings on stilts or utilizing only part of their plot area—and this open space demands increased design consideration of pavement patterns and materials.

Landscape architects traditionally have understood the importance of masonry ground cover as a component in the total design scheme. Texture, color, and pattern have been carefully used to complement the overall scheme harmoniously. Cobblestone, brick, terra-cotta, and asphalt block pavers have all been used with stunning effect. Other designers too have been concerned with the floor and its interface with housekeeping hardware. But the design solution oriented to the Renaissance marble court or church-yard green space is not always responsive to today's needs. What works for the Piazza San Marco doesn't necessarily work elsewhere. Consider what makes the plaza in the new Civic Center of Rochester, New York so stupefyingly dull and forbidding. Is it the lack of pigeons? Or is it the in-applicability of yesterday's materials to today's conditions? Another example is the White House east drive, where the carriageway cobblestones are now partially obscured by a skim coating of black asphalt.

The problems with using traditional elements in traditional patterns are threefold:

1. High product cost (piece production)
2. High installation cost (hand labor)
3. High maintenance cost (chewing-gum removal, salt damage, etc.)
4. High replacement cost (lack of availability of standard units)

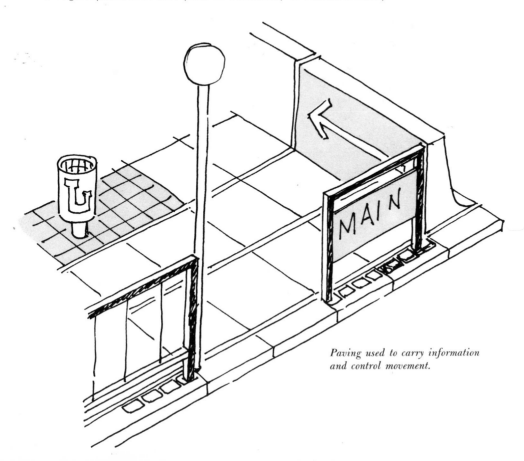

Paving used to carry information and control movement.

In interior design demand spurred industry to a fantastic increase in volume and innovation in resilient, woven, and hard floor coverings; the same can happen in exterior design. Prestige projects may continue to use handmade, hand-laid products. But industry will be required to develop mass-production techniques for new kinds of paving components and materials as designers weave the urban fabric by the mile.

Precast slabs are a beginning, but could be made more useful by greater use of cast-in-place inserts to pre-position and accept other hardware and components such as manholes, lamppost bases, planters, signpost sleeves, drains, etc. Machines could be developed for site use to continuously pour and emboss decorative patterns into concrete or synthetic materials for walks. Old sidewalks and paved surfaces could be rehabilitated by synthetic coatings machine-mixed and -applied.

The floor can be mechanically varied to offer change in reflectivity under artificial light. It can be programmed for sight and sound (visual inserts or add-ons, textural noisemakers) to provide cues and become a continuous information system:

1. To carry traffic or safety markings for motorist or pedestrian

2. To define parking areas

3. To identify "rooms" or special street spaces such as intersections or crossings

4. To provide a sense of territory, marking entrances to neighborhoods or commercial districts

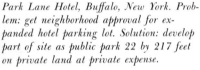

Park Lane Hotel, Buffalo, New York. Problem: get neighborhood approval for expanded hotel parking lot. Solution: develop part of site as public park 22 by 217 feet on private land at private expense.

By performing additional systems tasks, candidate designs offering similar new or additional options will be able to justify initial costs of development.

Barriers

Barriers are for separation. They may limit access and use, but growing complexity and density of spatial use demands better techniques and hardware for channelization and compartmentation. Barriers are sometimes inappropriate or misapplied because the function is not adequately assessed as security from people or safety from vehicles or space delineation. Dr. A. E. Parr has listed three types of barriers: prohibitive (chain-link fences), persuasive (bollards, railings), and suggestive (archways, lighting changes). Evaluation of the problem in broad terms will lead to consideration of many alternatives. Some will not be hardware solutions, but will lead to redesign of other elements to accomplish a dual purpose. Where barriers are essential, they should not be permitted to be stuck to the floor, but should be designed as an essential and integrated component of the urban furnishings.

Fences may serve two completely different functions which are often confused: security and space delineation. As an example of the latter, the genesis of the institution of turf in our cities was the appropriation of a street or housing project by a gang as its own territory. Members of other gangs could not enter without permission of the territory-owning gang. Jane Jacobs has described how this procedure of "fenceless," keeping the other gang out, evolved into middle-class turfs with literal fences to keep the other classes out. Soon high cyclone fences were built around the malls and plazas and playgrounds of developments and projects with signs saying KEEP OUT—NO TRESPASSING.

Now many people live in stockaded villages within a city. Fences are hostile. They are an invitation to attack and will seldom withstand a determined assault. If the function of the fence is to suggest a spatial division, other means such as markings or plantings should be considered.

Bollards are sturdy posts embedded in the floor either to protect some more fragile structure or to exclude vehicles from pedestrian precincts. Although they have an honorable history of traditional use in sculptured form, their use has languished except by highway engineers, who employ steel pipe or sometimes yellow-painted oil drums for the latter purpose.

It would seem, however, that their value in contributing to imagery and in providing an alternative to more formidable or massive constructions has been overlooked. Many materials and shapes can be employed in them which grow from, or integrate well with, floor textures and patterns. Bollards can by position and number act as "punctuation marks" as well as barriers. They can establish sign lines of varying scale and rhythms. They can simplify traffic- or parking-control procedures.

Birmingham University, Staff House, lighting bollards. Precast bollard contains bronze glareless light source. White tile provides reflected sparkle.

"Median" is the engineering nomenclature for a traffic separator, which usually appears as a flat raised curbing in the middle of the road separating opposing vehicles and marking no-man's-land. It's almost always an ugly and dangerous place to be. But thousands of miles of medians in many widths and shapes are poured each year, primarily in major urban roads.

Because of the significance of medians in the cityscape, funds have recently been made available for beautification. But many "beautified" medians are of routine design, with grass or trees at low elevation that are subject to noxious fumes and salt action on soil and plantings and do not provide headlight protection during winter months. Surely here is an opportunity for significant improvement in the public roadway. On-site or prefabricated median segments can be designed in infinite varieties of shape and material to mark *this* road as different from *that*. Shape can convey place, direction, and importance. Shape need not be low and flat, with curbs which require higher and uglier guardrails. The median can be formed of low walls which discourage pedestrians from crossing, mask out approaching headlights at night, and contain linear light sources for flooding the roadway with low-elevation glareless illumination.

WHEELS WITHOUT PEOPLE

The Problem and Goal

When most cities, recreational areas, and other public spaces were established, neither designer nor developer was concerned with the automobile. Existing streets and public transportation were adequate. Monumental buildings required only a carriage entrance; sports stadiums were serviced by trolley tracks. Most people lived near their jobs, frequently above the store or in the mill town. Students used mass transit to get to class; women walked to the neighborhood market. Cars were a luxury, not a necessity. Parking two generations ago was not a problem.

Now the city has exploded with people and pushed out its borders. Society is mobile, and business, shopping, and leisure activities are far-flung and numerous. Walking seems outmoded. Mass transit has lost and not yet regained status. Everyone wants cars and has the affluence to acquire them.

No single feature has so affected the appearance of towns as car parking along streets. The efficiency of streets, their ability to move vehicles and pedestrians, has been drastically reduced by the resulting congestion and disorder. And still there is not enough curb space for all parkers.

The automobile is extremely limited in mobility compared with a pedestrian. It cannot move sideways; it cannot enter restricted spaces. Because of this limited utility it must remain largely in storage. The average car is in motion only 500 hours per year; it is left parked on a paved surface the other 8,260 hours. The average person can stand with an armful of packages in 5 square feet. His whole wardrobe of clothes will take up no more than 2 square feet of closet space. But his car parked on the street will occupy approximately 150 square feet without counting the area required to maneuver him in and out of the resting space.

In simplifying the urban scene the removal of parking spaces with their signs and meters should be given special consideration. Well-organized parking facilities should be provided in accessible places.

Even in suburbia, where shopping-center lots may have a capacity of 8,000 cars, a number which turns over three to four times a day, getting in and out of these shopping-center or off-street lots has become a dangerous adventure. According to the nation's largest traffic insurers, parking-lot damage now appears to be the chief source of minor car claims. People seem to be careless, reckless, and thoughtless. Designers have not created new kinds of facilities that might reduce the consequences. Better layouts could lower the ratio of parking spaces to selling spaces. Better signing and control devices and markings would make more efficient the use of space.

Curb parking exists because businessmen and the bureaucracy regard it as suitable and sufficient. But nowhere in the urban scene is there more reliance on obsolete procedure and products and less on new ideas, techniques, devices, and signs and markings than in parking control. Moreover, it is expensive. In some middle-size cities the annual cost of parking signs and their installation exceeds $50,000, an amount greater than the cost of street-lighting replacement and maintenance.

More needs to be achieved than token observance of national standards for posting regulations, in themselves confusing and inadequate. Present procedure in the United States is for municipalities to post signs at each location where parking is prohibited. In the center city this practice has gone to the extreme of posting signs every 30 to 50 feet along the curb. Legends are long; typefaces and layout are illegible. Signs with complex schedules of authorized times are admissions of inadequate traffic solutions. The custom in England is to post signs only where parking is permitted. Parking is prohibited by negative information. The need for NO PARKING signs in profusion is deleted.

This procedure could be employed on private parking grounds, where the use of standard highway signs has no legal meaning. *Message sets should be simple, direct, and clear.* It is better to say NO ENTRY than AUTHORIZED VEHICLES ONLY. Messages such as SLOW or DRIVE CAREFULLY or CARS TOWED AWAY are of dubious value and should not be used.

Even on the public right-of-way, parking and similar regulatory signs that attempt to cite chapter and verse are futile. Signs should be designed to be explicit and directive, not legalistic.

This informative approach permits development of exciting concepts for communicating parking instructions. Parking areas can be identified with entertaining and memorable symbols, diagrams, or color. Community appearance can be enhanced through use of more pleasing sign panels and lettering materials. The parking authority can be presented as a helpful agency rather than the long arm of the law. By choice of alphabet and sign-panel materials, the identity of a community, urbane or rustic, commercial or residential, can be reemphasized.

Curb parking could also be optimized by greater and more sophisticated use of the floor for conveying messages. Properly used, curbing and paving can tell the driver much about when and how to use the space by means of surface changes and paint. This minimizes the need for sign "things" on poles. Messages or symbols can be set in or applied to the floor. This is not only less costly and more useful but also necessary in certain facilities or areas. While painting of stall lines has become accepted practice along curbs

Church Street Project. Color-coded aluminum parking signs fit in galvanized-steel light standards.

and in off-street parking facilities to define space and lanes, improved use of space and less car damage can be achieved with better-designed band widths and graphics and better placement.

Curb parking is frequently controlled on a time basis as the fair way to utilize space throughout the day. Parking meters, when accompanied by adequate-length stalls and timer restrictions appropriate to demand, may produce the following benefits:

1. Make a set number of spaces available for more parkers by encouraging a more rapid turnover.

2. Simplify enforcement and reduce police personnel required.

3. Liquidate their own cost.

However, these objectives are not always obtained with mechanical control aids. People need spaces for relatively long periods and find it more convenient to feed the device than find a space elsewhere. Frequently they will not use the meters or will resent paying for the "privilege" of parking in order to patronize a store or library or visit a campus. Enforcement requires expensive manpower.

There are a number of variables in meter-head selection, method of support, and siting that may produce either a pleasing installation or a visual disaster. Mechanically, industry classifies meters in two types, manual and automatic. The manual mechanism is wound by the user each time he inserts a coin and turns the handle. The automatic must be periodically wound by the coin collector.

Many of these products are difficult to operate, hard to read, and frequently malfunctional. Coin-operated meters freeze and jam. Many are expressly designed to be unreadable (unexpired time) by the space-seeking motorist in order to secure a higher payoff for the house. The general level of engineering and reliability is of such low order that few of the industry's products are currently useful. In 1966 the city of Buffalo had 3,166 parking meters; they needed maintenance attention in 16,347 instances. Such functional deficiencies make essential the design of new units that meet higher standards.

Perhaps a more fundamental consideration is the manner of installation of the devices. It seems wasteful to use a separate post for each meter for each car. Yet by far the greatest number of installations along curbs and in parking lots are made in this manner. Some have even an additional post embedded in the floor to protect the meter post! Clearly capital cost, maintenance cost, and visual pollution will be reduced by the sharing of one post by two units; even further savings will be made when one unit is made to serve two spaces.

But for truly greater synergetic benefits other techniques beyond post-mounted meters should be considered. The interface of the parking-control

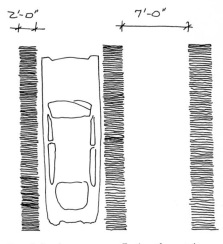

2'-0" 7'-0"

Broad bands are more effective than stripes in maintaining access space.

subsystem with other subsystems such as litter control and lighting offers an opportunity to share supports and installations. Many communities put waste receptacles on meter posts. Still other combinations are possible.

Parking meters are the literal modern equivalent of the old hitching post. The planner's problem is to keep them from being an imposition—to use them as punctuation rather than the statement of an old-fashioned environment.

Off-Street Parking

If downtown parking needs were met by ground-level car parks alone, they would cover nearly the whole area of the center city. Wheels without people can be more efficiently stored in multistory structures. The planning and design of these will not be covered here. Let us consider instead the furnishing of parking lots where essential.

Design parameters for off-street lots are derived from policy as well as traffic requirements and site conditions. An operating decision must be made on whether the lot is to be attendant or self-parking. If the lot is not to be free, then a pay procedure must be established; the alternatives include attendant collection, individual meters, and tollgate.

All lots, pay or free, require products, signing, and marking to improve utilization and reduce operating costs and mishaps. Their design and siting not only are dependent upon the parking concept but should be an integral part of it. Several studies published by the Eno Foundation for Highway Traffic Control detail lot planning for optimum speed of movement and maximum number of stall spaces. In order for this degree of efficiency to be achieved, various control devices frequently are necessary.

Use of space under North-South expressway for parking, Metropolitan Dade County, Justice Building.

In a pay unattended lot, a device is required for prevention of unauthorized entry or exit. Usually it is a lift arm, but it may be any form of gate or barrier. In some systems the car is driven onto a platform which must be shifted sideways in order for the car to proceed. In other systems entrance of the car into a space and over a treadle starts a timing device and raises the treadle to prevent car removal.

Treadles and moving floor surfaces have not proved satisfactory in cold-weather areas. Installation and maintenance costs are high. They require salting in winter, and are frequently damaged by snowplows. The more common device is the gate-arm barrier, which should contain the following features: thermostatically controlled heater for cold-weather operations, gate arm made of resilient material that will not damage a car on impact, and sensory device to retract the gate arm if it strikes the vehicle on descent. In addition, flexibility of mode of operation is desirable to provide options for free one-way traffic (for exit in single-lane operation of a small lot), two-way traffic, and controlled one-way traffic.

Unattended systems require insertion of coins, key, or card to activate the control station for operation of the barrier. Control (payment) may be established on entry or exit or both by buried presence sensors capable of directional sensing for automatic barrier actuation. Units should be positioned in advance of the barrier so the driver is not turning when alongside. Attended systems may issue parking checks manually or use a ticket dispenser. *A dispenser should issue one ticket per vehicle regardless of size or weight.* Entry lanes must be properly designed and marked. Widths have been increasing from 8 feet to as much as 13 feet. Stanchions or curbs may be necessary to keep motorists from damaging the equipment. These important visual elements should be carefully designed to assist the motorist in portal identification rather than merely act as barriers.

Traffic lanes may be established or delineated by low concrete islands separating stalls, or round plastic disks or pavement-mounted wheel barriers may be used. The front overhang of a car is approximately 3 feet; therefore a 6-foot median strip can be provided between parallel rows of parked cars without wasting space. Grass malls and trees can be used on the median. If medians are provided, 6-inch curbs are used for vehicle alignment. Without medians, raised guardrails are preferable to wheelstops, for easier snow removal.

The design of parking systems—efficient, esthetic, and integral with traffic systems—is a part of redeveloping the city. Parking areas must be linked to the places that generate the need for parking by direct and attractive pedestrian ways. The systems planning of facilities for parking access and storage will require systems design of supporting equipment also.

Chapter Six

Posts and Post Mortem

The most obvious and repetitive feature of the daytime environment is the array of poles, posts, and standards that support so many public products. We seem to want to put each light, signal, or sign on its own stick like a lollipop. But each pole is sited and installed without regard for the others or the total visual scene. Positioned along roads and walks the poles wall us in like a picket fence.

If well designed, these numerous elements can unify, organize, and provide continuity for the daytime image of the city. The lamppost can become the generative element of a new urban furniture system. Structure supporting necessary systems can be a handsome as well as useful linkage between man and his electromechanical environment.

But if lampposts are poorly designed, overcrowded, or inadequately chosen catalog items, they can make the city look slovenly and old-fashioned. Examination of their function and appearance, followed by redesign, is foremost in achieving overall environmental systems improvement.

Previous Practice

In the crudest form a light pole was (and in many areas still is) a pine tree with bark and branches lopped off and crossarm bolted on to support a lantern. Even when it was remotely fueled, its source of energy was carried externally until the late nineteenth century. Then the support assumed another function. It became additionally a hollowed, protective, housing carrier, or raceway, for distribution of the fuel—first gas, then electricity.

Posts and poles sprouted rapidly as cities grew. But their design parameters remained essentially the same. Function was still narrowly defined. The structure was still conceived as a tube, duct, or post with a single fixture perched on top or outthrust by bracket. Engineering was based on the manufacturers' traditional use of materials and the limited versatility of their production facilities.

As cities electrified, the light pole assumed still another function, that of image maker. It became a means of civic and business-district advertisement. In those cities using wood poles with overhead power distribution the message was "I am small, poor, or unaware." But the large, wealthy, sophisticated city displayed its preeminent position by installing custom-designed cast-iron columns.

The favored styles were based on classical motifs and usually featured an elaborately decorated pedestal supporting a fluted column terminating in an ogee-curve bracket; a most elegant variation of this style, the bishop's crook, is still seen and loved in some areas of Manhattan. As cities grew and took form, custom designs were installed downtown, with less expensive models doing service in the residential areas. Business districts vied with one another in efforts to have spectacular unique designs. In San Francisco one pridefully installed ornate-style lamppost, still treasured as a civic asset, was on Market Street, and another more appropriate style was displayed in Chinatown. Salt Lake City featured Indian heads on its posts.

Current Practice

Decorative styling is still the basis for the design of almost all downtown lampposts. In Chicago the brash commercialism of State Street is advertised with brutal, vulgar posts, while the style-aware North Michigan Avenue shopping district competes with more slender contemporary poles.

Although New York, with more than sixty-four different lamppost models in use, has attempted to standardize on the "Fifth Avenue standard," in most cities the installation of more single-purpose poles continues at an accel-

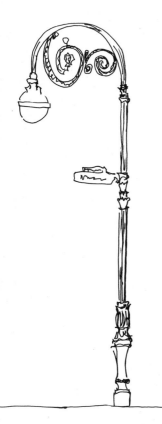

erated rate. Uncounted millions of single-function lampposts, signposts, and heavy-duty traffic poles to support span wire and signals are in use. Based on a nationwide survey by *The American City,* more than 5 million lighting poles alone are in use in American cities. And there are additional unknown millions of special-purpose poles and signposts. It is worth noting that residential streets account for 56 percent of the lighting poles, while business areas account for 16 percent. The balance are spread over highways, parks, and other undefined areas. Cities of exceptionally high density such as New York have only one-third the national average of poles per capita. But for other cities over 10,000 population, the density of light poles is about 48 per 1,000 people.

Clearly, lighting poles and other supports have become most significant and conspicuous elements in the cityscape. And concurrently their cost has increased. Over 500 thousand dollars was required to reequip the Downtown of Cincinnati, whose urban renewal project required 600 new light standards in 1969. Also, though lampposts are effective as machine-age totems, monumental symbols of city power, as long as this imagery remains unblemished and undiluted in impact, they have now been so festooned with signs and signals and other municipal junk that the imagery has changed to chaos and blight. Therefore the design problem now revolves about intensifying the community image, achieving synergetic benefits of cost savings, and reducing clutter. All three are not only desirable but essential.

Chinatown, San Francisco.

PLANNING PUBLIC IMPROVEMENTS

Systems Layout

No one plants a pole without cause. The installation is subsidiary to a primary need for some other subsystem, such as lighting, information, or communications. Thus the structure is valueless in itself. Its worth—economic, esthetic, or functional—has value only to the extent that it acts in concert with other components and contributes to the whole. Another component may be completely integrated into the support, in which case structure and message, for example, are one. In addition to posts, sidewalk and street surfaces or something else may be the message carrier. Curbs can carry linear messages. New electronic and optical devices can be used as multichannel carriers.

Early in the planning phase, then, before freezing on any specific support or carrier, it is desirable to determine the various subsystems requirements. The lighting plan will determine the number and location of necessary supports. The traffic signing, street signing, transit information, and other visual signage will also require support. So will fire and police and citizen

Lamp standard, Salt Lake City, Utah.

137

emergency-reporting equipment. All these composite needs should be shown on one overlay of the project site. The scope of support application will be evident. This "street-furniture plan" will show duplications and spatial overlaps. Improper locations can be adjusted and the plan revised to eliminate duplications and consolidate equipments on one support where possible.

Scale

Scale is not actual size, but apparent relative size, and most people instinctively sense this. A large overstuffed chair that appears gross and overimportant in a small room may appear opulent and appropriate in a larger space. Similar consumer reactions to size of fixtures should be considered in the furnishing of exterior space.

Scale of posts to the mass of nearby buildings can be predetermined. In certain areas of open spaces such as highway intersections and cloverleafs, few but high light towers may be appropriate. Along pedestrian walks posts should be small-scale, and the use of bollards could be considered. In any event a family relationship can be established between the various size units necessary to meet different needs throughout the city. Freeways, neighborhoods, and Downtown will each require light standards of different height and scale, but a continuity of community identity and greater sense of order can be provided by establishing a hierarchy of scale between posts, a related use of materials and color, and a continuity of shape.

SYSTEM DESIGN

Performance Criteria

The support components—foundation, base, shaft, and bracket, if any—should work as a unit, but their structural fundamentals will not be reviewed here. The relationship between structural behavior and structural form is important, but the relevant engineering data have been covered many times over elsewhere. Instead, systems criteria will be emphasized, with the following considered most meaningful. The support should:

1. Be multipurpose for utmost flexibility in accommodating varied component needs.

2. Be shaped to orient, index, and pre-position components for self-location and self-attachment.

3. Minimize wiring labor and facilitate plugging into.

4. Be producible by mass-production techniques.

After installation, continued systems performance demands a configuration adaptable to changing needs, thus minimizing the need for future poles and conserving space. Built-in flexibility versus immediate suitability poses the paradox of growth. The closer the designer gets to achieving the universal product grid, the farther he is from providing product spaces suited to specific needs. But signing needs will change. Lighting requirements are not static. Unknown devices to meet as yet unspecified needs will be installed in the next decade. Clearly the user will have less difficulty with the *multipurpose* pole in controlling equipment costs and maintaining integrity of environmental design.

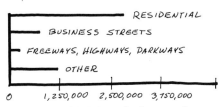

Distribution of lighting poles by area of city. Approximate national total 5 million units.

Other Design Goals

A favorable appearance is essential for consumer appeal, since the support structure's importance in shaping the urban synthetic environment is magnified by repetition as well as size. But what kind of imagery should the product have, and how is it to be achieved? Because of the need for precise component interface, cost control, and high-volume production, the most successful solutions will undoubtedly be shaped by machine tooling. Like consumer goods and private industrial products, public equipments must be attuned to the industrial process. And imaginative concepts need not be constricted. On the contrary, new dimensions for contemporary expression are made possible. Only the eclectic personalized designs requiring handcraft execution will be restricted.

Better design of the interface of support and sidewalk is essential. Present practice depends on the skill and interest of installation crews for adequate product placement and finished appearance. Excessive site work leads to crazy-quilt appearance of concrete work around post bases. The bolt-down hardware on catalog designs from industry is usually crude or poorly masked by decorative cover plates.

However, when floor interface is made part of the systems design, more ordered solutions become feasible. Fieldwork can be reduced through use of factory-made connectors. Where one-piece butt-base poles are inserted into the ground without concrete foundation, pre-positioning sleeves can be designed. Where posts are installed to transformer bases, anchor nuts can be tightened to studs within the vault. Where posts are bolted to concrete foundations, the installation can be recessed, with a flush cover making crisp and clean the intersection of post and floor. And numerous other possibilities, such as sliding collars, can be developed.

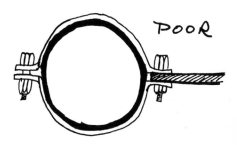

SOME CONCEPTS

Mast

Consider the soaring grace, economy of material, and sophistication of design embodied in the sailing-ship mast at the close of its history. Tall and

strong but light in weight, it withstood the stress of wind and wave. Although it was firmly rooted, its flexibility of rigging met the varying loads and needs of the wind power system. By comparison how clumsy is the assemblage of booms, brackets, and span wire attached to most street-corner masts!

However, there is growing recognition of the need to carefully integrate components into support. Although the great majority of traffic signals, signs, streetlights, and transmission wires are still attached by means of brackets and bolts, more consideration is being given to coordinated shape, scale, and color.

Vertical Matrix

In the vertical matrix components are indexed, pre-positioned, and mated to each other by means of the plug-in rather than bolt-on. Although the vertical support can be compartmented into even modules with each space reserved for one component, more flexibility may be achieved by plugging components into the vertical frame where needed.

The vertical matrix with precision-shaped section is well adapted to the needs of certain precision components and to the machine demands of mass production. More than the simple round pole, the matrix shape tends to simplify installation and order the visual scene.

Horizontal Module

Where the quantity of street-furniture components exceeds the capacity of a single vertical support, an array of posts can be used. These may be pre-ordered within a fixed grid. In this process both the vertical position of

(Below, left) *Lamppost, Century City, Los Angeles. Sliding collar conceals bolts.* (Center) *Thirty-foot tapered, natural-finish lamppost, Sheraton Hotel, Prudential Center, Boston. Sliding plate conceals recessed bolts.* (Right) *Flagpole base, Civic Center, Chicago.*

Mizzenmast, U.S.S. Constitution.

components on the posts and the horizontal location of posts on the side-walk are preestablished. Problems of growth and the need to add more components are solved by filling more horizontal spaces. In practice, a portion of the pedestrian walk parallel to the street can be reserved as a *collector strip* for street furniture. Division of the linear strip into compartments pre-positions each component.

This modular arrangement results in a formalized layout whose conventional approach has traditional appeal. But the emphasis remains on products, not people. The cityscape becomes rearranged for the convenience of machines, not according to use. And while this scheme may make more disciplined the visual scene, it has the disadvantage of perpetuating the use of great numbers of posts and separate units. Given the constant increase in number of equipments in the cityscape, this arrangement in not very skillful hands can result in the sidewalk fenced with an impenetrable picket of posts.

Rather than string supports along the curb, the designer may gather components together and gang-plug them into the floor. Each element or post remains separate and can be optimized to its most efficient diameter and height as well as position. Components such as waste receptacles or fire hydrants can be integrated into the cluster. Hopefully, these are all tied together by the design of equally expressive shapes and by the manner of their placement in a high-density relationship surrounded by open space. Although the arrangement is asymmetric, the position of each element within the cluster must be predetermined for repetitive use. However, this scheme may appear less formal and more dynamic than the more obviously regimented collector strip, as well as permit a higher density of components necessary at street corners.

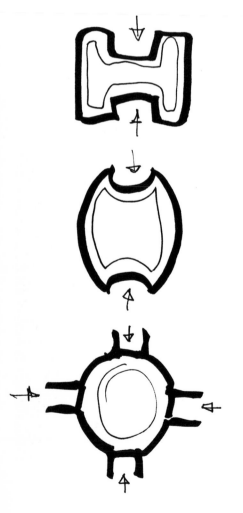

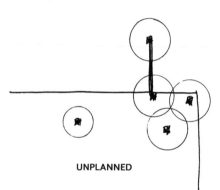

UNPLANNED

(Far left) *Possible pole sections that locate, index, and aid mounting of components.* (Left) *Same street intersection with different equipment arrangements.* (Below) *Street matrix that organizes cluster of poles.*

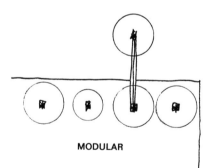

MODULAR

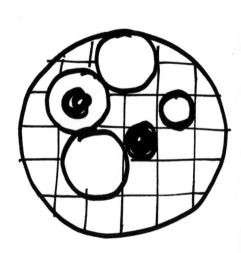

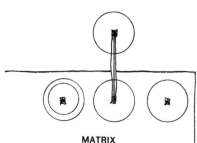

MATRIX

Multidimensional Space Frame

True spatial configurations will evolve from the analysis of the optimum spatial location of equipments, such as streetlights or traffic signals, and the development of a continuous structural shape, a multidimensional space frame, to support them there. This has already been tried on an experimental scale, and many variations can evolve and be used.

Such optimized use of three-dimensional space will become more frequent as designers, freed of conventional concepts of the static lamppost, exploit the full potential of technology and materials to place products in their appropriate place in space. In the nineteenth century new methods of calculation aided by improved ferrous metals conceived of structure as composed of linear elements. The behavior of forces moving in a prescribed direction could be measured and controlled in advance. But twentieth-century structural engineering is moving along other than linear paths. There is a tendency to activate every part of a structural system instead of concentrating the flow of forces into single channels—like posts. Designers can make these newer systems expand freely in all directions.

MATERIALS AND FINISHES

Evaluation Criteria

Contemporary technology affords the designer a wide choice of materials, the exotic as well as the traditional used in new ways. Previous criteria of

Model of space-frame experiment in stress-spun concrete, 1963.

choice have revolved about purchase and thirty-year maintenance costs. With growing recognition of the visual importance of the structural support and with a wider choice, the designer needs to select the appropriate material for the specific task based on additional criteria such as the following:

1. Compatibility with the reinforcement of community identity

2. Adaptability to mass production in achieving shape required by systems design

3. Compatibility with materials used in components to be supported

4. Resistance to destructive forces such as corrosion, vandalism, and vehicles

Safety

Most functional requirements for poles, such as roadway lighting or traffic signs, require placement at the curb in order to get most efficient use. This puts the lamp or sign where the action is but makes the pole hazardous to motorists. As an example, Buffalo, New York, a city of 500,000 population, experiences 600 ''breakaways'' per year when motorists strike steel light poles.

Previous engineering practice was to strengthen the pole to prevent damage. Since congressional hearings on highway safety have documented the hazard to motorists, emphasis has changed to protecting the driver. The designer now must relocate posts out of the way, choose a less rigid material, or integrate safety shear elements into the pole design.

Wood

About two-thirds of all poles in the city are presently wood, and this percentage may be as high as 80 percent in the smaller city. Each lasting about thirty-five years, wood poles still deliver 90 percent of the nation's electricity and are reportedly a 26-billion-dollar investment. Because the wood pole carrying a jungle of exposed wires typifies urban blight, development of more contemporary and less obtrusive support of overhead distribution wires has been sponsored by the American Wood Preservers Institute and the electric utilities.

OSAR (Overhead Systems Appearance Research) was one project dedicated to such development. Its goals were the esthetic improvement of poles and pole-top equipment. Systems criteria were proposed in order to assure economical and practical solutions to the goal of esthetic improvement in the residential environment. The criteria revolved about simplification and integration of wires to support. Desirable design practices dictated that the support structure should:

> Express its principal function.
> Reflect a visual integration of functional components.
> Express technological progress.
> Reflect provisions for special environmental conditions.

Many other innovative approaches to use of wood can be considered, such as lamination. Impregnated with resin and cured by heat and pressure, wood can be given additional properties that permit a greater variety of shape and section other than solid post. The potentiality of this machine-created material is largely unexplored, however, so cost is still high and acceptance low.

Cast Iron

The proportion of poles made of metal ranges from one-third in the larger cities to one-eighth in the smaller ones. Cast iron has been in use longer than any other noncombustible material. It offers many advantages, such as resistance to vandalism. The New York City Bureau of Gas and Electricity still uses it, for this reason, in the 10-foot pedestal size in the city parks. It can be produced in a variety of cross sections and shapes. It can be cast with integral butt end for easy ground installation and removal, and with integral collars and fixture adapters.

Park pedestals have been customarily painted in green enamel, a finish which is inexpensive and easy to maintain. But the designer should consider use of gray or other neutral colors when large posts are to be used on concrete walks or in urban settings.

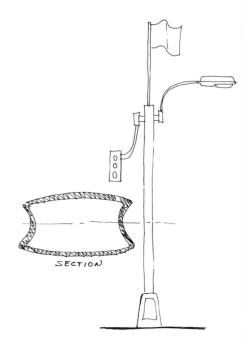

"Light tree" concept for downtown lighting.

(Right, above) *Fifth Avenue Standard with accessories.* (Below) *Fifth Avenue Standard, extruded aluminum shaft epoxy-welded to cast-aluminum base.*

Steel

Steel tubing is used almost three times as frequently as cast iron. Carbon steel offers low initial cost but possesses poor maintenance characteristics and shape potentiality. At greater cost, cold-rolled, fabricated, and welded sections of high-strength steel offer increased strength and configuration advantages. Color selection of paint on galvanized metal is good, and the post can be "painted out." An improved ten years life can be achieved by epoxy evaporation coatings, but these and similar films are subject to defacement. The "rusting" steels are a high-strength material, never need painting, and acquire a permanent patina of integral dark brown color expressive of the industrial process.

Aluminum

Presently used only half as frequently as cast iron, aluminum tubing is gaining acceptance for shopping centers, campuses, and civic areas as a single-purpose lamppost of contemporary appearance. The lamppost is most frequently seen as spun seamless tubing, tapered and/or bent. Utility has been limited by marginal structural characteristics. When davit shape has been used, motorist vertigo has been reported from observing pole sway induced by wind loading on the luminaire. Along with poor shear characteristics, electric conductivity may be a problem in areas of possible vehicular destruction. Thin-wall stems, supporting large globes, are vulnerable to vandalism.

The above deficiencies can be minimized through use of extruded shapes. And although the standard finishes seem obtrusive for most environments, other anodized or weather-resistant baked-enamel finishes could be used or developed. But the extensive systems possibilities of aluminum are largely unexplored, with the exception of the Fifth Avenue standard and an early 1959 prizewinning design by Jack Howe in England.

Concrete

Less than 10 percent of the poles in cities below 500,000 population are concrete, but the proportion rises to 27 percent in larger cities. Requiring no foundation, concrete poles are moderate in initial and maintenance costs and are therefore in greater use than steel in many residential areas and in areas where corrosion of steel is a problem. Older posts were made of reinforced static-cast concrete. By present-day criteria, these posts possess poor strength/weight and high water-absorption ratios. But concrete has been considerably improved in recent years, making it suitable for use in all areas of the city.

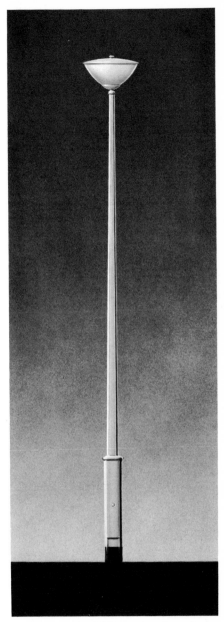

Fifteen-foot street-lighting unit, winner in 1959 competition by Aluminum Development Association. Features lightweight, tapered shaft made from parallel side extrusions cut diagonally, reversed, and epoxy-cemented together.

Trefoil shape produces lightweight column easily removed from concrete mold.

Centrifugal-cast concrete is one improvement. When the mix is pressure-pumped into a metal mold, then rotated at high speed, the mix is compacted. Excess water is spun to the center and removed, forming a nonconductive raceway for conduits. A dense, nonabsorbent surface, with integral color and aggregate effect, is obtained. Fittings may be cast as inserts. Also, the butt may be integral-cast, therefore eliminating cost of foundation work and anchoring.

Prestressed concrete makes possible an even stronger structure for severe applications. During manufacture of prestressed-concrete poles, high-tensile steel wires are attached to anchorages at either end and positioned in the mold. Predetermined stresses are introduced, directly opposed to those the mast or standard will receive. The mold is then revolved at high speed. Several manufacturers produce these poles, cost-competitive with steel and less costly than aluminum, in larger sizes.

Plastics

Fiber glass, filament-wound glass, and reinforced resin offer improved structural strength, integral color, and nonconductivity. Small-scale lampposts made of these materials are now in service in England and gaining increased acceptance on the Continent. The attraction of plastic for the designer is largely in the variety of contours possible for enhanced performance or imagery and achieved in mass production by use of mold or mandrel.

Chapter Seven

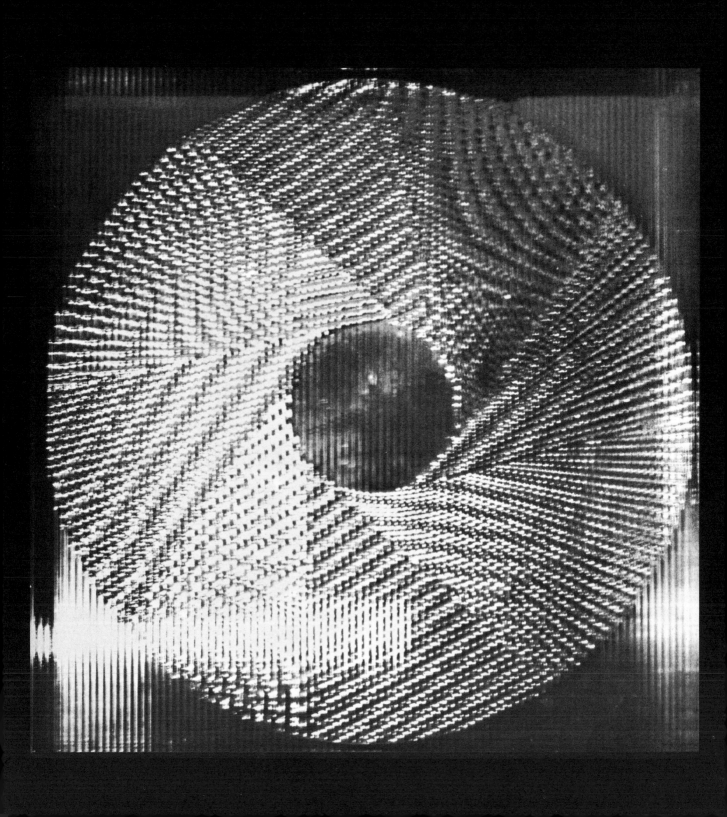

City Lights

Light is frequently referred to as a tool. It is not. Light is a raw material similar to space. The designer has to push it around. He has to determine what light is, how to use it, where to put it. His tools of manipulation are lamps and luminaires.

By day, sunlight covers all and sunlight is free. By night, artificial light is isolated, spotty, and costly. Artificial light is a commodity metered and dispensed by light fixtures which are the most obvious product in the nighttime environment.

Previously designers have been primarily concerned with improvement of lighting fixtures for interior use. There are now many instances where special designs for exterior use can be economically justified because of better interface with other products and systems or improvement of imagery.

Previous criteria of evaluation of light in public places have been based on a formula whose factors are dollars and footcandles. Historically, people have demanded (and paid for) more and more light to provide security and a sense of place. Reduction of vehicular accidents and speedup of traffic have recently been added as objectives. The engineer has always been concerned with amount and placement of light; now the designer has a role—to satisfy human needs through the lighting system.

A TALE OF TWO CITIES . . .
AND THEN SOME

Folklore is full of stories about cavemen finding fire to be a protection from prowling enemies and animals. Other legends tell us how more sophisticated uses of firelight evolved as society developed and moved into settlements and towns. Fire-filled iron baskets, oil lamps, then candles came into use. Each offered a bit more light or a bit less maintenance. The torchbearer or lantern bearer became a status symbol for those travelers who could afford him. The psychological and inspirational values of outdoor artificial light were recognized in towns; as early as 1417, the lord mayor of London ordered that lights be hung out on winter evenings between "Hallowtide and Candlemasse."

As the civilized world grew in size and sophistication, communities took over from the individual the responsibility for providing lanterns, for community safety and prestige. In 1666 Paris passed a street-lighting tax, whose proceeds provided 6,500 lanterns lighted twenty times a month (moonlight presumably illuminated the other ten nights). In 1738 London installed 15,000 oil lamps and in 1809 the first gas lamps. Gas was so superior and so much cheaper a fuel that the gas lamp quickly became the standard around the world, with the Baltimore installation of 1815 the first in America.

Other technical improvements followed, and cities quickly accepted them because of the increasing cost of lighting the increasing miles of residential streets as well as Downtown. Edison's carbon-filament arc light was more efficient than the gas lamp, and the tungsten-filament gas-filled incandescent lamp of 1915 was more economical than the arc light.

Spurred by citizen demand for status and/or crime prevention, our cities continued to add more and brighter lamps through the roaring twenties until the Great Depression. Now, forty years later, they still possess the same hodgepodge of posts, lamps, and luminaires—except for a few cities where aggressive merchants or public works people have upgraded lighting facilities to more contemporary levels. But even these special projects have usually had design parameters built around quantity, not quality, of light.

The story is told in Chicago that when State Street installed its glaring high-intensity lighting, "It became bright enough for you to read the serial number on the hoodlum's nickle-plated gun." Brightness alone does not cure crime. A more effective way to minimize crime on the streets is to get more people into an area, on the sidewalks, coming and going. And the way to achieve this is to build up the quality of the light and environment, not merely to put up more and more lights.

(Above) *Lexington, Massachusetts.* (Left)
Niagara Falls, New York.

152

Lighting can be, by its nature, an inherent shaper of urban form. Handsome lighting in an area attracts large numbers of people to it for work or play. Amusement parks and automobile sales agencies demonstrated the emotional magic and attraction of artificial light long ago. But until now lighting engineers have designed new systems by the narrow formula of dollars and footcandles. They have ignored the primeval potential of warm light to attract people and influence urban development as something beyond the scope of their responsibilities.

The urban designer or multidisciplinary team has no such limitations. But nothing constructive will happen until we realize that every true metropolis has two cities downtown—the daytime city and the nighttime city. Revitalization of the daytime city with new office buildings, banks, and plazas means nothing at five o'clock when everybody pours out and goes home to the suburbs. What happened to the nighttime city? It is dark and deserted. True urban areas like Tokyo, London, and Berlin have nighttime cities that are active and alive. Public lighting and signage contribute to that atmosphere. Making the nighttime city successful is a prime challenge for the environmental designer.

"Cherry Picker" is used to service high-mounted, high-output fluorescent lamps, State Street, Chicago.

THE HUMAN EXPERIENCE

How We See

There is so much emphasis on the quantity of light that it needs remembering that usually people don't see illumination at all—only brightness. As William M. C. Lam points out, "We all know that light is a form of energy which, when radiated to a given point, produces illumination at that point. The significant fact, though, is that we can't see this light until it is intercepted by our eyes." This means that unless the observer is looking directly at the light source, he sees only the light retransmitted, or reflected, by surfaces around him. This light is brightness, not illumination.

Accordingly, man interprets what he sees in terms of brightness. Obviously, then, this brightness is not an *absolute* but an *apparent* brightness of object or surface. It may be considerably modified by surrounding objects and surfaces as well as the total brightness of the scene—night or day.

Many of us forget to compensate for this effect when using the camera, for example, and ruin photographs. A great variation in lens opening or shutter speed is required for photographing a model on a grassy knoll as compared with a sandy beach, where overexposure usually prevails. The amount of light may be the same, but the reflectivity of sod is certainly much less than that of sand.

Carried to excess, brightness is glare. There is directed glare from an unshielded light source. There is reflected glare from glossy or shiny surfaces and objects in the environment. Glare interferes with vision and causes eye discomfort. In seeing, the effect of glare is a loss of contrast between detail and background. Contrast is important because the basis for seeing at any level of illumination is reasonable contrast in brightness or hue.

How Much Light

In full daylight, brightness differences of 2 to 4 percent can be discriminated. At dusk, the contrast has to be as much as 60 to 70 percent. This ability to distinguish fine details, or visual acuity, becomes important when reading, say, a traffic sign. Because committees that formulate lighting standards are task-oriented rather than people-oriented, the technical criteria frequently revolve about how high a degree of visual acuity is desirable and therefore how much illumination is necessary to ensure that level.

Are there any absolute criteria of value in designing outdoor lighting? First consider *indoor* lighting. Footcandle levels are based on the amount of illumination required to produce brightness that enables people to see their tasks clearly and comfortably. (A footcandle of illumination falling on a surface with 100 percent reflectance produces a footcandle of brightness.) The criteria for indoor needs relate to definition of task, task difficulty, and degree of required visibility. The illumination required for visibility is related to the size and contrast of the task, as well as its complexity. Therefore there are many variables of problems, which in turn pose many alternatives of solution.

But in discussions of *outdoor* lighting tasks have not been defined. Indeed, a survey of the literature indicates little consensus on the importance of the various factors involved in satisfying visibility requirements. It is not always known precisely how much illumination is required for each different mission. Selection of lighting levels is arbitrary. And artificial-light minimums have been rising as rapidly as the national gross product.

Example: State Street, Chicago. A 1958 merchant-sponsored project featured huge fluorescent fixtures producing 15 footcandles.

Example: City of Chicago. Voters approved a 20-million-dollar bond issue for more lighting to reduce crime. Then 51,000 mercury lights were

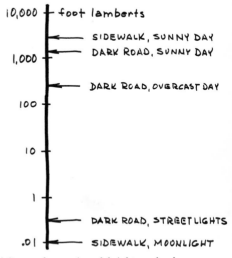

Commonly experienced brightness levels.

installed in 2,300 alley-miles, 1,800 lights on streets which had none, 3,800 additional lights on arterial-street approaches.

Example: New York City spent 65 million dollars through the 1960s to modernize 5,600 miles of streets and 500 miles of park footpaths. An attempt was made to standardize sixty-four different types of installations using 210,000 lamps of varied wattage.

Example: St. Louis in 1964 started a ten-year program to relamp 280 street-miles. Fixtures of 1926 vintage in 10 central business district (CBD)-miles were replaced with luminaires producing 12 foot-candles.

Example: Cedar Rapids, Iowa. Thousand-watt fixtures mounted at 30 feet, each providing 60,500 lumens and yielding 8 footcandles, replaced thirty-five-year-old fixtures in the CBD which had a delivery of 0.25 footcandles from 10,000 to 15,000 lumens light sources.

Example: Appleton, Wisconsin, relighted, changing from 0.8 footcandles to 12 footcandles with Lucalox luminaires 100 feet apart on two sides of street. Time clock turns off one side at midnight. Photocells turn off other side not on clock.

Example: Rockford, Illinois. Twenty square blocks of the central area were relighted to 18 footcandles.

A city whose Downtown has been illuminated at a level of 0.25 footcandles for thirty years may decide to install a new lighting system. But what level will be appropriate for the next twenty or thirty years—7 footcandles, 15 footcandles, 30 footcandles? Is the quantity of the utmost importance? I think not. For the important criterion really is how well the overall lighting system enhances the observer's appreciation of the nighttime city.

Outdoors at night we are constantly scanning our surroundings in order to orient ourselves. But usually there is not a specific viewing task at all. Therefore the primary need to be satisfied is the *comfort* of the viewer and his *pleasure* in seeing the environment.

Lam tells us that visual comfort in lighting has two main determinants, "the brightness ratio and what you are trying to see." This means that people can still walk in comfort and security on a dark night with a level of light which while low illuminates details and makes the objects around us brighter than the sky. We are interested in seeing these objects because they define the environment, and having just enough lighting to make this task easy also makes us more comfortable.

This may be why we are comfortable when viewing a city bathed in 10,000 footcandles of sunlight and yet prone to think a nighttime scene too bright if viewed at 15 footcandles. Perhaps the reason one street may seem too bright and harsh at 15 footcandles is that the adjacent street registers only little better than moonlight, 0.02 footcandles on the sidewalk. When mo-

Expo 67, Montreal. Projection lamps create interesting glow in filament-wound glass tubes and exciting patterns on adjustable plastic reflectors.

torists drive from commercial to residential street or pedestrians walk from space to space, the light they need to see by is affected by the previous brightness level.

The need for lighting must be established before it is designed or engineered. Imaginative and expansive lighting effects can do more than light the way for the observer. The influence of light on the culture and psychology of man is too great for it to be treated mechanically. The plastic value of artificial light should be used to sustain and enhance the imagery of structure and space. This requires a creative plan even more imaginative than the concept of "painting" with light, as in the theater.

Much can be learned from theatrical use of light and color to stimulate or control emotion and give pleasure. But flood-lighting of buildings, like stage lighting, is unidirectional, static, and not the answer. In the theater the audience sits in darkness and looks at the bright action. In the city the

157

audience *is* the action. Spatial needs of the nighttime environment require three-dimensional modeling of the public right-of-way and the people in it. The question is not only how the environment looks but also how the audience of observers looks and feels.

PROGRAMMING LIGHT

What Is the Problem?

Whether a nighttime scene looks bright or dark often depends on where you are. From an airplane the lights of Downtown and even the neighborhoods appear to be brilliant multicolored jewels strewn on the blue-velvet carpet of night. But on the ground and walking the same streets, the space may seem dark, drab, and colorless. Lighting is important for psychological and commercial persuasion—for convincing people that it really is all right to be *here,* for discouraging crime, for encouraging business—and in view of this it ought to be frankly designed more from the commercial and psychological point of view than the technical. Usually the need is to find a way to maximize nighttime use of space. The problem frequently is this: *how can the cost of light be made to buy a nighttime image of suitable consumer appeal?*

With the problem posed in this manner, the designer has more options. He is free to program the need for color, location, and variation in light as well as intensity. He can be more innovative in creating solutions that please people. Although certain features may lead to an increase in total project cost, it is entirely possible that this approach, by extending public usage of facilities, will result in a reduction in cost per participant.

The renewal of large segments of the city and building of new towns, campuses, shopping centers, and airports—these present unrivaled opportunities for character building through nighttime lighting. Each neighborhood in each city will have its own specific needs and problems, but a generalized lighting program might emphasize goals similar to the following:

1. Develop a system which expresses the unique character of the area and the ambitions of its people.

2. Define the organization of streets and circulation.

3. Provide essential information about the immediate area to all users of the public right-of-way.

4. Contribute to the overall orientation of the public in order to enable people to find their way about the city.

5. Achieve synergetic benefits by packaging other subsystems such as communications with lighting for structure and utility sharing.

The analysis of such goals will determine whether 10 footcandles of street lighting is too much or too little for, say, the city core. If the purpose is to emphasize and separate the main shopping street from the surrounding frame, this is not too much. If the goal is to prevent accidents, it may be too much.

Pedestrian Needs

Historically, in addition to crime prevention, the chief justification for public lighting has been to provide enough visual information for pedestrians to use the city at night with safety. Plainly put, at night the artificial-light pattern is the city, shopping center, or campus. When daytime visual cues are absent, the designer must determine the amount and kind of light material necessary to communicate facts to an observer regarding the organization and character of the space.

By this standard, the pedestrian requires far more guidance than he now gets from public lighting. Certain pedestrian points—crosswalks, bus stops, park exits—could be better identified. This cannot be achieved by rote in a mechanical way. Linear patterns of equally spaced light sources of equal

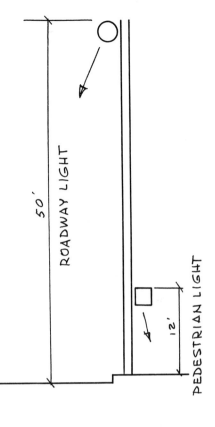

Oakland Mall, California. Cosmetic beautification.

intensity do not provide accents. The designer should analyze the space in terms of user needs and add these personalized improvements at small additional cost. The present monolithic single-purpose lighting system of most cities—high-mounted, roadway-oriented, high-wattage lamps—does not serve the dual needs of pedestrian and motorist. A multipurpose system can be evolved using a variety of lamps and components which will more realistically light city space in all its variations.

In the neighborhoods the pedestrian still requires light to illuminate his path and show obstacles, but his needs are primarily psychological. A sense of security is all-important. Shadowed areas may appear sinister. Whether in a large open space or in a narrow confined passage, there must be enough light to eliminate fear and provide reassurance.

Scale and design of pedestrian lighting are intimately related to human needs and directly influence emotions and actions. Warmth of light and a personalized atmosphere are essential. The use of indirect lighting or possibly low-wattage units closely spaced could be considered.

Formal plazas and courts may require psychological reinforcement of the active communal nature of the concourse or promenade. The basic concept of promoting activity may best be furthered by higher footcandle levels obtained from more frequent spacing of light sources.

Walks and stairs can be delineated with brighter lighting. But obtrusive fixtures or clusters on high stems are not essential. Optically engineered reflectors of hidden light can wash desired areas with light while leaving dramatic contrast in surrounding areas. Localized illumination can accent planter areas. Lighting may be recessed in steps, curbs, or balustrades where deep snow is not a problem.

In parks or on campus walks, the lighting problem is again psychological in nature. Warm accents of very low intensity are needed at close intervals to minimize shadows and therefore provide protection and a feeling of reassurance. Light sources should be low to maintain pedestrian scale. A linear line of light is desirable. However, intersections might have increased wattage for definition. The effect would be one of varying-size pools of light.

Motorist Needs

Roadway-lighting needs are not static. Even a single-purpose expressway has dynamic loading characteristics that change from hour to hour and mile to mile. A lighting system designed yesterday will surely not be adequate throughout its thirty-year life-span. The city is a kaleidoscope of lighting patterns. Design of the system requires analysis of the various land-use interfaces. Clearly the needs of various commercial and residential streets must be defined before performance criteria can be established and, finally,

Harvard Yard, Cambridge, Massachusetts.
Ever-popular scale and shape for pedestrian
precincts; 9 feet high.

Light, garden stairs, Lincoln Center, New York.

Lights, Habitat stairs, Expo 67, Montreal.

fixtures designed or selected. Strangely, this is not usual practice. Expressway lighting, for example, is a common need which seldom receives analysis and solutions according to changing road-use conditions.

The proper lighting of roadways can do much to provide the nighttime driver with visual cues and increase safety. Of especial importance are the entrances and exits onto highways, where consideration should be given to providing transitional lighting. The environmental change may be marked by color and/or intensity change. Doubled or different light sources may be used.

Forests of lampposts presently are used to light complex road junctions, producing a confusing array of light sources. This jumble of lights without clear pattern provides no visual cues, and the road is made hazardous by the great number of massive posts placed so close to the right-of-way. But in Europe, high-mast lighting schemes are being introduced to reduce the number of columns while maintaining good illumination. These are commonsense results of the correct analysis of, say, a cloverleaf as a spatial experience and not merely a node on a linear path.

One such system, supplied by Osram (GEC) Ltd., has been used for the Cumberland Basin Bridges scheme in Bristol. Conventionally about 160 lampposts would have been required. But only thirty masts, each one 82 feet high and equipped with four lanterns housing 1,000 watts of mercury lighting, were installed. The masts are of steel, the lanterns of aluminum. By use of winches (internal in the mast), lantern maintenance can be carried out at ground level.

Reduction of accidents on highways is a dramatic benefit of good lighting but not the only one. When an expressway is properly lighted, the safe driving speed at night can be 10 to 20 miles per hour higher. If the arterial speed limit is raised 15 miles per hour because of improved nighttime conditions, greater utilization of lanes can be achieved and significant savings can accrue in economic value of time saved per vehicle. Highway capacity is also increased by better motorist performance—for example, greater use of passing opportunities, improved utilization of interchanges, reduction in fatigue and tension.

Downtown

When the roadway enters the central business district, a new space is penetrated and new criteria must be established. The need is not just to increase brightness, but rather to create a mood of excitement and gaiety and an identity sufficiently unique to achieve a public response of commercial value.

Congested places of public activity such as downtown shopping or

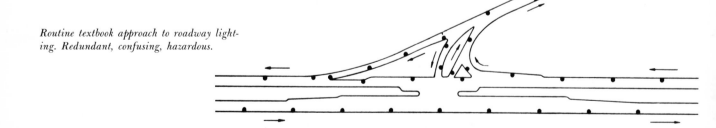

Routine textbook approach to roadway lighting. Redundant, confusing, hazardous.

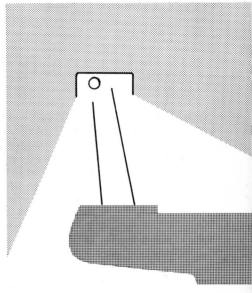

(Above, left) *Fort Washington Highway, Cincinnati, Ohio. Results of textbook approach. Redundant, confusing, hazardous.* (Opposite) *GEC system. English-designed light interchange with light fixtures clustered on four masts.* (Above) *Strip lighting integrated with center-median guardrail or bridge railing, as in San Mateo–Hayward Bridge or La Guardia Airport upper ramp.*

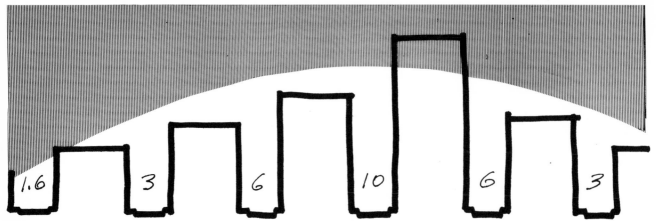

1.6 3 6 10 6 3

The nighttime city highlighted with transition from the 1.6 footcandles of Downtown to 10 footcandles in the Cincinnati core.

"Sun of the Sea," aluminum and glass.

amusement centers require a different design approach with even more emphasis on animation and mood. Characteristics of excitement, gaiety, opulence, and novelty may all have varying application. Very likely a lighting plan of only one brightness level will not be successful; variation is required to heighten the anticipation of the observer and to mark his arrival at the city's core.

At main intersections, changes in lighting can be purposefully and logically introduced. Light sources can be varied in height, color, intensity, or spacing to mark intersections and nodes. Monotony is relieved, identification achieved, and safety enhanced by manipulating light to signal potential danger points. And as the road changes and becomes residential in character, a new analysis is required which differs from that of arterial roads or Downtown.

I applied these principles in Cincinnati "Streetscape." Starting at an existing base level of 0.8 footcandles for the city at large, illumination was increased to 1.6 footcandles in the downtown frame, 2.5 footcandles in the inner ring of streets, 5 footcandles in the center city, and 10 in the city core of twelve blocks.

While those levels are not high by tomorrow's standards or even those of today, the variation provides transition. A balance is achieved between dramatic effects and pushing back the darkness.

The most significant changes and ideas, however, are yet to be tried. This will occur when a city is bold enough to program its downtown lighting for constantly changing kinetic effect. If the goal is truly the stimulation of the observer, then obviously static linear lighting, no matter how bright, is not enough. We should look to a more fluid use of lighting—enlarging, shrinking, twinkling—rather than fixed and constant street sources. There is a potential for instant beauty in urban lighting that can be achieved by projection of optical effects and colors on the public right-of-way and spaces. Lights can be *programmed* to tell time by flashing, the number of flashes corresponding to the hour. And even rhythm can be introduced, through programmed modulation or dimming of supplementary light sources, to create a sense of movement.

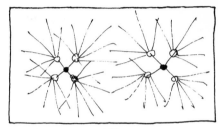

POOR

Parking

Since vehicle lights are directional and not always present, general illumination is required for security and safety in parking lots. Omnidirectional lighting tends to reduce shadows and concealment for vandalism. Center-post systems should be considered. Posts might be located within a distance twice the mounting height from the area perimeter. Post spacing does not normally exceed four times mounting height.

Parking garages present different problems, with consideration required for the effect of simultaneous viewing of interior and exterior. Programming can establish the need for, say, a dual electric system of fluorescent lighting which would give greater intensity during the day to avoid excessive contrast with the open sky.

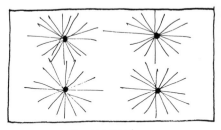

COMMON

DESIGNING THE URBAN LIGHTING PLAN

Scale

Both client and designer of interior space understand that various lighting techniques and tools are necessary to enhance interior space and make it work. Such understanding needs to prevail in relation to exterior space too. In furnishing this space, the creative designer will prepare a schematic concept which utilizes all possible techniques that best satisfy the functional criteria. The need is great. In contrast to the private sector, where the designer controls all building elements, in the public sector lighting is frequently the only means available for expression of the nighttime city.

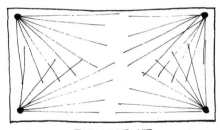

EFFICIENT

One approach would be to develop the design concept and then the fixturing according to a hierarchy of scale. In addition to brightness variation by means of different light sources, variation in mounting height might differentiate the nighttime use of major arteries, second-degree collector streets, commercial streets, residential streets, and parks.

It seems obvious that commercial-size poles and high-wattage lamps should not be used in residential streets. Yet in dozens of American cities old cast-iron low-scale units of pedestrian scale and charm are being replaced by commercial-size fixtures whose uncontrolled beams concentrate glare and high intensities under the pole. In the private sector, developers of housing tracts frequently select oversize commercial fixtures assuming them to be newer and more efficient. Or they may select underscaled mock-colonial gas lamps (electrified) under the assumption these are more esthetic. Clearly not enough emphasis has been placed on variation in mounting height and scale of fixtures to area or mass of buildings as a design factor as important as the luminaire itself.

Siting

Spacing is related directly to mounting height and scale. The present practice is to draft the lighting system by projecting light-distribution patterns on a plan at ground zero. When they overlap, the spacing between units is established. This is essentially a linear process of stringing equidistant light sources along a utility line parallel to a road or path. But this practice does not utilize to best advantage the essential three-dimensional characteristic of light. To do this, intervening space, people, and illuminated objects must be considered as well as the roadway. The designer tied to a post by a utility line is not free, but captive. He lacks the chance for independent design action.

A more satisfactory design approach would be to consider variation in lateral areas as well as make bright the longitudinal spacing along the road. Interesting lateral lighting can be achieved by varying the Illuminating Engineering Society (IES) light-distribution pattern of selected units at nominal cost or by adding supplementary units placed as spurs to the main line of lights. Or better yet, a more versatile and interesting arrangement can be secured through the development of a flexible lighting system whose lamps are variable and adjustable in position rather than fixed.

After preparation of the preliminary plan, locations should be checked against other subsystem plans (communication, traffic, etc.) for possibilities in sharing of structure, conduits, and other facilities.

Lightmarks

Punctuation marks make intelligible a sentence; "lightmarks" identify a space and clarify the confusion of the city. Lightmarks serve more as accents than as sources of illumination. They can denote changes in the spatial use with varying degrees of emphasis. They can serve as nighttime landmarks. Each designer can construct his own design vocabulary of symbols. I suggest only a few possibilities here.

Nodelights   Lights of distinctive color or shape can be repetitively used throughout the city to locate street intersections and guide drivers through them.

Pylons   Structures of great height can identify arterial interchanges by

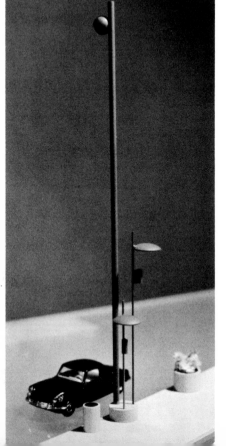

Schematic model of pedestrian and roadway lighting, streetscape program, Cincinnati, Ohio. Adjustable fixtures permit "trimming" the street for variable needs and effects.

166

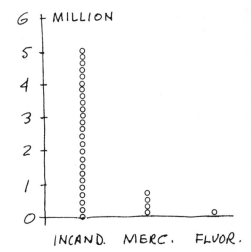

day and support illuminated route markers visible for great distances by night.

Twinning   Like quotation marks, paired lights before and after can set apart a particular area from the great mass of space.

Street-furniture identification   To provide counterpoint to the main lighting scheme, various street-furniture elements can be usefully illuminated. Street signs at intersections could be self-illuminated to advantage; fire-alarm and citizen emergency-reporting telephones should have distinctive lighting.

Directories   Information centers sited at strategic points can display data on large illuminated panels. Transit and street-layout maps can present information to motorists or pedestrians.

Bollards   Selection of light fixtures is not limited to stem-mounted sources. Light at low level, seen only in the immediate area, can define a parking area or special space reserved for pedestrians.

LIGHTING SYSTEM COMPONENTS

Lighting Sources

The terminus of the system, the component in direct relationship to the consumer, is the light source itself. Yet it is the least satisfying element both in daytime appearance and nighttime quality. Unlike the sun and moon, to whose purity and power men respond, artificial light sources are frequently cheapened by excessively styled luminaires and lamp holders.

Most of America is still lighted by products reflecting needs and tastes of thirty years ago. Historically a product attitude has prevailed in a situation where process has been the mode of activity. The designer must now find a way to meet the need of planner, developer, or bureaucrat for an environment which satisfies emerging urban patterns of life.

Let's start with basics. In the choice of a lamp to light the city, it seems reasonable to start with a light source whose makeup as closely as possible approximates natural daylight. Other lamps may be used for accents, special purposes, or supplementary lighting, but the prime goal should be a lighting system which both clarifies the environment and bathes people with light in a pleasant and healthful way. By these criteria the majority of lamps currently favored are inadequate and obsolete.

We know from recent medical research that light affects health. The spectral characteristics of the light source affect certain glands as well as contribute to the seeing process. Natural light containing vitamin D produces direct photobiological effects by skin absorption; it also produces indirect effects upon the neuroendrocrine system by entering the eye.

If we consider afresh what people are going to expect from their public environment in the future, the importance of these phenomena becomes clear. As the trend to urbanization continues and people continue to spend their workdays at indoor tasks, they will want additive light sources that promote health and suntanning at night. As medical knowledge warrants, the lighting industry will be required to provide ultraviolet wavelengths and full-spectrum sources simulating the beneficial effects of natural light.

But what lighting criteria actually prevail now, and what are their results? Go back to Edison's first carbonized-thread lamp. It burned forty hours. The big things then were lamp life and output. These are still the criteria. Incandescent, the most desired and liked source for its warm sunlight-like quality, is rapidly losing ground to more sterile sources less costly to operate. Although American cities are still lighted four-fifths by incandescent sources as compared with one-fifth by mercury-vapor and fluorescent, this ratio applies primarily in residential areas. Because downtown merchants want brighter illumination at low cost, they are given mercury-vapor lamps. Even

Chocolate and silver-foil kisses. Streetlights, Hershey, Pennsylvania.

in neighborhoods, because of fear of crime and vandalism, emphasis on brightness rather than quality prevails.

It remains for the designer, then, to encourage developments which will satisfy all aspects of our changing needs. Selection from existing sources might be based on consideration of the following product characteristics:

Incandescent lamps are a point from which light rays are directed. Objects are accentuated by highlights and shadows. Modeling and texture are revealed. The sparkling quality provides a psychologically satisfying buoyant effect.

Several types offer low initial cost of wiring, installation, and equipment. Axial or standard filament construction in clear or inside-frosted bulbs requires the use of appropriate reflectors or high mounting. White-bowl lamps improve lighting quality by reducing shadows and glare. Street-series lamps are used in systems operating a number of lamps in an electric series connection with a high-voltage source. Light output remains constant. Output is described in lumens rather than wattage, and lamp life is rated at 2,000 hours. Multiple-street lamps are used in systems operating a number of lamps in an electric parallel connection with a standard or low-voltage power source. Light output is indicated in wattage, and lamp life is usually rated at only 1,500 hours.

Quartz-iodine filament tubes are a newer form of incandescent tube typically used in 500-watt or 1,500-watt ratings for floodlighting. They should be considered for other applications as well because of high efficiency, longer lamp life, higher light output throughout lamp life, and overall costs lower than those of conventional bulbs.

Mercury-vapor lamps, like incandescent, are directional and have a sharp sparkling quality. High-intensity mercury lamps trade off a drop in light quality for lower operating and maintenance costs. These lamps have higher initial equipment and installation costs, and glare is difficult to control where low mounting is required.

But lamp life is much longer than that of incandescent lamps. Mercury-vapor lamps furnish up to 2.5 times more light per power consumed than incandescent lamps. Replacement is simple with their screw or plug-in base. Lamps of 400 watts in refracted glassware will produce 20,000 lumens output (such as may be required at nodes or important circulation areas). Lamps of 175 watts in open reflectors or plastic globes can produce 7,700 lumens, a quantity of light more suitable for dormitory and neighborhood areas. Moreover, a lamp rated at 16,000 hours will at the end of 8,000 hours still be producing at 90 percent rated lumen output. However, a ballast or transformer and a constant-current regulator are required. If a ballast is used, choice must be made between internal (transformer base or luminaire) and external location and housing.

Factors to be evaluated in selecting the mercury-vapor lamp as opposed to other sources are desired daytime configuration and installation and maintenance costs. Poor color quality has been a factor in the past, but the color-corrected (phosphorcoated) lamp has eliminated much of the unnatural color distortion of the standard silver-white lamp.

Fluorescent lamps produce lighting that is flat and dull; dark objects in particular do not show up in detail, but are seen only in silhouette. These lamps offer low surface brightness and therefore have particular application where low mounting heights are required. Light can be produced in all sections of the visible spectrum, and designs have improved color characteristics, but the standard tube produces a light deficient in reds and blues which exaggerates blues and greens. Fluorescent is essentially flat in quality because of the nondirectional source.

High-output lamps are used for street lighting. These range from 100 watts or 6,600 lumens to high-intensity 200 watts or 15,000 lumens. The operating cost is low, and the light-producing efficiency is high except in cold weather, when output drops. The tubes have a long-rated life, at 7,500 hours, and require minimal maintenance.

Metal-arc multivapor lamps produce a warm white directional light which is noticeably different from that of the fluorescent or sodium-vapor lamp. A translucent aluminum oxide ceramic tube may be used to activate metal vapors at higher temperatures than previously possible. A 400-watt lamp is rated at 105 lumens per watt, and life expectancy is 6,000 hours. The increased efficiency is achieved without increased operating cost as compared with the mercury-vapor lamp.

Luminaires

The luminaire packages and protects the light source; by night it may also perform some additional function such as modification or control of light.

Although the majority (68 percent) of fixtures are glass-enclosed (23 percent glass open bottom, 2 percent plastic-enclosed, 7 percent other), fixtures come in all sizes and shapes. As the most visible element of the daytime cityscape, they have an importance for imagery that has always been well recognized. The octagonal streetlamps in Trafalgar Square, London, originally were used as lanterns on Admiral Nelson's flagship in the Battle of Trafalgar. Streetlights are still the one element of street furniture which frequently arouses the interest of local groups such as businessmen, who sponsor distinctive designs. The package has become the product, and no shape seems too bizarre. The effect upon the public of these "Mickey Mouse" fixtures, sometimes shocking in their size or novelty, has been startling in intensity. Passions have been aroused. Letters to the editor are written. Street lighting, it seems, has often produced more heat than light. But why not these unique designs?

Some communities are noted for a particular feature which can be characterized or memorialized by a reminiscent or evocative shape. Some business districts may want unique designs which express to the consumer the particular nature and advantages of the area. When repeated in procession down the street, like packages on a shelf, the symbol assumes potent advertising value, presenting and then again presenting the desired image to consumers, local and transient alike.

Like banal supermarket packages, luminaires can also proclaim mediocrity. Murphy's law might be amended to read, "Whenever the wrong catalog design is available, it will be selected." But when the urban designer elects to join the technology team and becomes part of the decision-making process, he has greater and newer means to create a new esthetic. Luminaires and other devices, like landscape and paving materials, should be selected for their contribution to coordinated imagery. Housing developments and commercial areas alike can become a new nighttime experience when the scene is defined by regard for people-seeing rather than merely product-making.

Chapter Eight

People on Wheels

The problem with the automobile is that we haven't yet figured out how to get the mechanical monster into the electronic age. Although planners have been long concerned with the strangling of the urban environment by the network of highways and roads, the tightening process continues.

As the traffic jam on downtown streets, at airports, in factory parking lots, and at shopping centers thickens, so does the density of products used for traffic command, control, and communication. These usurp more and more of the sidewalk and airspace over the public right-of-way.

As long as traffic control is approached on a street-corner-by-street-corner basis rather than as a subsystem of city-wide control, we will have confusion. As long as traffic devices of limited capability are continually added to the already jumbled streetscape, we will have chaos. But when traffic-control components and techniques are better related to users and environmental conditions, as eventually they must be, then we will see a most dramatic improvement in the function and appearance of the urban scene.

SOME PROBLEMS

Congestion

In 1907, the horse-drawn vehicle moved through New York City streets at 11.5 miles per hour. In 1966, the average speed of the horseless carriage was 8.5 miles per hour. Abroad the problem is worse. In London 500,000 cars, 8,000 buses, and 6,000 taxis jam the streets every day; average speeds at peak periods are reduced to 2 miles per hour in, say, Old Kent Road.

Uniform control procedures have been developed and made standard over the years to regulate and speed up use of the road. However, there are 30,000 local highway and traffic agencies around the country, each of which may interpret standards in a different manner. Moreover, the standards are related to available products which were obsolete long ago.

Safety

The railroad is laid on a right-of-way placed so as to avoid crossings. Airplanes are separated from each other and people by altitude. Only the city street has no separation of vehicles and pedestrians.

A variety of techniques, devices, and regulations have developed to separate cars from cars and cars from people. Many of the devices and constructions, such as concrete medians and separators, are more hazardous to the driver than his own unrestricted actions.

Although not commonly recognized as such, traffic signals themselves are one of the most dangerous of road hazards. Many traffic engineers agree that traffic lights actually increase rather than decrease accidents. New York State statistics show that accidents at an intersection increase by 48 percent *after* the installation of a red light. Signals are installed at intersections to establish rights-of-way in order to regulate traffic volume. Like some medicines, this cure has unfortunate side effects. The fact that it causes accidental injury and death in significant numbers indicates that many faulty design and installation practices prevail.

Moreover, these products do not really do the job. As traffic counts increase, the proper and safe flow of vehicles becomes more critical and difficult to achieve. To aid efficient movement of traffic with a minimum of conflicts and delays, more traffic lights are installed. However, much programming of signal changes is static and fixed, frozen by a timing pattern based on previous flow. Therefore additional lights are not completely effective; motorists frequently wait for a red-light change at an empty corner. Studies show that this obsolete technique of traffic control may contribute to inefficient use of existing roadways as well as to a frustrating experience for the driver.

Concrete abutment with caution signal, sign, and light "protecting" trolley stop.

Visual Pollution

These traffic products are also the most ugly, numerous, and large-scale of the many urban furnishings in the visual scene.

Many traffic-control devices derive from railroad signals and look it. Present-day controls are still largely made by railroad-equipment manufacturers with large investments in older plant and technology. Although their engineers have achieved high reliability standards over the years, management has been slow to change from bulky electromechanic devices to small solid-state electronic ones. Established procedures impose standards of weight and mass more suited to the mechanical than the electronic age.

A factor leading to sign-product proliferation is the American custom of prohibitory design as a means of conveying instructions. Every city follows the procedure of posting signs along the curb prohibiting this, prohibiting that:

NO LEFT TURN
NO LITTERING
NO PARKING

The number of signs repeating the same admonishment in one block surpasses all sensible needs, and too many signs can be as dangerous as too

Traffic-control clutter on a campus.

Amherst, New York. If at first you don't succeed, try again, and again, and again. . . .

few. Nests of signs, sometimes as many as four and five on one post, challenge the comprehension ability of the most alert motorist. In Buffalo, New York, there are estimated to be 45,000 traffic signs displayed on light standards and makeshift supports. In a typical year, 1966, the city Bureau of Signs and Meters rehabilitated 5,304 traffic signs, fabricated 6,600 new signs, installed 963 concrete foundations, and erected 852 street-name signs. This pattern exists all over the country. Little Rock, Arkansas, established its own traffic-signing shop; in three years the shop brought some 2,000 old signs up to uniform standard and manufactured more than 13,000 new ones. According to a recent study by the Highway Research Board, in the District of Columbia alone there was an inventory of 34,100 parking signs estimated to carry over 51,000 parking messages.

Redundancy

When three, four, five, or ten traffic signals are required at one intersection to let motorists know who has the right-of-way, then it is clear that something is wrong with the design of the signal, the design of the installation, or the design of the intersection. Perhaps all three.

But this kind of design is deliberate. It results from the theory that communicating a message with more than one sign or signal helps minimize the background "noise" of all the competing stimuli on the urban scene. In other words, redundancy is considered desirable.

Although usual engineering practice tolerates some overdesign as a safety factor, redundancy may cause chaos and confusion in the hands of an unskillful engineer. Further, the acceptance of this theory leads to a hardened position that forecloses a number of other options and makes experimental progress much more difficult.

It has been said often enough that between now and the end of the century we must build as many structures as have been built since colonial times. This is possibly true. But it is an extension of colonial thought to suppose that we must therefore double the number of street products.

The theory of redundancy of products as a substitute for more efficient and economical systems design and siting is increasingly suspect. It is clearly evident that many oversignaled intersections are confusing and hazardous. Cities have begun to reject highway designs that carve choice property from city tax rolls or destroy valuable urban imagery. Similarly it is increasingly necessary that traffic-control products be evaluated by performance criteria which look at results achieved in terms of urban systems design objectives.

SYSTEMS COMPONENTS

One of the advantages of federal expenditure for research and development is that some lessons learned the hard and expensive way in one area have

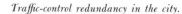

application in another. Progress made in human-engineering research for aerospace has application in public hardware. There should be design fallout.

An area of great potential improvement exists in reanalysis of the problem-solving capability of traffic-control devices. Present information processing and display systems use three components which are very much evident in the environment: detectors, controllers, and signals. How do they work? How can they be improved?

Surveillance: Detectors and Controllers

All-weather, real-time, low-error devices are required to count movements by lane and also to indicate vehicular speed and type. This includes automatic remote reporting. A variety of intelligence can be received, or sensed, by surveillance instruments adapted from military research, such as doppler radar.

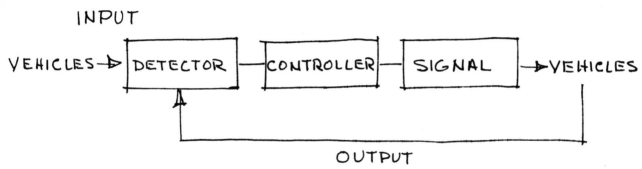

INPUT

VEHICLES → DETECTOR — CONTROLLER — SIGNAL → VEHICLES

OUTPUT

Feedback in a traffic-control system.

Space-age sensing, Victorian ironmongering.

Sensing units such as detectors determine vehicular movement and furnish information input on it to the traffic system. These presence-detection units may be vehicle-actuated by radar, ultrasonic, infrared, pressure-sensitive, magnetic, or other techniques. They may be installed under, over, or at the side of roads, depending upon the principle of operation. To minimize visual pollution, criteria of selection and installation should require miniaturization and integration into existing supports.

After receiving input data on vehicle count from sensing devices, controllers determine appropriate changes in the cycling of the system. They control the movement of vehicles by establishing which particular lane is to go. They may automatically recognize unbalance in opposing traffic and continually adjust the length of go time as the number of vehicles moving on each go signal changes. They can select time intervals as required. They vary the output accordingly in the form of changed signal display. Although the state of the art permits miniaturization of these cast-iron "caskets" which obstruct sidewalks, cities have not yet considered the matter sufficiently important to exert marketplace pressures upon producers.

Vehicle and Pedestrian Signals

The signal head is the display component of the system that the human being must scan. To display a simple go, no-go command, many combinations of colors have been tried:

```
RED     YELLOW   GREEN
GREEN   YELLOW   RED
RED     RED      YELLOW   GREEN
```

The obsolete four-deck configuration was based on the redundancy theory: "two reds are better than one." In delightfully ironic contrast, legal standards for signals have been known to be established and sanctified without benefit of *any* theory. Consider the size and shape of the signal lens. There are two sizes, the newer 12-inch and the traditional 8-inch, which really measures 8⅜ inches. The latter standard was established years ago when a manufacturer who received an order for a signal happened to have available a Corning glass mold measuring 8⅜ inches. Ever since, we have been sitting in our motor cars and staring at *trolley-car* headlamp lenses!

There is a special problem involving pedestrians in all this. Even the most advanced detectors provide data only on presence of vehicles, vehicle volume, and direction of travel. No indication is given of pedestrians. Therefore in areas of heavy foot traffic or at midblock locations manual push buttons may be required as an alternate mode for signal system actuation.

Obviously, more efficient display shapes could be created, given today's awareness of perceptual needs. Possibly a long rectangular display face horizontally mounted across the road would be more effective than vertical stacks of several lenses. Perhaps a round bull's-eye whose single face changed color and symbol would afford more target and recognition value. Further, the frequently employed practice of assembling separate signal decks for each approach should be reexamined. Since the geometry of the intersection does not change, flexibility of arrangement is not always a virtue—particularly if it unnecessarily confuses clarity of statement. The higher cost of additional units is unwarranted. Fixed heads are more compact and less wasteful of space than a cluster of stacks.

Also, serious consideration should be given to the painted color of the signal array. For years New York State practice was to paint the assembly "traffic yellow." Although this color obviously diminished the contrast and therefore legibility of the yellow light, the practice was not changed until recently, when the California practice of using neutral dark gray was adopted, making the signal colors much more visible.

Other factors such as climate and community identity should also be considered in choosing an equipment color, and where particularly difficult solar conditions exist, for example, where the signal faces east or west, the lens may be sun-shielded by a variety of visor shapes. If the surround or background is cluttered, a neutral panel can be applied to blank out the "noise."

As in all systems relationships, the first inquiry must be, "What are the goals? What purpose is the device to serve?" The purpose of pedestrian signals presently is not to expedite the movement of people, but to limit their passage so as to assign more roadbed time to cars.

This goal results in products which minimize social benefit and encourage killing and injuring people. After several pedestrians were killed at my street corner, I timed the pedestrian signal and found it to offer a WALK indication for eleven seconds. Eleven seconds for an elderly person or child—who else walks?—to cross a busy roadway! Clearly these people would be better off

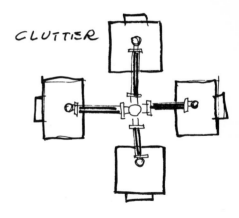

CLUTTER

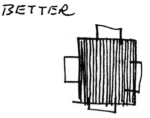

BETTER

Signal arrangements compared in plan view.

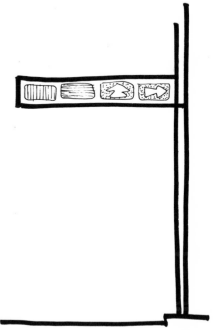

Signal arrangements compared in elevation.
Best.

Century City, California. Sheet-metal surround painted flat dark gray does not compete with signal colors, but separates signals from background.

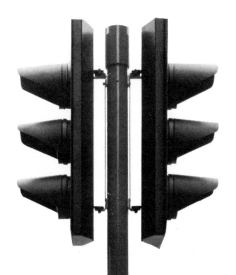

without this product and using their own native judgment in observing traffic conditions.

In addition to reexamination of device function and timing, consideration should be given to the use of symbols rather than legend. To get halfway across a street and see DON'T WALK is confusing and frightening. Far better to use, as in Canada, the sequence of flashing orange-colored hand, constant orange hand, green-colored man walking.

Today more and more cities are reprogramming and computerizing their city-wide traffic-control systems, particularly those controlling movement from high-speed expressways into downtown streets. The future New York City traffic-control system, for example, will include radar sensing of flow at many intersections, with real-time computer adjustment of traffic-light timing within the feedback loop. In Toronto, a large-scale Univac has already been hooked up to take data simultaneously on what ultimately will be a 1,000-intersection system. Detectors report on the passage of all the vehicles

New traffic-signal system for the Ministry of Transport. Molded-plastic signal shells are less obtrusive, costly, heavy.

in the system by scanning them at sixty-four pulses per second, and the data are fed into a central computer. The computer figures out the quantity, speed, and position of the traffic and activates the intersection lights to keep the traffic flowing smoothly.

Signaling systems controlled from a central point are also feasible when the mode of traffic detection is closed-circuit television. Cameras furnishing visual measurements that are interpreted by trained observers are a convenient and economical method of controlling a small system. These control systems are in use at military installations, parking garages, and central business districts. One large installation at Sydney, Australia, employs twelve 16-millimeter TV cameras, remotely controlled from the traffic-control center. Observers, using visual data from the cameras, may vary any established pattern of control. They select appropriate prepared programs for insertion into central control equipment. The programs specify the selection and arrangement of signal time intervals.

These innovative systems configurations will require sophisticated components. Some are already within the state of the art; others are yet to be designed; in each case better rapport must be achieved between people and signals. In the accomplishment, an unparalleled opportunity also exists for improved community pride and identity. This is achieved through consumer-oriented design. Shape that instills confidence. Color that promotes safety. Typeface and graphics that imply precision. Materials that demonstrate awareness. Visibility of message that demonstrates regard for the consumer. Components and installation that work together as coordinated units to demonstrate a feeling of municipal concern for the pedestrian and reassure him. In short, the design must involve the driver or pedestrian in a favorable way and make him want to cooperate.

SIGNS

Legend versus Symbol

At the moment, the city contains a big heap of signs dumped down in a most monotonous and dreary way. The planner-designer, through the technique of system design, must sort out the heap and give it order, pattern, and meaning.

Traffic-sign shapes, colors, symbols, lettering, etc., have been the subject of much research and discussion and many international meetings. The systems most used originated in the United Nations World Conference on Road and Motor Transport held in Geneva in 1949. This proposed a protocol on road signs and signals which could be adopted by those countries wishing to do so pending establishment of a worldwide system. The protocol sign

Experimental cellular traffic signal.

Swiss Pavilion, Lausanne Fair. Protocol sign and symbol exhibit.

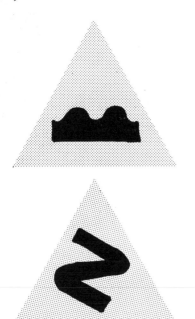

Pictorial symbols for uneven pavement and curve, first conventionalized in Paris, 1926.

system has since been adopted by approximately thirty countries, including most of Europe. The United States and the United Kingdom have not adopted the protocol.

After the 1949 Geneva conference, a group of six experts drawn from six countries, including the United States, attempted to devise a system acceptable to both the New World and the Old. This resulted in a United Nations Draft Convention in 1953. This also has not been accepted in the United States.

In England, the Anderson Committee Final Report of 1960 reflected the work of a professional designer, Jock Kinneir of London. For the first time anywhere "esthetic" and "amenity" considerations were stressed. A major change was adoption of an alphabet of initial capitals, with lowercase designed by Kinneir. Kinneir also developed arrows, which he further refined in the Worboys Committee Report, 1963.

The difference between United States and protocol signs is that the former use mainly words and the latter rely to a great extent on symbols only. United Kingdom practice is to use both symbols and words. In Canada more than 75 percent of the regulatory signs contained in the *Manual on Uniform Traffic Control* were symbolized to minimize the dual-language problem. The *United States Manual on Uniform Traffic Control Devices* is in process of major revision. The "Joint Committee" considered a wider adoption of symbols in preference to word messages as an important step toward greater safety and facilitation of traffic movement and control. In 1969, the Committee approved the use of over thirty symbols standardized by the United Nations, Vienna, 1968 Convention on Road Signs and Symbols.

The systems designer must decide the degree of abstraction to use in signing. There are three general approaches corresponding to three kinds of signs:

> Ionic—A sign which has resemblances to things it stands for (picture)
> Symbolic—A sign which uses abstracted devices (arrow)
> Alphabetical—A sign which uses letters or typography

The dual approach, a common procedure, is questionable since it promotes confusion and reduces message comprehension. The avoidance of use of words with symbols has the advantage that bigger letter forms or symbols, one or the other, can be used without increasing sign size.

The Message

Messages inform us and demand action. The designer must decide when communication with the driver is necessary to aid the safe and orderly movement of traffic. Information must be made apparent on special regulations which apply to specific places under specific conditions. The driver must be warned about hazards which are not self-evident.

Uniformity and consistency of application, standardization of design, and legibility are essential to safe and efficient traffic control. Various criteria for the alphabet, legend, size, and placement of signs are set forth in regulations of state traffic commissions. Within the traffic-communications vocabulary, however, value judgments must still be made. Needs must be determined. Appropriate installations must be designed and sited. The principal criterion should be clarity of command. If the system is poorly designed with frequent and confusing commands, people will ignore or unknowingly violate these orders.

The driver may be warned or directed to take some specific action by a number of instrumentalities classified as regulatory or warning.

Regulatory signs give the driver notice of city traffic laws or regulations that apply to a given place or time. They may be mandatory (do!), such as STOP or SQUEEZE LEFT. Or they may be prohibitory (do not!), such as NO PARKING or DO NOT ENTER.

Warning signs alert the driver to potentially hazardous conditions. Most of these signs reflect road conditions, such as a curve or bump, and have little urban use. However, warning signs whose need arises from the presence of other people, such as schoolchildren, are frequently seen.

United Kingdom traffic-sign alphabet.

Geneva, 1931

Geneva, 1949

Anderson Committee, 1960

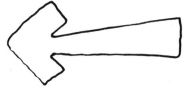

Worboys Committee, 1963

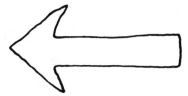

State Traffic Commission

Classic design for road marker which pre-dates Swiss system for organization of many bits of information, Illinois Division of Highways, 1925.

Shape

Clear distinction between regulatory or warning signs and those of guidance or orientation is necessary. The former require action—observance of a regulation or especially careful driving. The latter require no action; the signs are posed as an aid. This distinction in sign media may be achieved by shape, color, and/or message.

As a visual aid to recognition, shapes of signs have been coded to the sign vocabulary. The following shapes have a uniform meaning in all states:

> Octagon—STOP
> Equilateral Triangle (one point down)—YIELD
> Round—RAILROAD CROSSING
> Diamond—Hazard warning
> Rectangular (long dimension vertical)—Regulatory
> Rectangular (long dimension horizontal)—Guide

The full potential of shape as a recognition symbol has not yet been realized. A recent CBS TV presentation of the National Drivers Test revealed that only 25 percent of a national sampling of drivers scored a good or excellent rating. The majority of drivers even failed to identify an octagonal shape as a stop sign. The difficulty may be found to be that geometric sign shapes have been chosen by engineers without adequate regard for perception abilities of people. The United States shapes (and color and messages) may not be as successful as the protocol shapes and symbols. It is likely that no amount of redundancy will offset an inherently faulty premise.

Color

As a further aid to recognition, color coding has been standardized in an attempt to reinforce sign meaning. The following colors have a uniform meaning in all states:

> red, white legend—STOP
> yellow, black legend—Warning messages
> yellow, black legend—YIELD
> white, black legend—Regulatory messages

Current practice tends to reflectorization of almost all signs with reflective materials and delineators. As an alternative, signs may be self-illuminated in color.

MARKINGS

Under mandates of state traffic commissions all cities provide certain information to motorists by use of markings on the roadway. In 1966, the Buffalo, New York, Bureau of Signs and Meters logged 1.5 million linear feet of center and land markings—about 300 miles, covering less than half of the city's

650 miles of streets. The bureau also installed 17,492 feet of crosswalk markings, or about 3.5 miles.

In Little Rock, Arkansas, traffic-paint consumption recently spurted from 150 to 2,000 gallons per year. This provides 200 miles of center and land striping and 600 pedestrian crosswalks. Automated striping machines are now used which, by spraying preheated paint followed by reflective beads, eliminate the manual placement and removal of line-protective cones and thereby reduce costs from 7 to 3.5 cents per linear foot.

These painted lines or graphics on a two-dimensional surface can contribute to the look of the urban fabric. Correctly used, they can order and regulate traffic with a minimum of aboveground clutter of signing and signals. They can convey certain types of information without diverting the driver's attention from the roadway. Design application does, however, require consideration of snow or rain obliteration.

Color

Color codings are now used for pavement markings to signify meaning:

> white—aid to lane definition
> yellow—mandatory no passing or barrier definition

But other colors can also be used to provide a sense of identity to certain districts, such as Downtown, or even to encircle areas of historical heritage and significance.

Color should also be considered as a functional tool for simplifying night driving. Recent experiments reported by the Eno Foundation for Highway Traffic Control suggest the desirability of treating roadway surfaces with a reflective color to provide information. All roadway elements such as lanes, signs, and dividers having a common purpose could be treated in the same color. Blue has not been used for any major highway-traffic function and could be used as the identifying color. This technique could have application where velocities must change, as at arterial intersections with residential streets.

Even greater results can be achieved when texture is used in addition to color. Imbedded aggregates or applied materials can furnish the driver information by feel and sound as well as sight. Three-dimensional surfaces in combination with more advanced visual graphic designs can promote safer and more efficient traffic operations.

SITING

Goggled and gauntleted, sitting high on his horseless carriage, the early driver needed his signs high. Seventy years later the height hasn't changed. Most vertical signal decks are supported over the road, with at least 15 feet

Church Street project. Color-coded traffic signs relate to light standards.

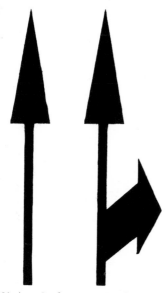

*United Nations Conference on Road Traffic,
Vienna, December, 1968. Pavement can
convey information. Arrow markings in
perspective indicate both the direction
straight ahead and a turn.*

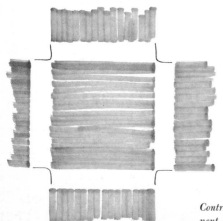

clearance over state highways. Yet the driver needs them lower. His sports-car windshield restricts upward vision from his bucket seat, and he can't see. When stopped for a light, he must crane his head to watch signals, their color is obscured by the sun, swaying from span wires strung between grossly overstated poles.

Clearly, new techniques for siting and support of signs and signals are essential. The most obvious refinements would seem to be integration of the information system into the support system so as to provide a more disciplined presentation at a more useful position relative to the driver.

The layout of sign and signal distribution is still very much an art. Inexpressive and contradictory signs hinder rather than help traffic flow, and may create a hazard. Certainly they create visual clutter. Traffic-control installation plans should be designed for the environment and require the engineer or designer imaginatively to sketch the system configuration in bold strokes, pick the proper products, and put them in the right place. Such a plan will be sensitive to the landscape, respect it, and contribute to the environmental imagery.

*Contrasting paving materials provide perma-
nent pedestrian lanes at street intersection.*

When People Need to Know or Talk

The old neighborhood was a close-knit unit of social relationships and personal contact. When you wanted information on how to get to such and such street, someone was there to tell you. When danger threatened, the group protected its own, or you could run to the corner and call a policeman.

Now there are more people, but there is less assistance. The megastructured city has become depersonalized. With everyone whizzing by on wheels, person-to-person talk is difficult. But more cars produce more accidents or mechanical breakdowns. More aging buildings multiply fire-protection needs. More crime and vandalism on the streets multiply citizen alarm needs.

Under normal circumstances, there is more social and business talk too. Today's teen-ager and businessman alike are affluent and want to have a great deal of communication. Much of this is impulse telephoning in public spaces. Adequate facilities must be provided.

Additionally, in an age of unparalleled literacy, the printed word has less value. An aware population is less responsive to the traditional communications techniques of the municipal establishment. Public signing telling people where to deposit trash, when to stop or go, where to park, is becoming less effective.

The public does want more information: "Where am I? Where do I want to go? How do I get there?" But when the city increases the sign inventory, city streets get more cluttered, and response to the chaotic stimuli diminishes. New information-display techniques of greater clarity and message-carrying capacity are required.

Successful meeting of all these needs can only be accomplished by employing a comprehensive public communications plan utilizing all appropriate media and carefully integrating them with other street facilities. This will also result in an enhanced imagery: in becoming a controlled element of the urban fabric, signage can make a positive contribution to community identity.

PERSON TO PERSON
Public Telephone

People want to talk—they will pay for use of a telephone and even stand and wait in line for the privilege. For example, recent New York Telephone Company studies at the State University of New York at Buffalo campus showed high utilization rates at the Student Union. Twenty-six thousand persons a day entered and left. They were served by only sixteen telephone booths inside, none outside. Lines of waiting patrons were the rule rather than exception.

This small talk adds up to big money. Coin-operated telephones are subject to tariff regulation and are usually known as Public Commission Paying Telephones. This means that the telephone is a vending machine which makes money for the property owner. There are 1,363,000 public booths in the United States, and they are under constant development and redesign for greater consumer satisfaction and better appearance. Changes are also made to incorporate contemporary materials offering improved maintenance and resistance to vandalism.

As a machine selling talk and performing a social need, the public telephone instrument can and should be packaged to contain the necessary components plus optional features geared to the functional, esthetic, and severity-of-use needs of the location. The package may be a complete booth shelter, or it may be a protective and acoustic screen enclosing various components.

Operating components have been engineered for flexibility of installation in a variety of assemblages. Packages can be designed to be used individually or grouped in modular multiples. The designer can choose from a great variety of enclosures or booths, making possible the reinforcement of the particular urban character. The selected configuration can thus make a significant cost-free contribution to imagery and identity.

Distinctive packages can be achieved without complete enclosure of components. In fact, the trend now is to phase out exterior use of the familiar square booth with folding door and even newer models with curved tempered glass, because enclosures present many problems when used outside. Maintenance costs are high. It is difficult to keep booths clean and free of snow, ice, or litter. Booths afford shelter for immoral activities. Booths encourage vandalism, such as cutting of receiver cords and removal of phone housings. Observation of coin-box pilferage is difficult. Above all, telephone booths occupy too much space on the public sidewalk, particularly when used in multiples.

One outdoor model without enclosure, designed by the Bell System with assistance by industrial design consultant Henry Dreyfuss and called "versatel shelves," resulted from a systems approach to solving these problems. Ver-

Familiar orange roof extends corporate image to public telephone.

Dynamic form identifies public telephone at Expo 67, Montreal.

satel shelves have been designed with a pie-shaped configuration (45 degrees) for greater versatility in installation. Up to four units can be arranged kiosk fashion around one post in a space 2 feet 6 inches square, the space required for a single full-size telephone booth. Wiring is concealed in the aluminum-closed structural-steel angle post. Capital requirements and leasing costs are lower. Units can be walk-up types or mounted lower for drive-up. An aluminum sandwich canopy overhangs the walk-up model, providing partial weather protection and additional sound insulation. (This is not necessary or desirable on the drive-up model.) Materials are smooth-surfaced; they clean easily and resist defacing. The stainless-steel coin-collector unit has a redesigned internal mechanism which is almost completely vandal-proof, including those who use cherry-bomb explosives, and the phone cable is steel-covered.

Phone-shelf units such as these can be integrated with other street furniture or into convenience centers such as bus shelters. They are a successful example of urban furnishings that are derived from analysis of environmental and functional needs.

Several factors are considered in deciding on whether or not to provide public telephone facilities and the number of units to be provided. The potential revenue produced by public telephones must be weighed against installation costs tempered by the public convenience factor. Exterior telephones in remote locations require costly trenching and long runs of service and electric cable. Exterior telephones are used less under conditions of cold or inclement weather. Good visibility is required for more frequent use and less vandalism. But more and more frequently the decision is made to install public telephones in all but the most formal outdoor public spaces.

Since all wiring should be underground, one of the important considerations in siting becomes the feed system. Planning for telephone lines should be done in context with other electric service and adjacent utilities. Sharing of costs of trenching and paving by all systems reduces installation costs.

HELP!

Fire

Turning in an alarm by running to the nearest fire-alarm box and pulling the handle is the oldest automated way for a public-spirited person to notify the authorities of a fire. It is also a current mode of leisure-time activity for those who like to play machines and hear fire bells and sirens. In 1967 alone, 48,000 false alarms were turned in in metropolitan New York, and 3,000 alarms were pulled during a seven-hour student rebellion in Paris. In Buffalo, the 1967 total of 3,400 jumped to 5,200 one year later and cost over $100 for each false alarm response.

Bell Telephone Laboratories. Four freestanding telephone modules interfaced to stanchion.

F Street Mall, Washington, D.C.

Fire-alarm equipment is nondiscriminating, single-channel, and without feedback. Whether false or not, the alarm is conveyed in the following manner. Any number of input devices—manually operated pull boxes, automatic sprinklers or fire detectors—can initiate a telegraph signal. The message provided by the signal box is single-purpose (fire protection) and coded (automatic identification of location). The signal is received by a master fire-alarm box, which automatically transmits it directly to the fire department for response to the emergency.

All this equipment is usually not leased as are telephones, but city-owned and -maintained. The location of input stations (fire-alarm boxes) along the public right-of-way is rather arbitrary and based on the estimated number of units required to minimize elapsed reporting time. Cincinnati, for example, has 1,549 fire-alarm terminal heads, using 5,880 conductor-miles of underground and aerial cable.

The tendency now is to use fewer boxes in residential areas, since most fire reporting is by private telephone. But in public areas boxes should be located in convenient and accessible positions of high visibility and left unlocked. For protection of major buildings they should be within line of sight of main exits. In order to reduce the fire hazard to circuit wires, mounting should be freestanding with all wires underground, rather than by attachment to a building.

Although sometimes touted as a piece of Americana, the Victorian alarm box never really aroused much esteem or nostalgia, and remains, simply, some archaic-looking junk on an ornate pedestal. In fact its appearance seems to invite ridicule and vandalism. The legend on many a box instructs the reader to BREAK GLASS. Youngsters do. The door cavities are filled with trash and glass shards. Jagged edges await the wrist veins of any citizen rash enough to reach into the box for the alarm handle during an emergency.

Ironically, this archaic appearance results not from happenstance, but by deliberate design. Although an inner stainless-steel or aluminum box houses electric circuits, the industry has tended to perpetuate the "cottage shape." The rationale for housing automation within an old-fashioned "cottage" is the very incongruity of appearance. The assumption is made that an archaic identity of such strangeness will aid public recognition of the device. Also, the past practice of painting the outer shell "signal red" for greater visibility has been continued. This simplistic practice requires reexamination. Very likely recognition ,and identity will be better secured by contrast of color and pattern than by uniformity.

The fire-alarm box really should be eliminated by merging its function into the emergency telephone system, but at the very least the environmental designer can effect considerable visual improvement in its siting and method of support. The typical cast-iron pedestal can frequently be deleted by uti-

lizing an existing nearby support in a multipurpose systems-sharing capacity. The multipurpose post could be given visual prominence by means of dynamic striping or color patterns. And the potential of nighttime marker lights should be exploited in shape, placement, or color.

In short, since by definition the fire alarm must be both accessible and properly used, design improvement in shape, color, and mounting is needed to promote recognition characteristics and respectful acceptance by the public.

Emergency-reporting Telephone System

Back in the days of the foot patrolman, a locked iron cabinet containing a telephone was essential for his emergency use and routine check-in. Then the "flatfoot" was made more mobile with wheels and equipped with sophisticated two-way radio which diminished the importance of the police call box as a communications tool. Now there is renewed interest in the telephone call box, which permits police or private citizens to report emergencies of any kind by voice transmission.

Although they have only recently been made available, there are already more than 200 public emergency systems leased from local telephone companies in the United States. Buffalo, New York, as a typical example, installed 467 units in 1967. Each is pedestal-mounted and, although the support is sometimes shared with a fire-alarm box, always has its own circuit. Unfortunately, little public use is made of these emergency telephones even though they are left unlocked, perhaps because the marking POLICE on the instrument conveys the notion they are locked or for police use only. Much more effective utilization would be made if the instrument were designed and identified as a public EMERGENCY system.

The great potential of the emergency telephone system for assuming new tasks is exemplified by new applications such as trouble reporting along expressways. Example: emergency telephones located at half-mile intervals along Interstate 87 (Albany, New York) reduce the labor costs of twenty-four-hour police or service-vehicle patrol.

Community Emergency Communications Center

The most efficient and economical way to receive such telephone input may be to establish a central communications center. In such an urban protection office an illuminated panelboard could serve as combined terminal point, recording instrument, and processing station for all low-voltage alarm devices and radio and telephone emergency communications. Through a console appropriately located in the dispatchers' center, incoming calls could be relayed to the appropriate local fire station, police station, or hospital or ambulance service. This office should be manned twenty-four hours a day and incorporate a "dead-man feature," whereby in case of lack of response to an alarm signal, the alarm would be "remoted" to the nearest fire or police station.

The planner of space, facilities, and services is necessarily involved in communications systems decision making. Careful design and location of exterior equipments should produce more useful communications systems featuring components better adapted to user needs. In fact, in view of the urgent need for improved communications between the public and the authorities, it seems reasonable to introduce use of picture phones. Such image-viewing equipment has been demonstrated frequently by the telephone companies. Technically, service could be made available now over existing circuits simply by modifying telephone switching equipment. Functionally, the initial equipment could be simplified by using fixed camera focus and making the viewing screen available only at the receiving switchboard. The system capability could be extended by the addition of picture-taking capability to the viewing camera, which might reduce the incidence of false-alarm reporting.

PUBLIC SIGNS

Public Nuisance

Ugly, confusing, obsolete public signing has been fodder for years for funny-paper jokes, satirical magazine covers, and serious editorials, yet change in traffic regulation, parking signing, transit information, and route marking is frustratingly slow. Even though simple low-cost improvements could have significant favorable impact on the public, meaningful experiments are rare.

The esthetic sign designs shown each year in graphics books almost invariably are product solutions to private building-identification needs and seldom information systems solutions to public signing needs. Such typographical niceties, no matter how handsome and delicious, do not make the city more viable or intelligible. A more organized wide-scope approach is required by bureaucracy and industry. In a nation of drivers most of us get lost: "What place is this? Where am I going? How do I get there?" The problem: too many places to go, too many ways to get there, too many people, not enough time, too many signs to look at. The sign has replaced the cop at the corner but does not serve as well. The sign remains silent and static and does not solve our problem. Public signing is not an infor-

Primitive but effective sign matrix.

197

mation system; it is a lash-up grown by accretion. Monostructural systems must take the place of discrete elements.

The Black-Box Bit

The sign painter has outlasted the lamplighter, but is on the way out. Existing sign techniques are inadequate in two major respects: not enough information is given, and there are too many signs for comprehension. Thus the message capacity of conventional signs is limited at a time when information needs increase.

For a time the designer's hope was symbolization. The Brookfield Zoo in Illinois pioneered the use of informal cutout animal symbols instead of complex legends. The Maryvale Shopping Center in Phoenix adopted turtles and alligators five times larger to distinguish zones in the parking lot. Now the designer of every outdoor spectacle feels impelled to use abstract pictographs rather than message sets.

These can be helpful; they may also create greater confusion in understanding than a simple legend. Better comprehension will develop from use of electronic media to meet circulation and information needs. Automated displays offer greater potential for leading one through the expressway maze, along the appropriate arterial, thence to the neighborhood, and finally to the desired local street and parking place.

These information channels are being tried. The Federal Highway Administration, for example, is experimenting with induction radio, triggered prerecorded audio messages, and visual displays on the vehicle controlled by external signals. And considerable potential for information presentation exists in the new science of holography based on optics.

Whatever the media selected, it now seems possible to look at men and automatic machines in interrelationship as information processing systems. In designing such a man-machine configuration, there might be three components:

> An input—The selection of a particular message at a given place or moment in time
>
> A process—The addition of this message to all previous messages that have been selected
>
> An output—a sequential selection of yes or no, go or no go, that is unique

Clearly the operational success of such a system depends on programming and translating data into inputs (language) which are acceptable and meaningful to the processor (human being or machine) and which can reasonably be transformed into useful output (action result). The public agency (transmitter) has a number of purposeful messages to be conveyed or communicated through media (carriers). These messages must first be encoded in a form the human observer (receiver) can understand.

"TURN ME ON" _____

*HAMLET*_____*"to be or not to be"*

*COMPUTER LANGUAGE*_____0—1

*COMIC BOOK*_____

*ARISTOTLE*_____either—or

*BIOLOGY*_____

*LIGHT GLOBE*_____

*SILVER CHLORIDE ON FILM*_

*AVIATION*_____flaps up—flaps down

*ASTRONAUTS*_____go—no go

*CRAP TABLE*_____come—no come

*CHARTIST*_____x, y

*CHESS*_____P-K4, P-Q3

It's a Barnum and Binary World
Just as ideatic as it can be,
But it would only be make-believe
If it wasn't for you and me.

Such messages must be uniformly displayed throughout the city. Messages should be simplified. Parking information, for example, must be presented on a city-block basis rather than store-frontage or foot-by-foot basis. Similar instructions must not be conveyed by different legends. The reinforcement techniques of classical psychology apply: if we wish uniform response, we must apply identical stimulus. Also the configuration of a word, or its "gestalt strength," plays an important part in perception. As in the new mathematics, we must deal with "sets" of symbols or images. We must recognize group effects. The format, or man-machine language, should be of wide application and adaptability that best satisfies human-component needs. The criteria of evaluation is not merely legibility, but *digestibility*.

To read these messages, the brain uses only dots, the number of which per second conveys all information. This is called "pulse-frequency modulation." It is the precursor of, and in many ways resembles, the work computing machines do with electric impulses, positive or negative. The physical world seems to be a yes-no universe. In practical terms messages can be a structured sequence of the dot-and-dash telegraph key, the on-off traffic light, the hole or no hole in a parking-lot pass card. Clearly, the simpler the message within a structure of yes-no choices, the better.

Pictographs, Tokyo Olympics, 1964. The name of the game is pictograph. How many can you identify?

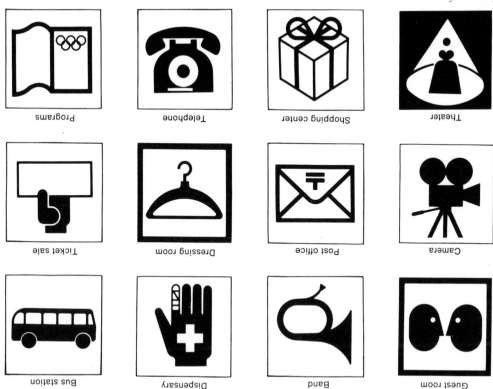

Programs

Telephone

Shopping center

Theater

Ticket sale

Dressing room

Post office

Camera

Bus station

Dispensary

Band

Guest room

Czech Pavilion, Expo 67, Montreal. Push-pull, on-off, variable-media matrix.

An essential component of the information system configuration is the message carrier. The carrier channel for a message need not be a conventional sign panel, but can be streets, curbs, walls, the sky. Whatever the choice, it is desirable that the display be capable of organizing a number of messages. In fact the most economical, space-saving, and versatile carriers will likely be those matrices that are variable and multichannel.

Program Elements

The greatest information systems successes to date have been in transportation, where the professional designer has sometimes worked for an aware public agency willing and able to implement the facility information system. The Montreal subway and several airports in America and abroad exemplify the results to be achieved when users' information needs are considered throughout the program planning and construction and not merely stuck on after the facility is complete. Such successful results with complex transportation facilities are almost invariably the product of disciplined design and management procedures.

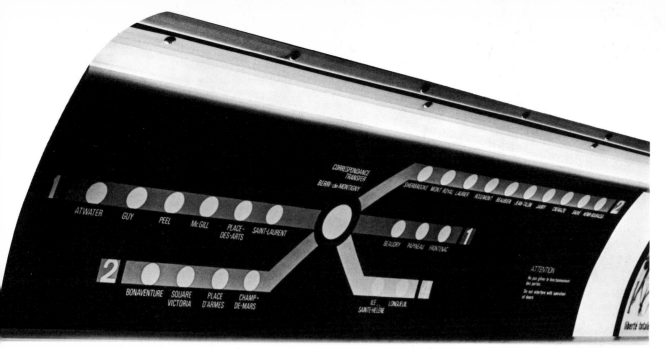

Map, Montreal subway.

West London Air Terminal.

not

When planning the information system for an airport, campus, shopping center, or entire city, four steps must be taken prior to hardware development: problem formulation, data collection, data analysis, design solution. To take these steps properly requires preparation of documents on the following:

Schematic Concept   The appropriate information scheme which best meets the unique communications requirements is visualized and presented in context with the specific environment.

Siting Plan and Schedule   The availability and sequence of information to the observer are shown on site drawings. All information, orientation, and control elements for motorist and pedestrian are precisely defined, located, and keyed to a list of carefully considered and authorized legends.

Component Specifications   The procurement drawings and descriptions of all elements which comprise the information-display system are gathered together. Included are specifications for panels, supports, typography, color, and other standardized components.

Sign Standards   A manual detailing the operating procedures and standards mandatory with administrative and shop personnel for consistent application of the system is prepared. This maintains the integrity of the original concept and assures uniform solutions.

SIGN SYSTEM COMPONENTS

Surround

The sign painter's period being past, the designer is less and less concerned with the gestural sign shape or idiosyncrasy of typography and more and more with the ordering device. This tends to be composed of panel modules which can be assembled in varying combinations and organized and positioned by a support matrix.

Whatever its form, the device derives from societal behavior and the industrial process. The surface of the data-display panel should be made uniform and innocuous. Because people are under continuous bombardment of stimuli, designers must eliminate unnecessary background or extraneous conditions detrimental to the central purpose. The designer first determines what is most relevant, then screens out the background "visual noise" that degrades the signal and destroys message comprehension.

In addition, the display system itself should have inherent flexibility, for change and expansion. It is a good rule not to chisel a name on a building. Nothing is permanent, not even a bank name or a college hall or a one-way-street designation.

And finally, the matrix system with plug-in panels imposes discipline

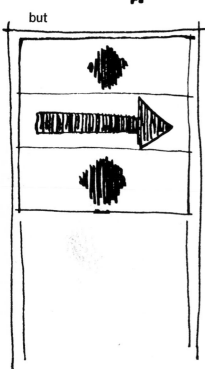

but

where a number of competing messages must be accommodated simultaneously in a limited space. Such a system can tolerate and even enhance differentiation of message between, say, traffic-control and parking information subsystems, by use of controlled family relationships of position, size, color, or texture. Such a family of color relationships for road signs was successfully developed by Jock Kinneir, consultant designer to the Road Research Laboratory in England. The panel color code was:

Motorways	Blue
A Through Routes	Green
B Routes	White
Local Streets	White with Blue Border

Alphabet

When considering legibility, other aspects besides content are concerned. Once the need for comprehensibility of message has been satisfied, the selection of typography for better legibility begins. Here size and shape of letter form, line width, and spacing between lines are involved. Beyond legibility, enhancement of the environment or of community identity partly depends upon choice of alphabet as well as development of sign surround and support. The letter form becomes part of the urban design vocabulary.

A readily available typeface should be selected or modified for standardized use for all city needs. Since different departments have different tasks requiring different emphasis, an alphabet offering a family of options (bold, italic, regular) may be advisable.

The technique of graphic design has been detailed in other books, but it might well be noted here that, as in corporate identity programs, the designer's choice of typeface is instrumental in expressing the public posture of the sponsoring agency. The selected alphabet can make the city or department appear naïve or knowledgeable, traditional or progressive, pompous or helpful.

Linear lettering casts linear shadows over linear wall pattern. Unreadable moiré.

Example: Parking Garage

Task: Develop a guidance system for staff and visitors using the parking facility of the Downstate Medical Center, State University of New York. The structure contains nine levels, none of which are horizontal. The site is in Brooklyn, New York.

Problem: Two parts: First, the facility has a confusingly great number of entrances, some restricted to staff. Second, the constant change of floor levels makes it difficult for a user to find his parked vehicle.

Analysis: First, it is necessary to provide identification of entrances and direction of travel—up and down, in and out. Second, there must be a constant visual cue to user's elevation.

Synthesis: Develop a concept that provides orientation information to user in four modes:

1. Legend coding of entrances
2. Numerical coding of floor levels
3. Color coding of floor levels
4. Pictorial presentation of user elevation above or below grade by means of "thermometer" concept

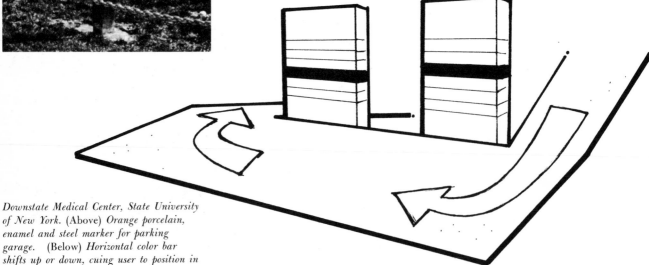

Downstate Medical Center, State University of New York. (Above) *Orange porcelain, enamel and steel marker for parking garage.* (Below) *Horizontal color bar shifts up or down, cuing user to position in parking garage.*

Chapter Ten

Good Housekeeping and the Good Life

Yesterday's luxury is today's necessity. The sparse rigors of Puritan living have long since lost attraction or even justification in an economy capable of producing endless conveniences and comforts.

Technology and industry have made available to the average homeowner a host of laborsaving appliances and leisure-enjoyment equipments. The public environment is an extension of the consumer's home and other private spaces. The standards of one must echo the standards of the other. Is the public willing to leave the climate-controlled environment of home or office to stand on a cold, wet street and wait for a bus? Failure to provide ordinary convenience has contributed to poor acceptance and economic failure of many mass-transportation systems. So it is with many aspects of our graceless cities.

Designers and industry have the challenge and opportunity to create new services and machines of attractive visual character that will make the city more pleasurable and habitable. What is required is the imaginative analysis of both environmental needs and peoples' wants, then their design articulation.

As Halprin pointed out, "kiosk" comes from the old Turkish word "kiūsch" and means "pavilion." The term and use have crept into our vernacular, and we tend to think favorably of the handsome Parisian structures covered with colorful collage.

Kiosks are particularly well suited to the leisurely European scene of plazas, open spaces, and broad walks, but have not transplanted well to the hustle-bustle of contemporary America. Still, street shelters are needed. They are needed not only as public bulletin board, street directory, newsstand, post office, or whatever, but also as dynamic punctuation and relief from the gray monotony of the streetscape. And since visibility to attract users and addition of color and gaiety to the street are compatible, clearly they should be designed with a sense of drama and flair.

Microarchitecture frequently produces more clutter than imagery.

Santa Monica Mall, California.

Bus Shelters

Transit companies often are still privately owned, but their routes and stops are publicly controlled, and the degree of service they provide at stops is of public concern. Considerations of service here include not only the length of waiting time but also the degree of protection and comfort provided the patron on the street. The trend now is to provide shelters, particularly at those locations where installation is obviously warranted by density of use.

In the past, few criteria have been available to the designer to help determine the extent of enclosure, area required per waiting patron, width/length ratio of floor plan, or need for amenities such as seating, route information, entertainment, and litter collection. Therefore bus shelters have tended to be site-built architectural features and frequently have been more affluence symbol than shelter. More recently, the trend has been to product design. But the concept remains architectural: curtain-wall building off-site-fabricated and on-site-erected, conventional framing with infilling of sandwich panels or glazing. When industry recognizes the market, however, then most certainly the next generation of street shelters will emerge as low-cost, mass-produced monostructures.

Magdalen Street, Norwich, England. Bus-stop shelter.

"Unit system shelter."

THE EFFLUENT SOCIETY

Litter-collection System

The disposable package is the symbol of the American economy. Americans produce a colossal amount of garbage and trash, an average of 4.5 pounds per capita per day not counting sewage. And a study of public disposal habits confirms that people will throw away on public sidewalks umbrellas, newspapers, beer cans, and almost anything else you can name. During an academic year, ten thousand students on a campus will throw away a million chewing-gum wrappers, candy cartons, and cigarette packs. The United States discards 440,000 tons of rubbish every day—an amount which has increased 60 percent since 1950, twice the rate of the United States population increase. The national cost of refuse disposal has reached $3 billion. Half of this is paid by municipalities, the rest by private consumers and commercial establishments. With every forecast of the packaging industry for increased sales, one can assume that the disposal problem will multiply correspondingly.

Many communities are increasing incinerator or dumping facilities. New emphasis is being placed on more efficient housekeeping procedures. More efficient materials-handling techniques are desirable. The container is the first component of the collection system, the one in direct relationship to man. Clearly, its manner and degree of use affect the complete system and warrant detailed study and design.

Criteria

Many communities still fail to provide public trash receptacles. Others provide receptacles that look as if they were made in a boiler factory. In these communities the product is considered a necessary evil, somewhat like a toilet, to be hidden away and used as inconspicuously as possible. Inevitably such a product will be designed in a superficial manner. It will repel the consumer who should be encouraged to use it. Or, conversely, the sanitation department may make an issue of litter control, threaten the public with monstrous fines, and, in so doing, encourage resistance or vandalism. Or occasionally the Downtown Businessmen's Association will act as prime mover in compelling the city to procure new off-the-shelf containers. Because these products are readily available and inexpensive relative to other street improvements, they seem a quick means of sprucing up Downtown for an impending fair, convention, or other event attracting many visitors. Unfortunately these products seldom match in color, shape, or scale other public products in the cityscape. The cosmetic freshening of Main Street fails to hide more serious blemishes. The new look is not really new and soon fades into obscurity.

Public trash receptacles must be seen to be used. But they must appear modest and utilitarian. Design or selection of containers must be based on performance criteria. The standards should derive from public refuse needs and the city's procedures for collection and disposal.

Frequently, public health authorities provide the impetus for a new or more critical analysis of these procedures. National standards of refuse control and collection are rising. Previously acceptable practices of burning trash and garbage in open containers such as those formerly used in Boston Common are now not tolerated. Even the boy scouts are no longer permitted by county health departments to burn refuse in open parkland, but must use disposable paper bags. So that the disposable inner liner has joined the two other acceptable modes of trash removal from receptacle, the self-dumping unit with hinged bottom or side and the inner container which is removed, dumped, and replaced.

But whatever the technique or procedure followed, the refuse-collection system will be successful only to the extent that the containers are used by the people. Greater utilization will be secured by, first, determination of the best receptacle locations, and second, choice of appropriate receptacle size and shape.

Siting

Enough trash receptacles (or litter bins) should be provided to be immediately visual and available. Sparse siting outdoors will be self-defeating. Units should be available near major path intersections. Receptacles should be placed near benches and be made available in areas of rest and recreation. On city streets, the usual procedure is to put out additional units on request for thirty-day trial. The city of Cincinnati, employing this procedure, usually maintains 600 units throughout the city.

Container

Studies or published standards validating optimum volumes for receptacles are not yet available, but the necessary capacity will depend on the ratio of desired frequency of removal to rate of use as determined by city agencies. The desired container volume can be secured with an infinite number of valid shapes varying from geometric to quite plastic. A suitable configuration might result from consideration of the performance criteria. Shape would be influenced by such factors as means of litter removal (liner, container, self-dump), installation technique (floor, wall, post), degree of weather protection and odor containment desired, and choice of material and industrial process.

Fresno Mall, California.

212

As can be seen on the city street, almost every material has been used for the outer container: cast concrete, fabricated steel, perforated or molded plastic. Each can work well. Perhaps the choice of material should derive not only from criteria of use and shape but also from compatibility with other components of the environment.

WATER TO PUT OUT FIRES WITH

Two Martians land on Earth. One walks up to a fire hydrant and says, "Take me to your leader." The other Martian says, "What are you talking to him for? He's only a kid."

This old joke has its point: the average fire hydrant is very noticeable on the sidewalk and does look like a mechanistic little out-of-this-world creature. Actually, the hydrant is nothing more than a water faucet which can be located anywhere along a pipeline and has a simple mechanism to turn on or off the flow of water. But as a piece of public plumbing, it needs analysis and design.

Early hydrants were primitive mechanical faucets with complicated and exposed valve linkage. Some are still in use. In Boston they have been enclosed in pressed-steel housings, and in Toronto cosmetic stainless-steel jackets have been applied. The concern here, however, is with the more recent hydrants in the public right-of-way, which are functionally classified in three types: wet barrel, dry barrel, and vault. The dry barrel has been preferred in the snow belt, where freezing conditions may prevail. In the recessed vault mode all operating mechanisms and hose connections are compactly enclosed in a covered cast-iron box installed flush with grade. Although the vault is not commonly used along roads, where snowplow burial or icing may render the unit invisible or inoperative, it can work well on a well-maintained plaza, street, or sidewalk.

The operating procedure is so simple small boys on hot city streets soon learn how. At the top a readily accessible large turning nut of any shape connects to and turns a plug (compression valve) which screws down into an elbow at the bottom. Then the water gushes up the barrel out of the elbow charged by the pipeline. To shut off the water, the stem nut is turned, the valve rises, and water pressure helps the valve seal the opening.

Flow measurement is the usual rating method for hydrants, which are classified according to capacity: class A, 1,000 gallons per minute or greater; B, 500 to 1,000 gallons per minute; C, less than 500 gallons per minute. Functional criteria have been developed by the American Water Works Association, and new products may be tested and standards evolved at the Underwriters Laboratories at Chicago.

Color has an important bearing upon the hydrant's obtrusiveness in the

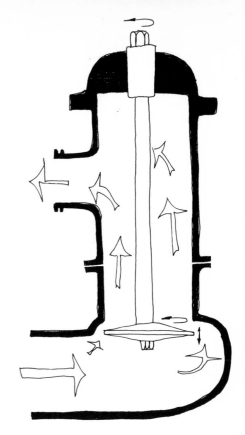

Fresno Mall, California.

visual scene. Some cities use a gray neutral color for the barrel in order to "paint out" the object. Some private developers paint hydrants in "corporate" colors, such as purple in the wine-making district of central New York or turquoise and orange in front of Howard Johnson's restaurants. However, many communities color-code hydrant capacity and paint the tops as follows: class A, green; B, orange; and C, red.

Material for hydrants may be cast iron because weight is not a critical factor; durability, resistance to water pressure, and vandalism are. The iron barrel should be of fail-safe construction with a shear device. Breakaway design permits the upper part of the unit to be carried away on impact without injury to the motorist or loss of water pressure.

Scale concerns the apparent size of the hydrant in relation to its surroundings. Customarily the hydrant has been decorated rather than designed, with dimensions and shapes arbitrary. Recent West Coast designs have shown that sculptural shapes can be modeled to use little sidewalk space and be less obtrusive and more handsome. The next steps in hydrant design may be in the direction of miniaturization and greater coordination with other urban furnishings in siting, shape, and color.

Santa Monica Mall, California.

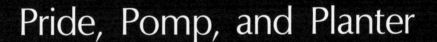

Chapter Eleven

Pride, Pomp, and Planter

In earlier times, even the meanest, dreariest crossroads hamlet was likely to have one grass square or traffic circle complete with granite-faced heroic figure and commemorative plaque, and this tombstone sculpture provided a sense of place. Or the public space may have been made musical by the sound of birds in a park or water from a fountain. Whatever the medium of accent was, you knew where you were and remembered where you had been.

Regardless of technological change, human needs remain the same. And when the city dweller has been provided the basic necessities, the furnishing of the city is not yet done. There remains the desire for an extra treat, an extravaganza, some touch of excitement to put pleasure in urban living.

Today, it's hard to find. Whether to visit or live in, many American cities are dull places indeed. Older neighborhoods are blighted and dying. Newer housing developments are at best bland and "solid." Blocks of new prime-rental office buildings such as those on Third or even Park Avenue in New York are monstrously monotonous. Large sections of the city have lost character and become gray and dispirited. Something is missing.

Color it green. Spark it red or orange. Make it sing or scream, but don't let it whimper.

WHERE YOU ARE
AND WHERE YOU'VE BEEN

Landmarks

When the commercial street, shopping plaza, or mall wants to identify its merchant area as different from all others, then memorable visual attractions are installed which offer inspirational or entertainment value. In fact, the art of producing a community attraction, like show business, is the art of touching people in some emotional way.

But what audience response is desired? Which particular character of the public place is to be enhanced? How much imagery is to be achieved? At what cost, paid by whom? The decision to entertain or move or inspire people requires precise definition of goals, constraints, and resources before seeking solutions. Only then can appropriate devices such as landmarks be developed which produce instant recognition, identification, excitement. At the same time, if worth is shallow, instant appeal may be followed by instant dismissal. It may be necessary for imagery to appear timeless and permanent as well as unique to a place.

From these criteria may come the opportunity to utilize something that already exists in the public space. One of the most spectacular European landmarks, Le Jet d'Eau de Genève in the middle of Lake Leman, sprays water

Northland Center, Detroit, Michigan. A landmark in imagery as well as graphics programming.

425 feet into the air. It was originally created to help equalize pressure changes in Geneva's water supply. Each imitation such as the smaller jet in the lake at Reston, Virginia, or the one in the Potomac River at Washington becomes more contrived and therefore less effective.

In small communities a common approach is to rehabilitate and dramatically light an old building of historical interest. Or an old memorial square or traffic circle can be freshly landscaped. But in many smaller communities the sole significant landmark is a church spire, a water tank, or a red-brick factory chimney. Then existing landmarks may need to be supplemented or supplanted because of obsolescence or because a more vital and appropriate identity is desired.

The large city has an intense competitive pressure to assert its importance, wealth, and vitality to the world at large. And its neighborhoods may each in turn require either an expression of economic health and desirability or a focal point around which to build community loyalty.

For any community, large or small, the expression of a contemporary identity could well be based on technological phenomena. In the past the most successful landmarks have been those structures which reflected unique or daring exploitation of new technical processes. The outstanding successes have been those which additionally enticed observer participation or involvement. And the mode of expression, depending upon the wealth and sophistication of the city, has ranged from revenue-producing utilitarian structures to huge playthings selling only *joie de vivre*. Examples: a bridge of daring engineering whose largeness of concept captures the public imagination; a sports stadium whose bulk and glittering dome are visible along a waterfront or mark an expressway interchange; a needle-shaped observation tower whose lofty rotating restaurant serves as a homing beacon.

Even more advanced techniques based on emotionally involving the observer with some form of contemporary technological experience are useful today. In fact, luminokinetic artists go so far in creation of landmarks as to work toward the total disappearance of the structure in the production of direct *effects*.

Derived from the kinetic art experiments of Duchamp, Man Ray, Gabo, and Moholy-Nagy and utilizing new techniques such as cybernetics, spectacular huge constructions and spatiodynamic towers are now associated with town planning. The resultant landmarks appear to be expressions of the contemporary environment. Designers such as Heinz Mack of Germany's experimental Group Zero and Nicholas Schöffer work in an elegant techno-scientific mode. Content is abandoned for the purely perceptual. At night multi-image moving projections transform the outdoors into a cinema nightscape. The dynamic effects are dazzling and supercharged; the sum of light and motion is more powerful than the parts.

The Mall, Fresno, California, 1964. Clock initially criticized for poor legibility, but now accepted and liked as total sculpture.

Triangular stressed-skin structure contains train of passenger cars traveling within to observation platform at top.

Cybernetic Tower, higher than the Eiffel Tower, functions as esthetic "governor" of Paris. Its luminokinetic elements include over 3,000 multicolored projectors, 2,000 electronic flashlights, 330 mirrors. Acting on data received from hygrometers, thermometers, anemometers, microphones, and photoelectric cells, a central computer constantly changes the rhythm of the elements to represent the esthetic condition of the city.

From Hero on Horseback to Nude with Hole in the Head

In Renaissance times human sculpture, often nude, in an Italian town center might identify the community or reinforce its image. For the time and place in history such sculpture made sense and was appropriate. The Italian city had a tradition of nude gods and goddesses; sculptors and marble were plentiful.

The tradition of representational sculpture was transplanted to America. National leaders were sculpted in togas or fig leaves. Military men were put astride rearing bronze beasts to kindle awe and respect in the breast of the local citizenry.

Representational sculptures of great men installed in public places symbolized the aspirations of growing cities; but the transplanted tradition did not always take root, and there was controversy. In 1783 Horatio Greenough carved a statue of Washington in marble for the Washington D.C., Mall which was rejected by the public, whose common sense could not accept the general of Valley Forge shown as a half-naked Greek god. The next try at memorializing George Washington was Robert Mills's design, an obelisk rising out of a colonnaded Greek temple. It was not built for lack of money for one hundred years; the obelisk part only was completed in 1884. This is the Washington Monument, now the American people's favorite "sculpture."

Today the need for symbolization and identification still exists. It exists in the corporate city, where boxy office skyscrapers raised on pilotis or stuck to the ground occupy a complete block and need something to announce the front entrance, and it exists in the civic or cultural center, whose pedestrian spaces seem to require art to look at.

Current practice for office skyscrapers is just to install a smaller complementary version of the building, a cube, say, which does not compete with the architecture. But today no first-class cultural center is complete without its Picasso, Calder, or Moore. The avant-garde pioneers of thirty years ago are now accepted as masters of middle-class modern. Unfortunately however, many of their selected or commissioned urban art works are still studio conceptions. They are overscaled and violate rather than adorn the urban environment. To these masters of the studio language the language of the streets is alien. When they speak, they only add to the general noise and confusion. Their image is not necessarily transferable. The space may only be decorated, not identified favorably to the consumer.

This view of the corporate and cultural sculptural scene becomes important when we turn to the public sector and note that it is now permissible to spend money for art in urban renewal or new town building. It is all right to budget 1 percent of project cost for amenities such as sculpture or fountains. For example, 5 million of the 480 million dollars put into the South Mall State Office Complex in Albany, New York was budgeted for art.

With government acceptance of art as a desirable and a project-reimbursable item comes the opportunity for employing these funds to secure greater entertainment and recreational value rather than mere adornment. Presently there is a prevailing emphasis on monumental and "conversational" sculpture. This Renaissance concept is expressed in welded steel rather than cast bronze, but remains static in concept. In the public space the designer might better provide a dynamic spatial experience. The user can be encouraged to enter, feel, sense a shape growing from the floor. He can be enveloped in a daytime environment of supergraphics. He can be given a nighttime environment of changing light and color whose programmed automated display excites and delights.

Lincoln Center, New York. Monumental, impersonal, "don't touch."

223

Expo 67, Montreal. Public art for people, not "experts."

Whether such public art is good or bad is immaterial. What counts is that it be accessible and not boring. It should be evocative rather than representational, humorous rather than pompous, imaginative rather than literary; and to be truly useful, it should be not merely decorative but inviting of public participation.

WATER TO WATCH AND HEAR

Like the flickering magic of fire, the wonder of water has always stimulated emotional response from man, and time and technology have not changed this natural response. In the country he never tires of watching and listening to water swirl in pools, leap over falls, crash on rocks. In his home, life-giving water offers him sensory satisfaction as he drinks or bathes. The visual and musical qualities of water can similarly stimulate people in the urban public space. They will play in it, eat in it, make music in it, use it as their urban source of refreshment. For, with increasing emphasis on conformance to

Reston, Virginia. Public art of human scale meant to be enjoyed.

codes, cost control, and quantification, water remains a commodity which can be not only essential but frivolous, playful, and organic, meeting human psychological needs in the synthetic city.

Clearly, then, the city dweller needs, wants, will pay for, and should have water integral to his environment. But clearer understanding of public needs and better definition of goals are required to achieve a useful and at the same time appropriate water product. Frequently, as things stand, the designer's client (the city) presents the product, and then the real client (the public) uses it in an unexpected, need-fulfilling way. Then comes outrage. Consider a typical reaction. The *Washington Post* recently reported in great detail that "Alexandria's City fathers made it a crime last night for anyone to play in a reflecting pool at City Hall. . . . [The city attorney] solemnly explained that violaters would be subject to fines and jail sentences of up to six months. . . . the 75 foot square reflecting pool, which contains seven fountains, has proved an attraction to many children. . . . The fountain is the central feature of the plaza, which cost $1.6 million and was built with urban renewal funds."

Every age has its ideals and needs and develops the technology to accommodate them. In Roman times precise, practical engineering brought water over the hills in aqueducts which provided an expression more bold and beautiful than the dispensing fountains themselves. In Renaissance times the Palladian grouping of fountains, pavings, and palazzo became an excellent expression of the preindustrial world, where people looked at things in fixed, primitive, one-point perspective. Symmetry, balance, formality—these were the ordering devices of design. In the city-beautiful era public art was puffed with pomp and plaster. Many examples are still around, singing their stilted old comic-light-opera song. A few have been relocated or revitalized and thereby serve as link between old and new, as in the fountain for the Cincinnati Fountain Square urban renewal project by Archibald Rogers. But many others are lifeless and should be reevaluated.

Whether old and refurbished or constructed anew, the successful public attraction will be the one that involves and stimulates the consumer. To achieve this objective, the designer needs to determine how best to use and intensify the various qualities of water. He can use its many unique properties to do so. Light reflection, for example, can be most distinctive. As water falls in droplets or sheets, it has different degrees of luminosity and brilliance. The effects that can be achieved range from sparkling jewels to shimmering sheets of molten metal.

Daylight penetrating to the paving texture of a shallow container can make water seem transparent and colorless. Or water can be made to look like the blue sky when light is reflected from a deep pool. And at night artificial light, programmed to be variable in color brightness and source, will enable people to experience a water of multiple moods.

Fountain, "Paul Revere" Church, Boston. Public art, dry, "don't touch."

Reston, Virginia.

Another strong quality of water is movement in infinite degree. To predetermine the activity and intensify the effect can make water fascinating, whether it is still, running, falling, spraying, or jetting high against the sky. Agitation of water will produce endless effects, depending on the method used. Projections rising from a channel can break and make choppy the surface of flowing water. An edge can aerate water falling over it, make it noisy and alive. If serrated, the edge will form water threads; if curled, it will make a sheet flow. Pumps and orifices of various pressures and apertures can make water bubble, foam, spray, or roar in a spectacular jet. In wintry air steamy vapor rising from heated water can add another dimension. With movement comes still another variable quality—sound. "Hsss," "plop plop plop plop," "fwooshhh."

Finally, containers, depending on their shape, size, and elevation, can offer the pedestrian elixir to drink, can encourage the young at heart to splash and wade, can be sculpture whose forms are animated by water.

The designer does not lack for drawing-board options. He can take his pick. But pick he must: the degree to which the public experience of water is to be intensified in each of its aspects—sound, movement, reflection, containers—should be predetermined. First, however, program management requires analysis of the suitability and entertainment value of water to the site, and then a decision on what degree of user involvement is desirable. Then comes the choice of approach and specific means making the experience of water a bigger thing in city dwellers' lives.

THE NEED FOR GREEN

A harsh synthetic environment makes people hunger for softness and living color. The more polluted the urban atmosphere, the more necessary are sweet odors. The more dehumanized the urban machine, the more essential are romantic expressions of nature. Surely the human animal wants contact with growing and ever-changing green things.

This need has been recognized in the past, as demonstrated by the development of greenbelts and park systems. Many Eastern and Midwestern cities not yet totally urbanized are saved from blight by their canopies of trees. And developers and businessmen accept plantings as a tool for dignifying stores, screening parking lots, beautification of gasoline stations, even the cosmetic concealment of parking meters.

Granted the latent demand and consumer acceptance and considering the demonstrated potential, why have not many more extensive and significant installations been created in our cities' shopping plazas, airports, campuses, and other public places?

Several difficulties, natural and man-made, inhibit successful plantings. Perishability of product is obvious. Climate can be severe. Many plant forms and methods of installation are not suitable for the polluted and synthetic urban environment. The average city loses more dead and diseased trees than are planted per year. Tree losses in Buffalo, New York, due to Dutch elm disease exceeded 7,700 for 1968, for a total of more than 50,000 trees since the disease was first spotted in 1951. And traditional budgets and procedures will not make a city green.

Vandalism is another problem. Of course, not all acts destructive to plant life are willful. Playing children can destroy unprotected plants or small trees

Fresno Mall.

without malicious intent. On the other hand, many plantings, formal in their isolation, set-apartness, and perfection, seem to be saying, "Look but don't touch," and like KEEP OFF THE GRASS signs may invite antisocial behavior.

Another problem in the cities may be poor subsurface conditions for trees. Basement vaults under sidewalks require expensive foundations and drainage for root balls. But an even greater problem inhibiting use of plant materials may be the design process itself. The potential of plants as urban furnishings of social utility and value has not been clearly demonstrated in a systematic way.

Greenery Systems Solutions

Even in the design of amenities, goals must be established. Before installing a planter or a fountain, it is necessary to ask what its symbiotic value is. That is, what will the proposed element of decoration do to enhance the environment as a whole? Greenery has traditionally been used to reduce urban harshness or to serve as a focal display point. What other, interrelated tasks can be accomplished?

Greenery can be additionally used as visual linkage to unify a varied streetscape. It can act as buffer between traffic and people. It can guide and control pedestrians. It can moderate the effects of climate and light. Depending on choice of plant form, it can reinforce the desired imagery of the community or area.

Atlanta, Georgia Plaza project. Multiuse art form: pool, pedestrian bridge, bandstand.

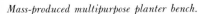

Mass-produced multipurpose planter bench.

All of these uses imply quantity consumption and therefore cost reduction through mass production and installation. But unless plant-life survivability is improved, natural landscape elements will still be increasingly replaced by simulated shapes in synthetic materials. Examples now abound of concrete parasols and aluminum space frames replacing live trees. Next will come artificial shrubs and trees. Some improvement in survivability can be expected through development and use of more hardy strains. But more progress will be made in lengthening the life-replacement cycle and reducing costs through design of more protective installations.

In order for greenery to compete with other media for providing pleasure or imagery, considerable improvement is required in choice of containers and method of siting. Placement may be obtrusive or awkward in the pedestrian area. When specially designed for a specific site, planters tend to be overdesigned, too decorative, monumental—a distraction rather than an enhancing use of plant life. Greater concern must be demonstrated for relationship of container to contents. Available off-the-shelf containers may be incompatible with the proposed plant life. Planter and plant must go together, in size, shape, color, and material. For greater plant variety, a family

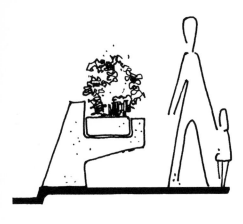

or hierarchy of planter sizes may be necessary. A container of well-chosen height, up-down, in-out, with respect to plane of floor, may make plantings more effective visually. Perhaps planters that would be not merely root containers, but capsules for all parts of the plant, leaves and all, might be introduced.

A system of self-regulating containers, although initially relatively costly, can substantially reduce vandalism, perishability, and maintenance labor. Ideally, such containers would be constructed with integral sprinkler heads and controls, would be connected to the city water supply and self-irrigating, would be climate-controlled by means of heating elements, and would be more completely enclosed for protection from wind, disease, pollution, and vandals.

To give the consumer the enjoyment of a sense of participation or involvement with plant life is obviously a more complex task than to secure his visual gratification. In the past the city provided the arboretum or zoological gardens as not only a showcase for exhibition of exotic plants but also a romantic place to be, to wander, to seek personal release and self-refreshment. Today the need is to take the gardens to the people and to make their overall effect more important than the individual objects in them. To achieve the latter, various components such as ground cover, shrubs, and trees should be assembled to interest and entice by overall sight, smell, sound, and movement. Experimentation might develop novel combinations of organic components or organic and synthetic components which would achieve previously unobtainable effects. Programmed movement and/or nighttime activation of light and shadow on leaf forms might give parks and gardens an altogether new appeal. Street lighting and supplementary light sources should be utilized that enhance plant colors. Variable controls and display trimmings would permit special effects and seasonal variation. These techniques will help make greenery competitive with other psyche-pleasing design options.

People no longer carry their own lanterns at night. The city provides light. People have been deprived of plant life. The city must give it back. When designers and industry develop more viable products and installation techniques, the city will be able to meet this responsibility.

HULLABALOO

The sight of Old Glory rippling in the breeze is great, but hearing seventy-six trombones with it is better. In marking a celebration or symbolizing a theme, there is no such thing as too much of a good thing. One must not only wave the flag but also shoot the works.

The techniques of pageantry have always produced favorable responses

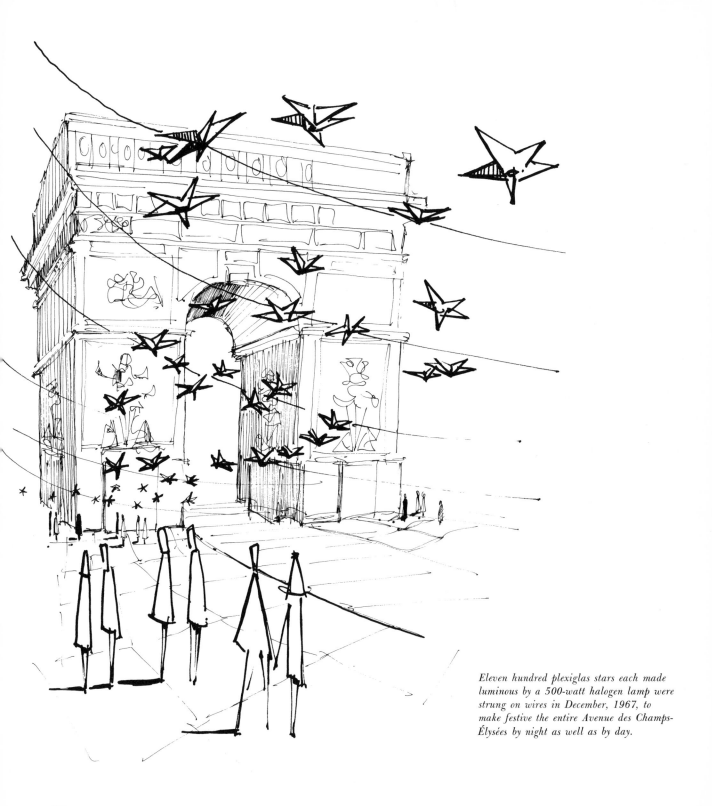

Eleven hundred plexiglas stars each made luminous by a 500-watt halogen lamp were strung on wires in December, 1967, to make festive the entire Avenue des Champs-Élysées by night as well as by day.

Church Street project. At Christmastime hoops of red bulbs are placed around the white lights, creating a halo effect.

in observers. Medieval social and political structure owed much of its glamour and acceptance to the proud symbols and brightly colored devices of heraldry on pennants and knightly trappings. When the town replaced the castle as the center of the civilized world, it also faced the need to provide crowd-pleasing excitement and set out to do so. In America innumerable spectacular attractions evolved in support of community events: bonfires and bands for political rallies, booths and bunting for fund-raising picnics, fireworks for the Fourth of July.

Pageantry, from the setting out of flags for parades to the use of festoons on streetlights to add yuletide spirit to the shopping season, has always been important in marking Main Street, but today the need for bright display in the public space is greater than ever. More restrictive codes and regulations regiment the appearance of the public right-of-way. The monotony and confusion of most downtown American streets call for the imaginative resources of the urban designer—it is no longer enough for him just to provide flagpole sockets along the curb.

A number of old techniques as well as contemporary devices can be used. Air is free, and the wind provides movement. Banners—big, bold, and ebullient—are always acceptable. New excitement can be provided by more experimental and aerodynamic shapes. Semirigid and new lightweight materials can be flown in eye-catching ways. Wild graphics and color patterns will prove again that the bizarre does things for any bazaar.

Light remains a largely unexploited resource. By day, sunlight can be caught, multiplied, patterned, directed by reflective, spinning disks or mirrors. By night, the common crisscross of searchlights on clouds can be supplemented at ground level by spectacular strobe or high-intensity light sources. Multicolored light sources with flashers can be used in clusters or in intriguing arrangements for pinpoint patterns. Banks of bulbs can be programmed to tell time, animate cartoons, or flash graphic images in coordination with time-phased prerecorded avant-garde music.

Whatever the medium, spontaneity and excitement are the qualities the designer needs to capture in the program. If he succeeds there, he will fulfill his opportunity to provide crowd-pleasing hullabaloo.

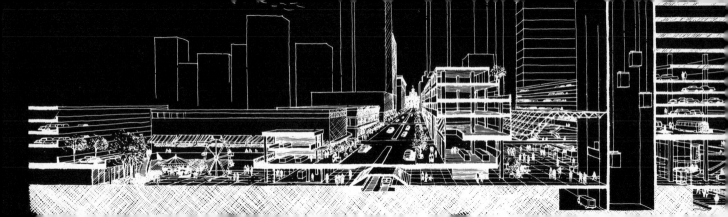

Put It All Together

In many creative efforts, book as well as song, the reprise restates the theme. Hopefully, it lingers as something to hum as well as to haunt. So it is with this chapter.

By now we know that the city is an artifact. The city is a product conceived, built, and inhabited by man.

By now we know this product is not only obsolete and ugly but also static and unresponsive to the changing needs of man. For the city is not yet a people-serving system. It is an accretion built by a fragmented industry. Unified direction has not been provided by the fragmented local bureaucracy. The urban environment has not been improved because the consumer too is fragmented. There has been an absence of a vocal consumer group with authority, responsibility, resources, and decision-making capability.

By now we know cosmetic tranquilizers do not cure more deep-rooted and harmful problem areas. Use of a better typeface for a "CURB YOUR DOG" sign indicates awareness, but. . . . But elimination of visual pollution requires far more sweeping solutions in all sectors of communications and control.

By now the essence of the systems approach—the interrelationship of site planning with public improvements and physical facilities whether for health and security or fun and games—is clear.

By now we know that whereas in 1900 only 30 percent of the people lived in urban areas, it won't be long before 80 percent of a vastly larger population will be living on only 1½ percent of the land. This is the challenge of our age.

Priorities are constantly being reordered. The national housing goal has been stated to be "a decent home and a suitable living environment for every American family." Although financial institutions and developers have been cautious in accepting site planning and design innovations, HUD has publicized well-designed federal-supported projects through the Design Awards Program and provided incentives to enable other cities to do the same. It remains to sing out loud and clear the new opportunities to plan, design, and furnish more liveable cities, to put it all together, to use subsoil rights as well as air rights, to achieve a cubic city.

With volume production of housing and environment as a national goal, with industrialization as the process, new techniques can be applied which spin off many benefits. With quantity output as a goal, more sophisticated design tooling and production techniques can produce lower unit costs. Cost reduction permits, for the first time in this country, the deflation of the popular notion that in the public environment good design costs more. Quantity can make quality available to everybody.

Additionally, the opportunity exists to create a new idiom, new forms of visual community identity and environmental imagery of appeal to the people. Although it is in the American tradition to pass over the old and to seek the new, the consumer has not been given a marketplace choice—until now.

ILLUSTRATION ON PPS. 234, 235:
Market Street East, Philadelphia. Multi-level, five-block transportation-shopping spine.

THE IMAGE IS MORE THAN SKIN DEEP
Up and Over/Down and Under

Economic forces increasingly act to optimize use of diminishing and expensive urban space. Rising costs have become the impetus for more technically innovative and comprehensive urban design solutions. Older precedents exist. Grand Central City in New York has been described by Douglas Haskell as "the world's finest interlocked multilevel demonstration of the futurist city." That complex was designed almost seventy-five years ago. It has been an obvious functional success engendering considerable consumer affection and loyalty in the process.

Surprisingly few functionally significant Center City complexes have been built since. Noteworthy among those few which successfully interrelate transportation, shopping, office, or hotel use are Midtown Plaza in Rochester, N. Y., Place Ville Marie, Montreal, Charles Center, Baltimore, and Capital Centre in St. Paul. More recent are The World Trade Center sponsored by the New York Port Authority and Market Street East, nurtured for some years by the Philadelphia City Planning Commission and Redevelopment Authority.

Each of these innovative complexes required design of subsystems such as floor, lighting, and signage of quality comparable with the basic structure. As stated in the 1966 Market Street East report by Skidmore, Owings & Merrill, "The plan demands physical integration of all parts of the Transportation–Commerce Center and shared structures and mechanical systems." In these comprehensively designed environments the failure of any subsystem is immediately self-evident and destructive to total system performance.

The commercial success of these and similar projects should redirect urban professionals and developers from a preoccupation with *appearance* to the exploitation of the potential of *design*. Such a fundamental omni-

Multiuse, multilevel World Trade Center, New York.

SUBWAYS   OFFICES

CONSULATES & TRADE CENTERS   PATH TERMINAL

PRODUCT DISPLAY   PARKING

MECHANICAL EQUIPMENT   STORAGE

TRUCK DOCKS   TOWER LOBBY ELEVATORS

CUSTOMS BLDG.   NORTH TOWER BUILDING   NORTHEAST PLAZA BUILDING

WEST ST.   PLAZA LEVEL   CHURCH ST.

CONCOURSE (CONNECTS ALL BLDGS.)

PATH TERMINAL

directional point of view must surely require a high order of technical innovation in physical site improvements as well as buildings. Constraints, such as traditional curb lines and subsurface systems (water, electricity, communications), which presently control the location of visible elements above, must be reevaluated. The place to begin is the site—not only terrain but utilities.

Utilities and service systems have been buried beneath the public street bit by bit until the earth has been repetetively punctured for pipes, conduit, and ductwork in an ever-changing mix of unknown composition and location. Manhole covers, meter and valve-box plates scattered all over the street and sidewalk signal the jumbled array below. Underneath the intersection of Fourth and Vine in downtown Cincinnati, for example, are: a 6-inch water main; an abandoned 6-inch gas main now carrying electric cable; a 10-inch gas main; the Cincinnati Gas and Electric Company's electric circuits for traffic lights, fire and burglar alarms; streetlights; telephone-company circuits; a Western Union electrical duct; Postal Telegraph lines; and underneath it all a great big sewer—*each in its separate trench.*

Typically, the arteriosclerosis of this aged plumbing barely keeping the city alive is ignored until the city street must be laid open. Then the numerous surgical scars crossing paving and walk remind us of the need for frequent repairs to the vital circulatory, communications, and waste systems pulsing below. Crowded, overloaded, and expensive to maintain, these networks cannot accept new functions. They are inadequate to meet rising standards of performance and the needs of a growing population.

Consider for example the need to separate storm and sanitary sewers which in combined form now serve 36 million people. It is well known that the overflow of storm water flushes raw sewage down the sewers and pollutes our streams. But the cost of correction has been estimated in a survey for the Interior Department at 48 billion dollars.

Despite such needs public spaces and streets are designed today by the same procedure used a hundred years ago. All too frequently the designer decides upon *visible* spatial relationships first and only then turns the work over to an engineer who tells him it can't be built that way because of the high capital cost of twisting and straining pipes and ducts into that configuration. Dozens of urban design studies with extensive street changes have remained paper studies because of the failure to tie above grade work to subsurface conditions, to design and fund adequately the *invisible* improvements as well as appearance factors. Rather that a constraint, the design of subsurface features can become an expressive element in the total design. Designs should be created that enable industry to produce with available technology standard units which, assembled in required combinations, can be the spatial utility lattice that supports our environmental needs. Thus an

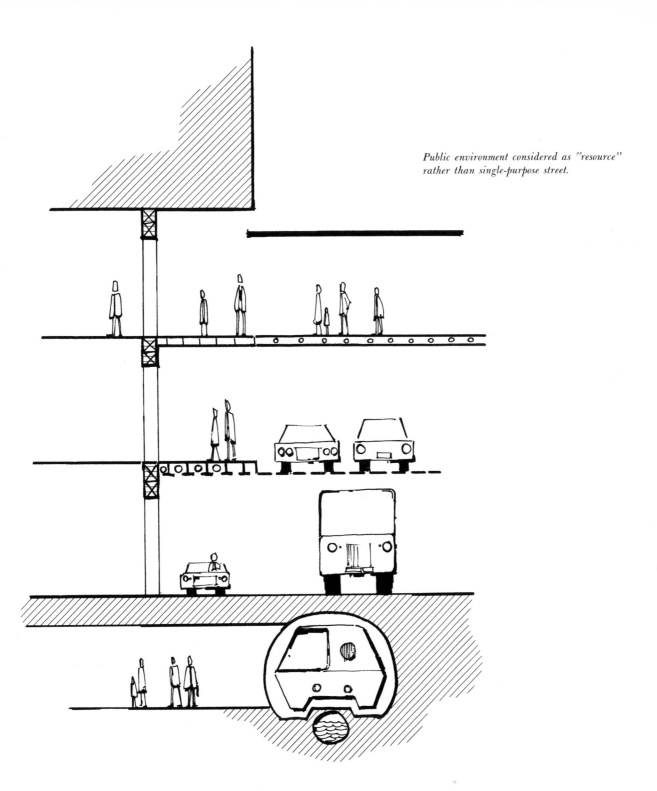

*Public environment considered as "resource"
rather than single-purpose street.*

industrialized approach leads to availability of appropriate elements to assemble utility networks which more economically and cooperatively locate and service the desired urban furnishings.

It is then possible to realign electrical distribution lines together in compact harness much like in the synthetic environment of aircraft. Many pipes and conduit can be grouped into a common duct or chase with a continuous access cover. In certain areas, such as Downtown, where access needs for service or change are greater a service tunnel would be useful. The tunnel should be large enough to accommodate service crews in special vehicles. Some such tunnels are in partial use in a few cities and even campuses. There they permit rapid access to and frequent change and expansion of services. They simplify inspection, maintenance, and repair of utilities without above-grade disturbance. The technology for the service vehicles exists as evidenced by the many special-purpose motorized units used by maintenance and ground crews at airports.

Downtown, if the below-grade utility raceway, the at-grade sidewalk, and the above-grade pedestrian pathway were all aligned as one total space, their separation could be achieved by horizontal partitions of new materials and function. New techniques could give these thin membranes other task potential and spin-off benefits. The separator or floor could contain mechanisms which move people automatically. Access, whether to service mechanical walkways above or utilities below, could be constant and linear, rather than through holes dug in the street. With a constant raceway, the plug-in and connection of street furnishings above to the service systems below is made less costly. Like gas lanterns, manhole covers would become decorative collectors' items, symbols of a bygone Victorian technology.

The potential can be even greater and more quickly achieved in new towns and housing developments of large scale or density.

The seventies will be noted for the significant flow reversal outward from the central business district to the surrounding neighborhoods. This residential environment represents a far greater marketing area and therefore increased potential to industry and the developer. It is assuredly of greater social importance to the individual resident. The residential neighborhood is being developed increasingly by technically innovative design and management techniques spurred by HUD incentives and the housing demand.

Although most shelter designs have followed conventional layout and appearance, economies of scale have shown that industrialized housing may offer more product for less money quicker. As shelter becomes industrialized the product will be further adapted to serial production which will promote greater change of form and materials.

Whatever form shelter takes, vertical stack or horizontal plug-in, the environmental designer must be the catalyst relating the technological prod-

Floating City. Industrialized shelter, stores, schools, roads, and utilities are fitted into a frame and replaced when obsolete.

uct to user needs. More advanced facilities underground are required to support the social environment of greater dimensions above.

Maintaining Environmental Integrity

When the change from product attitude to process behavior takes place, software such as programming instructions become necessary. Implementation of the urban systems design through the procurement, installation, operation, and maintenance phases of hardware will require development of standard procedures for the guidance of the various city agencies and departments. Availability of a *Street Furnishings Manual* is essential to the maintenance of a flexible system with many variables and the assurance of design and management control of quality standards as the system changes.

Many precedents exist in other disciplines and applications. The preparation of systems and components manuals is commonplace in the military–industrial establishment. And the integrity of corporate identity (communications) programs is protected by *Graphic Standards* manuals prepared by designers which show not only minutae such as typeface style and size but approved manner of utilization in all media including vehicles, buildings, and spaces.

Transportation systems too have their *Standards,* one of the foremost being that for the British Railway System prepared by Jock Kinneir.

Unique or complex environmental systems, such as fairs, required manuals prepared by designers for the use of construction and maintenance personnel.

Innovative site developments always required definitive construction documents. As the procedure becomes industrialized, the supporting software necessarily changes and assumes additional functions. Drawings and specifications in new formats describe interrelationships, specify performance standards for future construction or procurement purposes, predetermine possible configurations and combinations for most effective installation, advise optimum operation procedures, and mandate maintenance and change procedures which best protect the system integrity.

Thus we see that the systems view encompasses all phases of urban planning, design, installation, and operation. Nor should feedback from the consumer, as discussed earlier, be omitted. Such an approach can offer the consumer a more comprehensively furnished urban environment for his use and enjoyment.

Design the process, not the product.

Bibliography

There are many hard-cover works on urban design in general, but few that consider the street and its urban furnishings in depth. Only those standard works with some direct utility have been noted. The bulk of useful information appears in periodicals or project documents of limited circulation. When available, these have been noted. Each item is listed only once, under the chapter in which it was first used as a primary or secondary source.

GENERAL

Alexander, Christopher: "Relational Complexes in Architecture," *Architectural Record,* New York, September, 1966.

Chermayeff, Serge, and Christopher Alexander: *Community and Privacy,* Doubleday & Company, Inc., Garden City, N.Y., 1963.

Cullen, Gordon: *Townscape,* The Architectural Press, London, 1961.

Duke University, Caudill Rowlett Scott, Hewes Holz, and Willard: *Computer Aided Campus Planning,* interim report, Educational Facilities Laboratories, Inc., New York, 1967.

Ewald, William R., Jr.: *Environment for Man; Environment and Change; Environment and Policy, The Next Fifty Years* (3 vols.) Indiana University Press, Bloomington, 1968.

Goodman, William, and Eric Freund (eds.): *Principles and Practice of Urban Planning,* 4th ed., International City Managers' Association, Washington, D.C., 1969.

Malt, Harold Lewis: *Proceedings of the White House Conference on Natural Beauty,* Government Printing Office, Washington, D.C., 1966.

————: *Site Products,* interim report, State University Construction Fund, Albany, N.Y., 1966.

Nairn, Ian: *The American Landscape: A Critical View,* Random House, Inc., New York, 1965.

SCSD: The Project and the Schools, Educational Facilities Laboratories, Inc., New York, 1967.

Chapter 1 Our Hand-me-down Street Furniture

Bacon, Edmund N.: *Design of Cities,* The Viking Press, Inc., New York, 1967.

Giedion, Sigfried: *Space, Time and Architecture,* 4th ed., Harvard University Press, Cambridge, Mass., 1963.

Spreiregen, Paul D.: *Urban Design,* McGraw-Hill Book Company, New York, 1965.

Wolf, Peter M.: *Eugène Hénard and the Beginning of Urbanism in Paris* 1900–1914, International Federation for Housing and Planning, The Hague, 1969.

Chapter 2 The Problem

Doxiadis, C. A.: *Urban Renewal and the Future of the American City,* Public Administration Service, Chicago, 1966.

Pushkarev, Boris, Christopher Tunnard, and Ralph Warburton: *Man-made America: Chaos or Control?* Yale University Press, New Haven, Conn., 1963.

Starr, Roger: *The Living End,* Coward-McCann, Inc., New York, 1966.

Wolf, Von Eckardt: *A Place to Live: The Crisis of the Cities,* Delacorte Press, New York, 1967.

Chapter 3 The Systems Approach

Alexander, Christopher: *Notes on the Synthesis of Form,* Harvard University Press, Cambridge, Mass., 1964.

Campbell, Robert D., and Hugh L. LeBlank: *An Information System for Urban Planning,* U.S. Government Printing Office, Washington, D.C., 1967.

Eberhard, John P.: "Technology for the City," *International Science and Technology,* September, 1966, pp. 18–29.

Emerging Techniques of Architectural Practice, The American Institute of Architects, Washington, D.C., 1966.

Hall, Arthur D.: *Systems Engineering,* D. Van Nostrand Company, Inc., Princeton, N.J., 1962.

Metropolitan Data Center Project, Department of Housing and Urban Development, Housing and Home Finance Agency, Washington, D.C., 1966.

"Performance Design," *Progressive Architecture,* August, 1967, pp. 104–153.

State University Construction Fund: *Guide for Campus Planning,* Albany, N.Y., 1965.

Van Foerster, Heinz: "Logical Structure of Environment and Its Internal Representation," International Design Conference, Aspen, Colo., 1962.

Chapter 4   Consumer Is King

Alexander, Christopher: *The City as a Mechanism for Sustaining Human Contact,* Institute of Urban and Regional Development, University of California Press, Berkeley, 1966.

Gagne, Robert M., and Arthur W. Melton: *Psychological Principles in System Development,* Holt, Rinehart and Winston, Inc., New York, 1963.

Gibson, James J.: *The Perception of the Visual World,* Houghton Mifflin Company, Boston, 1950.

Hall, Edward T.: *The Hidden Dimension,* Doubleday & Company, Inc., Garden City, N.Y., 1966.

————: *The Silent Language,* Fawcett Publications, Inc., Greenwich, Conn., 1968.

Luckiesh, M.: *Visual Illusions,* 2d ed., Dover Publications, Inc., New York, 1965.

Chapter 5   Shaping the City Floor

Burrage, Robert H., and Edward G. Mogren: *Parking,* The Eno Foundation for Highway Traffic Control, Saugatuck, Conn., 1957.

Gruen, Victor, and Larry Smith: *Shopping Towns U.S.A.,* Reinhold Publishing Corporation, New York, 1960.

Halprin, Lawrence: *New York, New York,* Department of Housing and Urban Development, Washington, D.C., 1968.

Highway Research Board: *Automobile Parking: Selected References, 1962–1964,* Washington, D.C., 1965.

Lewis, David: *The Pedestrian in the City,* D. Van Nostrand Co., Inc., Princeton, N.J., 1966.

Lynch, Kevin: *The Image of the City,* The M.I.T. Press, Cambridge, Mass., 1966.

Metrotran-2000: A study of Future Concepts in Metropolitan Transportation for the Year 2000, Cornell Aeronautical Laboratory, Inc., Buffalo, N.Y., 1967.

Rudofsky, Bernard: *Streets for People: A Primer for Americans,* Doubleday & Company, Inc., Garden City, N.Y., 1969.

Chapter 6   Posts and Post Mortem

American Association of State Highway Officials: *Specifications for Design and Construction of Structural Supports for Highway Signs,* Bureau of Public Roads, Washington, D.C., 1968.

Chapter 7   City Lights

American Standards Association: *ASA Practice for Roadway Lighting,* IES, New York, 1964.

Cassel, Arno, and Douglas Medville: *Economic Study of Roadway Lighting,* Highway Research Board, Washington, D.C., 1966.

Lam, William M. C.: "The Lighting of Cities," *Architectural Record,* June, 1965, pp. 210–214.

Larson, Leslie: *Lighting and Its Design,* New York Whitney Library, New York, 1964.

Middleton, Michael, and Peter Whitworth: *Suiting the Setting,* conference paper no. 4, Brighton, 1965, The Association of Public Lighting Engineers, London, 1965.

Waldram, J. M.: "Surface, Seeing and Driving: Some Recent Studies," *Light and Lighting,* vol. 53, no. 11, p. 305, November, 1960.

Westermann, H. O.: "Planning Public Lighting for X-Town," *International Lighting Review,* vol. 17, no. 3, 1966.

Chapter 8   People on Wheels

AASHO: *Manual on Uniform Traffic Control Devices for Streets and Highways,* Bureau of Public Roads, Washington, D.C., 1961.

Froshaug, Anthony: "Road-side Traffic Signs," *Design,* no. 178, pp. 36–50, Oct. 1963.

Council on Uniform Traffic Control Devices for Canada: *Manual of Uniform Traffic Control Devices for Canada,* 2d ed., Canadian Good Roads Association, Ottawa, 1966.

Hanson, Daniel, et al.: "Curb Parking Sign Study," *Highway Research Record,* no. 151, pp. 18–40.

Kinneir, Jock: "Designing a System for Britain's Road Signs," *Design,* 221, May, 1967.

Ministry of Transport: *Traffic in Towns,* H. M. Stationery Office, London, 1963.

Ministry of Transport: *Traffic Signs for Motorways: Final Report of the Advisory Committee,* H. M. Stationery Office, London, 1962.

————: *Traffic Signs Manual,* H. M. Stationery Office, London, 1965.

———: *Traffic Signs Manual,* H. M. Stationary Office, London, 1965.

Ritter, Paul: *Planning for Man and Motor,* The Macmillan Company, New York, 1964.

Chapter 9   When People Need to Know or Talk

"Alarm Signal Systems," in *National Fire Codes,* National Fire Protection Association, Boston, 1965, vol. 7, secs. 71, 74.

Brinkley, John: *Lettering Today,* Reinhold Publishing Corporation, New York, 1965.

Krampen, Martin: "Signs and Symbols in Graphic Communication," *Design Quarterly,* Walker Art Center, Minneapolis, 1962.

Malt, Harold Lewis: "Systems for Civic Furnishings," *Industrial Design,* October, 1966, pp. 50–52.

Oster, G., and Y. Nishijima: "Moiré Patterns," *Scientific American,* 208, pp. 54–63, May, 1963.

Sutton, James: *Signs in Action,* Studio Vista, Ltd., London, 1965.

Chapter 10   Good Housekeeping and the Good Life

"Fire Hydrants," in *National Fire Codes,* National Fire Protection Association, Boston, 1965, vol. 7, sec. 29C.

Chapter 11   Pride, Pomp, and Planter

Halprin, Lawrence: *Cities,* Reinhold Publishing Corporation, New York, 1964.

Redstone, Louis G.: *Art in Architecture,* McGraw-Hill Book Company, New York, 1968.

Simonds, John Ormsbee: *Landscape Architecture: The Shaping of Man's Natural Environment,* F. W. Dodge Company, a Division of McGraw-Hill, Inc., New York, 1961.

Illustration Credits

All drawings and photographs not otherwise credited are the work of the author. Position on page is indicated as follows: T = top, B = bottom, L = left, R = right, M = middle.

Index

249

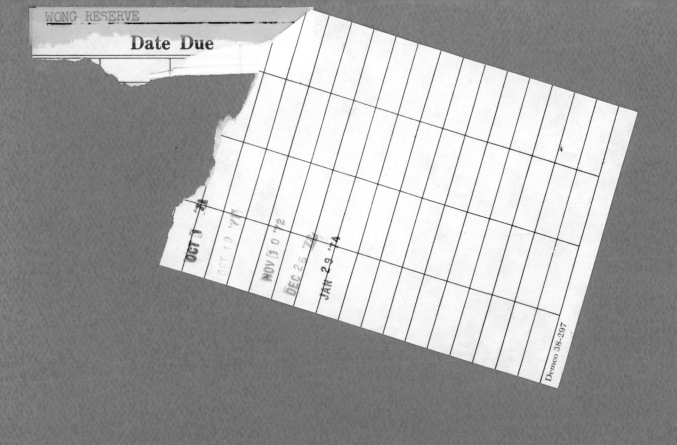